THE LIFE AND TIMES OF
ELIJAH MUHAMMAD

THE LIFE AND TIMES OF ELIJAH MUHAMMAD

CLAUDE ANDREW CLEGG III

The University of
North Carolina Press
Chapel Hill

© 1997 Claude A. Clegg III
All rights reserved
Designed by Gretchen Achilles

Originally published as *An Original Man: The Life and Times of Elijah Muhammad* by St. Martin's Press in 1997.
University of North Carolina Press edition published in 2014.

The paper in this book meets the guidelines for permanence and durability of the Committee on Production Guidelines for Book Longevity of the Council on Library Resources.

The University of North Carolina Press has been a member of the Green Press Initiative since 2003.

The Library of Congress has cataloged the original edition of this book as follows:

Clegg, Claude Andrew III.
An original man : the life and times of Elijah Muhammad / by Claude Andrew Clegg III—1st ed.
p. cm.
Includes bibliographical references and index.
1. Elijah Muhammad, 1897–1975. 2. Black Muslims—Biography. 3. Afro-Americans—Biography. I. Title.
BP223.Z8E42 1997
297'.87'092—dc20
[B]   96—44692
CIP
ISBN 978-1-4696-1805-0 (pbk.: alk. paper)
ISBN 978-1-4696-1806-7 (ebook)

Publication of this book

is enabled by a grant from

Figure Foundation

To the ending of man's
inhumanity to man

GENEALOGY OF
ELIJAH (POOLE) MUHAMMAD[1]

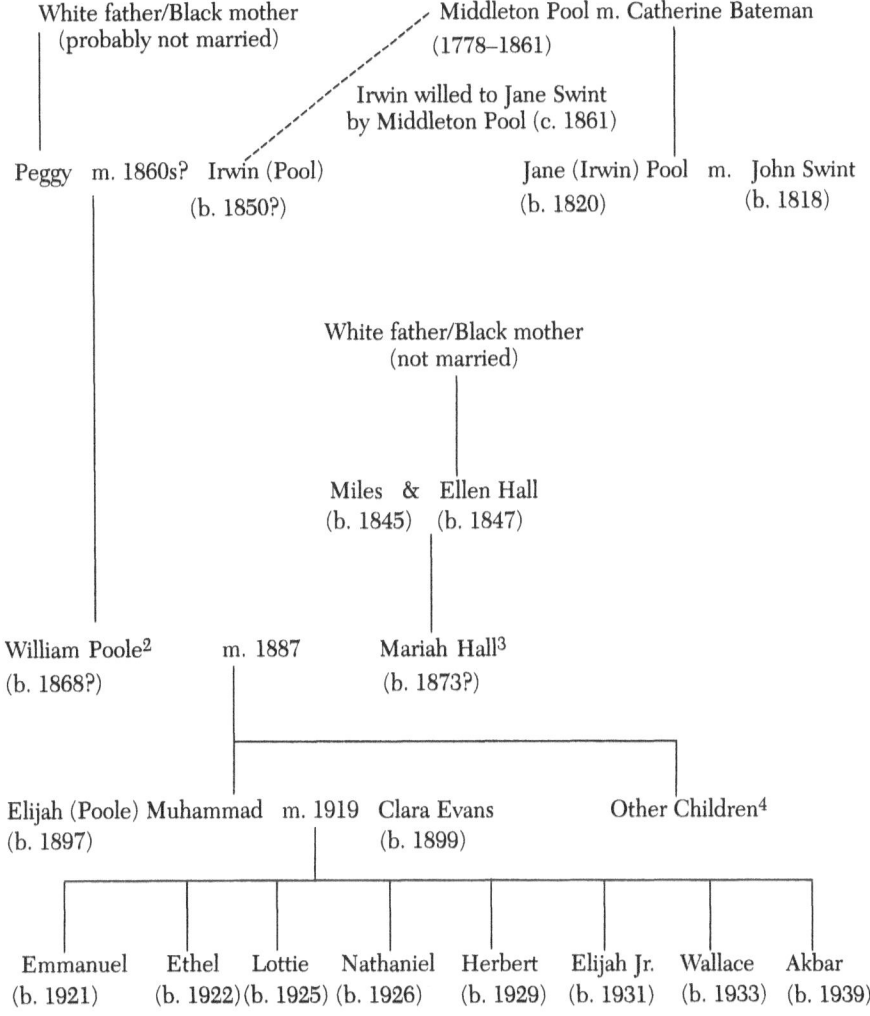

[1]This genealogical sketch of Elijah Muhammad's lineage includes only married adults and their legitimate offspring, except where noted otherwise.

[2]William Poole is listed as a mulatto in the 1880 census, though his father Irwin, is listed as black. It may be that the census enumerator based his assessment on skin color and not genealogy.

[3]Mariah Hall is listed as nine years old in the 1880 census, which would have made her twenty-nine in 1900. The census for the later date lists her as twenty-six years old. FBI records describe her as seventy-two around 1945, which supports the findings of the 1900 census.

[4]Annie (b. 1889?), William Jr. (b. 1890s), Hattie (b. 1890s), Lula (b. 1890s), Tommie (b. 1894), Kalot (b. 1904), Emma (b. 1906), Jonnie (b. 1907), James (b. 1910), John (b. 1910), Sam (b. ?), and Charles (b. ?).

CONTENTS

Preface ... xi
Acknowledgments ... xv

Part I: Genesis

1. 26,000 Years ... 3
2. An Original Man, Lost and Found ... 14
3. The Knowledge of Self and Others ... 41

Part II: The Wilderness

4. Tabernacle in the Wilderness ... 77
5. Public Enemy ... 88
6. Messenger of Allah ... 109

Part III: The Keys to the Kingdom

7. Trials and Tribulations ... 149
8. Rumors of War ... 190
9. A Nation of Shopkeepers ... 235

Part IV: Judgment

10. In the Last Days ... 269

Epilogue: Elijah Muhammad in American Memory ... 285
Appendix: Terminology of the Nation of Islam ... 289
Notes ... 291
Bibliography ... 345
Index ... 367

PREFACE

His followers knew him as the Messenger of Allah. His detractors, none of whom could ignore his profound influence on others, denounced him as a cult leader, a black supremacist, and a hate teacher. Those who admired him but would not follow him called him the Honorable Elijah Muhammad. Reporters typically addressed him as either Mr. Muhammad or by his surname alone, even when they wrote unflattering stories about him and his movement. The numerous other cognomens and aliases by which he went served mostly utilitarian purposes, such as confusing government surveillance agencies or shielding the leader from undesirable public scrutiny. Only his most bitter enemies referred to him as simply "Elijah" or by his "slave name" of Poole—insults resorted to most often by his religious opponents.

Each of these names, labels, and salutations conjured up particular images of Elijah Muhammad and his leadership. Some of the images were meant to stigmatize him and diminish his influence; others were self-serving illusions that he had created and fostered for certain purposes. Despite this range of designations, no single term or phrase completely captured the essence of his life or significance. He was much larger and more complex than mere names and phrases, notwithstanding the countless attempts to reduce him to such.

Given his relevance to the evolution of black nationalist and religious thought in the twentieth century, Elijah Muhammad has unfortunately been the subject of few monograph-length studies. Until now, his life and work have been mired in simplistic popular images and distortions. To be sure, Muhammad has not entirely escaped the historian's attention. Several works, including books, articles, and dissertations, have examined the Nation of Islam. However, Muhammad and his historical importance have still suffered, in many ways, from a surprising degree of scholarly neglect, which has often vitiated his role in shaping American Islam and African-American racial consciousness. The earliest books on the movement appeared in the early 1960s, followed by a spate of articles and other writings, which made the Muslims a somewhat vogue, if controversial, topic of discussion, not unlike the explosion of interest that the image and words of Malcolm X enjoy today. Yet, following the departure of Malcolm X from the Nation in the winter of 1963–64, scholarly and journalistic interest in the movement markedly declined. From then until the present, academic and nonmember writers have studied, almost without exception, the separatist organization only in reference to the life and experiences of Malcolm X and, to a lesser degree, Louis Farrakhan—the Nation of Islam inspiring little of the literature in and of itself. None of the later works have dealt at length with the impact of Muhammad's early experiences on his leadership style and ideological moorings during the 1960s and 1970s.

Consequently, this biography seeks to capture the life and meaning of Elijah Muhammad, the man and the leader, and to understand him within his historical context. Toward these ends, this critical analysis advances three major themes of crucial importance in explaining the leader's life, views, and leadership. The first of these is his seminal role in the evolution of black nationalism and Islam as an alternative religion among African-Americans in the twentieth century. In particular, *An Original Man* will not only show that Muhammad was the most prominent icon of the quasi-Islamic and racial separatist movements that developed among blacks following World War II, but also that he personally was the main guiding force behind the beliefs, rituals, and functions of the Nation of Islam for over four decades. From his feeling of personal persecution, which he acquired early in life, to the organizational triumphs and crises of the 1960s and 1970s, the experiences and philosophy of Muhammad were fundamental to the fashioning of the Nation of Islam as a significant separatist movement in the United States. In sum, to understand the nature and appeal of varieties of Islam and black nationalism to African-Americans over the past fifty years, one must examine the life and work of Elijah Muhammad. His leadership illuminates the importance of leaders before him, such as Marcus Garvey and Noble Drew Ali, and those who came after him, including Louis Farrakhan and Warith D. Mohammed.

Secondly, economic factors had a crucial impact on both Muhammad's leadership and the maturation of the Nation of Islam. Circumstances and conditions, such as Muhammad's agrarian background and experiences in depressed Detroit during the 1920s and 1930s, were directly tied to his later attraction to the Nation of Islam as a vehicle of financial uplift as well as spiritual and racial empowerment. Furthermore, material considerations progressively overshadowed purely spiritual matters, which led to conservatism in the movement. The emphasis on economics was not necessarily a contradictory element in the ideological development of the Nation of Islam and can be traced to the founding of the organization during the Great Depression. In fact, thousands of African-Americans were attracted to the movement because of its willingness to address both eschatological and earthly concerns. However, the experiments of the Muslims in real estate and entrepreneurship after World War II had a drastic impact on both the fortunes and ideological underpinnings of the movement. The fiscal dealings of the Muslim leadership led, by the 1950s, to individual acquisitiveness, even avarice, that routinely consumed growing amounts of the group's resources. Consequently, the imperative to maintain economic expansion resulted in an aversion to both doctrinal innovation and various forms of activism. While this book does not maintain that Elijah Muhammad's role in the Nation of Islam was solely motivated by materialism, his leadership, and the movement in general, were increasingly shaped by both a stress on material concerns and the larger economic patterns behind American society.

Thirdly, to understand the life of Elijah Muhammad demands that he be placed in his historical environment. His rural Georgian background and acclimation to urban life will be detailed, as well as important national and international events and conditions. The various ideological influences and organizational dynamics that helped shape his philosophy and leadership will be assayed. The pervasive influence of government censure on Muhammad's leadership is also of special interest, especially since state repression so proscribed the activism and protest strategies of the Nation.

An Original Man is not intended as an exhaustive study of the Nation of Islam. The author hopes that this work will inspire further research on Elijah Muhammad as well as the Muslim movement. Much remains to be said and written about Muhammad and his important role in twentieth-century American history.

ACKNOWLEDGMENTS

This book was first conceived as a doctoral dissertation during my graduate studies at the University of Michigan at Ann Arbor. A number of individuals in academia helped facilitate the research and writing of this biography, and I am especially grateful for their assistance. First of all, my interest in the historical profession was primarily ignited by Drs. Colin Palmer, J. Lee Green, and Harold Woodard, three fine scholars who instructed me during my undergraduate years at the University of North Carolina at Chapel Hill. During my Ph.D work at Michigan, I was particularly indebted to Dr. Keletso Atkins for her scholarly guidance and the many times she allowed me to use up her office hours talking about black nationalism and other topics. Dr. Robin Kelley, now at New York University, also provided me with valuable academic advice while at Michigan. Additionally, various members of the library staff and history department of North Carolina A&T State University have been extremely supportive regarding this project, and their enthusiasm has been very encouraging. Special thanks to Dr. Ernest Allen of the University of Massachusetts at Amherst. His insight and generosity have never failed to amaze me, and several of the sources used in this work were brought to my attention by him. Many others could be mentioned here, and to them I also extend my gratitude.

A number of institutions were instrumental in the completion of this book. Many thanks to the Rackham Graduate School of the University of Michigan for funding my graduate studies and research. The archival staff of Clark Atlanta University Library graciously allowed me to review documents that had not yet been prepared for public scrutiny. The probate courts of Cook County, Chicago, and Washington County, Georgia, granted me access to many important documents related to the life of Elijah Muhammad. John W. Roberts of the Bureau of Prisons helped me to reconstruct the prison experience of the Muslim leader at Milan, Michigan, by bringing several governmental records to my attention. Other institutions and repositories that contributed to the success of this project include the Schomburg Center of the New York Public Library, the Library of Congress, the Michigan Historical Collection, the reading room of the Federal Bureau of Investigation, the John Fitzgerald Kennedy Library, the Lyndon Baines Johnson Library, the Oral History Research Office of Columbia University, the Washington County Historical Society, the Georgia Department of Archives and History, and the staff of St. Martin's Press (particularly, Senior Editor Robert Weil).

Many other individuals who helped me during my research and writing deserve mention. Grace Poole, Lydia Pool, and Katie Smith Poole were very useful in helping me with the family background of Elijah Muhammad. Fahim Knight and Adib Rashad assisted me in establishing contact with people who had interesting stories to tell regarding their membership in the Nation of Islam. Seifullah A. Shabazz graciously provided me with sources that I would not otherwise have seen. Additionally, "my boys" helped sustain my confidence (and sense of humor) with their excitement about this work, especially Jerome Lucky and Kevin Martin, who helped defray the cost of photographs. I am most indebted to my wife, Alfreda, whose patience and understanding made this work possible. Likewise, my mother and father never wavered in their support of my academic pursuits and other endeavors. Of course, any mistakes that this book may contain are my sole responsibility.

C. A. C.
Greensboro, North Carolina
September 1996

PART ONE

GENESIS

CHAPTER 1

26,000 YEARS

That which does not kill us makes us stronger.
—Friedrich Nietzsche

On the eve of the Civil War, Sandersville was a dusty village nestled in east-central Georgia. With a population of about five hundred people, the hamlet was a typical small Georgian settlement with roots in the colonial period. The first white settlers in the area started as yeomen, scouring the land of trees and verdure to create farms and homesteads. Increased European immigration into the region during the late eighteenth century led to frontier conflicts with Native Americans, who quickly found the early treaties—and their observance by white settlers—disappointing. Sandersville, as an official unit of government, was not legislated into existence until the 1790s when a Mr. Saunders, in response to an act of the state government, donated part of his plantation to Washington County for the establishment of the county seat, Saundersville. By 1812, the village, now known as Sandersville, had become a stagecoach stop and relay station, its importance largely tied to its proximity to the state capital in nearby Milledgeville.[1]

During the early nineteenth century, Middleton Pool Jr., a white immigrant from North Carolina, was among the more notable settlers to arrive in Sandersville. Pool, along with his father, Middleton Sr., and brother, James, had come to the area primarily to claim land that was being doled out by the Georgian land lottery in 1805. Although the senior Pool died in that same year, Middleton Jr. and James subsequently settled near Bold Springs in Washington County.[2]

By the standards of the antebellum rural South, Middleton Pool Jr. fared well in the social and political milieu of central Georgia. In 1820, he was commissioned justice of the peace for the one hundredth Georgia Militia District and, four years later, served as an extra member of the Georgian House of Representatives. An attendee of the Darien Baptist Church, Pool had by the 1830s acquired a venerable status in the community and, commensurate with his influence, was one of five commissioners selected to supervise the construction of a new bridge in the area. His most significant achievements, however, were in finance and real estate, which undoubtedly enhanced his political and social prestige in Washington County.

According to the 1850 census, Pool, at age seventy-two, owned thousands of dollars in assets, not the least of which were twenty-two slaves.[3]

Only weeks after the State of Georgia formally seceded from the United States on January 19, 1861, Middleton Pool died and bequeathed the lion's share of his estate to his children. Among his survivors was his forty-one-year-old daughter, Jane Irwin Swint, who had become a widow following the death of her husband, John Swint, sometime earlier. Pool's will provided well for Jane and the others; she received 215 acres of land valued at $1,184.62. Additionally, Jane was given other valuables for her upkeep and comfort, including "Lucky a woman and her increase [or offspring,] one horse saddle and bridle two cows and calves a bed and furniture and also a negro woman named Easter and a boy named Irwin." The whole transaction, along with its financial and human implications, was a common one in the pre–Civil War South. Casually listed with cows and furniture, slaves and their prospective progeny were routinely passed from owner to owner just as other properties were. Georgian slavery was already a century old when Jane Swint received her inheritance. Nonetheless, she lived in interesting times when such perfunctory events as the reading of the wills of slaveholders fed the fires of sectional crisis and national disunity.[4]

The Southern ancien régime that had allowed people such as Jane Swint to own people such as Lucky, Easter, and Irwin collapsed under the stress of four years of war. The denouement for Georgia's house of bondage came in the spring of 1864. With the avowed intention of making Confederates "so sick of war that generations would pass away before they would again appeal to it," Gen. William Sherman and his Union Army blazed a fiery swath from northern Georgia to Savannah, stopping in tiny Sandersville to impress upon rebels there the futility of resistance. When Sherman arrived in the village on November 25, he found only a handful of wooden shops, a few homes, three brick buildings, and a courthouse square. A Confederate cavalry unit under Joe Wheeler launched a brief defensive action, and Union prisoners taken from rebel stockades were massacred. Federal troops led by Sherman, however, brought superior force to bear on the town, compelling the defenders to quit Sandersville altogether on November 26. The triumphant Union general, who had frequently visited brutality and suffering upon civilians—ranging from freed blacks to ardent Confederate sympathizers—his army had encountered during the campaign, abstained from burning dwellings, but did allow his men to raze the courthouse ("a handsome Greek Revival building of stuccoed brick"), the local jail, and the railroad depot in the adjacent town of Tennille. Like so many other parts of Georgia, Sandersville was simply another refrain in Sherman's anthem to total war.[5]

Irwin, the black youth passed down to Jane Swint as a perpetual servant, was fourteen years old when the army of General Sherman brought hell to

Georgia. His experiences in slavery are lost to history, but he did apparently exhibit a pious disposition in his early adulthood and would eventually be "called" to preach. Following emancipation, Irwin courted and married a fair-skinned mulatto woman named Peggy, who bore him a son, William. At this time, African-Americans in Georgia, as well as the South in general, were testing the limits of their newly acquired freedom. Seven hundred blacks attended a Sandersville rally on July 4, 1867, organized by John T. Costin, an African-American minister, and Macon politician Jefferson Long for the purpose of shoring up support for the Republican Party. The presence of Union troops coupled with federal legislation made black suffrage, for the first time in Georgian history, a reality, though brief in duration and limited in scope. For Irwin Pool and other freedpeople in the South, however, freedom and power in an agrarian society stripped of liquid capital by four years of war were not so much based on access to the ballot box as on land ownership, credit, and markets. These prerequisites of economic empowerment and social mobility were, for the vast majority of African-Americans, unattainable given the federal government's lack of commitment to sweeping land reform. Even though the price of land in Georgia in 1870 was half that of 1860, hostile local governments, indifferent banks, and the smoldering ashes of white supremacy still managed to limit ex-slaves in almost all spheres of economic activity. Ten years after Sherman torched the Peach State, blacks, who constituted over 40 percent of the population, owned just 338,769 acres of Georgian land, or less than 1 percent.[6]

Reconstruction was stumped out of Georgia by the Ku Klux Klan and other white redeemers by the early 1870s. Facing a future of closed ballot boxes and empty pockets, most African-Americans were forced into some kind of labor arrangement with either their former masters or other propertied whites. The Pools sharecropped as did 90 percent of black Georgians by 1890, when cotton production experienced a resurgence. William, like his father before him, received the call to preach sometime during the close of the nineteenth century and, for the next several decades, ministered to the spiritual needs of blacks who would listen. On January 9, 1887, William married Mariah Hall, a local woman whose family had roots in Washington County. Mariah's mother, Ellen, was a mulatto, fathered by a slave master who had raped her enslaved mother. Very light in complexion, Ellen had been separated from her mother through sale during slavery. Her white half-brother was reportedly a state senator in Georgia, and though she avoided discussing her lineage, later in life she periodically visited her white relatives. In describing her affinity for her father's descendants, one black relative said of Ellen, "She was half and half, and she looked it, and act it."[7]

In a cosmetic way, Sandersville seemed to prosper during the turn of the century. Though a fire ravaged the downtown area in 1888 and again in 1893, many of the town's buildings were redesigned in brick, and several residents rebuilt their homes with second floors. These architectural touches hardly masked the gnawing poverty that gripped the majority of the 25,237 inhabitants of Washington County, especially the African-American community, which made up 59 percent of the population. For them, the emergence of Jim Crow, a devastating depression, and lynching turned poor prospects into an even worse predicament. Declining cotton prices strengthened the chains of peonage and penury for both sharecropper and cash renter alike. While a few more blacks managed to secure titles to land, their share of Georgian real estate, even at its peak in 1920, never accounted for more than 5 percent of the available land, though African-Americans made up over two-fifths of the state's population. As a morbid exclamation point to the misery endured by its black majority, Washington County experienced a record amount of snowfall and low temperatures in the winter of 1899. During February 12–13, twelve inches of snow blanketed the rustic town accompanied by temperatures below zero. In that same year, the state of Georgia itself set another kind of record: twenty-eight people lost their lives through lynchings, a ten-year high.[8]

Mariah Poole believed in dreams.[9] When she was seven years old, she claimed to have had a vision that one day she would give birth to a male child of preeminent stature and importance. During his lifetime, this youth would come into contact with "a great power," perhaps a divine presence, which would change the course of human affairs. While life was hard in Sandersville, and matters of divine destiny seemed to carry little weight compared to the material reality of deprivation around her, Mariah held on to this preternatural vision, this prophecy, for a lifetime.[10]

The Poole family grew quickly during the 1890s. First, there was Annie, born in 1889, followed by William Jr. (Billie), Fornie (Tommie), Hattie, and Lula. A second male baby was born in October 1897, a child who seemed somehow different from the rest and who, at least temporarily, eased the rather vapid lives of the Pooles in bucolic Sandersville. The newborn, named Elijah by his grandfather, was pampered from the beginning and became the favorite among the other children. When Annie first held him a week after his birth, she was enamored of his appearance. "He was a beautiful baby," she recalled some years later. "He had beautiful black eyes. I just loved him." His grandfather teasingly called baby Elijah "the Prophet" and predicted that he would one day be just that.[11]

As necessity required, William and Mariah labored assiduously to provide for their children. Between sharecropping for various local farmers and working in sawmills, William pastored Bold Spring Baptist Church and Union Baptist Church. His wife, like so many other black women, worked as a domestic for local white families, receiving only a fraction of the wages that working males commanded. Mariah was often paid in kind for her labor, and many days she came home with pig's feet, chitterlings, and other less desirable parts of slaughtered animals, instead of the cash wages that the family so sorely needed. By 1900, she was pregnant again with a seventh child.[12]

For unknown reasons, the Pooles left Sandersville in 1900, probably during the latter part of the year. The departure, which was not necessarily abrupt, was perhaps related to William's occupation as a minister as well as conflicts in his personal life. Possibly the family relocated because of prospects for a more comfortable lifestyle elsewhere. William might simply have paid the family's debts, secured a pastorate in the new locale, and moved the family at the first opportunity. Unfortunately, it is equally possible that the family left Sandersville amidst rumor and scandal. Sometime during the turn of the century, William allegedly fathered a male child, Lonnie, by a local woman named Vinnie Poole. The details of the affair are elusive, but it seems substantiated by some evidence. The resulting opprobrium, highlighted by a sparser attendance at church meetings and peculiar stares from neighbors and others, probably forced William's hand and led to a voluntary exile from Sandersville. Whatever the reasons for the move, the Pooles left Washington County for good and set out for more verdant pastures in south-central Georgia.[13]

When the Poole family arrived in Cordele in 1900, the small town, located in Dooly (later Crisp) County, was undergoing significant changes. Incorporated in 1888 with a population of three hundred, Cordele attracted both a national highway and a railway. By World War I, it boasted a Telephone Exchange building, a well-constructed water and sewerage system, electric lights, three newspapers, and other amenities as well as an expanding downtown area that included two cottonseed-oil mills, an ice factory, four hotels, three fertilizer plants, and two bottling plants, which serviced and employed the city's growing population of 8,250. Segregation in Cordele, as it had been in Sandersville, was de rigueur, and the African-American community was, of course, the worse off for it. Sharecropping and renting were the typical occupations of Cordele's black majority, but some limited opportunities in mills and factories attracted men like William Poole. The move to Cordele does not seem to have greatly improved the Pooles' economic status, but it perhaps rehabilitated the social standing of William Poole. Accordingly, the pastor found a new niche among the black Baptists of Cordele and mounted the pulpit once again.[14]

Church attendance for the Poole children was mandatory and, for at least Elijah, often pleasurable. By age four, he was allowed to sit in the "preacher set," where he was admired by members of the congregation as his father delivered his sermons. Elijah was deeply impressed by his father's orations and even more enraptured by the concept of "Hell's Fire," which the minister seemed to stress. On occasion, the younger Poole would find his father's messages "so frightening until I, Myself, being his son, would tremble.... I would think and wonder, 'Will I live to get to Heaven before this comes?'" Over time, Elijah acquired a will to preach and evangelize. Moreover, he was also determined to become a "corrector" of the discrepancies and non sequiturs he sometimes discerned in the lessons of his father and other ministers. Eventually, he found himself so emboldened that Monday mornings saw theological duels between father and son, the latter armed with scriptural proof for his arguments. When possible, William avoided the youth, commenting to his wife, Mariah, "You know, that boy gets on my nerves." While Elijah enjoyed his father's "jackleg" preaching and the power that he projected from the chancel, he felt that something was missing from the presentations, some hidden truth that had not been made clear.[15]

Elijah's early interest in Christian doctrine and church affairs stemmed from a sincere curiosity about God, salvation, and the place of man in both the panorama of history and the larger divine plan. Having lost some confidence in his father's teachings, not to mention his qualifications as a minister, Elijah often pored over the Bible in solitude, looking for those gems of arcane knowledge that his father had missed the prior Sunday. Still unsure of his comprehension of the Scripture, he made himself two promises. First, he would not become an official member of the church before the understanding that he sought was revealed to him. Second, he would never allow those he suspected of insincerely presenting themselves as believers to continue to do so without an abrasive challenge from him.

In fact, after one of his younger brothers joined the church, Elijah confronted him and taunted, "You say God told you to go and join the church?" The younger boy answered affirmatively. Elijah replied sardonically, "Man, you ought to stop lying.... You do everything you did before you joined the church. How can you tell the preacher a lie and say you got a religion. Why didn't the religion stop you from doing the evil that you used to do?"

At about age fourteen, Elijah did finally join the church, but not of his own volition. Apparently, he was pressured into doing so by the conformity of the other children or by his father, who had simply had enough of Elijah's interrogations and equivocation. Even though he was now "convinced" that he should become a member of the body of Christ, Elijah found it difficult to deceive the church into believing he was saved. Unlike his younger brother, who claimed God had told him to join, Elijah, deep in his conscience, was still nagged by what he knew to be the truth: "God had not told Me anything."[16]

During his youthful struggles with theology, Elijah did manage to acquire some education, though incomplete and brief. He attended the public school for blacks in Cordele, walking as far as five miles to get to the languishing facilities provided for the less fortunate of Crisp County. Sources disagree on when Elijah left school, perhaps as early as the fourth grade but definitely not past the eighth. Like other African-American children in Cordele, Elijah had to work at home to help with the family's survival. For the foreseeable future, he would have to be satisfied with the rudimentary lessons one of his sisters taught him at night. In the end, Elijah numbered among the 25 percent of Cordele blacks who stood at the chasm of illiteracy.[17]

Elijah's experiences as a laborer started as early as age ten, when he and one of his sisters chopped firewood and sold it for fifty cents to customers in town. The work was time-consuming, and their pay hardly compensated them for their efforts. The family, however, needed whatever hard currency it could get, including the coins earned by the children. Poverty was a constant for the Pooles regardless of whether they were in Sandersville or Cordele. During the winter months when their business prospered most, Elijah and his sister, as well as their other siblings, still knew well the face of privation. Typically, they each wore the same "rough garment for the whole season," even when they made their periodic treks into town to sell firewood.[18]

The excursions into town not only exposed Elijah and the other children to a quasi-urban setting distinct from the countryside they were used to, but also marked the beginning of their training in the harsh school of Southern race relations. Elijah had already learned much about blacks and their history in Georgia from his parents and grandparents. On several occasions, he had sat and paid rapt attention to his grandmother's tales of beatings that her sister had received during slavery. His grandfather shared poignant details about how religion had been used to reconcile slaves with their bondage and thus make them more manageable. During his early years, Elijah heard of systems of debt slavery and peonage that still existed throughout Georgia where whole families could not leave their white creditors' farms for years due to unsettled accounts. Worse still were the macabre rumors that "certain rivers, lakes, and wooded wilderness-like places carry the bones and skulls of many Black slaves from these plantations in so-called freedom times." All of these stories sickened and grieved Elijah to the point that he promised himself to do something for his people when he became a man.[19]

For a while, Elijah was able to ignore—or at least keep himself from overtly responding to—the racial slurs and discrimination that he and his siblings encountered both in town and in rural areas. Most blacks, to exist within the uneasy peace of Crisp County, learned to cope with the hostile white community that dominated here. The family's needs necessitated that all the able-bodied Poole children work and thus face white Cordele at least periodically. For Elijah, however, the necessary journeys to Cordele and its environs became, over time, unsafe and outright horrifying. Some threats became commonplace and even tolerable; yet, other instances of intimidation, such as when a white man coolly revealed to him the severed ear of a black person, were unnerving, not only in themselves but also due to the level of hatred and barbarity underlying them.[20]

Few things in the history of the South set off the kind of shock waves in the black community that lynchings did. Emerging as a phenomenon during Reconstruction and lasting well into the civil rights era of the 1950s and 1960s, mob murders of African-Americans crested at the turn of the century. In Georgia, there had been 159 lynchings during the 1890s, and as late as 1916, when blacks began leaving the state in droves, 16 people lost their lives to vigilante violence. Tales of lynchings and indiscriminate brutality unleashed upon blacks were plentiful in south-central Georgia, but Cordele seems to have had a special reputation for midnight kidnappings and mob violence. Just three years following the Pooles' arrival in Cordele, a black man was found hanging from a tree on a public road close to the city. In time, Elijah Poole came face-to-face with the worst of the South's crimes.[21]

The unspeakable happened sometime around the winter of 1907, when Elijah, now ten, had first begun taking firewood to Cordele for sale. As he approached the African-American section of town, he encountered a large crowd of whites. He moved closer to see what the crowd saw. There, for all who cared to see, the corpse of an eighteen-year-old black youth whom Elijah had known was "dangling from a tree limb." He had been accused of raping a white woman and, without a trial, was seized and summarily reeled up a willow tree by the neck and riddled with bullets. Though a most savage object lesson, Elijah could not understand how this could have happen to a young man "in the midst of his own people" while "all our grown men right there in the section" watched and dared not intervene. The murder and the subdued reaction of the African-American community repulsed him, and his tears flowed unencumbered. He cried for the dead youth and the rest of the blacks of Cordele, who had, in his view, allowed the killing to take place. No firewood was sold that day, and the pellucid impression of the hanging man gripped his entire consciousness as he made the four-mile trip back home.[22]

This traumatic experience stayed with Elijah for the rest of his life and certainly made him more susceptible to black separatist doctrines. For now, his response was to get out of Cordele, or at least to avoid it as much as possible. At age sixteen, Elijah left home to find work in Macon, Georgia, perhaps directly influenced by the lynchings of two African-American men in Cordele during 1912. Over the next few years, he worked in a variety of occupations, from laboring in sawmills to overseeing workers at the Cherokee Brick Company, where he served as a tramroad foreman and builder. His real desire was to become a dining boy for the railroad, and to achieve this goal, he sought employment with a white farmer who turned out to be little more than a relic of the antebellum South. Elijah worked "from sun to sun" to save enough money to pay for the training necessary for the railroad job. Within a six-month period, however, he found the farmwork unbearable, having seen laborers flogged at gunpoint and offered only eight dollars a month in wages. The breaking point came when the farmer threatened to beat Elijah with a six-foot staff if he did not submit to every command. Elijah warned that if he was struck, he "would have no better sense than to strike him [the farmer] back." Elijah, who had been favored and looked up to for leadership by his siblings and others, never became used to either ceding absolute authority to others or being cursed by employers who knew he needed the job. Ordered to leave this farmer's premises, he turned his back forever on working for white farm owners.[23]

During the second decade of the twentieth century, black life in many Georgian cities underwent a series of adjustments in response to new circumstances. Poverty, racism, lynchings, and political disfranchisement remained relatively constant, but the outbreak of World War I in 1914 and the swelling demand for labor in Northern industrial centers began pulling thousands of hopeful black migrants north. African-Americans began leaving Georgia in a trickle that eventually resembled a flood, as ten thousand left in late 1916, followed by at least fifty thousand more the next year. The loss of labor severely damaged Georgia's agrarian economy, the greatest blow perhaps coming during the period between 1920 and 1922 when over 150,000 blacks quit the Peach State. The migration continued for decades, and the ill effects were not quickly absorbed.[24]

The boll weevil, regarded by many as a plague of biblical proportions, helped many blacks to make up their minds about leaving Georgia. The infestation struck hard and extensively, forcing Georgians to pay the price for depending so heavily upon a cotton monoculture. Immediately prior to the attack in 1916, Georgia's fields averaged 230 pounds of cotton per acre, and afterward 117 pounds. During the Great Migration, the destruction of cotton fields seemed to correlate with the departure of African-Americans from the state, with 10 percent of crops being damaged in 1918 and 40 percent by 1923, when the migration declined temporarily. To negate the effects of the boll weevil and the demands of wartime production in Northern cities on Georgia's demography, local governments placed restrictions on labor recruiters and intimidated blacks bent upon leaving the region. When these efforts proved largely ineffectual, politicians and editors resorted to antilynching lip service to superficially address one of the real causes of the migration. All to little avail. In a matter of years the largest

African-American communities in the United States would be found in Northern and Midwestern cities, owing to the pestilence of war, boll weevils, and odious Southern traditions.[25]

Like thousands of other blacks, Elijah switched from agricultural to industrial employment just as the United States decided that armed neutrality was impossible and that participation in the war in Europe was unavoidable. In 1918, he barely missed being among the thirty-four thousand Georgian blacks drafted for service in the conflict, the war having ended "one day before they were calling up the group that I was in." The following year, the Southern Railroad Company hired Elijah in Macon as a gang laborer on a section of the track. The Southern, which invested millions of dollars in trackage at that time, had a reputation for hiring African-Americans as firemen and brakemen as well as common laborers. It also, like many other white-owned corporations in the South, was known for racial discrimination, as evidenced by its agreement to pay blacks 35 percent less than whites in order to avoid a strike in 1911. Notwithstanding their vulnerability to the pressure of local whites, the Southern and other Georgian railroads employed eleven thousand African-Americans by 1925, more than in any other state, and even met on common ground with the newly formed International Railroadmen's Benevolent Industrial Aid Association, which organized black workers and established locals in Macon, Augusta, and Savannah. Whether Elijah ever joined the union during his four years of employment with the Southern is unknown; however, at least in his first year on the job, much of his time was probably spent courting a woman he had met named Clara Evans, whom he married in Cordele on March 17, 1919.[26]

Clara was born in Georgia on November 2, 1898. A petite woman with a deep brown complexion, she was soft-spoken and devoutly Christian, having been raised in a Holiness environment. Elijah was perhaps impressed by both her piety and her willingness to accommodate his intermittent trips between Macon and Cordele. Her companionship and comfort after long days on the railroad helped him to deal with his bouts of ennui. Their first child, Emmanuel, was born in February 1921, followed by Ethel in October of the next year. Elijah now had his own family and the attendant responsibilities, and the job on the railroad meant more than any other he had ever held.[27]

The predictable, though stressful, patterns of work in industrializing Georgia disillusioned Elijah less than the sporadic atrocities, which sent tremors of horror through his soul. Like others, he grieved for the victims he heard about, but learned to cope with the reality of racism and brutality that underlay Southern culture, without becoming paranoid. He learned to survive. However, firsthand knowledge of savage events always repulsed him and again, as an adult, he was privy to the unspeakable. During a Saturday evening in 1920 or 1921, Elijah and one of his brothers traveled to Macon on business. As they covered the nine miles from their home to the city, African-Americans leaving the area warned them of a lynching. The body of the victim had been tied to a pickup truck and dragged through the streets. The Poole brothers could not turn back, and anticipating the encounter was probably as morose and disgusting as actually seeing the mangled black body. In the tragic walk past yet another crowd of sanguinary white Southerners, Elijah, indeed, saw what he had been warned about, and "returned back home with this image of lynching."[28]

With the addition of this last graphic episode, Elijah had endured too much in Georgia to stay. The lynchings, racist employers, marginal wages, boll weevils, and other social and economic maladies all formed an equation that seemed to have only one answer. Whether Elijah's departure from Georgia was triggered by obscene words from a railroad boss, inviting letters from relatives who had already fled the state, or some combination of influences, the burdens of race and class placed upon blacks in general were the primary causes for the Poole exodus. In April 1923, Elijah, Clara, and their two children migrated, probably by railway, to Detroit, Michigan. They were accompanied by Elijah's parents and siblings, who had apparently arrived at the same solution for their lives in Georgia. In the years to come, Elijah would make few trips back to the South and would have even fewer pleasant things to say about Georgia in particular. His bitterness, which was now an inherent part of his consciousness, would later be contagious and galvanize thousands of African-Americans throughout the country behind his leadership. But for the present, Elijah left the Peach State without looking back, having seen "enough of the white man's brutality in Georgia to last me for 26,000 years."[29]

CHAPTER 2

AN ORIGINAL MAN, LOST AND FOUND

*Most people ... [are] born followers, wanderers in search
of guides.... [If] a visionary man had great drive and
determination, and was smart enough to remain sufficiently
vague and elusive so that other people could superimpose
upon him their ideals and fantasies, he would sooner or
later attract his share of followers.*
      —Gay Talese[1]

During World War I and succeeding decades, Detroit was a popular destination for African-American refugees from the South. The first trickle of migrants began in mid-1915 when one thousand blacks arrived each month from such states as Georgia, Alabama, South Carolina, and Arkansas. Traveling primarily on overcrowded railroad cars, they flowed into the city looking for a better life. A larger wave occurred in 1916–17 in response to the rapid expansion of Detroit's wartime industries and the subsequent demand for African-American labor. During this period, perhaps a total of twenty-five thousand to thirty-five thousand blacks entered the city. Although the recession of 1920–21 discouraged many of the newcomers—especially the seventeen thousand unemployed, who often had to migrate to other cities for work—the impact of decreased immigration, as a result of new quotas placed on foreigners, on the labor market initiated a second wave of black migration from the South during the mid-1920s. In 1923, almost fourteen thousand African-Americans arrived in the city, many poor and without employment or residential prospects. Whereas only 5,741 blacks lived in the city in 1910, comprising a little over 1 percent of the total population, by 1920 the African-American community had swelled to 40,838, or 4.1 percent of the aggregate. By 1930 with the onset of the Depression and the temporary cessation of the Great Migration, 120,066 blacks resided in Detroit, forming 7.6 percent of the populace.[2]

As one of many minority groups, African-Americans found their niche in Detroit within an uneasy mosaic of different peoples. Potentially explosive, the city's population mix included native whites, Jews, Poles, Italians, and Greeks, many of whom had migrated there during the latter part of the nineteenth century. Predictably, competition, especially on the economic front, was intense and sometimes violent between the groups. While Detroit did not experience a full-blown race riot comparable to those that took place in Chicago, Tulsa, and other cities following World War I, employers and real estate agents knew the limits of the city's racial, ethnic, and religious tolerance.

African-Americans in early-twentieth-century Detroit were employed in a range of occupations. On the eve of the Great Depression, a significant minority of blacks were self-employed and operated a number of businesses, among which were eighteen drugstores, fifty-one groceries and markets, ninety-one barbershops, sixteen hotels, and two loan associations. The majority of African-Americans, however, were common laborers who worked for wages ranging from an average of sixty-four cents an hour in soda companies to twenty-four cents an hour in hotels. In 1929, according to one estimate, forty thousand black Detroiters worked in automotive-related industries, three thousand in building construction, and two thousand in public works. Overall, African-Americans filled about 10 percent of the city's blue-collar jobs. In step with the times, many white employers practiced wage discrimination and were usually more inclined to hire white laborers than black. Moreover, African-Americans were almost entirely excluded from white-collar employment. Since whites, for the most part, controlled the economic sphere of the city, the black unemployment and turnover rates were always higher than those of white groups. By the time the stock market plunged in October 1929, African-Americans, who were "on the fringes of industry," were already facing economic conditions beyond their control.[3]

Along with unemployment, a housing shortage affected all of Detroit's migrant populations. Like most major Northern cities, Detroit had a tradition of segregated housing. Restrictive covenants and other surreptitious devices usually maintained patterns of segregation; and when these measures were not enough, violence and intimidation were used to keep neighborhoods homogeneous. At the high point of the migration during the war years, only 20 percent of the African-American population in Detroit was buying homes. Although a few middle-class blacks ventured—at their own risk, of course—into white areas for housing during the 1910s and 1920s, the majority were confined to unattractive, poorly constructed tenements in areas customarily designated for African-Americans.[4]

It was this kind of world the Pooles entered in the 1920s, and they found their niche in Hamtramck, an independent municipality in the Detroit area. In many ways, this community was simply a transplanted Polish town where the mother tongue was as frequently heard as English. In other ways, Hamtramck, and Detroit, were similar to Southern towns such as Macon, where a man could wander around for years, from job to job, never really achieving anything. Elijah and his father, William, fell into this pattern as did thousands of other blacks who had neither the skills nor social connections necessary to avoid job-hopping. The elder Poole, after finding preachers in high supply and low demand in Detroit, secured employment with the city and labored on public works. While Elijah's will to preach was blooming, nurtured by the belief that "I should be a better man, and I should do what I always longed to do," the same compunctions that had made him dread joining the church in Cordele were now blocking his ascent to the pulpit in Detroit. As he explained to his mother, Mariah, who had become one of his most trusted confidants, the desire to preach was almost overwhelming, yet "I cannot see my way to going to the church telling the preacher that I want to preach the Christian religion as they are preaching . . . [which] is not right." His conscience, coupled with the low demand for ministers in the city, steered Elijah into the swelling unskilled labor pool and the cycle of job-hopping that he had experienced in Georgia. His pastoral aspiration, nonetheless, stayed with him and would eventually find release years later.[5]

Survival in Detroit for Elijah, Clara, and the children rested largely upon Elijah's shoulders, given his wife's child-rearing responsibilities at home. With the addition of three other children (Lottie, January 1925; Nathaniel, June 1926; and Herbert, April 1929) to the household by the time of the stock market crash of 1929, the search for jobs and sustenance consumed nearly all of Elijah's time and energy. At first, he worked at something familiar, namely, selling firewood for fifty cents per bundle. This seasonal work, however, was not enough to support his burgeoning family, making it necessary for Elijah to seek employment in the industrial world. His first factory job in Detroit, with the American Nut Company, lasted for perhaps several weeks. Sometime in 1923, he secured a second job with the American Wire and Brass Company and was responsible for "separating steel shavings and cleaning nuts and bolts for 60 cents an hour." The work was monotonous and the hours long, but the wages were the highest he had ever earned, and the money was desperately needed. His job with this company lasted until 1925, and at least for these two years, steady employment was the norm for Elijah.[6]

Over the next several years, Elijah's work record became nothing more than a dispiriting chronicle of hirings and firings, layoffs and walkouts. For a while, he worked for the Detroit Copper Company, then for the Briggs Body and Chevrolet Axle Company. Like most of the small numbers of blacks who secured jobs with the latter corporation, Elijah probably worked in a foundry where metal was processed for automobile construction. His job with Chevrolet, which lasted for six months, was followed by a period of extended unemployment and the downward spiral of industrial Detroit into the depths of the Depression.[7]

Elijah's struggle with joblessness in the late 1920s and early 1930s debilitated him emotionally. Like most other men, his self-esteem was inextricably tied to his ability to feed and take care of his wife and the children. The role of provider conferred both authority and responsibility, and lacking steady employment, Elijah felt as though he had failed to live up to this ideal of manhood. As weeks without work turned into months, Elijah lost the resolve to confront the dilemma that he and his household faced. His pride would not allow him to stay at home and face the hard questions that Clara posed about survival or inquisitive looks from the children. Moreover, when the family finally started receiving public assistance, he was frequently absent from home, forced out by the shame of having to appeal to outsiders to fulfill his obligations. He coped best when drunk on alcohol—which temporarily liberated him from cruel reality. In time, Elijah could routinely be found in the gutter, incessantly inebriated with cheap liquor and disillusionment. In only seven years, he had seen the worst that the Motor City had to offer, from the harsh vagaries of industrial capitalism to "our people killed on the street by the police without any justice whatsoever." On occasion, he would ignore the odds against finding gainful employment and spend days beseeching employers for any kind of work. At other times, he drank to unconsciousness in alleyways, where Clara would find him and "bring him in off the streets on her shoulders."[8]

Elijah's malaise did not appear to ease until 1931. Chronically unemployed, he often found himself sitting at home discussing religion with his oldest brother, Billie. Informal sermonizing and theological debates became a pastime for Elijah, which helped him to maintain his hunger for the ministry and deal with the frustration and apparent meaninglessness of life in Detroit. During one of their many theological sessions in the spring, the Poole brothers were joined by their father, William, who mentioned an interesting encounter he had had with one of his friends, a Brother Abdul Muhammad. The latter, who had formerly answered to the name Brown Eel during his membership in a quasi-Islamic movement called the Moorish-Americans, had spoken to William about a Mr. W. D. Fard (pronounced Far-rod), who had taught him about Islam and bestowed upon him his new "original" name, Abdul Muhammad. The elder Poole's summation of the discussion was sketchy, but titillating enough to spark curiosity among his sons, especially Elijah, who exclaimed, "I like to hear that man! . . . That is good what Abdul Mohammed told you." The bits and pieces of Fard's message revealed to them by their father soon took the two Poole brothers to the home of Abdul Muhammad, who, over the course of several subsequent visits, disclosed to them the essence of Islam as Fard had taught it to him.[9]

Months passed between the first mention of Islam to Elijah and his actual attendance at one of Fard's gatherings. His hesitancy regarding meeting this man was not so much rooted in his opposition to what the religious teacher was saying about the origins of man and the universe, the nature of good and evil, and the path to salvation; rather, it was based upon his own notions about Islam as a faith. Elijah, along with other African-American Christians, believed that Islam was a "heathen religion," something foreign and sinister that played into man's impure desires for multiple sex partners, war-making, and other hedonistic passions. In his mind, elements of voodoo, which encompassed everything that was strange and esoteric, bolstered Islam and contradicted the Christian tradition. However, lacking a firm grasp on the faith of his father, which he had agonized over for years, Elijah eventually concluded that he had little to lose in giving Mr. Fard a hearing. After being partially prodded by his younger brother Charlie, who had come home one evening euphoric over what he had heard, Elijah decided that he would listen to this "Islam," despite his intolerance of heathenism.[10]

The history of Islam in the United States went back further than Elijah might have imagined. The arrival of the first African Muslims in Spanish Florida and French Louisiana by way of the slave trade predated the settlement of English colonists in North America. Before 1808, when the transatlantic trade was still legal in what was by then the United States, possibly tens of thousands of Muslims from Senegambia and other Islamic parts of West Africa were transported to North America as slaves. Numerous notices in Georgian and South Carolinian newspapers for runaway slaves with Arabic names confirmed the presence of a significant Muslim minority among African-American slaves. Even after emancipation, some blacks could still trace their ancestry to a Muslim past.[11]

Despite the existence of Islamic Africans in America during slavery, generations of bondage had largely destroyed their ability to perpetuate their religion, especially among descendants. The rigors of slavery and the submergence of most blacks into a European culture that esteemed only Christianity as a religion, discouraged basic practices of Muslims such as circumcision, Islamic educational instruction, avoidance of pork, and the passing on of traditional Arabic names to children. Insofar as legal statutes did not recognize the legitimacy of the slave family, familial instability among slaves was commonplace and could only have hindered the preservation, not to mention the spread, of Islamic beliefs and practices among African-Americans. Thus, by the turn of the nineteenth century, one would have been hard-pressed to find indigenous traces of Islam among blacks in any part of the country. Similarly, those few individuals who embraced the Muslim faith at this time were almost always new converts with no direct link to Islamic antecedents.[12]

Interestingly, the first significant encounter between African-Americans and Islam in the twentieth century was initiated by Ahmadiyya missionaries from the Punjab, a region of what is now Pakistan. This Muslim group was founded in 1889 by Mirza Ghulam Ahmad, who taught that he was the promised Mahdi (or messiah) spoken of in Christian and Islamic holy texts.

Though his movement was surrounded by hostile critics and questions of doctrinal legitimacy, his followers carried his message to different parts of the world over the next twenty years. In 1918, the Ahmadiyyas split into two major sects: one believes that Ahmad was, indeed, the awaited savior; the other relegated him to the status of a great reformer and thus maintained a tie to orthodox Islam. By the 1920s, the movement had established cells in various cities in the United States including Chicago, its headquarters, Detroit, Kansas City, and Cincinnati.[13]

The American leader, Sufi Mutiur Rahman Bengalee, attempted to make Ahmadiyya Islam appealing to blacks by emphasizing the premium it placed on interracial brotherhood and its accessibility to all regardless of color. In spite of multicity speaking tours and inviting editorials in their official organ, *The Moslem Sunrise,* the Ahmadiyyas were largely unsuccessful in converting even a marginal minority of African-Americans to their faith. Their failure partially reflected that their prospective black constituencies in urban areas were predominantly poor, Southern-born immigrants with little formal education—at least not enough to place them within the perimeters of the literate audience that the Ahmadiyyas were appealing to. Perhaps more importantly, the Islam that the Ahmadiyyas offered neither adequately addressed the material reality of the emerging ghettos nor satisfied the psychological need of many blacks to have their basic humanity and particular destiny as a people forcefully affirmed by religious doctrine. In sum, Bengalee could not convince African-Americans that he had something to bestow upon them more valuable than Christianity, which had much deeper roots in the black community.[14]

Where the imported beliefs of the Ahmadiyyas failed, the homegrown Islam of the Moorish Science Temple of America (MSTA) enjoyed limited success. The MSTA, or Moorish-Americans, was organized in Newark, New Jersey, by Noble Drew Ali (formerly Timothy Drew), a black mystic from North Carolina. Between its founding in 1913 and the death of Ali—the prophet of the movement—in March 1929, the group established temples in a number of urban centers, including Chicago, Detroit, and Harlem. According to one estimate, as many as thirty thousand African-Americans may have passed through the ranks of the organization prior to the Great Depression. Unlike the Ahmadiyyas, Ali and his followers offered blacks a new "Moorish" (or Moroccan) identity outside of the constraints of their status as Negroes and attempted to socialize them into a spiritual world in which a mythical "Asiatic" past was the central focus. In addition to constructing a nationality for blacks, the Moorish-Americans tried to rid African-Americans of those vices, such as alcohol consumption and extramarital relations, that undermined the moral fabric of their communities. Tailored to fit into ideological trends already present in black America, such as black nationalism, the MSTA was perhaps the preeminent Islamic group among

African-Americans during the decade following World War I. Consequently, while the group declined sharply in membership and appeal during the 1930s, the religious foundation it had laid—which was partially borrowed from the Ahmadiyyas, the Garvey movement, and other sources—lasted long enough to be exploited by others.[15]

With much of the ideological groundwork already in place as a result of the influence of the MSTA, Marcus Garvey, and the black church, W. D. Fard began his ministry of preaching a peculiar variety of Islam among black Detroiters during 1930. The teachings that he promoted—discussed and analyzed in detail in Chapter 3—were a mix of a number of philosophies, but did not wholly embrace any single system of beliefs. Like black separatists, he spoke of African-Americans emigrating back East to avoid extermination and continuing deprivation in America. Similar to Noble Drew Ali, he attempted to transform blacks into Asiatic "Original People" whose roots were trillions of years old and who had once ruled the earth under the righteous banner of Islam. Additionally, like Mirza Ghulam Ahmad, he presented himself as an intermediary between man and God and later, as Allah in person. However, unlike these other movements, Fard taught a form of racial chauvinism that labeled whites as "devils" by nature and blacks inherently righteous. He perhaps did this believing that such a doctrine would be effective in recruiting African-Americans who had little else to believe in and longed for a sense of importance and a rationale for their oppression. Apocalyptic predictions by Fard of the divine destruction of the white world and the subsequent heaven on earth for his followers increased the appeal of his teachings. So did his claim that he was from Mecca, Saudi Arabia, and of royal parentage. Along with his ascetic lifestyle, his explanation of the black race's past history, present condition, and destiny, based on allegorical interpretations of the Bible and the Qur'an, gave him an almost saintly aura in the eyes of some African-Americans. In time, he would attract a significant following in depressed black Detroit.[16]

Adding to the mystery surrounding Fard's operation in Detroit, a less flattering, though somewhat credible, depiction of his background and character emerges from various police-department and FBI inquiries. According to law enforcement records of the period, Fard was born in New Zealand or Portland, Oregon, on February 25, 1891, to either Hawaiian or British and Polynesian parents. Using the aliases Fred Dodd and Wallace Ford, Fard married, fathered a son, and abandoned his family prior to moving to Los Angeles during World War I. His education was minimal (he "had trouble with his correspondence") and his temperament made him difficult to get along with; nonetheless, he still managed to open a café during the early 1920s. About this time, Fard apparently slipped into a life of crime. As early as November 1918, he was arrested for assault with a deadly weapon. Ultimately, nothing became of the charge, and he was later released. On January 20, 1926, Fard was arrested for violating the California Prohibition law and, a month later, was again detained, along with a "half-Chinese" associate, for selling narcotics in his restaurant at 803 West Third Street. On May 28, 1926, he was sentenced to a prison term of six months to six years at San Quentin, where he worked in a jute mill and in road construction while serving his time. Following his release on May 27, 1929, he departed from Los Angeles in a Model A Ford coupe. Before journeying to Detroit, Fard apparently stopped in Chicago, where he perhaps came into contact with the Ahmadiyya movement (possibly not for the first time), followers of Noble Drew Ali, Garveyites, and other groups. His sojourn in Chicago was brief, and he departed for the Motor City during mid-1930 with his own plans for blacks there.[17]

Fard started out as a retail salesman among African-Americans in Detroit, though few had any money to spend. Desperately mired by the severity of the Great Depression, blacks could afford little beyond the necessities. Even the essentials, such as housing, food, and employment, could be elusive. To gain entry into the homes of blacks, Fard would typically display his wares and tell prospective buyers that the clothing he sold "was the same kind that the Negro people use in their home country in the East." Having aroused the interest of his hosts, Fard would then deliver his sales pitch on the history and future of African-Americans. The tactic worked well, and eventually he honed it to the point that meetings of curious blacks were held in private homes. Later, public halls were rented for his orations, and an organizational structure for his "Nation of Islam" began to take shape in the midst of poverty-stricken Detroit.[18]

During his first visit to one of Fard's meetings in the fall of 1931, Elijah realized that he had underestimated the popularity of the man and his message. The basement in which the teacher was delivering his oration overflowed with African-Americans. Elijah and others could not gain entrance and had to be satisfied with the few audible words that occasionally streamed through the basement's window. Undaunted, Elijah made a second attempt to hear Fard during his lecture in a hall at 3408 Hastings Street, but ran into the same problem. According to Elijah, thousands of people had appeared for this meeting, and he, like others, could only hear parts of the teacher's speech. Nevertheless, he was still able to hear enough of the message to gain a sense of Fard's Islam and what it meant to him and the black community in Detroit. For Elijah, the teachings "did so much good just to think about them" that he resolved to meet the teacher after the gathering.[19]

As usual, a long line of people formed after the lesson to shake hands with and greet Fard. A short, fair-skinned man with dark, straight hair, the Islamic instructor was difficult to distinguish from a white man yet appeared comfortable among large crowds of Detroit blacks. According to one of

Elijah's sons, Fard's European features, despite the fact that he presented himself as a mulatto, perhaps made him and his message more palatable to his African-American followers. His light complexion and willingness to take the time to counsel blacks in matters of race and religion probably impressed them more than a similar program sponsored by a conspicuously black man would have. Besides these factors, Fard certainly possessed a flare for the dramatic fueled by a powerful imagination, both packaged in a charismatic delivery. In him, hundreds of African-Americans saw pristine power and divine omniscience, qualities that their Christian ministers had never possessed. Elijah saw even more and could not help but express it.[20]

Fard was probably shocked by what Elijah told him when they shook hands. Fard was quite used to well-wishers thanking him for his expositions and pledging future support, but without using biblical allegories or metaphors, Elijah candidly stated, "You are that one we read in the Bible that he would come in the last day under the name Jesus.... You are that one?" Caught off guard, Fard paused and looked deep into Elijah's eyes with a "very serious" gaze. He then smiled and whispered into Elijah's ear, "Yes, I am the One, but who knows that but yourself, and be quiet." In an almost paternal way, he touched Elijah on the shoulder and gently pushed him away, ostensibly unconcerned with whether others may have overheard them. As the teacher waded farther down the line of extended black hands, Elijah stood motionless, paralyzed by the colossal importance of the revelation. He had met the man he believed to be Christ returned, and the whole world did not know him.[21]

That evening, Elijah went back home to Hamtramck, his head pounding with the "knowledge of self and others" that Fard had laid out for all to see and examine. Using the Christian Bible and other texts, the teacher had illuminated much that had been shrouded in total darkness ever since Elijah sat in the pulpit of his father's church in Cordele. With this revelation, everything was becoming clear. With the fervor of the newly converted, he described to his relatives and others the truth he gleaned from Fard's teachings about the history of the black Nation of Islam and biblical prophecy. Future meetings of the faithful (or "Muslims") were attended by Elijah as often as possible, and eventually the teacher presented himself to the whole congregation as the new Jesus, independent of the one who had been crucified two thousand years ago, "but the one we had been expecting." In a private moment with Fard, Elijah asked, perhaps simply to hear again what he already believed, "Who are you, and what is your real name?" He was hardly disappointed when the revered Muslim replied, "My name is Mahdi; I am God, I came to guide you into the right path that you may be successful and see the hereafter." At home, Elijah and other converts discussed the message (Truth as they called it) that their fair-skinned savior had brought them and rejoiced in its power to redeem. On many occasions, Elijah would prostrate himself alone in his clothes closet and pray to Fard, asking to see the day when the righteous Muslims would set up the kingdom of God and punish the white man for his evil against the black people.[22]

Throughout his entire life, Elijah always believed that he was destined to preach. Not simply because his grandfather and father were ministers, but according to Elijah, because he saw the need to correct the teachings of such men. The savior who had called Irwin and William Poole to preach never spoke to him, much less called him to the ministry. Their God, Elijah now believed, had no such power anyway, for there did not exist any kind of noncorporeal, spiritual deity. The only redeemer the world was in touch with now was Fard, and he alone had the power to call ministers.

According to Elijah, this honor was bestowed upon him by "the Mahdi" in a quite interesting manner. Only weeks after having been brought into the Muslim fold, Elijah stayed home to tend to the children while Clara attended Fard's meeting. Following his regular lesson, the teacher asked the congregation, "Anyone here in this hall know the little man who lives in Hamtramck?" Clara, surprised by the question, replied, "Yes, he is my husband." Speaking directly to her, Fard gave the call that would start the forty-four-year career of his most faithful minister, stating confidently, "You tell him that he can go ahead . . . and start teaching [Islam], and I will back [him] up." Elijah, who had been in correspondence with the teacher, was ecstatic upon hearing the news. At age thirty-three, he felt that he could finally begin his life's work. Shortly after the appointment, he began in earnest to talk about Truth with every African-American who showed an interest.[23]

In time, Elijah received an original surname, Karriem, and dropped forever the name that the slave master Middleton Pool had passed along to his human chattel. The formal call to the ministry of Fard came during a meeting that is both noteworthy for its irregularity as well as the dissension that overshadowed it. Ordinarily, the teacher had allowed the ministers in training to select a head minister from among their ranks. However, to affirm his faith in Karriem's ability to evangelize, the Muslim leader called him up before the class and, embracing him, proclaimed, "From now on this is my minister." Fard went even further and named Karriem "Supreme Minister" with authority second only to his own. The jealousy and animosity of men more articulate and better educated than the appointee were apparent during the ceremony, and immediately following the meeting battle lines would secretly be drawn between supporters and opponents of both Fard and Karriem. However, for the time being, the humble Supreme Minister graciously accepted the honors extended to him and continued to teach Islam as it was revealed by his master.[24]

The conversion experience of Elijah Karriem in particular must be examined in the ideological context of Detroit's black community as etched above (and elaborated in Chapter 3), tempered by other factors. According to Karriem, since the Cordele debates with his father, he had been on a quest for spiritual fulfillment for most of his life prior to meeting Fard. Christianity, at least as he had known it in Georgia, was defective and did not appeal to him enough to satiate his need for understanding. When Fard found him in the doldrums in Detroit, Karriem was spiritually an open book with almost blank pages for the teacher to write on. In many ways, he had been primed for his acceptance of Nation of Islam theology in 1931. Exposure to the naked brutality of Georgian whites and Detroit policemen must have contributed greatly to Karriem's attraction to the white-devil theory of the Muslims. The adjustment to urban industrial life and the stress and disorientation that many Southern migrants experienced following their arrival in large cities certainly gave a tempting glow to closed, ascetic, secret societies such as Fard's group, which rationalized the predicament of the black race as being the result of an ancient white conspiracy and promised a new identity for those willing to socially withdraw from a doomed America. This, along with Fard's allegorical use of biblical scripture to lend credibility to many of his claims, makes the susceptibility of Karriem to Muslim doctrine understandable.

To maintain that Karriem was duped by Fard or was overly naive in his uncritical acceptance of the leader's ideas oversimplifies the complex interaction between the two men. While in Cordele, Elijah had been privy to the "jackleg" Christianity of his father and grandfather and had been the victim of foul dealings perpetrated by whites time and time again. Undoubtedly, he had also been aware of the emigrationist, Islamic, and nationalist movements among blacks in Georgia and Detroit. Thus, based on his early life experiences, little evidence suggests that Karriem was ignorant enough to fall for every con artist's line or to join every organization that promised miraculous deliverance from oppression. However, his encounter with Fard was different, but not in an absolute sense. If he had met Fard in Cordele while gainfully employed, he may not have given him the time of day, not that Georgia whites would have tolerated the teachings of the Nation of Islam in the first place. Yet, in urban Detroit during the severest depression in American history, unemployed, and addicted to alcohol, Karriem was mesmerized by the ideas of the Muslim leader regarding the originality and superiority of blackness, moral living, proper dieting, and the new world to come. But still, this message alone was probably not enough to enthrall him for over four decades. Under the surface of his "hundred percent" conversion were other more practical factors that made him "a righteous Muslim."[25]

Eliminating naïveté as the primary reason behind his joining the Muslims, Karriem perhaps ultimately saw the organization as a propitious financial opportunity, in addition to its being a vehicle for spiritual empowerment and cultural resurrection. Considering his popularity, Fard probably made thousands of dollars from preaching his brand of Islam to black Detroit during the early 1930s. Through collections and donations, the marketing of clothes to potential and actual followers—who he incidentally encouraged to dress extravagantly—and the possible sale of "original names" to believers, the leader had ample occasion to amass considerable wealth. Karriem and other African-Americans were surely cognizant of this situation. Unemployed with "no hope in anything else," the Georgia migrant probably believed that loyalty to Fard and his teachings was a small price to pay as long as he would be remembered when the rewards were given. This observation, of course, is not meant to imply that Karriem's attachment to the Muslims was solely material in motivation; from the available evidence, his conversion experience seems genuine. Nonetheless, his joblessness and the prospects for advancement in the movement, especially considering his appointment as Supreme Minister and its implications for status and self-esteem, must be counted as factors that contributed to his long-term commitment to the Nation. In the final analysis, the relationship between Karriem and Fard was a symbiotic one in which the former gained a much needed sense of self-importance, spiritual enlightenment, and sustenance for a growing family. In return, his mentor attained both an intermediary between himself and his darker constituency and a faithful disciple who would share the persecution that the authorities and the black clergy were inflicting upon the movement by 1932.[26]

After his conversion and promotion to Supreme Minister, Karriem gave his first sermon before a gathering of the faithful at the Muslim meeting place or "temple." The hour-long talk was difficult for him, especially given his initial "bashful" demeanor before crowds. In the address, which he had prepared himself, he praised his teacher and reminded his audience that the Muslim leader was the one they had searched for. Fard, who was seated behind him, excused himself during the meeting, aware that his presence was a distraction for his novice minister. With the rostrum to himself, Karriem relaxed and spoke more confidently about the savior who had come to gather the Original People in America and reveal to them his wisdom. Overall, the initial sermon was a success, though not a rousing performance. Fard, pleased by the panegyric, detected enough sincerity in the new minister to send him on excursions to Chicago to preach Truth there. By late 1931, Karriem, from the platform of a rented building at 37 Wentworth Avenue, was imparting to believers in the Windy City the knowledge of self and others. In one meeting, he proclaimed, "Fard is Allah, who came to save the dark people." To shore up support, the teacher himself made appearances before Chicago converts to show them what God looked like in person.[27]

Fard and his pupil Karriem were constant companions for the next nine months. The teacher visited the minister's home almost daily to instruct him in his brand of Islam and the rituals of the Nation. In many instances the leader would talk all night about various subjects until the light of dawn reminded him of the hour. Sometimes when he departed, Karriem could only wish that his absence would be "long enough for Me to get a little sleep." On other occasions, the two cruised across the poverty-afflicted landscape of black Detroit in Fard's Chevy coupe, parking on the outskirts of town to talk at length about the universe and the black man's place in it. Over time, Karriem would not only esteem the Muslim teacher as a savior but also as a trusted friend to whom "I gave My last dime" while family members were "sitting at home hungry."[28]

The mysterious ways of his teacher convinced Karriem and others that his presence was, indeed, supernatural. While usually humble and "always happy" in public forums, Fard was in touch with the pulse of his movement to an uncanny degree and often amazed his Supreme Minister with his insight into the circumstances that promoted and hindered the organization. For example, when the leader detected that Karriem's portrayal of him as the second Jesus turned off some potential converts (and perhaps aroused the ire of African-American Christians), he decided to downplay his putative divinity, telling his chief lieutenant, "Give them a little milk. . . . You cannot give babies meat!" To stress to Karriem his alleged omniscience, Fard sometimes revealed to him before meetings who would come to harm the minister, and even the chair in which the person would be seated. In all likelihood these revelations were staged by Fard, who would certainly have been aware of enemies in the movement; nonetheless, episodes of this nature impressed his protégé greatly. Other actions of the teacher, such as the sporadic changes in his hair color, fascinated his followers, and the whole air of unpredictability and quiet confidence that Fard exuded was hard for some blacks to resist. To Karriem, the magnetism of the teacher went far beyond parlor tricks and what he believed to be the leader's psychic powers. What inspired him most with awe and a sense of heartfelt loyalty was the stated willingness of Fard to die for his cause, the salvation of the black people. Mindful of the expectations of his premier minister, the teacher frequently assured him that while "I can't destroy the Nations [of the Earth] . . . I will die trying to teach them . . . [for] Jesus didn't do anything; no more than any Believer."[29]

Karriem's advancement in the Nation of Islam was swift, but not so accelerated that Fard exempted him from the initiation rituals that others had to perform. To officially join the movement, the interested observer had to first write out a letter stating that he or she had accepted the teachings of the Muslims and would like to be given an original name. If the letter contained grammatical or spelling errors, it would be returned to the applicant for rewriting. After an acceptable correspondence was submitted, the new convert would have to memorize and learn, to the satisfaction of the leadership, a number of lessons that dealt with the philosophy of the Nation. The first lesson, "Student Enrollment," is a list of ten questions and answers about various population groups, the size of the earth, and the "Original Man." The next lesson, "Actual Facts," consists of eighteen statements on the natural features of the earth (such as mountains, oceans, and deserts) and their measurements. "English Lesson No. C1," part three, is a series of thirty-six questions and answers that focus on Fard's mission and the predicament of African-Americans. The last teachings, "Lost Found Moslem Lessons No. 1 and 2," are a battery of fifty-four queries and solutions that concentrate on geographic statistics as well as the history of black people, the "white devils," and the end of the white world. Taken together, the lessons were taught in classes attended by initiates fed up with their plight in America.[30]

Learning the lessons could be tedious, and perhaps the initial interest in the organization of many individuals was lost on this requirement. For those who persevered, however, the repetition in the lessons and the pronouncements of Muslim officials guaranteed that at least some of the information was committed to memory. In many ways, the Nation of Islam was organized in a fashion conducive to the recruitment of disenchanted Christians. Passages from known texts such as the Bible, which was ironically transformed into a cudgel against the "icemakers" (or the Christian clergy, who froze the minds of the people in ignorance), as well as less familiar books such as the Qur'an, which Fard had supposedly interpreted from the original Arabic, supplemented the lessons and sermons of ministers. Additionally, other trappings of the African-American church, such as the collection of offerings and an initial fixation on Fard as a second Jesus, made the transition from Christianity to Islam smoother for many believers and gave the temple a less alien atmosphere. While the ex–"icehouse" member could definitely look forward to a heavy dose of anti-Christian rhetoric upon joining the Nation, the movement was, nevertheless, deeply rooted in the traditions of the black church.[31]

Once a pupil had mastered the lessons, he or she was given an "original" Arabic name or an X, which represented the surnames of unknown ancestors as well as the fact that the person had given up the vices of the world and was now an ex-alcoholic, ex-prostitute, ex–drug addict, ex–Uncle Tom, and/or ex-slave. The X was meant to be a temporary name until Fard, and later Karriem, bestowed upon the follower an Arabic name such as Ali, Muhammad, or Sharrieff. Yet, a number of Muslims would go years or even a lifetime before the X was replaced. Typically, believers would be identified by their first names followed by an X. For example, John Smith became John X. If there was more than one John in the temple, subsequent members with that name would be identified as John 2X, John 3X, and so on.

Often, to avoid confusion, Muslims would keep their "slave names" and simply insert an X before the surnames, e.g., John X Smith. The new name, whatever it turned out to be, symbolized the new identity of the convert as a restored member of the original Black Nation. The granting of original names and Xs represented a psychological break with the "blind, deaf, and dumb" previous existence of the convert and a submergence into the collective identity of the Nation of Islam and knowledge of self and others. In the eyes of the believers, the name change was ultimately a liberating experience akin to an emancipation from slavery.[32]

From the beginning, the new convert's role in temple life was determined by a structured arrangement of authority and obligations. As much as possible, the Nation isolated the individual Muslim from those outside influences it deemed destructive and attempted to redefine the values of followers within the context of Fardian Islam. To do this, the leadership of the temple waged a propaganda war against white America to the extent that it was clear to all who entered the temple that they were surely in another world. Nothing in Western society was sacred or revered, and the symbols of the white world were singled out for scorn. On a blackboard in the temple Fard had drawn pictures of the American flag, the Islamic star and crescent (or "the National"), and a cross. The sketches were initially used to illustrate the life-giving qualities of Islam and the evil and deleterious effects of Americanism and Christianity. Later, the question "Which one will survive? The War of Armageddon" was added to remind the Muslims of the impending fall of America. Along with the wearing of fezzes and miniature National pins, the new convert was channeled away from the ways of the world during the initial stages of membership.[33]

In addition to psychological conditioning, the early incorporation of new members into the organizational structure of the movement was a primary concern of the leadership, and a number of positions and institutions were created to address this issue. At the top of the Nation's hierarchy were, of course, Fard and his Supreme Minister, Elijah Karriem, who ruled the movement in a monarchical manner. Serving at the pleasure of "the savior," a cadre of assistant ministers dedicated to clean living and spreading Truth administered the temple's everyday affairs and instructed the believers. Next was the Fruit of Islam, which was established among the men in the Nation to maintain order and decorum in the temple. Under Supreme Captain Kalot Muhammad (Elijah's younger brother), the Fruit enforced the laws of the movement through example first but by coercion when necessary. The men in this wing of the organization were trained in fighting tactics, drilled along military lines, and looked to for protection in the event of outside interference in temple affairs. An intelligence service, adjunctive to the Fruit of Islam, was formed among loyal members to keep up with the activities of those suspected of breaking temple laws.[34]

As a counterpart to the Muslim police force, the Muslim Girls' Training and General Civilization Class (MGT-GCC) was founded to instruct women in domestic affairs such as cooking, sewing, and cleaning as well as in the proper role of a Muslim woman in family and temple life. This women's sphere of the Nation was also headed by a female Supreme Captain, who was assisted by lieutenants in the enforcement of organizational policies regarding females. Also, for the benefit of children in the movement, a University of Islam, which was actually a grade school, was set up to instruct minors in a variety of subjects, including mathematics, astronomy, and the "general knowledge of ending spook [white] civilization." As evidenced by the elaboration of authority and functions, the leadership of the Nation believed in a holistic approach to organization building and strove hard to reduce the attractiveness of the outside world by providing meaningful associations and activities for the new converts, the segment of the membership that was the most transient.[35]

During 1932, it became increasingly clear that backsliding among new initiates was not the biggest problem facing the Nation of Islam. Rather, rivalries within the leadership surfaced as the major source of organizational instability. As mentioned earlier, by the time of Elijah Karriem's promotion to Supreme Minister, tensions started to emerge in the movement along personal and ideological lines. Karriem was not the first individual to be appointed Fard's chief lieutenant; two other members, Abdul Muhammad and Othman Ali, had previously served as the leader's right-hand men. More so than the latter, however, Muhammad was apparently appalled by the selection of Karriem and expressed his dismay by exacerbating divisions in the movement. A former member of the MSTA, he began to emphasize primarily the teachings of Noble Drew Ali and only touched on Fard's lessons when they served his purpose. Possibly, Muhammad may have even exploited the membership for financial aggrandizement. According to Satokata Takahashi, a Japanese propagandist who encouraged the Nation's view of Imperial Japan as a champion of the darker races, the Muslim dissenter was "a fraud" not really concerned about the salvation of African-Americans or much else. Consequently, following Karriem's appointment, Fard's first assignment for the new minister was to take notes on what Muhammad preached and report back.[36]

Over the next several months, animosities within the movement continued to boil and would perhaps have exploded if it had not been for an incident that abruptly interrupted the proselytizing and growth of the Nation. At one time, Fard dealt with outside scrutiny of the movement by simply paying off those law enforcement officials who voiced concern about Muslim activities. Routinely, he brushed aside black Christian leaders who were bold enough to confront him with "baffling questions and [demands for] proof about his prophecy." By the fall of 1932, these remedies were no longer effective, as events placed him in the midst of a scandal that threatened to topple his leadership and movement.[37]

On November 20, Robert Harris, a forty-four-year-old black migrant from Tennessee, invited a neighbor, James Smith, into his home around nine o'clock in the morning. According to his later confession, Harris informed his guest that Harris had been "commanded to kill some one by the Gods of Islam" and that the order was based on a fifteen-hundred-year-old prophecy. Smith, uncooperative at first, later resigned himself to be the sacrificial victim after being told that death would make him "the saviour of the world." At noon, the appointed time for the immolation, Harris forced his wife, the "queen" Bertha, to hold a clock while Smith was positioned in a chair before an altar. As stipulated by the gods, the killing could not take place before the victim freely consented. The executioner asked his guest, "Smith, do you still want to die?" The seated man nodded and replied, "Yes," but apparently thought better of the situation and put up some resistance. Harris, "to quiet him," seized a conveniently placed rear-wheel axle and struck Smith, crushing his skull. Discarding the seventy-five-pound auto part, Harris hoisted the fallen man onto the altar. Methodically and with conviction, he impaled "the saviour" in the heart with an eight-inch knife, "thrust to the hilt." Smith died on the improvised altar, and the sacrificial instrument was left in him for hours. When the body was discovered by neighbors later in the day, Harris and his wife, the prime suspects, were immediately taken into police custody. The crime, premeditated and heinous, would have convulsive ramifications for the Nation of Islam.[38]

The relationship of Harris to Fard's Muslims was vague, although there was probably some connection between the suspect, the Nation, and the Moorish-Americans. During interrogations, Harris claimed that he was the "king" of the Order of Islam, a small cell of one hundred people who had probably broken with the Nation of Islam or the MSTA. In their investigation, the Detroit police appear to have erroneously concluded that the Nation of Islam, followers of Noble Drew Ali, and Harris's organization were one and the same and persecuted in general African-Americans with Islamic leanings. The killing turned out to be as much a pretext for an anti-Muslim propaganda crusade launched by the black clergy as it was for law enforcement repression. Shortly after the murder, ministers were quick to condemn what they believed to be the "fanatical teachings and barbarous practices" of the Muslims and implored the citizens of the city not to hold the entire black community "responsible for the development of the cult." While they expressed "a feeling of pity . . . for those who have so grievously been misled," they, nonetheless, allied themselves with the police department to assist "in combating the sinister influences of voodooism."[39]

Adding to the hysteria, social workers came forward with tales of how

Harris had threatened their lives and how he and other African-Americans openly talked about "the infidels perishing and the 'beys' taking over the country." A hit list, disclosed to police by Harris himself, revealed a larger plot to murder Mayor Frank Murphy, Judge Edward J. Jeffries, and other public officials. The more information about Harris made available to the press, which unduly sensationalized the story, the more intense the pressure on Fard and the Nation of Islam. The implication of the group in the murder actually occurred during a newspaper interview with Edward Harris, the suspect's brother, who ironically was trying to defend the Muslims against the charges that the police and others were leveling against them. Armed with a pretense and a warrant to arrest one W. D. Fard, Detroit authorities knew whom they were looking for but did not know whether they would find a Moroccan who taught sixty-six-trillion-year-old histories, a "Mohammedan" who sold Turkish names to blacks, or some other individual who fitted the strange descriptions that were cropping up in press reports daily.[40]

On Wednesday morning, November 23, Fard was apprehended while leaving his hotel room at 1 West Jefferson Street. He had probably guessed that the arrest would come and did not resist the police officers who seized him. During the incident, he remained cognizant of the role he was playing as the savior of black Detroit, and for the consumption of his followers who looked on, he smiled "enigmatically" as he left with law enforcement officials. Once at police headquarters, he answered questions circumspectly and in his typical messianic vein. According to police and press transcripts, Fard identified himself as the "supreme being on earth" and claimed responsibility for starting the Nation of Islam, assisted by Ugan Ali, who was also arrested. To support himself and the activities of the group, he took up collections from followers and sold each new member an "identification card." Though he received a commission from a printing house for the cards, Fard stated that the organization's treasury was empty and that "I have had to ask the brethren to contribute a fund for the payment of an overdue electric bill in the temple." Despite the insolvency of the Detroit Muslims, the "Oriental fakir" boasted of other branches of the Nation of Islam in cities such as Chicago, New York, and Philadelphia where he supposedly had "large followings."[41]

In regard to Harris's deed, Fard categorically denied having instructed anyone to sacrifice human beings in the name of religion, although he did suggest death for those guilty of "disturb[ing] the peace in our temples." In light of evidence independent of that discovered by the police inquiry, the Muslim leader was perhaps not entirely honest in his statement on the matter. It is probably true that Harris was not a member of the Nation of Islam when he killed James Smith. Also, Fard more than likely did not give him a direct order to kill; it may even be that the two men had never actually met. However, the belief in blood sacrifices was definitely a part of early Muslim doctrine, notwithstanding Fard's denial. To give an example, in the organization's lessons, one of the question-answer exchanges that new initiates had to memorize reads as follows:

QUESTION: Why does Muhammed and any Moslem murder the devil? What is the duty of each Moslem in regards to four devils? What reward does a Moslem receive by presenting the four devils at one time?

ANSWER: Because he is one hundred percent wicked, and will not keep and obey the laws of Islam. His ways and actions are like a snake of the grafted type. So Mohammed learned that he could not reform the devils, so they had to be murdered. All Moslems will murder the devil because they know he is a snake and also if he be allowed to live, he would sting someone else. Each Moslem is required to bring four devils, and by bringing and presenting four at one time, his reward is a button to wear on the lapel of his coat, also free transportation to the holy city of Mecca to see Brother Mohammed.

In the absence of instructions to the contrary, this part of the catechism could be interpreted as it is presented verbatim: the killing of four "devils" (whites) would gain one entrance into Mecca. Arguably, Robert Harris, in his own distorted way, was trying to carry out the literal essence of this teaching. Elijah Karriem, in a later interview, admitted that Fard had actually instructed Muslims to kill four whites in order "to take the fear of the white man out of the hearts of the followers." However, it is possible that the purpose of the lesson was more symbolic than it appears. Whatever the case may be, the shadow of "voodooism" hung over the Nation for years because of this teaching and the perhaps unrelated murder of James Smith. As far as its immediate effects, Fard, following the police interrogation, was admitted to the psychopathic ward of Receiving Hospital for observation, along with Harris and Ugan Ali.[42]

Events over the next two weeks seemed to happen too quickly and unpredictably even for a witch-hunt. Harris, whose sanity was suspect from the beginning, staged a two-day hunger strike, hallucinated, attacked his jailers, and finally was declared mentally unbalanced and committed to Ionia State Hospital for the Criminal Insane. Ugan Ali, an early associate of Fard's, recanted his support for the movement and "promised to use his influence in disbanding the group." As a reward for his cooperation with the authorities, he was released from Receiving Hospital on December 6.

On that same day, Fard was also freed from detention, but under different conditions. His followers, by the hundreds, had protested his arrest at rallies before the First Precinct—which was in charge of investigating "voodooism" in Detroit, the courthouse, and various other places, where a few were arrested by nervous policemen. According to some law enforcement and newspaper reports, the number of African-American Muslims in the city ranged from five to eight thousand. The one thousand letters of support seized from Fard's residence revealed many more in "all sections of the country." If anything, the arrest of the Muslim leader had caused only a minute, localized decline in the number of people affiliated with the Nation of Islam.[43]

In combating the Muslims with overt repression, the police learned that their actions had caused many black Detroiters to view the whole situation as a racist assault on their community instead of an issue of law and order. As bystanders while African-Americans exercised religious freedom, the police learned that organizations such as Fard's expanded what the press called their "menacing grip." As an alternative short of making a martyr of the leader, the Detroit police department decided to banish him from the city permanently, hoping that this would demoralize his followers and fracture the group's strength. Again posing no resistance to his captors, Fard agreed to leave the Motor City and promised never to return. *The Detroit Free Press,* believing as the police did that the matter was settled, reported the agreement in an article entitled "Voodoo's Reign Here Is Broken."[44]

But the matter was not settled. Over the next few months, in the early part of 1933, Fard continued to secretly guide the Nation of Islam, working mostly behind the scenes and through his loyal Supreme Minister. Because of the lingering vigilance of the authorities and black Christians, he was aware that in time they would find out about his presence. In the meantime, he tried to groom Elijah Karriem for the leadership of the organization. During the winter and spring of 1933, Fard tied up doctrinal loose ends with his chief lieutenant and instituted some cosmetic changes that were designed to make Karriem more palatable to the believers as their new custodian. According to the Supreme Minister, Fard began by first adopting a new name for himself, Wallace Fard Muhammad, and started placing a renewed emphasis on his divinity. The teacher then offered Karriem the new "big name," Abdul, but was dismayed when his lieutenant declined the proposed change, because it reminded him of the heretical Abdul Muhammad. In response, Fard Muhammad supposedly told his disciple, "I will give you a better name than Karriem. . . . You take Muhammad, My name." Henceforth, Elijah Karriem, formerly Elijah Poole of Georgia, became Elijah Muhammad, the Supreme Minister of the Nation of Islam. The honor was, of course, not lost on Elijah, who immediately convinced most of his relatives in Detroit to adopt the new surname, including his father and mother, who became Wali and Marie Muhammad. For the most part, activities such as the fine-tuning of doctrine and the transfer of administrative power to Elijah occupied Fard Muhammad's last months in the city. Ultimately, it was all meant to prepare the Muslims for the inevitable day when their beloved messiah would be permanently exiled from their midst.[45]

On May 25, the awaited arrest, on charges of disturbing the peace, came as the Muslim leader knew it would. He, as before, complied with the routine interrogation at the police station and patiently answered more questions about Islam and human sacrifice. According to the police transcript, Fard Muhammad was more candid than before about his presence in the Motor City and stated for the record that the Nation of Islam, its teachings, and Muslim activities in general were "a racket" from the start. His whole purpose behind organizing the black community in Detroit was reportedly to get "all the money out of it he could." Whether the statement was simply a case of Fard Muhammad's telling the police what they wanted to hear, a canard concocted by his interrogators, or the ugly truth, his real motives were now, as far as the authorities were concerned, a moot point. In unambiguous terms, the law enforcement officials again ordered the Muslim leader to leave the city and perhaps intimated the severity of the consequences if he reneged a second time on his promise. Fard Muhammad quietly assented to the demand, and for the good of peace, his captors agreed to allow him to speak to his followers before his departure, a last request that no doubt benefited both parties. It was, nonetheless, made abundantly clear that he was forever unwelcome in the city, even among the African-American population of the swelling ghetto.[46]

The scene of Fard Muhammad's sorrowful farewell to his followers can be compared to the trauma that Garveyites endured during the deportation of their "Black Moses" in 1927. According to Elijah Muhammad, he had already been prepared for the event during one of his theological huddles with the leader. Using the words of martyrs, the teacher had reassured him that "I love them [black people]. I will destroy the Nations of the Earth to save them and then die Myself." Elijah, touched as usual by Fard Muhammad's sacrificial remarks, agreed, "I'll do the same." For the crowd that gathered to see his departure, the leader stood poised before his car and consoled them with words of defiance and encouragement. Some openly wept for their teacher, and others crowded around his car to see and touch him one last time. During the send-off, the leader's sense for the dramatic did not fail him, and his last words were still quoted years later. "Don't worry," he asserted confidently to well-wishers. "I am with you; I will be back to you in the near future to lead you out of this hell." With these parting words, Fard Muhammad, "the savior" of the Nation of Islam, sped away in his car, leaving behind memories that would become legend.[47]

In some ways, the departure of Fard Muhammad from Detroit was the end of the beginning. Now, the believers themselves would have to teach and guide each other without the benefit of what they believed to be a divine presence. In other ways, the leader's banishment was the beginning of the end, at least in regard to organizational unity. Internal challenges to the leadership of Elijah Muhammad bubbled to the surface quickly, along both personal and doctrinal lines. Unable to hold the movement together for more than a few months, the Supreme Minister could only helplessly watch as splinter groups siphoned off members. Abdul Muhammad, who was now openly preaching Moorish-American Islam, started a rival organization whose distinguishing features were its sworn loyalty to the U.S. constitution and avowed hatred for Elijah and his followers. Another group, perhaps irreverently referred to as "Rebels against the Will of Allah," was also formed by Muslims seeking to escape the stigma that rumors of human sacrifice had smeared upon the parent organization. Police crackdowns and persecution were a constant throughout 1933 and succeeded in scaring away many members who could ill afford entanglements with the law. Communism and the African-American church even claimed a number of believers who had become disillusioned by the infighting. By the early months of the following year, the situation had deteriorated to the degree that Elijah Muhammad feared for his life. Sometimes accompanied by his wife, Clara, who had just given birth to their seventh child, Wallace (named by and after Fard Muhammad in utero), the Supreme Minister began making periodic trips to Nation of Islam Temple No. 2 in Chicago in search of refuge from those he called "the hypocrites."[48]

During one of these getaways to Chicago, Elijah and Fard Muhammad apparently had their last encounter. According to Elijah's version of events, before he disappeared for good in June 1934, the teacher gave him a list of 104 books to read and a copy of the Qur'an written in both Arabic and English. As Elijah pondered over the tome, it became more apparent to him that his mentor was, indeed, "Allah himself incarnated." Fard Muhammad, fearful of staying in one place too long, wrote his disciple letters when he left town, instructing him in religious and organizational matters. When the Chicago police arrested him one last time in mid-1934, the leader summoned Elijah, as he had during previous detentions, so that he "may see and learn the price of TRUTH for us (the so-called Negroes)." According to the Supreme Minister, around this time Fard Muhammad completed the transfer of power over the Temple People, the faction of the Nation of Islam that had remained loyal to Elijah and the lessons of his teacher. As the ultimate honor, the teacher supposedly bestowed the title of "Messenger of Allah" upon his chief lieutenant and promised to give him a book authored by himself at some future date. Though Elijah implored him to stay following his release, Fard Muhammad demurred and assured him, "You don't need Me anymore," since a messenger had been raised by Allah to teach the people. When asked whether he would return, the leader equivocated and told his follower to search the Bible for the answer, for it was sealed in prophecy. The last words and handshakes were exchanged in an airport terminal, following over thirty months of instruction and friendship. For Elijah, the final moments were as pregnant with mystery and symbolism as the first, as the man he knew as Fard Muhammad, the second Jesus, the Mahdi, the Son of Man, and Allah in Person soared into the Chicago sky.[49]

Elijah Muhammad's interpretation of the brief, shadowy history of Fard Muhammad's leadership in Detroit established a foundation for his ultimate ascension to the head of the Nation of Islam. During his tenure as "the savior," Fard Muhammad had, indeed, favored Elijah and allowed him to reign with him in the subordinate role of Supreme Minister. Gradually, over the course of three years, the two invented W. D. Fard (later Fard Muhammad) as the messiah of the Black Nation and then eventually as Allah in the flesh. Propaganda in the form of rhetoric and symbols was instrumental in this transformation. Moreover, the ideological landscape of Detroit, shaped by Garvey, Noble Drew Ali, the black church, and other forces, made the messianism, nationalism, and millenarianism of the Nation of Islam acceptable to a certain segment of the African-American community. White racism and the weight of the Depression went a long way toward making the self-styled savior attractive to some, and the financial opportunities that the organization presented to others, such as Elijah Muhammad and Abdul Muhammad, supplemented its theological appeal. The Supreme Minister would over the next several years skillfully package the history of his teacher's sojourn in Detroit in divine terms and characterize his own leadership, as the Messenger of Allah, as flowing directly from Fard Muhammad. In a real sense, the mythology that he (and his mentor) had created was necessary to his continuing primacy in the organization. In the future, the legitimacy of his leadership would be dependent upon convincing others that he alone had been favored by God in person and was uniquely privy to his will.

Back in Detroit, the Temple People continued to skirmish with other Muslim groups for legitimacy and converts. When Elijah Muhammad made his messengership known in the city and openly deified his teacher, angry rivals heaped ridicule upon him and his followers and insisted upon calling him Karriem. The authorities, who were interested in rooting out African-American Muslims in general, intensified their campaign against the Temple People in April 1934 by interrupting classes at the University of Islam. The Michigan State Board of Education, under the pretense that Muslim children were being illegally deprived of the benefits of public education, ordered the arrests of teachers at the school. When law enforcement officials attempted to close the facility, the instructors resisted and a scuffle ensued.

Although there were no deaths, a number of the police officers and Muslims were injured.[50]

Law enforcement officials arrested Muhammad himself on April 17 in the temple on Hastings Street and charged him with "contributing to the delinquency of a minor child and voodooism." Most of the charges against the thirteen other individuals apprehended were dropped following protests by the Muslims; but Muhammad was found guilty and sentenced either to pay a ten-dollar fine or to spend ten days in jail. He was also placed on six months' probation, during which time he had to see to it that Muslim children were put back into the public schools. His philosophical differences with the school board and what the Muslims called "spook" education would not allow him to comply with the order, and apparently the state did not press the issue. However, mounting interference in temple affairs by the police, an unsuccessful attempt by an Ethiopian nationalist, Wyxzewixard S. J. Challouehliczilczese, to channel the group's funds to Haile Selassie's empire, and a five-hundred-dollar contract on his life issued by a Muslim opponent forced Muhammad to leave the city anyway in September. In his absence, he appointed Theodore Rozier, a trusted Haitian assistant, to supervise Temple No. 1 in Detroit while he relocated the headquarters of the movement to less hostile Chicago.[51]

In only three decades, the Great Migration had brought tens of thousands of black Southerners to Chicago looking for better, more humane conditions than existed in the Southern United States. By the time Elijah Muhammad arrived there in 1934, the Windy City had one of the largest urban communities of African-Americans in the country, second only to New York's. At the turn of the century, Chicago, like Detroit, Milwaukee, and other Midwestern industrial centers, had had few black residents. In 1910, they numbered only 44,103, 78 percent of whom lived on the South Side. By 1940, the number had swelled to 277,731, accounting for over 8 percent of the population. In contrast to its agrarian Southern counterpart, the Black Belt of Chicago was an industrial proletariat incorporated into the city's economy, albeit at its lowest rungs. However, like depressed rural areas of the black South, the expanding ghettos of Chicago were no mere accidents of history and reflected systematic efforts by those who controlled the city to keep African-Americans on the fringes of power.[52]

Despite the similarities, Chicago was by no means simply a Southern town in a Northern milieu. The city offered opportunities for blacks to become more than sharecroppers and low-wage workers, and black access to the hallmarks of citizenship became commonplace early on. For example, African-Americans routinely voted for their own local politicians. In 1915, they succeeded in electing Oscar DePriest alderman and thirteen years later had gained the electoral strength to make him the first black U.S. congressman since 1901. In education, black children, for a time, attended schools with whites, which guaranteed a level of quality in and funding for these institutions. Additionally, a modest degree of upward mobility even resulted in class tensions among middle- and working-class African-Americans on the South Side and in other smaller black areas of Englewood, the West Side, and the North and Near North Sides. Still, "industrial democracy" in Chicago had its limits, and racism in the city was all too easy to find.[53]

The housing and employment situations demonstrated most cogently the impact of race on the city's evolution. Like many urban centers, Chicago was a town of tenants, and most people of both races were renters in 1940. African-Americans, nevertheless, were more likely to be leasing their residences than whites and were restricted to the poorest and most crowded areas of the metropolis. On the eve of the American military buildup for World War II, job prospects for black and white Chicagoans continued to show gross disparities. The black unemployment rate, or more accurately, the percentage "seeking work," stood at 19.3 percent in 1940, compared to 10.6 percent among both native and immigrant whites. In the same year, 16.4 percent of African-American laborers worked on public emergency relief projects, compared to only 2.8 percent of whites. Although the nightlife of State Street may have soothed the economic bruises that the black community received during the Depression, gaps between the two races in terms of jobs, housing, and social status in Chicago would remain an open sore for decades to come.[54]

The move to the Windy City in 1934 was difficult for Muhammad and his family, not to mention the Temple People in Detroit, who had come to esteem their "Holy Apostle." The Chicago group, though vigorous in its search for new converts, was not able to maintain its leader financially or do much else. Islamic and separatist teachings among blacks were not new in Chicago, and long days of "fishing," or searching, for new initiates often turned out disappointing. On a number of occasions when the movement's coffers were empty, Muhammad found working in packinghouses and other businesses a necessary evil to support his family. To facilitate recruitment, the Muslims started a newspaper called *The Final Call to Islam*, which praised their savior, Fard Muhammad, and warned non-Muslims of the coming "destruction of the Caucasian world by God Almighty." Services were held wherever the Temple People could worship before black Christians, the police, or the FBI convinced the landlord to evict them. Unfortunately for the Muslims, their newspaper floundered and eventually became too expensive to continue. Depressed Chicago, like economically devastated Detroit, seemed to produce too few African-Americans who were willing or able to support the grand vision of the Nation of Islam.[55]

Two incidents in Chicago during early 1935 brought the Temple People again into direct confrontation with municipal authorities. In the first, which occurred on March 5, fifty to sixty believers, following a three-day fast, appeared at the Central Police Headquarters on Eleventh Street to support Rosie Hassan, who had been charged with allegedly striking a white woman on a streetcar. The charge was dubious from the start and, following a brief hearing, was dismissed by the mediator of Women's Court. Pleased by the results of the case, the fez-topped Muslims "rose with military precision" and proceeded to leave the courtroom. By accident, the group moved toward the wrong door and was forcibly redirected by bailiffs to the proper exit. In an already tense situation, one of the white guards spoke to or touched a Muslim woman in a manner that was perceived as insulting. In short order, a pushing match began between the Temple People and the bailiffs. A challenge issued by one of the female believers to a court official ("Take off your glasses and I'll whip you") preceded the throwing of chairs by the unarmed Muslims and the firing of guns by the guards. When the commotion ended, police captain Joseph Palczynski had died of a heart attack, two members of the Nation of Islam and one policeman (a victim of friendly fire) had been shot, and thirty-eight others, mostly Muslims, suffered injuries. In the two-day trial that followed, forty of the Muslims who stood their ground against the bailiffs were sentenced to jail; the sixteen men convicted of contempt of court received six-month terms, and twenty-four women were given thirty-day sentences.[56]

In April, a second clash with law enforcement officials occurred over the lawfulness of the Muslims' University of Islam in Chicago. Similar to the earlier Detroit episode, a legal complaint against one of the temple members who had sent his children to the Nation's grade school brought the Muslims to court en masse. The air of disciplined defiance that had characterized previous appearances of the Temple People in court was again present, along with the nervous defensiveness of white bailiffs and other court officials, who were not used to dealing with orderly, yet proud, groups of blacks. As the courtroom became packed with observers, a few of the Muslim women were manhandled by two court deputies, and at least one of the female believers was pushed through the courtroom door. Predictably, their male escorts, sworn to protect black womanhood, intervened and engaged the guards in fistfights. In the chaos, the deputies fired a fusillade of bullets at the Muslims, wounding a number of them. In addition to injuries, the indirect costs of resistance in this case were not negligible, for a number of people left the movement after this encounter with the law. The University of Islam, nevertheless, remained open, and the Muslims continued to insist upon being allowed to "shape our children first."[57]

Despite their opposition, city officials and even rival Muslim groups were not the most serious threats to the leadership of Elijah Muhammad in Chicago. Rather, an internal clique of contenders who rose up against him in late 1935 created the most dire situation to date. This movement to oust the leader was spearheaded by his younger brother Kalot and an assistant minister named Augustus Muhammad, both of whom lived with the Muslim chief. The mutiny seems to have been caused by Elijah's refusal to allow note-taking in the minister training course and by the attainment of "a little wisdom" by the emboldened dissenters. Actually, internecine opposition to Elijah Muhammad's messengership had accumulated over months and eventually reached the stage where "over 75 per cent of [the Temple People] were hypocrites." When the fifth column decided to strike, enough followers had sided with the rebels to turn the odds clearly against the leader's remaining in power. The dissenters issued warnings, even death threats, and Elijah Muhammad was ultimately compelled to flee Chicago to save his life. Organizational and personal arrangements made before his departure were necessarily improvised and hastily put into place. From among the loyal followers, whose numbers had shrunk from four hundred to thirteen by September, the deposed leader selected Malik X to instruct the faithful during his absence. At home, he regretfully passed the reins over the household to his wife, Clara, who had suffered along with him during the whole succession ordeal. Following a few precious moments with his family, which would henceforth have to depend largely on Muslim charity for support, Muhammad slipped out of Chicago and traveled to Milwaukee, Wisconsin.[58]

The successful revolt among dissidents in the Allah Temple of Islam No. 2 nearly destroyed everything Muhammad had held sacred over the past four years. The realization of having failed to hold together the legacy that Fard Muhammad had bestowed upon him along with the humiliation of being rejected (and hunted) by once faithful adherents must have left the leader both distraught and depressed as he began his hegira in late 1935. Despite the desperation of his circumstances, his failure in Chicago helped build character and resolve in both Muhammad and among his few partisans. Moreover, the rebellion also instilled in the ousted head minister a greater sense of mission, self-righteousness, and persecution that sometimes bordered on paranoia. In the scheme of things, Muhammad's flight from Chicago in 1935 concluded the loss of a major battle in a lifelong war against orthodox Muslims, quasi-Islamic groups, and Nation of Islam apostates. Of the three groups, the latter became a permanent symbol of evil for Muhammad, who referred to them henceforth with scorn as "the hypocrites."

CHAPTER 3

THE KNOWLEDGE OF SELF AND OTHERS

*We believed . . . in some of the most fantastic things
that you could ever imagine.*
—Malcolm X[1]

"The Truth" that attracted Elijah Muhammad and eventually tens of thousands of other blacks to Fard Muhammad and his legacy was obviously influenced by Christianity, orthodox Islam, black nationalism, and other faiths and doctrines. However, its originality and power to proselytize lay in its unique appeal to race and racial destiny as well as its attempt to explain in religious terms the history of the world and its impact on the present. Broken down into its constituent theories, the teachings of Fard Muhammad address everything from the origins of God(s) and the nature of heaven and hell to the prescribed diet and attire of Muslims. What Elijah Muhammad and others taught on the streets of Detroit and Chicago during the Great Depression was, indeed, a religion that dealt with all of the major questions that people have posed about their place in the universe since time immemorial.

Rooted in Fard Muhammad's teachings, the development of the Muslims' theology remained remarkably consistent with the original lessons until the death of Elijah Muhammad in 1975, save for a few theological alterations made by the latter. The ideological influences of the Garvey Movement, the MSTA, the African-American church, and other groups also remained a constant over the four decades of Muhammad's leadership. Since a complete exposition and analysis of the Truth, in all of its complexity and absurdity, is necessary at this point before the admiration (and repulsion) that it later enjoyed (and suffered) can be fully comprehended, the following discussion provides a path to understanding its inner meanings and the ideological influences behind it.

According to Nation of Islam lore, 76 trillion years ago, before the existence of temporal and material reality, the universe was dark and motionless, void of life. Out of the womb of total darkness was issued an atom that rotated into being and thus began the concept of time. Still spinning, the atom of life matured and developed flesh and blood, brains and power. A corporeal entity, later known as Earth, incubated the dark, growing body until it achieved self-awareness and the power to create. The body, which was once an atom, became a man, a Black Man, "the Original Man," and lord over all that which was engulfed in universal night. In time, the self-created man took on the name Allah or God and proceeded to create others like him in his own dark, majestic image.[2]

Allah, still expanding in knowledge, discovered the secrets of light and fire and kindled a ball of gas that he called sun. The other gods emulated him and threw spheres of flame (stars) into the darkness, some of which traveled to the outer edges of the infinite universe. At his leisure, Allah created a wreath of stars 600 million miles from Earth—his home and favorite celestial body—to separate it from the other bodies. Planets, or masses similar to his beloved Earth, were created and named, seven of which were even endowed with life. On Mars, the inhabitants, though inferior to the Original People of Earth in knowledge and intelligence, eventually created a civilization and became noted for their life expectancy of up to twelve hundred Earth years. In contrast, Pluto (or Pluton, meaning "a little fool") was hurled 4.6 billion miles to the periphery of "the power of the Sunlight" and never became a notable haven of humanoid life, but rather served as a testament to the strength of Allah's sun, which was still able to bathe the tiny planet in light and dictate its orbit even at such great distance.[3]

After lighting their universe and adorning it with planets, Allah and the other gods concentrated their efforts on developing their homeland of Earth. The black people, the first and sole human residents of the planet, were organized into thirteen tribes, which formed a Nation united by skin color (black), religion (Islam), and natural disposition (righteousness). Since Allah, the first man and founder of the Black Nation, was born at the beginning of time and no written documents were kept until 6 trillion years later, the black people, or Nation of Islam, had no birth record nor knowledge of any history prior to Allah's ascendancy. Ruling the earth from the sprawling continent of Asia, the black people prided themselves on being the original "Asiatic blackman, the maker, the owner, the cream of the planet earth, God of the universe." Indeed, their feats seemed to affirm as much. For instance, although other life-forms on earth, such as lower animals, appear to have always been present and were perhaps not fashioned by the black man, the mountains, along with other features of the planet, were products of the Nation's ingenuity. To create these massive mounds of dirt and rock, black god-scientists used motorized bombs tipped with drills and packed with dynamite to burrow into the earth (which at one time was smooth) and blast up mountains as high as six miles. While a miraculous triumph by any standard, other wonders would follow on an even larger scale.[4]

As described above, the creation myth of the Muslims was closely tied to Judeo-Christian and Quranic traditions, but there are interesting variations. The birth and anthropomorphic character of the God of the Nation and his fashioning of other gods in his own image is analogous to the creation of Adam and Eve in the Bible. Furthermore, the glorification of man as being black, naturally righteous, and linked to God is metaphorically connected to the Quranic description of man as being created from mud and animated by the breath and spirit of Allah (Surahs 6:28 and 95:4). For those believers with Christian backgrounds who came into the movement, Fard Muhammad's description of the beginning of time was familiar and perhaps helped them to digest other parts of the Nation's cosmology.

The portrayal of God as a black man served two purposes, both designed to facilitate the recruitment of members. First, the depiction stressed that African-Americans were as close to being divine as any other group and had a history that went back further than slavery in the United States. Second, the portrayal of God as man, made of flesh and blood, and his construction of the universe conveyed the idea that human beings had the power to affect their environments, for better or for worse. The use of dynamite and drills by the gods of the Nation of Islam to create mountains and other natural wonders illustrates this point and relates the story of the creation to contemporary technologies and conditions. The main purposes of this description of the theogony of black gods and the "Original People" were to give African-Americans a sense of pride in a glorious, pristine past that stretched back trillions of years and to prime them for Fard Muhammad's declaration that he was the Mahdi, and later, God in person. Without veering too far off course from the Judeo-Christian and Quranic versions, the cosmology of the Muslims was in large part intended to attract black Christians to the Nation, who would find the racial core of the story inviting and the biblical shell of the message comforting.

The contention of Fard Muhammad that there was intelligent life on Mars, though absurd on the surface, utilized a popular theme in early-twentieth-century cinema to convince blacks that sovereign worlds existed outside of white control. Throughout this period, many Westerners exhibited a general fascination with both the prospect of extraterrestrial life and the possibility of an alien invasion. Sporadic reports of UFO sightings and the advent of the airplane fueled interest in Mars and inspired a panoply of motion pictures including *A Trip to Mars* (1903), *England Invaded* (1909), *A Message from Mars* (1921), and *Mars Calling* (1923). Of course, the ultimate Martian thriller would be the radio adaptation in 1938 of H. G. Wells's, *The War of the Worlds*, which frightened thousands of listeners due to its realism. Fard Muhammad capitalized on popular images of Mars as a mysterious and possibly inhabited planet in an effort to emphasize the power of his black God and to portray white hegemony on earth as limited. While certainly steeped in fiction, this tactic was perhaps quite effective in attracting some blacks to the Nation, especially in the era of zeppelins and high-tech entertainment.[5]

To continue the narrative, after the discovery of writing the gods of the Nation of Islam decided that it was necessary to chronicle the future. This was due to both the people's need for predictability and the mortality of the gods. The deities of the Black Nation, being mere men of flesh and blood but exercising great power and insight, lived and died as others did. Some would die from the boredom caused by knowledge of the future; others would simply perish from poor diets. To make the transition from the reign of one god to another smoother for the Original People, twenty-three god-scientists were impaneled to write the future history of the Nation covering the subsequent twenty-five thousand years, and a twenty-fourth was responsible for "the analyzation and calculation" of what was written. The latter god-scientist also served as the paramount deity (or Allah) of the black people, and it was his knowledge and vision that filled the pages of the chronicle. Typically, a god did not live longer than one or two hundred years, and no one in the recorded history of the Black Nation lived longer than a millennium. Despite their life spans, the knowledge of each paramount god guided the affairs of the black people for twenty-five thousand years, a legacy that guaranteed his place in the Asiatic pantheon. Occasionally, prophets arose from the midst of the Original People to reveal to them the will of Allah, but only after the book authored by the god-scientists (whether it be a Qur'an, the Torah, or the Bible) was ten thousand years old. Following the time covered by each tome and the expiration of the spiritual vision of each paramount god, another deity was selected from among the god-scientists to write a new book, based on his own knowledge, for the next twenty-five-thousand-year cycle.[6]

The intimate relationship between the Black Nation and divine power made righteous Muslims out of the Original People. Their religion of Islam was incorporated into their very nature, and a love of peace, freedom, and justice was instinctual to them. In a sense, every black person was a deity insofar as their inherent goodness brought them close to the essence of God, whose proper name was Allah. Free of sin and iniquity, the world that the black man had constructed in Asia was nothing less than paradise.[7]

Sixty-six trillion years ago, a renegade god-scientist tried to pull the curtain on the golden age of the black man. An iconoclast, this deity was dismayed by the multilingual civilization that the black people had built and endeavored to introduce a lingua franca to replace regional dialects. The atmosphere of the planet, however, foiled his attempts to standardize the language, and failing in his efforts, he decided to destroy the earth along with the thirteen tribes "to satisfy His mind." The feat required tremendous destructive power, and the god-scientist almost mustered enough force to do it. Single-minded, he drilled a hole to the center of the earth and packed it with dynamite more powerful than that in use today. The explosion that he set off disrupted mountains and displaced whole oceans, ultimately dividing the earth into two pieces. The larger part, earth, was jolted thirty-six thousand miles out of its original "pocket" before it settled into another niche and began revolving again. The smaller planetary chunk, the moon, lost all of its water to the earth and was propelled twelve thousand miles. Though the cataclysm, later referred to as "the deportation of the moon," happened in a matter of split seconds, it changed the course of the Black Nation's history forever. The divine demolitionist failed in his goal of destroying the black people, but he did extinguish one of the thirteen tribes. Apparently, the unlucky tribe was either a victim of the blast or had been unfortunate enough to be marooned on the waterless moon where life could not be sustained.[8]

The postexplosion earth was abundant enough in resources to maintain the recuperating Black Nation, which probably suffered a decline in its standard of living, at least for a while. The most resilient of the remaining twelve tribes proved to be the Tribe of Shabazz (pronounced Sha-boz), a black-skinned, straight-haired people whose features were "soft and delicate, fine." Their search for arable land and sparkling waters led them to the Nile River Valley in East Asia (Africa) where they would eventually form a glorious civilization called Egypt and a sister civilization in Mecca, Arabia. Again, the Nation of Islam had created something from nothing and showed the universe that a righteous people could accomplish anything they wished. For the next several trillion years, the Tribe of Shabazz, protected and guided by their God, Allah, governed the black people of the earth with a magnanimous hand, ruling mostly by example.[9]

This part of Fard Muhammad's tale is loaded with meaning and feeds into his creation myth and humanized depiction of God. Again, the mortality, even fallibility, of the gods is stressed in an attempt to disassociate African-Americans from the belief that their creator is eternal, flawless, and noncorporeal. The description of gods as scientists was aimed at giving the myth a rational, calculated veneer, and the tale of the use of modern explosives to "deport" the moon was designed to tie Fard Muhammad's black gods to the twentieth-century world of his black followers. More than anywhere else in the story, the purpose here was to invent a mythical past that would appeal to African-Americans more than the tales of African savagery and American bondage that many believed to be their sole roots.

Thus, Fard Muhammad created the fantasyland of "East Asia" to connect black Americans—whose ancestors were predominantly West Afri-

can—to the ancient civilization of Egypt and the Islamic culture of Arabia. As with his creation story, biblical precedents were relied upon to give credence to the account, exemplified by the twelve "original" black tribes, which symbolized the twelve tribes of Israel mentioned in Revelation 21: 12. However, a doctrinal tension builds here as the narrative progresses. Fard Muhammad has introduced the concept that African-Americans were Islamic by nature, a direct challenge to the Christian leanings of potential converts. Using terms suggestive of the Old Testament, the leader attempts to make the primordial paradise of East Asia even more appealing than the Garden of Eden in order to subvert the foundations of the Judeo-Christian description of paradise and its origin.

Resuming Fard Muhammad's story, fifty thousand years ago an eccentric black scientist named Shabazz proposed that the Tribe of Shabazz explore the rest of Africa, which heretofore had been uninhabited by humans. He theorized that if the tribe lived in the jungles of the continent long enough, it would become tougher and better able to deal with the rigors of life in any setting. The idea was not well received by Shabazz's compatriots, who wrote it off as nonsense. Undiscouraged, the scientist relocated his family to the tropical rain forests of Africa to prove his point. Others, whether inspired by wanderlust or bored with idyllic life on the Nile, followed. Over thousands of years, the immigrants changed phenotypically, only vaguely resembling their ancestors. Their hair, which had been straight, coiled and became kinky; their thin lips swelled, and their noses became broader. The Original People who settled in the jungles of Africa did, indeed, become more rugged physically, but at a cost: they lost the cultural legacy of their forefathers, which resulted in a precipitous decline in their level of civilization. In the end, the scientist Shabazz had made a monumental mistake in leading his people into the woodlands of Africa. For the next several thousand years, the black man would live "a jungle life" in the interior of East Asia, allowing "the weaker of himself to rule."[10]

Following the settlement of East Asia and the resultant deterioration of black culture, the Black Nation faced a number of philosophical crises that almost rended it apart. Originating in the part of Asia known as India about thirty-five thousand years ago, two great religions gained popularity among selected tribes of the Original People. Heretical and contrary to the truth of Allah, these faiths led many of the black people away from the path of Islam. The first doctrine, called Buddhism, tarnished the innate righteousness of its black converts by encouraging them to believe in reincarnation and other "ignorant practices." Even more threatening to the Black Nation than the Buddhist was the believer in Hinduism, who had wandered so far from the timeless religion of Islam that he was content in worshiping "more gods than he can mention." If the Muslims had a natural enemy at this time, it was the Hindus, who quickly became persona non grata in Islamic Asia. Over time, the righteous black people, if forced to choose, would believe it preferable to kill a Hindu and spare a Christian, though the latter would cause the Muslims much grief in the future. Despite the animosities, the Nation of Islam, perhaps due to its love of peace, chose to coexist with the heretics rather than eradicate them from the face of the earth through warfare.[11]

Over the next several millennia, India continued to boil with religious strife until one group, the red-skinned Indians, stepped too far outside the bounds of theological orthodoxy. This sect, which flourished in India sixteen thousand years ago, refused to acknowledge the existence of Allah and discarded Islam completely. The extreme nature of their dissidence was offensive even to the Indians, who had become accustomed to living in a diverse religious community. As a lesson to those who would deny his power and presence, Allah banished the rebels from the Black Nation of Asia, forcing them to travel thousands of miles across the Bering Strait into the uninhabited wilderness later known as America. Still unrepentant, the exiles built idols to worship and prostrated before "the work of their own hands." From his throne on the Nile, Allah completed his chastisement of the red people by later sending to America another group of outcasts, the white people, "to chase . . . and give the Indians another whipping" for their arrogant disobedience.[12]

Here the narrative reveals some of the more disturbing elements of the mythology of the Nation. Strands of anti-Africanism and religious intolerance creep into open view and are made the more pernicious by the guise of religion that cloaks them. Though the Muslims glorified blackness, sub-Saharan Africa was depicted as a savage place populated with uncivilized people. Actually, Fard Muhammad argued that the use of the word *Africa* to denote what he called East Asia was a method of whites to divide people of color who were, in his view, all Asiatics. The repudiation of the terms *Africa* and *Africans* by the early Muslims, starting with Fard Muhammad, was by inference an attempt by the group to rid itself of the Western stereotypes and negative associations that the words attached to blackness. Transforming Africa into "East Asia" made the continent more palatable to those converts who harbored a sense of shame in having roots in Africa. Yet, in a regrettable way, the attempt of Fard Muhammad to rationalize the origins of Negroid features denigrated natural characteristics of blacks from tropical Africa. To depict this part of the continent as uncivilized enough to strip away both the Caucasian features and Islamic culture of the Original People reinforced the myths and racist stereotypes about Africa that were already popular in the Western world.

Added to the anti-African bias inherent in his portrait of the continent, Fard Muhammad's depiction of Hinduism and Buddhism as doctrinal aberrations and Native Americans as a people in revolt against God did little toward giving his followers a realistic view of Asian and Amerindian history. The purpose here was both to steer blacks away from the two religions (and toward the Nation's Islam) and to explain, in terms of religious banishment, the populating of the Americas by immigrants from Asia. Unfortunately, inventing a mythical Asiatic past perpetuated among African-Americans an ignorance of the histories of religions much older than Islam. This part of Fard Muhammad's tale was not constructive in any manner, though his intentions were probably not as insidious as the psychological effects of his story.

According to the Nation's chronology, while the expulsion of undesirable elements such as the red Indians tended to remedy the disunity among the Original People, tensions within the tribes, especially in regard to the Shabazz, crescendoed about sixty-six hundred years ago. Increasing discontent seemed to overshadow many of the positive achievements of the Egyptians and Meccans, though the god-scientists could still arguably maintain that life in Asia was heaven on earth. Perhaps due in part to the expanding population, which now numbered 5 billion, "demand for a change" became the rallying cry for black radicals disillusioned with the divine government of East Asia. Revolutionary violence against the ruling class was, of course, unheard of, for that was not the way of the peace-loving Nation of Islam. However, according to prophecy, the black people were definitely preordained to suffer an upheaval that would have grave consequences for their ancient civilization. Eighty-four hundred years into the current twenty-five-thousand-year cycle of history, a new god, Yacub (pronounced Yak-coob), was born twenty miles outside of the Holy City of Mecca. His sole destiny would be to destroy his own people.[13]

Yacub had a superior intellect and a thirst for knowledge. He began school at age four and early on displayed a penchant for scientific inquiry. Known as the "big head scientist" on account of his unusually large cranium, which symbolized his vanity as well as his mental powers, he earned degrees from all of the colleges and universities in the land by age eighteen. Though one of the preeminent scholars of the Nation of Islam, his greatest achievement took place outside of school when he was just six years old. While toying with two pieces of steel, he learned the secret of magnetism, that opposites attract. The larger lesson for Yacub was that if he could create a race of people completely different from the Original People, that race could attract and dominate the Black Nation through tricknology—tricks, lies, and deception. The essence of the black man, which consisted of a black and a brown germ, was the key to creating such a race. If he could simply graft, or separate, these germs until none of the original black genetic code was left, he would be able to create a species of man, called "mankind," who would rule the earth forever. Sinister and seditious, the idea, which he broached only to his uncle, stayed with him until he was able, as a young man, to lure the 30 percent of dissatisfied Meccans into his scheme.[14]

In times of trouble, charlatans fare well. Yacub, charismatic and visionary, tapped into the discontent in Mecca and preached an Islam that stressed wealth and luxury for those who adhered to it. The dispossessed, the frustrated, and the opportunistic flocked to him and made Yacub their champion against the government of Mecca. The authorities, incensed by Yacub's manipulation of the original religion and fearful of his popularity, persecuted the preacher and his followers. In days, jails and prisons became glutted with the dissidents, and the king of Mecca was forced to come to terms with Yacub, who was also arrested. To avoid bloodshed on the streets of the Holy City, the monarch cut a deal with Yacub, which included passage by ship for the Yacubians to the island of Pelan in the Aegean Sea. The arrangement also provided for twenty years of assistance for the exiles to help them to construct a civilization. Yacub, along with his 59,999 followers, disembarked for the island en masse, banished like the red Indians from the halls of paradise.[15]

To outsiders, the story of the exploits of Yacub has traditionally been the most peculiar part of the Muslims' theology. The tale suggests a fascination among Nation of Islam members with the bizarre. Nonetheless, the myth is at least partially anchored in both Judeo-Christian and Islamic theology. Two major themes of scriptural origin were exploited here by Fard Muhammad, and his purpose was again to allegorize religious traditions familiar to potential followers. The dissatisfaction of the Meccans and the preordained rise of Yacub are symbolic of the fall of Adam and Eve from grace and the advent of original sin. In essence, the birth of Yacub is analogous to the success of the serpent in the Garden of Eden. The expulsion of the evil scientist and his followers from Arabia is metaphorically related to the ouster of the vain Lucifer from heaven as described in both the Bible (Isaiah 14:12–17) and the Qur'an (Surah 7:11–18). The modern trappings that Fard Muhammad bestowed upon his version of ancient Mecca, from universities and colleges to sophisticated government and genetic experimentation, again give his story a facade of rationality for African-Americans in twentieth-century Detroit. Ironically enough, the Yacub myth, while having no place in Christian or orthodox Islamic doctrine, is allegorically more connected to the holy texts of both religious traditions than many other parts of the Nation's theology.

In line with Muslim lore, once on Pelan, Yacub was finally able to rule as he had always wanted to. He was also able to carry out his experiments using the germ of the black man to create a race genetically independent of its original host. From his laboratories, Yacub used murder, deceit, and lies to keep blacks from reproducing, thus decimating the number of Original People on the island. His plan was a vicious form of unnatural selection. Women who gave birth to black babies lost them to infanticide, the nurses claiming that the newborn had become an "angel child" who lived at peace in heaven. Only brown-skinned people were allowed to mate, and only babies of similar hue were spared. In two hundred years' time, the people of Pelan were all brown. Over the next two centuries, the brown people, through genetic engineering, or "grafting," and selective birth control, or racial genocide, gave way to the rise of red and yellow peoples on the island. By this time, Yacub's followers—the great scientist himself, whose rule had become murderous and dictatorial, died during his initial experiments at 150 years of age—had mastered the knowledge required to create the race that Yacub had envisioned as a boy while playing with steel: a white race. Containing none of the original germ of the black people, the creation of a white people was a testament to both Yacub's supreme intelligence and his legendary evil. His blue-eyed, artificial man was born of lies, homicide, and treachery, all of which became part of the very character of the emerging white race. In six hundred years, Yacub and his servants had turned a completely black people into a population of "white devils," genetically programmed to oppose freedom, justice, and equality. From the beginning, they were made to be the natural enemies of the righteous Tribe of Shabazz.[16]

In physiological terms, the white race was both similar to and quite different from its parent race. Their bones were fragile and their blood thin, resulting in an overall physical strength one-third that of blacks. Weak bodies made Yacub's man susceptible to disease, and most future ailments, "from social diseases to cancer," would be attributable to his presence on earth. Additionally, six-ounce brains made whites inherently inferior in mental capacity to the Original People, whose gray matter weighed an ounce and a half more. Though he would later prove his creativity by founding a civilization largely structured on the black model, the white man simply lacked the acumen of the black man. Actually, the grafting process had made the white race both incapable of righteousness and biologically subordinate to the black people. Yacub, aware that prophecy accorded his ersatz man only six thousand years to achieve his evil purpose, created the white people in haste and even mandated that they marry at age fifteen or sixteen in order to accelerate their birth rate. Products of the racial holocaust on Pelan, the white devils were clearly at a disadvantage in terms of strength and brainpower when compared to the Nation of Islam; however, for at least a while, the all-important factors of time and destiny were on their side.[17]

The white assault on Mecca that took place in 4000 B.C.E., 600 years after Yacub's expulsion, was among the first exercises in "tricknology," or treachery, for which the race of devils would become notorious. They planned to conquer the Original People by causing dissension through rumor and deceit. In the midst of the distrust and turmoil that followed, the whites would offer to serve as mediators between the disputants and eventually rule over the Black Nation altogether. The scheme worked for six months and even led to a cultural deterioration among the pyramid-building Egyptians—due to the "devil-stuff" introduced by white Turks—and a full-blown civil war in Mecca. The king of the Holy City, however, was much wiser than the white people had anticipated and immediately addressed the crises with a flurry of edicts. "Gather every one of the devils up and strip them of our costume," he demanded. "Put an apron on them to hide their nakedness. Take all literature from them and take them by way of the desert. Send a caravan, armed with rifles, to keep the devils going westward. Don't allow one of them to turn back; and, if they are lucky enough to get across the Arabian Desert, let them go into the hills of West Asia." In accordance with the monarch's wishes, the whites were herded together, manacled, and driven across the desert into West Asia, or Europe, where they were roped in to keep them from returning to paradise. Fruit of Islam, or Muslim guards, were stationed at the border to maintain the territorial integrity of the Black Nation. In the event of conflict, their orders were to decapitate any white person who dared break the peace again. Yacub's children, secluded in the land of Europe, which was given to them by Allah himself, lost touch with the radiant civilization of the Original People. Lacking a viable cultural heritage of their own, they rapidly plunged into the dark pit of savagery.[18]

The myth of Yacub's creation of the white race and the murderous, deceitful, and evil nature attributed to whites by the Nation of Islam has given it the distinction, with some justification, of being the most racially chauvinistic black organization in the history of the United States. Fard Muhammad's description of the alleged mental and physical inferiority of whites, resulting from "grafting" on Pelan, suggests that his doctrines were a tragic variation of the ideas of Hitler, racist eugenicists, and other racial purists of his day. Although their ultimate objectives were quite different, the Muslim leader, like the Nazis and others, understood the power of hatred in mobilizing a people. Through symbols and rhetoric, he purposefully portrayed whites as subhuman both to explain white racism and past abuses of blacks by Europeans and to exploit latent nationalist sentiments in the African-American community.

As was the case with many of the teachings of Fard Muhammad, his tale of genocide on Pelan and the return of whites to Mecca contained hidden meanings. Beyond imaginatively inventing a Caucasian "race of devils," his story also explained, in a pseudo-scientific way, the origins of other races and their genetic links to blacks and whites. Characteristic of the Nation's creation story, allusions to biblical scripture were again used by Fard Muhammad to draw parallels between the early experiences of Yacub's whites and Judeo-Christian beliefs. The expulsion of the "white devils" from Mecca into Europe was a figurative portrayal of the defeat of Satan by the forces of God and his banishment from heaven (Revelation 12:7–10). Just as the creation story of Fard Muhammad was aimed at humanizing God and making paradise earthly, the Yacub myth sought to personify evil, as the white race, and to make hell a geographic location, Europe. The ultimate purpose of the Muslim leader in this instance was to portray man as the master of his own destiny and African-Americans as the victims of evil, mortal men who could be challenged, not of unseen forces beyond human comprehension.

Returning to the tale, over the next two thousand years (4,000–2,000 B.C.E.), the white tribe degenerated to the degree that it no longer resembled the Original People or even the creatures that Yacub had developed. The knowledge of walking on two legs, food preparation, and civilized behavior in general died in the hills of Europe, as did any notions of decorum that the whites may have picked up in Mecca or Egypt. Bestiality reigned among the outcasts, and many evolved, or regressed, into gorillas, apes, and monkeys. Others became hairy, grew tails that "came out from the end of their spines," and walked on all fours like beasts. Those few who retained a semblance of humanoid features and mannerisms wore animal skins, fought off wild predators with clubs and stones, and lived in caves during the harsh European winters. But even these few who remained humanlike could not help but express their innately savage and evil nature in other ways. White women, according to the legend, began commonly copulating with their most cherished pet, the canine, and would over time acknowledge to anyone curious enough to ask that "there is nothing she loves better than a dog."[19]

If the Nation of Islam was heaven on earth, then West Asia was a veritable hell. The whole scene in Europe was quite pathetic, with its wild animals, blistering winters, and fiendish white devils. The degrading situation finally became so morbid and bestial that Allah himself was touched by the suffering and decided to send a mulatto prophet, Musa (or Moses), in 2000 B.C.E. to assist in reforming the white race and free it from the clutches of barbarism. The prophet's mission was to raise the whites to a level of civilization that would allow them to rule as prophecy had ordained. The task was enormous and a lesser man would have failed completely; but Musa, who became the leader of the whites, worked wonders where only savagery had reigned. He first brought the devils out of their caves, taught them about Allah, and explained the benefits of wearing clothes. Next, he ended their custom of eating raw meat, especially their beloved swine, and disclosed to them the secret of fire, which they greatly feared. Under the stewardship of Musa, the light of civilization slowly filtered into Europe, which the prophet called Israel, but not without some difficulty.[20]

During his work, Musa was aware the specter of atavism was always present. He was constantly reminded through the devil's unrighteous propensity that he could trust the white man only at his peril. At night, the prophet slept in a ring of fire to ward off those whites who sought to injure him or still retained an appetite for human flesh. At other times, he rejoiced over signs that his mission was bearing fruit. Over the years, Musa noticed that some among Yacub's progeny were more religious than others, though all were by nature incapable of goodness. One group in particular among the whites, the Jews, forsook idolatry and the temptations of the hog and were steadfast in their faith in Musa and his teachings. In the centuries to come, they would be closer to the Original People in their manner of worship than any other people. Yet, despite the perseverance of the Jews, many of the whites did not even pretend to aspire to holiness, and Musa chastised them accordingly. In one instance, the prophet became so disappointed in their lack of respect for Islam that he mined a mountainside with dynamite, invited three hundred devils to "stand there on the edge of this mountain and . . . hear the voice of God," and ignited the explosives. For Musa, the resulting carnage was therapeutic and relieved the sense of failure that he endured due to the refusal of the white people to become good Muslims.[21]

This section of Fard Muhammad's story was tailored to accomplish two objectives. First, by portraying whites as subhuman, even animalistic, in the bowels of a savage Europe, the Muslim leader sought to strip away the white mystique that Caucasians had invented over the past four hundred years to convince people of color of the supposed moral and intellectual superiority of Europeans. The tale of the cultural collapse of whites in the hills of "West Asia" intentionally omitted any mention of institutions of higher learning, artistic endeavors, governmental structures, or other cornerstones of civilization. In describing Europe as a wasteland and whites as waste, Fard Muhammad hoped to bolster notions of black superiority among his African-American audiences and to depict twentieth-century Western civilization as decadent and founded on weak antecedents.

As a second objective, this part of Muslim mythology was also designed to bring Moses within the realm of Islamic prophets, thus attracting converts to the Nation whose Christian backgrounds emphasized the centrality of this biblical leader to the ancient world. This portrayal of the Hebrew leader as a prophet is generally consistent with his position in orthodox Islam. However, the deeds attributed to him, such as civilizing whites and bombing dissenters, were, of course, products of the imagination of Fard Muhammad. In an obvious effort to shore up his own claims to divinity, the Muslim leader described Moses as a mulatto, a racial heritage that he claimed was responsible for his own light complexion. Interestingly, though the Jews as a group were defined as part of the white race, Fard Muhammad characterized them as marginally faithful to the word of Allah, probably because of their observance of dietary restrictions similar to those of Muslims. In sum, the depth of white suffering in Europe as detailed in the Nation's mythology was meant to depreciate the value of Western civilization in the minds of African-Americans and to encourage them to seek refuge in the ranks of the Muslim movement.

In the Nation's version of history, the influence of Musa held sway over the white race for two millennia, although the nascent civilization he had started among the Europeans was crushed by Nimrod, "the evil demon of the white race," who rose up against him in the fourth century B.C.E. Again without a guide or a culture vibrant enough to survive the hostile environment of Europe, the whites sank into the mire of savagery. For the second time, Allah and the Black Nation showed mercy and sent to them another prophet, Jesus, around two thousand years ago. The illegitimate son of Joseph and Mary, the black prophet preached the essence of the original Islam to the whites—freedom, justice, and equality. He built the city of Jerusalem as a sanctuary for those who would follow the path of righteousness. Notwithstanding his efforts to reform the devils, Jesus met his fate at the hands of those who feared his sanctity. Jews who had despised the prophet for having pointed out their evil origins turned him over to bounty hunters, who skewered him with a knife. The force of the blow pinned Jesus to a wooden wall and projected his arms into the air, his whole body forming a cross until his father, Joseph, claimed his corpse. The prophet was prepared for burial by Egyptians and interred in Jerusalem. His sepulchre, guarded by Fruit of Islam, could be freely visited and viewed by Muslims; however, others would have to pay six thousand dollars and secure a certificate from the pope of Rome to gain entrance to the site. Again, the whites were without spiritual direction largely as a result of their own doing.[22]

The white people who killed Jesus had acted out of fear. Their apprehension was not so much caused by Jesus himself as by his message of peace and the legacy of righteousness he might have left behind to prospective white Muslims. Following his murder, a conspiracy was formulated to make sure that the true teachings of Jesus (Islam) would not become a part of the popular consciousness of the white race. Jesus, who had been simply a mortal man of flesh and blood, was deified by the conspirators, who sought to obscure the reality of Allah. December 25, the birthday of the wicked Nimrod, was designated Christmas, or the date of birth for Jesus, who was actually born in September. Additionally, a book, the Bible, that mixed spiritual truth and secular falsehood was promulgated as the authoritative text regarding the history of God and the creation, the life of Jesus and other prophets, and the nature of heaven and hell. The unholy conspiracy, later known as Christianity, was spearheaded by the pope of Rome, who is symbolized in the Book of Revelation as the dragon or devil. The Christian church, a masterpiece of tricknology, was organized to worship the pope, though communicants believed that they were honoring Jesus, the dead prophet. Beyond the treachery behind it, the beauty of the conspiracy lay in the way it effectively used symbols associated with Jesus, such as Jerusalem, the cross, and the Bible, "to shield [the] dirty religion" of Christianity. As an indicator of its early impact, the gullible among the Nation of Islam pointed to the new faith as evidence that Yacub's people were capable of goodness. The more wary, however, held the doctrinal innovation up to high ridicule and compared its advent to the murder, lies, and turpitude that accompanied the creation of the white race four thousand years earlier.[23]

As revised by Fard Muhammad, the life and death of Jesus and the rise of Christianity were a pivotal part of the religious doctrines of the Nation of Islam. In many ways, this tale was the centerpiece of the attempt to make African-Americans susceptible to Fard Muhammad's claims of his own divinity. The portrayal of Jesus as the product of an illicit affair between

Joseph and Mary was intended to humanize him and eliminate, or at least downplay, the aura of sanctity that Christians associated with him. As he is portrayed in orthodox Islam, Jesus was thoroughly co-opted into the Nation's belief system as a prophet, as opposed to being depicted as the son of God. However, unlike the version of his departure from human existence generally accepted by orthodox Muslims—that is, that Jesus did not die a physical death—Fard Muhammad described him as being murdered in a rather common manner in an attempt to contradict the significance of the crucifixion in Christian theology and to reduce him to basic human terms. Similarly, the denial of a physical resurrection was meant to further separate African-Americans from the Christian beliefs of life after death and the transcendence of Christ. Thus, the humanization of Jesus by Fard Muhammad, from his allegedly illegitimate birth to his burial under Islamic protection, was aimed at limiting divine power to flesh and blood. In doing so, the Muslim leader sought to place himself on the level of major Judeo-Christian and Islamic personalities, even God himself, in the eyes of his followers.[24]

For many prospective converts, this part of the Nation's doctrines, the repudiation of Jesus as the son of God and as rising from the grave, was the biggest obstacle to embracing the movement. Although the portrayal of God as man by Fard Muhammad was meant to make the acceptance of the humanity of Jesus easier, the limiting of Christ to flesh and blood surely turned off many African-Americans who could not imagine him as less than immortal, perfect, and the essence of God. However, for those individuals who were persuaded to doubt the idea of an eternal, noncorporeal God and the traditional depiction of Jesus as divine, convincing them that Christianity was a hoax was probably an easy step for Fard Muhammad. Having established that Jesus was solely the son of man, the Muslim leader could deduce that any attempts to deify him as an omnipotent spirit or to worship him as such, whether through observing Christmas or believing in biblical accounts of his resurrection, were part of a conspiracy by the unrighteous to camouflage true Islam. Viewed this way, pretexts for both the selective use of the Bible (or Poison Book as the Muslim movement called it) and the promulgation of anti-Christian sentiments became readily available to Fard Muhammad. Drawing again on an allegorical interpretation of the Scriptures, the characterization of the pope as the dragon in Revelation 12:3–9 not only labeled Christianity as erroneous, but also as founded on the evil intentions of white conspirators and impostors who supposedly sought to lead the Black Nation astray. In recruiting members, when Fard Muhammad convinced African-American listeners to break with Christianity, the odds of their embracing the rest of his story increased dramatically.[25]

To proceed with the tale of Fard Muhammad, insofar as the Tribe of Shabazz was not known for giving up, a third prophet, Muhammad ibn

Abdullah, was sent to the white people in the seventh century C.E. to reintroduce Islam and to counter the falsehoods on which Christianity was based. The latter religion had had its way with Europe for over six hundred years and to a large extent had supplanted what little traces of Islam Musa and Jesus had left behind. Before Muhammad started his mission, he had been warned by the scientists of the Black Nation that the white man was incorrigible and instinctively evil. The prophet ignored his colleagues and preached Islam to the Europeans anyway, as Allah had commanded. Like Muslim teachers before him, Muhammad's message of righteousness fell mostly on deaf ears, for Christianity and its parent, Judaism, had over the years made the Europeans virtually impervious to Muslim influence. Before the prophet died of grief at age sixty-two in 632, he lashed out at the whites for his poor reception and denied them the use of the Arabic language and Islamic garb. The prohibitions, which set the Christians back a thousand years culturally, along with territorial ambitions led to protracted wars between the two faiths and a dreadful loss of life on both sides. In the end, the Muslim crusaders were able to penetrate the very heart of Europe during the centuries of fighting. With the capture of Jerusalem in 1187 and the fall of Constantinople in 1453, Yacub's madmen had to look elsewhere for a place to practice their evil.[26]

This part of the Nation's history of the world is generally more accurate than others, but fits neatly into the overall effort of Fard Muhammad to pull African-Americans away from Christianity and American society and into his movement. Muhammad ibn Abdullah, honored as the last prophet of Allah by orthodox Muslims, was portrayed as simply an emissary to Europe whose task was to reintroduce Islam to whites there. He was viewed as neither the final messenger nor the most important one—Fard Muhammad reserved those distinctions for himself and later for Elijah Muhammad. The depiction of Europeans as dependent upon the Islamic world for language, dress, and culture in general minimized the significance of Western civilization and Christianity vis-à-vis the Middle East, making the latter even more attractive to prospective followers. His description of the Crusades as a triumph of Islam aimed to explain a historical event in propagandistic terms, but was also designed to underscore the aggressive, sinister nature Fard Muhammad attributed to whites. This part of the tale set the stage for his final and most powerful appeal to the racial consciousness of the prospective convert. To arouse the ire of his black audiences to an even higher pitch—and to attract them into the ranks of the Nation—he followed his discussion of the Crusades with the history of the enslavement of the Original People in America.

According to Fard Muhammad, the Europeans, forced to turn westward by conquering Muslim armies, found a new land to defile across the Atlantic Ocean. They also found a new people to defile: the exiled Indians of America. The whites who made the voyages to the Western Hemisphere during the sixteenth century and onward did not leave Europe to push plows in America. They had come to get rich, preferably with little self-exertion or, even better, off the labor of others. The Indians proved a sufficient labor pool for a while, but when a greater supply of workers was needed, the whites turned to East Asians, their age-old enemies, for slaves. Through tricknology and coercion, the Europeans brought Original People from Mecca and other parts of the Black Nation to America to serve as bondmen. Sailing from East Asia in 1555, the white transatlantic slave trader John Hawkins was the first to bring members of the Tribe of Shabazz to the "New World." In his ship *Jesus*, the Englishman deposited his black captives in the wilderness of North America, "a place of sin and evil doings," for labor on plantations. In line with the character of Yacub's people, the first generation of Original People in America were murdered so that their children would not be able to draw inspiration from the history of the Black Nation. Ignorant of their past, the second and subsequent generations of blacks in the wilderness had to rely upon their white slave masters for knowledge and, in a short time, became "blind, deaf, and dumb to the knowledge of self or anyone else."[27]

Like the six-thousand-year rule of the white race, the enslavement of black people in America was prophesied and was to last four hundred years. During this time, Europeans stripped away from their slaves as much of their original culture as possible. For example, the slave master renamed his chattel *Negro*, which meant "something dead, lifeless, neutral (not that nor this)." He took the black man's flag, the National, in an attempt to deny him a national origin. Above all, he thrust upon the black slave Christianity and the Bible, which the slave master had tailored to keep the slave's mode of thinking servile. The Tribe of Shabazz in America, having lost the true knowledge of Allah, began to pray to a mystery God who was invisible and remote while the white man became wealthy from its toil. Over four centuries—from the sixteenth through much of the nineteenth—the slave master continued to kidnap, murder, rape, and mutilate the black people in America as his sinful nature dictated. Indicative of their wicked mission, by the end of their six millennia of rule over nine-tenths of the Black Nation on earth (which includes brown, red, and yellow people), Yacub's children had managed to kill a shocking 600 million people, a crime of catastrophic proportions.[28]

The divinely decreed year for the end of the white man's rule was 1914, but Allah extended the time by fifty to seventy years so the black people in America could regain the knowledge of self and Islam. The expiration of white domination came none too soon. Four hundred years of slavery had killed the black man in America mentally and led him to believe that European names, the Christian religion (and its "spook" god), and the American government and flag were his own. The enslavement period had actually made the "so-called Negroes" in America no longer Original People, but instead, individuals "wrecked, robbed, and spoiled" by the slave master's brutality and useful only "as a tool for whatever purpose the white man sees fit." The black man partook of swine as the savage whites of Europe did during the cave days. He fornicated, drank alcohol, swore, fought his brother over nonsense, mistreated his women, lived on credit and handouts (like the biblical Lazarus), forsook his God (Allah), and loved the devil. The Tribe of Shabazz in America had become no more than Yacub's race in black skin. Uncivilized and stranded in the wilderness, the black people were in need of a savior as much as the white man had been centuries earlier.[29]

The major themes that pervade this segment of Fard Muhammad's narrative are those of white brutality and black cultural devastation. Arguably, the primary attractiveness to blacks of his entire mythology of the Original Man and the white devil lies within his description of these four hundred years. Though plagued by self-serving inaccuracies and creative license, the Nation's history of African-American enslavement aroused indignation in perhaps every black listener who heard the story. As a recruiting tool, tales of slavery were both recent enough to elicit a reaction and significant enough to guarantee that at least some African-Americans would give Fard Muhammad a hearing.

Evil, again, was not a concept for the Muslim leader, but real individuals who were visible and mortal. John Hawkins, a historical personality, epitomized in the view of the Muslims the malevolent and deceitful nature of whites. By pointing out an individual white man who had, indeed, been important in transporting Africans to the Americas as slaves, Fard Muhammad attempted to offer verifiable proof that his theories about Caucasians were correct. Moreover, he sought to do this often at the expense of historical accuracy. Conventional histories of John Hawkins's first voyage describe him as arriving in Hispaniola in 1563, not in North America in 1555, as part of the English effort to break the Spanish monopoly on the slave trade. The slave ship *Jesus of Lubeck* perhaps did not make the trip across the Atlantic until Hawkins's third voyage in 1567. Despite the known facts about Hawkins's activities, the Muslims would stick by their original story, adding only that there was a "hidden history" of sixty-four years of slavery between 1555 and 1619, the generally accepted date for the arrival of African-American bondmen in English North America. The revision added to the poignancy of the story and was, of course, designed to give more credibility to Fard Muhammad's claim that whites were a "race of devils."[30]

As part of his effort to invent a new black identity, Fard Muhammad wrapped his history of slavery in religious and nationalist terms familiar to African-Americans. Analogous to the four-hundred-year bondage of Israelites in Egypt, the servitude of blacks in America was presented as preordained, supporting the complementary notion that African-Americans were God's chosen people. However, it would not be a Christian God who would deliver blacks from bondage, but instead, the God of their alleged Muslim ancestors. Fard Muhammad introduced the unfamiliar religion of Islam to the known historical setting of slavery hoping that his chronicle of the stripping of blacks of their "originality" by whites would be enough to make their imagined 76-trillion-year Islamic past believable. Symbols such as a flag, a language, and a homeland (East Asia) were invented to inspire nationalist sentiments in prospective converts who were unhappy with their identity as simply the descendants of former "Negro" slaves.

Though Christianity and the Bible were held responsible for the psychological enslavement of African-Americans, Fard Muhammad made metaphorical use of biblical scripture to again characterize whites as evil by nature. For example, the number 6 runs throughout the mythology of the Muslims in a manner that links whites to the Mark of the Beast referred to in Revelation 13:18. From the six hundred years it took Yacub's henchmen to make white people and their predestined six-thousand-year reign to the 600 million members of the Black Nation killed by whites and the sixty-four hidden years of slavery, this particular number was used by Fard Muhammad to denote the innate wickedness of whites. While used for mythical purposes, the number 6, along with the Nation's history of Europeans, evoked in black Christians the kinds of negative images that the Muslim leader hoped would lead them to believe that he was their savior.

Proceeding with the narrative, the black man's messiah, Wallace D. Fard (later Fard Muhammad), was born on February 26, 1877, in the Holy City of Mecca in line with the Nation's prophecy. His mission was to redeem or mentally resurrect the American so-called Negro before the destruction of the white world. Just as Yacub before him, this god of the Nation of Islam was groomed from birth for his divine work, and like most saviors, his background is enshrined in mystery. Interestingly, his father, Alphonso, was an ebony-colored man of the Tribe of Shabazz, and his mother, Baby Gee, was "a Caucasian lady, a devil." Fard's father met his mother in the hills of Asia where she lived as other whites lived, semicivilized and content with a wicked existence. During their initial acquaintance, Alphonso saw potential in the woman and taught her the ways of the righteous until she became a holy Muslim, not by nature but by belief and practice. Since Fard's father knew scripture and was aware that his future son would be destined to explore the world to find a lost portion of the Tribe of Shabazz, he believed that it would be best to have a male offspring whose skin color would allow him "to deal with both [white and black] peoples justly and righteously." Thus, the savior was to be a mulatto as was Musa before him. The couple's first baby was a girl, who was ineligible for the mission of resurrecting the so-called Negroes. The second child was male, maroon-eyed and pale like his mother. A precocious dreamer, the boy, Wallace, had a vision of his destiny as early as age six. From that time forward, he knew that his purpose as the new Allah of the Black Nation would be to overthrow the white race, gather his people in America, and give back to the so-called Negro the knowledge of self and Islam.[31]

For Wallace, the temptation to become prosperous and famous in the white world was formidable and, during his early life, eclipsed his more noble aspirations. Many factors, from the royal blood in his veins to his membership in the Koreish tribe of the Prophet Muhammad, influenced him to pursue a career that would lead to status and comfort, even if it was among his mother's people. To broaden his prospects, he roamed the globe and studied every educational system in every civilized country. A natural polyglot, he learned to speak sixteen languages fluently. Eventually, his oratorical gifts and intellect would take him to places such as England, where he was trained to be a diplomat. In the end, these wanderings were unfulfilling, and Wallace's conscience pressured him back on track. On the eve of the First World War, he made the journey to the wilderness of North America, knowing that the white man's time had run out and that only he could bring "freedom, justice, and equality" to the lost Tribe of Shabazz in the United States. The prophecy had been made fifteen thousand years ago, and not even he, the messiah, could alter it.[32]

While white men shot, bombed, and gassed each other in the trenches of Europe, Fard secured a room with a white family in California, perhaps in Los Angeles, and enrolled in one of the local universities. The American so-called Negroes, whom he often referred to collectively as "his uncle," were in as bad a shape as he had imagined. Though they picked cotton and made automobiles, migrated and soldiered, they were still as out of place in America as lambs among wolves. Careful not to reveal himself as the savior to either the so-called Negroes or whites, Fard entered and left the country freely for the next several years. Perhaps during his absences he reported back to Mecca or gained another degree at some famed college or picked up a new language. Whatever the case, he finally decided to start his work among the Tribe of Shabazz of Detroit, Michigan, and on July 4, 1930, appeared there as a clothes retailer peddling silks from the East. His arrival in the Motor City marked the emergence of the Nation of Islam in America.[33]

Fard Muhammad stressed this part of the mythology to invent himself as a messiah for the blacks oppressed in America, fabricating his credentials as such. To place himself, in the eyes of his followers, on the same level as Moses and Jesus (and later God), such an embellishment was necessary. The story's elements of prophecy and extreme sacrifice on behalf of the "so-called Negroes" by Fard Muhammad were aimed at convincing African-

Americans that his stated mission among them was important enough to force him to repudiate a life of comfort. Along with religious undertones, this self-glorification by the Muslim leader played upon the most familiar symbol of Americanism, Independence Day, co-opting it into the theology of the Nation of Islam. Finally, Fard Muhammad was careful not to go too far in his use of Western symbols, such as university degrees and English diplomatic training, to create for himself a reputation of accomplishment. Cognizant of the incongruity between his racial teachings and Caucasian features, he portrayed himself as a mulatto to assure his black audiences that he was one of them—indeed, their nephew. Beyond inventing himself as a messiah, this part of Fard Muhammad's tale utilized modern terms and meanings to connect the mythical past of the Black Nation to the Muslim leader and his twentieth-century mission to "mentally resurrect" African-Americans.

To continue the tale, the work of Fard among blacks in Detroit was to last only three years. This was just long enough to establish the rudiments of a Muslim organization among African-Americans there and to reveal himself as the awaited savior. As prophecy mandated, Fard had to raise a messenger from among the so-called Negroes to preach the knowledge of self and others to the once lost, but now found, Muslims. The designated bearer of Truth would be none other than Elijah Poole, a former country boy from Georgia. Appointed Supreme Minister of the Nation, Elijah, christened Elijah Karriem and later Elijah Muhammad, arose as the Messenger of Allah just as the preordained period of Fard's divine presence in America came to an end.[34]

Elijah Muhammad was not a prophet in the biblical sense, but simply a courier of Islam. Commissioned by God himself (Fard Muhammad), he was the last in the line of men, or scientists, to be sent to disseminate Truth to the so-called Negro before the end of the white man's "spook" civilization. In the tradition of Musa, Jesus, and Muhammad ibn Abdullah, his duty was that of the civilized man, which entailed teaching "spiritual civilization" and cleansing his people of the vices and sins that Yacub's race had filled them with. His place in the divine plan was of such significance that at least two-thirds of the Bible was written about him. Moreover, Elijah Muhammad's centrality to the mental resurrection of the so-called Negro made him an intermediary between the Black Nation and Allah, making it impossible for anyone to "get a prayer through to Allah (God) unless you mention me [Elijah Muhammad] in your prayers." As in all matters, great power produced great responsibility, and during the Judgment, the Messenger of Allah would be judged first. But given the urgency of his mission, Muhammad was more than willing to accept this condition.[35]

Culture, Muslim morality, and cosmology were among the many precepts that Allah taught his messenger. To get back to the ways of the Original People, the so-called Negroes would, first and foremost, have to renounce their Christian affiliations and promise fealty to Allah and his apostle Elijah Muhammad. Next, the new convert had to drop the names of the white man and take on one of the one hundred names, or "attributes," of God. (In the time of the Judgment, the Muslims believed that anyone answering to a European name would be shunned by Allah.) In preparation for the destruction of the white world, the righteous "lost-founds" (or new converts) were required to keep their bodies physically fit and properly nourished. Observance of the major dietary rules of Islam was mandatory and included the consumption of one meal a day, or in some instances, every other day, which preserved health and prolonged life, the eating of only kosher meats, and the absolute elimination of pork from the diet, especially since the pig was "grafted from rat, cat, and dog" and carried 999 poisonous germs. Only after they had regained their original religion of Islam, their original (Arabic) names, and their original strength and vitality could the members of the Tribe of Shabazz prepare themselves for the Judgment, which would soon befall America.[36]

This section of the narrative was as much—perhaps entirely—the creation of Elijah Muhammad as it was of his teacher. Its purpose was to give ideological support to Elijah's claim of being the Messenger of Allah and to establish him as the intermediary between the movement and its God. Once converts came to believe that Elijah was, in fact, the instrument of a deity, his words and actions became the will of Allah in their eyes. His emphasis upon the uniqueness of his position in relationship to the God of the Nation (Fard Muhammad) and the claim that he was the last messenger were intended to put to rest questions of succession and to take away from potential competitors any philosophical basis for challenges to his leadership. Those who challenged him were readily labeled hypocrites and against the will of Allah. Along with providing a doctrinal defense for the role of Elijah Muhammad in the group, this part of the Muslims' story also encouraged the adoption of certain orthodox Islamic practices by followers, using myths about names and the contents of swine flesh to ensure adherence. This discussion explained to believers why they should follow Elijah Muhammad and how they should live under his leadership.

In accordance with Muslim doctrine, heaven and hell were not places that could be reached only through death or life after death. Rather, paradise and perdition were conditions of life on earth. According to the wise scientists of the Black Nation, the earth was and will always be the home of the black man and his creation, the white man, and life on the planet was what they made it. A heavenly state of being could be achieved through the embracing of Islam, which would satisfy the so-called Negroes' most basic desires for "good homes, money, and friendship in all walks of life." The resurrection that the Bible refers to is not a physical resurrection—for there is no life after the grave—but a mental resurrection in which "the mentally dead, the ignorant, whom the devil's falsehood has killed" are taken from the benighted tomb into the garden of divine truth. Like heaven, a state of hell could also be reached while one was still alive on earth. As Allah had decreed, such a frightful destiny, indeed, awaited all who insisted upon following the devil and succumbing to his tricknology at the time of the Judgment.[37]

Before the final destruction of the white world, Allah would send a warning to the so-called Negroes who had not accepted Islam. In the form of natural disasters, like the biblical plagues in Egypt, these warnings would consist of storms, earthquakes, drought, unusually cold temperatures, crop failure, and the like. This period, which was to start around 1965–66, would be known as the first hell, which both black and white would suffer together. Similar to Babylon, Sodom, and Gomorrah, America would be the victim of the wrath of God for the mistreatment of his chosen people. But unlike his biblical predecessors, the so-called Negro would be able to avoid the carnage through territorial separation from his former slave master. Whether this escape took the form of a partition of the United States or a great migration to Africa, blacks would have the opportunity to survive the second, more destructive hell to come. Actually, even "a remnant" of whites would be saved, but only those who strove against their evil nature by doing good and submitting to Islam, which was not their natural religion, though they would be allowed to practice it. Those few whites who were Muslims and were just to the so-called Negroes would see a hereafter, but not the same afterworld the Black Nation would inherit. These whites would simply survive "the great world destruction," but would not achieve the new birth or immortality that the black people would experience. For the most part, the question of white redemption was academic insofar as so few would be able to contradict their wicked nature and save America by extending freedom, justice, and equality to the so-called Negro.[38]

In this portion of the tale of Fard Muhammad, his materialist, earthly definition of heaven and hell complemented the larger themes of his teachings, which stressed the power of man to mold his environment and destiny. By again denying the possibility of physical rebirth, he reduced the concept of resurrection to a mental enlightenment that could occur only among those who followed him. Interestingly, he drew upon the black separatist tradition and biblical examples of divine retribution to encourage African-Americans to seek sanctuary in his Nation of Islam, but remained rather vague about the logistics of territorial separation, not to mention a precise destination. As one of the few major changes that Elijah Muhammad introduced into the Nation's overall belief system, over time white Muslims became eligible for salvation; however, their hereafter would supposedly be qualitatively inferior to that of blacks. Unlike his teacher, Elijah Muham-

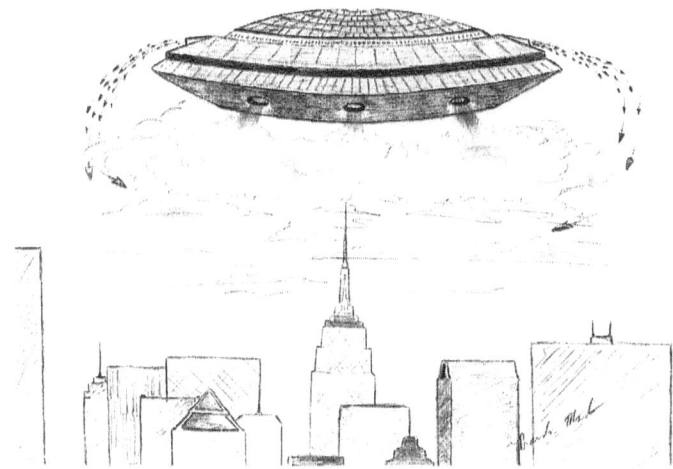

mad, older and mellower, was willing to offer the "devil" an out by the early 1970s, although as late as the 1950s he had maintained that Allah "will not accept any white people in His kingdom."[39]

In the view of the Nation, the destruction of the white world—variously known as the Judgment, Armageddon, the fall of America, and the second hell—would be carried out by a technological monstrosity called the Mother Plane. This wheel-shaped spaceship would take the form of a small human-built planet a half mile in diameter, capable of staying above the earth's atmosphere for six months to a year before reentering for oxygen and hydrogen. Over twenty-two years, Allah (Fard Muhammad) would build the ship in Japan and integrate into its structure fifteen hundred smaller ships, each equipped with three of the same drill bombs that were used to raise the earth's mountains. Black scientists with psychic abilities would pilot the Mother Plane, which could not be attacked but "can hide behind . . . stars and make herself invisible to the eye." On the day of destruction, Fard Muhammad prophesied that two black scientists on every other street corner would direct the righteous black people to the only two safe havens on earth prior to the commencement of Allah's terrible work.[40]

At the time of the Judgment, this "masterpiece of mechanics," hovering twenty miles above the earth, would dispatch the smaller planes, which would drop their incendiaries on America and England. Each bomb would rip into the earth and produce a mountain one mile high and columns of flame twelve miles high, destroying everything within fifty square miles. The strafing of America by the planes, though horrific, would not conclude the destruction. The coup de grâce would come when Allah himself would annihilate the earth by creating an explosion in its atmosphere resulting from a shortage cut into its atoms by Allah. In an instant, the "whole heavens will be blotted out...and the atmosphere of the earth will melt with fervent heat." America would burn in a great lake of fire for 390 years and would be fit for human habitation only after cooling for an additional 610 years. For the Black Nation, the event would be comparable in significance only to the deportation of the moon and the creation of the white man.[41]

Perhaps second only to the Yacub myth, the Mother Plane story was the most peculiar element of the theology of the Nation. Unless one was predisposed to believe in flying saucers, this tale could hardly be told without raising doubts even among the most open-minded of listeners. Nonetheless, the story, of course, served a purpose and was not simply a random piece of bizarreness inserted into the larger puzzle of Fard Muhammad. Like his contention that Mars was inhabited, the Mother Plane tale was rooted in a historical context that lent it credibility. Also, it was metaphorically associated with biblical scripture in a manner that maximized its appeal among prospective converts with Christian backgrounds. This aerial aircraft carrier of Fard Muhammad's played into both the science fiction films that, as mentioned earlier, were extremely popular during the early twentieth century and actual technological developments. It was probably no coincidence that Fard Muhammad described the Mother Plane as being constructed in Japan, where the world's largest dreadnoughts, the Yamato class, were being designed in the 1930s. Here, his intention was to thoroughly exploit the popular image of Japan among some African-Americans as the champion of people of color in order to give his story a gloss of realism.[42]

In essence, Fard Muhammad's fictional plane simply combined the mythical spaceships of the Martian movies with the superbattleships and aircraft carriers that were filling the ranks of every major navy in a weapon of divine retribution that was virtually invincible. To make his vision more palatable to his audience, he allegorized passages from Ezekiel 10:2–11 to confirm the circular appearance of the Mother Plane and extracted the lake-of-fire scenario directly from Revelation 19:20 to illustrate its destructive capabilities.[43]

To conclude the Nation's depiction of the Judgment, the Black Nation would construct a new world upon the smoldering ashes of the dead civilization of the Caucasians. A new people, numbering a bit more than the 144,000 prophesied in Revelation, would build a new government "based upon truth, freedom, justice, and equality," which would live forever under the guidance of Allah. Sickness, fear, grief, and the vices of the old world would be eliminated, as would the language and names of Yacub's people. In twenty years time, even the memory of American civilization would be erased from the minds of the saved. Amidst the new spawning of trees, vegetation, and sparkling waters, the Original People themselves would look different, clearly better. Physically fitter and "clothed in silk interwoven with gold," the lost-found black people would appear sixteen years of age and would be able to live a thousand years or longer, just as the black god-scientists had trillions of years earlier. After the Judgment, the reason for Allah's creation of the devil would be clear, and his righteous people would know that he gave the white man "power to rule the earth for six thousand years" to show that he could "destroy the devil in one day without falling a victim." The new paradise, more than anything else, would be a testament to God's omnipotence and his new Islam.[44]

The afterworld of the Muslims was an almost standard version of the hereafter of millenarian groups. The absence of evil and sickness and the enjoyment of abundant resources and extraordinary longevity, if not immortality, was not unlike heaven in Judeo-Christian theology or paradise as described in the Qur'an. Fard Muhammad's depiction of the white world as irredeemably evil and doomed set the stage for an afterlife that was perfectly divine. Even the memory of the former wicked world was supposedly lost among the faithful believers after the Judgment, which emphasized the lack of value that the Nation attached to Western civilization. Like many other millenarian organizations, the Nation's view of the end of the world, while revolutionary in a superficial sense, was an essentially conservative approach to changing the conditions of black oppression. Their belief that God would, in the future, intervene in human affairs both to destroy evil nations and to set up a global theocracy under his direct control freed the Muslims from having to commit themselves to an activist program, especially one based on violence, to address the status quo. Ultimately, his depiction of the Judgment and the afterworld allowed Fard Muhammad, and later Elijah Muhammad, to attract African-Americans into the Nation of Islam without having to actively deliver them from their oppression beyond a partial withdrawal of believers into temple life. Conveniently, the burden of deliverance was left to God, who would act in his own good time.[45]

The whole story of Fard Muhammad was both incredible and disturbing. Only a rare person could hear it told without being momentarily struck speechless. To some, the Muslim history of the Black Nation made perfect sense and explained a great many things; to others, it was sheer lunacy born of a depraved mind. Whatever responses it evoked, the philosophical moorings of the Nation of Islam were not all new and were, indeed, rooted in ideological influences present in black America during the early twentieth century. The disparate theoretical elements were drawn both from familiar sources (such as the African-American church, Masonry, black nationalism, etc.) as well as from sources that were *en vogue* (e.g., Islam) in black urban communities in the 1920s and 1930s. Amalgamated and modified by Fard Muhammad and the Muslims, these ideas were crystallized into what they called Truth, or "the knowledge of self and others."

In regard to traditional or orthodox Islam, the Nation of Islam was heterodox in many of its views and practices; however, it was arguably a legitimate Muslim sect given its marginal adherence to central tenets of the Islamic faith. The differences between the two theological traditions were substantial, but not to the point of mutual exclusiveness. For example, while God, according to orthodox Muslims, is immortal, noncorporeal, and flawless, the Nation of Islam portrayed Allah as a successive incarnation of divine power in the guise of flesh and blood. The feats attributed to both versions of God, such as the creation of the universe and man, are the same, though the nature of his presence and appearance is described differently. For both the Nation of Islam and orthodox Muslims, the Bible and the Qur'an are authoritative texts. However, the former believed that these two tomes "must soon give way to that Holy Book which man as yet but Allah has seen." Additionally, Fard Muhammad and his followers believed that parts of the Bible had been tampered with by whites to mislead blacks, while their orthodox counterparts held a similar, but nonracial, view that the holy book could not be taken literally on some topics, such as the crucifixion and resurrection of Jesus.[46]

The similarities and dissonances between the Nation of Islam and traditional adherents of Islam can be discerned in other beliefs and rituals. For instance, unlike Fard Muhammad and his black advocates, orthodox Muslims believe that all people, including whites, were created by Allah "from mud moulded into clay," not by "grafting" performed by Yacub or any other human beings (Surah 15:26–29). In common with the Nation of Islam, Muslim religious tradition incorporates Moses, Jesus, and Muhammad ibn Abdullah into Islamic doctrine as prophets, but it does not recognize Elijah Muhammad or anyone else who has lived during the past thirteen hundred years as a "messenger of Allah." Furthermore, the leadership structure of conventional Islam is different from that of the Nation of Islam. In the case of the orthodox Muslims, the *ulema* (a group of scholars) and the *imam* (a prayer leader) interpret Islamic doctrine and guide the worship of the *umma* (the Muslim community). In the Nation of Islam, Fard Muhammad, and later Elijah Muhammad, ruled the organization in a dictatorial manner, assisted by an elaborate hierarchy of ministers and other officials who controlled temple affairs.

Finally, in matters of proper living, ritual, and eschatology, the two groups were more alike than different, though not uniform. The Muslims of the Nation and their orthodox cousins were most alike in eschewing pork and immodest dress. However, the Nation of Islam at best only marginally recognized the traditional Islamic prayer rituals and the observance of Ramadan, and it banned polygamy altogether. Only in a rudimentary way is the Judgment and afterworld of the Nation rooted in orthodox Islam. The ultimate punishment and elimination of evil and evildoers and the resultant paradise for the righteous are prominent themes in both doctrines. But, of course, the Mother Plane and the racially biased Judgment depicted by Fard Muhammad have no place in traditional Islamic theology. Overall, the basic outlines of both religious traditions do appear to overlap enough to allow the black organization to reasonably claim membership in the body of Islam, albeit as a heretical limb.[47]

As stated earlier, the most salient Islamic precursor of the Nation of Islam was the Moorish Science Temple of America (MSTA), which flourished in the 1920s. In many ways, the Moorish-Americans were quite comparable to the Nation of Islam, for both groups insisted upon similar dietary restrictions; shunned sports, gambling, motion pictures, and other secular entertainment; and banned the use of alcohol, tobacco, and hair-straightening products, which they believed were indicative of how the white world had vitiated blacks. Moreover, the MSTA, like the Muslims, embraced Islam as their natural religion and repudiated Christianity and such labels as *colored* and *Negro,* which were deemed inappropriate for Moors, whose "Asiatic" roots lay in the ancient land of Canaan (or East Asia, according to the Nation of Islam). Both groups met in temples under the Islamic star and crescent and seated members in sex-segregated pews, the women dressed in pants or the traditional full-body garb of Muslims in the East, the men in Western-style suits and ties. Monogamy was emphasized and divorce discouraged, along with intermarriage. Additionally, worshipers were given Nation of Islam original names or MSTA national cognomens, the former sometimes consisting of an Arabic name but more often an X, which represented the lost, unknown surname of the new convert before the enslavement of his/her ancestors, or in the latter case, the surname *Bey* or *El,* which signified membership in the Moorish nation.[48]

Divergences between the Muslims and the Moors are most apparent regarding doctrinal matters. Both groups conceived God as a terrestrial entity intimately connected to the material world of man. In the Nation of Islam, the god-scientists who created the universe and wrote the history of the world were mortal in almost every sense, living and dying as other men do. In MSTA theology, however, concepts of good and evil are all internal; Allah and the devil are simply states of mind. The higher self, or the part of man that is spiritual and eternal, is in touch with the nobler principles of truth, love, mercy, and justice and is the essence of the "human spirit clothed with soul, in the form of Allah." The lower self, steeped in carnality and desire, is the devil, which man must purge from within. This part of man is given to falsehood and "the murky ethers of the flesh" and ultimately stands between humanity and salvation. Although both conceptions of the divine and the wicked are centered around man, the views of the Nation of Islam and the Moorish-Americans in regard to deities and demons differ, the former opting for a more racially chauvinistic, materialist approach to explaining the world.[49]

Along with these dissimilarities, the two groups held different opinions regarding the nature of their presence in the United States. The Muslims in general believed that their stay in "the wilderness of North America" was temporary until they could migrate back to "their own" in East Asia. Accordingly, they rejected U.S. citizenship along with its obligations, such as military service in times of war, and claimed to be "registered with the nation of Islam." In contrast, the Moorish-Americans, who over time gained a reputation for being hostile to whites, honored citizenship in both America and their "homeland," Morocco, and carried around nationality cards that stressed the latter affiliation. Regardless of these doctrinal variations, the Nation of Islam undoubtedly emerged from the same waters of quasi-Islam as had the MSTA. For many individuals, membership in this latter group had preceded their association with Fard Muhammad's Muslims.[50]

The black separatist trend in Muslim ideology can be traced to ideas and programs that have their origins in the midnineteenth century. The most pertinent source of the Nation's form of nationalism was the Universal Negro Improvement Association (UNIA), based in Harlem. Started by Marcus Garvey, who arrived from Jamaica in the United States in 1916, this organization nurtured back-to-Africa and Pan-Africanist sentiments among African-Americans more than any other group prior to the decolonization of Africa. During the peak of his popularity in the early 1920s, Garvey stressed emigration as well as respect for blackness and economic self-help. Like the Muslims, who paid tribute to his legacy, he often emphasized that blacks should give up otherworldly views of religion and wrote at length about what he comprehensively called "the tragedy of white injustice." While he did not go so far as to embrace the racial determinism of the Nation of Islam, he did share with them an animosity toward Jews, whom the UNIA leader viewed as a people living "inconsistent with the broader human principles that go to make all people homogeneous."[51]

In a sense, the UNIA was as much a religious movement as it was a political force. The desire of Garveyites to achieve the "redemption of Africa" from white imperial control often took on spiritual significance. Moreover, many of the hundreds of thousands of individuals who joined the movement described their attraction to Garvey's ideas as akin to a conversion experience. Indeed, Garvey, like Fard Muhammad, utilized the symbols of Christianity to draw African-Americans into his organization. The God of the UNIA was portrayed as black, and each chapter of the organization was authorized to select a chaplain to attend to the spiritual needs of members.

The favorite rallying cry of the movement ("One God! One aim! One destiny!") summed up both its nationalist and religious underpinnings, and editorials in the UNIA organ, the *Negro World,* were read aloud at Sunday meetings as if they were the words of God. Largely rooted in the contagion of nationalism that swept the Western world between the world wars, Garveyism was an integral part of Muslim doctrine as it evolved during the 1930s.[52]

The similarities between the Nation of Islam and the Peace Mission movement of Father Divine (George Baker Jr.) seem to be more superficial and coincidental than imitative. Like the Muslims, Father Divine advocated black self-help, prohibited indulgences such as smoking, alcohol drinking, and fornication among his followers, and achieved a degree of notoriety in the midst of the Great Depression. His God, similar to that of Elijah Muhammad, was an anthropomorphic being, a spirit that could be expressed in flesh and blood. Initially, he assumed the title of "Messenger, God in the Sonship degree," deferring only to his spiritual mentor, Father Jehovia (Samuel Morris). By the First World War, he had promoted himself to God, and his followers began to revere him as such. Aside from these resemblances, there appear to be no other notable similarities between the Muslims and the Peace Mission.[53]

The most striking difference between the two religious groups was in regard to perceptions of race. While Fard Muhammad promoted a racially chauvinistic Islam and prohibited "white devils" from joining the Nation, Father Divine supported integration and welcomed whites into his fold. Underscoring his belief in racial liberalism, he married a white follower in 1946 and dubbed her "Sweet Angel the Spotless Virgin Bride." In further contrast to the Muslims, Father Divine's following was largely confined to the East and West Coasts, with strongholds in Seattle, Los Angeles, New York, and Newark. His movement even attracted a few professionals and wealthy contributors; the Muslims would not make significant inroads into the middle class until the late 1950s. It is possible that Fard Muhammad, who established his Nation of Islam in the Midwest, may have come into contact with the Los Angeles branch of the Peace Mission before arriving in Detroit. If he did, he apparently absorbed little, if any, of its ideology besides the self-help teachings and messianism, which many other groups had also embraced.[54]

Besides Islam, nationalism, and self-help philosophies, the influence of Freemasonry, present in the black community since at least the eighteenth century, was also evident in the ideology of the Nation of Islam. Many of the early converts, including Elijah Muhammad, had been Masons prior to their membership in the Muslim movement and found the exclusivity of the lost-founds, as well as their esoteric ways and privileged knowledge of Truth, familiar and attractive. Similar to the Masons and other black fraternal organizations, the Nation affirmed that people of African descent had an honorable past worthy of positive reflection. Also, the group stressed the importance of the present experiences of African-Americans and how current events were linked to momentous developments in the future. The Muslims, like the Masons, primarily attracted those blacks who simply desired to be a part of something larger than themselves; something that gave them a new identity and helped them to forget about the unpleasantness of the world around them.[55]

At least for some Masons, membership in the Nation represented a spiritual graduation to a new level of knowledge even more intriguing and coveted than the thirty-three degrees of Masonic secrets. The Muslims believed that their gnosis was superior to the knowledge of the Masons in philosophical breadth and practical utility. It was not so much that they felt that the Nation's theology was radically different from Masonic doctrines, though it was in many ways, but instead, that the beliefs of the Muslims were "original" formulations from which Freemasonry flowed as a sort of doctrinal distributary. Both the Muslims and the Masons shared an affinity for mystical symbolism, biblical allegories, and numerology, but the former considered themselves superior custodians of arcane knowledge. Whatever their ultimate motives for becoming Muslims, Masons did number among the early converts of the Nation of Islam. In subsequent years, leaders of the organization actively recruited Masons by evoking the language and symbolism of the order itself. As late as 1972, Elijah Muhammad advised Masons "to come over [to the Nation of Islam] because we give you more than what the devil has given you."[56]

To a greater extent than commonly acknowledged, the millenarian beliefs of the Jehovah's Witnesses made an indelible impression on the Muslims' version of the Judgment. The year 1914 is central to both religions as the date marking the fall of the gentile nations (and Satan) and the establishment of a new order under God himself on earth. Similar to how the Jehovah's Witnesses pushed back the year in which the battle of Armageddon was to start to the fall of 1975, the Nation of Islam gave the white world, and the "so-called Negro," a grace period that would end between 1965 and 1984. Both groups believed that God would punish the world with natural disasters and that only the elect, which numbered 144,000 according to a literal interpretation of Revelation, would enjoy paradise after the Judgment. However, others might achieve a form of salvation through good deeds and faith. The heaven of the Muslims would be remarkably similar to that of the Witnesses, in which "perfect food" would lead to perfect health, lost teeth would be regenerated, and all of the righteous "will be as beautiful as you were in your youth." In preparation for the end of the current wicked world, members of the two religions repudiated all allegiances outside of the faith and discouraged saluting the American flag and military service. Like Judge Rutherford, the leader of the Witnesses between 1917 and 1942, Elijah Muhammad and other Muslims would choose prison sentences rather than comply with the draft during World War II.[57]

In common with the Jehovah's Witnesses, the Nation of Islam advocated the kind of anti-Catholicism that flourished among nativist groups during the interwar period. The Muslim critique of the papacy and the Catholic Church was actually derived directly from the writings of Judge Rutherford and other Christian theorists. The typical characterization of the Church by both movements focused on the Pope himself and only secondarily on Catholics as a group. Pointing to Revelation for scriptural proof, the leaders of the Nation of Islam and the Witnesses identified the pontiff as the dragon (Satan), guilty of having deceived the ignorant. To them, the Pope was the head of a conspiracy to ensnare the righteous and drag them to hell. Elijah Muhammad, like Rutherford, would have little positive to say of loyal followers of Rome, writing them all off as "Beasts" in the Revelation sense of the term. Though the criticisms were, of course, self-serving, the Nation of Islam, like the Witnesses, reserved special invectives for the Catholics and their leader in contrast to their milder fulminations against other religious opponents. In sum, the Muslims, for good or for ill, owed a number of their convictions to the Jehovah's Witnesses. Blended with Islam, nationalism, Freemasonry, and other Christian ideas, the theology of the Witnesses would assist Fard Muhammad (and Elijah Muhammad) in portraying membership in the Nation as an imperative for African-Americans seeking to escape the fall of America.[58]

Constructed on an eclectic foundation yet unique in many ways, the theosophy of Fard Muhammad was carefully tailored to appeal to blacks who had fallen by the wayside of America and were susceptible to the rhetoric of messianism. The cosmology, separatism, and moral code of the Muslims were all suited to the recruitment of African-Americans who had Christian roots and bore the burden of white racism and discrimination. The tales invented by Fard Muhammad to explain everything from the origins of the universe to the destiny of the Western world drew from many different sources, and little was too outrageous to be included if it would attract followers. At least for a segment of African-Americans, many of the myths and ideas that Fard Muhammad used to stir up support in Detroit during the Depression were still appealing as late as the 1990s. Ultimately, the whole story of the Tribe of Shabazz leaves one awed by the leader's ability to package the bizarre and esoteric in the wrappings of logic and rationality. Seemingly, Fard Muhammad's, and later Elijah Muhammad's, appeal may have lay as much in his presentation as in the message itself.

PART TWO

THE
WILDERNESS

CHAPTER 4

TABERNACLE IN THE WILDERNESS

And verily this Brotherhood of yours is a single Brotherhood, and I am your Lord and Cherisher: therefore fear Me (and no other).

But people have cut off their affair (of unity), between them, into sects: each party rejoices in that which is with itself.

But leave them in their confused ignorance for a time.
—The Qur'an
(Surah 23:52–54)[1]

Contrasted with the African-American communities of Detroit and Chicago in the 1930s, black Milwaukee was tiny. During the Great Depression, the city's black community grew at a higher rate than the general population, yet by 1940, only 8,721, or less than 2 percent, of the city's residents were African-Americans. Many of the black people who migrated to Wisconsin were from the lower South and had passed through larger urban areas such as Chicago before settling in Milwaukee. Once in the "beer town," however, their place in the city's life resembled that of blacks in other industrial centers. As in Detroit and Chicago, the African-American community of Milwaukee was not hard to find. Over 93 percent of the city's blacks resided in the Sixth and Tenth Wards in 1940, immured within four streets in the northern Near Downtown district. Their homes were obviously among the oldest in the city, and according to one source, 67.7 percent of them were due for serious repairs or were simply "unfit for use," while 6.5 percent of white homes were in the same category. On average, the residence of a black homeowner was worth only half that of his white counterpart, and only 5.7 percent of African-Americans were homeowners in 1940 as opposed to 32.6 percent of whites. The housing situation was not the only indicator that a little ghetto was blossoming in Milwaukee; the tragic economic plight of the black community was perhaps the most salient symptom.²

For a while during 1933–34, Milwaukee appeared to be slowly recovering from the Depression, due in large part to New Deal programs and the repeal of Prohibition. These hopeful signs, however, proved deceiving, and in the fall of 1937, massive layoffs occurred in all major industries in response to the city's plunge into another recession. Two years later, 20 percent of the families in Milwaukee County were receiving public assistance. While bleak, the economic situation of the city in general was simply hard compared to the abysmal poverty that descended upon the African-American community throughout the Depression. In 1937, blacks, accounting for only 1.5 percent of the population, comprised 3.9 percent of Milwaukee's "totally unemployed" and 6.9 percent of the laborers working on public emergency relief projects. Milwaukee's African-American community actually suffered a relatively unique kind of deprivation compared to the experiences of blacks in many other depressed industrial centers. For example, the unemployment rates of Milwaukee and Detroit after the stock market crash were about the same. By 1940, however, almost a third of the African-American men in the former city were looking for work in contrast to 15.7 percent in the Motor City. Of course, many factors contributed to the high level of misery in Milwaukee's black community, but racial discrimination in the workplace was certainly among the most important. The opposition of white workers and unions to the hiring of African-Americans by breweries and other industries helped employers keep wages down and kept the black unemployment rate up. The use of African-American workers as strikebreakers further strengthened racial antagonisms within the workforce. Consequently, even as Milwaukee blacks were being proletarianized by the demands of urban industrial life during the 1930s, they were also being ghettoized by patterns of residential segregation and economic exclusion.³

The small, destitute black section of Milwaukee in all likelihood reminded Elijah Muhammad as much of the Southern towns of Cordele and Macon, where he had become well acquainted with hard times, as it did the large black areas of Detroit and Chicago's South Side. Though the city was more industrialized and whiter than most Georgian urban centers, many of the same racial and class-based proscriptions that afflicted the Black Belt in the South produced ghettos in Northern cities.

In Milwaukee, Muhammad found temporary refuge in Temple No. 3 on McKinley Boulevard, thanks to a Muslim named Ali who had facilitated his escape from Chicago. The Milwaukee cell of lost-founds, organized by Fard Muhammad and his messenger a few years earlier, was perhaps as old as that of Chicago, but probably much smaller given the size of the black section there. Muhammad's purpose in visiting Milwaukee is not altogether clear, but he probably used the opportunity to fish for new members as well as to make sure that the contagion of hypocrisy, which had decimated his following in Detroit and Chicago, had not reached Wisconsin. Overall, his stay in Milwaukee was brief, only lasting a few weeks at most. The visit was, in fact, a mere stopover in a longer journey that would take him to the East Coast. The members of the Nation of Islam in the penurious Sixth Ward were no doubt pleased to see their leader, but unlike Temples No. 1 and 2, they had from the beginning existed without the day-to-day presence of either Fard Muhammad or Elijah Muhammad. After the departure of their messenger, they would continue under the leadership of a "laborer" (or faithful member) by the name of Sultan Muhammad, who was appointed around this time. In late 1935, Elijah Muhammad concluded his business in the city and bid his followers farewell. Discreetly, he boarded a train for Washington, D.C.[4]

Muhammad's flight from Chicago was likely meant to be only temporary until things cooled down at Temple No. 2. However, the departure from Milwaukee, possibly occasioned by an appearance of some of his enemies in the city, would begin a seven-year exile of Muhammad to the Eastern states. He would infrequently visit his family and followers, checking on Clara and the children and offering words of advice and encouragement to those Muslims who remained loyal to him. Yet, he did not risk staying in Chicago too long during these visits, lest he become a victim of his rivals. While he was away from the nerve center of the movement, certain consistencies made his wanderings both tolerable and difficult. For example, the shadow of persecution followed him everywhere and was at least partially responsible for his rather erratic movement from city to city. Also, deprivation was a constant companion, and on many days Muhammad went without food or shelter. Despite the uncertainty and suffering, the experience probably solidified his support of the teachings of the Nation of Islam and his belief in the legitimacy of his messengership. He claimed that he received annual mental messages from Fard Muhammad, akin to telepathy, which bolstered his loyalty to the man he knew as God. His "knowledge of self and others" and faith in his deity probably made life bearable during his seven-year hegira.[5]

Muhammad made Washington, D.C., his adopted home during his absence from Chicago, but was rarely in town long enough to become attached to the city. Under the name Mr. Evans, he rented a room with a man named Benjamin Mitchell, who had advertised for a boarder to help out him and his wife financially. During his stay, Muhammad became quite fond of his hosts and even disclosed to them that he was engaged in "missionary work among our people . . . , had met with God," and was currently attempting to resurrect the so-called Negro. Benjamin, after hearing the teachings, became one of the first converts in the capital, proving to Muhammad that the black section of the city had potential as a recruiting ground for the Nation. The African-American community of the capital was much larger than that of Milwaukee, forming a significant minority of the population. But the familiar patterns of housing discrimination, unemployment, and racial tensions made life for the over 187,000 black people in the city similar to the situation of African-Americans in the Midwestern towns Muhammad had lived in. Even though it was the seat of the ostensibly liberal New Deal, Washington was still a Southern city with all the trimmings, notwithstanding Roosevelt's "black cabinet" and the less rigid Jim Crow system. Muhammad found his niche in the capital within the black community, of course, and ventured across the tracks only when absolutely necessary.[6]

Most of Muhammad's time in white Washington was spent in the Congressional Library reading books from the list of 104 titles that Fard Muhammad had given him. Some of the works were on Islam and the life of Muhammad ibn Abdullah. Others were simply "different pieces of truth that devil white man had recorded, but which were not in books generally available to the public." Whole days were often consumed by reading, and Muhammad's life in Washington seemed to revolve around the library and the study of religion. The knowledge that he acquired in Washington was put to good use and shared with African-Americans he met while traveling to such places as Newark, Baltimore, Providence, Pittsburgh, Cleveland, and Atlanta. During one encounter with Moorish-Americans in Hartford, Connecticut, his grasp and presentation of Nation of Islam doctrine impressed the MSTA members to the extent that they implored him to instruct them over the objections of their leader. Muhammad's education in spiritual matters was largely a product of his attempts during this period to build upon the foundation that Fard Muhammad had laid. His penury—perhaps only partially relieved by menial jobs and funds received from followers in Chicago—reinforced the appeal of the asceticism that coursed through Muslim teachings. This philosophy ultimately fortified the sense of sacrifice on behalf of the "so-called Negro" that Muhammad had cultivated since 1931. In addition to the books assigned by his savior, he delved deep into biblical scripture and the surahs of the Qur'an, finding those elements of wisdom that had eluded him during his life as a Christian. By 1939 when Hitler unleashed blitzkrieg on Europe, Muhammad felt the time was ripe to open Temple No. 4 in the capital of the wilderness of North America.[7]

During their leader's exile, Muslims in Chicago gradually resuscitated the nearly collapsed structure of Temple No. 2. When Muhammad left in late 1935, only thirteen members were in his corner, not even enough to effectively carry out the all-important tasks of fishing on the South Side and administering organizational affairs. In fact, the movement had become merely a collection of officers with no general body. There was a general secretary, a recorder secretary, a Fruit secretary, a registrar, a captain, a minister, an assistant minister, and six lieutenants, but no rank-and-file following. Also, as usual, the treasury was in poor shape. To feed their families and to fund temple activities, the male members often collected and sold whatever salvable refuse they could find in alleys. Muslim women worked as day laborers and performed odd jobs to supplement household and temple income. Some lost-founds, such as Pauline Bahar, who fixed meals for the Fruit of Islam, became known among the Temple People as exemplary altruists and model Muslims. Others were ostracized for using the teachings to gain a quick dollar from the gullible.[8]

Actually, the responses of Muslims to economic conditions could be quite diverse. Some members of the Nation gained reputations as disciplined, honest workers and were often hired over other blacks because of their strict moral code and dependability. A number of the more millenarian followers even went as far as to heed the advice of their leaders and dispensed with their worldly possessions in 1936 in preparation for the fall of America. In contrast, many lost-founds, in the midst of hard times, acquired expensive tastes in clothing, furniture, and cars and used their hard-earned paychecks to purchase luxury items that "represented a restoration of original high status and an escape from slavery." Some became thoroughly bourgeois in their outlook and were known for living beyond their means, especially during the brief economic respite of the mid-1930s. Despite these millenarian and secular tensions in the movement, recruitment drives did eventually produce new members, and income, and allowed the Nation of Islam in Chicago to move its meetings from the houses of the faithful to a building at 51 Michigan Avenue. As an indicator of their moderate success, the Muslims of the flagship temple could boast a membership of 150 to 300 lost-founds by the time of their messenger's return in the summer of 1942.[9]

As the members of Temple No. 2 began its reconstruction, the Nation of Islam as a tristate organization continued to splinter during the late 1930s. Before his departure, Elijah Muhammad had tried to reduce the likelihood of further offshoots by claiming his teacher's mantle and purging dissident elements from the movement. He even went so far as to ban the wearing of fezzes by Temple People since this practice made his group appear indistinguishable from MSTA members and other Islamic groups that "smoke, drink and misbehave." His efforts, however, availed him little, and a new rival temple seemed to appear on almost every street corner. Notably, a former minister of the Nation named Azzim Shah established an independent congregation in 1936, followed two years later by the secession of Theodore Rozier, the appointed custodian of Detroit Temple No. 1, who founded his own movement based on a doctrinal variant of the original teachings of Fard Muhammad. In Detroit in particular, leadership coups and ideological schisms were the order of the day prior to the Second World War. Various cliques within the temple rose and receded every year, and Muslim rhetoric could change from anti–New Deal to pro-socialist without adequate conditioning of the membership. Though Elijah Muhammad appointed his eldest brother, William Jr., to replace the apostate Rozier, special-interest groups—only secondarily concerned with Islam—used the Nation repeatedly as a platform for their agendas. On the whole, the decade between 1932 and 1942 is most memorable for the Muslims as a time of destructive disunity, overly competitive leadership, law enforcement harassment, and organizational penury.[10]

Elijah Muhammad instructed Muslims in the newly formed Temple No. 4 under the name of Muhammad Rassoull, one of his many aliases at this time. His teachings were generally in line with what Fard Muhammad had revealed to him, yet a bit more politicized due to the world war. The membership of the Washington temple grew steadily under Muhammad's leadership to the point that it was noticed by law enforcement officials, who wasted little time in infiltrating the group. The statements that informants heard in temple meetings were standard elements of Muslim rhetoric, but were not quite acceptable to law enforcement agencies obsessed with wartime domestic security. During gatherings in 1941, Muhammad prophesied that a conflict would erupt involving the United States. Early in the following year, he preached against black participation in the American war effort and even predicted that the Japanese would cross the Pacific Ocean in the Mother Plane to herald the occasion "when the white devils will be destroyed by dark mankind." Whether it was for the consumption of his followers or the federal agents he knew attended his meetings, Muhammad lambasted white America, the draft, and the country's racist practices. Around this time, hints of an impending impressment of Muslims into the U.S. armed forces must have reached the leader, for preparations were apparently made by some lost-founds to circumvent the selective service law. Muhammad, who was forty-four years old and still eligible for conscription, began a fast with the objective of reducing his body weight below 112 pounds. If it ever became necessary, he hoped to be able to grin in the faces of white draft-board officials as they determined that he was much too thin to fight tyranny in Europe.[11]

An able-bodied man could legally do little to counter the Selective Training and Service Act of 1940. The law was broadly inclusive and allowed for the induction of men between the ages of eighteen and forty-five. Educational requirements were lowered in May 1941 to permit individuals with fourth-grade scholastic ability and below to serve, despite some official concerns regarding the acceptance of illiterate soldiers into "a modern mechanized army." As of 1940, African-Americans comprised 10.4 percent of the 29,029,125 registrants, with the largest number (230,511) coming from Muhammad's home state of Georgia. Age, which the leader hoped to use as a trump card, would not necessarily exempt one from service, for some 54,913 blacks age forty-four were required to register for the draft, 1,128 of whom lived in the District of Columbia. Additionally, conscientious objection was no sure way of avoiding the demands of selective service. At best, those who challenged the war on religious and moral grounds could look forward to either a Class I-A-O assignment in noncombatant service "as defined by the President" or Class IV-E duty with the Civilian Public Service Camp. The unsuccessful objector could appeal his case, but the law did not recognize the right of anyone, regardless of ethical compunctions, to be exempt from "service to the Nation in its time of peril." For those African-Americans who claimed affiliation with the Muslims, the Hebrews, or other religious groups and failed to honor the requirements of the conscription act, prison sentences of up to five years were liberally passed out as an object lesson to others. By the end of 1943, 167 black men had been convicted for various draft violations under the 1940 law.[12]

Beyond his religious beliefs and advancing age, Muhammad's aversion to military service is understandable given that racial discrimination affected every branch of the armed services. To be sure, the U.S. military of the 1940s was not the same force that fought the Spanish-American War during Muhammad's childhood or that defeated Germany in 1918. By World War II, the U.S. military was much more open to African-American enlistment than during any other time in the country's history. Black aviators, trained at Tuskegee Army Air Field in Alabama, flew missions in some of the world's finest aircraft. African-American soldiers fought in artillery units and tank battalions and served in a variety of support organizations, from the signal corps to the medical corps. As a result of both necessity and changing attitudes, four thousand black women volunteered for the Women's Army Corps, and five hundred others served as nurses in the wartime army. Altogether, about 1 million blacks were enlisted during World War II, half of whom saw service overseas. Although segregation and menial jobs were still the order of the day for most black soldiers, with these advances military service was palatable enough to African-Americans to ensure that draft evasion was rare.

Despite the reforms of the Roosevelt administration, as always, black units were led by white officers, though some junior officers were black. Many white leaders were startlingly insensitive to the feelings and aspirations of their men and had little confidence in the character and intelligence of African-American troops. At least in the European theater, blacks were held to a higher standard of conduct than their white counterparts, resulting in a disproportionately high number of African-Americans being sentenced to death following courts-martial. Segregation in the military was strictly enforced throughout the war, sometimes to a ridiculous degree. Barracks, medical facilities, and training centers were routinely designated by race. Ironically, the American Red Cross went so far as to separate blood plasma by skin color, though Dr. Charles R. Drew, a black physician, pioneered the use of plasma for transfusions. An extension of civilian society, the military was not immune to the racial conflicts that tore through places like Detroit and Harlem during the war. Outbreaks of violence near army bases in Fayetteville, North Carolina, and Gurdon, Arkansas, in 1942 surprised no one who knew how much white Southerners detested black troops stationed in their midst. More than any other profession, military service was an extreme sacrifice for African-Americans. Black recruits, already demoralized by the domestic situation, went off to fight fascism and intolerance in Europe and the Pacific knowing that their own rights and freedoms were not secure at home.[13]

As early as 1931 when Muhammad "registered with the nation of Islam in Detroit," the leader had already decided that "under no circumstances" would he allow himself to be inducted into the American military. The day on which he was supposed to register, February 16, 1942, came and went, and Muhammad remained resolute in his refusal to fight white men on behalf of other white men. As it had for perhaps months, the FBI continued to keep Temple No. 4 under surveillance and did not make a move on the organization until midspring. On Friday, May 8, bureau agents finally arrested Muhammad, under the alias Gulam Bogans, at his home on 1306 Girard Street, N.W., charging him with failure to register with selective service. Like Fard Muhammad before him, the leader went peacefully, the arrest not wholly unexpected given the presence of photographers at the scene.[14]

Once in federal custody, Muhammad was grilled all night not about his unwillingness to serve, but about his political and religious beliefs. To support claims that the Nation of Islam was subversive, Muslim literature taken from a bag that the FBI had seized at his home was used by his interrogators as evidence against him. During the session, he tried to answer all the queries posed by his interviewers, but did not risk implicating himself with completely honest responses. The purpose of the fourteen-hour interrogation, which did not end until eight or nine o'clock Saturday morning, was to wear the detainee down physically as well as to secure an incriminating confession regarding his views on the war and the U.S. government. At one point, the questioning became so tormenting that a physician was called in to check Muhammad's mental state. To avoid indulging them in argument, he repeatedly responded to their questions with the refrain that he had come from Chicago to conduct business in the capital. Regarding his failure to register for the draft, he advised his interrogators that they would have to be satisfied with the explanation that his adherence to Islam prohibited him from taking part in a war against Hitler, Tojo, or anyone else. The interviewing agents, apparently unsatisfied with Muhammad's responses, detained him further in a Washington, D.C., jail under a five-thousand-dollar bond.[15]

Muhammad's arrest rallied Muslims not only in the capital but also in the Midwestern temples. As their messenger, his imprisonment was synonymous with their own incarceration, and as expressed by one member of the Nation, the lost-founds generally "believed that if our Brother Rassoull . . . was guilty of anything, we all were equally guilty." Anticipating an organized attempt by the Muslims both to come to Muhammad's aid and to violate the selective service law, the FBI used his arrest as a pretext for conducting a multistate assault on the Temple People. When William Muhammad and Sultan Muhammad, ministers of Temples No. 1 and 3 respectively, arrived in the capital to consult with their leader, they were quickly arrested at the Washington temple in the 1500 block of Ninth Street, N.W. The Wisconsin laborer was sent back to Milwaukee to face federal hearings for his failure to register for the draft. The Michigan minister was detained under a two-thousand-dollar bond pending extradition to Detroit to stand trial for the same charge. Around May 16, federal officials searched Temple No. 3 and found a number of records of interest, including instructional letters from Clara Muhammad. Three days later, the Detroit temple was raided, and eleven Muslims were apprehended. Though pleased "that there was no Japanese influence apparent" among them, the federal agents were dismayed, but probably not surprised, that the six men arrested had refused to register for the draft because it "was contrary to the law of Allah."[16]

In the end, the FBI's calculated sweep of the Nation of Islam was effective in enforcing the draft law of 1940, but not in depriving Elijah Muhammad of the moral support and loyalty of his followers. At the moment, however, more than fidelity from his partisans, the leader needed their financial support. Unfortunately for him, the raids on the Milwaukee and Detroit temples made monetary assistance from these quarters unlikely. Exercising his last option, the imprisoned messenger of the lost-founds appealed to the headquarters of the movement for desperately needed funds, hoping that the government's net had not also been cast over Chicago.

While Muslims in the Windy City scoured the South Side for money to send to their messenger, the Washington believers started a campaign to publicize what they felt was an outrage against Islam. Photographs of Muhammad and other Muslims in police custody were circulated by the faithful, and a protest march was organized by parents and children, who circled the District jail in support of the man who had convinced them to give up the white man's religion, names, and school system. Unlike in the demonstrations of the mid-1930s, there were apparently no outbreaks of violence between the Muslims and the police. But again, a price was to be paid for their demands for "freedom, justice, and equality." Anti-Muslim landlords, probably inspired by the FBI and local law enforcement officials, evicted African-Americans who were identified as active supporters of Muhammad, and a number of other lost-founds were arrested for draft resistance. Despite these trials, many of the Temple People of Washington continued to stand firm behind their leader. Consequently, when the emissary from Chicago arrived in the capital with the awaited bail money, she found a group of Muslims who were as devoted as any to their Holy Apostle and his cause.[17]

For Muhammad, the appearance of his wife, Clara, at his Washington jail cell must have been uplifting. He had seen her too infrequently over the past seven years, and many nights he had gone to bed depressed about the life he had left behind in Chicago. In 1939, when the Detroit temple was rent by ideological warfare and ministerial intrigue, she was giving birth to their eighth child, Akbar, and raising the family almost single-handedly. Her spirituality guided her through the trauma of having to care for small children in the midst of a worldwide economic catastrophe. To Muhammad and others, she was a genuine hero, and her arrival in the capital, bearing a suitcase full of one-dollar bills, to rescue her husband from his enemies simply affirmed this fact. In the years to come, Sister Clara would continue to endure the pain of familial separation and poverty, but would not neglect her responsibilities to her children or fail to live up to the demands that her husband's mission placed upon their marriage. For these reasons, Muslims throughout the country would come to esteem her as a "truly original" black woman.[18]

Clara arrived in Washington none too soon. According to a vision of Fard Muhammad that Elijah allegedly experienced in his cell, the FBI's plans for him were not pleasant and might even have involved bodily injury or extreme deprivation. At his arraignment, the leader waived the right to be represented by an attorney, but later reconsidered his predicament and hired an English lawyer. Before Clara's arrival, his counsel had informed him that the government had no intention of giving him a trial and was satisfied in having him "out of the public." This news bothered Muhammad greatly, and for two and a half months he paced his cell wondering "whether they were going to have a trial or anything—or let me sit [here] and mold." Once his bond was finally paid on July 23, he and Clara were barely beyond the shadow of the District jailhouse before his attorney found them and warned, "For God's sake, leave the city. They are planning to get you tonight." Later that evening while Muhammad was perhaps taking care of business at the temple, a white man approached Clara and requested information regarding her husband's whereabouts. Careful not to give Muhammad away, she was fully aware that what she said could lead to further jail time for her husband. Clara then related the encounter to Elijah, who wasted no time in making arrangements for them to leave on the next Pennsylvania-limited train to Chicago.[19]

Muhammad's seven-year journey along the East Coast strengthened his emotional and physical endurance as he interacted with African-Americans from many different cities who had a thirst for the knowledge of self and others. The hours spent in the Congressional Library added a bit of refinement to Muhammad's crude formal education, and Washington Temple No. 4 would in time become one of the more important strongholds of the Nation. In general, he became more confident in his mission and ability to lead through the establishment of the Washington temple. Nonetheless, like the succession conflict of 1933–35, the hegira heightened his feelings of persecution and sacrifice, which would become even more accentuated by events in the near future.

When he arrived in Chicago in late July 1942, the Messenger of Allah was not the same man who had slipped away in 1935, and the circumstances under which he left had changed. He had gained new followers, and "the hypocrites" who had chased him out of Chicago were apparently out of the picture. Perhaps some of his enemies simply lost interest in the Nation, especially after its drastic decline in membership and resources. Perhaps some were taken away by the draft or had migrated to other cities in search of employment. Whatever the case, Muhammad was able to return to Chicago without fearing immediate reprisals from his rivals. However, he now had to worry about more powerful enemies who had the will and resources to pursue him indefinitely. Having preached against white America in the midst of war and broken the stipulations of his bail, Elijah Muhammad was now "public enemy number one" in the draconian era of J. Edgar Hoover. He would soon "learn the price of TRUTH for . . . the so-called Negroes."[20]

CHAPTER 5

PUBLIC ENEMY

Was not Christ crucified?
—Nat Turner[1]

In 1942, the average temperature in Chicago for the month of July was the hottest it had been in six years. In fact, the average had been unusually high for the past decade. African-American migrants in the city, both newcomers and "Old Settlers," found it somewhat reminiscent of the scorching summers that annually baked their Southern home states. Upon his return to the city, Elijah Muhammad was definitely reminded of the oppressive Georgia heat that he had endured for twenty-five years. The exile of the leader in 1935 and his subsequent reappearance in July 1942 went virtually unnoticed by the vast majority of the black population of the South Side, which was much more concerned about subsistence and the draft than developments on the religious periphery of the African-American community. Yet, for those intimately associated with the affairs of the Nation of Islam headquarters at 104 East Fifty-first Street, the Temple People subculture was definitely going through important changes at this time. Meetings held on Wednesdays and Fridays at seven o'clock in the evening and Sunday afternoons at two o'clock routinely attracted two hundred people. During the periodic talks of Muhammad at the temple, attendance was sometimes higher. Overall, however, the leader was disappointed with the performance of those he had left in charge and wished that a greater number of so-called Negroes had realized the importance of the Nation's work in Chicago during his absence. Though they had come to his rescue in Washington, D.C., the accomplishments of the believers in the Windy City, in Muhammad's estimate, left much to be desired.[2]

To a large extent, circumstances beyond the control of the Chicago laborers, such as the Depression and police harassment, had made the job of recruiting difficult even for the most devoted and articulate of the lost-founds. Likewise, Muhammad's long absences and the shaky finances of the group did not aid expansion. Nonetheless, as the first order of business, the leader rearranged the hierarchy of the temple, replacing the minister and captains of the Fruit of Islam and MGT-GCC with members he believed more trustworthy. A follower named Len Karriem became the new ministerial head of Temple No. 2, and Raymond Sharrieff, Muhammad's son-in-law, was selected as the new "chief of police." The effect of these promotions and demotions are hard to trace, although the national membership figure of nine thousand, which Muhammad cited in August 1942, was probably inflated. However, the Chicago cell of Muslims had no problem attracting the attention of the FBI and other law enforcement agencies. In fact, federal agents had been spying on Temple No. 2 since its leader's return in July and was "waiting only on the go-ahead from Washington" to pounce.[3]

This go-ahead came on September 20. A two-pronged assault was launched against the Chicago Temple People, and the results this time were even more successful than the May raids. Muhammad and his followers were perhaps privy to the plans of the FBI prior to their execution, but had little opportunity to prepare. The Fifty-first Street temple was ransacked by agents searching for weapons, claiming that the group was under Japanese influence, but neither weapons nor any links to the Japanese were found. The most interesting piece of evidence the FBI confiscated turned out to be a blackboard with a blueprint of the Mother Plane on it. Several Muslims were present in the temple during the raid, and a number of officials were arrested on charges of sedition, conspiracy, and draft violations. According to observers, the lost-founds were treated respectfully, and the women, whose mistreatment would surely have provoked a clash, were not handled inappropriately. However, the temple was closed and services there discontinued indefinitely.[4]

Muhammad, who was perhaps tipped off by his followers, sought refuge at his mother's house, where he resided anyway, in hope of avoiding the sweep. But by this time the government's knowledge was thorough, and there were few places he could hide where his pursuers would not find him. The raid on the home produced a mother lode of materials for the federal agents, which would later be used to prosecute Muhammad and others. Among other things, the pillagers seized an old copy of the Muslims' defunct newspaper, the minutes of a February 1935 meeting, pictures and typewritten teachings of Fard Muhammad, and a red sign bearing the statement "There is no God but Allah, Master W. D. Fard, Elijah, his prophet." Muhammad was also apprehended at the scene, according to the FBI's version of events, found "under his mother's bed . . . wrapped in a carpet." In view of later events, the two raids were preliminary and small in scale. But in terms of significance, the arrests were quite pertinent to the government's wartime program of quelling African-American dissent, regardless of how peaceful or legal its manifestations. Instantly, the capture of "Takahashi's Blacks" became national news, and the Messenger of Allah was at the center of it all.[5]

Over the next few days, the first vague details of the FBI offensive became known to the general public. At the very least, three black groups had been targeted by the government, including the Peace Movement of Ethiopia and the Brotherhood of Liberty for Black People of America. Moreover, though initial roundups led to the arrests of twelve leaders, subsequent persecutions netted as many as eighty-five members of the three groups in Chicago alone. The charges of sedition and "conspiracy to promote the success of the enemy," on which the government hoped to build a case, were questionable at best and, even in the midst of a war involving real and perceived threats to domestic peace, would scarcely justify a conviction in an apolitical court of law. Nevertheless, the government, assisted by the black and white press, succeeded in stigmatizing African-American dissent and portraying the accused as fanatics, traitors, and charlatans whose leaders aroused "the most gullible and least literate fringe of their race into a fanatic hatred of the white race."[6]

The strongest charge that the government could levy against the Muslims and others was draft evasion. However, this count was downplayed in favor of the more serious and sensational accusations of subversion and conspiracy. Such distortion was commonplace in the Hoover-led FBI of this era, whether for gangsters like Dillinger, Robin Hood bandits like Pretty Boy Floyd, or black groups. In the end, the first appearance of sixty-five Muslims in court would reveal that for many, the exact nature of the charges were irrelevant and at best secondary to their real concerns. Illustratively, one lost-found, Allah Ben Aiken, after stating the standard Muslim reasons for opposing the war, requested that the adjudicating commissioner "sentence me to fifty years if you want. The white man is reaching the end of his rope after six thousand years and I won't do anything to stop him." In a courtroom where the Muslim presence was marked by the "blind, bitter defiance" that had become characteristic of the group's appearances before white bars of justice, observers could only be awed and perhaps frightened by the willingness of black men and women to go to jail, and even prison, for Allah and the so-called Negro.[7]

For Elijah Muhammad, the stint in the Cook County jail was an extension of his confinement experience in Washington, D.C. As before, the authorities bombarded him with many questions about the Nation of Islam, and in particular the drawing of the Mother Plane that had been confiscated during the raids. His failure to appear before the draft board in February was only of passing interest to the FBI interrogators; the beliefs and teachings of the Muslims were their main concern. While interviewing Muhammad, the government agents were apparently candid about their reasons for arresting him and conceded that "President Roosevelt doesn't want you out there in the public with that kind of Teaching while America is trying to prosecute a war between her, Germany, and Japan. That's all we are putting you in jail for, to keep you out of the public." The rationale genuinely perturbed Muhammad. He had never viewed himself or his group as a threat to the internal security of the United States, although the prophesied downfall of the country at the hands of Allah was wished for by all faithful Muslims. To the reasons that the FBI gave for jailing him, the leader could only reply, "Well . . . it is a terrible thing to set a man up in jail until the war ends to free him."[8]

The persecution and imprisonment of the Muslims seemed to confirm to Muhammad the white man's innate adverseness to truth and fairness. In his view, he and his followers had done nothing to deserve incarceration except teach the knowledge of self and others to the so-called Negroes. No lost-found had joined the German or Japanese armed forces, turned American top-secret documents over to Hitler or Hirohito, or cached weapons for a fifth-column offensive. They had simply practiced their religion of peace and asked for freedom, justice, and equality. Having failed to persuade his jailers of the unaggressive nature of the Nation of Islam, Muhammad decided to occupy his time constructively behind bars and requested a copy of the Qur'an to study. The warden, who had little respect for the Muslims and their claims to religious freedom, laughed at the request and denied him access to the book since "that is what we put them in prison for." His advice to Muhammad was to "read the Bible." Apparently, the leader chose to do without until his next scheduled court appearance on September 29, when he would presumably be able to defend his plea of not guilty. In the interim, he contemplated ways to secure the money needed to satisfy his ten-thousand-dollar bond.[9]

"Justice" for the Muslims would be swift and comprehensive. On the date of their arraignment, thirty-eight lost-founds appeared before the court shrouded in their typical air of silent aloofness. The main charge against them was failure to comply with the selective service law of 1940. Asked to clarify their refusal to serve in the armed forces, the defendants responded that they were not American citizens and could not participate in the draft because they had already "registered with Allah," whose will was revealed through Elijah Muhammad. Furthermore, since the Japanese were Asiatics and descendants of the black Original People, to go to war against the emperor would be fratricidal. The hearing was, of course, a perfunctory ritual aimed at satisfying the Muslims' constitutional rights to a trial. At the end of the session, all thirty-eight defendants were indicted for draft violations and remanded back into police custody until a later court date.[10]

On October 5, the accused Muslims appeared again in court to hear the decision of the U.S. government regarding their stated allegiance to Allah. Several of the accused were dressed in robes and were indifferent enough about the proceedings to decline legal counsel. In fact, most believed that carrying out their religious obligations, even at the risk of incarceration, was an honorable exercise in righteousness. Of the defendants, thirty pleaded guilty to the charge of violating the draft law and were sentenced to three-year prison sentences. Emmanuel Muhammad, Elijah's eldest son, received a five-year term, which led him to announce to the court, "I hope the Japs win the war. Then all the Negroes will be free!" Insofar as the majority of the defendants could not be convicted of the more serious charge of sedition, only Elijah Muhammad, Len Karriem, and Pauline Bahar (the secretary of the temple) were scheduled to be tried on this charge. In almost every regard, the government's case against them was weak, and even with assorted documents seized in another raid on Temple No. 2 on September 30, the state would have a difficult time proving that the leadership of the Nation was subversive. The records taken by the FBI raiders revealed no Japanese influence in the Muslim movement since the early 1930s, and the director of selective service himself admitted that black resistance to the draft "was purely a problem of individuals and not due to any organized effort or propaganda." Nevertheless, on October 23, Muhammad was indicted on eight counts of sedition, and Karriem, Bahar, Sultan Muhammad of Milwaukee, and David Jones of the Washington temple were charged with "conspiracy to commit sedition." To achieve its wartime political objectives, the government readily used dubious legal evidence.[11]

The prosecution of Muhammad's case by the Roosevelt administration would be much more thorough and systematic than in typical instances of draft violations. In addition to the October sedition indictments, the leader was also convicted of three counts of draft evasion on November 24, then immediately extradited to Washington, D.C., to await sentencing in a District jail. On December 18, before a tribunal in the capital, he was sentenced to one to five years in prison on charges of violating the Selective Training and Service Act of 1940. For the next seven weeks, Muhammad was detained until his scheduled removal back to Chicago in early February. His experiences over these months further solidified his notions of destiny and martyrdom, which were inherent ideological underpinnings of his messengership. Shuffled between the courts and jails of white America, he had come to view his persecution as solely designed to keep him "from teaching my people the truth during the war between America, Germany, and Japan." For the next three decades, he would continue to perceive all state harassment in this light and resign himself to the role of public enemy in which the U.S. government had cast him at this time.[12]

While the government's pursuit of Muhammad bolstered his faith in his mission, the response of the Muslims to the federal onslaught encouraged his faith in the Nation of Islam. Back in September during the raids, he had heard of lost-founds anxiously turning themselves over to the police so that they could be numbered among the "persecuted." In October he had personally witnessed defiant Muslims, including his son Emmanuel, stand before their accusers and talk frankly about the destruction of the white world and their loyalty to the Messenger of Allah. These episodes strengthened his resolve to resurrect the so-called Negro and to preach Truth as it had been revealed to him by Fard Muhammad. For Elijah, going to prison for what he believed in was akin to the ultimate sacrifice Jesus had made two thousand years ago when he preached Islam. Like the crucified prophet, Muhammad was determined to talk "to the white man like he was the white man's daddy" and willingly accept the consequences as Jesus had done following his castigation of the Jews. The events of 1942–43 earned Muhammad a permanent place in Muslim hagiography. His name would henceforth be inscribed in the annals of the Nation of Islam as one of the many prophets and messengers who had submitted themselves to the torments of "the devil" to spread the word of Allah to the people.[13]

On February 4, 1943, Muhammad was back in Chicago for the final ruling on the eight counts of sedition that he had been charged with in October. Since the successful conviction of the leader for draft violations guaranteed that he would be going to prison for at least a year, the U.S. attorney in Chicago entered a motion in late May to have the rather weak allegations of subversion dropped. The request was granted, and Muhammad vegetated in a Chicago jail cell for another two months awaiting his ultimate fate. The American war effort, in which he had tried so hard to avoid participation, appeared to be gaining momentum at this time. Throughout the fourth year of the global conflict, island-hopping U.S. Marines steadily conquered the various enclaves of the Japanese Pacific empire. In Southern Europe, the Italians began to see the folly of their ways and jettisoned Mussolini just as an Allied invasion force assembled for the campaign against Sicily. Additionally, by late July, the firebombing of Hamburg by the Royal Air Force claimed up to one hundred thousand German lives and served as a precursor of the destruction to come. Overall, the winds of fortune were blowing westward, and the Allies were in a much better position by the end of 1943 than they had been a year earlier.[14]

Meanwhile, as it led the crusade against fascism in Europe and Asia, America itself was seized in 1943 by the worst racial violence the country had experienced since the Red Summer of 1919. Detroit, the birthplace of the Nation of Islam, was by far the bloodiest battleground of the races, and the racial tensions that exploded there on June 20 claimed the lives of twenty-five African-Americans and nine whites. Other incidents in such places as Beaumont, Texas, and Marianna, Florida, added to the death toll, and in the month of June 1943, at least thirty blacks were murdered in racist assaults. When Elijah Muhammad entered the Federal Correctional Institution (FCI) at Milan, Michigan, to begin his prison term on July 23, the world appeared in flames, and America was at the center of the fire both domestically and abroad. The worldwide violence of 1943 seemed to once again confirm what Elijah had subconsciously believed since his boyhood in the lynch town of Cordele: at the end of the day, the white man, whether in Georgia, Detroit, Chicago, or Berlin, had nothing to offer but slavery and death.[15]

FCI Milan opened as a state-of-the-art prison for federal offenders on April 11, 1933. Many of the first inmates incarcerated there were minor offenders who served terms of one year or less. Seven months later, the institution opened its gates to female criminals who had been convicted of federal offenses. Later, other male prisoners were relocated to Milan "for various reasons." In October 1939, the women's wing of the facility was eliminated, making FCI Milan a single-sex prison. The inmate population stood at 444 when Elijah Muhammad arrived in 1943. The average prisoner was thirty-seven years old, a recidivist, and had a sixth-grade education (the average black inmate had not passed the fifth grade). By the American entry into World War II, FCI Milan housed a variety of criminals—from car thieves and WPA check forgers to narcotics offenders and selective service violators—and was considered one of the more innovative institutions of the period. Promotional literature described it as a prison without walls, and it consisted of a rectangular grouping of buildings surrounded by a fence and guard towers and was tailored for holding inmates who were regarded as "improvable." Despite this characterization, Milan, like its federal counterparts in Leavenworth and Atlanta, strictly adhered to societal patterns of racial segregation as well as contemporary theories of prison discipline, punishment, and rehabilitation. In many ways, the Michigan institution was a mixture of the creative and the conventional, not unlike many other facilities and programs established during the Roosevelt era.[16]

As part of their rehabilitation, all inmates who were physically able to had to work a regular job. In fact, the American war effort had mandated that federal penal institutions produce useful items for the armed forces. At Milan, double-decker beds were the major product supplied to the Navy, Coast Guard, and Marine Corps during the war. Inmates not involved in bed-making were employed in various other occupations such as carpentry, brick masonry, welding, and electrical work. A number of prisoners labored on the institution's three-hundred-acre farm, which raised cows, pigs, chickens, and other animals. The rest worked in other areas such as food service, construction, administration, and "general maintenance and garage mechanical service." The daily routine started at 6:30 A.M. and did not end until 10:30 P.M. Inmates were required to work at least eight hours each day, compensated by a few cents an hour and "industrial good time," which shortened their sentences.[17]

FCI Milan, like most American prisons, maintained discipline and obedience among inmates through a system of rewards and punishments. Correspondence and visitors were probably the most valued avenues of contact that most prisoners had with the outside world, and the threat of losing these links was perhaps enough to keep many inmates out of trouble. After composing a list of correspondents' names, each prisoner was allowed to receive seven pieces of mail each week and to mail three letters. Noncontact visits were limited to one per month for a duration of two hours, and only authorized immediate family members and others who passed a background check could call on an inmate. Educational opportunities available to prisoners included English, typing, writing, business-economics, and other classes; correspondence-school courses; and vocational training. Recreational outlets at Milan included such team sports as softball, basketball, and volleyball. For the less athletic, leisure time could be spent in the facility's small library or in one's cell or dormitory listening to selected radio broadcasts. One of the most popular sources of recreation at the prison was the weekly movies, which were supposedly "the top grade of newer releases," excluding "gangster or crime stories."[18]

During his imprisonment at FCI Milan, Elijah Muhammad was a model inmate and "caused no difficulty." Upon his arrival on July 23, he was admitted to the facility as Gulam Bogans (prisoner number 10039-MM), fingerprinted, and allowed to make out a list of people with whom he wished to correspond. After submitting his personal possessions to prison officials, he was permitted to wash and exchanged his civilian clothes for inmate attire. The first thirty days of his incarceration were spent in the admissions unit, where he was familiarized with the rules and culture of the institution. In a way, this early period of indoctrination resembled a kind of psychological war between Muhammad and his jailers. On the day after his arrival, he was registered for selective service by "a special board" and officially detailed to draft board ten in Chicago. This insult to Muhammad's religion-inspired stance on the war surely piqued him, but probably not as badly as the mental evaluation that followed.[19]

As was customary, he was interviewed by the resident psychiatrist, who asked several probing questions about his childhood and self-concept. The interrogation was aimed at appraising Muhammad's psychological age as well as his intellectual capacity. While the conclusions of the psychiatrist are interesting to contemplate, their accuracy and usefulness are dubious. Muhammad was diagnosed by his evaluator as being afflicted by dementia praecox, "paranoid type." Though he had made "an adjustment to his psychosis," he was still not very intelligent and had an IQ between 70 and 79 and a mental age between 10.6 and 11.9 years. According to the psychiatrist, Muhammad exhibited "a marked persecutory trend both against himself and his race" and, on occasion, felt as though he were being pursued and slandered by enemies. Additionally, the interviewer labeled as schizophrenic Muhammad's claim that Allah had communicated with him "in visual and auditory form." On the whole, the report contained both elements of truth (the sense of persecution) and fiction (the false assessment of schizophrenia and mental age). Nonetheless, for the next two years, he would be exposed to further sessions with psychiatrists, who would try to prove that he was psychologically unbalanced. In the meantime, he cooperated with prison officials, even taking English classes after his limited formal education was confirmed by standardized testing. However, his stay at the facility would continue to be one long mind game in which his captors would make his life almost unbearable.[20]

The administration at Milan did little to accommodate Muhammad and other Muslim prisoners. There were services for Protestants, Catholics, and Jews, but no allotment of time or space for Islamic ritual and worship. The Qur'an was again not accessible behind bars, though a sympathetic guard tried in vain to secure a copy for Muhammad. Moreover, as he feared, pork was used to season many of the dishes served in the prison, and the Muslims were forced to eat bread and white potatoes until they could arrange for a lost-found named Leonard X to prepare their meals. Poor eating habits, inadequate living space, and other problems caused Muhammad to become regularly ill and probably led to the bronchial asthma that would cause him pain and grief for the next three decades. Despite the deprivation and suffering of prison life, he resolved to continue to teach the knowledge of self and others to any African-American inmate who sought Truth. Since FCI Milan already had a small core of Muslims that included Muhammad, his son Emmanuel, and a few others, support for three meetings a week—Wednesday and Friday evenings and Sunday afternoons—was immediately forthcoming, and a makeshift temple was organized within the institution. The number of African-American prisoners who joined the Nation of Islam while at Milan is difficult to estimate, yet enough attended Muhammad's talks to attract the attention of guards. Curiously, when he became eligible for parole on December 17, 1943, the leader failed to file the proper documents requesting early release from prison. Perhaps he felt a greater need at this time to instruct lost-founds in the belly of the whale than to leave them and return to his Chicago tabernacle in the wilderness.[21]

Throughout his detention in Milan, Muhammad's main connection with the outside world was through his wife, Clara. She proved again to be his most faithful advocate and, by way of "considerable and regular correspondence," kept him abreast of developments in the temples. As the Supreme Secretary of the Nation, she was the conduit through which his directives reached the ministers and the laborers and was second only to Muhammad during this time. Often, she went beyond the call of duty, copying and mailing verses from the Qur'an to the imprisoned Muslim leader and her eldest son, Emmanuel. Trips to Milan were probably infrequent given her household responsibilities and cost. Nonetheless, her role as liaison was crucial to the survival of the movement, which was slowly recuperating from the FBI assault of 1942.[22]

The wartime incarceration of Muhammad and many of his followers caused a noticeable decline in the numbers of Muslims attending temple services and openly affiliating with the group. Predictably, the Chicago headquarters was hardest hit by the membership losses; still, other temples suffered almost commensurately. After the government raids of May and September 1942, Temple No. 1 in Detroit could attract only thirty-five active members, twenty-one of whom were women and children. In Chicago, the persecution and imprisonment of lost-founds forced the group to revert back to holding services in the homes of believers until money could be collected to rent a temporary meeting place on Wentworth Avenue in 1943. By the time World War II reached its atomic climax, Muslims who had been incarcerated on draft-related charges began to slowly trickle out of prison and back into temple life. Unfortunately for the Nation, Muhammad was not among those released, for his May application for parole was flatly denied on June 18, 1945. Another year would pass before the Holy Apostle was a free man again, but the movement was gradually regaining its vitality. After purchasing a former animal hospital at 824 East Forty-third Street, Chicago Muslims embarked upon their first major postwar task of constructing a new place worthy of the title Temple No. 2.[23]

Over one full year after the cessation of war in the Asian Theater, Elijah Muhammad walked out of FCI Milan on August 24, 1946, on conditional release. No cheering crowds greeted him nor did Fruit of Islam escort him. A parole officer dropped him off in the Loop in Chicago and told him to "teach what you always have been teaching and nobody will bother you anymore." To this, Muhammad replied that he intended to resume his ministry among the so-called Negroes as soon as possible. Four years in jails and prisons did more toward consolidating his authority over the Nation of Islam than a decade of bickering, purges, and wandering could ever have done. The FBI had, in fact, enhanced his power rather than diminished it. During the period between 1931 and 1942, he was simply the embattled Supreme Minister of a schismatic movement that had too many conflicting and ambitious personalities disputing his claim to the messengership. After 1942 and especially following his release from prison, he had unquestionably become the premier martyr of the Muslims—their "little lamb" and saintly "Messenger of Allah." Competition for the reins of power in the organization had ceased, and Muhammad, through his adherence to Nation of Islam doctrine and subsequent persecution, now commanded an almost immeasurable loyalty from his small, but growing, following. When he resumed the rostrum in late 1946, he did so with a new confidence. Henceforth, the days of running were over, and his leadership was more secure than ever before.[24]

Though more evident in later years, Muhammad's persecution and incarceration by federal authorities subverted many of the activist tendencies that he had exhibited during the 1930s. Over the next three decades, the Nation of Islam under his leadership would increasingly avoid activities that could evoke government censure and reprisal. The basic teachings of the movement remained the same: racial separatism, white devilry, and the coming Armaggedon. Yet, a growing aversion to conflict with state and national authorities became a major consideration in the tailoring of his postwar strategy to bring African-Americans into the Nation.

The whole prison experience, and the events leading up to it, had been extremely unpleasant for Muhammad in many ways. His family and followers were, of course, devastated by the lengthy ordeal. His children had for the most part grown up without the benefit of his parental guidance. In fact, he scarcely knew his youngest sons, Wallace and Akbar, who had been born in the midst of his protracted clashes with federal and organizational enemies. Muhammad dreaded exposing himself to further persecution and detention and clearly avoided creating circumstances that might lead to future difficulties with the state. Other factors, too, would later push him toward a less activist, even conservative, style of leadership, such as a desire to minimize political and legal pressures that could inhibit the economic expansion of the movement. Consequently, courtroom brawls, protest rallies at police stations, and extremely vocal draft resistance were largely things of the past. Now, the Nation's program for black mental resurrection would consist mainly of self-help experiments and rhetorical opposition to white America, both of which would keep it in the public, and government, eye.[25]

The prison experience of Muhammad also exposed him to new ideas and more modern ways of doing things. Prior to 1942, the Muslims had been taught to shun radios and other items and trends that were reminiscent of the grave, or secular life, and its culture. All of the knowledge and training of the believers were to be obtained from the temples and the Universities of Islam. However, upon returning from prison, Muhammad encouraged his followers to purchase these items and even offered to demonstrate their operation. In four years of captivity, Muhammad had witnessed how radio brought news of baseball, consumerism, and warfare even into the confines of a Midwestern prison. He heard Roosevelt and war-bond commercials on the radio as well as Count Basie's big-band hits. He was perhaps most impressed by the relative self-sufficiency of the prison, particularly in food production. The institution's three-hundred-acre farm reminded him of every Southern black's desire to own his own property independent of sharecropping, tenancy, and other arrangements that made black people beholden to whites. Indeed, to own land had been his father's dream for decades and his grandfather's, too. When he returned to the helm of the Nation of Islam in 1946, Muhammad was thinking innovatively about the future. In his view, if the white man could use radios and farm technology to bring the world to Milan, he could use these same tools to bring the so-called Negro into the temple.[26]

The idea to take the Nation of Islam into the realm of finance and business cannot be credited to Muhammad alone. Actually, the new economic impetus was the product of round-table talks among Muslims incarcerated at Milan during the war. The prison served as a model of agrarian productivity and collectivization, but the Southern background of most of the believers definitely made the dream of black ownership and self-sufficiency that much more enticing. In 1945, the Muslims, under Muhammad's direction, pooled their finances and purchased a 140-acre farm and some cattle in White Cloud, Michigan. Two years later in July 1947, the Chicago Muslims launched a grocery store, Shabazz restaurant, and a bakery at 3117 South Wentworth Avenue. The fledgling enterprises were modest and heavily dependent upon African-American patronage and the volunteer work of the faithful. Insofar as most of the Muslims had meager educational and vocational backgrounds, Muhammad himself performed many of the tasks necessary to keep the businesses afloat, from instructing women in baking to serving as the butcher at the grocery store. Over time, the administrative demands of the Nation's stores encroached upon his religious commitments to his followers, and many weeks he could only make one appearance at the temple. Though the grocery store, restaurant, and bakery were small concerns and employed only a handful of the Muslims, they were still heralded as examples of what blacks could do for themselves without having "to demand [anything of] the devil or resort to him."[27]

While the first stores of the Nation were minor enterprises, the implications of their advent for the development of the movement and the leadership of Elijah Muhammad cannot be overstated. Economic tensions in the organization had been a factor in its evolution since the early 1930s. Arguably, Fard Muhammad himself was responsible for both the thrift and consumerism among the early Muslims. In the postwar period, finance and entrepreneurship became major issues that overshadowed at least some of the religious and doctrinal foundations on which the movement had been based. Traditional themes of emigration and antisecularism were deemphasized in favor of heaven-on-earth rhetoric and consumer loyalty. The opening of Shabazz restaurant and other businesses and the mandate issued by Muhammad that Muslims should shop only at these establishments transformed the believers from a following into a clientele. The donations policy, which may have required as many as ten contributions per week to various projects and funds, underscored the centrality of economic considerations in the movement. During this period, the Muslims continued to secure jobs more easily than other African-Americans and subsequently did much to fatten the treasury of the Nation.[28]

Of major importance, Muhammad and others inadvertently became more bureaucratic and money-minded so as to maintain both the organization's businesses and the administrative framework of a multistate movement. The Muslims purchased and gave freely, and Muhammad and others in the leadership sold and received freely. Though elements of overt corruption in the Nation were hard to find at this time, the roots of future financial misconduct and resource mismanagement among some in the hierarchy of the group can definitely be traced to the growing prosperity of Muhammad and his chief lieutenants in the years immediately following World War II. By 1952, the Nation's messenger would be worth an estimated $75,000, not including his home and other real estate owned by the temple. His annual income was approximately $25,000, largely derived from donations and sales receipts.[29]

The Muslims of Temple No. 2, who served as the backbone of this economic shift in the Nation, numbered only 286 around 1950. The backgrounds of most of the believers were quite similar to that of Muhammad. The average convert was between thirty and sixty; originally from a rural area of Georgia, Alabama, Virginia, Mississippi, or some other Southern state; not formally educated beyond the eighth grade; and exposed to some familial crises—whether parental separation, desertion, fights, or death—early in life. After migrating to Chicago, the prospective Muslim generally lived a life at the bottom rungs of the city's socioeconomic ladder, working at unskilled labor and indulging in such activities as gambling, petty crime, and premarital and extramarital sex. Upon becoming a member of the Nation, the typical believers, however, experienced a dramatic change in lifestyle and outlook.[30]

Drinking, smoking, dancing, swearing, and a list of other indulgences labeled vices were given up by the new convert for the virtues of manhood as epitomized by the Fruit of Islam, womanhood as portrayed by the MGT-GCC, and childhood scholarship as taught in the University of Islam. The types of jobs available to the majority of Muslims did not change substantially upon membership in the temple; however, the disciplined laborers, as mentioned earlier, did secure work as bellboys, factory workers, laundresses, and waitresses with ease compared to other blacks. Temple No. 2 and its auxiliary businesses employed a total of forty-five Muslims, the majority of whom worked in Shabazz restaurant, on the Nation's farm, or held official positions in the organization. Those not employed by the group found other ways of participating in temple life, such as fishing for new converts in the expanding stretches of black Chicago. Small and insular, the membership of Temple No. 2 would become the model upon which the Nation of Islam of the 1950s would be based.[31]

Recreational activities sanctioned by Temple No. 2 were limited, but perhaps fulfilling considering the new philosophy that governed Muslim converts. Since believers were discouraged from fraternizing with nonmembers, "socialization" usually centered around Unity Night (Tuesdays) at Shabazz restaurant or group study sessions in the homes of laborers, where hours would be spent analyzing the Bible, the Qur'an, or Nation of Islam lessons. Some members used spare time to train in gymnastics, and a number of athletic Muslims practiced amateur sports. Other converts visited their brethren in other cities or stayed at home poring over Arabic script in efforts to regain their "original language." The favorite pastime of most members of the group were the periodic contests held by the University of Islam, which spotlighted the talent that the movement was cultivating among the young. The fifty-six students (twenty-seven boys and twenty-nine girls) who attended the school in 1950 were taught most of the basic subjects that were commonplace in public schools, including language arts, arithmetic, physical science, and Arabic, along with a Muslim course called "Chronological History from 13,000 B.C., Solar System, Spook Being Displayed for 6,000 Years, Ending of the Spook Civilization, and Chronology," which was not taught in any other institution. From the time of Fard Muhammad's stewardship over the Nation of Islam through the Cold War, the University of Islam remained a center of Muslim social life and a showpiece of the potentialities of black self-help. Generally, for the believers, recreation was equivalent to self-improvement and was often simply an extension of their quest for the knowledge of self and others.[32]

Although the majority of believers were male, women were a significant group within the Muslim fold. Black womanhood, and the images of purity, domesticity, and piety that the believers associated with it, continued to remain a prominent part of Muslim doctrine throughout the postwar period. Likewise, the training of women and girls who aspired to the Nation's standards of feminine grace and cultured refinement was a mainstay of the organization even during its decline in the early 1940s. In addition to the mandatory meetings on Wednesdays, Fridays, and Sundays that all Muslims attended, female believers also participated in a nursing class on Tuesday nights and a "culture and civilization" course on Thursday nights. The MGT-GCC, the comprehensive women's program, taught gymnastics, cooking, sewing, and household management as well as child rearing and the proper approach to gender relations. Attired in long dresses and turbans, Muslim women were placed on pedestals and jealously guarded, as attested by their segregation in open meetings and the prohibition against their shaking hands with men or intermingling with the opposite sex "as the Christians do." Yet, their position in the temple, as these gestures suggest, was clearly secondary to that of men, who conducted the services, decided how funds would be spent, and made the more important decisions for individual Muslim families and the organization in general.[33]

Sometimes, women joined the movement at great costs to themselves, including loss of status in the community and problems at home with parents and other loved ones who detested "the cult." In the case of Sister Sylvia, a sixteen-year-old convert born in Chicago, her Catholic parents characterized her engagement to one of Muhammad's sons as "the greatest disgrace that threatens the name of the family in the Catholic community." Ironically, for some women the sword also cut the other way, and at least four men divorced their wives during this period because of the women's refusals to join the Nation. The image of virtuous black womanhood presented to the public through Muslim displays of chivalry and propaganda often gave outsiders the impression that female believers actually held a superior place in the temple. However, the reality of Muslim power arrangements and gender relations confirmed for the insider and the keen observer that the pedestals on which women were placed had been constructed by men and could be cast aside when a female believer needed a good "smack in the face" for challenging the will of her male counterpart. In future decades, women would continue to play an ambiguous role in the Nation and would be both the beneficiaries of glorification and the victims of objectification.[34]

Many of the people who had passed through the ranks of other religious and nationalistic movements found something unique in the Nation of Islam. The Muslims' conception of morality added order and a sense of dignity to the lives of African-Americans who had consumed tobacco, burglarized neighbors, and fornicated. Moreover and perhaps just as important, the rituals and symbols of the group impressed upon the new convert that he or she was a significant part of a larger entity destined for some great purpose.[35]

The trappings of moral authority and this intense notion of togetherness, or nationalism, were all evident in temple affairs, from the Muslim star and crescent to the divinely commissioned potentate, Elijah Muhammad. The power of these images convinced many African-Americans from various backgrounds that the Nation of Islam was, in fact, their nation, and the world outside its boundaries was, indeed, the grave. The leaders of the movement manipulated symbols in such a way as to submerge gender, age, and personality conflicts that caused organizational divisions in favor of racial, socioeconomic, and educational commonalities that served to bond members together. The result was a quasi-national culture and consciousness among converts that stressed absolute loyalty to the Messenger of Allah and selfless service to the Nation of Islam.

A national flag was as much a part of Muslim group identity as it is for contemporary territorial states. The standard of the Nation of Islam, the National, was pregnant with symbolism and evoked emotions not unlike patriotism. The background of the flag was red, the color of the sun, which emits "light and life." The star and crescent moon were white, the former representing the five senses and the latter standing for the equilibrium of the earth's water. At the four corners of the flag were printed the letters *F, J, E,* and *I,* which meant "Freedom, Justice, and Equality you and I own." The National was not only believed to be of symbolic importance, but was also felt to have an almost magical, protective quality, and all members were encouraged to wear it and have it in their homes. Important printed matter distributed by the organization usually contained a representation of the flag, and every temple displayed it proudly at every meeting.[36]

Along with having a national standard, members sang a national anthem as part of the temple ritual. Up until the mid-1940s, this had not been the case, for singing had been prohibited during services. However, when one of the older believers wrote this anthem and convinced Muhammad to lead the group in a few strains, the favorable response earned the song a place in temple worship. Eventually, it was sung prior to prayer. The song itself was one of a superior, martial people. Its liberating tone played upon the inherent racial pride of the Muslim movement. The rousing spirit of the anthem is captured in the refrain, "So let us rise ye moslems, Fight for Your Own."[37]

The organizational hierarchy of the Nation resembled more than anything else a kind of military theocracy arranged along dictatorial lines. The structure of offices and positions in the movement were in many ways designed to convey a sense of order and a respect for stratified authority. The reverence and pomp surrounding important officials in the group conferred a certain mystique upon both the office and the officeholder. For African-Americans who had rarely, if ever, seen black civilians conduct themselves with discipline and confident aloofness, a procession of Muslim officials, replete with orderly, militaristic marches, salutes, and other mannerisms, served as an excellent device for recruitment.

The postwar Fruit of Islam, consisting of all males in the temple, exuded martial precision and was organized on the Western military model. Along with its ceremonial duties, the Fruit of Islam wielded formidable power in the Nation, acting as close-contact bodyguards for Muhammad and his ministers and providing security at services against unwelcome outsiders and agents provocateurs. Additionally, it enforced punishments meted out to Muslims who had been convicted by a gathering of believers of breaking temple law. Penalties ranged from Class C duty, which required the offender to clean up the temple for a stated time, to Class F suspensions, which could last thirty, sixty, or ninety days and prohibited contact and communication between active Muslims and the suspended individual. For adultery, fornication, and other serious infractions, violators could be "isolated" (cut off utterly from the temple and its activities) for up to seven years or until they could prove themselves worthy of renewed active membership in the Nation. On the whole, the Fruit of Islam used symbols and display to instill both admiration and fear in followers. Its role in the organization, both in image and in substance, was second only to that of the messenger in importance and, in a real sense, supplemented his power and authority over the group.[38]

By the early 1950s, Elijah Muhammad had become the most salient icon in all the strands of Islam among American blacks. Within the Nation of Islam, he continued to be intimately involved in administrative and fiscal decisions, but gradually his position in the movement was becoming more ceremonial and removed from the everyday affairs of the temple. This is not to say that he became a mere figurehead; his words were still law and would continue to be so until the 1970s. However, other men and women of talent were now providing leadership in areas that he had at one time manned alone. The prosperity and growth of the Nation were largely responsible for this development, for by May 1954 eight other temples had cropped up in various cities, such as New York, Baltimore, and San Diego, making the movement necessarily more bureaucratic and institutionalized.[39]

Other considerations that led to Muhammad's greater reliance upon his lieutenants were his advancing age—he was fifty-seven in October 1954—bronchial asthma, and affluent lifestyle, all of which mellowed him. Quite significantly, the proven loyalty of his followers and the relative absence of internal strife in the organization allowed him to delegate responsibility more freely. Muhammad's adherents, from the increasingly powerful Supreme Captain, Raymond Sharrieff, to the rank-and-file believer, had affirmed to his satisfaction that they could weather internal civil wars, abject poverty, police harassment, and even the imprisonment of their Holy Apostle and still serve him and the cause of the Nation without question or hesitation. The brotherhood, enthusiasm, and fealty that the leader had always sought to promote among the believers was finally becoming apparent after years of trials. Consequently, in 1950, when North Korean Communists were pinning down U.N. and South Korean forces at the port of Pusan, some Muslims were more than happy to tell curious outsiders that they would shed blood on behalf of Muhammad if he determined that it was the will of Allah. While most of their demonstrations of loyalty were not so extreme, the believers frequently assured Muhammad and others that they would do anything he desired when the word was given.[40]

The most important collective expressions of the fidelity of Muslims to their messenger took place every February on Saviour's Day. Beginning in 1950, these annual conventions in Chicago were meant to honor and commemorate the God of the Nation of Islam, Fard Muhammad, and outline his teachings for the benefit of believers and non-Muslim visitors alike. The celebrations would usually start around February 26 and last a few days, during which Muslims from various temples would arrive by the busload to hear their leader. By the time of the first Saviour's Day, Elijah Muhammad had taken the Nation of Islam lessons out of circulation so that he could "interpret . . . and put the emphasis where he wanted the emphasis to be." Though this did not change the fundamental teachings that Fard Muhammad had left behind, it did give the leader the ideological leeway to portray the affairs and destiny of the Muslim movement in a manner that suited him from year to year. Over time, the conventions would actually become as much praise sessions for Elijah Muhammad as they were for his savior.[41]

Consistent with the economic themes behind the movement, Muslims who attended the 1950 convention were ordered to give a minimum of fifty dollars to their messenger as a tribute to his leadership and wisdom. A number of temples competed with each other to raise the most money for this. In exchange for the loyalty and generosity of his followers, Muhammad commonly addressed the meetings for an hour or so, discussing the creation story of the Muslims, the mission of Fard Muhammad, the legitimacy of his own messengership, and the prophesied destruction of the white world. Other issues of timely importance would also be mentioned, such as the opposition of the Nation of Islam to African-American participation in the Korean War and the ongoing persecution of the Muslims by the government. The Saviour's Day address of 1954 was typical of Muhammad's early talks, which tended to stress the religious elements of the Nation's message as opposed to the later preoccupation with territorial demands and criticisms of integration and its proponents. This particular speech, delivered in vernacular rather than in more formal English, evoked constant ovations from the believers in attendance, and possibly no one applauded louder than the head of the New York Muslim delegation, a twenty-eight-year-old convert of promising potential named Malcolm X.[42]

Elijah Muhammad first heard of Malcolm Little, as he was known, through his brothers, Philbert and Reginald, who had joined the Nation during the 1940s. The first direct contact between the two men was through a 1949 letter Malcolm had scrawled while serving a seventy-seven-month sentence for breaking and entering and larceny in Norfolk Prison Colony, Massachusetts. On the surface, Malcolm was no different from other imprisoned converts of the postwar period. Like many believers, he had come from a poor, broken home; his father had been killed when Malcolm was quite young, and his mother had been committed to a mental institution in 1939. His formal eighth-grade education had been of little use to him in the urban wilderness of North America, and by his late-teenage years, he had sunk to the lower depths of urban cesspools in Detroit, Boston, and Harlem. While in the grave, he procured women for prostitution, used narcotics heavily, and organized burglary rings. Before his day of reckoning on February 27, 1946, Malcolm had lost faith in all forms of authority and entered prison an avowed atheist, despite his Baptist upbringing. Barely literate and addicted to various drugs, the teachings of the Nation of Islam reached him during his most desperate hour when he believed in nothing at all.[43]

Encouraged by his brothers, Malcolm gave up cigarettes and pork and refrained from using the foul language of his otherwise limited vocabulary. Reading and writing skills were enhanced through tedious practice, and correspondence courses and prison debates nurtured his growing fondness of etymology and elocution. His biggest thrust toward reform and salvation came from the letters and other printed literature that relatives sent him regarding the Nation of Islam and its leader, Elijah Muhammad. The teachings outlined in the materials seemed to place his life into a larger, more comprehensible framework, just as Fard Muhammad's message had beckoned so brightly to Elijah Poole. The past glory of the original black man, the Yacub story, American slavery, and his own tragic life appeared to be a continuum that flowed logically together. Everything that had happened to him, his parents, and every other black person had occurred as a result, directly or indirectly, of the actions of whites. All of the evil he had done in Harlem and other places was perpetrated in full view of a Christian America, which in many ways had restricted his chances for success in life and forced him "to be realistic about being a nigger." His dope peddling, his mother's impairment, and his father's possible death at the hands of racists could no longer be explained as mere misfortune or bad luck. After his mental resurrection behind bars less than forty miles north of Plymouth Rock, Malcolm had only one thing left to say. In fact, Reginald said it for him during one of his many visits to the prison in 1948: "The white man is the devil." As Malcolm would later write, the statement was "a perfect echo of . . . [my] lifelong experience."[44]

Malcolm wrote Muhammad regularly until his parole on August 7, 1952. During this time, his letters gradually became more intelligible and filled with the faith of the true believer. Replies were encouraging, even "electrical" in effect, and sometimes contained a sorely needed five-dollar bill. When Malcolm was released from prison, the nature of his loyalty and gratitude to Muhammad was very much akin to that of other Muslims who idolized him to the point that they were willing to die and take lives upon his command. In time, Malcolm would be genuinely awed by his teacher and would even turn his back on his brother Reginald after Muhammad suspended him for improper sexual relations with a Muslim woman. On occasion, this extreme reverence lapsed into fear, but as he explained, "not fear such as of a man with a gun, but the fear such as one has of the power of the sun." Three weeks after his parole, Malcolm would personally meet Muhammad. In the interim, he worked as a salesman at the Detroit furniture store of his brother Wilfred and attended the services of Temple No. 1 conducted by Minister Lemuel Hassan.[45]

The kindness and understanding that Muhammad had extended to Malcolm while in prison were not unusual, for he had shown the same concern for numerous other African-American convicts who sought to turn their lives around. His years in FCI Milan had definitely made him more sympathetic to the plight of incarcerated members of the race and permanently reserved for them a place in his heart. Additionally, his detention had also taught him that prisons were fertile recruitment grounds for the Nation of Islam. For simply showing compassion and concern for their well-being, the movement would eventually succeed in transforming hundreds of convicts into loyal and sometimes lifelong dues-paying members. The Nation benefited from the increased membership, and the inmates profited from the moral empowerment of the teachings, which helped them shed the vices and criminal behaviors they had picked up while floundering in the grave. In essence, recruiting black convicts into the movement was a win-win situation, and the Muslims touted their success among imprisoned African-Americans.[46]

On August 31, 1952, a cavalcade of Muslims from Detroit arrived at Temple No. 2 in Chicago to hear Muhammad speak. The gathering was small, the two hundred people present indicative of the size of the movement. Still, the same ceremonial air and military pomp that would characterize the mass meetings of the 1960s were apparent. Flanked by Fruit of Islam bodyguards and wearing a gold-embroidered fez, Muhammad entered the temple to applause and cheers and took his place behind the podium. His speech dwelled on standard themes such as his persecution and imprisonment, the effect of the white man's tricknology on the so-called Negro, and how "the true knowledge of ourselves would lift up the black man." During a pause in his talk, Muhammad, without looking in his direction, called Malcolm Little to his feet. Humble and shocked, the convert stood and was praised by his teacher for his faithful letter-writing in prison and the strength he exhibited while incarcerated. Muhammad also issued a challenge to the youthful Muslim. Comparing Malcolm to the biblical Job, Muhammad told the congregation, "Well, now, our good brother Malcolm's hedge [prison cell] is removed and we will see how he does. . . . I believe that he is going to remain faithful." Standing before the Messenger of Allah, Malcolm felt as though he had encountered his maker. The vote of confidence caused him to freeze in veneration, and he could only respond with meek silence, "feeling the eyes of two hundred Muslims upon me."[47]

After the assembly at the temple, Malcolm and a number of others gathered at Muhammad's new nineteen-room house at 4847 Woodlawn Avenue, which he had recently moved into supposedly at the insistence of the believers. The dinner and conversation that followed were actually devoted more to strategy than the further exposition of Muslim doctrine by Muhammad. The major issue discussed was how to enlarge the membership of the temples. Muhammad's solution was simple: "Go after the young people.... Once you get them, the older ones will follow through shame." Though unbeknownst to him at the time, this charge would define the role and significance of Malcolm to the organization for the next twelve years. Once back in Detroit, he fished in the ghetto for prospective converts every chance he could. Largely through his proselytizing efforts, temple services drew larger and younger crowds, and the cavalcades to Temple No. 2 increased in length. Knowledge of these fruitful struggles of Malcolm's reached Chicago, where Muhammad became even more aware of the asset he had found in the young laborer. Over the next several months, Malcolm and his teacher developed a relationship not unlike that between father and son. The first honors were bestowed by the summer of 1953 as a reward for the proselytizing work. Dubbed Malcolm X, the diligent young Muslim was appointed assistant minister of Temple No. 1 after a number of rousing preliminary sermons.[48]

Malcolm's sincerity, talent, and perseverance inspired Muhammad to send him on further missions to organize new temples and revive older ones that were faltering. He went first to Boston to work among blacks in Roxbury, where he had once hustled before his imprisonment in 1946. The initial meetings of new converts were held in the home of Lloyd X at 5 Wellington Street. Three months of trials in the wilderness were necessary before the small cell of Muslims in the city were able to afford a tiny temple with rented chairs. The Boston believers were designated Temple No. 11, and a local laborer named Ulysses X was appointed minister. When it appeared that the new group could stand on its own, Muhammad moved Malcolm to Philadelphia in March 1954, where he laid the foundation for Temple No. 12 within just three months. Again, Muhammad recognized the importance of Malcolm's contributions and rewarded him with another promotion. In June, he was named minister of Temple No. 7 in New York City, which had a potential constituency of over a million African-Americans, the move signaling his meteoric rise.[49]

These early triumphs of the roving minister were due largely to the message he imparted, whether he talked about the antidraft sentiments of the Nation of Islam, criticized the "white devils" and Christianity, or praised the Mau Mau of Kenya. However, his delivery of the teachings—facilitated by an ever-expanding vocabulary and a natural charisma—was also part of the formula for success and netted many wavering younger individuals. For the Muslims and the world in general, 1954 would prove an eventful year. While it was probably too early for most people to discern, Malcolm X was on his way to becoming the best minister Elijah Muhammad would have, ever.[50]

CHAPTER 6

MESSENGER OF ALLAH

*I have a sinking feeling that
Elijah Muhammad is very significant.*
—Edwin C. Berry, Director,
Chicago Urban League, 1959[1]

To a world accustomed to the hegemony of the West, the year 1954 seemed to inaugurate a period of decline in European imperial power around the globe. Events of that year did not portend an immediate destruction of colonialism in foreign lands or even a significant reduction of Western influence in international affairs. However, the changes ushered in by the Cold War did not result in a reconstruction of prewar conditions. Egypt, which had been granted independence in 1922, fell under the sway of Gamal Nasser, who wasted little time in getting the British to sign a pact ending seventy-two years of military occupation in the Suez Canal Zone. On May 7, the French war effort in Vietnam was abruptly terminated following a shattering defeat of colonial forces at Dien Bien Phu. After basically handing their problems in Southeast Asia over to the Americans, the French engaged in another bloodletting in Algeria in November, which would ultimately lead to the demise of the Fourth Republic and Algerian independence in 1962. The United States, indisputably the most powerful country on the planet, would also have to deal with resistance in its imperial domain, and the halls of power themselves would not be safe from anti-American protests. On March 1, Puerto Rican separatists wounded five members of Congress in a hail of anticolonial gunfire that foreshadowed later, more serious resistance by Caribbean countries against American policies in the area. Over the next two decades, nationalist conflagrations would erupt like spreading wildfires in colonized areas, and the tide of Western dominance would be forced to recede, at least in its most blatant noncultural manifestations.[2]

Domestically, fractures, even faults, were beginning to appear in the very bedrock of American traditions. On May 17, 1954, in a landmark decision the Supreme Court officially outlawed racial segregation in public schools, which provoked an avalanche of "massive resistance" from racists, epitomized by the founding of the first White Citizens Council in Indianola,

Mississippi, in July. As the Civil Rights Movement turned the South into a battlefield, individual blacks enjoyed access to positions of power that had hitherto been closed to them. On August 19, Ralph J. Bunche was appointed undersecretary of the United Nations, and two months later, Benjamin O. Davis Jr. was named the first African-American general of the U.S. Air Force. In politics, in the large November turnout of voters, the Democrats gained control of the Congress, and Charles C. Diggs Jr. became the first black congressman from the state of Michigan. In many ways, 1954 marked the beginning of a new age in which blacks and American society in general would struggle to redefine themselves outside of conventional restraints. In other ways, the year began an era of hesitation, uncertainty, and inconsistency in American life, exemplified by the banning of the U.S. Communist Party in August and the senatorial censuring of its worst critic, Joseph McCarthy, on December 2.[3]

As mentioned earlier, the Nation of Islam steadily grew in size and influence during the 1950s, owing mostly to white intransigence regarding desegregation and the skillful recruitment efforts of laborers like Malcolm X. Just as the White Citizens Councils would thrive on federal successes in implementing civil rights laws, the Muslims would increase in number and popularity due to government failures to satisfy African-American demands. To accommodate his growing fold, Muhammad purchased a synagogue at 5335 South Greenwood Avenue with a seating capacity of five hundred and converted it into the new Temple No. 2. The movement was incorporated on November 28, 1955, under the title "Holy Temple of Islam," and Muhammad and John Hassan, a faithful veteran of the organization, were named trustees. Bylaws for the incorporated Nation of Islam were passed three years later, defining the requirements of membership and the arrangement of offices in the movement. Theoretically, blacks who were devoted to "leading an Islamic life" would be eligible to join the group, and membership could be terminated by death, written dismissal, or exclusion. The administrative hierarchy of the temple placed Muhammad at the top, followed by a three-member board of trustees, a clerk, a treasurer, and other subordinate officials. The tenure of all officers expired after a year's service, and ideally, all positions (except that of messenger) were reassigned during annual elections on December 31. The movement offered opportunities for advancement based on talent and hard work. However, by the late 1950s, the more important offices were dominated by a nepotistic network, reminiscent of Middle Eastern sheikhdoms, which emphasized familial connections to Muhammad as much as ability.[4]

The entrepreneurship that had first emerged in the Nation of Islam following World War II played an even larger role in the development of the movement during the 1950s. Businesses started by Muslims serviced the needs of the believers in a number of ways and were maintained by perpetual "buy black" campaigns sponsored by the group in African-American communities, auguring more widespread trends that would occur in subsequent decades. Along with the bakery, restaurant, and grocery store, enterprises associated with Temple No. 2 by 1958 included a car-repair and paint shop, a laundry, a cleaning plant, a dress shop, and a haberdashery. Big projects of the Chicago Muslims at this time, such as an apartment building at 8201-07 South Vernon Avenue and the temple and University of Islam, involved investments amounting to tens of thousands of dollars and were truly an indicator of the ability of the movement's leadership to mobilize the financial wherewithal of a largely lower-class following. Interestingly, the net profits reaped by the businesses of the Nation—approximately four hundred thousand dollars in 1958 value—were used mostly to support elderly members of the organization as well as to underwrite the activities of the Chicago headquarters and smaller temples that were operating in the red. The reinvestment of profits in businesses became less frequent over time, and on average, a quarter of the annual earnings of the group were earmarked for the Muslims' school and educational program alone. By the 1950s, the economic enterprises of the movement were still primarily a symbolic statement about what the Tribe of Shabazz could do for itself if it only tried. Nonetheless, as an organization, the Nation of Islam was beginning to handle more money and inspire more blacks through its financial initiatives than most of its counterparts in the African-American Christian community.[5]

During this period, the economic character of the Nation's membership underwent changes as well. Whereas the vast majority of believers were solidly anchored in the lower class during the early years, increasing numbers of professionals and educated individuals began to join the movement by 1956. Many blacks who held "positions in the white man's world" did not openly discuss their affiliation with the group and were content with being Muslims incognito. Yet, others who by day were civil servants, salesmen, nurses, and secretaries, but in the evening, committed members of the Nation, devoted their time openly to temple affairs.[6]

To Muhammad, the success of the Nation in attracting African-Americans depended upon striking a balance between economic classes in the black community. Moreover, this formula often required that one class of African-Americans be subjected to reprobation in order for the movement to appeal to another group. For example, the Muslim leader was well aware that his power base was built on the lower class. He could not alienate this class by accusing it of being anything but the innocent victim of white America. Many blacks in ghettos and other depressed areas already suffered from low self-esteem and would undoubtedly have found little enticing about a movement that labeled them Uncle Toms or stooges of the white man. But Muhammad felt that professional and middle-class groups were deserving of such criticism, and in remarks he underscored both their dependency on white patronage and their potential value to their community. In a sense, he played upon class tensions among African-Americans to make the Nation appear to be the champion of the ignorant, downtrodden lower class and the redeemer of the wily, bourgeois black who had shirked his responsibility to the race.[7]

The leader believed that African-American professionals had erred in "giving their knowledge back to their [white] teacher." More distressing, since the American educational system had not exposed them to the knowledge of self and others, the economically successful among the race had no desire to seek an existence separate "from the slavemasters' children." Degrees from renowned colleges and universities could not change the fact that the middle-class black was still merely "a free slave to serve them [whites] or others than your own." Also, the scarcity of black-owned businesses seemed to testify to the lack of initiative on the part of the professionals. Despite this situation, it was not too late, according to Muhammad, for the well-placed "free slave" to make himself useful to the African-American masses.[8]

Muhammad praised the talent of the engineers, professors, doctors, and artists of the race and encouraged them to "practice ... [their] wisdom among our people to help elevate." He believed that if the educated and the middle class of the race were taught the value of economic self-help and injected with "only one dose of Islam," they would no longer have to depend on whites for jobs and would embark upon business ventures that would employ black resources and manpower. Of course, the economic advancements of the Nation were to serve as the ultimate example of the possibilities of African-American entrepreneurship, and Muhammad used the organization's financial endeavors as propaganda to attract educated, professional, and middle-class blacks into the movement. The tactics worked to a moderate degree and did attract some well-educated and middle-class African-Americans. In some cases, business-minded professionals came into the movement to tap into the ready-made clientele and were perhaps only secondarily concerned with the theology of the Nation. Nonetheless, Muhammad recognized that even the most profit-oriented of the middle class could serve a purpose and pointed to the membership of professionals in the group as evidence of the broad appeal of the Muslims.[9]

Young ministers, articulate and passionate, were essential to the appeal of the group to middle-class youths and social climbers. Ironically, these same laborers were also instrumental in tightening the grip of the Muhammad clan on the reins of the movement. It was actually Malcolm X who suggested that Muhammad appoint his children to positions of authority in the Nation. Over time, the advice was heeded, and the Chicago headquarters, more than any other temple, became the preserve of the "royal family," supported by unrelated officials who had exhibited needed talents. As of the early 1960s, Raymond Sharrieff was the Supreme Captain of the Fruit of Islam; his wife, Ethel Sharrieff, was Sister Instructor of the University of Islam; Elijah Muhammad Jr. was second to Sharrieff as the Assistant Supreme Captain; Herbert Muhammad served as public relations director; and Akbar Muhammad was employed as secretary of Temple No. 2. These individuals would eventually exercise considerable influence over the movement, especially concerning its finances. As for Malcolm X, who had first broached the idea, he would later view the employment of Muhammad's family by the movement as a mistake that he would live long enough to regret.[10]

As the architect of the fiscal policies of the Muslim movement, Elijah Muhammad prospered greatly from the gradual economic expansion of the organization. Officially, and for tax purposes, he did not receive a salary from the group's coffers and subsisted only on funds periodically withdrawn from the Poor Treasury of the Nation. Despite this stated arrangement, he was to live a wealthy and luxurious lifestyle for the next two decades, and his view of heaven as a condition of life encouraged acquisitiveness among the leadership. The growing amount of property owned by Muhammad is most revealing on this score. By 1958, he personally held the title to two apartments at 7123 Indiana Avenue worth twenty-five thousand dollars and had transferred his temple-purchased home (worth sixty-five thousand dollars) into his own name, along with the Chicago bakery and grocery store and the Michigan farm, which now comprised 160 acres. Muhammad's first Cadillac was purchased in 1955, followed by a second in 1956 for Clara, a third a year later, and a fourth in 1959. The following year, he could be seen cruising the South Side in a Lincoln. This spirit of materialism was not only exhibited by Muhammad; his son-in-law, Supreme Captain Raymond Sharrieff, also drove a black 1954 Cadillac. Yet, the leader set the tone of the movement and ultimately validated, by example, a trend toward materialism, even avarice, that would hamper the Nation as a religious organization in the future.[11]

The affluence of Muhammad, derived from both donations and business profits, did not adversely affect his personal image in the organization. If anything, his thoroughly middle-class outlook, which emphasized "money, homes, and friendship in all walks of life," lured many blacks into the movement. However, juxtaposed with this theme was a message of frugality that Muhammad from time to time issued to his followers. "If you must have a car," he occasionally counseled, "buy the low-priced car, or a rich man's used car, and not his used Cadillacs and Rolls-Royces. I hope that you will begin leaving off the use of these things which you do not need to buy." Seemingly contradictory, the images of extravagance and thrift conveyed by the statements, and the practices of Muhammad took into consideration both the desire of African-Americans to secure the trappings of middle-class America and the financial constraints that made this dream unattainable for the majority of them. In essence, the Nation once again used symbols and rhetoric to enhance the attractiveness of the group to a variety of prospective recruits, including the big spender and the penny-pincher. The call by Muhammad for the exemption of blacks from taxation was also motivated by an understanding of the importance of economic concerns to his constituents. His declaration that donations by believers would be divinely paid back in multiple returns was in this same vein. Finance and religion in the movement, not unlike the situation in the larger Christian community, were tightly intertwined by the late 1950s. Consequently, evolving patterns of economic growth, entrepreneurship, and personal enrichment guaranteed the Nation of Islam a certain appeal, beyond its nationalism and religious doctrines, in poverty-soaked areas such as Chicago's South Side, where African-Americans and Cadillacs were rarely mentioned in the same sentence.[12]

The ultimate indicator of the influence of the Muslim message among blacks was membership figures. Unfortunately, the number of the National-wearing believers in the United States was difficult to tally. During the late 1950s, the Chicago temple had an active membership of about 400 to 600 Muslims. Temple No. 4 in Washington, D.C., could boast 300 to 500 members; the recently established Los Angeles cell, 300 followers; and the Detroit home of the Nation, 100 to 175 believers. Temple No. 7 in New York City, with a membership of 350, was probably the fastest-growing temple and would soon consist of three separate meeting houses: Temple No. 7A in Harlem, Temple No. 7B in Corona, and Temple No. 7C in Brooklyn. Other branches of the movement were scattered throughout the country, with memberships ranging from 12 to 100 believers. By March 1959, there may have been as many as thirty different temples in fifteen states and the District of Columbia. The explosion of interest that the Nation experienced after it came to the attention of the national media resulted in a mushrooming of the membership and the number of temples in various states. According to one source, over fifty temples in twenty-two states revolved around Muhammad's Chicago headquarters in December 1959, a figure that is not unreasonable if it included temples operating out of rented facilities and private residences.[13]

In 1960, estimates of the national total of "official" Muslims varied so widely that no authoritative figures can be given. Researchers, members of the press, and laymen have arrived at a range of guesses. The uppermost number of African-Americans affiliated with the Nation was between 100,000 and 250,000, figures reported by scholars such as C. Eric Lincoln and E. U. Essien-Udom and newsmen such as Louis Lomax and Mike Wallace. Moderate projections place the figure between 40,000 and 50,000, the former figure cited by Malcolm X during his tenure as minister of Temple No. 7. Conservative guesses suggest that the membership of the Nation never reached more than 25,000 and it has even been posited that no more than 5,000 blacks were ever in the movement at one time. Muhammad and other Muslim officials were skeptical about disclosing membership rolls to the public and were content with allowing the media to frighten white America with bloated estimates. The common response of Malcolm X to questions about numbers—"Those who know aren't saying, and those who say don't know!"—was typical of the attitude of the leadership.[14]

Based on the memberships of the major temples, 20,000 members may have been the high point of the recruitment drive of the Nation of Islam during the early 1960s. However, thousands, perhaps tens of thousands, of non-Muslim African-Americans sympathized with the teachings of the movement and would perhaps have been willing to supplement the ranks of the believers in the event of a national race war. Exact membership figures were shrouded by organizational secrecy, unpredictable patterns of conversion and apostasy, and the sensationalized estimates of the press and others. The mystery of their numbers served the interests of the Muslims well and added to the potential power and influence that some perceived in the movement.

Essential to the growth of the Nation of Islam was its public image. Beyond the message of moral reform, economic self-help, and separatism, the couriers of Muhammad's message were as important to its appeal as the message itself. Better than anyone else, Malcolm X conveyed those elements of style and charisma that captivated curious youths and convinced many to join the Nation so that they, too, could be transformed from so-called Negroes into Original People. A lean, towering man with fair skin and a boyish countenance, Malcolm had a natural, or at least exceptionally cultivated, gift for eloquence and was a tireless recruiter for the movement. Having lived the street life for years, the New York minister effortlessly related to the plight and mannerisms of the urban African-American and, over time, became just as comfortable among intellectuals and middle-class individuals, whom he debated on some of America's most prestigious college campuses.

The demographics of the Nation reflected and bolstered his appeal among the membership, which by 1960 was predominantly male and between the ages of seventeen and thirty-five. Even among the ministers, men of Malcolm's age and younger were becoming the norm, and some patterned their ministerial style after his. In an era when television shaped people's perceptions of almost every public event and personality, the Nation could do little better than be represented by Malcolm X. His blistering debate performances on talk shows made adherents proud to be Muslims, and his bold critiques of white America from Harlem soapboxes made blacks discontented with being just so-called Negroes. Fishing in the grave and organizing were his favorite organizational endeavors, but hypnotic orations and cold, hard logic were his specialities.[15]

Malcolm X continued to represent to Elijah Muhammad what the latter had been to Fard Muhammad. The New York minister was the liaison between the Messenger of Allah and young blacks who found little appealing about the tactics and objectives of the Civil Rights Movement. As Muhammad had deified his teacher as "Allah in Person," Malcolm worshiped his mentor as "the Honorable Elijah Muhammad." His loyalty and talent earned him the position of ambassador during the movement's Goodwill Tour (recruitment drive) in Atlanta in the late summer of 1956. Most of the Muslims' preliminary attempts to publicize their teachings through newspapers and magazines were placed in the hands of the New York minister, who wrote the editorial column "God's Angry Men" for the *Los Angeles Herald Dispatch* and played a role in beginning the short-lived publications *The Messenger Magazine* and *The Islamic News*. His influence may also have been behind Muhammad's own printed message, "Mr. Muhammad Speaks," which appeared in weekly newspapers such as *The Pittsburgh Courier* and the *Amsterdam News,* and most certainly was responsible for the founding of the official organ of the Nation, *Muhammad Speaks*, in 1960. As Fard Muhammad had done in 1933, Elijah Muhammad was slowly receding into the background while his faithful pupil carried on the business of making African-Americans aware of the Nation.[16]

Malcolm was both Muhammad's sword against critics and main workhorse within the movement. When the leader unsuccessfully invited Dr. Martin Luther King Jr. to speaking engagements to discuss the merits of integration, it was Malcolm X who was called upon to let the world know how much of "a traitor to the black people" the reverend was. The disciplined vigil of Malcolm and five hundred Muslims outside Harlem's 123rd Street police precinct to protest the April 1957 beating of Johnson Hinton by New York's finest shored up the reputation of the Nation for action, though the demonstration was much tamer than Muslim-police confrontations of the 1930s. Ultimately, when it came to fund-raising, the lifeblood of the movement, Malcolm X was without equal and regularly surpassed rival temples in generating donations, as he did during Saviour's Day, 1960. Despite ugly rumors of Malcolm's ambitions and whispers regarding Muhammad's private life, the two men constantly tried to repay the debts that they owed each other. Muhammad had saved Malcolm from the grave and given him "the wings" to fly. In return, the minister had in large part saved the Nation by reflecting its core conservatism in a more militant and youthful light. For the time being, teacher and student rode the crest of the Nation's popularity together and looked forward to a future of continued growth and success among the so-called Negroes.[17]

Unlike Malcolm, Muhammad was not charismatic in the conventional sense and had neither a flare for dynamic oratory nor an impressive command of the English language. In appearance, he was an unimposing man, standing five and a half feet tall and weighing less than 150 pounds. Balding, the leader was a fair-skinned man with a disarming gentleness. His slender body was almost delicate in form and, according to a contemporary, appeared "tiny and transparent and breakable as a china doll." Like his slow gait, his countenance complemented his small stature. To some, Muhammad's thin lips, pronounced cheekbones, and deep-set brown eyes were reminiscent of Oriental features. His appearances in fezzes, indeed, gave him a decidedly Eastern look. To others, his petiteness was part of his charm and underscored the meekness and humility of Allah's chosen one. Beyond his jovial comportment, one could sometimes detect in Muhammad's facial expressions the burdens that his work placed upon him—a "pain so old and deep and black that it becomes personal and particular only when he smiles." His sense of persecution, which was an integral part of his character, continued to overshadow his public addresses and was best expressed through the conspicuous appearance of watchful Fruit of Islam at every Muslim function. Despite these appearances, his public demeanor tended to emphasize strength, as did the dark suits he wore, the oversize Qur'an he often carried, and his calculated approach to the podium. If nothing else, his lean physique and pleasant face attracted the attention and sympathy of many African-Americans who found the tremendous message of the small Messenger of Allah irresistible.[18]

Orations by Muhammad always evoked thunderous applause and cheers from the believers. The uninitiated, however, responded to his speaking style in a variety of ways. Typically, he spoke in a deliberate fashion; that is, "in soft, measured cadences" that stressed his Southern accent. When bouts of bronchial asthma did not hinder his delivery, his pronouncements sometimes contained the passion of the black Baptist minister, a feature traceable to his father's oratorical style. Many non-Muslim observers were wholly unimpressed by his sermons and marveled at his ability to inspire standing ovations, "especially in the light of his barely literate oral delivery." Nonetheless, the simplicity of his speaking style and his improvised syntax conveyed sincerity and high purpose, which permeated even his dining-room talks. In fact, conversations in the privacy of his home were commonly marked by a graciousness and kindness that pleasantly surprised even his most skeptical guests. Still, the Muslim fanfare that preceded his public speeches seemed to many people to be incongruous with the addresses themselves. The high expectations of numerous visitors were often crushed by both his diminutive appearance and peculiar grammatical style. "To be able to listen to Muhammad for any length of time," one observer noted, "you had to be a believer, convinced in advance." Another contemporary who would eventually join the Nation was less charitable in his preliminary appraisal of the leader and admitted, "His voice was a bigger letdown than his size. It was squeaky and hard to follow. . . . He stumbled over words that I had been taught in the third grade of elementary school." Observers of the movement who pondered his popularity could not dismiss Muhammad as either grossly overrated or insignificant. Something ineffable about this "squeaky, little man teaching hate" attracted African-Americans for an entire generation as few other leaders could.[19]

The appeal of Muhammad to the black masses was largely based on his iconic image in the Nation and his ability to harness talented men such as Malcolm X to sing his praises. As the Messenger of Allah, his words carried weight among both believers who attributed their spiritual salvation to him and interested African-Americans who knew little about Islam. His confidence in his message and apparent sincerity attracted many converts to the movement, and the racial strife and civil rights upheaval of the period facilitated recruitment. Moreover, the paternal, custodial role of Muhammad in the organization appealed to many blacks who sought order and a symbol of authority in which they could believe. The leader, who was sixty-two in October 1959, provided this patriarchal presence for thousands of African-Americans and furnished rules, rewards, punishments, and a sense of belonging that many associated with parental guidance. To a great extent, his charisma lay in his fatherly image, which was attractive to Malcolm X, Cassius Clay, and a number of individuals who joined the Nation after World War II. Also, his young, talented ministers, who attributed all of their knowledge and achievements to Muhammad, extended his charismatic aura and further enhanced his authority within the movement. More important than fiery oratory or a dynamic stage presence, he had the power to command the loyalty, services, and resources of others. On the whole, his appeal was tied to both his organizational image and concrete actions he had taken on behalf of blacks whose self-esteem had been shattered by life in the grave.[20]

The year 1959 was the most pivotal period in the development of the Nation as a nationally recognized phenomenon among African-Americans. Not charisma, the Muslim program, or even their increasing numbers was decisive in bringing the group to the attention of the American public. As had been the case in the 1930s, the white media issued the clarion call that made the Nation an overnight sensation. Prior to the new notoriety of the movement, Muhammad had tried to publicize his program through his column, "Mr. Muhammad Speaks," and by word of mouth. During 1958, he had undertaken a limited speaking tour, traveling to a number of cities to spread the Muslim message. In January, he gave a law-and-order speech in Detroit's Temple No. 1 to discourage Muslims from retaliating against abusive policemen whom "God himself is about to remove from the planet." In July, he spoke at a two-day Unity Feast in Harlem, which was attended by as many as thirteen thousand people, including the Manhattan borough president, Hulan Jack, and city councilman Earl Brown. His talk emphasized the merits of the Nation's economic program and, according to one estimate, netted five hundred new converts. An early-August speech in Pittsburgh's Temple No. 22 was attended by three thousand people, whom Muhammad challenged to unite under Islam. What he did not have time to say in public addresses he stated in editorial columns, and the themes of separatism, white devilry, economic self-help, and Christian chicanery appeared regularly in his writings. In December, due to extremely high blood pressure, Muhammad was bedridden and was even forced to request that Clara, who was visiting in Cordele, return to Chicago. As he recuperated, he could reflect on 1958 as a year of progress and growth in the Nation. Unknown to him, the new year would bring even greater advancements.[21]

The year 1959 opened as had many years in the past with preparations for the annual Saviour's Day convention in late February. Muhammad's address for this occasion was one of his more rousing orations, which touched on a number of themes. The traditional motifs were most prominent, and integration along with the "race of devils" were both roundly criticized. The leader encouraged black men to protect their women from the advances of whites and even suggested that they lock up and slap around those females who insisted upon socializing with Caucasian men. The talk centered around separatism, as did many of his addresses during the late 1950s. Though he supported African independence from colonial rule, he warned audience members not to get too caught up in decolonization movements thousands of miles away before securing their own freedom at home. Specifically, Muhammad called for a place in the Western Hemisphere for African-Americans to establish an independent state. He admitted that the American government would probably not accede to this demand, but retorted that its likely refusal would not "hinder you and I from asking for it." The overall tone of the speech was defiant, and the inevitable friction between the races was underscored as a reason for blacks to seek their own before it was too late.[22]

Usually, the Saviour's Day address of Muhammad was the most important speech that the leader would deliver during the year. However, in 1959, his most notable talk would be given before an enthusiastic crowd of ten thousand people in Uline Arena, Washington, D.C. When the leader arrived in the city on May 31, he was met at the airport by ten police motorcyclists who escorted him to the Roosevelt Hotel. Security precautions could hardly have been tighter. The building was surrounded by law enforcement officers, and the eighth-floor suite of Muhammad was guarded by two hundred Fruit of Islam. Compared to his treatment by the FBI in May 1942, his reception in Washington was akin to that extended to a foreign dignitary, which in many respects he believed he was. The leader was moved by the concern shown for his safety by the District police department. He even felt comfortable enough to rest and gather his thoughts before the speech.[23]

Despite his friendly welcome to Washington, D.C., by law enforcement officials, Muhammad harbored no illusions about the attitude of the Eisenhower administration toward him or his organization. He knew from experience the lengths to which the federal government would go to curb "radical" black dissent. (Around this time, FBI director J. Edgar Hoover made an unsuccessful attempt to prosecute the Muslim movement or at least have it officially labeled a subversive organization. However, for the present, the director had to be satisfied with the electronic surveillance device placed on the home telephone of Muhammad in January 1957.) Over the years, the leader had come to detest government operations against the Nation and was prepared to use whatever means available to prevent a recrudescence of the chaos that government operatives and law enforcement officials had inflicted upon the movement during the 1930s and 1940s. To him, if this meant that "the intelligent of our people would [have to] sacrifice a few heads of the informing [stool] pigeons and Toms among the white-scared Negroes" to achieve unity, so be it. With the possible exception of Muslim apostates ("the hypocrites"), no other group would draw the hostility of the Nation more easily and consistently than the U.S. government and its agents. The cordial interaction between law enforcement officials and Muslims during Muhammad's speaking engagement in Washington masked tensions and animosities that even then were over a quarter century old. When he arrived at Uline Arena among watchful white policemen, the peculiarity of the scene—the "devil" escorting the Messenger of Allah—was not lost on him or his followers.[24]

The overflow crowd, having been searched by Muslim guards and warmed up by Malcolm X, received Muhammad with a ten-minute ovation. The leader had not been in the city for eight years, and it was quite a welcome. There were probably as many non-Muslims in the audience as there were believers. Therefore, the prepared speech of Muhammad was tailored to stress African-American concerns as opposed to purely Islamic issues. As was common for Muslim orators, the leader began his talk with a depiction of the plight of the American so-called Negro as a form of bondage. He emotionally described the sexual abuse of black women and the lynching of the race's men by whites. In his view, the former slave master had, indeed, produced a hell for his ex-slave in the wilderness of North America, and his "turn the other cheek" religion of Christianity was no more than "a key to your [the black race's] slavery." Following his outline of the racial situation, Muhammad castigated other groups and programs that desperate African-Americans had embraced in their search for civil rights. "Everybody has failed the Negro," he reminded the gathering. "The government has failed; the FBI has failed; Christianity has failed. All we can do now is throw these things in the garbage can and then use the garbage can to fight back!" Ecstatic applause and laughter erupted following these statements, and the audience seemed ripe for a speech of messianic import.[25]

Confidently, Muhammad proclaimed his messengership to the crowd and stated that his "mission is from the Lord of the World." Since America was already facing the Day of Judgment, he warned that blacks would have to prepare themselves to suffer extreme casualties to enjoy "freedom, justice, and equality." He concluded his fiery speech by discussing his solution to the race question, which entailed armed self-defense against white aggression, the abandonment of Christianity for Islam, and separation of the races. He demanded that whites turn over to African-Americans "three or four or more states" for the establishment of a sovereign black nation and provide them with assistance for the next twenty-five years. To him, this was the least the white man could do since the ex-slave had "well earned" twenty-five states. Above all, he encouraged blacks to "demand something! Don't demand a job—demand some earth."

The speech, which lasted two hours and twenty minutes, ended in a dizzying ovation. The Muslim leader had given the crowd what it had come to hear and succeeded in picking up a number of converts along the way.[26]

Muhammad and his entourage were escorted by police back to the Roosevelt Hotel. Before departing for Chicago by plane, he agreed to participate in his first filmed interview. The reporter, who represented station WNTA of New York, was apparently most concerned about the implications of the Nation of Islam for white America. The Muslim leader flatly told him that by 1970 there would be no white America, for the time of Allah's vengeance was close at hand. Muhammad left Washington, D.C., from National Airport, well guarded by policemen and the Fruit of Islam. By any standard, his presentation at Uline Arena had been a success and would add to the growing popularity (and infamy) that the movement was generating.[27]

By this time, the separatist beliefs of the Nation of Islam had become more pronounced in the statements of spokesmen, usually at the expense of integration and its African-American and white advocates. The independence of Ghana in 1957 had much to do with Muhammad's renewed emphasis on emigration; however, the growing influence of Christian black civil rights leaders and the resistance of white Southerners to desegregation were pivotal in resuscitating the latent separatist sentiments of the movement. In writings and speeches, Muslim ministers stressed that "separation of the so-called Negroes," whether in an all-black state in North America or through migration to Africa, "is a MUST," and independence and its benefits could not be attained "under the slavemaster's children and their flag." The biblical example of the departure of the Israelites from their Egyptian masters was the precedent most frequently cited by the Muslims to justify their demands. On a less theological level, the economic opportunities that a separate state would supposedly provide for educated and untutored African-Americans alike were also stressed by Muhammad and his adherents.[28]

In addition to a national territory, Muhammad and his followers demanded reparations as payment for centuries of slavery in order to establish the rudiments of a black civilization at a remove from the orbit of Western culture. Furthermore, the Muslims never ceased to lambast nonviolence as a ploy to make black integrationists acquiesce to any treatment by white racists. Self-defense, to the Muslims, was a right mandated by the laws of Allah and required even the "peace-loving people" of the Nation of Islam to protect themselves and their families from aggression. While the right did not excuse the believers from abiding by the laws of the United States, it did emphasize the Old Testament adage "an eye for an eye" in interpersonal and interracial relations. The elements of separatism and self-defense, individually, did not make the Muslim movement appealing to African-Americans who desired empowerment. Instead, the combination of these two factors, plus the movement's critique of Christianity and white America, led many casual observers to become devoted followers.[29]

During his address in the capital, Muhammad had stressed that his organization was not receiving foreign aid. Insofar as Islam was not a creature of Americanism and black discontent was viewed by some as inspired by outsiders, the leader felt it necessary to address rumors regarding his alleged tie, even dependency, on the Arab-Islamic world. It is reasonable to assume that the Nation of Islam did not receive any financial assistance from Middle Eastern countries during this period; however, the leadership of the movement had definitely made contact with a number of Arab nations by the time of the Uline Arena speech. As early as December 1957, Muhammad had written Gamal Nasser an open letter expressing solidarity and Godspeed in attending the African-Asian Conference in Cairo. The Egyptian leader responded to "these noble sentiments" in gracious terms and offered "best wishes to our brothers of Africa and Asia living in the West." The dialogue established by the letters continued mostly by phone during the next few years. Yet, the importance of this connection would grow over time as the Nation sought recognition in the Islamic world and the Arabs struggled for influence in the industrialized West.[30]

Related to these links with the Middle East, the Nation of Islam of the 1950s flirted, in fact, with orthodox Islam. Mostly due to the influence of Jamil Diab, a Palestinian Arab who taught Arabic at the Chicago University of Islam, the beliefs and practices of Eastern Muslims were perhaps more evident in temple ritual during this period than at any previous time. Diab tutored Muhammad in Islamic doctrine and instructed him in the prayers of orthodox Muslims as well as the significance of Muhammad ibn Abdullah.

The Arab was even credited by one source as having taught the leader the correct pronunciation of the name *Muhammad,* which he had allegedly mispronounced as "Mudd Mudd" (or "Muck Muck") for over two decades. Before leaving the movement due to philosophical differences, Diab spoke at Saviour's Day conventions during the early 1950s and perhaps influenced a few of the ideas included in Muhammad's first major booklet on Nation of Islam theology, *The Supreme Wisdom,* which appeared in two editions in 1957. Nonetheless, the strands of variance in the ideology of the movement still outweighed strands of orthodoxy and would continue to do so until the 1970s.[31]

Fundamentally, Muhammad remained faithful to the teachings of Fard Muhammad, and the organization continued to reflect the eclecticism on which it was based. Christian elements remained central to the Muslim experience, as exemplified by the title of *minister* given to temple leaders and the heavy reliance upon selected passages of the Bible to support the group's views of history and the future. Moreover, the unique features of Elijah Muhammad's brand of Islam did not change, such as the belief that his teacher had been Allah in person and that whites were evil by nature. Additionally, rituals of the Nation of Islam generally remained stable despite the contributions of Diab. Meetings were still proceeded by extensive weapons searches; the Lost-Found Moslem Lessons supplemented the Qur'an; and pictures of a racial Armageddon remained in the homes of the believers. As illustrated by their funerary practices, the Muslims did not cease shaping Islam to fit their African-American cultural context and psychological needs. If the last rites of Muhammad's mother, Marie, who died in May 1958, were performed in the typical manner, the gathered mourners did not shed tears or bring flowers to the ceremony, but instead, listened to the presiding minister read two passages from the book of Job and contributed to a fund for the family of the deceased.[32]

Generally, Muhammad's view of Eastern Islam and Arabic culture was an idealistic one. He believed, based on the teachings of Fard Muhammad, that the Middle East was a kind of multiracial utopia in which all people lived as brothers, "regardless of how black the skin or how kinked the hair." In his often naive view, "East Asia" was very different from America where the "slavemasters' religion does not recognize equality of brotherhood." Arabs and blacks, in addition to the Japanese, Chinese, and Indians, were one people—a black people—who were connected by a common racial identity and natural fraternity. Muhammad was vaguely aware of tales of slavery in the Arab world. (Saudi Arabia, the cradle of Islam, would not officially emancipate its one hundred thousand plus African bondmen until November 1962.) However, he rationalized anecdotal evidence and was satisfied in letting the Arabs "answer for themselves." For the past twenty-eight years, he had firmly believed in the maxim that the so-called Negro and all

Muslims were brothers and "that no Muslim will enslave a Muslim." To admit that he and his followers had abandoned the beliefs and values of one slave master to adopt the names and religion of another was perhaps too much for him to do at this time. Thus, despite the reality of slavery and racial discrimination in the Islamic world, Muhammad sent his lieutenant, Malcolm X, on a three-week tour of Muslim countries in June 1959. The mission was designed both to illustrate the brotherly love that supposedly existed between all Muslims and to familiarize the East with the Nation of Islam of America.[33]

Malcolm departed for Egypt on July 5. His stay in the land of the pharaohs was three days longer than intended, but was the most pleasurable part of the trip. He was constantly in the company of Anwar Sadat and other important officials and attended a number of gatherings until he developed an acute case of diarrhea. Malcolm declined an opportunity to meet with President Nasser, for he believed that this privilege should be reserved for his teacher, Elijah Muhammad. The minister next made brief stops in Jerusalem and Damascus before moving on to Saudi Arabia. Malcolm had originally planned to visit Mecca, but due to illness and poor airline scheduling, was forced to leave the country after a two-day stay in Jidda. Much of his African itinerary, which included trips to Ethiopia and Nigeria, was abandoned due to various difficulties, and he was en route back to New York after only an abbreviated tour of Muslim lands. Malcolm was not in the Middle East long enough to convey more than a rudimentary awareness of the Nation of Islam to selected Arab and African Muslims. Nonetheless, he still learned a great deal from his ambassadorial journey.[34]

Malcolm's mission specifically revealed to him the differences between Nation of Islam attitudes and doctrines regarding Islam and the practices and cultural outlook of Eastern Muslims. The Mideast was not the mecca for blacks that had been portrayed. In fact, a number of circumstances that he encountered while abroad actually caught him off guard. For example, his lack of even basic training in the Arabic language embarrassed him during prayer rituals in Egypt. Also, he saw that "East Asia" was not nearly as prosperous and heavenly as it was portrayed in the teachings of the Muslim movement. Most significantly, he learned of events and situations that challenged the very foundations of Elijah Muhammad's message. In Saudi Arabia and the Holy City itself, African blacks were being legally held as slaves by Arab Muslims. Whether Malcolm actually witnessed bondage in the Middle East is impossible to determine from available sources. But given the longevity of the tradition, the large number of bondmen, and the minister's own studious nature, it would have been almost impossible for him not to know of this situation even before his journey. Later, after leaving the Nation of Islam, he would make a few comments against "slavery, no matter who it's carried on by." Yet, for the present, he dispatched glowing accounts of his trip to African-American newspapers, claiming that "no color prejudice [existed] among Moslems," and equality and brotherhood were practiced as "a way of life" in the Islamic world.[35]

Religious and political motives were surely behind Malcolm's less than sincere portrayal of race relations in Arab lands. His continuing adherence to the Nation's white-devil thesis, though he more than likely met racially tolerant white Muslims while in the Middle East, can be attributed to these factors. In a way, Malcolm's trip placed him in a difficult position. Now, he could either challenge everything that the Nation of Islam taught that was not consistent with the teachings and practices of Eastern Muslims, or he could pretend that everything he witnessed and heard while abroad was in line with the message of his teacher. He, of course, chose the latter option. He understood better than anyone that the ministry of Elijah Muhammad had been founded on certain racial and historical "truths" that appealed to many American blacks. Moreover, to jettison these truths would lead to a loss in the movement's popularity among the race-conscious "Original People" of the United States. Except for a few slips that revealed that he did not wholeheartedly embrace all of the Nation's doctrines, Malcolm resigned himself to being the chief propagator of the traditional Muslim line, until his return to the Middle East in April 1964. To him, the status quo was simply an easier, more predictable path to follow.[36]

Ironically, it was during Malcolm's absence from the country that the Nation of Islam was thrust into the consciousness of the American public. A sensational five-part documentary on the movement entitled "The Hate That Hate Produced" was aired by WNTA-TV of New York, which outlined, in a distorted way, the Muslim organization and program. Produced by *News Beat* reporters Mike Wallace and Louis Lomax, the series was televised July 13–17 with a reprise a few days later. This piece of yellow journalism was not only notable for the images it captured; the loaded terminology used by the reporters created a sense of impending conflict and destruction. Wallace prefaced the story with only negative terms, such as "black racism," "black supremacy," and "gospel of hate," thus setting an ominous tone for the entire series. Film footage of a Muslim meeting where *The Trial*—a play in which the white race is prosecuted for its mistreatment of blacks—was being performed appeared next on the screen, followed by shots of the Chicago University of Islam "where Muslim children are taught to hate the white man." The only positive statements made about the movement were in relation to the businesses it had started to service the Muslim and African-American communities. Wallace even opted to cite the extremely high membership figure of 250,000, no doubt to enhance the shock value of the documentary.[37]

An interview with Muhammad partially clarified the Muslims' position, but the questions asked always seemed to intimate the prospects for a race war. Clips of his speech in Uline Arena were shown in which he denounced Christianity and the U.S. government for failing blacks. Beseeched by Lomax for an exposition of the Nation's ideology, the leader confirmed for the record that he believed the white man was the devil, that the so-called Negro would be resurrected by 1970, and that there would be some bloodshed when the white world was destroyed. To Lomax's question as to whether he was preaching hate, the self-assured Muhammad replied that he was only teaching truth. The filmed segment of the interview with the Muslim chief was brief and edited to emphasize the movement's hostility to whites. It was obvious that the show had been rushed into production and irreparably tainted by anti-Muslim views. Illustratively, the News Beat researchers had not even bothered to verify the birthplace of Muhammad, allowing Wallace to report that he hailed from Hawkinsville, Georgia. Such a program was the harbinger of more frequent white media treatment in the 1960s.[38]

But it was not the Muslim leader but Malcolm X who was covered most by the series. The New York minister was not necessarily portrayed as the superior or equal of Muhammad in the movement, but his role as chief spokesman for the Nation was definitely emphasized over that of his teacher. More of his introductory speech in Uline Arena was aired than Muhammad's keynote address, and his interview with Lomax commanded much more film footage. The creators of the series may not have intended to stress the importance of Malcolm to the Nation above the centrality of his mentor. Yet, the documentary, as other press reports would in the future, revealed how much more newsmen were drawn to the oratorical fire of the youthful minister than to the theological simmerings of his sexagenarian teacher. For the time being, the appeal of Malcolm X to the media was viewed by Muhammad and most of his followers as in the interest of the movement. On occasion, the Muslim chief publicly "thank[ed] Allah for my Brother Minister Malcolm." Later, when leadership intrigue and questions of succession began to surface in the Nation, many top officials would take offense when the head of Temple No. 7 uttered even the most innocuous comments before microphones and klieg lights.[39]

"The Hate That Hate Produced" did much for (and to) the Muslims. The numbers of temples and African-Americans attending services increased dramatically over the next year or so, thanks in part to the series. Also, the power of television and radio to bring the images and teachings of the group's leadership instantly into the living rooms of Americans went a long way toward making the movement a familiar, if controversial, topic of conversation. The publicized Muslim program injected the group into the civil rights dialogue, at least in an adversarial, rhetorical sense. On a less positive note, the opposition of the Nation to integration gave white racists the stark evidence that they had been looking for to prove that not all blacks favored the methods and goals of Dr. King and other opponents of racial separatism. Mass media coverage of the Muslims from mid-1959 onward differed significantly in emphasis and content compared to the stories that had seized headlines during the 1930s. No longer did the "Black Muslim" threat simply consist of a parochial cult practicing "voodooism" and human sacrifice among African-American migrants in Depression-racked Detroit. The Nation of Islam was now portrayed as a national phenomenon that embraced a kind of "reverse racism" (or "black supremacy") and was bent upon starting a racial Armageddon when Elijah Muhammad gave the word. In many ways, the ideology of the Muslims, with its ringing denunciation of whites and their institutions and its prophecies of destruction, had helped the press to create this image. Still, Muhammad and his followers saw only the divisive tactics of the white man behind the media's largely negative representation of the Nation and its leaders.[40]

During a speech in St. Nicholas Arena, New York, on July 26, Muhammad returned the salvo launched by Wallace and Lomax. A Whites Barred sign was posted outside the building to ensure that only blacks made up the audience of six thousand people. After the usual body searches, Malcolm X spoke briefly about his recent trip to Africa and the Middle East and introduced his teacher to the crowd. The Muslim leader, following a long ovation, called for unity among "the darker peoples on earth" and underscored the necessity of black emigration in the days to come. "Allah has spoken to me," he exhorted, "and he has chosen the so-called Negro to be his people. You are the lost sheep. . . . You must be restored to your people." At the rally, the defense of the Nation against the *News Beat* documentary was actually left to the minister of Philadelphia's Temple No. 12, Wallace Muhammad, the leader's twenty-five-year-old son. Though not the most eloquent spokesman in the movement, the young minister certainly captured the sentiments of the leadership regarding the Wallace-Lomax report. "They say we are preaching hate, but they never said what the teachings of Elijah are." In a persecutory vein reminiscent of his father, he went on to charge the white man in general with attempting to "split Elijah's followers . . . [because] he wants to put a stop to him. . . . He's too afraid of what he is saying."[41]

The young minister's counterattack against the media, of course, evoked applause and enthusiastic support from the all-black audience and was reported in newspapers and magazines. Nonetheless, the war between the Nation and the mass media over the group's public image was still being won by the latter, which had access to greater resources and a larger audience. The almost perverted fascination of the press with the "black supremacists" continued, and unflattering stories appeared in major publications such as *Time* and *U.S. News & World Report* throughout the remainder of the year. Because of the violence-prone, antiwhite reputation that the movement was being saddled with, the black-owned newspaper *The Pittsburgh Courier* decided to drop the Muslim chief's column, "Mr. Muhammad Speaks," after three years of regularly printing it. Apparently, the new, more conservative owners of the publication found it expedient to rid themselves of the column to avoid serving as a platform for, as *Time* described him, the "purveyor of this cold black hatred."[42]

Regardless of the odds against success, the Nation continued its battle against anti-Muslim bias in the press. For a while, the two seemed to be going blow for blow, with the media striking at the most venerated institutions of the Nation. On August 15, the city of Detroit, following leads from the *Detroit Free Press,* ordered the closing of the University of Islam operated by Temple No. 1. State and city officials had "swarmed over" the facility the day before and concluded that "the building [was] poorly ventilated, dimly lighted, and inadequate in fire prevention measures." As a result of "a *Free Press* inquiry," the 102 pupils who attended the school were forced to relocate elsewhere. Despite the outcry of the Muslims, a newspaper report had succeeded in shattering a pillar of the Nation's superstructure.[43]

In defense against the press, Malcolm X and Wallace Muhammad castigated *Time* magazine before an August gathering of six thousand people at Rockland Palace, New York. They accused the periodical of "purposely twisting" Elijah Muhammad's words to make the movement appear seditious. Though the attendance at the meeting itself attested to the growing clout of the Muslims despite the bad press, vocal opposition to the movement began to emanate from other quarters around this time, in addition to the media. Abruptly, the attention of the Nation's leadership was shifted away from hostile news organizations to individuals and groups whose criticisms were potentially more harmful.[44]

Many African-American leaders struggling for desegregation and civil rights enforcement in the South believed that the program and philosophy of the Muslims were inimical to the achievement of full citizenship for the race. Biting tirades against the U.S. government, Christianity, and integration by Nation of Islam spokesmen were often viewed as personal assaults by those blacks who had risked life and limb to vote, secure better educational opportunities for their children, and pursue the American dream. While some of the group's rhetoric struck a chord of sympathy even among African-Americans optimistic about future race relations, most black leaders involved in the Civil Rights Movement in the early 1960s felt it necessary to publicly oppose the Muslims, especially after the Wallace-Lomax documentary. Philosophical differences with the Nation at least partially inspired the opposition of African-American leaders to the movement; however, fear of the group's growing notoriety and membership was probably the decisive factor behind many of the attacks of detractors. Conflict between the civil rights leadership and the Muslims had been mostly a one-sided affair before mid-1959, with Muhammad levying editorial and verbal charges of "Uncle Tomism," which often went unanswered. Once the organization was propelled onto the world stage by the media, prominent black activists and organizers wasted little time denouncing the "black racism" of Muhammad and his followers.[45]

The first broadsides were fired by the NAACP. In an August statement to the press, executive secretary Roy Wilkins declared that his organization "opposes and regards as dangerous any group, white or black, political or religious, that preaches hatred among men." Wilkins conceded in his announcement that the popularity of the "so-called Moslems who preach black supremacy" was predicated on the lack of government commitment to passing a strong civil rights bill or protecting African-Americans from persecution. Yet, he made it clear that his group was against "hate white" teachings and went on to imply that the Nation of Islam would fade away once the Civil Rights Movement began to bear more fruit. Two months after Wilkins's repudiation of the Muslims, Thurgood Marshall, the top attorney of the NAACP Legal Defense and Education Fund, delivered a more scathing critique of the movement. The lawyer, before an audience at Princeton University, characterized the Nation as "run by a bunch of thugs organized from prisons and jails, and financed, I am sure, by Nasser or some Arab group." Not satisfied with being just another "vicious" collection of blacks who could not wait until Southern racists ended their "massive resistance" to integration, the Nation, in Marshall's view, posed a formidable challenge to the FBI, the NAACP, and law and order in the states. The leaders of the NAACP, the organization at the forefront of the legal struggle for African-American rights, apparently felt compelled to speak out against the Muslims, not only for the sake of minimizing the appeal of Muhammad's separatist program, but also to affirm that they had not spent thousands of dollars in litigation for goals that were not attainable. In the interest of black unity, the response of the Nation to the NAACP offensive was muted, at least for the time being. Among rank-and-file believers, however, Marshall began to be derisively referred to as "the Ugly American."[46]

The most significant, but not the worst, barrage of black faultfinding came from Dr. Martin Luther King Jr., who had already become the symbol of the Civil Rights Movement. The leader's first major public statement regarding the Muslims was not from an official capacity as Wilkins's remarks had been nor as vitriolic as Marshall's assertions were. Still, his stance against Muhammad and his followers added greatly to the rising barrier of hostility and the spirit of uncooperativeness that hindered the development of amicable relations between the Muslims and the mainstream civil rights leadership. During a Milwaukee address before the National Bar Association in August 1959, King cited the Nation as being among the "hate groups arising in our midst which would preach a doctrine of black supremacy." Like Wilkins and others, the leader acknowledged the reluctance of the government to force the integration issue, but warned African-Americans not to "stoop to the low and primitive methods of some of our opponents." King lumped the Muslims together with white racist groups and made no effort to discern differences between the programs of the two. In future comments on the Nation, King would select his words carefully and would usually offer remarks only after being solicited by an interviewer or a curious reporter. At best, his adherence to nonviolence, faith in Christianity, and desire for racial conciliation would allow him to be no more than a silent admirer of the articulate Malcolm X, whom he would meet only once, and then briefly, in March 1964.[47]

The attacks of prominent blacks affected Muhammad in a way much different from those of the media. While he and his ministers had partially drawn the fire of these leaders through their own criticisms of integration and Christianity, the charges made by King, the NAACP, and others seemed to fall beyond the boundaries of fair play. The Nation had already been sensitized to unfavorable scrutiny by the press. The harangues of civil rights leaders, as far as Muhammad was concerned, appeared to add salt to the wound and reeked of a pernicious kind of racial disloyalty. In response to their public disapproval of the Nation, he collectively denounced African-American leaders as "hungry for a place among the white race instead of their own race" and held them responsible for having "brought the Negroes to the present conditions." He condemned the clergy of the race in particular for serving as "the white man's right hand over the so-called Negroes" and "teaching the white man's slavery religion called Christianity." His disparagement of black leadership was bitter and became more frequent over time. During the late 1950s, however, he tended to speak only in general about this class and avoided mentioning specific names, at least in public, hoping to secure a broad appeal for the Nation among the black masses and among certain black groups.[48]

In not criticizing specific black civil rights leaders, Muhammad was undoubtedly conscious of the dominant role that the educated middle class of the race played in the national struggle for integration. Moreover, he more than likely knew that criticism that was too caustic could backfire and not only isolate potential black converts who admired spokesmen like King and Wilkins, but also deny the Nation the sympathy and support of African-American leaders during this period of intense media scrutiny and ongoing government harassment. A more farseeing and less confrontational approach seemed best, at least at present, and the Muslims adopted a strategy of coexistence with the integrationists. Speaking invitations futilely extended to King and attempts by the movement to attract professionals were designed, in part, to achieve a certain measure of respectability that was associated with both the mainstream leadership of the civil rights struggle and the values and outlook of the middle class in general.

Despite Muslim efforts, an alliance between the Nation and other major black organizations did not materialize. Indeed, abrasive criticism of the movement continued to the point that Muhammad, fearing the repercussions of suffering in silence at the hands of opponents, finally gave Malcolm X and other spokesmen permission to respond directly to individual critics. Integration, nonviolent protest, and Christianity all came under fire from Muslim orators and writers, and there was little that was too harsh for them to say about the major personalities behind the Civil Rights Movement. To Muhammad, Christian ministers such as Dr. King served as a crutch for the dying white world and "turned many potential freedom-fighting Negroes into contented, docile slaves." Furthermore, prominent leaders such as Thurgood Marshall who spoke against the Nation were, in the leader's words, "the most unfit, and worse enemy of all to the real cause of freedom, justice, and equality for the so-called Negro." The verbal and editorial thrashing of critics by the Muslims evoked more charges of black supremacy and hate-mongering from integrationists. However, no major leader was prepared to face the agile intellect of Malcolm X in debates or to present his case before Muhammad at an open meeting of the Muslims. On the contrary, well-known black opponents of the Nation were usually satisfied with sniping at the organization from a distance. Only infrequently would they come close enough to hear Muslim spokesmen ridicule them as "black bodies with white heads!"[49]

As the rhetorical war between Muhammad and his African-American critics heated up, another group began assailing the theological roots of the movement. Prior to the late 1950s, orthodox Muslims had never posed a formidable or consistent challenge to the Nation. There had been occasional friction between Muhammad's followers and individual Muslims with Sunni or other affiliations, but no full-blown rivalries akin to the organizational challenges launched by splinter groups during the 1930s. Yet, by the time the movement began responding to its black civil rights opponents, cracks in its near monopoly over Islamic sentiments in the African-American community were quite evident. The challenges were not only external assaults; internal tensions tugged at the doctrinal seams of the Nation as well. For example, Jamil Diab, the Palestinian Muslim who had introduced elements of orthodox Islam into the movement during the mid-1950s, broke with Muhammad once their philosophical differences proved irreconcilable. Diab established his own Islamic Center of Chicago and became one of the Nation's most vocal ideological enemies. In a statement published in late 1959, the Palestinian rebuked Muhammad and his followers as "totally lacking in the requisites which constitutes any Muslim group.... They start controversies everywhere, carry on ... propaganda in an aggressive manner and continuously strive to swell their numbers at the expense of Islam." Unlike Thurgood Marshall, Diab did not see the hand of Gamal Nasser behind the movement and, in fact, conceded that the Nation had "every right to exist." Still, he repudiated the movement for turning the "very cornerstone of Islam, universal brotherhood of man, black as well as white . . . into hatred." He concluded that Muhammad's organization "is not now, nor has it ever been, a part" of Islam.[50]

Diab's rejection of the Nation, though definitely among the most vociferous, was not the first by a previous insider of orthodox ilk. A year earlier, Hamaas Abdul Khaalis, the secretary of Temple No. 2, had left the fold of the believers ostensibly over favoritism shown to Muhammad's family members and the refusal of the leader to embrace Sunni Islam. According to Khaalis's version of events, he joined the movement in 1951 for the sole purpose of bringing Muhammad closer to orthodox Islam and saving his followers from "being deceived." After being appointed secretary in 1956, he came to realize that two sets of rules governed temple affairs—one for the rank-and-file membership and another for Muhammad and his relatives. Also, those in the inner circles of power at the Chicago headquarters "were not following the way of the Musselman." Khaalis left after an unsuccessful confrontation with the leadership and journeyed to New York where he reportedly met with Malcolm X, who tried to convince him, at Muhammad's behest, to rejoin the Nation. The dissenter declined the invitation and became affiliated with Sunni Muslims, eventually organizing his own Islamic movement. Not until the early 1970s would the paths of Khaalis's Hanafi Muslims and Muhammad's Original People cross again. This later confrontation would be a most unfortunate demonstration of the tragic potential of the open hostilities that arose between the Nation and its orthodox opponents during the late 1950s.[51]

By far, Talib Ahmad Dawud, a black Muslim from Antigua, was the most belligerent critic of the legitimacy of the Nation of Islam as an Islamic movement. Married to jazz vocalist Dakota Staton, Dawud was instrumental in organizing the Muslim Brotherhood, Inc., in 1950, which established branches in Philadelphia, Detroit, and Harlem. His most stinging comments came in the wake of the Rockland Palace gathering of Nation of Islam supporters during August 1959. In the pages of a Chicago weekly, Dawud denounced Muhammad as a fraud and convicted criminal who taught racial hatred contrary to the true teachings of Islam, which seek to "unify mankind." The Antiguan, who had just completed the hajj, held that the Nation was not accepted as a valid expression of Islam by Middle Eastern Muslims and thus "neither Elijah Muhammad nor his followers can get into Mecca." More so than that of many other critics, the disapproval expressed by Dawud took on personal overtones that went beyond organizational rivalry.[52]

Muhammad, aware that the theological legitimacy of the Nation was at stake, responded to the charges of Dawud immediately instead of allowing him the grace period that African-American civil rights leaders had been given. In an open letter, the leader accused Dawud and "his TV blues-singing" wife of breathing "their venomous poison against me" and of being "jealous of the progress with which Allah . . . is blessing me and my followers." Muhammad scorned his rival's spouse for singing "filthy blues and love songs" and "publicly serving the devil in the theatrical world." Aware of the efforts of the Dawuds to discredit him internationally, the leader stated that his Muslim opponents were only doing themselves a disservice by slandering him at the embassies of Muslim countries. Dawud, in reply, labeled Muhammad and his followers "phonies" with "no connection whatsoever" to true Muslims. Over the next few months, the charges and countercharges went back and forth. Added to the pressures of unfavorable media coverage, government surveillance, and the censure by black leaders, the antagonistic dialogue between Muhammad and Dawud and other orthodox Muslims represented the opening of a fourth front in the Nation's war over its public image.[53]

On the surface, the conflict between the Muslim movement and its orthodox rivals was doctrinal in nature. The critics, aroused by the spotlighting of the Nation by the media, accused Muhammad of distorting Islam with racial hatred, while the leader maintained that "slavery and systematic brainwashing by the slavemasters" required that the so-called Negro embrace a race-conscious interpretation of Islam. At its core, however, the clash between Muhammad and his opponents was primarily fueled by the desires of each to appeal to different constituencies, domestically and abroad. Each of the groups craved recognition from Middle Eastern Muslims to bolster its claims of being the preeminent Islamic movement in the United States, and to tap into patronage from Arab leaders. The emergence of Arab Muslim nations as significant players in international affairs had everything to do with the rhetorical battles of American Muslim sects. Muhammad's criticism of Dakota Staton, the "filthy blues" singer, and Dawud's smearing of the reputation of the Nation at various embassies must be viewed as a struggle over the trappings of legitimacy as well as interpretations of the Islamic message. In a world shrunk by television, radio, and the media in general, the combatants could hardly have afforded to overlook the importance of image in shaping opinions.[54]

The Muslim movement of Elijah Muhammad, even before its heyday in the 1960s and 1970s, was the main custodian of black nationalist sentiment in the United States. Many African-Americans who joined the Nation found its separatism and critique of white America at least as appealing as its purely religious and ritual aspects. Since the organization had become so popular *because* of its heterodox brand of Islam and racial chauvinism, to eliminate these features of the Nation's doctrine would have alienated many of those blacks who clung, with aloof pride, to beliefs in the original black man, the imminent destruction of the white world, and so on. As Muhammad certainly knew, doctrinal rapprochement with orthodox Muslims would lessen the loyalty of a membership that had responded to the nationalistic features of the movement, such as the call for a black territory and the attempts to construct an internal economy. In recruiting followers, the known benefits of black separatism and a race-based Islam far outweighed the risks of accepting orthodoxy, and thus revolutionizing the theology of the Nation was unattractive. Consequently, if Muhammad never embraced Eastern Islam nor paid it the slightest lip service, he could be assured that "in a society where there are too many White Muslims [or nationalists]," his movement would continue to thrive.[55]

Orthodox rivals of the Nation of Islam attempted to appeal to those African-Americans who were spiritually unfulfilled by Christianity but could not force themselves to write off as impractical or undesirable the goals of the Civil Rights Movement and the larger struggle for a brotherhood of man. The attacks of Sunni Muslims and others on the white-devil theory and racial separatism of the Nation were solidly supported by traditional readings of the Qur'an and other Muslim texts, which stressed the relatedness of humanity regardless of race. To Dawud, Diab, and Khaalis, the scriptural high ground belonged to them, and the accessibility of Islam to all was its best selling point. The goals of equality, desegregation, and enfranchisement that motivated the black push for civil rights were reflected in these tenets of Islam and gave the orthodox version of the religion that much more potential in some African-American communities. At least doctrinally, the theological rivals of the Nation were already in tune with most of the Middle Eastern world and did not have to discourage their American followers, as Muhammad allegedly did, from visiting the region for fear of bringing the ideological foundations of their organizations into question. On another level, the orthodox Muslims would never have to deal with the stigma of black supremacy, which both attracted and repelled blacks to whom Muhammad had reached out.[56]

Despite the efforts of its orthodox rivals, the Nation of Islam more easily won African-Americans over to its cause for a number of reasons. Primarily, its Sunni opponents and others joined the game late and had over the years allowed Muhammad, with the help of the press, to define Islam for a significant number of blacks. The Nation had seized the initiative, and the media simply tightened that grasp. Also, historical timing was a factor in the appeal of Elijah Muhammad. The Southern "massive resistance" campaign against integration along with de facto segregation in Northern and Midwestern cities fed the flames of black discontent and made millenarianism and black separatism, even in their most extreme forms, an almost natural response for many African-Americans living under some of the worst

CG 100-35635

It is requested that Washington Field contact the Passport Office, Department of State, Washington, D.C., and arrange to place a stop on ELIJAH MUHAMMAD, CLARA MUHAMMAD, his wife; WALLACE D. MUHAMMAD, his son; and RAYMOND SHARRIEFF, his son-in-law, in the event they make application for a passport. It is requested further that this stop be placed for a three month period and that it be allowed to expire automatically at that time. Chicago bases this request upon the above information as furnished by ▓▓▓▓. Chicago is also including the other three named individuals as it has in the past been indicated that MUHAMMAD will be accompanied by an entourage and the above three would be the more likely persons selected to accompany him. Chicago is also of the opinion that MUHAMMAD might take some action in this matter if he visits Washington, D.C., on May 31, 1959 as planned.

conditions in the industrialized world. Moreover, anticolonial movements throughout Africa were gaining momentum and inspired pride and nationalistic feelings in the most devastated of American ghettos. In black America as well as in the Middle East, Islam was already being fused with nationalism in order to reduce Western influence. Given these factors, plus the tailoring of Muhammad's message to attract the postwar generation of angry urban youths, orthodox Muslims would have to wait for more settled times before they could pose a serious challenge to the popularity of the Nation of Islam. In the meanwhile, Muhammad fully exploited the situation and attempted to deliver the coup de grâce that would silence his Muslim critics. In late November 1959, he embarked upon a hajj, the pilgrimage to the holy city of Mecca that all believers in Islam are encouraged to undertake.

Though orthodox critics made the journey more urgent, Muhammad had actually been planning to visit the Middle East as early as February 1959. Originally, he had intended to begin his travels in April, but did not get around to filing his passport application until late May. The FBI, apparently fearful of the implications of his trip for American propaganda efforts in the region, secretly tried to place a three-month stop on his application in hope of delaying his departure. Impatient, Muhammad called the Passport Office in Washington, D.C., on June 4 and demanded that appropriate documents be granted to him by the following day. After being told that his application would take five or six additional weeks to process, he contacted his attorney. The tap placed on his telephone allowed the FBI to hear incoming and outgoing calls, and perhaps to avoid litigation on account of the delay, Muhammad was issued a passport on June 24. Around this time, Malcolm X was preparing to take a preliminary tour of the Middle East to set the stage for his teacher. Yet, unforeseen events such as the

Wallace-Lomax documentary and the resultant explosion of interest in the Nation of Islam forced Muhammad to put his travel plans temporarily on hold even after his protégé returned with warm greetings from Nasser and others.[57]

The denunciation of his movement by Dawud and other orthodox Muslims more than anything else convinced Muhammad of the necessity of making the hajj before the end of the 1950s. His desire to settle nagging questions concerning the legitimacy of the Nation as an Islamic entity spurred a special fund-raising drive led by New York's Temple No. 7 to finance the trip. Once informed by Malcolm X of what to expect in the Islamic world, Muhammad, accompanied by his sons Herbert and Akbar, departed by plane from New York City on November 21 after a one-day stopover. The three Muslims made connections in Copenhagen, Denmark, following a twelve-hour flight and were in Istanbul, Turkey, by the early afternoon of November 22.[58]

Since the breakup of the Ottoman Empire in 1923 following its defeat in World War I, Turkey had experienced a cultural revolution of sorts. In many areas, an upheaval against the traditional—or more accurately, an alignment toward the West—took place that greatly changed the face of the former seat of Islamic power. While a modernizing nationalism had been instrumental in powering the transition of the country from an imperial caliphate to a Western-style nation-state, conservative and progressive forces were both responsible for the character of the Turkish republic of the 1950s. Under the nation's first president, Mustafa Kemal (1923–38) and his successor, Gen. Ismet Inonu (1938–50), the country shed or altered many practices and institutions associated with the Ottoman period. Most significantly, the influence of Islam in Turkey was greatly reduced by state decrees in favor of a clearer dichotomy between government and religious affairs. Women, traditionally subordinate to men in all realms of society, were given the franchise and the power to initiate divorces. Additionally, polygamy, a mainstay of Turkish life, was banned as were the wearing of red fezzes by men and religious education. Symbolic of the conscious efforts of the modernizing rulers of Turkey to graft European features onto the traditionally Asiatic face of the country, Arabic script was replaced by an alphabet based on the Roman model, and the Hagia Sophia, a sixth-century church-turned-mosque in Constantinople, was converted into a museum.[59]

In politics and economics, Turkey also followed the lead of Western Europe. In 1923, the capital of the country was moved from the religious center of Constantinople, renamed Istanbul in 1930, to Ankara in central Anatolia where a national bureaucracy was established. Turkish republicanism became more sophisticated during the Second World War to the point that the ruling People's Party allowed an electoral challenge by the Democratic Party to unseat it in a 1950 vote. The new leaders of Turkey promised a greater role for private enterprise in the country's development, an acceleration of agrarian reform and industrialization, and more political freedoms for the nation's 21 million people. Internationally, they shunned Communism and settled into a Western orbit marked by aid from the United States and membership in NATO in 1952. Despite their efforts to further develop the country along European lines, the Democrats were hampered by political unrest caused in large part by their own reactionism, conflict with Greece over Cyprus, and a revival of Islam and traditional customs. When Elijah Muhammad and his sons arrived in the country in late November 1959, the Turkish republic was teetering on the brink of collapse with the military preparing to push it over the edge.[60]

The Muhammads were in Turkey for only three days. Their visit was largely confined to the Islamic center of Istanbul and its environs. Straddling the Bosporus, the city was a major trading and industrial entrepôt as well as a center of religious importance. Muhammad and his sons most likely visited holy places and tourist attractions such as the Hagia Sophia, the Blue Mosque, and the city's three universities, the oldest dating back to the fifteenth century. Three days was just enough for them to get a taste of the ancient flavor of the city.

In religious matters, Muhammad found the Turkish people to be good Muslims by practice, although their whiteness precluded them from being Muslims by nature as the so-called Negroes putatively were. Visits to mosques certainly revealed to Muhammad the ideological gap between the doctrines of the Nation and orthodox Islam. Unlike his temples in America, Turkish places of worship had no altars, sanctuaries, or chairs. No rigid hierarchy of officials conducted mosque affairs, and no living messengers mediated between Muslims and their God, Allah. Like the Nation of Islam, Islamic Turkey did not allow music or dancing in places of worship, but orthodox Turks believed in "submission to the One, remote, and immaterial God," not Fard Muhammad, the Nation's "God in person." Few of the disparities between his brand of Islam and that of the Turks could have surprised Muhammad, for he had been exposed to elements of orthodox Islam for years. In minimizing the differences, the leader drew inspiration from selected features of Turkish worship and history, such as the Turkish massacres of Armenian Christians in 1894–96 and 1915. As he always had in the past, Muhammad continued to count the Nation of Islam among the millions of Muslims in the world. To him, ideological consistency was less important than the imperatives of unity and brotherhood among those who adhered to some version of the Islamic faith.[61]

Departing from Istanbul on November 25, Muhammad and his sons journeyed next into the heart of the Arab-Islamic world. After four quick days in Damascus, Beirut, and Jordanian Jerusalem, they reached Cairo, Egypt, on November 29. Since 1958, the land of the pharaohs had been federated with Syria and Yemen as the United Arab Republic. Firmly under the military rule of charismatic Arab nationalist Gamal Nasser, Egypt in the 1950s had witnessed significant social and political changes. The Bandung Conference of 1955 had lionized the Egyptian president as a staunch opponent of British imperialism as well as a progressive statesman who had ousted a decadent monarch. It set the stage for the more dramatic event of the ensuing year. The Suez Canal crisis of 1956 enhanced this idealized image, especially among Muslims who felt humiliated by Israeli participation in the assault on Egypt. The state-sponsored expulsion of British and French nationals along with Jews went a long way toward making Nasser the object of hero worship throughout the Arab world. For the common Egyptian, land-reform measures that broke up the larger estates were a welcome adjustment in a desert nation well accustomed to absolute monarchy and aristocratic privilege. Nasser's Egypt was a rising star in 1959, and few other third-world countries had futures so seemingly bright.[62]

Muhammad's visit to Cairo had almost certainly been prearranged with Egyptian officials, and according to his version of his two-week stay, the hospitality extended to him underscored his political clout more than that of his hosts. As had been the case in Istanbul, there was much to see in Africa's largest city, and Muhammad and his sons had ample time to explore. The leader made it a priority to visit the major holy places, such as the tenth-century mosque and university at Al-Azhar, where he had tea with the chief imam, Grand Sheikh Shaltuat. He probably made the trip to Giza, or even the Valley of the Kings, to see the famed pyramids that the Nation of Islam attributed to the craftsmanship of the Tribe of Shabazz. The most significant episode in Muhammad's stay in Egypt was, of course, his meeting with Nasser. The event is shrouded in legend, and the later recollections of Muhammad were likely embellished to aggrandize his claims of organizational legitimacy. Nonetheless, the encounter was important for both men, particularly for Muhammad, whose position vis-à-vis his American orthodox critics was fortified.[63]

According to Muhammad, the Egyptian president graciously received him in his palace home, hoisting him into his arms "like a father meeting his son." After welcoming him to Egypt, Nasser reportedly made strenuous attempts to convince Muhammad to teach Islam to the people of French West Africa who "were having a lot of trouble." Muhammad politely turned down the offer, but his host was insistent. "These are the places where you need to spend your time," the Arab beseeched, "because America is not going to pay any attention to you." Put on the spot, the Muslim leader again declined the invitation, arguing, "But that is why God gave me the job of bringing our people to life: because they live in the crossfire." To make his proposition more attractive, Nasser allegedly offered a seventy-five-room palace to Muhammad in Cairo and encouraged him to take a look at it. Escorted by cabinet officials, he agreed to the showing and was assured that "if you don't like it, we will build you [another] one." Muhammad was impressed by the offer and the palace itself but could not accept it. Though the Egyptian president did not believe that the majority of blacks in the United States would ever adopt Islam, the African-American Muslim was apparently too convinced of the sanctity of his mission to abandon it. Regardless of their disagreement, the two men, both fierce nationalists, parted company amicably after the conference, never to meet again. For Muhammad, his appointment with the most popular man in the Islamic world was a propaganda coup of enormous proportions.[64]

While parts of Muhammad's account of the generosity of Nasser may be apocryphal, the importance of the meeting was not lost on enemies of the Nation of Islam. During the leader's stay in Cairo, the FBI, through its office in Madrid, Spain, attempted to place stops on the visas of Muhammad and his sons in the event that they tried to enter Morocco from Algeria. The plan had evidently been designed to keep the Muslims from traveling to Senegal in French West Africa and discussing the American racial situation among African blacks there. Regardless of the ultimate purpose of the FBI, Muhammad and his sons did not visit any areas west of Egypt, though they may originally have intended to do so.[65]

On another front, another opponent of the Nation was working hard to discredit Muhammad's movement in America. Talib Dawud, apparently aware of the meeting between Muhammad and Nasser, reported to *The Pittsburgh Courier* that the leader had been requested by Egyptian officials to cut his visit short "because he was posing as a Muslim" and had visited Israel before arriving in Cairo. The newspaper seemingly took the words of Dawud, the chief orthodox rival of Muhammad, at face value and did not confirm the report, which was likely erroneous. Whatever the case may be, there was very little that either he or the FBI could do to keep the leader from reaching Mecca. To their dismay, their wars against Muhammad and the Nation of Islam would have to be placed on hold until he returned to the United States in 1960.[66]

After departing from Cairo, the Muhammads arrived in Khartoum, Sudan, on December 16 for a three-day stopover. The exact nature of their visit here is unclear, but an outline of Sudanese affairs might lend some insight into the impact of the brief stay on the travelers. Like Egypt, Sudan had already experienced a military takeover, in November 1958, which had led to the banning of political parties, the abrogation of the right to assemble, and the silencing of the press. The political fallout of the coup did not only alter institutions; it affected the chances for social stability under a federal government. The northern part of the country, far more economically backward than Egypt, was primarily Arab and Muslim, and the southern area was populated by African blacks who embraced Christian and traditional beliefs as well as Islam. The prospects for cultural pluralism suffered greatly after the ascendancy of the military, and the often forcible methods used by the new government to ensure the political and cultural conformity of the South exacerbated longstanding animosities. Although his visit was probably confined to the capital, located at the confluence of the Blue and White Nile Rivers, Muhammad was perhaps made aware of the coercive means employed by Muslim Arabs of the developing North against non-Islamic Africans in the even poorer South. If nothing else, he more than likely recognized the religious and racial tensions in the country, even within Khartoum. In this instance, Islam had not been a unifying force, at least not in the manner in which it was inflicted on the South. As a result of a history of divisive British policies and later military rule, the Sudan, beginning as early as 1955, was spiraling steadily into the trauma of civil war.[67]

The reality of disunity and conflict among African peoples of various racial, ethnic, and religious backgrounds was further illustrated to Muhammad upon his arrival in Ethiopia on December 19. An ancient kingdom stretching back to biblical times, the nation was one of the many countries in Africa on the verge of dissolution. Emperor Haile Selassie had succeeded, despite scarce resources and the Italian occupation of 1936–41, in constructing a modern bureaucracy and even ridding the thirteen provinces of some of their more feudal elements. Yet, he had failed to create an Ethiopian nationality or consciousness that could harmonize relations between the various ethnic populations of the empire. The traditionally dominant Amharic people still firmly controlled the political system. However, the period up to 1959 was actually the quiet before the storm. In less than a year, an unsuccessful assassination attempt would be made against the aging emperor, and a full-fledged war of independence would later be launched by Eritrean nationalists against their Ethiopian masters. More so than even Sudan, the last black empire in Africa was coming apart at the seams. In the end, imperial Ethiopia, mired in the hostilities of an ancient past, would serve as a poor model of nation-building for the younger countries of the continent.[68]

The month-long stay of Muhammad in Africa exposed him to circumstances and conditions that the Nation of Islam's history of "East Asia" had not prepared him for. The pyramids and Islam were there, but so were conflicts and cleavages that even he could detect during his brief travels. Such observations were disillusioning. Extremes of wealth and poverty, power and powerlessness, were abundant in Egypt, Sudan, and Ethiopia. Also in bountiful supply was a capacity of African peoples, whether the northern Sudanese or the Amhara of Ethiopia, to exploit other Africans for political, economic, and social gain. These conflicts were perhaps most exasperating for Muhammad because they contradicted his belief that African and Asian people were a common stock, righteous and fraternal. Perhaps, he was not aware of the Arab slave trade in Sudan during the nineteenth century or the slave markets of modern Ethiopia; however, the legacies of ethnic hostility and economic inequality in postemancipation societies were still there for everyone to see. In the midst of it all, Islam was not the absolute positive force that Muhammad and the Nation of Islam believed it had been in Africa. Nor was it the only ideological current stirring in the region, for it had coexisted with Coptic Christianity and Islamic derivatives such as Sufism for centuries. The African trek of Muhammad was surely a learning experience, albeit a difficult one. When he and his sons departed from Ethiopia in late December with Saudi Arabian visas obtained in Addis Ababa, the leader's idealized image of "East Asia" had been eroded by African realities.[69]

On December 23, the Muhammads reached the busy port of Jidda in the coastal Hejaz region of Saudi Arabia. Known for its humidity, the city was one of the most important urban areas in the country due to its ancient trade networks and proximity to the Red Sea. Its role as a port of entry for Muslim pilgrims bolstered its economy and diversified the racial and ethnic composition of its population. Though officially not one of the holy cities of Islam, the importance of Jidda to the region is surpassed by few other cities. Muhammad and his sons, like most prospective hajjis, stayed only briefly in Jidda. Local officials had arranged for them to be driven the roughly forty-five miles to Mecca the following day. Dressed in "sandal-like slippers" and the traditional *ihram,* or two-piece toweling that covers the upper and lower body of the pilgrim, they arrived in Mecca without incident on Thursday, Christmas Eve.[70]

Since Muhammad's pilgrimage was not during the first half of Dhu'l-Hijja, he could only make the *umra,* or minor hajj, an abbreviated journey to the more important holy sites of Mecca. After checking into a local hotel, Muhammad washed his hands and face, a ritual cleansing before the actual hajj. An older man had been appointed to guide him through the pilgrimage and, "like a father leading his child," took the leader to the Great Mosque of Mecca. Along the way, Muhammad and his sons were directed in Arabic prayer by their escort and were led to the Kaaba, the cube-shaped structure in the center of the mosque, believed to have been erected by Abraham and Ishmael. With thousands of others, Muhammad, barefoot, performed the sevenfold *tawah,* or the circumambulation of the Kaaba. Chants of *"Allah-u-Akbar"* ("Allah is the greatest") were repeated in reverence by the pilgrims, and each kissed the sacred Black Stone in the southeast corner of the building. To Muhammad, the Black Stone was more than an object of Islamic ritual. It symbolized his mission among the so-called American Negroes and his belief that ultimately "the people will bow to the real Black Man."[71]

After the circling of the Kaaba, the pilgrims drank water from the well of Zamzam. Muhammad, curious about the water, imbibed "cupful after cupful." To his amazement, he found the lukewarm water to be "very light and easy to digest in the body." The last major part of the ritual involved running between the holy hills of Marwah and Al Safa, which represented Hagar's search for water to quench the thirst of her son, Ishmael. Muhammad's elderly guide, as he had throughout most of the ritual, held the hand of the leader as they completed the approximately one-thousand-foot run. At this point, the pilgrimage and its requirements were satisfied, and Muhammad's new status was official. He was now El-hajj Elijah Muhammad, recognized as a true Muslim by the custodians of Islam's holiest city. When he left the mosque and its environs, he immediately cabled his followers in America to inform them of his successful pilgrimage. In his mind, the question of the legitimacy of his movement and teachings was finally moot.[72]

After a brief stop in Medina, the first city to accept Islam, Muhammad and his sons departed from Saudi Arabia and arrived in Karachi, Pakistan, on January 1, 1960, just as a new decade began. As in Egypt and Sudan, the country's constitution had already been shelved by martial rule, declared by Ayub Khan in October 1958. The coup was more reformist than revolutionary, and its planners had acted to preclude a scheduled election in February 1959, which they feared would have led to the dissolution of the new state. Typical of military interventions of the period, civil liberties, such as the right to assemble and freedom of the press, were curbed, and political parties were banned altogether. To garner popular support, the usurpers established a land commission soon after seizing power and introduced reforms that reduced the influence of landlords. The redistribution of land was slow, except in West Pakistan, where as much as one-third of the property of wealthy landowners was expropriated. In major urban areas such as Karachi, gradual land reform did little for refugees seeking housing and jobs after the partition from India of 1947. Only after the relocation of the capital to Islamabad in 1959 did overcrowding ease to a limited extent in some of the larger cities.[73]

While in Pakistan, Muhammad spent much of his time in Lahore, the chief city of the Punjab region. Close to the Indian border, the city did not possess the architectural wonders of Istanbul or Cairo, nor the religious significance of Mecca or Jerusalem. Still, it did contain enough of interest to engage Muhammad for two or three days. Lahore was primarily a railroad and economic center. In 1960, the Pakistan University of Engineering and Technology was being completed, which would make the city a focal point for the country's educated elite. The Badshahi Mosque, one of the largest in Pakistan, was located here, as were the famed Shalimar Gardens (Sanskrit for "Gardens of Bliss"), which covered over eighty acres of land east of the city. The Gardens had been created by the Emperor Shah Jahan in 1641 as a testament to the imperial greatness of the Mogul dynasty. Adorned with trees, canals, pavilions, and fountains, the site was one of the main tourist attractions of the area. The beauty of the Gardens did not mask the recent history of political violence that was an integral part of Lahore's evolution, but did symbolize the continuing importance of the city. Illustratively, Lahore was also the headquarters of the Muslim League, the party responsible for securing the independence of Pakistan from India.

Muhammad's visit to the Punjab perhaps had something to do with its being the birthplace of the Ahmadiyya movement, the unorthodox Islamic sect whose leader, Mirza Ghulam Ahmad, presented himself as the Mahdi during the late nineteenth century. While very different from most of the teachings of the Nation of Islam, the doctrines of the Ahmadiyyas were ideological precursors of the Muslim movement of Fard Muhammad and probably did have an impact on the early development of the organization (see Chapter 2). Either in Lahore or Karachi, Elijah Muhammad and his sons attended at least one prayer service in a mosque that accommodated thousands of worshipers. As he had reportedly done in other Muslim countries, the leader debated issues such as the nature of God and "the natural humanity of European-Americans" with Islamic scholars. Leaving the country on January 5, Muhammad concluded a remarkable tour of the Islamic East, which internationalized his image as a significant Muslim leader of the Western world.[74]

On a more profound level, the travels of Muhammad through Asia and Africa affected the program and ideological premises on which the Muslim movement was based. One of the minor changes resulting from the trip was the decision to rename the temples of the Nation *mosques* in line with the designation used throughout the Middle East for places of worship. A more significant consequence of the excursion was that it forced Muhammad to reevaluate his views of Eastern Muslims and their world. Prior to making his pilgrimage, he had believed and taught that Mecca and Saudi Arabia in general were part of a primordial paradise constructed trillions of years ago and righteously ruled by the Original People. In essence, he had hoped to find a place much better than the North American wilderness. When he arrived in Turkey and journeyed south to Addis Ababa and then farther east to Mecca and Lahore, he, indeed, did witness some of the most renowned architectural wonders and extravagant displays of wealth. Yet, he also saw, on a more frequent basis, the grossest forms of poverty and deprivation that the modern world had to offer. Whether in Cairo, Medina, or Khartoum, conditions much worse than he had experienced in Sandersville or Detroit prevailed, often in the midst of fiscal mismanagement and political corruption. Even the hajj to Mecca was not free of sanitary problems, which the affluent Muhammad was surely not accustomed to, and tales of the existence of slavery haunted him for years. The whole experience convinced him that African-Americans would have to make their own way in the world. The East, with its economic malaise and social problems, proved not to be as heavenly as he had once preached.[75]

Muhammad's disappointment with the Middle East caused him to deemphasize the importance of making overtures to Arab and African Muslims and to stress traditional elements of the Nation's doctrines. To a large degree, he lost respect for those he had esteemed as the Tribe of Shabazz in East Asia. While Muhammad had enjoyed discussing religious matters with Islamic intellectuals and appreciated the kindness extended to him during his tour, he, with his attraction to material comforts, was critical of the poverty of Eastern countries, sometimes to the point of ridicule. The penury and suffering he saw encouraged him to stress even more the economic message of the Nation. This change in direction may have led to a gradual breakdown in organizational controls against avarice and corruption in the upper echelons of the movement and to later crises caused by overindulgence in the earthly. After his trip, Muhammad became far more attached to the teachings of Fard Muhammad and would not look seriously to the East again until the 1970s, when the Nation sought Arab financial assistance. Interestingly, the Afro-Asian tour had afforded him credibility and validation, but also instilled in him a measure of disillusionment that reinforced the very beliefs and practices for which orthodox Muslims had scorned him.[76]

The decade of the 1950s saw change and maturation in Elijah Muhammad and the Nation of Islam. Membership, as low as a few hundred during the beginning of the decade, boomed into the thousands by late 1959. Moreover, the socioeconomic mix of the rank and file was diversified by an influx of disaffected, and opportunistic, professionals and educated converts, and the leader's family became a prominent part of the administrative hierarchy. Ideologically, flirtations with orthodox Islam, which culminated in the hajj of Elijah Muhammad, gave the Nation an aura of doctrinal legitimacy but ultimately confirmed that the popularity of the movement did not derive primarily from religious conformity. Black separatism, economic entrepreneurship, and the charisma of young ministers were behind the successes of the Muslims as much as the opposition of the South to integration and the emergence of a decolonized Africa. Discovering the Nation, the mainstream media tagged it with the "black supremacy" label and in a real sense invented a "Muslim threat," which would even evoke the corrosive criticism of African-American civil rights leaders in addition to the increasing hostility of the U.S. government. Regardless of negative publicity and state surveillance, Elijah Muhammad, at the start of the 1960s, had found his niche as the head of a religious and economic empire envied and feared by blacks and whites alike. He had come a long way since his hungry, deprived childhood in rural Georgia and intended to go even further in the future as the Messenger of Allah.

PART THREE

THE KEYS TO THE KINGDOM

CHAPTER 7

TRIALS AND TRIBULATIONS

The measure of man is what he does with power.
—Pittacus[1]

The 1960s was perhaps the most pivotal decade in the twentieth century in the struggle for black rights in the United States and elsewhere. The sit-in movement, begun by four college students in Greensboro, North Carolina, on February 1, 1960, made nonviolence more confrontational, providing mainstream civil rights activism with a more youthful face. With the founding of the Student Nonviolent Coordinating Committee (SNCC) that spring, young militants, frustrated with the slow pace of social change, finally came into their own, albeit to the discomfort of some older, more conservative elements in the Civil Rights Movement. During the following year, the Congress of Racial Equality (CORE), headed by James Farmer, organized Freedom Rides, which challenged not only racial segregation in the South but also Pres. John F. Kennedy's commitment to the enforcement of civil rights laws. Across the Atlantic, colonialism in Africa and Asia, in Nasser's words, was "retreat[ing] like a prostitute," having been confronted by opponents vowing "to sacrifice their lives and face force with force." If the early 1960s were a period of change and readjustment in American race relations and international affairs, the backdrop against which these and other events were taking place remained remarkably similar to that of past decades.[2]

In the United States, significant civil rights legislation, though promised by the Democratic Party during the 1960 election campaign, was not forthcoming. Even as late as 1962, racists in small towns such as Albany, Georgia, could rest assured that they could violate established civil rights statutes and pack their jails with demonstrators—including Dr. King—without the intervention of the federal government. In parallel anticolonial struggles in Africa, imperial interests proved more resilient than many may have imagined, as exemplified by the murder of Patrice Lumumba and the emergence of the white-ruled Republic of South Africa in 1961. Every major area of conflict in the world, from Cuba and Vietnam to Soweto and Birmingham, seemed to reiterate what Du Bois had said about the color line sixty years earlier. To Elijah Muhammad and his Muslims, all of these struggles against white privilege confirmed what they believed to be the sole source of the dilemma: the dominance and very existence of the white man.[3]

Following his return from the Islamic East on January 6, Muhammad settled back into the familiar routine of speaking tours, interviews, and organizational administration. Much of his attention was devoted to publicizing and defending the Nation of Islam and its program across the country. For the next several weeks, his sojourn through the Muslim world was a frequent topic of discussion, as was the legitimacy that the trip had supposedly conferred on his group. For example, during a Los Angeles press conference in February attended by reporters representing *Time, Life, Newsweek*, and a host of other publications, Muhammad described his followers as genuine members of the Islamic faith, recognized by orthodox Muslims in the East. In similar forums during early 1960, Muhammad tried to get as much mileage out of the Middle Eastern tour as possible. At least for a while, his more vocal Islamic opponents were not as quick to challenge his "Muslim-ness" in newspaper articles or from rostrums. Perhaps, they, like others, were waiting to see if Muhammad had actually altered his stance regarding race and other issues that alienated the Nation of Islam from orthodox rivals.[4]

No one had to wait long to find out where Muhammad stood philosophically. During a speaking tour of major cities, such as Boston, Philadelphia, New York, and Cleveland, he delivered his standard message of black separatism, economic uplift, and white devilry. By midsummer, it was clear that little had changed in the ideology of the Nation. If anything, a willingness to abandon even lip service to orthodox Islam was becoming more apparent. With the Civil Rights Movement becoming more militant, thanks in large part to the rising impatience and expectations of younger activists, the Nation appeared more concerned about keeping pace with mainstream developments and refining its own reputation for militancy than satisfying orthodox standards of proper Muslim conduct and belief. Muhammad, like his counterparts in the integration struggle, was quite aware of the importance of maintaining the interest of the growing number of African-American youth in his constituency. To him, a continuing adherence to black nationalism and a race-oriented religious ethos was the best way to accomplish this.[5]

Throughout the early 1960s, the idea of a separate black state was Muhammad's biggest drawing card. In fact, the national notoriety of the Nation of Islam was largely due to its avowed willingness to territorially withdraw from the United States if it persisted in denying blacks "freedom, justice, and equality." The notion of a black nation administered by a black government, protected by black armies, and maintained by black businesses had been around since the antebellum period and, depending on socioeconomic and racial conditions, enjoyed varying support in some quarters of the African-American community. The ideas and programs of earlier black separatists such as Martin R. Delany, Bishop Henry McNeal Turner, and Marcus Garvey were precursors of the Nation of Islam. In ways similar to his ideological predecessors, Elijah Muhammad held up to blacks the ideal of nationality as the ultimate expression of power and security in a world where the nation-state defined the distinctiveness of a people. In his view, to seek statehood was to seek protection from racist brutality (and extermination), a voice in world affairs, and financial independence. Though he wavered between demanding a return of blacks to Africa and favoring the cession to blacks of "seven or eight states . . . in the deep South where it is nice and warm for farming," Muhammad's rhetoric focused on a great separation of the races sometime in the future.[6]

In practical terms, emigration to Africa and the carving of a black state out of "the wilderness of North America" were problematic. More so than in earlier times, such programs faced obstacles that were virtually insurmountable. A return to Africa raised immediate questions of transportation (and its costs), cultural dissonance between the returnees and their African hosts, and the political and demographic impact of African-American immigrants on societies already under varying degrees of social and ethnic stress. Added to these dilemmas was the likelihood that most of the prospective emigrants would be from the lower end of the American class structure—the poor, the uneducated, the hopeless, or in general, individuals who had nothing to lose from relocating to Africa but possessed few of the skills or resources so desperately needed by newly independent African countries. Ironically, those educated, middle-class, entrepreneurial black Americans who would have been most welcomed as immigrants would have been least enamored with the prospect of giving up a tolerable existence in the United States for possible hardship and uncertainty in underdeveloped Africa. The whole proposition was a catch-22 that doomed even the most skillfully packaged emigrationist plans to failure.

As to a black state in the American South, the federal government, not to mention state governments, was not likely to invest billions of dollars in the movement of populations to give blacks national independence on North American soil. Moreover, blacks were too few in number and lacked the organization to wage more than a fleeting armed struggle for "national liberation" against white Southerners who were all too willing to use violence to control and subjugate African-Americans in even the backwater regions of the South. Of course, Elijah Muhammad was aware of these impediments to a black state in Africa or the United States and actually made few efforts outside of verbal and editorial demands to make either a reality. As early as 1959, he even admitted to an audience that "they [white Americans] will never give us three or four states. That I probably know." Still, the idea of a black American homeland took on religious overtones for the Muslims, who believed that Allah would one day will it into being. Until then, Muhammad counseled patience and faith and used the allure of a black state as an instrument for recruiting disaffected blacks into the Nation.[7]

During this period of increasing militancy on the part of civil rights activists, Muhammad's nationalism and ideological disposition in general were conservative or even reactionary. On the surface, the Muslims were at the cutting edge of black radicalism—defiant, candid, and fiercely proud. The reputations of Muhammad, Malcolm X, and the movement itself were very much tethered to their ability to recruit African-Americans using the "knowledge of self and others." However, just under the doctrinal skin of the Nation of Islam were philosophical seeds that were suggestive of the most disturbing trends in Western thought. Indeed, what sometimes passed as religion among the faithful was no more than recycled racial dogma objectionable to most African-Americans in its original form. The similarities between Muhammad's ideas and those of white racists, in some instances, could be quite chilling.

Illustrative of this trend in Muhammad's thought are his views on race mixing, a favorite topic of his at this time. Muhammad spoke of interracial sexual relations as morally depraved, especially if black women submitted to the overtures of white men. He also viewed miscegenation as destructive in a genetic or biological sense. In a 1962 speech, he described white opponents of race mixing as "wise." Additionally, Muhammad noted that the white segregationist "don't intend to destroy his people—not with your [black] blood. . . . I don't blame them for wanting to keep you out of their family. I don't blame them for [not] wanting the integration law to be passed. Because they know what will be the result." During a 1965 interview, Muhammad described what he believed the result would be. Miscegenation, he concluded, "only ruins the races to mongrelize themselves, it just ruins and destroys a people, and it's also indecency to even think about these things like that." Though in these instances Muhammad was probably trying to advance his own separatist program by inverting the language of the Ku Klux Klan and other racist groups to support his notions of black superiority, his mocking imitations here unfortunately had the effect of legitimizing beliefs in racial determinism and the alleged "evils" of integration and miscegenation that the Klan and others posited.[8]

Interestingly, the relationship between the Nation of Islam and its closest ideological counterparts in the white community went beyond common ideology and rhetoric. During a secret meeting in Atlanta on the night of January 28, 1961, Malcolm X and Jeremiah X, the local Muslim minister, met with members of the KKK to discuss their mutual hostility toward integration. According to the accounts of Malcolm X and an FBI informant present at the conference, the two sides exchanged views on race, and the New York minister went so far as to attribute the whole struggle for integration to a Jewish conspiracy carried out by unsuspecting blacks. He also intimated that the Klan should kill those whites who advocated integration. Besides swapping platitudes with segregationists, the ultimate reason for the attendance of Muhammad's representatives at the gathering appears to have been to protect Southern mosques from the threat of destruction at the hands of a revitalized Klan. Toward this purpose, they negotiated a non-aggression pact with the Klansmen specifying that Muslim affairs in the South would not be censured by the KKK as long as the Nation did not aid civil rights activists there.[9]

The KKK's motive for meeting with the Muslims was apparently to maintain segregation by bolstering the Nation of Islam as a viable vehicle of nationhood for African-Americans. Klan negotiators, according to one source, may have offered the Muslims as much as twenty thousand acres of Georgian land for use as a settlement for black separatists. In general, the nocturnal dealings of the Nation of Islam and the Invisible Empire were mutually advantageous, and to some extent both sides seem to have kept their promises. Following the conference, Malcolm X, who would later regret his collusion with Klansmen, dutifully reported to Chicago the land offer made by the KKK. As for Jeremiah X, the Atlanta minister was now in good standing with the powerful Klan of the Peace State. He would later be warmly received at KKK meetings as the Southern representative of the Nation of Islam.[10]

While the Klan and the Nation made strange bedfellows, Muhammad's flirtations with American Nazi Party leader George Lincoln Rockwell were an even darker episode in fringe politics. Like the Klan, Rockwell made no secret of his hatred of integration, black rights, and African-Americans in general. He and his small following looked to Hitler for their ideology, which was rabidly segregationist and anti-Jewish. Yet, the Nazi leader believed that "Muhammad has the answer for my people" and concurred with him on the inadvisability of integration and racial conciliation. Some evidence suggests that Muhammad and "Commander" Rockwell exchanged correspondence and apparently even met and "worked out an agreement of mutual assistance." Though specific joint ventures were perhaps not arranged, Muhammad did acquiesce to Rockwell's desire to make an appearance at a Muslim meeting.[11]

During a gathering of eight thousand people at Uline Arena on June 25, 1961, Rockwell and twenty of his "storm troopers," in full Nazi regalia, sat among Muslims to hear Malcolm X deliver a talk entitled "Separation or Death." Muhammad himself did not show up for this Washington, D.C., meeting; he was reportedly fighting off a cold in Chicago. However, he would get a chance to address Rockwell and the Nazis at the 1962 Saviour's Day convention held at the Chicago International Amphitheater on February 25. His speech touched on all of the familiar Muslim themes, including a separate territory for blacks, economic self-help, and respect for black womanhood. The talk also included a prediction that Allah would kill the whites in accordance with Nation of Islam prophecy. At least in regard to racial separation, Rockwell liked what Muhammad had to say and placed about twenty dollars in the collection plate. Given an opportunity to speak, he stood and conceded Muhammad's point, announcing to the twelve thousand gathered "that no American white desires to intermix with black people."[12]

Despite appearances, Muhammad, of course, had no love for the KKK or the Nazis. Individuals of their ilk were responsible for many of the lynchings and other atrocities against blacks that had disturbed him since he was a youth in rural Georgia. As recently as 1957, he had received a letter from Jesse B. Stoner, the head of the Christian Anti-Jewish Party. The correspondence was heavily laden with white supremacist rhetoric, describing Islam as "a nigger religion" and blacks as racially inferior. The letter ended on an ominous note, which should not have been taken too lightly since Stoner would later be convicted of bombing the black Bethel Baptist Church of Montgomery, Alabama, in 1958. "We will not tolerate your infidelic Christ-hating religion on American soil," the former Klansman warned. "We will drive Islam into the ocean. America isn't big enough for the Christian Party and Black Islam, so Islam must go." Given that Muhammad had no illusions regarding the intentions of the Nazis, the Klan, the Christian Party, or any other white racist group, his willingness to deal with such organizations hints at deeper themes within his philosophy and perception of these groups.[13]

The interactions between the Muslims and white supremacists can only be explained in relation to the political context of the early 1960s and the organizational interests of the Nation of Islam. These contacts were probably not intended to result in any kind of working partnerships with segregationists, but instead, to preclude confrontations between Muslims and white racists and to increase membership. Muhammad recognized the growing strength of the Klan in the South and, like Marcus Garvey, chose to negotiate a truce before a war could break out between mosques and klaverns. In the event of hostilities, the outnumbered Muslims could not fight off a Klan onslaught, not to mention their silent supporters in Southern police departments and the general population. The options were between extinction and adjustment, and Muhammad chose the latter.[14]

In regard to Rockwell, the decision to sanction his appearance at Muslim meetings was actually a recruitment ploy. The Nazi leader was supposed to represent a brutally honest white man who spoke "for all white[s]." He was a sort of bugbear that Muhammad used to scare blacks into the Nation of Islam. While these tactics perhaps gained the group some immediate benefits, cooperation between Muslims and white racists, albeit perhaps pragmatic at the time, certainly carried a price, as it had for Garvey's UNIA. Arguably, black nationalism as a philosophy and a program is potentially progressive when aimed at eliminating or minimizing the influence of those institutions, forces, and groups that have traditionally oppressed African-Americans. However, when black separatists seek accommodation and rapprochement with racists and reactionary elements of a society, they compromise the moral force behind their struggle for liberation regardless of how noble their intentions may be. To a certain extent, Muhammad had done exactly that by entertaining the Georgia Klan and countenancing Rockwell. Even worse, he had allowed the Nation to stray dangerously close to the ideological pathway of white supremacy.[15]

Actually, the dealings of the Muslims with segregationists highlighted the conservative core of the movement. Far from being radical or revolutionary, the Nation was more evolutionary than anything else, adapting to circumstances and opportunities that could expand its domain without provoking, if possible, those forces that could hamper its continued existence. A number of the doctrines of the movement belied the militant rhetoric and image that Muslim spokesmen offered for public consumption. First, the Nation was autocratic in authority and structure, with power concentrated in a few hands. Over time, the Muhammad family increasingly dominated decision-making at various levels, especially regarding finances, and few democratic pretenses counterbalanced this influence. Second, the Nation pursued a purely capitalistic model of economic organization that mostly enriched the Chicago elite. As mentioned earlier, many of the enterprises purchased with donations and profits were later placed in Muhammad's name or those of family members and close associates. Third, the theology of the Muslims actually rationalized the state of race relations in America by portraying the status quo as predestined since whites were believed to be "devils" by nature and Allah had given them six thousand years to rule, plus a grace period. Unlike nationalists in Africa and Asia who advocated armed struggle and political opposition to white domination, Muhammad advised blacks to unite and wait for divine intervention to settle the score between the races. In essence, the theology of the Nation placed the burden of altering race relations on Allah and discounted human attempts to change the distribution of power in America, though self-help was encouraged for the sake of survival. Altogether, these and other conservative tendencies minimized the potential activism of the Muslim movement.[16]

The parallels between the beliefs of the Muslims and white reactionaries should not be overstated. The Nation of Islam, though racially chauvinistic and hostile toward Jews, was not fascist according to traditional definitions of the term. Yet, striking consistencies cannot be denied. For example, Elijah Muhammad was the object of a cult of personality arguably as strong as those that embraced Hitler, Mussolini, and others. The position of Messenger of Allah was not only an office in the movement but a very real expression of how the Nation was tied to the person of Muhammad and the romanticized image of his leadership created and refined by him and others over the past three decades. From the messenger flowed the sole source of authority in the organization. Unlike other officials, he was irreplaceable, having been allegedly appointed by Allah himself and allowed to exercise power in God's name.

In addition to a fixation on an individual leader, the Nation also had a quasi-military component, the Fruit of Islam, which was responsible for enforcing the moral code of the movement and the dictates of Muhammad. By the early 1960s, the policing apparatus of the movement had gained quite a reputation for discipline and ensuring conformity among the rank and file of the Nation. In some mosques it had also acquired, like the Blackshirts and Brownshirts, a penchant for harshness, even brutality. Muslims in Anniston, Alabama, told horror stories about beatings of errant members, inflicted by the Fruit, that included razors and rubber hoses. According to Aubrey Barnette, a former member who was severely injured for leaving the organization, the Boston mosque sponsored a "terror squad" that corporally punished Muslims who failed to adequately support the economic program of the Nation. Malcolm X himself, whose vilification and murder following his departure from the Nation would implicate some members of the Fruit of Islam, even confessed to having witnessed a beating administered by Muslims that he "wasn't too far from" and could probably have stopped. While the purposeful use of force to ensure obedience was apparently not widespread in the Nation, enough Muslims had perhaps either observed or heard of individuals being subjected to physical cruelty to suggest such violent incidents were more than just isolated occurrences.[17]

Finally, the Nation was proudly anti-Communist, but not for the same reasons as the typical fascist movement. Muhammad believed that Communism was an abomination because it did not recognize God or a divine presence in human history or contemporary affairs. Even among third-world revolutionaries, Muhammad opposed any Marxist leanings and was outraged by a chance meeting of Fidel Castro and Malcolm during a visit of the Cuban leader to the United Nations in September 1960. Despite its atheistic component, Communism, according to Muhammad, was a part of the divine plan. "It was raised to destroy the whites," he concluded. Nonetheless, he still shunned any alliance with Communists of any race for fear of the public and state hostility that it would incite against the Muslim movement. Indeed, he went so far as to offer the United States help in fighting Red armies if his territorial demands were ever satisfied.[18]

While anti-Communism and a few other elements of fascist ideology seem to resemble the philosophy and program of the Muslims, fascism was not a defining characteristic of the movement and would be a misleading label to attach to it. Unlike fascists, Muhammad and his Muslims did not glorify the exercise of force and violence for its own sake. Nor did they rely upon politics and military power to accomplish their goals, but rather, religion and economics. They never advocated or resorted to the use of force to seize state power or to exterminate "inferior" populations. The conservatism of the Muslims was a depoliticized phenomenon that was expressed through capitalist endeavors, the mythology of racial superiority, and monarchical/militaristic organizational structures. The Nation, the white supremacists, and the Nazis were not simply different sides of the same coin, though they shared some distinct qualities.

Economic imperatives largely overrode any particular political philosophy during this period, and the Muslims undertook new areas of growth and administrative development. With the advent of a few modest businesses and a drastic increase in membership and donations during the 1950s, Muhammad and his followers were able to showcase to the black community in Chicago and elsewhere the potential of African-Americans who pooled their resources. Ironically, the same economic nationalism and fiscal advancements that made the self-help program of the Muslims appear progressive, even radical, also thinly veiled tendencies toward materialism and a self-centered management style on the part of Muhammad and the national leadership. Prosperity, while good for the image and recruitment efforts of the Nation, gnawed at the ethical fiber of men (and women) in the Chicago elite. By the early 1960s, a consuming preoccupation with making money and conspicuous display was quite evident among the high command, though not all highly placed individuals used membership donations and business profits for their own benefit and ends.

The cancer was a slow one and had been present, but to a much lesser degree, since the days when Fard Muhammad sold names and peddled his wares among Original People in depressed Detroit. In the 1950s, Muhammad's Cadillacs and Lincolns were modest personal investments compared with those of the following decades. The explosion in Muslim membership during the late 1950s and early 1960s greatly enhanced the financial wherewithal of the movement and enriched the leadership to the extent that it jealously guarded the new prosperity. Some policies of the group now reflected Chicago interests more than anything else, and concerns regarding recruitment, donations, and profits virtually became doctrine. Notwithstanding the occasional disillusionment and defection of recruits appalled by this, avarice was not fatal to the movement. Many rank-and-file Muslims believed that Muhammad and his family should live well, even at their expense. Other believers bore the financial burden of membership in the Nation apparently convinced that its benefits outweighed the misfortune of returning to the grave, regardless of how much of their money flowed to

Mosque No. 2. If it did nothing else, the rhetoric of black self-sufficiency and economic nationalism soothed those who still believed that the Muslim movement was on the verge of going toe-to-toe with the white world over territory, reparations, and everything else they felt was owed to African-Americans. In fact, even in the view of many non-Muslim blacks, the Nation was saying exactly what the race needed to hear regarding community economic empowerment.

The official economic philosophy and goals of the Muslims were certainly grandiose and inspiring. The group's fiscal program for the black community was one of the few topics that Muhammad wrote and spoke about concisely, without the nebulous coating of religious doctrine. His ideas regarding economic advancement were delineated in his "Economic Blueprint" and "Program for Self-Development," which urged blacks to "pool your resources, physically and financially"; "stop wanton criticism of everything that is black-owned and black-operated"; "build your own homes, schools, hospitals, and factories"; and "spend your money among yourselves." Above all, he advised African-Americans not to be adverse to taking lessons from other minorities and even the white man himself. "Observe the operations of the white man," he counseled. "He is successful. He makes no excuses for his failures. He works hard in a collective manner. You do the same."[19]

To implement these ideas, Muhammad announced a "Three-Year Economic Program for the Black Nation in America" during the early 1960s, which requested that blacks send twenty-five cents a week (or a dollar a month) to the Muslims' headquarters in Chicago. During the three-year period, African-Americans were to live frugally. No one was to purchase more than three outfits a year in excess of sixty-five dollars each, eat "extravagant" foods, or waste money on luxuries such as "fine automobiles . . . whiskey, beer, wine, cigarettes, tobacco, and drugs." Once the program produced a million dollars in savings, the Nation would begin laying the groundwork for a banking system to service the financial needs of African-Americans. This kind of black economic nationalism had been around since at least the midnineteenth century and was embraced by both the industrial-education and self-help doctrines of Booker T. Washington and the financial ventures of Marcus Garvey. Yet, in a climate in which blacks were becoming economically worse off relative to whites despite their rising expectations, the Nation appeared to be constructively addressing the plight of blacks without "begging and praying to the white man." For many members and admirers of the Muslim movement, Muhammad's slogan of "Do something for self" was as much a rallying cry as "We shall overcome" was for civil rights activists.[20]

During the early 1960s, the Muslims' business and real estate empire continued to expand, due almost entirely to the faith (and generosity) that believers exhibited toward the economic vision of Muhammad. One of the most noteworthy investments made at this time was a new mosque in Washington, D.C., which was dedicated by Muhammad in December 1960 and reportedly cost $150,000. As had become customary in cities with large Muslim followings, the local minister, Lucius X, a former Seventh-Day Adventist elder, was given the use of a house on Staple Street valued at $6,200 and in Elijah Muhammad's name. Generally, when good fortune shone on the Nation, it also shone on its leader. In July 1961, Muhammad purchased two more houses, an office, and accompanying real estate in Phoenix, Arizona, which were valued at $100,000 by 1965. Though Muhammad primarily used the house at 2118 East Violet Drive as his winter retreat when the Chicago cold exacerbated his bronchial asthma, he purchased other Phoenix properties in his name in mid-1963, including a $18,500 home that he gave, in usage and in title, to his chauffeur and "houseman," Antonne Williams, and his wife, Ruby.[21]

The pet project of Muhammad during this time was a proposed $20-million Islamic Center, which was to consist of a school, mosque, hospital, and library—a miniature Mecca in the midst of the Windy City. Donations and profits never did, however, amount to enough to make this dream a reality, and Muhammad had to settle for smaller successes. One achievement was groundbreaking for an "ultramodern" restaurant in Chicago during January 1963. This particular property was purchased for $15,950 by a newly formed corporation run by Muhammad's son-in-law Raymond Sharrieff, twenty-year associate and minister of the Chicago mosque James 3X, and John Hassan. Another accomplishment of even greater value was the founding of the Muslims' official organ, *Muhammad Speaks*, which first came off the press in September 1960.[22]

The founding of *Muhammad Speaks* was a turning point for the Nation in a number of ways. First and foremost, it gave the Muslims an independent platform from which to proclaim their beliefs and program to the world. No longer did Muhammad have to rely solely upon the black press or the white media for publicity and a chance to be heard. Secondly, *Muhammad Speaks*, besides its propaganda value, was an invaluable newspaper that proved that the Muslims did have journalistic talent among them and could produce informative stories ranging from insightful discussions of nationalist struggles in Africa to cogent critiques of the American economy and political system. More than any other Muslim institution, the newspaper was the Nation's bridge to the non-Islamic black community and was as good a recruitment device as any.

Of utmost importance, the newspaper brought in large amounts of revenue, due primarily to the manner in which it was marketed. Typically, each Muslim male was required to purchase a set number of each new issue at fifteen cents per copy (newsstand value). Those members who could not sell all of the newspapers that they had purchased had to take a loss and hope for better results next time. This arrangement may not have been extremely taxing during the early years of the paper; however, after *Muhammad Speaks* became a biweekly publication in July 1962 and followers were called upon to buy as much as forty-four dollars' worth of each edition to sell, the financial pressure on Muslim hawkers escalated greatly. Eventually, the Nation's mouthpiece became the best-selling black newspaper in the country, its publisher claiming a circulation of six hundred thousand. Yet, this figure was deceiving and did not account for the untold number of papers that ended up in the closets or car trunks of hapless Muslim vendors who were counseled, in any event, to "think, eat, and breathe, sleep and live *MUHAMMAD SPEAKS!!!*"[23]

Muslim businesses such as the newspaper were largely successful because they had a captive market. Muslim males *had* to buy copies of *Muhammad Speaks* for distribution to the larger black community. Similarly, Muslim women *had* to buy the traditional angle-length robe and headpiece that were standard attire for female members. According to one source, women in the Nation were required to buy a minimum of three outfits in different colors (white, beige, and red), which in total could cost as much as two hundred dollars. One of Muhammad's daughters, despite the appearance of impropriety, controlled the shop that produced the garments. These monopolistic practices were justified by Muhammad as consistent with both the need to patronize black businesses and to keep "black money" in the African-American community. Taken to its logical conclusion, this policy resulted in members even being prohibited from buying copies of the Qur'an other than from a Muslim in the Newark mosque who imported them from Pakistan.[24]

The centralized economy of the Nation, though beneficial to the Muhammad family and a few others in the movement, was generally not strong enough to produce profits regularly. Problems included the selection of managers based on kinship and not merit, being too small to achieve economies of scale, poor bookkeeping, and diversion of profits that should have been reinvested in capital improvements. These drawbacks did not doom all Muslim businesses to failure; indeed, *Muhammad Speaks* prospered as did several other enterprises. However, because of these impediments a number of stores owned and controlled by Muhammad and others in the Nation operated at a deficit, in spite of the "buy black" policy. If his own Chicago concerns lost money, Muhammad reportedly poured emergency funds into their coffers from his personal finances.[25]

In addition to the profits from the more robust enterprises of the Nation, the Muhammad family during the 1960s and 1970s was heavily dependent upon the contributions of the Muslim membership. Officially, the family was supported by the "No. 2 Poor Treasury," which consisted of donations from different mosques "designed to see to it that our leader and teacher and his family want for nothing," as the new-member "Orientation Brochure" put it. Along with this fund, gifts from followers supplemented the leader's income. He usually received the most presents from the membership during Saviour's Day conventions in February. At the 1961 annual commemoration of Fard Muhammad's birthday, the roughly seven thousand Muslims in attendance were requested to donate $125 each to cover the living expenses of Muhammad and his kin. These donations were also supposed to compensate the national treasury for the twenty-five thousand dollars that was allegedly disbursed for traveling expenses during 1960 and the cost of renting the amphitheater for the gathering, set at eight thousand dollars. That each of the followers in attendance gave the requested $125 is doubtful, especially considering their generally low incomes and the various donations that they were required to give to both their local mosques and the national headquarters during the year. Nonetheless, Saviour's Days never failed to inject thousands of dollars into the Nation's treasury and the private exchequer of the Muhammad family.[26]

While it raked in basketfuls of money at mass meetings, the Chicago leadership kept its finances secret. No official records were kept for accountability, and few believers would have dared to ask their superiors for written proof of anything. To be sure, an occasional Muslim would question the funding of projects seemingly unrelated to the stated economic mission of the Nation, such as the purchase of expensive homes for Muhammad's family members. However, these individuals were labeled "seed planters," whose inquisitiveness was divisive and inimical to the interests of the organization. In one instance, even Malcolm X was rebuked by John Ali, the national secretary of the Nation, when he asked about what had become of several thousand dollars raised by the New York mosque for the proposed Islamic Center in Chicago. All Muslims were encouraged to give what they could and to let the leadership handle financial affairs. As the "Orientation Brochure" once again advised, "For a man who has given his very soul and health to see to it that his people hear the truth, we can not give too much."[27]

Though the Muslim membership and the general public were led to believe that the Nation was funded entirely by blacks, a rumor alleging another source of support surfaced during the early 1960s and persisted for years. Haroldson L. Hunt, a Texas billionaire oilman and sponsor of the ultraconservative radio talk show *Life Line*, reportedly subsidized a range of right-wing and extremist causes, including the John Birch Society and the Minutemen. From his Mount Vernon–style home in Dallas, Hunt supposedly funneled an unknown sum into the Nation of Islam to boost its separatist program. That such funding had the potential to discredit the Muslims by tying them to conservative, even white supremacist, forces was quite clear to those privy to the report.[28]

As a policy, Muhammad and his representatives rarely discussed private contributions publicly. In this instance, the leader neither conceded nor denied the validity of the rumor. Of course, even if the Nation had received funding from Hunt and other white admirers, these contributions would not necessarily have made Muhammad beholden to the interests of these donors. Arguably, the contributors were simply endorsing beliefs and practices that the leader had embraced decades before. However, to people who subscribed to the black-original-man-versus-the-white-devil rhetoric of the Muslims, the rumors about Hunt's patronage, along with the Rockwell and KKK episodes, must have been perplexing, if not disheartening. Critics of the movement who labeled it racist and extreme could certainly have scandalized it by association. Muhammad—if the rumor was accurate—was probably being pragmatic in accepting money from Hunt, perhaps believing that no discernible strings were attached and the general public would never know. But the rumor did circulate beyond Muhammad's inner circle and did not make for flattering publicity.

Secret dealings with white supremacists, while troubling for some, did not draw the attention of Muslims and others as much as the tales of corruption and materialism in the Chicago leadership. Those most closely affiliated with Muhammad, such as his sons and top advisers, knew firsthand of financial indulgences by officials. In some cases, Muhammad and some family members were the perpetrators. According to Wallace Muhammad, individuals in the Chicago leadership "presented my father as a holy image" while misusing "thousands of dollars." Akbar, the leader's youngest son, who left the movement in 1965, supposedly knew of officials in the Nation who had lost faith in the Messenger of Allah but remained loyal to him to stay on the payroll. Hints of opulence and frivolous spending were not hard to find in and around Mosque No. 2, whether one listened to gossip regarding the private Swiss bank accounts of Muhammad or caught a glimpse of his daughter, Ethel Sharrieff, adorned in furs and jewels. Contrary to what some followers believed, the avarice that tainted the national headquarters was not limited to everyone *except* Muhammad. Nor did his illnesses and temporary escapes to Phoenix keep him in the dark. Indeed, Muhammad was at the center of it all, and his own acquisitiveness may even have served as a model for others.[29]

Illustratively, during a conversation with his attorney about taxes in March 1963, the leader spoke frankly about his financial interests in the Muslim movement. Among other topics, the two discussed ways of shielding personal and organizational income from taxation by emphasizing "gifts" and the religious nature of the Nation of Islam. Muhammad wanted the

IRS to take as little as possible, if anything at all, from the income of the Nation and its individual leaders, a subject that made him "about sick almost" to contemplate. Ideally, he hoped to transfer the group's property that was not already in his name into his children's names "as fast as possible" so that they would not suffer upon his death. In practice, many of the businesses were already possessions of the family except in title. As he told his lawyer, "You see we run it and we are just using [the organization's name] as a trade name.... See nobody knows anything about it." In the long run, Muhammad wanted his heirs to swim even if the Nation drowned by transfering its economy into the hands of relatives.[30]

In some respects, the Nation of the early 1960s resembled a "money-grabbing scheme," which was how one disenchanted former member described it. Certainly, the preoccupation with financial matters and materialism among the Chicago leadership makes the monopoly capitalism and social conservatism of the Muslims more understandable. But to say that money and an ideology of political passivism were solely responsible for what the Nation became would be an incomplete assessment. Other forces at work in the larger society had a significant impact on Muhammad and his followers.[31]

Stretching back to its founding in the early 1930s, the Nation had been indelibly influenced by the power of the state and its ability to censure and repress. From the municipal to the federal level, government involvement in Muslim affairs was a constant reminder of the state's hostility toward the brand of Islam that Elijah Muhammad promulgated. During the early years, Muslims had been imprisoned, forced out of mosques, branded as traitors, and denied constitutional guarantees regarding freedom of religion. This official persecution nearly caused the collapse of the Nation during the Second World War. Lulls occurred in the state's war against the Nation, such as immediately after Muhammad's release from prison. However, respites became much rarer once the Muslims attracted national media attention in 1959 and experienced a resultant upsurge in membership.

The campaign of the U.S. government against the Nation in the 1960s encouraged political disengagement and anti-activism within the ideology and program of Elijah Muhammad. Whereas militant protest during the interwar years had led to courtroom scuffles, mass arrests, and sometimes long prison sentences, the capitalist pursuits and passive separatism of the postwar Nation allowed it to appear revolutionary and progressive to many onlookers but at the same time traditional and even conservative to others. Muhammad, being once again pragmatic, desired to have it both ways. He wanted to gain the allegiance of young African-Americans looking for a radical answer to America's race question, while avoiding the gaze of state agencies on the lookout for Communists, subversives, and other forces that were being singled out as the alleged orchestrators of the Civil Rights Movement. In the end, regardless of Muhammad's assurances that the Muslims were law-abiding and respected "the rulers of the land," various strata of government still took an interest in the movement. Subsequently, during the Kennedy administration, the state stepped up efforts to curtail the growth and prominence of Muhammad's following, sometimes using clearly illegal means.[32]

On the local level, the relationship between Muslims and government depended on both regional and national factors. In the case of the Chicago headquarters, official pressure on Mosque No. 2 could definitely be termed harassment, but was modest compared to the experiences of Muslims elsewhere. The political machine of Richard Daley and the Chicago police department appear to have reached an accommodation with Muhammad and his followers by the 1960s. Whether or not a mutually beneficial quid pro quo had secretly been arranged between the parties, the Chicago Muslims hardly ever experienced the periodic raids, police brutality, denials of permits to gather, and other affronts that were common features of Muslim life in other major cities. Of course, the names of Elijah Muhammad and a number of his followers were on the list of 117,000 "local individuals" that the security unit of the police department had compiled by 1960 for surveillance purposes. Yet, the national headquarters of the Nation coexisted with the power elite of the city for years without any major conflicts.[33]

To explain this, one can reasonably rule out any kind of natural benevolence toward Muhammad and his followers on the part of the Daley administration. The city's history of dissident activism—ranging from black nationalism and Communism to syndicalism and anarchism—and its ongoing ethnic and racial divisions made politicians sensitive to forces, real or imagined, that threatened to shatter the uneasy peace. But Muhammad and Daley apparently shared common ground that minimized the chances of confrontation between them. Perhaps the Muslims greased the machine with money from time to time. Possibly the mayor feared offending the black electorate of Chicago by openly persecuting Muhammad, who was definitely one of the more influential and affluent African-Americans in the city. Whatever the case, the result was a political symbiosis that lasted until Muhammad's death in 1975.[34]

Notwithstanding the mayor's office, some individuals and groups in Chicago and Illinois did openly challenge both the growth and legitimacy of the Nation of Islam. For example, in May 1962, state senators Arthur Gottschalk and Edward Eberspacher attacked, in separate instances, the University of Islam No. 2 for teaching hate and contributing to truancy since the school had not been accredited since 1959. Robert Hayes, the assistant superintendent of Cook County schools, concurred with the senators and went so far as to encourage the Chicago Board of Education to bring charges against parents who were supposedly "contributing to the delinquency of a minor and not complying with the state's compulsory attendance law." The issue was then passed around like a political football, with the state remanding the case to the county. Cook County superintendent Noble J. Puffer in turn denied having jurisdiction in the matter and passed it over to the City of Chicago. Likewise, Benjamin C. Willis, the Chicago superintendent of schools, declared the dilemma "a question of accreditation" and handed it back to the Illinois Office of Public Instruction. To the chagrin of Gottschalk and his allies, no one seemed to want to take responsibility for following through with the attack on the Muslim school.[35]

To defend the school and its right to exist, Muhammad dispatched John Ali, the national secretary of the Nation. At a public hearing, Ali dismissed the charges against the University of Islam as "ridiculous" and an effort "to intimidate blacks to surrendering their rights to train and educate their children . . . as accorded to Catholic, Jewish, and other parochial school systems." Shortly after the hearing, the issue evanesced into the fog of Illinois politics, perhaps an acknowledgment of the Muslims' growing influence, the "vague and unclear" laws governing private schools (as Hayes put it), behind-the-scenes compromises, or some combination of factors. To Muhammad, the whole affair was "a perfect insult to my followers" and a question of truth being taught, not hate. The senators and the school officials had again aroused the ire of the Chicago Muslims with tactics that had been used to discredit the organization in earlier years. Still, considering the trials that other believers faced in other regions, the members of Mosque No. 2 had simply been inconvenienced by Gottschalk and the others. Their problems in this instance paled in comparison to those encountered by Louisiana Muslims a year earlier.[36]

The Nation had just begun to expand into the Deep South during the 1960s. Historically, it had been an urban movement confined to Northern and Midwestern cities, though its members often had Southern roots. Mosques in Atlanta (No. 15) and Miami (No. 29) were the first to be organized in the Black Belt and beyond, but in other cities, such as Dallas and Jacksonville, Florida, interest in the Nation had given rise to pockets of believers. Major urban areas in the Upper South, such as Washington, D.C., and Baltimore, had much older Muslim cells, and even Richmond, once the Confederate capital, hosted a mosque at 2116 North Avenue. Undoubtedly, a number of blacks in the South saw the Nation of Islam as a viable separatist alternative to the mainstream Civil Rights Movement, which seemed to require sacrifices that some were not prepared to make.[37]

When Elijah Muhammad exhorted people to "stop forcing yourselves into places where you are not wanted" and to "do something for self," many black Southerners perhaps compared his words to those of Booker T. Washington, who had near the beginning of the century pushed for the economic empowerment of the race and conceded, "In all things that are purely social we [blacks and whites] can be as separate as the fingers." In some ways, the message of the Muslims was not wholly alien to the South and in fact, was at least partially rooted in Southern black culture. The Islamic ideology of the Nation was not familiar in its entirety to African-Americans in Dixie, but the Muslim movement had historically drawn on the black church for both doctrine and rituals, as discussed earlier. Moreover, the black separatist tradition in the South had remained active and could be traced back at least to the late 1870s when "Liberia fever" swept parts of the region following Reconstruction. Henry McNeal Turner, the foremost black separatist at the turn of the century, encouraged emigration to Africa and made Georgia his base of operations. Similarly, the Garvey Movement, headquartered in New York City, boasted a large Southern membership during the 1920s, with Louisiana and Virginia leading all other states in local chapters and divisions of the UNIA. The Muslim movement, while active in the South, did remain primarily a Northern-Midwestern phenomenon during the 1960s and 1970s. However, for those blacks in Louisiana, Georgia, and other Southern states who embraced its beliefs and agenda, their conversions to Islamic separatism cannot be dismissed simply as a historical anomaly, despite the growing influence of the Civil Rights Movement.[38]

Much of the white South, feeling threatened by the assertiveness of civil rights activists and selected federal agencies, wanted no part of the Nation of Islam and was prepared to terminate its influence in the region. This was clearly the case in Monroe, a small city in northeastern Louisiana, where a group of Muslims had begun holding meetings. On March 5, 1961, as many as thirty local policemen armed with rifles, riot sticks, and tear gas invaded a gathering of the believers, allegedly in search of subversion. Initially, the Muslims resisted the assault in a melee, but eventually succumbed to arrest. After the confrontation, nine of the worshipers, including Minister Troy X, were charged with "aggravated assault and battery" and imprisoned under a $11,500 bail.

As soon as the news of the raid and arrests reached Chicago, the case became a cause célèbre. Muhammad, using Raymond Sharrieff and John Ali, then known as John X, as couriers, forwarded funds to Monroe to satisfy the bail. He then hired James Venable, a white lawyer from Atlanta, to defend the accused, who had been handled in "an inhuman manner" as Venable described the encounter in a complaint to U.S. attorney general Robert Kennedy. Despite the rapid response of the national headquarters, the Muslims went to court on April 4 convinced that the chances of a fair trial were already beyond their reach. Rather predictably, the U.S. Department of Justice was not interested in intervening to ensure an impartial hearing.[39]

The jury that heard the case convicted all nine defendants of assault on police officers and sentenced them to a total of twelve years in the Louisiana

State Prison. Muhammad, directing the defense from Chicago, had Venable appeal the cases to the State Supreme Court and doled out the money needed to pay the $12,000 bond. The Muslims walked free for the next several months, but the State of Louisiana was hardly finished with its offensive against the Nation. In late May, Troy X was indicted by an all-white jury of "criminal anarchy and flag desecration" for allegedly advocating the annihilation of the national and Louisiana state governments, encouraging black territorial separatism, and displaying a picture of the American flag with the caption "hell, slavery and death." The minister was briefly imprisoned in the local jail under a $12,000 bond, but was freed after Muhammad again channeled funds to Monroe. On November 7, Troy X, represented by three attorneys supplied by Chicago, was tried and convicted by another all-white jury of instructing Muslims to overthrow the U.S. government. This time, the sentence was much stiffer—ten years in prison, and the defense could only promise further appeals. In the end, seven Muslims served time in prison for the March 5 incident, having been denied a hearing by the State Supreme Court. The whole affair ultimately destroyed the Muslim mosque of Monroe, Louisiana.[40]

The State of Louisiana tried to tie up the loose ends of its campaign against the Muslims by launching an investigation sponsored by the legislative Committee on Un-American Activities in Baton Rouge. The inquiry was probably no surprise to anyone; however, its conclusions were fanciful and revealed just how involved Louisiana was in the shadowy world of Communist-hunting. The committee resolved that the Nation of Islam was a threat to the internal security of the state and the country for several reasons. First, "the total control exercised over the minds and lives of the cult members by Elijah Muhammad" was believed to be "extremely dangerous." Especially since the organization tended to be successful in recruiting followers from among "the larger cities, and in jails and penitentiaries," state security could be compromised by a group that already had 750 to 1,000 members in Louisiana (according to the estimate of the Monroe police chief, James C. Kelly Jr.). Second, the committee discerned a "Communist conspiracy in the Nation of Islam [which] appears to be significant and dangerous." Echoing the McCarthyite jargon of the previous decade, the committee declared that the Muslim movement was a conduit for Reds who endeavored to cause "progressive disillusionment, dissatisfaction, disaffection and disloyalty." If allowed to continue in its activities, the Nation, and the Communists, would supposedly destroy the very institutions of the country. Finally, the committee saw the Muslim movement as "a cruel sham and deceit, based upon gross ignorance and superstition" and camouflaged by the "protective coloring of 'religion' to give credence and dignity to . . . racial hatred."

In addition to these charges, the committee pointed out other themes to support its decision to investigate the Muslims, but concerns regarding Communism, treason, and the well-being of "the white race in particular" were the main focus of the legislators.[41]

Testimony from an assortment of witnesses, ranging from Chief Kelly to members of the Nation, was solicited to bolster the state's case against the Muslims and "the Communist conspiracy." Literature and printed statements of the group's beliefs were also entered as evidence. Still, despite pretenses of impartiality, the entire investigation seemed adversarial. Many of the questions asked by committee members were leading and revealed a strong anti-Muslim bias. Moreover, the words of self-interested witnesses such as Chief Kelly were taken at face value. Against the background of the Civil Rights Movement and a national witch-hunt for "subversives," the Louisiana legislature concluded that the Muslim movement was, indeed, "a Subversive Organization" as defined by the state's Subversive Activities and Communist Control Law. Nonetheless, this determination and the anti-Muslim frenzy that it stirred up in Baton Rouge did not succeed in ridding Louisiana of Muslims. Confrontations between believers and state law enforcement officials would reoccur. If nothing else, the report of the legislature, dated January 9, 1963, did give state and local agencies broad powers to scrutinize and intervene in Muslim affairs. Now, the tactics of the Monroe police department were officially and publicly sanctioned.[42]

The experiences of Elijah Muhammad's followers in Louisiana were not isolated. A national pattern of harassment and repression was beginning to emerge, even in Chicago. The trials of California Muslims are instructive both for what they reveal about the concerns and goals of the state and the impact of official persecution on Muhammad and his leadership. The difficulties that Los Angeles Mosque No. 27 faced affected the political trajectory of the Muslim movement as much as any other singular series of events during the early 1960s.

Unlike the Louisiana Muslims, members of the Los Angeles mosque at 1480 West Jefferson Boulevard were first labeled "un-American" in 1961 and then assailed. Since the Second World War, countersubversive investigations were a fashionable pursuit for ambitious politicians in the state legislature in Sacramento. No other state had a legislative committee more committed to exposing Communists and chasing subversives, nor one with the longevity of California's body, which would last over three decades (1940–71). The first tribunal organized to gather political intelligence and root out alleged Communists and others was the Yorty Committee, started in 1940 under state assemblyman Samuel W. Yorty of Los Angeles. This body did not last long—only a year—before Yorty sought higher political office and was succeeded first by Jack Tenney and the Fact Finding Committee on Un-American Activities (1941–49) and later by Richard E. Combs and the Burns Committee. An indefatigable nativist, Combs belonged to a nationwide network of Communist hunters and was a reputed expert on subversion. For twenty-one years he was the top investigator and "senior analyst" of the Burns Committee. In 1961, he and his colleagues took an interest in the Nation of Islam as a possible threat to the internal security of the Golden State and subsequently launched an investigation into its activities.[43]

National press coverage of the movement and its beliefs was at least partially responsible for the attention that the Burns Committee focused on the Muslims. Yet, the proliferation of mosques in the state was probably a more decisive factor. Since the late 1950s, three local cells had surfaced among blacks in California: one in San Francisco (No. 26), another in Oakland (No. 26-B), and of course the Los Angeles group (No. 27). The latter cell was especially active in proselytizing youth in the state's largest city and, under Minister John Shabazz, had mushroomed to over one thousand members by the early 1960s. The campaign of the Burns Committee against the Muslims was not unlike past governmental assaults, and even the strategy of the legislators mirrored methods previously employed elsewhere. In their "Eleventh Report" to the California legislature, the investigators found the "Negro Muslims" to be "un-American" purveyors of racial hatred who ran a school that specialized in inculcating antiwhite sentiments in African-American children. The report went on to draw parallels between the Nation and the Communist Party and included a factually inaccurate summary of Elijah Muhammad's early life. Muslim literature, such as the "Twelve-Point" program that outlined the beliefs and goals of the Nation, was reprinted by the committee as evidence of the subversive nature of the movement.[44]

The Chicago leadership, already under pressure from Monroe, Louisiana, responded immediately to the report of the Burns Committee, publishing an extensive rebuttal in the December 1961 edition of *Muhammad Speaks*. In his article "What Is Un-American?" Muhammad critiqued the committee report and concluded that "if you are black or a member of the Black Nation you are un-American. If you want equal justice and a decent way of life to live, or have love for the black people, you are un-American." Similar to the 1963 report of the Louisiana state legislature, the findings of the Burns Committee laid the groundwork for more intensive surveillance and repression of the California Muslim movement. Almost inevitably, the Los Angeles mosque, the largest in the state, became the flash point.[45]

Local operations against censured groups were spearheaded by the intelligence unit of the Los Angeles Police Department. Chief William Parker, a former infiltrator of radical groups, had been the guiding force in the department since 1950 and worked closely with the FBI and the Burns Committee in the prosecution of the war against subversion. To Parker, the city of Los Angeles and the country in general were polarized into two camps consisting of conservative, patriotic, hardworking Americans who guarded the gates of Western civilization and radical, Communist-inspired, disloyal "un-Americans" who sought to revolutionize and undermine the very traditions of the United States. The John Birch Society, the Christian Anti-Communist Crusade, and other ultraright groups passed the chief's litmus test of "American-ness" and loyalty. He and a number of the members of his department actually had close ties with these organizations. As for the forces of evil, they could be anywhere and spanned an ideological spectrum broad enough to include black nationalists in Watts and the liberal element in the Hollywood community.[46]

The strategy of Parker and his intelligence unit against "subversives" went well beyond monitoring behavior. The Cold War and the paranoid political culture of the United States had made ideology and belief legitimate targets of police action. With both state and federal support, the LAPD secretly amassed countless files on individuals and groups suspected of "un-American activities" and employed vast resources in the persecution of both the real and the imagined. Surveillance was now an end in itself and had a punitive aspect about it. Within this atmosphere of political intolerance and police license, Mosque No. 27 encountered Parker's "Red squad," a force that could do almost anything and have it rationalized as in the interest of municipal (and national) security.[47]

On April 27, 1962, a pair of policemen approached two Muslims for questioning outside the Los Angeles mosque. One of the Muslims, apparently a worker at a cleaning company, had been either selling or storing clothes in his car. According to the story of the LAPD, the two Muslims were hostile to questioning and attacked the policemen. In self-defense, one of the officers fired at the Muslims, who were quickly reinforced by a massive wave of "black-suited" worshipers from the mosque. More policemen arrived and more shots were fired until the Muslims, faced by as many as seventy-five well-armed patrolmen, backed off. In the Muslim version of events, the policemen were the aggressors from the beginning, manhandling their detainees. When one of the Muslims tried to explain that he was in the cleaning business by gesturing at the clothes, one of the officers grabbed his hand. Next, the policemen drew pistols and started firing. Muslims in the temple, alerted by the shots, came out to see what was going on. To their horror, several of their unarmed brethren were lying on the ground, all bleeding and at least two immobilized. In the end, Ronald Stokes, a twenty-eight-year-old Korean veteran and the mosque's secretary, was killed; another believer, William Rogers, was paralyzed from the waist down by a gunshot to the back; and five other Muslims were wounded by gunfire and blows from policemen, a number of whom were also hospitalized for injuries. Reminiscent of the Monroe incident a year earlier, nine Muslims on the scene were promptly charged with assaulting law enforcement officers and each jailed under a $10,000 bond.[48]

The Stokes killing came as a complete surprise to Elijah Muhammad. In his thirty-one years of membership in the Nation of Islam, no Muslim had ever been murdered by law enforcement officials. There had historically been repression and abuse of all sorts, including beatings and imprisonment, but no deaths caused by agents of the state. Muhammad, who was in Phoenix at the time, was both incensed and shaken. "Every one of the Muslims," he would later say in private conversation, "should have died before they allowed an aggressor to come into their mosque." Muhammad dispatched Malcolm X and John Ali to Los Angeles as representatives of the national headquarters to assist the Muslims there and to publicize the shootings. Over the next few weeks, tensions between the Los Angeles believers and city officials threatened to erupt into a major civil crisis, especially after the city launched a grand jury investigation into the Muslim movement and dismissed the killing of Ronald Stokes as "justifiable homicide."[49]

Charges and countercharges were issued by both sides. Malcolm X and John Shabazz lambasted Parker's LAPD as "well-armed storm troopers" comparable to the Gestapo and described Mayor Sam Yorty (the former head of the California Un-American Activities Committee) as "a professional liar." In turn, the mayor labeled the Nation of Islam "a Nazi type of movement preaching hate." The invectives were tossed around well into July. Some Muslims were anxious to inflict bloody retribution against whites in Los Angeles, but Muhammad directed them to "Hold fast to Islam" and avoid further confrontations with the police. He even warned Malcolm X "to cool it" regarding his bruising criticism of Yorty—who had telephoned Muhammad in Phoenix—and eventually ordered the minister back to New York. Subsequent violence in connection with the Stokes killing was minimal, except for a few instances in which renegade Muslims ambushed and assaulted drunken whites along skid row on Fifth Street.[50]

The response of Muhammad to events in Los Angeles underscored both his increasingly pragmatic, conservative leadership style and ideological fault lines that were developing within the Nation. His attempts to defuse the conflict surrounding Mosque No. 27 were quite understandable to those who could look beyond the rhetoric of the Nation and see the nepotism, materialism, and fear of government censure that were shaping Muhammad's policies. But for those Muslims who devoured the movement's official program and ideology at face value, Muhammad's call for discipline and perseverance in the face of police brutality and murder was confusing. Underneath most of the Nation's beliefs lay the themes of retribution, justice, and redemption. Members were actually primed by the militarized structure of the Fruit of Islam and the principle of self-defense it supposedly embraced to expect some response to abuse, especially when perpetrated by "white devils." Instead, in the case of the April 27 shootings, Muhammad encouraged them to trust in Allah and to sell more newspapers "to let the world know he [the white man] is the devil."[51]

Many believers who were attracted to the Nation because of its facade of militancy were disillusioned by the whole affair. To their amazement, Muslims were being encouraged to be nonviolent in the face of beatings and murder. At least in Los Angeles, a number of believers parted ways with the Nation; a few even organized themselves into a "band of angels" and attempted to carry out their own brand of justice against unsuspecting whites. Most, however, stayed in the Nation, but were forced to reexamine their expectations of the movement. Malcolm X, who had been the Muslims' mouthpiece during the Stokes tragedy, summed up the dilemma that the more militant followers of Elijah Muhammad faced. "We spout our militant revolutionary rhetoric and we preach Armageddon," the minister indignantly told confidants after he returned to New York. "[But] when our own brothers are brutalized or killed, we do nothing.... We just sit on our hands."[52]

Muhammad's caution and nonconfrontational tactics during the Los Angeles ordeal were also motivated by the national headquarters' involvement, financial as well as organizational, in the Monroe incident of the previous year. Moreover, Muhammad, as discussed earlier, had a number of business transactions in Chicago and Phoenix absorbing his attention. At this time, too, Gottschalk and others were on the warpath against "hate teaching" at the University of Islam No. 2, and Muslim prisoners, who could ill afford the bad publicity that a race war in Los Angeles would surely bring, still had cases pending before various courts throughout the country regarding the practice of their religion behind bars. To say the least, a radical response by Muslims to the Stokes killing was inconvenient at the time, as would have been the inevitable counterresponse of the government.[53]

To complicate matters even further, Muhammad was experiencing crises in his personal life that made the likelihood of a West Coast jihad remote. His bronchial asthma and other maladies were worsening, requiring extended trips to Phoenix and frequent bed rest. Marital discord resulting from a series of indiscretions undoubtedly took a tremendous emotional toll, as did the imprisonment of his son Wallace, who had been convicted of draft evasion a year earlier. To Muhammad, little was to be gained in taking a stand in Los Angeles where the odds were clearly on the side of the Yorty administration and Parker's LAPD. A Muslim offensive against the "City of Angels" would simply be a pretense for the government to utterly destroy Mosque No. 27 and the organizational strength, financial potential, and prestige that it conferred upon the national body. At bottom, Muhammad well understood the unevenness of power relations between

Muslims and the State of California and decided to keep the peace rather than start a calamitous miniwar. Though he privately expressed outrage about the April 27 shootings, his policy was one of forbearance.[54]

The role of the state in curbing the potential activism of the Muslim movement went far beyond the events that took place in Los Angeles, where eleven believers were eventually convicted of charges ranging from interfering with law officers to felony assault. The ongoing anti-Muslim campaign of the federal government played a decisive part in hindering the expansion of the movement and discouraging activities that could be labeled "un-American" or in some way noxious to state security. Washington's interest in the Muslims had been most intense during times of war and national stress such as the Depression and World War II. The 1960s witnessed an increase in government scrutiny and harassment of the Muslims due in large part to the Civil Rights Movement and the national hysteria over Communism, subversion, and other challenges to the status quo from unconventional sources. Though President Kennedy could report to concerned citizens as late as August 1963 that the "Justice Department has not received any reliable information that the 'Black Muslims' are violating any federal law," he still allowed the FBI to conduct open-ended surveillance and counterintelligence operations against the organization until his death three months later. As had always been the case, J. Edgar Hoover personally prosecuted the war against Elijah Muhammad and his followers, often using illegal tactics.[55]

The motives and strategy behind the pursuit of the Nation of Islam by the FBI were rooted in Hoover's Cold War attitudes and racial prejudices. The director believed that the advocacy of racial justice itself was inextricably tied to Communist infiltration of the United States. He could not conceive of domestic conditions that would lead blacks to follow Martin Luther King Jr. or to join the Muslim movement. He felt that African-Americans had little to complain about and that the Civil Rights Movement and other social protest movements were inventions of Reds who sought to use gullible blacks as a medium through which to saturate American society with Communism. The breach that civil rights activism caused in traditional race relations supposedly afforded Communists—a broad, flexible label for dissenters rather than a purely ideological grouping—the opportunity and leverage needed to subvert the institutions of the country.

In line with this reasoning, Hoover held that his agency and others that took Communists seriously were the last line of defense between traditional America and a Marxist revolution on North American soil. He felt personally responsible for chasing "the Red Kite's tail wherever it led." If fulfilling this mandate meant ordering FBI operatives to break the law, Hoover was willing to do that, especially in regard to black organizations that he believed unnecessarily challenged the racial status quo. Ultimately, the director was prepared to sacrifice the ideals of American democracy to construct a national-security state that valued domestic conformity over constitutionally guaranteed freedoms.[56]

During the early 1960s, the countersubversive operations of the FBI against the Nation of Islam were mainly aimed at exposing the organization as a dangerous, unpatriotic fraud to blacks and others who were otherwise believed to be too ignorant to see it for what it really was. The surveillance machinery at Hoover's disposal was diverse and nationwide. At the top of a pyramid of spies and informants, the FBI was plugged into local and state counterintelligence activities through its links with police departments, state legislative committees, and other agencies. Files on alleged subversives were routinely made available to Hoover by state and city governments, which in turn drew on federal funds to pay informants. Along with these connections, the national office of the FBI supervised a web of field offices that kept the director abreast of even minute matters under surveillance.

In regard to the Nation of Islam, the field offices were constantly occupied with monitoring the activities of important officials. Informants were placed at almost every level of decision-making in the movement. The Chicago office, which kept an intimate watch of Elijah Muhammad, was one of the more diligent of the field agencies dedicated to "efforts to disrupt and curb [the] growth" of the Nation. On the eve of Saviour's Day, 1963, its agents were conducting a search for Fard Muhammad in hope of exposing the organization as a hoax and making Elijah Muhammad "appear ridiculous." Of all the government agencies that could "disrupt and curb" the activities of individuals and groups, the FBI was as powerful as any and used its many resources to accomplish goals that often exceeded its authority.[57]

Hoover commonly leaked information from bureau files to other government departments and agencies, particularly when he wanted a subject or an organization to receive a heavy dose of countersubversion. In the early 1960s, the director almost certainly passed files on the Muslim movement to the House Un-American Activities Committee, among other government agencies, hoping that Elijah Muhammad, Malcolm X, and others would have to answer questions from hostile congressmen in the halls of power in Washington. A formal, public investigation never occurred, but the Muslims did come close to being victims of the kind of interrogations involving blinding camera lights, subpoenas, and contempt citations that the committee had become notorious for. In August 1962, the chairman of the federal HUAC, Francis E. Walter, publicly announced plans to launch "a very extensive investigation" into the Nation of Islam once it was determined whether the committee had the legal wherewithal to do so. A resolution was even placed on the House calendar authorizing a vote on the committee's proposal. In the end, the HUAC did nothing, but the Muslims would again be mentioned as detestable during future floor debates on black extremism and national security.[58]

As the head of the Nation of Islam, Elijah Muhammad was not interested in arousing further state repression. Accordingly, the readership of *Muhammad Speaks*, which included the FBI, was once again reminded in the October 15 edition that the Muslims were law-abiding and unaggressive. Given his age and illnesses, Muhammad probably could not have handled the abuse of a congressional grilling or any more time in prison. Considering, too, the financial dealings and personal problems the leader was involved in at the time, more entanglements with local and national authorities would have been disastrous and thus, were to be avoided. When he left Chicago for the warmer clime of Phoenix on October 18, Muhammad had much to think about regarding the hostility of the U.S. government, and its many tentacles, toward his movement. Perhaps known to him by this time, his getaways to Arizona were not really an escape from the intense scrutiny and harassment of the American countersubversion community. In fact, his residential telephone in Phoenix had been tapped for over a year, courtesy of J. Edgar Hoover.[59]

Phoenix, located in the south-central part of Arizona, felt as if it were on fire for most of the year. Summer daytime temperatures routinely exceeded one hundred degrees, and even the nights provided scant relief when temperatures in the low eighties were the best that one could expect in July. Low average annual rainfall—less than eight inches—did little to relieve the climate. When Muhammad arrived at his seven-bedroom home on East Violet Drive that October of 1962, Phoenix was already basking in the lower temperatures of autumn. Yet, daily temperatures hovered around the mid to upper eighties, roughly equivalent to steamy Chicago in July.[60]

Phoenix had become a familiar destination in Muhammad's continuing journey through urban America. Like Chicago, Detroit, Sandersville, and other places he had lived in, the Arizona capital was not impervious to racial problems. During the early 1960s, segregation was a fact of life in the city, enforced by custom in theaters, restaurants, and hotels and by statute in schools. The African-American population of Phoenix, which numbered 25,119 in 1960 and comprised 3.8 percent of the metropolitan total, was concentrated in racially homogeneous neighborhoods south of the downtown area, away from the more affluent white communities of North Phoenix. Unemployment, poor housing, and deficient educational institutions relegated blacks to the bottom of the socioeconomic ladder alongside Native Americans, who had struggled with whites over control of Arizona since the days of Geronimo. On the surface, Phoenix seemed like a Southwestern oasis separate from the larger United States. Beneath its sunburnt skin, however, the city exhibited the racial norms that prevailed in other major urban centers.[61]

Beginning in 1961, Muhammad had come to Phoenix to avoid the brutal Chicago winters, which exacerbated his bronchial asthma. The dry, temperate Arizona winters helped him to cope with an illness that robbed him of the precious energy and stamina that a man his age needed to accomplish even modest tasks. During his trips to Phoenix, Muhammad usually stayed close to home. Much of his time was spent entertaining visitors and directing the Chicago headquarters as best he could through couriers, letters, and phone calls. Occasionally, property acquisitions and proselytizing work broke this routine. In January 1962, he gave a speech in the Phoenix Madison Square Garden that reportedly netted three hundred converts, including the entire congregation of the Mount Zion Baptist Church. Also around this time, Mosque No. 32 was established in the city for the further propagation of the Muslim cause in Arizona. For the most part, though, Muhammad's stays in Phoenix were restful occasions devoid of many of the pressures associated with life in the Nation's nerve center in Chicago.[62]

Muhammad's absence from Mosque No. 2 made it necessary for him to delegate more authority to those in the hierarchy there, such as John Ali, Raymond Sharrieff, Minister James Shabazz, and his own sons Herbert and Elijah Jr. The headquarters had to function without his physical presence, and these were the people he left in charge. Yet, as always, he made every effort to keep the movement under his control while in Arizona, even if it meant some long days at the office. He loathed being out of touch with the affairs of the Nation and sometimes sacrificed his health to stay at the center of things.

On a typical day, whether in Chicago or Phoenix, Muhammad arose early in the morning to eat breakfast and to sort through the piles of mail that he received daily. Secretaries wrote down the letters, speeches, and editorials that he dictated. The telephone rang incessantly, and Muhammad spent hours consulting with close advisers, ministers, and other laborers who were responsible for informing him of the day-to-day affairs of the various Muslim mosques. Between telephone conversations and dictation, he signed business and salary contracts and met with scheduled visitors. One of the more important tasks that he attended to each week was the taping of speeches to be broadcast by radio stations throughout the country. In December 1962, over 150 stations were broadcasting Sunday addresses by Muhammad, making his views almost as accessible as the Christian message. Though only modestly educated, the leader was fully aware of the power of the written and spoken word in a society in which the media increasingly shaped public perceptions and values.[63]

During the 1960s, news reporters and book writers were a major source of publicity for the movement. Even before "The Hate That Hate Produced" documentary made the Muslims a media phenomenon in 1959, certain black newspapers had already discovered that the Nation of Islam was newsworthy. But once film footage of Muhammad and Malcolm X espousing their racial beliefs was aired on television, plans for books, magazine articles, extensive newspaper stories, and future documentaries were made by editors and authors across the country. Naturally, Muhammad welcomed the interest. He granted interviews, allowed reporters to film his speeches, and even entertained white writers in his home. In time, though, he came to realize that many who expressed a desire to report on the movement's activities were motivated by self-interest. Misquotes, quotes out of context, and slanted stories were all too common, and writers and announcers were rarely objective in their work on the Nation. Muhammad, after being lied to enough by reporters, eventually restricted journalists to fifteen minutes of inquiries and picture-taking. To guard against misquotes, he made his own audio recordings of interviews. Despite these precautions, vicious criticism of Muhammad and the Muslims never ceased to appear in newspapers and magazines. For many news agencies, sensationalized reports were simply more interesting and sold more newspapers than the sometimes bland truth. Nevertheless, the Muslims both benefitted and suffered from media exposure, and Muhammad's willingness to give an occasional interview even up to the last years of his life testifies to his recognition of the Nation's dependency on the media for delivering its message to the general public.[64]

During the early 1960s, four books that became seminal works on the Muslim movement were written. Charles Eric Lincoln, then a graduate student in the School of Theology at Boston University, devoted his doctoral dissertation to the Nation of Islam, or "the Black Muslims" as he called the group, and the social conditions that encouraged its growth. Lincoln traveled back and forth to Chicago, New York, Boston, and other cities to talk with key leaders in the movement, most notably Muhammad, Malcolm X, and Louis X, the Boston minister. He published the first monograph on the Nation, entitled *The Black Muslims in America*, in 1961. The following year saw a second work on the Muslims, called *Black Nationalism: A Search for an Identity in America*, an ethnographic study that complemented Lincoln's sociological work. The author, E. U. Essien-Udom, was a Nigerian scholar who had arrived in the United States ten years earlier and had spent much of the following decade earning a doctorate at the University of Chicago. Like Lincoln, the African writer had collected organizational materials, newspaper articles, and other vital sources, but devoted much of his time to interviewing rank-and-file Muslims and attending organizational gatherings. The interest of academia in his movement pleased Muhammad, who believed that "one of our [race's] worst needs is writers." Yet, he did not generally agree with the conclusions of Lincoln and Essien-Udom, who pointed out both flaws and positive elements in the Nation and its leadership. Consequently, Muhammad stated in a later interview that while "both books have very good things in it," they still "show undeveloped knowledge of just what's what." He criticized the authors as "people who want to write" simply to get something "on the market."[65]

Sometime in early 1963, Alex Haley, an African-American reporter, approached Muhammad for permission to write a book on the Nation. The work was not to be a strictly academic study of the movement, but an autobiographical account of the public persona of the Nation—Malcolm X. Apparently unfamiliar with the rigid hierarchy of authority in the movement, the reporter had approached the New York minister first for permission to write the book. But Malcolm, who had worked with Haley previously on an interview for *Playboy* magazine, dutifully directed him to make his request to the master of the Nation of Islam, Elijah Muhammad. Haley caught up with the leader during one of his Phoenix retreats and was welcomed in the gracious manner that he typically greeted guests. If Muhammad was dismayed or offended by Haley's request to write a one-hundred-thousand-word account of his chief lieutenant's life and not his own, he did not express it. In fact, he sanctioned the project with the phrase "Allah approves" and added that "Malcolm is one of my most outstanding ministers." Undoubtedly, Muhammad saw the proposed autobiography as a vehicle by which the beliefs and program of the Nation could be further transmitted to potential followers. He trusted that Malcolm would make the account amenable to the Muslim cause. The book would not actually become available until 1965 following the assassination of the by then repudiated New York minister. But regardless of the bitterness that later existed between Malcolm and his former teacher, *The Autobiography of Malcolm X*, more than any other work by any other follower of Elijah Muhammad, cogently describes the inner workings, philosophy, and appeal of the Nation of Islam. It is an extraordinary account of how the Muslim movement attracted and maintained the loyalty and admiration of men like Malcolm for virtually all of their adult lives.[66]

Muhammad's own magnum opus, *Message to the Blackman in America*, was published in late 1965, shortly after—and at least partially in reaction to—the publication of Malcolm's autobiography. Originally, the leader had planned to publish a fifty-to-sixty-page booklet of speeches to coincide with the 1963 Saviour's Day convention, but persistent illness and other problems distracted him and nothing became of his plans. By design, the book is not a study of the interior operations and functions of the Nation. It is not autobiographical, except for a brief, sketchy depiction of Muhammad's early life, and cannot really be considered a history of the Nation in the chronological sense. In essence, it is a purely religious guidepost for a religious movement; that is, there are no pretenses toward objectivity. *Message*, moreover, is not an original work, but a compilation of newspaper articles, letters, and *Muhammad Speaks* editorials previously published. The common Muslim themes of racial separatism, economic self-help, white devilry, and divine deliverance hold the chapters together, and the Nation's program and theology are expounded upon at length. Over three hundred pages long, *Message* replaced the shorter and less nationalistic *The Supreme Wisdom* (1957) as the main canon of the Nation and, like *The Autobiography of Malcolm X,* became required reading for Black Power advocates during the late 1960s. Insofar as it came out later and was written in the same propagandistic vein as *Muhammad Speaks, Message* simply supplemented the publicity that the earlier writings of Lincoln, Essien-Udom, and Malcolm X (and Alex Haley) had brought to the movement.[67]

Despite his doctor's advice to rest in Phoenix, Muhammad kept in touch with officials in Chicago and continued to actively push his program into the spotlight of the media. His daily routine during his winter escapes to Arizona sometimes turned out to be as rigorous as his organizational activities at the Mosque No. 2 headquarters, even though his bronchial asthma had been diagnosed as acute in 1961, and since then, his health had steadily declined. His deteriorating condition was no secret to members of the Nation or to anyone who knew him. When Alex Haley visited him in Phoenix in early 1963, Muhammad literally coughed the whole time, and the writer left quite disturbed about the leader's health. In Chicago and throughout the national organization, Muslims became greatly concerned about their messenger's illness. The question of succession was openly discussed in the media, though prematurely. Muhammad's ailments and extended stays in Arizona fueled rumors of ambitions and jealousies among the upper echelon of the Muslim leadership. It also revealed fractures in the organizational unity that Muhammad had so desperately tried to foster ever since the destructive schisms of the 1930s.[68]

The succession question was especially sensitive for the Nation, as it is for any organization in which the leader claims a divine right to rule. No official mechanism existed to effect a transfer of power and authority in the event of Muhammad's death. To complicate matters, Muhammad repeatedly proclaimed in public that he was the last "Messenger of Allah" and after his death "come God himself." He refused to openly address the issue of a successor in any other way, even up to his passing in 1975. Among national leaders and the Muhammad family, an informal choice had apparently been made as early as 1960 regarding the heir apparent of the movement. Wallace Muhammad, Elijah's seventh child and the one named by Fard Muhammad, was to take his father's place, presumably taking on some title other than messenger. But this decision was not without drawbacks and consequences, and it did not address other concerns of some top officials in the movement. In a real sense, the succession question drew battle lines in the organization that would never really disappear.[69]

Ever since the Nation attracted national media attention in 1959, Malcolm X and the Muslim elite, including the Muhammad family, at the Chicago headquarters had been at the center of the struggle for influence in the organization. The conflict flowed and ebbed depending on the health of Muhammad and other factors, but did not cease to sour relations between Mosque No. 7 and national officials. The tensions were largely over Malcolm's growing presence in the movement, and his larger-than-life image in the media as the key figure in the Nation. Malcolm routinely denied assertions by reporters and others that he was Muhammad's successor or the vice messenger of the movement. However, the minister's passionate orations and photogenic appearance, which so easily attracted the press, often left this impression. Though he would later be concerned about Malcolm's towering image in the movement and the media, Muhammad favored Malcolm above all other ministers and consistently called upon him to represent the Nation before the world. As mentioned earlier, the relationship between the two was like father and son, and it could reasonably be said that they loved each other as such.[70]

This situation exacerbated the envy and jealousy of Chicago officials who desired Muhammad's favor. Family members and close associates perhaps felt that Malcolm's closeness to Muhammad was depriving them of both his paternal attention and the kind of authority that Malcolm commanded in the organization. Also, philosophical differences apparently pushed Chicago leaders away from Malcolm. While the New York minister flirted with a more activist black nationalism that would lead the Nation into militant participation in the Civil Rights Movement, many Chicago officials, comfortable with their affluence and effete program of territorial separatism, shunned the kind of political agitation that might adversely affect the economic well-being, especially the tax-exempt status, of the movement. The Muslim elite, including Muhammad, stressed divine remedies to the black man's problems. Malcolm and others saw political protest and the practical application of the Muslims' belief in self-defense as the future of the Nation.[71]

At no time during his tenure as minister of Mosque No. 7 was Malcolm in open revolt against Elijah Muhammad or adversaries at the Chicago headquarters. If anything, he pandered to Muhammad more as the hostility of national officials toward him grew. When he was instructed to turn down invitations to speak, he obliged his teacher. He raised and turned over annually to Chicago more money than most mosques could dream of generating. In July 1962, he even honored Muhammad by naming his third daughter Ilyasah, a feminized Arabic version of Elijah. Muhammad knew that Malcolm had been one of the single most important reasons for the popularity of the Nation among African-Americans and, despite resistance in Chicago, appointed him national minister in 1963. Yet, the leader knew also, as did his inner circle, that any attempt by Malcolm to seize control of the movement—particularly in the event of Muhammad's death—could be catastrophic and thus sought to impose parameters around his influence. As early as 1961, Muhammad made local captains of the Fruit of Islam directly responsible to him, a decision that Malcolm found difficult to live with over time. A year later, Malcolm started fading away from the pages of *Muhammad Speaks,* which he had helped create. Muhammad, if he did not initiate them, at least acquiesced to these and other measures designed to curb the influence of the New York minister and to appease the high council in Chicago. Still, according to Wallace Muhammad, some around the Messenger of Allah wanted nothing less than Malcolm's resignation.[72]

The question of succession, and all of the jealousies and tensions that surrounded it, carried even greater weight since the heir apparent, Wallace Muhammad, faced problems that would have made it difficult for him to assume the mantle of his father. On March 23, 1960, the Philadelphia minister was convicted in a federal court of evading the draft and was sentenced to three years in prison in June. The case was appealed by Wallace's attorney, who cited conscientious objection. Elijah Muhammad, who personally opposed the impressment of Muslims, reportedly advised his son to make the decision for himself whether to report to Elgin State Hospital in compliance with his draft orders. Ultimately, Wallace decided that serving at the hospital aided American war efforts and thus did not appear for induction. During an October 1961 hearing, his earlier appeal was dismissed, and the Muslim minister was ordered to turn himself over to authorities for immediate imprisonment. Wallace surrendered to federal officials on October 30, his twenty-eighth birthday, and began serving a three-year sentence for violating the selective service law in the Federal Correctional Institution at Sandstone, Minnesota.[73]

In addition to his physical isolation from mosque life, Wallace underwent an ideological divorce from the Nation of Islam during this period. He had apparently been struggling for some time with the contradictions and inconsistencies between Sunni Islam and the teachings of his father. Having read the Qur'an and studied Arabic at the University of Islam under such teachers as Jamil Diab, Wallace questioned the theological legitimacy of the Muslim movement. He continued to believe that the Nation was related to the larger Islamic world in some way, but could not reconcile himself with the incongruity between his father's beliefs and those of orthodox Muslims. When he approached Elijah with questions, the senior Muhammad, already sensitized to criticism by Muslim rivals and the press, became suspicious. "You're not with me," he told his inquisitive son. Wallace, aware that his father had in essence called him a hypocrite, took exception and argued that he meant no offense by his query. Indeed, he just wanted to be honest about his feelings and doubts. At the time of their discussion, Wallace was about to be imprisoned for violating induction orders, and as it turned out, he had little time to further discuss philosophical matters with his father before leaving for Minnesota. Regretfully, he went off to prison before he could resolve the issues he had presented to Elijah.[74]

Wallace's incarceration was a period of soul-searching and spiritual enlightenment. He spent much of his time in prison poring through the Bible and the Qur'an for answers to those elements of the Nation's doctrine that puzzled him. He questioned his father's messengership and "a lot of those experiences from the past" that had heretofore been unclear. To be sure, an awareness of theological differences between orthodox Muslims and followers of Elijah Muhammad was not new for Wallace. For anyone who had bothered even to superficially study the beliefs and rituals of the two groups, the inconsistencies were easy to find and were blaring. However, actually reading the Bible and the Qur'an over fourteen months behind bars highlighted for Wallace just how divergent the teachings of his father were from traditional Sunni Islam. Whereas he had claimed to be "a hundred percent" behind his father's leadership prior to his jailing, months of isolated study behind prison walls had given him the chance to look critically at the teachings of the Nation of Islam without the pressures of conformity that radiated throughout every mosque in the country.[75]

At the end of his spiritual odyssey at FCI Sandstone, Wallace concluded that neither the messengership that his father claimed nor many of the doctrines of the Nation of Islam were supported by strong scriptural evidence. To him, the movement was embracing a religion that was at odds with the very holy books from which it was supposedly derived. When he was paroled on January 10, 1963, Wallace resumed his ministerial duties at Mosque No. 12 in Philadelphia. He still had his doubts, but he did not openly break with his father. Instead, he stayed in the Nation and quietly worked for reform from the inside. By this time, a few members of the Nation showed discernible signs of discontent, and Wallace perhaps took comfort in the possibilities.[76]

With Wallace's imprisonment and theological wavering, the succession issue and related conflicts festered. Adding to the personal and ideological tensions within the Nation, brutal criticisms from a familiar outside source started again during the early 1960s to gnaw away at the doctrinal legitimacy of the movement. Hostile attacks by orthodox Muslims had never really ended following the anti-Nation offensive launched by Diab, Dawud, and others in 1959. But 1962 seemed a particularly bitter year in the continuing war of words between Elijah Muhammad and his Islamic rivals. During a press conference in late May, Talib Dawud announced plans to file a lawsuit against Muhammad to bar him from using the words *Islam* or *Muslims* in reference to the Nation of Islam. He also challenged Muhammad to a debate intended to expose him as a "phony." Dawud's wife, Dakota Staton, claimed that her singing career had "suffered irreparable harm as a result of the fact that the press has linked us with the Elijah organization." Dawud himself may also have felt the repercussions of the anti-Muslim mood of the government following the arrest of Muhammad's followers during the police assault on Los Angeles Mosque No. 27 in April.[77]

Malcolm X had barely uttered his typically blistering response to Dawud's attack when Abdul Ghefoor Soofi, president of the Ahmadiyya Muslims of the USA, reviled the Nation in September as "a hate cult [that] uses for its hymn of hate the name plate of Islam." Speaking before a small crowd at the Centre Avenue YMCA in Pittsburgh, Soofi further denounced Muhammad's movement as a "deliberate and wicked act of fraud and unabashed theft of priceless treasure." The criticism directed against his organization by the Dawuds and the Ahmadiyyas came as little surprise to Muhammad. Yet, at a time when so many other pressures were confronting the movement, such as the Los Angeles disturbance and the threatened HUAC probe, the charges of Muslim opponents were especially harmful to the Nation's image—as they were no doubt intended to be.[78]

Muhammad, of course, had to respond charge-by-charge to the attacks of Muslim rivals. His reputation and the legitimacy of the Nation as a truly Islamic movement were at stake, and losing the propaganda war could only adversely affect recruitment. As early as the fall of 1961, he had planned a second trip to Karachi in response to an invitation reportedly extended by the Educational Department of Pakistan. He never made it to Karachi, but the trip would surely have been played up by Muhammad as further evidence that he and his followers were respected in the East. A year later, he responded to the verbal assaults of orthodox Muslims by barring members of the National Muslim Improvement Association of America and the Muslim Brotherhood from attending his October talk, "Islam vs. Christianity," in Philadelphia Arena. In an open letter to one Muslim critic, he went so far as to place his messengership beyond the authority of even Middle Eastern centers of Islam: "I will say that neither Jeddah nor Mecca have sent me! . . . There is no Muslim in Arabia that has authority to stop me from delivering this message." Defiantly, he argued that "I am not taking orders from them, I am taking orders from Allah (God) Himself." The conflict between the Nation and its critics did not end with these words, nor were the messengership claims of Muhammad any more acceptable to orthodox Muslims. In fact, Dawud later escalated the war to a level that had previously been avoided by both sides of the conflict.[79]

In a December 27, 1963, letter to newly sworn-in president Lyndon B. Johnson, Dawud libeled Muhammad, calling him the son of a Japanese spy "who was never apprehended" and accusing him of having been involved in at least five murders, the most famous victim being Noble Drew Ali, the founder of the Moorish Science Temple of America. Though Johnson's White House—assisted by Hoover's FBI—picked up where the Kennedy administration had left off in regard to the surveillance and censure of the Nation, Dawud's insistence that the president have Elijah Muhammad arrested for his alleged crimes as a serial killer was not heeded. Certainly, Johnson would have had Muhammad apprehended posthaste if any of the accusations were true or rooted in the thinnest circumstantial evidence. But they were not, and the government—and Dawud—had to be satisfied with spying on the movement and exacerbating tensions within it.[80]

Muhammad probably never learned of Dawud's letter to Johnson, although he more than likely felt the effects of it. These smear tactics and others like them dismayed him since he believed that his Muslim rivals should have been in solidarity with the Nation. Muhammad was not affected by criticism to the point that he would sacrifice his reputation and leadership for the sake of religious peace. He and Malcolm shoveled dirt into the tents of opponents as often as filth was heaped into their own camp. Muhammad, nonetheless, felt that a larger white hand was behind the whole conflict. Moreover, he believed that someday it would be exposed and that his Islamic opponents would see the error of their ways. While quite significant, the clashes between the Messenger of Allah and his religious antagonists were overshadowed during the early 1960s by a self-inflicted wound that jeopardized the cohesion and popularity of the Chicago-based movement. Ironically, the private activities of Elijah Muhammad himself proved to be one of the biggest threats to the future of the Nation of Islam.[81]

Shortly after Muhammad returned from his tour of the Islamic world in January 1960, one of his secretaries gave birth to a baby girl at St. Francis Hospital in Lynwood, California. The woman, young and unmarried, had worked closely with the leader in Chicago, but had relocated to the West Coast to have her child, which was born on March 30. As the Muslim moral code stipulated, she was sentenced to isolation for having a child out of wedlock, presumably by Muhammad himself, and not allowed to interact with other members in good standing with the organization. This pattern of events was repeated at least twice, with unmarried secretaries of the leader giving birth to babies followed by isolation and forced withdrawal from Muslim affairs. The astonishing feature of these stories was not that women in the movement had children out of wedlock; this had certainly happened before, along with the meting out of punishment. The real surprise was that these three women, and eventually at least four others, pointed to a common denominator in their pregnancies: their romantic involvement with Elijah Muhammad.[82]

Perhaps as early as the mid-1950s, Muhammad had secretly been carrying on relations with a number of young women employed by the Nation of Islam. The relationships were apparently short-term and discreet, and in spite of the leader's debilitating asthma, they frequently produced children, which he tended not to claim publicly. These trysts were apparently most common in the years 1961–62, but they also likely took place during earlier, less documented times. In the end, seven women who had been personal secretaries of Muhammad would claim to have given birth to a total of thirteen children fathered by the leader. Possibly others were intimate with Muhammad but bore no children. By early 1963, the extramarital exploits of the leader had become the worst-kept secret in the Nation. However, it appears that his philandering had tapered off significantly by the previous autumn. Undoubtedly, Muhammad was aware of the potential explosiveness of his activities. Indiscretions smaller in number and magnitude had ruined much more powerful men. In some instances, he appears to have been cautious and conscious of the implications of public disclosure. In others, he displayed a startlingly cavalier attitude toward the consequences of his actions and left behind evidence that could easily have led to his undoing.[83]

Whatever benefits Muhammad derived from the liaisons, the costs were often high. First, the fear of public exposure and scrutiny made the relationships secretive and often inconvenient to maintain. Secondly, he found himself spending in just a few months thousands of dollars on child support, rent, furniture, and other expenses incidental to his extramarital activities. Of course, he accused a few women of attempting to make "a fool" of him by using their love children for extortion. Ultimately, the unwary membership of the Nation of Islam paid for Muhammad's affairs and the children he sired. He had no income independent of the Muslim movement and its adjunctive businesses.[84]

Thirdly, and perhaps most importantly, the relationships carried an emotional toll for everyone involved. Muhammad had to live a lie with Clara and could not acknowledge his flesh and blood in public. He bickered constantly with mistresses, who were sometimes bold enough to leave their children on his doorstep and to threaten to call his family members and inform them "just how he was." These women, who at one time believed in the Messenger of Allah, were exposed to a side of him that sought carnal knowledge of unmarried believers in contradiction to laws he imposed upon others. Moreover, they were tarnished by his forbidden advances, robbed of his spousal presence in their lives, and sentenced to isolation for his convenience. Their children, too, were negatively affected by the circumstances surrounding their births, growing up under the shadow of illegitimacy and its implications. Muhammad, however, desired that the children be raised together under one roof and disported himself with them during secret moments together. Yet, his position in the Nation of Islam and his life with Clara prohibited him from playing the fatherly role in their lives that they really deserved. The emotional ramifications of the various relationships that he engaged in must at times have seriously distracted him from managing the religious and administrative affairs of the Nation. The romances may have started off as infatuations that were psychologically liberating, but appear to have become mentally burdensome by the summer of 1962. The cumulative weight of the women, the babies, the secrecy, the illnesses, and the ideological and personal turmoil within the movement could only have been debilitating in the end.[85]

Muhammad's extramarital activities affirmed and contradicted many of his stated religious and moral beliefs regarding women. Over the past three decades, he had taught that black women were both the mothers of civilization and "man's field to produce his nation." They were extremely important as the nurturers and first teachers of the children who would eventually inherit the movement. Their modest attire and makeup denoted their respected place in the black race, and their avoidance of men other than their (monogamous) husbands and relatives symbolized their purity and integrity. Inherent in Muhammad's view of women were issues of power and control. Black women were to be discouraged, by coercion if necessary, from fraternizing with white men, behaving promiscuously, or committing adultery. He opposed birth control and abortion for religious reasons and because he felt that these lowered the African-American birthrate, playing into the hands of whites. Some of Muhammad's opinions of women were obviously sexist, such as his contention that men had "more powerful brains" than women since the former was "made to rule." Also, he felt that the husband necessarily "had to have something above and beyond the wife" to ensure her comfort and psychological well-being. In its totality, his official view of women and their place in the Nation of Islam emphasized the themes of beauty, purity, and domesticity, bound together by the vigilance and domination of men.[86]

It is not enough to say that Muhammad repeatedly risked his leadership, marriage, and credibility simply for the carnal pleasures of his relationships with young secretaries. The character of these affairs and their inconsistency with some of his stated beliefs suggest that deeper issues were involved. No one except Muhammad can ever be sure of his exact motivation(s); however, reasoned speculation does suggest a few possible influences. At least at the outset, the affairs acted as a release, however unethical, for the pressures that had accumulated in his life by 1960. In addition, they perhaps added adventure and excitement to a routine of policy-making, crisis management, and administrative minutiae. The conquests of young secretaries, who were so worshipful of him, arguably gave him a renewed sense of power and control in the face of mounting government and religious opposition to his program and leadership. His love children themselves sometimes mitigated his mental burdens, and one in particular made him laugh "till he almost cried" during Wallace's draft-evasion ordeal in October 1961.[87]

The affairs may have been a response to his fear of mortality. The numerous children whom he fathered, not to mention the young women themselves, likely helped him to forget about, or at least better cope with, his advancing age and declining health. Each relationship and the concomitant offspring may have confirmed his stamina and sexual virility. The affairs, and the attendant issues of age, paternalism, and authority, were clearly tied in with his burgeoning sense of self. They satisfied some critical need that had emerged at this important juncture in his life and leadership.

The affairs must also be viewed keeping the culture of the Chicago headquarters in mind. The casual attitude toward the materialism of the Muhammad family and other top officials may well explain Elijah's willingness to test the boundaries of self-indulgence. His position of Messenger of Allah and its attendant privileges and immunities offered incentives—and possible rationalizations—to behave in ways forbidden to the rank and file of the organization. After all, who in the movement had the authority to question his actions even if they did contradict the stated rules? Certainly, many of the people in his inner circle in Chicago would think twice before biting the hand that fed them. Thus, offending the sensibilities of selected family members, close advisers, and others who depended upon him for their sustenance probably was not a major concern. The only people whom he perhaps feared alienating were those who could call him a hypocrite and make the label stick or Muslims outside of the Chicago elite who could not cope with imagining Muhammad hypererotic. If, in fact, the leader's infidelities were tolerated within the moral ethos of Mosque No. 2, this would have had parallels in black organizations dedicated to the Civil Rights Movement. Regardless of his seeming hypocrisy, Muhammad was able to engage in intimate relations with a number of women over a period of years without losing the basic loyalty of those around him.[88]

Muhammad's efforts at discretion were fooling no one by 1962. His attraction to both his paramours and their children was sometimes too intimate to conceal. His son Wallace was aware of his relationships with various secretaries and had even witnessed Muhammad and the women together. For a while, Wallace tried to ignore the obvious and refused to deal with the implications of his father's behavior, but eventually conceded that "somewhere in my consciousness, I'm sure it was registering that that was his family." Since Wallace was living in Philadelphia—or in prison—when he became aware of the affairs, his siblings in Chicago could hardly have been able to avoid the evidence of their father's indiscretions. Actually, anyone, including ministers, reporters, and others, who visited Muhammad often enough might discern hints of what was going on. By early 1962, a number of the women might show up at any time to demand child support or to cause a scene.[89]

Malcolm X, Muhammad's chief lieutenant, had heard rumors as early as 1955, but had discounted them as baseless gossip. However, by 1962 when Muslims started defecting from Mosque No. 2 in droves due to tales of Muhammad's adultery, the minister sought reliable information. He talked with Muslims and nonbelievers around New York and Chicago who had heard the rumors. He mentioned the reports to Wallace, who verified them and suggested that Malcolm not confront Muhammad about the issue. Malcolm went so far as to visit three of the isolated secretaries, against Muslim rules, to hear it from their own mouths and to personally see the love children of the Messenger of Allah.[90]

More so than the typical believer, Malcolm was distraught over all that he had learned. He felt betrayed in the most cruel sense because he had trusted so deeply. For the past decade he had presented the Chicago leader to the world as "the Honorable Elijah Muhammad," the premier moral and religious leader of the black race. Now, he could envision headlines that would damn Muhammad and everyone in the Nation to ignominy. Malcolm could do little besides search the scriptures for precedents while toning down the moral themes in his speeches. To soften the impact of the reports on members of his own mosque, Malcolm stressed that the achievements of their messenger outweighed "his personal, human weaknesses." For clarification regarding the official Muslim position on the matter, he penned a letter to Muhammad, who replied that they would talk it out during their next meeting. The minister did ultimately confront his teacher months later about the rumors, but not before going through an emotional crisis. Until their fateful encounter in April 1963, Malcolm, convinced that his brain actually had been damaged by the news of the affairs, coped with the situation as best he could.[91]

Clara Muhammad may have found out about the extramarital activities of her husband as early as January 1960. By this time, Elijah was reportedly spending whole nights away from home and had grown distant toward his wife. At times she would break down while talking to confidants over the telephone, complaining that she was "sick of being treated like a dog" by her husband of over forty years. Over several months, some of the details of the affairs became clearer to her, including the existence of the love children. Tensions in the couple's home sometimes erupted into open strife, and by April 1962, Clara was seriously contemplating leaving Muhammad. In the end, she could not bring herself to take that step, though Elijah was making a mockery of their marriage. Too many obstacles prevented her from leading an independent life, not to mention the time and emotions she had invested in the relationship since 1919. She did, nonetheless, have to get away, at least for a while. Around June, she and son Herbert flew to Egypt for several weeks to visit her youngest son, Akbar, who was attending Al-Azhar University in Cairo. While away, she probably made her decision to stay with Elijah. In her absence, the FBI, which had meticulously chronicled Muhammad's romances, prepared anonymous letters to send to Clara and others containing explicit information about her husband and various women. Hoover hoped to drag the entire mess into public view so as to "expose Elijah Muhammad's lack of character to members of the NOI."[92]

By year's end, Muhammad's romantic escapades had decreased sharply in frequency and intensity. A new awareness of the real possibility of public exposure, along with a heart-to-heart talk with Clara following her return to the United States, probably influenced him. Despite his altered behavior, the damage was done, with too much evidence to deny what had occurred. Some followers adjusted to knowledge of the affairs and took for granted the rationalizations that Muhammad's damage controllers offered later. Others left the Nation forever, distressed by the marred image of the Messenger of Allah. Muhammad never gave a public accounting for his actions. No one expected him to. To have done so would have been an admission of guilt that could have destroyed the Nation or plunged it into factional war. Nor were such mea culpas his style. However, his intimacies with secretaries would come back to haunt him in ways that he could perhaps not imagine at the time. Indeed, the scandal, along with growing organizational strife and external pressures, portended ill for the future of the entire Nation.[93]

CHAPTER 8

RUMORS OF WAR

And there was war in heaven.
—Revelation 12:7

In 1963, for the first time in the history of Saviour's Day, Elijah Muhammad was not present to preside over the event or to give the keynote address. Well into the spring, he was still afflicted with bronchial asthma to a crippling degree and could not leave Phoenix even for the celebration of Fard Muhammad's birthday, the holiest day of the Nation of Islam. Having lost much weight due to his illness, by late March, after regaining a few pounds, Muhammad still weighed only 126—over twenty pounds under his usual weight of 150. Despite his suffering, Muhammad wanted his followers to know that they were in his thoughts, and through a telegram read at the Saviour's Day gathering, he expressed his sorrow over his absence: "Due to persistent illness, my grievous regret of not seeing you who are there.... The cold weather produced several setbacks." Concluding on an optimistic note, he assured his followers that "I am with you in spirit, hoping and praying to Almighty (God) Allah's richest blessing for success, peace, happiness to you, and the unity of 20 million black people." Though ailing fourteen hundred miles away, Muhammad continued to keep his hand on the pulse of the movement and knew exactly what words to use to inspire the believers gathered in Chicago.[1]

In his absence, Muhammad's family and close associates were well represented at the convention. Many of those who were officials sat on the coliseum stage behind the rostrum. Clara sat in her usual front-row seat next to other honored guests, and Malcolm X served as the master of ceremonies. Malcolm, in a vein similar to his teacher's, talked about a range of subjects including racial separation and the glory of Islam, but most notably called for blacks to support the NAACP, CORE, and other groups dedicated to the empowerment of African-Americans.

Despite the celebratory nature of the occasion, the tension between the New York minister and members of the Chicago elite was quite discernible, especially after Malcolm, due to time constraints, repeatedly turned down requests to allow Wallace to speak. A certain coolness on the part of audience members toward the Muhammad family was also evident, undoubtedly resulting from the financial and other indulgences that selected officials were rumored to be involved in. Following Malcolm's speech, a number of other guests, including Minister James Shabazz, Dr. Lonnie X Cross of the Atlanta mosque, John Ali, and columnist Tynetta Deanar, briefly addressed the crowd of four thousand, which was predominantly Muslim but included the typical complement of interested observers. After the first session of the convention ended sometime during the afternoon of Tuesday, February 26, an unprecedented second meeting convened around 8 P.M., attracting many of those who worked during the day and could not attend the earlier gathering.[2]

The 1963 Saviour's Day convention proved to be a microcosmic depiction of the Nation of Islam at the time. The central role of Malcolm X in the celebration, underscored by Muhammad's absence, reflected his growing prominence in the movement. Moreover, the escalating jealousy of him among top officials was quite clear to many onlookers, as was the dissatisfaction of rank-and-file Muslims, whose numbers were rather low for a Saviour's Day gathering. The atypical 8 P.M. meeting may have been arranged to solicit further donations for a movement that had become so fiscally motivated over the past decade. Of course, the audience was riddled with undercover agents, who were playing an increasingly destructive role in the organization. By this time in 1963, the difficult questions of succession, personal and ideological rivalries, and Muhammad's own fallibility could no longer be ignored. Only the wishful could not see the storm clouds gathering over the Nation, and Elijah Muhammad was not among them.

Even in faraway Phoenix, Muhammad had to deal with the spiraling crises, one of the most visible being the decline of Mosque No. 32. Muhammad himself had been instrumental in organizing a cell of Muslims in Phoenix and had devoted more time to nurturing the mosque there than in any other city, save the older Midwestern strongholds. Yet, despite his physical presence in Phoenix, Mosque No. 32 had collapsed to the point that by March only a third of the one hundred seats in the sanctuary were filled on any given occasion. Rumors regarding the extramarital activities of Muhammad had repulsed a number of Muslims who had formerly attended services in Phoenix. Harassment by local authorities may also have been responsible for diverting prospective followers away from the Nation. Regardless of the range of factors, Muhammad knew that the successes and failures of his ministers in Chicago and Phoenix reflected more directly on him than did the actions of laborers in other cities. Consequently, the dismissal of the Phoenix minister as incompetent was among his first major administrative decisions of the new year.[3]

To resolve another crisis, sometime in April Malcolm X flew to the Phoenix home of his mentor. Muhammad, in his usual paternal way, received his star pupil with an embrace and escorted him to the swimming pool, where they could talk freely, out of earshot of Clara and others. Malcolm had ostensibly come to the leader to get his response to the unflattering news that was circulating regarding his personal life, but actually ended up proposing a plan to cover up Muhammad's indiscretions by shrouding them in biblical allegories. The New York minister told the leader how he and Wallace had combed through the Bible and the Qur'an looking for precedents to explain the affairs and pregnancies. He suggested that, "if it became necessary," officials in the movement could be instructed to portray the leader's intimacies with secretaries as "the fulfillment of prophecy." According to Malcolm's recollection of the meeting, Muhammad went along with this scriptural characterization of the situation and complimented Malcolm for having "a good understanding of prophecy, and of spiritual things." Muhammad then elaborated further for his protégé and put the finishing touches on what would become an official rationalization for the liaisons. "I'm David," he reportedly told Malcolm. "When you read about how David took another man's wife, I'm that David. You read about Noah, who got drunk—that's me. You read about Lot, who went and laid up with his own daughters. I have to fulfill all of those things."[4]

This explanation was probably not wholly convincing to Malcolm, though he had broached it to Muhammad himself. In essence, the Messenger of Allah was saying that he had to repeat the errors and sins of ancient deliverers in order to carry out Allah's divine plan for the salvation of the so-called Negroes. This reasoning sounded too convenient and shallow and could only generate further questions among the more thoughtful believers. In fact, Malcolm saw the potential for an epidemic of apostasies if the reports were allowed to spread throughout the Nation, checked only by the thin prophetic justifications of Muhammad.

Back in New York, Malcolm subtly tried to prepare other East Coast Muslim leaders for the inevitable blow to their faith that would result from knowledge of the affairs. To his surprise, he found that several, including Louis X of Boston, already knew. Malcolm probably did not realize until later that his efforts to "inoculate" Muslims against news of Muhammad's transgressions provided his rivals in Chicago with even more weapons in the fight against his ascendancy in the movement. Almost overnight, a number of top officials began portraying the New York minister as the initiator of the rumors, despite the existence of women and babies who substantiated Muhammad's conduct more than anything Malcolm could have said. His actions to save the group from embarrassment would soon be depicted as treachery by his antagonists in the "royal family" and the Muslim hierarchy. Over the next several months, forces within and outside of the Muslim movement—inadvertently assisted by the minister himself—began laying the groundwork for the downfall of Malcolm X as the head of the second most powerful mosque in the Nation of Islam.[5]

Starting with the rationalization concocted by Malcolm, Wallace, and Muhammad, a few official reasons were, and still are, offered by Muslims to explain away the otherwise blatant violations of Muslim morality committed by Muhammad. None of the arguments are convincing even within the framework of the Nation's theology; however, two major excuses were invoked most often. The first, which cited prophecy for support, was actually contrary to earlier teachings of Muhammad regarding biblical leaders. As early as 1957, he had challenged the accuracy of the Bible for depicting Noah and Lot as sinners. "The Bible charges all of its great Prophets with evil," he wrote in *The Supreme Wisdom*. "It charges Noah and Lot with drunkenness and Lot [with] getting children by his daughter. What a poison book!" Prophecy is not mentioned as guiding the actions of these biblical personalities, nor does Muhammad claim for himself a right to emulate the indulgences that they are portrayed as participating in. Indeed, though he saw some elements of truth in the Bible, he generally denounced the tome as "the graveyard of my poor people" and "not quite as holy as they first thought it was."[6]

Not until Muhammad committed acts similar to those of Lot did the coloring of prophecy conveniently come into play. Over the next several years, the leader eventually claimed that he was destined to sample "a little of everything, evil and good." From his private liaisons to his bronchial asthma, everything about him that revealed weakness and fallibility was presented as part of a divine plan that stretched back to the days of Lot and Job. Whatever improprieties he engaged in supposedly had the divine sanction of Allah. For those who still found this rationalization hard to swallow, Muhammad and his proponents simply enjoined, "We just cannot be the judges of Divine Messengers. Obeying them is what Allah warns us to do." In the end, this argument becomes the nonargument that the Messenger of Allah can define (and redefine) the moral vision of the Nation for his own purposes.[7]

The second—and in recent years, most often cited—justification for Muhammad's numerous romances depicts all of the women with whom the leader was intimate as his wives. Ironically, this popular justification has less credible support than most other rationales. Typically, partisans of Muhammad's would point to the Qur'an, which allows Muslim men to have up to four wives if they can treat each one fairly. But the pattern of Muhammad's affairs veered sharply from Quranic definitions of matrimony, and many others. Firstly, the leader did not restrict himself to just four "wives." Within four to five years, he had relationships with at least eight women, including Clara, with no public marriage or divorce ceremonies as was customary among his followers. Secondly, his sexual relationships with female followers were secretive and informal. He did not live openly with them as he lived with Clara, nor did he claim them as wives in public. He refused to confirm he was the father of their babies well after the affairs had made the headlines of major newspapers. He even went so far as to allow one of his ministers, Isaiah Karriem, to describe two of the women as "prostitutes" in the pages of *Muhammad Speaks*.[8]

In addition to his public repudiation of the women and their children, Muhammad left no legal traces of even private nuptials. For example, the women did not take on the Muhammad surname until the last years of the leader's life, when a struggle over his estate seemed imminent. At least three never did make the change. Moreover, the courts had no knowledge of any wives of Muhammad besides Clara, and upon his passing, his death certificate described him as widowed with no surviving spouse. The leader himself always stressed that the Muslims were law-abiding and would ideally have been opposed to polygamy if not for the mere fact that it was illegal in the United States. Thus, as far as the evidence—or lack thereof—suggests, Clara Muhammad was the only woman whom Elijah ever married.

Nonetheless, the notion that these other women were wives of Muhammad died hard among some believers. As late as 1993, Louis Farrakhan, formerly Louis X, presented four of the former secretaries as "wives" of Muhammad before a Saviour's Day audience. The minister and the women talked of marriages to "the Honorable Elijah Muhammad" without a shred of corroborating evidence. The extraordinary efforts of a number of Muslims to maintain this fiction twenty years after Muhammad's death would probably have bemused him, for he would never have presented the women before any public gathering. Still, that they were presented as "wives" by Farrakhan suggests that some still have an interest in portraying the affairs as a legitimate, even divine, part of the mission of Elijah Muhammad.[9]

Prior to June 1964, when the extramarital activities of Muhammad became public knowledge, the leader was at a clear disadvantage in relation to those around him who knew about his indiscretions. Rationalizations aside, Malcolm X and other high-ranking Muslims knew that being privy to unflattering details about Muhammad's private life, given the specter of public exposure, might make the leader more amenable to their agendas. At the same time, they also knew that one risked life and limb by going to the press or overtly using the information for personal gain. The vulnerability that his actions had produced in his leadership and the reputation of the Nation in general must have distressed Muhammad as well as others. Especially at a time when the movement was confronting so many other problems, any traces of moral decadence in Chicago simply eroded the organization's defenses against outside criticism and internal divisions.

Muhammad, in an attempt to maintain stability in the Nation, allowed many things to go on as before. The Chicago elite became even wealthier and more influential, the rank and file continued to be pressed for tithes, and the movement kept clear of any entanglements in Birmingham and other civil rights battle grounds. Muhammad did, however, endeavor to end the tense standoff that existed between Malcolm X and the Muhammad family. In response to a deferential letter from the New York minister designed to downplay his towering stature in the media, Muhammad assured Malcolm that he would continue to work along with him despite efforts by others to divide the two men. During this time the minister's power in the movement was actually enhanced by Muhammad, no doubt as compensation for his continuing obedience and silence on private matters. In May 1963, Malcolm was appointed minister over the Washington, D.C., Muslims to reorganize the group. He replaced Lucius X, who had apparently failed to manage the affairs of Mosque No. 4 to Muhammad's liking. From Phoenix, the leader tried to both mediate the rivalries in the Nation of Islam and recast the image of his leadership in a way that would preclude an organizational crisis in the future.[10]

Though preoccupied with the problems of the insular world of the Nation of Islam, Muhammad kept abreast of developments in the Civil Rights Movement, often deriding them in favor of his own goals. Media-covered attacks on segregation, such as the sit-in movement, consistently drew the criticism of Muhammad, who characterized the protesters as "ignorant" individuals whose behavior had made him "ashamed of them." The admission of James Meredith, under armed escort, to the University of Mississippi in October 1962 drew similar fire from the Muslim leader, who believed that it was a "crazy idea" for a black man to attempt to "force himself into a school where it is 100 percent white." He felt that if the army was needed to secure the entry of African-Americans into places where they were unwanted, that was reason enough for them to avoid such places. Token desegregation of white schools and lunch counters, in his view, did not address the fundamental relationship between race and power in the United States. As long as whites controlled the schools and owned the restaurants, black demands for access amounted to nothing more than begging whites for the right to be tolerated in institutions and businesses that were not established by or for African-Americans.[11]

During the spring of 1963, most of Muhammad's criticisms of the Civil Rights Movement were directed at the Birmingham demonstrators, who had grabbed headlines around the country. In keeping with his earlier positions on civil rights protests, the leader denounced Dr. King as "a fool" in an interview that appeared in the April 30 edition of the *New York Herald Tribune*. He especially opposed the integrationist goals of the protests and compared King to a dog that "just waddles all around the door" in hope of gaining the favor of its master. Interestingly, Muhammad also questioned the restraint exhibited by protesters in the face of abusive law enforcement officials and police dogs. He asserted that the besieged demonstrators "would have been justified by God and the Divine law of self-defense" in retaliating against the attacks, although he had counseled Los Angeles Muslims to be nonviolent in a similar situation a year earlier. In addition, Muhammad found President Kennedy's dispatch of federal troops to Alabama detestable, since the administration had acted only after blacks began to respond violently to the assaults and bombings by whites. Overall, Muhammad and his followers had nothing but contempt for activists who "put their children on the firing line" before the rifles, clubs, and fire hoses of racist policemen and a seemingly indifferent government.[12]

In later writings and interviews, Muhammad was more ambivalent about his appraisal of King's leadership during the early 1960s. In a 1964 Phoenix interview, he conceded that the civil rights leader "has the desire to see his people dealt with according to justice," but denied that King was equipped to guide the struggles of black people since he had not been divinely appointed to do so. Generally, Muhammad believed that King was too infatuated with white people to be an effective African-American leader. To him, the Baptist minister could have made a much-needed statement of independence if he had refused the Nobel Peace Prize medal that was bestowed upon him in 1964, but kept the prize money for "his followers who really need financial help." King did, in fact, use the award to fund further civil rights activities. However, this gesture alone did not satisfy Muhammad, who retorted in *Message to the Blackman in America* "He won neither peace nor justice for his people." Insofar as King had not endorsed the program of the Nation of Islam and demanded "a place on this earth," Muhammad viewed him primarily as an ideological rival whose popularity was largely undeserved.[13]

However, Muhammad was, at times, quite complimentary toward other individuals and groups involved in the Civil Rights Movement. For instance, he had dinner with Edwin Berry, the executive director of the Chicago Urban League, during early 1962. When the NAACP closed ranks with the Muslims in response to the killing of Ronald Stokes, Muhammad expressed his gratitude to Roy Wilkins and others "for their love and sympathy shown for their people." In May 1963, the Muslims of Trenton, New Jersey, purchased their mosque—a defunct store—from S. Howard Woodson, the New Jersey president of the NAACP and ironically, a Baptist minister. When it suited his purposes, Muhammad could be gracious in his dealing with other black organizations. Of course, when he found it advantageous to highlight the distinctions between the Muslim program and the agendas of civil rights groups, his rhetoric was as venomous as anything that his critics could write or say.[14]

Perhaps no other civil rights figure received the consistent praise of Muhammad more than Harlem congressman Adam Clayton Powell Jr. During 1964–65, the Muslim leader began to acknowledge that blacks might be able to achieve some progress "through the judicious use of the ballot box." He avoided openly endorsing politicians or speaking specifically on the topic of politics, but did attach some importance to the national elections of 1964. Nonetheless, Muhammad did not consider blacks to be citizens of the United States. He was skeptical that whites would ever extend to blacks, in theory or in practice, the same rights that they exercised themselves. Ultimately, he viewed the territorial separation of the races as the true solution to the problems of black people. Yet, for the time being, he cautiously encouraged African-Americans to elect their own representatives and championed Adam Clayton Powell, an outspoken advocate of civil rights, as the "strongest politician of our kind." Muhammad believed that the best politicians would be Muslim in faith, but lauded Powell as a respectable alternative.[15]

On the rarest occasions, Muhammad even made favorable remarks about liberal whites, but always with reservations. At a time when young people of both races were sacrificing their lives in Mississippi and other places during the climax of the Civil Rights Movement, the Muslim leader recognized a need to "give the white people credit. They do the best they can in some instances." However, in his characteristic way, he was quick to remind blacks to remain wary of Caucasians, since "at the same time, I cannot say that they are angels." Gradually, Muhammad's views of whites would become a bit more moderate, but not before the 1970s when some of the gains of the Civil Rights Movement were more evident.[16]

Undoubtedly, some whites could not be compared to angels in any sense. Foremost among them were J. Edgar Hoover and his cronies in the FBI. Since at least early 1962, the director and his field agents had been trying to determine the best way to expose Elijah Muhammad and the Nation of Islam as frauds. Over three decades, the agency had amassed considerable information on the movement and had discovered enough credible evidence to embarrass a number of top officials. However, Hoover and his operatives faced a formidable dilemma. How could the questionable, behind-the-scenes activities of Muhammad and others be exposed to the public without bringing highly placed undercover agents under suspicion or revealing the wiretaps and other infringements of privacy by the FBI? To act too hastily might in the end lead to the curbing of Hoover's extraordinary influence in the American intelligence community. To fail to act at all could, in his view, give subversives opportunities. Backed implicitly by his superiors, the director chose to act in the summer of 1963.

With the cooperation of sympathetic editors, Hoover leaked an exposé on Fard Muhammad, based on both semifactual and false information, to a few newspapers. In the July 28 editions of the *Los Angeles Herald-Examiner* and the *Boston Record American*, the report, under the byline of Ed Montgomery, described the Nation of Islam's founder as "a white man masquerading as a Negro." His alleged criminal background was discussed as were his time in prison and his appearance in Detroit as a deliverer of the black race in the 1930s. The article cynically portrayed Fard Muhammad as a hustler who had fooled gullible Depression-stricken African-Americans into the ranks of his racket, "the black supremacy cult" better known as the Nation of Islam. It also characterized his early followers as "primitive" and inclined toward ritualistic homicide. To stress at least one claim of the report, the *Herald-Examiner* reprinted a large photo of Elijah Muhammad and his son Wallace with an imposing portrait of their beige-skinned savior in the background.[17]

Muhammad had no choice but to respond immediately to the accusations. In the August 16 edition of *Muhammad Speaks*, he challenged the claim of the *Herald-Examiner* that Fard Muhammad (referred to as "Wallace Dodd" in the Montgomery article) was white. He asserted that neither he nor his followers were "liars and worshippers of white devils." Muhammad went on to dispute other aspects of the physical description of "our Saviour" given in the report, such as the alleged height and weight of Fard Muhammad. He also denied that early Nation of Islam members had paid money to the founder for his services. Elijah did concede that some believers had given Fard Muhammad items such as topcoats, shirts, ties, and other gifts, but maintained that they had not been mulcted by the leader since "money was so scarce in those days that we just did not have any." The tenor of Muhammad's extremely defensive rebuttal was one of outrage and incredulity. Mainly for the consumption of his followers, the Muslim leader publicly offered to give one hundred thousand dollars to the *Herald-Examiner* if it could prove the truth of the report. While the FBI, the source of the information in the article, worked on tracking down Fard Muhammad to verify its claims, Elijah seriously contemplated suing the Los Angeles paper, instructing John Ali to seek an attorney who was "one hundred percent for us."[18]

The report of the *Herald-Examiner* gradually faded from public consciousness as had so many other malicious news stories on the Nation published during the past thirty years. Nothing became of the lawsuit proposed by Muhammad, and the FBI was never able to produce its Wallace Dodd. In subsequent months, however, law enforcement agencies became even bolder in their censuring of the Nation, convinced that religious freedoms were secondary to official concerns over subversion. To cite one example, Muhammad himself was interrupted by a ruckus provoked by two white policemen during an October lecture in Flint, Michigan. The officers had been dispatched by Edward Joseph, the city attorney, to observe the four thousand believers in attendance. Apparently, the Muslim leader did not object to their presence, but did demur when the policemen would not allow Fruit of Islam to disarm them. As his later comments attest, Muhammad was infuriated by the refusal of the officers to obey Muslim protocol. To avoid an ugly confrontation that might have turned violent, he abruptly ended the meeting only halfway through the scheduled agenda. After the gathering, he vowed to "never again permit white people to sit in our meeting—armed or unarmed." At least for a short while, he rigidly adhered to this pledge.[19]

The Flint incident, like the *Herald-Examiner* report, put Muhammad in a litigious mood. As soon as he returned to his winter estate in Phoenix, he contacted a lawyer for advice regarding a lawsuit. The attorney encouraged legal action and was given permission to file both a civil rights motion with the U.S. District Court and a breach-of-contract suit against the Michigan auditorium. Though he was scheduled to make only two other public appearances for the year, Muhammad intended to let state agencies know that unwarranted government interference in Muslim affairs would carry a price. However, lawsuits by disaffected black separatists would quickly become one of the last things that the law enforcement community would be concerned about, for nothing could have quite prepared the world for what was about to take place in Dallas, Texas.[20]

The early afternoon of Friday, November 22, 1963, was a typical day for Elijah Muhammad. For the past few days, he had been absorbed in administrative matters, such as designing a strategy for boosting the sales of *Muhammad Speaks,* and had spent hours on the telephone with laborers around the country. He was also working on scheduling a trip to South Africa during 1964. He was aware that the U.S. Passport Office might try to hinder his plans as it had done in 1959. Yet, he was prepared to secretly leave the country through Mexico or Canada if governmental stalling became a problem. He believed, somewhat naively, that he had made "enough friends in the world to go anywhere" undetected by "any of the enemies." The FBI, which was closely monitoring his proposed travel plans, awaited the opportunity to prove him wrong. When President Kennedy fell prey to an assassin in Dallas, the attention of Muhammad, and the rest of America, was torn away from all other matters.[21]

Muhammad, contrary to his public position on whites, grudgingly admired Kennedy. Of all the administrations that he had lived through, he probably respected the Kennedy White House more than any other. That is not, of course, to say that the Muslim leader was not critical of the president and his policies. He was aware that the Kennedy administration had allowed the FBI to intrude upon the affairs of the Nation. Moreover, he knew that white racists routinely went unpunished for committing atrocities against civil rights activists—crimes sometimes perpetrated in the presence of Justice Department officials. As far as he was concerned, every abuse inflicted upon blacks that did not result in presidential action was simply more evidence that Kennedy was not entirely sincere about extending freedom, justice, and equality to African-Americans. Muhammad did believe that Kennedy had distinguished himself from past executives by saying "something favorable for the so-called Negro." Years after the assassination, he would characterize Kennedy as a man "of value" who had been the victim of "thieves and robbers" as well as poor security arrangements. Muhammad felt that the killing was primarily caused by the putative racial liberalism of the president, but also believed—like his chief lieutenant—that the Dallas tragedy "shows to the world that the government of America and its people are actually given to such outlaw and violent action."[22]

Like many other blacks, Muhammad expressed shock over "the loss of our President." He saw nothing positive in the killing. Actually, he was deeply concerned that the Nation would be falsely implicated, especially since he and his spokesmen had been among the worst critics of Kennedy's New Frontier. To protect the movement from suspicion, he ordered Muslim ministers to refrain from commenting publicly on the murder. He even canceled a scheduled speaking engagement in New York City perhaps in part to avoid the temptation himself. In his place, he sent Malcolm X to address the crowd of seven hundred people who gathered at the Manhattan Center on December 1. The topic was "God's Judgment on White America," and the minister's prepared speech was as provocative as the title hinted. Malcolm was careful, however, not to cross the boundary that his teacher had set and made no direct references to Kennedy's death during his talk. But during the question-and-answer session, which Muhammad would likely have avoided, the situation became explosive.[23]

Malcolm X, John Ali, and other Muslims at the gathering knew that many people wanted to hear what the national minister of the Nation of Islam had to say about the killing. No one knew, except for perhaps Malcolm, how he would answer until he was queried by one of the reporters present. Malcolm, despite the directive of Muhammad, characterized the killing as a case of evildoers reaping the iniquities they had sown. To him, Kennedy had merely become a victim of the foul and violent status quo that his administration had tolerated, even nurtured, in Vietnam, the Congo, and Alabama. To some, it appeared that Malcolm was reveling in the assassination when he stated that "being an old farm boy myself, chickens coming home to roost never did make me sad; they've always made me glad." To others, the statement was more about authority, rivalry, and betrayal in the Muslim movement than about roosting chickens and dead presidents. The news of Malcolm's comments reached Chicago fast, probably first relayed by John Ali, who had not smiled when the crowd applauded and laughed deliriously over the statements of the minister. Shortly after the meeting ended, Malcolm was summoned to Chicago to give an accounting for his disobedience.[24]

Malcolm's remarks on the Kennedy murder were probably not a calculated act of defiance designed to challenge the supremacy of the Messenger of Allah in the Nation. His subsequent efforts to make amends for his actions belie such a notion, though his adversaries and detractors noted the clarity of Muhammad's instructions and the enormity of Malcolm's error. The minister said what he did about Kennedy for at least two major reasons. First, Malcolm, over the past several years, had cultivated a knack for making impolitic statements to attract media attention. Like many men of his stature, Malcolm loved the spotlight and the attendant benefits of being the main spokesman for a controversial organization. He genuinely relished his rather bugbearish image in the media. The press, of course, had developed the complementary knack for quoting, and misquoting, Malcolm for the pure shock value of some of his statements. He was good for newspaper sales and broadcast ratings. When asked about the president's assassination, he responded both out of a sense of obligation to the press (as well as to the assembled Muslims), which he believed should know his position on the matter, and out of an inability to shun the opportunity to make headlines. He certainly did not intend to provoke further government repression of the movement or to necessarily incite the wrath of Elijah Muhammad. But his comments do seem to reveal a lack of appreciation for the range of consequences that resulted.

Malcolm's statement must, secondly, be viewed within the continuum of his experiences within the Muslim movement. In past instances, he had said and done several things that were much more insensitive than his comments on Kennedy without arousing notable resistance from Muhammad. For example, when an airplane carrying 121 "leading citizens" from Georgia crashed on June 3, 1962, Malcolm publicly described the deaths as "a very beautiful thing" and hoped that other planes would fall on a daily basis as a sign of Allah's displeasure with whites. As noted earlier, Malcolm, against Muslim rules, had talked to at least three of the women who had been isolated by the father of their children, Elijah Muhammad. Similarly, as late as November 1963, the minister had described in his "Message to the Grassroots" speech the virtues of political violence in terms that surely did nothing toward reducing state suspicion of the movement as subversive and potentially violent. These few examples do not amount to a broad pattern of reckless behavior and commentary on Malcolm's part, but they do shed light on why the minister may have made his statements about Kennedy.[25]

Apparently, Malcolm did not believe that he would be penalized by Muhammad, at least not as severely as he actually was. In the past, the Muslim leader had tolerated, maybe even encouraged, off-color remarks by

Malcolm and had certainly allowed selected high-ranking officials to indulge in practices that were strictly prohibited among the rank and file. Malcolm may have believed that his knowledge of Muhammad's romantic affairs and other unpleasant reports coming out of Chicago made him somewhat immune to censure. Whatever the case, he was astonished to find that Muhammad had taken very seriously the implications of his "chickens" statement, especially since Kennedy had for years been "white devil" number one in Muslim circles.

The meeting on December 2 between Muhammad and Malcolm X was laden with tensions. It started with the usual embrace and persiflage, but was conspicuously missing the element of closeness that had always existed between the men. The Muslim chieftain first raised the Kennedy matter by asking if Malcolm had seen his comments on the assassination in the morning paper. The minister acknowledged that he had. "That was a very bad statement," Muhammad chided. "That was very ill-timed." He reminded Malcolm that Kennedy had been loved by blacks and whites alike, and to criticize him in death was inimical to the interests of the Muslims. "The president of the country is our president, too," Muhammad stated in an almost patriotic vein, though neither of the men had voted in the 1960 election. The Muslim leader intimated that he was less concerned about the substance of Malcolm's remarks than their timing. The country was still mourning the death of the president, and insensitive statements by the national spokesman of the movement reflected negatively "on Muslims in general." During their talk, Muhammad did not appear to be angry with Malcolm; he was more disappointed than anything else. Even when he meted out punishment, he spoke as if Malcolm had forced his hand and as if the penalty was mandated by some strict guideline—as opposed to being the arbitrary dictate that it actually was. "I'll have to silence you for the next ninety days—so that the Muslims everywhere can be disassociated from the blunder." The minister, crestfallen, agreed that the sentence was warranted and assured Muhammad that he was in "one hundred percent" submission.[26]

Following Malcolm's departure, national officials telegraphed every press organization in New York City about the silencing. Using *Muhammad Speaks,* they distanced themselves from Malcolm's comments on the assassination. They also contacted Mosque No. 7 and enhanced the authority of Captain Joseph X, the head of the Fruit of Islam. Muhammad intended for the punishment to be both public and humbling. The sentence itself, a prohibition against public speaking, was not particularly harsh considering that the Muslim leader could have penalized Malcolm according to his whims. However, the prominence of the offender and the swiftness of corrective action were meant to impress upon all believers that the center of power and authority was in Chicago, and not New York. No one was to be left with any false impressions regarding who actually led the Nation of Islam. Undoubtedly, the majority of Muslims agreed with the punishment; even Malcolm himself routinely instructed assistants on the occasional need to discipline those who exercise power over others. Yet, during the next four weeks, Muhammad's perception of the chastised minister would change to the extent that a complete restoration of Malcolm to his former position would become improbable.[27]

Over the next several days, Muhammad talked about the suspension regularly with a number of people. According to FBI transcripts of telephone conversations, his tone was subject to change depending on his audience. For example, he told one adviser that the action was required to keep him from looking "like a fool" and getting "into trouble," presumably with the HUAC or some other federal tribunal. On a few other occasions, Muhammad described the disciplining of Malcolm in parental terms, stating to one confidant that "papa" had been forced to whip his errant child, who would be punished even worse "if he sticks out his lip and starts popping off." When talking to the silenced minister himself, the Muslim leader was conciliatory, assuring him that only his public speaking privilege had been revoked. He even told Malcolm that the suspension was for "no definite time set," hinting that his sentence could be commuted before ninety days had passed.[28]

Sometime during mid-December, however, Muhammad became much more suspicious of Malcolm and decided against putting Mosque No. 7 back into his hands. Around this time, he warned one follower "to be very careful about this poison" that had allegedly been spread by Malcolm, whom he characterized as both disobedient and selfish. In another instance, Muhammad reportedly told one ambitious minister, who would have been "more than happy to" become the new head of Mosque No. 7, that he intended to purge the Nation of pro-Malcolm elements and strip the silenced national spokesman "of everything." As 1964 began, the Muslim leader privately expressed a hostility toward his erstwhile protégé that would have surprised people who believed that the two were inseparable. By the time they met again in early January, Muhammad had broadened the silencing to prohibit Malcolm from teaching in Mosque No. 7 and talking with the press.[29]

Several reasons were behind the change in Muhammad's attitude toward Malcolm and his place in the Nation. Over the last couple of years, the leader had been trying to mediate rivalries between the New York minister, members of the Muhammad family, and national officials. All were competing for the favor of the Messenger of Allah and for influence in the organization. Malcolm's comments regarding the Kennedy assassination and his subsequent silencing gave his adversaries an excellent opportunity to exploit the friction between Muhammad and the chastened minister. Raymond Sharrieff and John Ali, according to one report, encouraged Captain

Joseph X and assistant ministers in the New York mosque to openly criticize Malcolm, instructions that were contrary to the Muslim honor system. Others in Chicago were portraying the faux pas at the Manhattan Center as treachery that should have been more severely punished. The change in Muhammad's views on the silenced minister were definitely influenced by the anti-Malcolm biases of Sharrieff, Ali, and other officials who believed that the suspension afforded them a chance to rid the Nation of the New York minister and perhaps a number of his partisans. While Muhammad was ultimately responsible for the official policy of the movement toward Malcolm, his inner circle of advisers and family members were instrumental in creating paranoia regarding the loyalty of the minister, which accentuated any doubts that the Muslim leader already harbored.[30]

Additionally, Muhammad became more antagonistic toward Malcolm due to his own insecurity over the prominence of the minister. Malcolm's defiance, regardless of his intentions, *was* a challenge to the organizational hegemony of Muhammad, as was the stature of the minister in the media, on the East Coast, and in black America in general. To make that challenge more serious, Malcolm knew things about Muhammad that could potentially devastate the movement. It is difficult to overstate the delicacy of this situation. If anyone else told the world about financial abuses, sexual licentiousness, and corporal punishment in the Nation, he or she might be ignored by the media as simply one of thousands of detractors who sought to get their agenda into print. If the national spokesman revealed these things, his words would make headlines from Chicago to Mecca. Well into his suspension, Malcolm could still attract the attention of the press, which thrived on such revelations. Muhammad, of course, had no illusions about the irreparable damage that the minister could cause if he decided to go to the media with an inside story.

After some reflection, and coaxing from others, the Muslim leader concluded that Malcolm had become too powerful and knew too much to remain in his high office in the Nation. Muhammad also concluded that he might increase his own stock with his followers, the media, and others by humiliating Malcolm to the extent that no one would again question his supremacy in the Nation. Perhaps recalling the destructive schisms of the 1930s, Muhammad intended to use Malcolm's fall from grace as a vehicle to reclaim the prestige that he had lost to the New York minister. In so doing, he hoped to safeguard himself against any future challenges to his leadership, though he fully expected to lose many followers if Malcolm openly revolted. While some have argued that Muhammad and others had been waiting to oust Malcolm from the organization and that his "chickens" statement made that possible, it appears that Muhammad only began to consider this scenario a week after the suspension. Even then, it is unclear whether the Muslim leader meant to eventually force the minister out of the movement or to merely push him out of the spotlight for the time being. Unfortunately for Malcolm, he had played right into the hands of enemies who favored the former option and who happened to have Muhammad's ear. After such a public display of disregard for an important Muslim edict, it was just a question of Muhammad giving in to his insecurities and the pressures of top officials, which had both increased dramatically since December 1.[31]

Finally, the growing opposition of Muhammad toward Malcolm's return to power in Mosque No. 7 cannot be fully understood without an awareness of the role of the FBI in events. Few people were happier to see discord in the Nation than J. Edgar Hoover, and fewer were in a better position to encourage it than his agents. Many of the Nation's meetings and virtually all of its telephone calls between New York, Chicago, and Phoenix were monitored by operatives, who passed on their information to countersubversive strategists in the bureau. In fact, bureau agents were candid enough about their interest in the issue to approach the New York minister during his suspension to find out if he would join their ranks as an informant. While the FBI has been careful to cover its role in the drama by redacting declassified files, its previous efforts to expose Fard Muhammad, Elijah Muhammad, and others arguably implicate it in the heightening tensions between the Muslim leader and Malcolm X.[32]

The culpability of the FBI in the widening conflict between Muhammad and his national minister should not be exaggerated. As late as 1973, the bureau admittedly found the Nation to be the "most disciplined" black separatist group in the country, and its efforts to infiltrate the movement were greatly hindered by the believers' pronounced suspicions of whites and the American government. Also, Muhammad, Malcolm, and other officials had for years been aware of the bureau's meddling and had presumably learned how to guard themselves to some extent against its tactics. Regardless of Muslim defenses against infiltration, the FBI still made "efforts to disrupt and curb [the] growth" of the Nation, and it would be difficult to believe that the silencing of Malcolm X was not actively exploited by Hoover for these purposes.[33]

On January 2, Muhammad telephoned Malcolm to discuss various matters related to the suspension. The Muslim leader allowed two other persons, probably John Ali and Raymond Sharrieff, to listen in on the conversation, which made it more tense than it would otherwise have been. Muhammad opened with a short sermon about parables, linking his own ministry to the will of Allah. Afterward, he lectured Malcolm on issues that had soured his opinion of the minister since early December. Much of the conversation focused on Malcolm's broaching of the private affairs of Muhammad to a number of Muslim officials. The older man expressed both surprise and displeasure with the minister's attempts to prepare believers for a media frenzy and apparently could not fathom why Malcolm would have discussed such matters with others. Muhammad, correctly, compared the reports of his extramarital indiscretions to "fire" and "poison" that could ravage the Nation if they ever became public knowledge. Citing letters from other laborers, Muhammad charged Malcolm with maliciously not trying to "put out this fire." Hinting at his own worst fears, Muhammad assured Malcolm that he was his "property" and that, in the end, he "could not prove any of this." The suspended minister, seemingly shocked by the tirade of his mentor, was obsequious throughout the whole conversation, repeatedly apologizing for what he believed to be a misunderstanding between the two men.[34]

Besides his intimacies with secretaries, the Muslim leader explored other sensitive topics with Malcolm. The rivalries in the Nation were underscored by Muhammad as a real problem in the movement. He acknowledged that not all of his family members were "angels," and that the silenced minister could do little without making "this one and that one" jealous. He also revealed that a few relatives had even become adversarial toward him. In a moment of introspection, he conceded a need "to clear [myself] with Allah" and asserted that he was "just a man as the rest of them." Still, he spoke against Malcolm's being involved in "family matters" and, in a veiled reference to the minister's relationship with his son Wallace, intimated that Malcolm should keep his distance since he was an outsider. This latter statement must have hurt Malcolm, who had always viewed Muhammad as a second father. To hear "the messenger" refer to him as an outsider created distinctions that he was not used to. Nonetheless, the conversation centered less on how Malcolm felt than on how ungrateful he had allegedly been. Muhammad reminded the minister that he had reached out to him when he was still behind bars in Massachusetts. Moreover, he was careful to mention that he paid Malcolm one thousand dollars monthly for his work as head of Mosque No. 7. Sounding a more ominous note, Muhammad reiterated that the minister's suspension was open-ended, this time implying that it might last for more than ninety days. To this, Malcolm replied that he had, indeed, benefited from the older man's generosity and that he would continue to pray for forgiveness for his mistakes.[35]

Unknown to Malcolm, Muhammad had already decided to end his career as the national minister of the Nation of Islam before their talk on January 2. During the next week, this decision became clearer to everyone. On the day after the telephone discussion, the Muslim leader handed Mosque No. 7 over to Captain Joseph X, divesting Malcolm of all authority. He also sent a message to his son Wallace, who was then openly wavering in his faith, that said that the silenced minister had implicated him when called to account for his actions. Around this time, Chicago officials appear to have told New York Muslims that Malcolm had not only been suspended, but also indefinitely isolated—deprived of contact with other believers as the disgraced secretaries had been. On January 5, Muhammad put the final touches on the power play and promoted Minister James Shabazz of the Newark mosque to the top position in the Muslim citadel in Harlem. To make it all official, Muhammad summoned Malcolm to Phoenix for a private "hearing," which was contrary to the usual airing of accusations before a gathering of the believers. He also scheduled a separate informal trial for his orthodox-leaning son Wallace, who in turn demanded an opportunity to confront his foes. Muhammad, of course, wanted no part of a hearing in Philadelphia that would give his own son a chance to publicly embrace Sunni Islam. Nor did he plan to give his demoted national minister a Harlem platform from which to drag out the nasty business regarding the secretaries. "Malcolm X is not facing his accusers either," Muhammad told Wallace. "We're talking to you separately."[36]

The January 6 "trial" of Malcolm X in Phoenix does not appear to have been substantially different from the tongue-lashing that he had received four days earlier. In fact, it was only perfunctory. With John Ali and Raymond Sharrieff present, Muhammad grilled Malcolm about his alleged role in disseminating rumors regarding the leader's extramarital activities. According to Malcolm, the older man was irate over the reports he had received from Captain Joseph X, but apparently more concerned about the possible consequences of his own actions. "Go back and put out the fire you started," Muhammad ordered. By this time, he believed that since Malcolm was the primary source of the rumors, he was the person best able to convince Muslims that they were not true, despite the evidence to the contrary. He still felt that the conflagration, which had really grown beyond the control of any one person, could be extinguished with parables and lies. With his instructions, the suspended minister departed for Harlem, concluding what would be his last meeting with the Messenger of Allah.[37]

Following the departure of Malcolm X, the Muslim leader made plans to have Wallace flown to Phoenix. In Muhammad's mind, Malcolm and the Philadelphia minister were possibly in collusion. He felt that both intended to undermine him, but neither was prepared to acknowledge his treachery. Previously, Muhammad had secretly sought to divide the two men by creating tensions between them. Yet, he was not wholly successful, at least not to the extent that he felt comfortable meeting with them together. Though Wallace could not make his way to Arizona due to objections by his parole officer, Muhammad had probably already made up his mind to suspend the minister, especially after Malcolm had claimed that Wallace's loss of faith had adversely affected his own fervor. "I'm so disgusted now, I'm not particular now," the Muslim leader reportedly said about meeting with Wallace. He resolved to deal in due course with what he saw as his son's hypocrisy.[38]

In the weeks following the January 6 meeting, Muhammad became more callous toward Malcolm and his alleged perfidy. According to a number of sources, he began even to condone the use of violence to reduce the lingering influence in the Nation of the suspended minister. "Death-talk," as Malcolm called it, had been in the air since December, and attempts—orchestrated from Chicago—to stigmatize him as an ambitious traitor deserving of death were starting to have effects on some members of Mosque No. 7. For example, while assistant minister Henry X smeared Malcolm from the podium of the Harlem mosque, another believer, evidently under orders of superiors, made plans to attach a bomb to the ignition system of Malcolm's car. The ostracized minister was only saved from a fiery end by the conscience of his would-be executioner, who disclosed his mission at the last moment. Once informed of the indulgences and machinations of the Chicago leadership, that believer, according to Malcolm, "was stunned almost beyond belief." Of course, Muhammad was careful not to publicly implicate himself in any scheme designed to physically harm Malcolm, but he did over time become amenable to punishing him with more than words. The Muslim leader reportedly made veiled threats against the suspended minister during a January telephone conversation with a confidant, stating that the Muslims "had better close his eyes."[39]

Malcolm, not without reason, attributed this early effort to take his life to the will of Elijah Muhammad. Based on his knowledge of the inner operation of the Nation, he did not believe that such a tremendous undertaking—the killing of a top official by Fruit of Islam—could take place without the explicit consent of the Messenger of Allah. It was a sad realization for Malcolm; in his autobiography, he states that this "death-order was how, finally, I began to arrive at my psychological divorce from the Nation of Islam." To be sure, he did not break with the movement at this time or denounce his persecutors publicly. Nonetheless, he had certainly come to recognize his expendability in the wake of intense organizational rivalries and scandal. Responding to the pressures and perils of his isolation, Malcolm left New York City temporarily. As a guest of heavyweight contender Cassius Clay, he made a couple of trips to Miami to support the boxer in his title match against Sonny Liston on February 25. His absence from Harlem may have saved him from a mental breakdown and possibly a violent death.[40]

Predictably, nothing in the Saviour's Day address of Elijah Muhammad in 1964 hinted at the unsavory plotting that was taking place in Chicago and Harlem. The lecture dwelled mostly on the biblical Israel and how the devil had deprived blacks of the truth. As he had at other Saviour's Day gatherings, the Muslim leader recited the Nation's history of the universe and the significance of Fard Muhammad to the salvation of the Original People. He issued his trademark calls for racial separation and for self-help among African-Americans. No comments addressed the state of affairs within the Nation, despite the conspicuous absence of the isolated national minister. Moreover, the complex issues that had driven Muhammad to sanction, or at least acquiesce to, attempts to terminate the life of Malcolm X were not even alluded to. Yet, a murderous climate was definitely coming into being in certain quarters of the movement, and Muhammad was quite aware of this potentially tragic development.[41]

The pursuit of Malcolm X by some Muslims was not surprising given the history of the Fruit of Islam and its role as an internal police force in the Nation. As mentioned earlier, corporal punishment of Muslims for perceived wrongdoing was common in some mosques, even though some excesses probably took place without the approval of top officials. Likewise, the willingness of Muhammad to allow, perhaps even order, his followers to kill Malcolm X must also be viewed in light of the history of the movement. Having come so far from the schisms and infighting of the 1930s, the leader did not want to see Malcolm X, Wallace, or anyone else walk off with even a portion of the membership, financial resources, or message that had made his Nation the richest and longest-lived black separatist organization in history. Especially when government surveillance and suppression were so pronounced, public divisions among Muslims would surely give the FBI, orthodox Muslims, and others the opportunity needed to hack the movement to pieces. Knowing this, Muhammad acted to discourage dissent and secessions. He, more than anyone else, did not intend to stand by while outside forces, in conjunction with a splinter group under someone like Malcolm X, demolished thirty years of Nation-building.

Since his imprisonment, Muhammad had worked primarily to keep the Nation together under his autocratic control. He had learned well the lessons of past challenges and apostasies by high-level officials, such as Abdul Muhammad and his own brother Kalot Muhammad, and had no intention of fleeing from his rivals as he had done between 1935 and 1942. He was much too old for that now; anyway, he still had more than enough support in the movement and resources at his disposal to preclude a forced abdication. But to maintain his advantage, Muhammad, perhaps out of paranoia and his decades-old sense of persecution, came to believe that extreme measures were warranted when internecine challenges to his leadership emerged. If that meant eliminating the "hypocrites" (now defined as anyone he believed to be a threat to his supremacy in the Nation) through suspensions, isolations, or even death, he was willing to do what was necessary. In the case of Malcolm X, it was clear that by Saviour's Day 1964 Mosque No. 7 had not collapsed with James Shabazz at the helm and that the Nation in general had not experienced any noticeable loss of membership despite the downfall of the national minister. The apparent lack of repercussions regarding the suspension perhaps encouraged Muhammad to place the isolated spokesman into a permanent state of organizational limbo—far enough away from Muslim affairs to allow the spotlight to fall once again on "the messenger," but close enough at hand to control or even eliminate altogether. Hostile propaganda had already prepared the Muslims as a group for the indefinite isolation of Malcolm X. By late February, it was beginning to appear as if Muhammad could do anything he pleased to the suspended minister without risking a serious backlash among his followers.

An important, though ironic, factor that played a role in the willingness of Muhammad to jettison Malcolm X was the upset victory of Cassius Clay over the seasoned heavyweight boxing champion Sonny Liston. Born in Kentucky in 1942, Clay grew up in the segregated South, mindful of the limitations that racial discrimination placed on African-American youths. Through hard work and determination, he earned a place on the U.S. Olympic boxing team and won a gold medal at the 1960 games in Rome. However, upon his return to Kentucky, Clay found that little had changed. Racism still circumscribed the potential of blacks in almost all aspects of life, and even Olympic athletes were not immune to its effects. Exasperated, the boxer hurled his gold medal into the Ohio River one night—a symbolic protest against the country's hypocrisy. From that point on, he actively sought a vehicle through which to publicly express his disenchantment with American society.

The young fighter, raised Baptist, had been attracted to the Nation's message of black pride, self-sufficiency, and independence as early as 1961. On occasion, he had secretly attended mosque meetings in Atlanta to hear "the knowledge of self and others," which had attracted so many other young black males to the movement. Minister Jeremiah X reported Clay's interest to Chicago, but was denounced for becoming involved in sports, which was prohibited by the Muslim code of behavior. Muhammad reminded the minister that his work in the South should be tailored "to make converts, not to fool around with fighters." Ostensibly, Jeremiah X and others informally encouraged Clay to maintain ties with the mosque, regardless of his repudiation by Chicago. Malcolm X hobnobbed openly with the boxer during early 1964, bringing him even closer to a public embrace of the Nation. All the while, Muhammad remained staunch in his opposition to the courting of Clay by Muslims, even after he had secured a title bout with Sonny Liston. Like many others, the leader wrote Clay off as a loudmouthed icon of the sports world who would soon be quieted by his widely favored opponent. Muhammad simply saw nothing worthwhile coming out of the association of the Nation of Islam with a loser—albeit a Muslim loser. Predictably, *Muhammad Speaks* did not cover the fight at all.[42]

On February 26, the day after Clay stunningly defeated Liston in six rounds, Muhammad changed his tune altogether regarding both the new champion and the sport of boxing. "I'm so glad that Cassius Clay admits he's a Muslim," the leader crowed before followers gathered for Saviour's

Day. "He was able, by confessing that Allah was the God and by following Muhammad, to whip a much tougher man. . . . Clay has confidence in Allah, and in me as his only messenger." The sudden embrace was as opportunistic as it appeared. Notwithstanding the Muslim proscription against sports, Muhammad now viewed the twenty-two-year-old boxer as a timely addition to the Nation. In a number of ways, he was just that. Having publicly announced his affiliation with the movement, Clay brought instant, but not always favorable, press coverage to the program of Muhammad and his followers. He also brought to the coffers of the Nation tithes that would make the remittance of the average believer appear paltry. Most importantly, Clay was invaluable for recruitment. He revitalized the appeal of the movement among angry urban youth as well as college students, young professionals, and sports enthusiasts. His outspoken media image, though it perhaps bristled some conservative believers, was exactly the portrait of defiant black manhood that many African-Americans found refreshing, especially as the Civil Rights Movement headed toward a bloody Freedom Summer. In short, Clay was the perfect poster boy.[43]

To Muhammad, Clay was possibly that missing transitional link between a Nation mesmerized by Malcolm X and a new paradise in which the fallen minister played no role whatsoever. Conceivably, Clay could help the Muslim leader retain the loyalties of at least a significant portion of the young, activist element that would almost surely leave the movement if Malcolm revolted or was killed. The key would be to package the boxer in a way that accentuated his racial consciousness and loyalty to Muhammad, while minimizing his boxing career and ties to the white world of entertainment.

Easily enthralled by the Muslim message, Clay proved pliant in the hands of Elijah Muhammad and was amenable to playing whatever role in the movement was delegated to him. He freely allowed the Muslim leader to use him as a diversion for believers who were dismayed by some of the things that were going on within the Nation. Not unimportantly, the fighter seemed to have no qualms about publicly giving homage to his fatherly patron, "the Honorable Elijah Muhammad," or subjecting himself to the kind of media hostility that the Nation had lived with for years. The Muslim leader, aware of Clay's potential value to the movement, quickly bestowed an *X* upon him, welcomed him into his home, and set aside whole pages of *Muhammad Speaks* to shore up the fighter's reputation among the faithful. Within a month of his victory over Liston, the boxer was given an "original name," an honor that some lifelong believers had not received. So thorough was the embrace of Clay by Muhammad that it soon became difficult to imagine the boxer outside of the ranks of the Nation. On the front page of the April 10 edition of the group's newspaper appeared a large picture of the Muslim leader with his newest prize disciple, Muhammad Ali (literally, "one who is worthy of praise").[44]

Muhammad Ali had initially been Malcolm X's ace in the hole. The isolated minister had planned to use the boxer as leverage in his attempt to get reinstated in Mosque No. 7. However, by the time Ali became a valuable pawn in the game, that is, after the triumph over Liston, Muhammad had made his own overtures to the fighter, no less from his Saviour's Day podium. To Malcolm's dismay, Ali was immediately responsive and gave the Muslim leader direct access to him. At this point, Malcolm, who did not pressure the boxer to become loyal to him personally, no longer figured into the equation. Before long, Ali was in Chicago playing with the grandchildren of Muhammad, while the former national spokesman languished in purgatory hundreds of miles away. It all seemed so strange. Perhaps only after seeing a boxer, whom he had tutored in spiritual matters, groomed to stand at the right side of the Messenger of Allah did Malcolm finally realize that he could never wait, plead, or maneuver long enough to get back into the good graces of Elijah Muhammad. Actually, the Muslim leader seemed distracted when the ninety-day suspension expired on March 2. He perhaps had stopped counting back in December. No edicts were issued regarding the matter, and the Muslim world in general seemed unconcerned with the stalemate. Muhammad, confident that he held the upper hand, allowed Malcolm to fade further into the fog of isolation.[45]

Malcolm had probably made the decision to leave the Nation of Islam prior to March 2. He had suffered too many indignities over the past three months to stay. Death threats, private inquisitions, and protracted public humiliation had convinced him that further endurance would be no more than masochism. Malcolm, of course, knew that his response to the silencing had not been perfect. He had on occasion strayed too close to the spotlight of the media and bent the Muslim code of conduct, such as his dabbling in the sports world. Nonetheless, these infractions appeared minor to him compared to what some top officials were getting away with in Chicago. As it turned out, his small errors did not seem to make much difference in the long term. By late February, it was apparent that he could do nothing right in the eyes of Elijah Muhammad. Thus, he was finally left with two rather extreme options. He could either fully capitulate to the arbitrary penal power of his mentor and ignominiously exit into the recesses of oblivion, or he could secede from the Muslim movement and end months of demoralizing isolation. Malcolm ultimately chose to leave, concluding his seventeen-year membership in the Lost-Found Nation of Islam in the Wilderness of North America.

Malcolm, being the quintessential public man that he was, announced his break in well-reported stages. The declaration of independence was released to the press on March 8. Though not a diatribe against Muhammad or the Nation as a whole, it did allude to the jealousies that had made it difficult for him to stay in the movement. Malcolm was careful not to criticize his former teacher, lest he start a war in Harlem. He actually encouraged believers to "stay in the Nation of Islam under the spiritual guidance of the Honorable Elijah Muhammad." Reassuringly, he stated, "I remain a Muslim." However, he emphasized that his loyalties had, indeed, changed. "I have reached the conclusion . . . that I can best spread Mr. Muhammad's message by staying out of the Nation of Islam and continuing to work on my own among America's 22 million non-Muslim Negroes." The severance of ties was delicately done. One could easily have gotten the impression that Malcolm was still somehow under the wing of "the messenger," though outside of his grasp. At the time, this was probably what he wanted people to believe.[46]

The March 8 statement did, however, make a few things clear that undoubtedly confirmed that Malcolm was no longer with the Muslim movement. Firstly, he proposed to start a "black nationalist party" to engage in political activities and "social action against the oppressor." Next, he planned to align himself with civil rights organizations and "fight wherever Negroes ask for my help." Finally, he made himself again available for speaking engagements at institutions of higher learning, "because I find that most white students are more attuned to the times than their parents and realize that something is fundamentally wrong in this country."

None of these programmatic goals were entirely consistent with the teachings of Elijah Muhammad. They revealed the extent to which the break carried both personal and ideological undertones. Over the next few days, Malcolm made television appearances, granted interviews, and sent an open telegram to his former mentor to formalize his new autonomy. Again careful not to blame Muhammad for his departure, Malcolm's transmittal singled out "national officials there at the Chicago headquarters," in cahoots with Captain Joseph X, as being responsible for the conspiracy "to pressure me out of the Nation." He still credited the separatist program of "the messenger" as "the best solution" to the racial strife in the United States, but behind his conciliatory words was the implicit assertion that things could never go back to the way they were before. That is, he was no longer beholden to Elijah Muhammad.[47]

In Phoenix, Muhammad took the news of Malcolm's departure hard. He sincerely believed that the disgraced national minister would not leave the Nation even under the mortifying and dangerous conditions that surrounded him in Harlem. The loyalty and deference that Malcolm had shown him since the late 1940s simply left Muhammad unprepared for such an event. "I never dreamed this man would deviate from the Nation of Islam," the Muslim leader told reporters. "Every one of the Muslims admired him." This last statement was not exactly true, for there were those, arguably including Muhammad, who would have preferred to see Malcolm disconnected from the believers and their affairs far into the future. But the leader was "stunned" and "shocked" enough by the split to cry openly in the presence of newsmen.[48]

His tears expressed two emotions—paternal affection and a fear of rivalry—which had been a source of inner conflict since December. Muhammad, at least until the first days of the suspension, loved Malcolm as a son. Even in the face of his family's opposition, he had embraced him and given him authority in the movement that was second only to his own. Malcolm's break from the Nation certainly had familial undertones for the Muslim leader, who probably felt as if his own flesh and blood had deserted him. Additionally, the rift also carried with it serious implications for the future of the Muslim movement. Muhammad was keenly aware of the monumental challenge that Malcolm could pose to the organization if he left. While still within the Nation, his public stature had overshadowed that of his mentor, heightening rivalries and hostility among top officials. The Muslim leader had reportedly whispered to others, including a mistress, that Malcolm might possibly leave him one day and thus was "dangerous." When that day finally arrived, Muhammad was forced to face the very situation that he had hoped would never come into being—a loss of control over his best minister and open competition for recruits.[49]

Initially, Muhammad tried to head off the crisis with diplomacy. He evidently believed that Malcolm could be coaxed back into the Muslim fold through a conciliatory gesture. He contacted Malcolm's brother, Minister Philbert X of the Lansing, Michigan, mosque and instructed him to talk things over with his younger sibling. During their discussion, Malcolm assured Philbert that he had not lost faith in Islam, but remained adamant in his decision to leave the Nation. From this point on, any chances of an amicable resolution of the brewing conflict became progressively more remote. Rebuffed through his surrogate, Philbert, Muhammad ordered the leadership of Mosque No. 7 to pen a letter to Malcolm demanding that he vacate his Nation-owned home and return other property that belonged to the movement. The correspondence was polite in tone, but Muhammad had clearly taken offense at Malcolm's departure and intended to sever all ties with him. The shock and displeasure that the Muslim leader had experienced from the break had quickly turned into vindictiveness aimed at discrediting the former minister. Initially, Muhammad seemed sure that Malcolm would eventually come back sniveling for forgiveness, but until then, he intended to use him as an object lesson to others who were considering apostasy.[50]

In his escalating duel with Malcolm X, Muhammad had certain preliminary advantages that his erstwhile protégé did not have. For example, he had the personnel and financial backing of one of the best-organized black groups in the history of the United States. His authority over the Muslim movement reached from Los Angeles to Harlem, and dozens of local cadres of Fruit of Islam awaited eagerly to do his bidding. Also, Muhammad had a platform within the black community that would allow him to define at least some of the terms by which his miniwar with Malcolm would be played out. In particular, *Muhammad Speaks*, with an audience well into the tens of thousands, would be a most useful tool for the vilification of Malcolm X and the incitement of Muslim hostility against the former favorite son of the movement. Insofar as Muhammad's words were divine utterances to the believers, the anti-Malcolm editorials that would appear in the newspaper throughout 1964—with the approval of Muhammad—probably turned more Muslims against the former minister than anything else.

The national perception of Malcolm and the Muslim movement in general benefited Muhammad greatly. Over the years, Malcolm had made too many enemies outside of the Nation to secure immediate sanctuary elsewhere. Like Muhammad, Malcolm was a bête noire with civil rights leaders and philosophically isolated from orthodox Muslims. Needless to say, white America probably paid little attention to the conflict aside from the drama value that the press attached to it. Government agencies, such as the FBI and the New York Police Department, that were in the best position to check the open hatred and violence that would eventually characterize Malcolm-Nation relations watched from the sidelines. If anything, these forces silently delighted in the increasing destructiveness of the rivalry. Malcolm was, in effect, out of his element after leaving the movement and forced into the awkward position of building a power base from scratch, without the personnel and funding necessary for instant results. As long as no one really cared about what happened to the former national minister, Muhammad was free to use an assortment of weapons in battling him, from threatening editorials to open violence against his supporters. In this setting of indifference, he carefully primed his followers for a jihad against Malcolm, who was fast becoming known in Muslim circles as "the chief hypocrite."[51]

Though at a relative disadvantage, Malcolm was not without assets in his struggle for survival and relevance outside of Muhammad's Nation. According to one Mosque No. 7 insider, he had taken as many as one-third of the three thousand New York City Muslims with him when he declared independence. In contrast to Elijah Muhammad, Malcolm was a younger man with a popular image as a defiant, uncompromising black nationalist who was not afraid to remind the white world of everything it had done wrong from time immemorial. Even when he was given to rhetorical excess, he exuded charisma and power. Elijah Muhammad had made him, but he was not responsible for all that Malcolm had become.[52]

The politicized intelligence of the former minister had breached the outer boundaries of Muhammad's racial theology sometime before. Malcolm's trenchant analyses of colonialism, third-world nationalisms, and the American political process in his "Ballot or the Bullet" speeches should have come as no surprise to anyone who had followed his ideological development over the past decade. His endorsement of voting, boycotts, rent strikes, and other traditional tactics of African-American civil rights activists should also have caught few off guard given his tutelage under a master of pragmatism, Elijah Muhammad. In modifying his philosophy, Malcolm sought to tap into a constituency within the black community that had become disenchanted with mainstream advocacy groups and nonviolence, but remained too American to write off the country totally as the Nation had done. To gain the attention of this group, Malcolm pushed into the background the less flattering elements of his "Black Muslim" past and brought to the foreground a program that both emphasized his fundamental genius for verbalizing the plight of blacks and posed realistic solutions to their problems. With only marginal success, Malcolm worked on these formidable tasks for what was left of his life.[53]

After breaking away from the Nation, Malcolm searched for credibility and a place within the black struggle that would fracture the apolitical mold that Elijah Muhammad had attempted to confine him to, yet would not compromise basic principles of his Muslim past that he still believed in, beliefs such as racial pride, economic nationalism, and self-defense. With little hesitation, Malcolm extended an open hand to Dr. King, the NAACP, and others whom he had bitterly criticized for years. He had not now embraced all of the strategies and agendas of integrationists, but he saw a niche for himself and other militants within the broader civil (and human) rights struggle. He genuinely believed that he had something to contribute to the struggles of black people that would broaden, even internationalize, their search for solutions.

Malcolm did not, in fact, come up with any new answers after departing from the Nation, though his philosophy became more flexible. His "new program" consisted simply of old questions (regarding the role of violence and revolution, the connection between African-Americans and third-world anticolonialism, and the applicability of socialist economics) that were stifled by Elijah Muhammad and traditional tactics adopted from civil rights organizations (such as bloc voting, self-help, and cooperation with sympathetic whites). The most novel part of Malcolm's program was his attempt to build an ideological bridge that would connect him to the heart of the Civil Rights Movement without separating him from his black nationalist roots and internationalist agenda. He hoped that his Organization of Afro-American Unity, organized in June of 1964, might serve as that bridge. However, subsequent events would preclude the group from emerging beyond the paper it was written on.[54]

In his attempt to reconstruct himself as a credible leader outside of the Nation of Islam, Malcolm tried to break with his religious past as well as his history of nonactivism. In mid-April, as *Muhammad Speaks* was attacking him at every turn, Malcolm embarked on a tour of the Middle East that began with a hajj to Mecca. In open letters to the press and later statements, Malcolm portrayed the pilgrimage as a sort of conversion experience in which he discovered that true al-Islam was a universalist doctrine that emphasized the brotherhood of man over the parochialism of race. The trip to the holy city, despite his efforts to make it appear otherwise, was actually a calculated move in both his struggle for legitimacy and the war against Elijah Muhammad.

Probably as early as his first trip to the Middle East in 1959, Malcolm had questioned the theological basis of the Nation of Islam. Encounters with orthodox Muslims then and upon his return to America surely did not leave him unaffected philosophically. At times he even openly contradicted the racial chauvinism of Elijah Muhammad, but in ways that did not result in chastisement from his mentor. "Many people in this country think we are against the white man because he is white," he once stated in May 1963 during a radio interview. "No, as a Muslim we don't look at the color of a man's skin; we are against the white man because of what he has done to the black man." In other instances as well, Malcolm hinted that he was preaching, and altering, doctrines that he did not wholly believe in. Yet as he confessed later, "Many of my own views that I had from personal experience I kept to myself." To stay in good standing with the Messenger of Allah, he knew that this was his only option.[55]

The hajj gave Malcolm an out. It saved him from appearing opportunistic, pretending to believe in something simply to satisfy peers, attract media attention, or maintain a steady income. By portraying the journey as a spiritual awakening, he laid the burden of his Nation of Islam past at the feet of Elijah Muhammad. According to his story, he had been fooled by the Muslim leader for almost two decades, being gullible and acting in good faith. But having seen "the *color-blindness* of the Muslim world's human society," Malcolm could now discard the racial Islam that he had promulgated in the past, especially since "I have always kept an open mind ... [in my] intelligent search for truth." It was a self-serving account, and those who were closest to him knew that. Nonetheless, for those who had traditionally ignored him as a racist bent on ushering in the Armageddon, the liberalization of his views was a welcome change. Conceivably, he could now have the best of both worlds: a new image untainted by the "black supremacy" label that the press and others had stuck on the Muslim movement and a ready-made constituency of black nationalists and disgruntled civil rights activists.[56]

While Malcolm was busy re-creating his public image, Elijah Muhammad, who saw the conflict as nothing short of a struggle for survival, and his followers were digging trenches for the propaganda war. From the start, the Muslim leader knew that an open conflict with Malcolm would be grueling and potentially embarrassing. Nevertheless, he was determined to extricate his followers from the sway of the former minister in order to protect his own power base within the movement. In the opening volley of recriminations, Muhammad had three carefully selected ministers spearhead the attack against Malcolm. In the April 10 edition of *Muhammad Speaks*, Philbert X compared his brother to Judas and other historical figures "who betrayed the relationship between them and their leaders." He accused Malcolm of being motivated by selfishness and a hunger for media attention. Philbert even suggested that the former minister had been stricken with a mental illness similar to that which had afflicted their mother. The editorial contained several references to Malcolm as a hypocrite, a buzzword designed to spark animosity among the believers. The most ominous part of the message, however, was a prediction of things to come. "I see where the reckless efforts of my brother Malcolm will cause many of our unsuspecting people who listen and follow him unnecessary loss of blood and life." Ironically, Malcolm's own brother played an instrumental role in creating the atmosphere that would lead to a number of tragedies over the next several months.[57]

Besides Philbert, others also defamed Malcolm in *Muhammad Speaks*. James Shabazz, the Chicago minister, denounced him as coveting "worldly praise" and the messengership of his teacher. He, like Philbert, expressed pity "for the poor fools who refuse to trust the God of the Honorable Elijah Muhammad, and choose to follow Malcolm for self-victory." A feature of his diatribe that would become standard in Muslim writings against alleged hypocrites was an allusion to retribution and death. "I am sure that Malcolm has not believed the Honorable Elijah Muhammad to be the Messenger of Allah," Shabazz insisted. "If he did, he would be afraid for his future."

In May and June issues of the Muslim newspaper, these dark notes were again sounded by Louis X in a two-part editorial. Claiming to have been a close associate of Malcolm's, the Boston minister portrayed the former national spokesman as an innate hypocrite who had used the Kennedy assassination as an opportunity "to bring discredit and needlessly endanger and expose our followers." Louis went on to state that he was shocked by the "almost unbelievable treachery and defection" of his former mentor, whose recent hajj did nothing toward rectifying his "monumental blunder." At the end of his tirade, the Boston minister concluded that Malcolm was now concerned about being physically harmed by Muslims because of "his evil and vicious attack on the Messenger and his family." Louis said nothing, of course, that might have abated these fears he attributed to Malcolm.[58]

At the helm of the Nation, Muhammad, with the help of his ministers, set the tone of the increasingly bitter confrontation with Malcolm. Before his followers and the general public, he tried to appear above the dirty business of smearing the reputation of a former minister. None of the early editorials about Malcolm were in his name, though he certainly endorsed all of them before they went into print. In private, however, he was thoroughly engrossed in the campaign to make Malcolm the most detested black man since the mythological Yacub. For instance, during a telephone conversation with a Boston follower in March, Muhammad referred to his former protégé as "that no-good long-legged Malcolm," who deserved to be handled as "Moses and others did their bad ones." Talking in parental tones, he stressed how he had loved and cared for the former minister, but had been taken advantage of because of his generosity. "With these hypocrites," he warned, "when you find them, cut their heads off." For those who understood the authority behind Muhammad's messengership in the Nation, such a comment was more of a directive than an observation. Most Muslims would not have had to be told twice what this statement meant. A cartoon of the deed was included in the April 10 edition of *Muhammad Speaks*. On the same page with the editorials of Philbert X and James Shabazz was a sketch entitled "On My Own," showing Malcolm's severed head chattering excuses for his departure as it bounced toward a heap of skulls labeled "Judas, Brutus, Benedict Arnold, Malcolm 'Little Red.'"[59]

Following the macabre propaganda war of the spring, the conflict nearly became violent during the summer of 1964. On the night of June 16, six armed partisans of Malcolm X were arrested after a confrontation with thirty-five Fruit of Islam. While no shots were fired, Malcolm was shaken enough by the event to temporarily go into hiding. The situation became more acrimonious toward the end of the month. Perhaps coincidentally, Elijah Muhammad had planned to speak at the 369th Armory in New York City on June 28, the same day that Malcolm had scheduled the founding meeting of his Organization of Afro-American Unity in Harlem. Perhaps, it was no coincidence. Each of the men, aware of the other's schedule, took pains to show that he could bring out a crowd. Neither was disappointed.[60]

Muhammad's seventy-five-minute harangue on racial separation was attended by over six thousand people. During his talk, he made no direct reference to his former national minister, but did allude to him. "Some person wants to be what I am," the Muslim leader told the audience, "but that person is not able to be what I am because he has not been revealed what has been told to me." Primarily, the meeting was a demonstration to the faithful that Muhammad was still their master and that he continued to command a substantial following in New York, Malcolm's home turf. In a brutal illustration of his authority, Muslim guards beat two alleged followers of Malcolm X who had attempted to attend the gathering. After his speech, Muhammad left for the airport under a heavy escort of Muslims and law enforcement officers. He had no illusions about the danger that he had placed himself in by coming to Harlem. Yet, in his effort to reduce the influence of Malcolm X in his own stronghold, the Muslim leader apparently felt that the appearance was worth the risk.[61]

Before Muhammad's visit to New York on June 28, Malcolm had been trying to deliver a knockout blow to the Muslim leader's credibility among believers and non-Muslims alike. His trump card—the reports of Muhammad's numerous affairs and illegitimate children—had up to that point been too sensitive for the press to print, at least without solid proof. In early July, Malcolm convinced two of the women, Evelyn Williams and Lucille Rosary, to file paternity suits in a Los Angeles court against Muhammad, which would enable reporters to make the disclosures front-page news. The coverage of the *Amsterdam News*, a weekly African-American newspaper based in New York, was probably the most thorough and revealing. According to a July 11 article, Williams was charging Muhammad with siring her four-year-old daughter, Eva Marie, who was born in Lynbrook, California, but was conceived during her employment as a secretary for the Muslim leader. Rosary told a similar story, charging the leader with fathering her three daughters: four-year-old Saudi, two-year-old Lisha, and a baby girl born in early July. Page two of the newspaper displayed a picture of the two women with three of the love children; Ms. Rosary, in sunglasses and a housedress, was still bloated with her third child when the photo was taken.[62]

The story contained official denials by Raymond Sharrieff and John Ali, who stated that their leader "would not dignify the charges by answering them." Aware that Malcolm X had encouraged the women, the Muslim officials insinuated that the former minister may have fathered the children himself, though Mosque No. 2 was currently providing support for the families. Along with paternity suits, the women took the precaution of submitting affidavits in Superior Court claiming that "fanatic followers" of Muhammad might try to take their lives in response to their charges. Perhaps better than anyone else, they knew that by giving their stories to the press they had entered a war zone that would likely produce casualties.[63]

In addition to the news stories generated by Williams and Rosary, Malcolm X disclosed information about the extramarital activities of Muhammad to every reporter and confidant who would listen. His account seemed to contain a different shocking element each time he retold it. In an appearance on the Jerry Williams radio show in early June, he described infidelities of the Muslim leader that extended back to 1955. While he was in Egypt during August, he told *The Egyptian Gazette* that Muhammad had confided in him that he could have nine wives. In the most disturbing story, Malcolm related to a female confidant by phone that his erstwhile messenger had seduced a relative and then accused her of adultery. The reports of marital indiscretions and bastardy, undeniable at this point in their basic veracity, were bombshells that left many paralyzed in disbelief.[64]

Most Muslims viewed the reports as a vicious attempt by Malcolm X to impugn the character of their sacred leader. Perhaps to his surprise, when he pulled back the curtain in mid-1964, Malcolm had been so demonized by Muslim spokesmen and *Muhammad Speaks* that many of the believers saw his actions as a ploy to divert attention from his own apostasy, or "hypocrisy," and unwillingness to accept the chastisement of Muhammad. Most of the believers who could not reconcile themselves with the news of the infidelities had left after the first rumors surfaced in 1962. Probably very few departed due to the public revelations of Williams, Rosary, or Malcolm X. Those who remained in the movement were not necessarily die-hard believers in Muhammad's putative sanctity or Malcolm's alleged treachery. Indeed, some continued to revere Malcolm X but, for whatever reason, could not follow him. Ultimately, many of the faithful stayed because they saw redeeming qualities in the Nation and their leader. Despite his frailties, they simply could not bring themselves to abandon the man they had credited with saving them from a "blind, deaf, and dumb" existence in the grave.[65]

Malcolm had pushed for public exposure of the affairs for a couple of reasons. First, he desired to discredit Muhammad to lure disaffected Muslims into his own organization. Since he had baptized himself in the waters of Sunni Islam and fashioned a more activist black nationalist program, he felt that a heavy dose of anti-Nation propaganda might pay off for him. Second, and more important, he wanted to stay alive. He probably felt that by seeking the spotlight of the media, he would be somewhat protected from Fruit of Islam, who were becoming increasingly persistent, and physical, in their harassment of him and his followers. If that meant telling the press, the police, and the public that Muslims were threatening his life, that Elijah Muhammad was immoral, or that he himself was a changed man philosophically, he was prepared to do so. In his battle against his former teacher, Malcolm used the only weapons available to him. He had no *Muhammad Speaks*, Fruit of Islam, or national organizational base to support his assault upon the ramparts of the Messenger of Allah. He was more or less left with exposing the scandals and unorthodox religious teachings of the Muslim movement. There was plenty to talk about, from Muhammad's secret nights with inamoratas to gross financial irregularities; but in the end, these reports would run their course and the media would lose interest. Until then, Malcolm turned his oratorical barrels toward the Nation and opened fire, hoping that he would not run out of ammunition before he perfected a more permanent plan for survival.[66]

Though he had tried to appear above the Muslim war against Malcolm X, Muhammad found it necessary to descend into the fray and respond directly to the charges. "I will not acknowledge the hypocrites' charges against me," he announced in the September 11 edition of *Muhammad*

Speaks. As was common in such editorials, he hinted at the infliction of retribution and suffering upon his opponents, who would find "that they might be playing with fire and a very hot fire at that." The public stance of Muhammad regarding Malcolm X tended to be more moderate than the statements of some of his ministers. He had even written in July, when reports of his extramarital affairs were selling thousands of newspapers, that "hypocrites" were not to be murdered, though the "Messenger is warned . . . to be hard against them." In private conversations, however, Muhammad was as malevolent as any of his followers who hated "the chief hypocrite." According to one adviser of Malcolm X who had access to the Nation's inner circle, orders to have him murdered were issued from Chicago around the time that reporters were printing the Williams-Rosary stories.[67]

Whether Muhammad actually handed down an edict calling for the assassination of Malcolm X can never be confirmed. Still, he had clearly sanctioned the pursuit of the former minister and his followers by his network of Fruit of Islam and had allowed his representatives to say and write things that were no more than thinly veiled death threats. While he sought to lead the public to believe otherwise, Muhammad felt the sting of Malcolm's words and hoped to eventually be able to silence him. According to Malcolm, Elijah Jr. told New York Muslims in June that their former minister should already have been killed and his tongue removed and mailed to Chicago. These sentiments were becoming more common in some quarters of the Nation. In a number of ways and through various mediums, Muhammad had encouraged them.[68]

Just when Muhammad was ordering Muslims to close ranks against Malcolm X, another front opened in his ongoing conflict with "the hypocrites." His son Wallace, who had been a source of grief since his imprisonment and embrace of Sunni Islam in 1961, began to publicly oppose the teachings of his father during the summer of 1964. In a letter, Wallace informed his father that "I find your helpers, your followers and the family withering like dying flowers," devoid of the righteousness that had at one time been an integral part of Muhammad's leadership. Unlike many of his relatives and other Muslims, Wallace could no longer excuse the "explosive situation" that his father's philandering had created or the corruption at the headquarters that had been financed by the "excessive contributions" of hardworking believers. Beyond personally criticizing his father, Wallace also attempted to influence his siblings to oppose unethical conduct within the leadership of the movement. Few of them sided with Wallace; actually, he was derided for not resisting the devil white man. But even without their support, the Philadelphia minister was determined to be the voice of reform—a choice that would put him into direct conflict with the Messenger of Allah.[69]

Wallace, of course, knew that his revolt was a dangerous endeavor. At a moment's notice, "punch-your-teeth-out" squads, as he called the Fruit of Islam, could be called out to deal with his dissent as they were currently handling Malcolm X and his partisans. Nonetheless, Wallace's disapproval of the teachings and leadership of his father had become irrepressible, culminating out of years of personal agony under the strict patriarchal rule of Muhammad. In the past, the Muslim leader had never been close to his children. Wallace was hardly two years old when his father fled from Chicago in 1935. His incarceration during the 1940s separated him from his family, and even when he returned from FCI Milan, he spent little time with his children. His attention had been drawn to the world of business and the revitalization of the Nation of Islam. When Muhammad *was* around, he was the sternest of disciplinarians. He often embarrassed his children at temple meetings when they misbehaved and rarely showed paternal affection for even his grandchildren. "He was building a nation and people were the material you threw in," Wallace said in a 1980 interview. "Their sentiments, their hearts, their naked souls, were only the nails and the mortar to build the building." Thus, beyond just repudiating his father's religious views and organizational leadership, Wallace was in revolt against the paternal dominance and neglect that Muhammad had imposed upon him. Though it appeared that he would have to go it alone, save for the allegiance of his nephew Hassan Sharrieff, who routinely ridiculed his grandfather in private, Wallace concluded that joining the ranks of "the hypocrites" was the best way to address the creeping decadence of the Nation of Islam.[70]

Harassment started immediately. Following excommunication by his father, Wallace claimed that he was stalked by Fruit of Islam, who threatened to kill him on several occasions. Hassan, whose close relationship with his uncle led to his suspension, was also a victim of a mini-jihad. Muhammad terminated his grandson's stipend and attempted to repossess his home. Aroused Muslim crusaders menaced the house from cars parked along the curb and occasionally lobbed bricks through its windows. Tagged as hypocrites of the worst sort, Wallace and Hassan were subjected to the brunt of Muhammad's vengeance. By early July, according to Wallace and Hassan, their lives—or at least physical health—were in jeopardy. Like Malcolm X, Wallace came to believe that staying alive meant staying in the public consciousness. Unless he could gain the sympathy of the non-Muslim world, he felt that he would either be killed off quietly or forced to live in fear for the rest of his days.[71]

In desperation, Wallace went to the local press and told everything. Nothing was too sensitive to disclose. In an exposé for *The Chicago Defender*, he accused the national leadership of the Nation of being "ruthless and frantic" and not beyond murdering dissidents. "The members of my father's staff are guilty of some or all of these evils," including adultery and alcohol consumption. He went on to describe the "beatings, lies, and hypocrisy" that had marred the image of Elijah Muhammad and his organization. Cognizant that press attention was a temporary refuge at best, Wallace did not stop with just informing the local media. On August 4, he contacted the FBI and told them of his precarious earthly existence. He also talked to Chicago police officials and his parole officer about the matter. After he took these measures, the intimidation and pursuit of the Fruit of Islam abated. But now, Wallace had a new set of problems. To pay his bills, he worked as a painter or welder when jobs became available. As the ultimate declaration of freedom from his father's authority, Wallace formed the Afro-Descendant Society of Upliftment for the propagation of his views and program. Short on resources and momentum, the group never became a viable vehicle of Sunni Islam or much else. Consequently, Wallace, outside of the Muslim fold for the first time in his life, learned quickly that independence brought responsibility and hardship. His isolation from family and all that was familiar proved to be a trial.[72]

For Muhammad, Wallace's dissent was predictable, but the extent to which he would go to free himself from the Nation, and to save his life, was not. In this instance, the Muslim leader had been too quick to ostracize and abuse apostates, whose bitterness could cause problems in the future, especially if they went to the press or the FBI. Like the Williams-Rosary paternity suits, the publicized stories of Wallace and Hassan were a further embarrassment to Muhammad and made the Nation even less attractive to individuals turned off by reports of graft and sexual immorality. Rumors and secrets that the movement had suppressed for years were now regularly making headlines.[73]

Meanwhile, thousands of miles away, Muhammad's youngest son, Akbar, was paying rapt attention to the drama unfolding at Mosque No. 2. Though still studying abroad at Al-Azhar University in Cairo, he had kept abreast of developments in the Nation through correspondence with Wallace. Around the time that his brother was being banished from the movement, Akbar wrote Muhammad for clarification regarding the many sordid tales of corruption and immorality that had reached him in Egypt. The Muslim leader, either unable or unwilling to answer the query, did not reply. Consequently, Akbar thought the worst. In August, he contacted press officials in the United States and announced his decision to follow Wallace out of the Nation. When officials of United Press International telephoned Muhammad regarding Akbar, the leader acknowledged that he had received the earlier letter of his son and "would answer it shortly," but insisted that he had "no knowledge" of a break. After speaking with the press, Muhammad apparently contacted Akbar and tried to resolve the differences between them. However, the gap between his religious teachings and what his youngest son had learned in Cairo was as wide as the rift between Muhammad and Wallace. Perhaps for the sake of stability in the family and the movement, Akbar did not leave the Nation immediately. Instead, he returned to the United States in late 1964 and engaged in "fruitless arguments" with Muhammad over the meaning of Islam. By early December, Akbar had resolved to leave the movement quietly without the publicity that had accompanied the departures of Malcolm X and Wallace. No one outside of the high command of the Nation was to know that his father had lost another son to Sunni Islam.[74]

However, while reading the January 1 edition of *Muhammad Speaks,* Akbar learned that his father had labeled him "a hypocrite" and had cast him out of the Nation of Islam. According to the decree, the action had been taken in response to a talk that Akbar had given at Mosque No. 7 on November 29, 1964. Muhammad did not elaborate on what had offended him in the lecture, but merely stated that it included "statements and views which were not in keeping with the teachings and principles" of the movement. The public ouster of Akbar suggests that Muhammad already knew that his son was leaving the movement and that New York Muslims had reported his Wallace-like behavior to Chicago in expectation of punitive action. Whatever the case, the Muslim leader felt it necessary to denounce his son publicly and to let the world know that he was "no longer regarded as a follower of his father."[75]

Akbar was incensed by the announcement and went straight to the press. In an interview with *The New York Times,* in January 1965 he roundly criticized much of what his father stood for. Everything from Muhammad's "concocted religious teachings" to his "politically sterile" separatism came under fire. Like Wallace, Akbar revealed unflattering information about the movement such as dissatisfaction among the believers (who he said numbered only seven thousand) and avarice among national officials. He rejected his father's teachings regarding white devils and, most significantly, sided with Malcolm X in his call for African-Americans to embrace orthodox Islam. Of the three apostates, Akbar's departure from the Nation was the least complicated or antagonistic. He was never subjected to a protracted smear campaign in *Muhammad Speaks* or hunted by Fruit of Islam. His father, who appears to have favored Akbar among his children, allowed him to walk away relatively unmolested. Muhammad still occasionally referred to Akbar's putative ungratefulness and hypocrisy as late as the 1970s, but not in the caustic terms that he reserved for Malcolm X and other notable dissenters.[76]

By the fall of 1964, catastrophe appeared to be closing in on Muhammad. Already, his finest minister and his heir apparent had fallen prey to "hypocrisy," followed by his youngest child. Who was next, Clara? The whole uncomfortable, humiliating ordeal affected Muhammad physiologically. In late October 1964, suffering from a nervous condition and insomnia, he decided to take ninety days off. He delegated decision-making powers to Minister James Shabazz of Chicago, John Ali, and Raymond Sharrieff, but despite his retreat from the helm, the broadsides kept coming.[77]

Throughout the fall, Malcolm X took every opportunity to denounce Muhammad and the Nation as he traveled through the Middle East and Africa. In an open letter from Saudi Arabia, he disparaged his former mentor as "a religious faker" who had "fooled and misused" unsuspecting blacks. To enhance his own legitimacy as an Islamic leader, Malcolm journeyed to Mecca to receive an endorsement from the World Muslim Council, the top religious authority in the Islamic world. While he was abroad in the East, Malcolm was virtually untouchable. The Fruit of Islam had no international network to intimidate him, and he was more at home ideologically in the Middle East than Muhammad would ever be. Predictably, he took full advantage of Muhammad's lack of influence there. Unable to silence Malcolm's voice from Chicago, the Muslim leader withdrew to his winter home in Phoenix and contemplated making a trip to Jamaica in late November, the need to get away from it all appearing overwhelming.[78]

Muhammad canceled his Caribbean vacation plans around the time (November 24) Malcolm X returned to the United States. The Muslim leader did not want to be out of the country while "the chief hypocrite" was again seizing headlines. Despite his four-month absence, Malcolm's trip to the Middle East and Africa had not led to a noticeable lull in the Muslim war. On the legal front, Muhammad had secured a September court order requiring that Malcolm vacate his Nation-owned home in Queens by January 31, 1965. On the battlefield, Fruit of Islam from the Bronx pummeled to death one of his sympathizers only days before Malcolm arrived back in New York.

As always, *Muhammad Speaks* nurtured the violent tone of the anti-Malcolm crusade. In a December 4 article, Louis X editorialized darkly about "the cowardly hypocritical dog" who had at one time been a big brother to him. "The die is set, and Malcolm shall not escape, especially after such evil, foolish talk about his benefactor," the Boston minister warned. "Such a man as Malcolm is worthy of death, and would have met death if it had not been for Muhammad's confidence in Allah for victory over the enemies." For those who did not peruse *Muhammad Speaks* on a regular basis, a similar message was circulated among the non-Muslim press. In an open telegram dated December 7, Raymond Sharrieff "officially" notified Malcolm X that the Nation "shall no longer tolerate" further criticism of its leader. Seemingly, the conflict was headed toward a climax.[79]

The first salvos fired in 1965 presaged a violent year indeed. Muhammad's rhetoric, tailored to stir up his followers, continued to dwell on the alleged hypocrisy of Malcolm X. Ad hominem attacks in interviews and editorials characterized the former national minister as an upstart contender for a position that had been divinely reserved for Muhammad. "This chief hypocrite is not with Allah," he wrote in January. ". . . If he were with Allah, he would be with me." Addressing his apostate critics collectively during a Phoenix interview, Muhammad noted that "they cannot yet say I am not the Messenger of Allah. They can't take that away from me." Adeptly, the Muslim leader portrayed his vilification by antagonists as a form of persecution akin to that endured by biblical prophets. His audience, the believers, were conditioned to respond to these images as if they, too, were under siege. Muhammad carefully baited editorials in *Muhammad Speaks* with the necessary hints and buzzwords to produce a crusading frenzy among his readers. For example, the January 29 issue of the Muslim organ hailed 1965 as "a year in which the most out-spoken opponents of the Honorable Elijah Muhammad will slink into ignoble silence." More sinister things were being said behind the scenes, unbeknownst to many of the believers. According to inside sources of Malcolm X, his tongue was still wanted in Chicago before Saviour's Day in February. If this information was true, the "ignoble silence" that Muhammad hoped for was actively being pursued, and the deadline for its realization was fast approaching.[80]

Minus the allusions to violence and death, the verbal assaults of Malcolm X were becoming as corrosive as those of his Muslim adversaries. One reason for this was the failure of one of his earlier tactics to discredit Muhammad. Evelyn Williams and Lucille Rosary declined to show up at a January 11 court hearing in Los Angeles on their paternity suits. Muhammad had never even been served legal papers. More than likely, the Muslim leader convinced the women not to appear, using either the stick (threats of reprisal) or the carrot (enhanced financial support) to guarantee their absence. Whatever the case, the matter was conveniently dropped from the court calendar and from public view altogether.

In addition to this debacle, the growing physical threat that he was experiencing made Malcolm more vocal in his denunciation of the Muslims. During the early morning hours of February 14, Malcolm's home was firebombed by unknown arsonists. Malcolm suspected that Muslims had acted "upon the orders of Elijah Muhammad." In retaliation, Malcolm subjected his former teacher to a blistering attack before a Detroit crowd the following afternoon. "The man has gone insane, absolutely out of his mind," Malcolm said of Muhammad. The Muslim movement "has gotten into the possession of a man who's become senile in his old age and perhaps doesn't realize it." He excoriated the Muslim leader for allegedly sanctioning "murder, acts of maiming and crippling other people," and blamed his children for misusing the finances of the movement. Over the next few days, Malcolm berated the Nation and its "senile" chief as never before.[81]

Despite the harshness of recriminations, there was a window of opportunity that could have served as a safety valve for the rising tensions between Muhammad and Malcolm. The window may have always been there; however, it was definitely closing by February 1965. It is probable that the only compromise that could have been worked out at this time would have been a limited, mutual agreement to disagree and a truce to end the fighting between the followers of the two men. There was really no possibility of a complete reconciliation. Unquestionably, Muhammad had no intention of converting to Sunni Islam or becoming a civil rights activist. His power base was built on black nationalism and a race-sensitive theology. Likewise, Malcolm had moved too close to Mecca and the Civil Rights Movement to go back to the "strait-jacket" world of the Nation. To return to Muhammad would have meant a complete loss of credibility.

Regardless of these obstacles, the two men were not irreversibly divided. On at least one occasion, the Muslim leader had stated that the apostasies of Malcolm, Wallace, and Hassan were all forgivable, though amnesty would presumably be conditional. Similarly, Malcolm, as late as mid-February, had expressed regret over the prospect of "two Black groups [having] to fight and kill each other off" and called on Muhammad to end the feud. In the absence of a pact to halt the conflict, an escalation of hostilities proved virtually inevitable. In the worse-case scenario, mounting casualties would lead to a national crisis in which African-Americans in general only stood to lose.[82]

Muhammad was in his Chicago office when assassins silenced Malcolm X on February 21 in New York's Audubon Ballroom. According to one of his grandsons who was with him at the time, the Muslim leader seemed genuinely shocked, even disturbed, when the assassination of Malcolm X was announced over a nearby radio. "Oh my, God!" was reportedly his first reaction as he fell back into his chair. "Um, um, um!" The deed, which he had meticulously set the stage for, had finally been accomplished. His split with his former national minister had been finalized for eternity. Muhammad contemplated the news solemnly for the next half hour until he personally felt unsafe. "You know," he confessed to his grandson, "I really want to go home now." As the two sought a more secure haven, news of the murder spread quickly around the globe. It seemed that few people, including Muhammad, could truly comprehend the enormity of the tragedy until later, when the significance of Malcolm X came into clearer focus.[83]

If Elijah Muhammad had not given the explicit order that resulted in the gangland-style assassination of Malcolm X, he had made it quite clear through editorials, telephone conversations, and tolerance of Fruit of Islam violence and intimidation that the slaying of the former minister had his implicit support. For many Muslims, his acquiescence to—indeed, engineering of—the escalating hostility toward Malcolm during 1964 and early 1965 had been synonymous to an order to have Malcolm killed as "the chief hypocrite." As Louis X admitted years later, "There was not a Muslim who loved the Honorable Elijah Muhammad that did not want to kill Malcolm," a testament, albeit exaggerated, to the success of the Nation's propaganda war.[84]

The actual assassins were a shadowy crew; only one, Talmadge Hayer, was captured at the scene of the crime in the Audubon Ballroom. Two others, Thomas 15X Johnson and Norman 3X Butler of Mosque No. 7, were later arrested and also convicted of the killing. To this day, the contours of any conspiracy to kill Malcolm X remain vague. Except for the parties who may have been involved, no one can discern with certainty the forces that made the assassination possible on that winter day in February.[85]

Without question, the FBI and the NYPD share partial culpability for the murder. Hoover and his field offices knew months earlier that the Muslim leader had mentioned in telephone conversations that he wished to close Malcolm's eyes and chop off his head. Still, the agency did nothing, besides maybe exacerbating the conflict with counterintelligence tricks. Arguably, the NYPD had as much information about the feud as the FBI; regarding events in New York, it probably had more. Yet, it only acted after the fact, rarely taking preventive measures to protect Malcolm X and others. If nothing else is certain, the meaning of the assassination is clear. The sponsor(s) intended to make an unequivocal statement. The assassins killed Malcolm while he spoke before his supporters, on his own turf, in public. The conspirators wanted to emphasize that Malcolm was hardly untouchable; in fact, he could be killed even in his own element. Beyond assigning blame, that was the chilling lesson of the murder. No one could mistake the grim symbolism of the event.[86]

Predictably, calls and visits from reporters and others tied up the agenda of Elijah Muhammad for the next few days. Everyone wanted to know how he felt about the death of his former protégé Malcolm X. In televised sessions from the living room of his Chicago mansion, the Muslim leader appeared relaxed, faintly smug, when asked about the killing, but was conspicuously flanked by close advisers concerned about his safety. "I don't have any knowledge of anyone trying to kill Malcolm," he stated plainly to a group of assembled journalists. "We have never resorted to no such thing as violence." When asked about Talmadge Hayer, known then to the press as Thomas Hagan, Muhammad denied knowing the assassin but promised to initiate an internal investigation of the Nation to find out if any of his followers were involved in the killing. Though his denials of prior knowledge regarding efforts to kill Malcolm X were probably feigned, the Muslim leader was acutely aware of the need to distance himself and his movement from the murder. In private quarters, some believers perhaps boasted of planning to kill Malcolm X. His widow, Betty Shabazz, later stated that complicity was believed to be a "badge of honor" among some Muslims. However, for the public, Muhammad claimed that the murder was "a shock and surprise to us," though he added that Malcolm was a victim of the violence he preached. Adroitly, he refrained from making statements that were inflammatory or subject to press manipulation, but unsurprisingly, stressed the themes of "divine chastisement" and the sanctity of his self-proclaimed messengership.

While Malcolm X had failed in a year since leaving the Nation to muster a significant following, some sympathizers outraged by his murder would have avenged him if given the opportunity. The press, of course, sensationalized the possibility of retribution against the Muslim movement. A headline of the *Pittsburgh Courier* asked, "Black War Eminent?" Gloomily, the *Charlotte Observer* forecasted, "Black Nationalist Civil War Looms." In an exasperated tone, the title of an article in *U.S. News & World Report* read, "Now It's Negroes Vs. Negroes in America's Racial Violence." Other reports contained more dire news, such as a rumor that "a brigade of up to 1,000 Black Nationalists" was headed to Chicago to dispatch Muhammad, and the prediction of one of Malcolm's lieutenants that the Muslim leader might be killed before month's end. In retrospect, the stories of retaliation were blown out of proportion and were indicative of the cupidity of some news organizations. Still, during the immediate aftermath of the assassination of Malcolm X, enough anti-Muhammad incidents occurred to suggest that the life of Muslim leader was in real danger. Not without reason, those around him spared no expense in making sure that none of the gruesome rumors came to fruition.[87]

On February 23, Mosque No. 7 at Lenox Avenue and 116th Street was destroyed by an unknown arsonist in apparent retaliation against Muhammad and his Muslims. The San Francisco mosque narrowly escaped the same fate and was saved only by policemen who happened to be in the area. Hate mail began to pour into the Chicago headquarters. Within a couple of weeks, the large volume of written death threats against Muhammad necessitated a statement in *Muhammad Speaks* demanding that the anonymous authors "stop writing their poison pen notes and planning threats against [the] Messenger." The most serious incident took place in March when someone fired shots at the Phoenix home of the Muslim leader. Fortunately for him, he was out of town when the shooting occurred.

On the eve of Saviour's Day in 1965, security for Muhammad was tight. Fruit of Islam patrolled his nineteen-room home, and a large complement of Chicago policemen guarded Muslim properties and O'Hare International Airport. In the end, no one came for Muhammad—no black nationalist brigade, no carload of avengers from New York. The only real cause for panic was a mysterious crate that arrived at his Chicago home on February 24; it turned out to be the casing for a grandfather clock that had been sent as a gift by Philadelphia believers. The Muslim leader was certainly comforted by the thousands of followers who arrived in Chicago at this time for the annual celebration of Fard Muhammad's birth. Based on the harrowing events of the past few days, his keynote address promised to be unlike any other.[88]

The three-day 1965 Saviour's Day convention actually resembled more of a rehearsed melodrama than a religious event. Before speaking on the last day of the commemoration, February 26, Muhammad presented Wilfred X, who briefly commented on his brother's assassination. In an attempt to downplay the culpability of the Nation, the Detroit minister advised the audience not to lose sight of the real enemy in the wake of the tragedy. He also reiterated the official Muslim line that Malcolm had asked for death by taking "a reckless path" of action. Coming from almost anyone else, this statement would easily have meshed with the prevailing mood of the gathering. Coming from Malcolm's oldest sibling, however, it appeared ill-timed and callous, at least to those who had not quite reached the point of hating the former minister before his death. Muhammad was obviously using Wilfred to soothe the consciences of believers who may have felt remorseful about the Muslim role in the killing of Malcolm X. Ironically, Muhammad had used Philbert X a year earlier to inaugurate the propaganda campaign that contributed to the demise of his younger brother. For maximum effect, the Muslim leader used the next speaker, Wallace Muhammad, to accomplish yet another goal. Before the thousands gathered, he was to affirm the validity of the same teachings that he, Akbar, Hassan Sharrieff, and others had publicly ridiculed earlier.[89]

Wallace's "confession of guilt" was done swiftly, as if he feared taking up too much of the crowd's time. In five minutes of pathetic groveling, he tried to prove to the audience that he now realized that publicizing the flaws of his father and the Nation had been "a great mistake." The admission of fault must have been hard for Wallace, who had only months earlier upbraided the national leadership for its corruption and immorality. As his later actions would prove, he had not completely reconciled himself with the teachings of his father. Apparently, Wallace had been forced back into the Muslim movement due to financial difficulties; principle had to give way to survival. In concluding his recantation, he pleaded for forgiveness in the hope of convincing the assembly to "accept me and permit me back in your midst as a brother." Now, virtually prostrate before his triumphant father, Wallace was pardoned for his offenses and received back into the fold with warm applause. Ostensibly, Muhammad had achieved an undisputed victory in the theological duel with his son. Little did he know, however, that the tide of orthodox Islam had only temporarily receded. Following Wallace's spectacle, the master of ceremonies stirred up the crowd for the main event. To the sound of a roaring ovation, the Messenger of Allah assumed the rostrum to deliver his annual address to the Nation.[90]

Muhammad's speech was both a vainglorious tribute to his own leadership and a self-serving farewell to the slain Malcolm X. It would be the last time that he would publicly talk at length about his relationship with his former protégé. Not surprisingly, the address was heavily laden with biblical allegories. The Muslim world, according to Muhammad, was a Manichaean construct in which he, a messenger of God like Moses, Noah, and Lot before him, existed in polar opposition to the purveyors of evil. Within this world, people had the freedom of choice. They could either gravitate toward the righteous (Muhammad and his followers) or take the path of the devil white man and the hypocrite. To illustrate his schema, the Muslim leader examined the life of Malcolm X. As long as he was with the messenger, the New York minister was "a light, a star among his people." He was loved by the righteous and protected by Allah. However, when he departed from the Muslim fold and denounced its beliefs, he sank back into the grave to be used by the devil to divide black people. Not satisfied with just being a hypocrite, he made war against the divinely protected messenger and the "well-armed" white man, evidence that he "had lost his mind" and was foolish enough to embrace "bloodbath" teachings. According to Muhammad, it was not necessary for the Muslims to kill Malcolm.

"We didn't want to kill Malcolm and didn't try to kill him," he asserted. "We know such ignorant, foolish teachings would bring him to his own end." Muhammad held up Malcolm X as the ultimate example of what could happen to an individual once he was outside of the ranks of the believers. "The Holy Qur'an forbids the Messenger even to stand beside the grave of a hypocrite," he declared tersely. The Muslims in attendance, dutifully deferential to their leader, applauded.[91]

Over the next decade, Muhammad would publicly refer to Malcolm only on rare occasions and always derisively. To him, Malcolm X was the premier hypocrite among the Muslims, and nothing could change that. He was not to be missed or idolized. In fact, his absence was believed to be good for morale and unity among the faithful. In a sense, the assassination of Malcolm X did represent a turning point in the history of the Nation of Islam. Perhaps more accurately, his death symbolized the culmination of several developments that had been influencing the movement over the past several years.[92]

The forces of orthodox Islam within Muslim circles almost petered out completely after Malcolm's death and the "reconversion" of Wallace Muhammad at the 1965 Saviour's Day convention. During the 1970s, orthodox pressures upon the Nation would again emerge, but for the time being, the person perhaps best able to make al-Islam appealing to large numbers of African-Americans was dead. Moreover, the death of Malcolm X quieted many of the more activist-minded Muslims within the Nation. That is not to say that politicized believers suddenly became conservative separatists content with waiting on Allah. Instead, many discontented black nationalists who had not left with Malcolm left shortly after his death to join new groups such as the Black Panthers and the radicalized remnants of the Civil Rights Movement such as Stokely Carmichael's SNCC and James Farmer's CORE. The conservative, fiscally oriented, theological faction of the Nation headed by Elijah Muhammad had triumphed over the challenge of the younger political element, but not without costs in terms of membership and credibility.

Additionally, the assassination was a watershed in the government's ongoing manipulation of the stresses within the Muslim movement and the black community in general. A complete accounting of the roles of the FBI, NYPD, and other state agencies in amplifying the strife between Muhammad and Malcolm X may never become public knowledge. Nonetheless, the counterintelligence programs that literally destroyed groups such as the Black Panthers during the late 1960s and early 1970s were almost certainly based on the early anti-Muslim surveillance programs of Hoover and his agents.

Though he definitely tried, Muhammad could not dismiss the significance of Malcolm X in a single speech. The term *hypocrite,* while damning in Muslim quarters, could not begin to capture the depth of his impact on African-Americans even three decades after his murder. Malcolm's contribution to the ethos and spiritual evolution of the black community endured on several levels. Primarily, he made black nationalism in its various forms appealing to the angry generation of black youths who came of age just as American segregation and European colonial empires were collapsing, albeit slowly. Malcolm articulated sentiments that had historically been balled up in the hearts of African-Americans and dared the world to dispute them. Even when he was in the Nation, his analysis was cogent enough to make a politically effete organization appear radical. Once he left, his vibrant intellect laid the theoretical foundations of the Black Power Movement.

Malcolm was an extraordinary teacher and grassroots scholar. He was not afraid to engage in the murky intellectual debates that all true leaders must immerse themselves in while searching for real solutions to complicated problems. When he perished on February 21, 1965, he had not yet built a solid ideological framework for addressing the plight of African-Americans. However, he had relentlessly investigated every major system of thought available to him, including black nationalism, al-Islam, and socialism, for useful facets of knowledge. Skillfully, he interpreted complex ideas in a vernacular that the man on the street could digest. When his life was tragically cut short at age thirty-nine, Malcolm had touched more people than he had perhaps realized. The twenty-five or so "truly saddened" Nation of Islam members who attended his funeral understood his significance as did a growing number of African-Americans who had earlier discounted him as irrelevant. In fact, his life and message would later take on mythical attributes. "I'll tell you this," one Harlem woman declared on the day of his death. "We're going to get another Malcolm X." Without delay, his canonization had already begun.[93]

The Muslim campaign to vilify, harass, and ultimately silence Malcolm X did not have a precedent. During the early years of the movement, some people were defamed and physically intimidated so as to effect changes in the leadership and direction of the Nation, but nothing was as coordinated and sustained as the pursuit of Malcolm X. The lengths to which Muhammad went to arouse animosity against the former minister and his tolerance, and likely approval, of the use of violence against him and his followers were unique in the Muslim experience. More than anything else, the campaign revealed the innermost fears of Muhammad regarding schisms, personal persecution, and the loss of his sizable financial empire. As was intended, the crusade against Malcolm X and other alleged hypocrites diverted attention away from the increasingly publicized shortcomings of the national leadership and onto the trail of apostate scapegoats who would serve as object lessons. As the end result, the Nation, despite the denials of its spokesmen, would have the blood of a major black leader on its hands. The forces that created the murderous atmosphere of 1964-65 would do the same in the 1970s over similar issues. Tragically, the assassination of Malcolm X may have institutionalized violence as a means of resolving conflict in some Muslim quarters. Nonetheless, following the turbulent years of the early 1960s, the Nation was on a course of expansion and enhanced popularity. Black Power was on the horizon, and Elijah Muhammad would bask in its glow.[94]

CHAPTER 9

A NATION OF SHOPKEEPERS

Do something for self.
—Elijah Muhammad

The year 1965 was a watershed for black Americans. Few could dispute the importance of civil rights gains in the realms of voting and social equality. The Civil Rights Act of 1964 and the Voting Rights Act of 1965 brought federal authority to bear upon the century-old practices of segregation and electoral disfranchisement. Desegregation plans for schools throughout the country heralded the repudiation of Jim Crow in education, and antidiscrimination laws banned statutory segregation in public accommodations, residential areas, and even bedrooms. As they had during Reconstruction, African-Americans trickled into local and state governments throughout the South, largely as a result of the elimination of poll taxes and tedious literacy tests, which, along with political violence, had suppressed black voting strength since the 1870s. The high point would not come until three years later, in 1968, when a record ten African-Americans, including Shirley Chisholm, the first black female U.S. representative, entered the Congress. To many, it appeared, even in the midst of the Vietnam era, that white America was finally poised to extend the open hand of brotherhood and citizenship to that part of America that had historically been dispossessed. Undeniably some had given all to bring America to this point. In fact, suffering and brutality had become routine for many civil rights workers as the Selma demonstrations illustrated. Nonetheless, 1965 was arguably a turning point in the black struggle for equality in the United States. From this historical vantage point, the suffering of countless protesters, sympathizers, and common folks did not appear to have been in vain.

Along with being a time of political and social renewal for black America, 1965 proved also to be a year of fire and disillusionment. Racial explosions in Watts and Chicago during August revealed just how impervious many quarters of the country were to congressional civil rights bills and court decisions. Ghettos sprawling over parts of New York City, Los Angeles, Washington, D.C., and many other cities were only marginally affected by the racial liberalism of the Johnson administration. Chronic unemployment, economic chaos, inadequate educational facilities, colonial-style police policies, and indifferent political machines could not be altered without fundamental changes in the distribution of power and resources in the cities and states. To the chagrin of many Americans, racism permeated the school systems and housing patterns of cities such as Boston and Chicago as thoroughly as it did in Birmingham and Little Rock. The Civil Rights Movement and the legislation it spawned had been important steps toward the realization of America's core values of freedom, equality, and democracy, but were no panacea. Slums and slum dwellers had been created over a period of decades and could not be eradicated overnight.

In several regards, the country continued to live up to its Janus-faced past during the mid-1960s, contradicting itself at almost every turn. While writing federal civil rights laws, the government intensified its pursuit of radicals and subversives, and Hoover's FBI wielded greater authority over national security matters than ever before. The domestic War on Poverty took second stage to another war, a tragic conflict that decimated countless people in Southeast Asia. Nothing was truly as it seemed; there was always another, often darker side to everything the United States was involved in. As black people began dying on the streets of Watts and in the jungles of Vietnam, the Civil Rights Movement was in its twilight, coming to a triumphant, though arguably premature, end. This three-to-four year period in which black activism gradually lost its effectiveness proved to be a lull between the era of nonviolent protest and the ascendancy of Black Power. For some, 1965 marked the beginning of the end—the last gasps of the integrationist dreamers. For others, the year was the last in which the American bastille could contain the black revolution.

On the eve of the Black Power Movement, Elijah Muhammad, the most prominent icon of black nationalism, was again forced to cope with life-threatening illnesses, which had become permanent features of his precarious physical condition. In March, he dismissed plans to visit Pakistan, aware that "a good rest" was in order following the stressful, protracted battles against Malcolm X and other apostates. Two months later, he learned that he had diabetes, which his physician deemed "pretty bad" since Muhammad's blood sugar was elevated well beyond normal. The doctor prescribed immediate doses of insulin and fluid to fight off the possibility of diabetic coma. He also suggested hospitalization as a way to prevent further complications. Despite his condition, the Muslim leader refused to abide by the advice. He was perhaps becoming more cynical regarding the capacity of modern medicine to address his growing health problems. After all, good doctors and sophisticated facilities had done little to relieve his primary affliction, bronchial asthma. Only bed rest and frequent trips to Phoenix proved somewhat effective. In June, large amounts of salt in his system resulted in swollen ankles, and high blood pressure continued to be a cause of concern. By summer, it was clear that 1965 would be a year of confinement and recuperation for the Messenger of Allah.[1]

If he was not actually at the helm of the Nation, Muhammad was still in command and made it a point to keep up with organizational and national developments. His own physical problems made him more sensitive to the necessity of maintaining stability within the movement, as did his tendency toward avoiding actions that jeopardized Muslim financial growth or invited further government scrutiny. When civil disturbances erupted in Chicago and Los Angeles, Muhammad predictably forbade his followers from participating in any demonstrations or illegal activity. In fact, he expressly prohibited Fruit of Islam from selling papers in Watts and counseled them to withdraw from the affected areas altogether. Under the pretense of searching for stashed weapons, fifty policemen assailed a group of Muslims at the Los Angeles mosque, arresting fifty-nine people and sending four others to the hospital. Reminiscent of the 1962 episode, Muhammad did not call for retaliation against the LAPD, but did issue a statement of protest. His September 1 press release excoriated the "evil" Chief Parker and Mayor Yorty for sending "an army of policemen against the Mosque to shoot it up and kill Negroes." Though he likely expressed greater outrage in private, this was as far as his public condemnation went. Typically, he was more delicate in sanctioning the misdeeds of whites, particularly state officials, compared to the more stringent methods he used to punish perceived offenses committed by blacks, especially "hypocrites."[2]

Muhammad's aversion to provoking interracial violence ironically made possible a long-awaited meeting with his erstwhile civil rights rival, Dr. Martin Luther King Jr., in early 1966. King was trying to transplant the Civil Rights Movement to Northern cities, where its impact had been negligible relative to the successes in the South. Muhammad and King had been in contact since at least February 1965, but scheduling conflicts had apparently derailed efforts at arranging a conference between the two. When they finally met at the Muslim leader's mansion in Chicago, neither had any illusions about the irreconcilable nature of their ideologies and much of their programs. King's visit was largely an act of courtesy—homage paid to the older man on whose territory he hoped to reinvent the Civil Rights Movement. While no complete public transcript exists, their talk on February 23 appears to have been a general discussion of the plight of black America. In broad terms, the two men agreed to cooperate more in the future and to form a "common front" against those forces that had traditionally oppressed black people. According to Muhammad, King conceded the similarities between the racial situation in America and the colonial conditions of Africans under European rule. When King asked the Muslim leader whether he believed that *all* whites were devils, the older man reportedly resorted to an analogy to illustrate his position. "Dr. King, you and me both grew up in Georgia," Muhammad asserted, "and we know there are many different kinds of snakes. The rattlesnake was poisonous and the king snake was friendly. But they both are snakes." Disarmed, King found the comparison witty, even humorous. Though he did not buy into the demonology of the Nation, he and Muhammad shared a roaring laugh.[3]

Despite their amicable encounter, Muhammad and King were on different courses. King, whose analysis of American society came to reflect as much issues of class as race, was losing his position as the central figure of the civil rights struggle. After Selma, his role in the dialogue between oppressed and oppressor became much more complex as he took on broader issues such as capitalist excesses in America, imperialism in Southeast Asia, and other global currents that complicated the race question. He remained the venerable icon of the fight against racism, but became progressively less audible and convincing on a stage on which other, younger actors were claiming the spotlight and passionately articulating demands for Black Power. Admirably, he attempted to adjust to the new situation without compromising his beliefs in nonviolence and racial reconciliation. However, by the time Stokely Carmichael and others began raising the new standard of revolt in the summer of 1966, the political center of the black community had shifted in a way that made King appear to be a compromising moderate as opposed to the liberal moralist he had previously been cast as. The urban rebellions that took place in the wake of his murder in April 1968 would certainly not have had his blessing. Arguably, the protests were indicative of just how irrelevant civil disobedience seemed to African-Americans in the midst of desperate, violent times.

In a sense, King had become a victim of his own success. The codification of the Civil Rights Movement in legislation and court decisions forced him to focus on the informal and customary forces that were still impeding African-American progress. De jure obstacles that had historically united activists behind his leadership and given them clear-cut targets for their crusade no longer existed. Aware of these realities, King attempted to change his approach. Yet the costs of his shift from racial politics to a more internationalist, macroeconomic vision of the United States would prove great. His increasingly vocal criticism of the Vietnam War gradually dissolved his working relationship with the Johnson administration. His call for a Poor People's Campaign challenged the core values underlying the structure and operation of American capitalism. King certainly had not joined the New Left or applied for membership in the Black Panther Party; however, many of his former allies in government and white America were taken aback by his new ventures. Without question, King's contributions to the discourse on race in America had been valuable. Nonetheless, by the time he met Muhammad in 1966 (and definitely by the time of his death two years later), his influence on both black demands and white responsiveness were waning due mostly to fast-changing circumstances beyond his control.[4]

As King and others were salvaging the remnants of the Civil Rights Movement during the late 1960s, Elijah Muhammad's star was on the rise as never before. The ability of the Muslim leader to maintain a reputation as a stalwart champion of black pride, initiative, and self-reliance, despite organizational factionalism, scandals, and corruption that had become public knowledge, testified to the success of the image-building efforts of Muslim spokesmen. Muhammad and his ministers were able to propagandize the Muslim program and point to tangible results, such as business enterprises, tracts of real estate, a well-circulated newspaper, and thousands of redeemed convicts, prostitutes, and drug addicts. All of these achievements shored up the image of Muhammad as a savior of sorts, even if one did not accept him as the Messenger of Allah. The Black Power Movement, at least partially inspired by the Nation of Islam, enhanced Muhammad's image as a kind of godfather of modern black nationalism.

In image-building, Muhammad and his advocates were able to erase many of the stains that had tarnished the leader's reputation by pointing to biblical and Quranic passages to rationalize behavior and policies that smacked of selfishness, graft, or even hypocrisy. Those stains that were difficult to erase from the image of Muhammad and the movement, such as complicity of some Muslims in the killing of Malcolm X, were explained away as the work or influence of enemies—the FBI, "Uncle Tom Negroes," the hypocrites, and so on. On the whole, the Muslims were quite thorough in refining the image of their messenger to downplay his flaws and frailties and overstate his immaculacy and omniscience. Given the political tenor of the times, the Nation of Islam was perfectly positioned to benefit from the explosion of popularity that all things black enjoyed during the late 1960s.

Ideologically, the racial and religious views of Muhammad remained consistent. The territorial separation of blacks into their own country in the continental United States or through emigration to Africa continued to be advanced as the best solution to the ongoing racial dilemma in America. In his eyes, whites were still the devils they had been since their creation by Yacub six millennia earlier, and the United States was still destined for divine destruction within the next few years. "Do something for self" remained the rallying cry of the Muslims and, in many ways, the main source of their appeal among blacks.

Diversification of the Nation's financial holdings was stepped up during the Black Power era to show members and prospective converts the power of unity (and the dollar). The Universities of Islam associated with some of the larger and older mosques continued to generate support and respect from the larger black community, which applauded the Muslims for taking on the tasks of educating African-American children. Along with the business dealings of the movement, the educational program of the Nation commanded a sizable portion of its finances. "You must teach and train your boys and girls in your own schools and colleges," Muhammad continued to counsel as he had since the 1930s. "Keep your little children, especially your little girls, from mixing with white children." Like his traditional teachings against drinking, smoking, gambling, swearing, and other vices, the theology of Muhammad did not undergo any significant revisions during this period. If anything, it stayed remarkably stable considering the shifting political center of the African-American community.[5]

The black nationalism of Muhammad and his followers, while attractive to many during the late 1960s, often diverged from the various philosophical strains that comprised the Black Power Movement. The separatism, cultural revivalism, and self-help doctrines of the Muslims were mainstays of the era, but other elements of the ideology of the Nation were at odds with the basic beliefs of many radicalized black activists. The most glaring incongruity lay in the portrayal of Africa and Africans in Muslim teachings. Ever since the days when Fard Muhammad led the Nation, African civilizations were not characterized as being particularly meaningful in and of themselves, outside of their contact with the Islamic world. At times during the leadership of Elijah Muhammad, an appreciation of Africa was exhibited by himself and various spokesmen, especially Malcolm X; however, it was usually limited to an admiration of national independence movements and not cultural developments on the continent. During a decade when interest in African history and indigenous cultures was burgeoning among black Americans, Muhammad was still clinging to stereotypes and myths about the continent that were both inaccurate and denigrating.

As late as the 1970s, Muhammad believed that non-Islamic Africa was desperately in need of a "civilizing" influence. He was critical of the "near nude" African who was too "savage to hide his nakedness," and those who wore Afros and lived a "jungle life . . . the way you see in some uncivilized parts of Africa today." In addition to depicting "bushy hair [as] the style of savages," Muhammad also denounced traditional African attire, languages, religions, and customs, which black Americans would supposedly "be degrading themselves to adopt." The Muslim leader believed that only African Muslims and educated Christians had risen above the level of barbarians; all others were benighted and without dignity. Similar to westernized black nationalists of the nineteenth century, Muhammad had a missionary complex regarding Africans. On several occasions, he spoke of going to Africa to bestow upon its inhabitants civilization and decency. "We have got to civilize people," he declared during a lecture in late 1972. "We must go to Africa. . . . I am already civilized and I am ready to civilize Africa." Despite his stated intentions, Muhammad never returned to Africa following his tour of the East in 1959. Still, until his death in 1975, he clearly discerned a need to save Africans from themselves and the savagery that had supposedly stymied their development.[6]

The contempt that Muhammad occasionally displayed toward African traditions was indicative of his acceptance of Western, modernist definitions of cultural refinement and civilization. Possibly, the contradiction between the glorification of blackness and the vilification of traditional Africa in Nation of Islam theology did not register in the minds of Muhammad and many of his followers. After all, their search for the pristine origins of the Black Nation had led them to revise geography and history so as to depict Africa as an extension of Asia and Arab-Islamic culture as inextricably tied to the black psyche. Nonetheless, the persistence of unflattering myths regarding the continent and its people, at bottom, revealed a fundamental reluctance to discard long-held views despite the expanding availability of informed scholarly works and black studies programs designed to dispel ignorance of Africa and Africans.

The personal conservatism of Muhammad, which had always dictated Muslim mannerisms and values, separated the Nation even further from the attitudes and lifestyles of radicalized activists who were attracted to the nonconventional elements of the counterculture. The generational gap between Muhammad and the largely youth-oriented Black Power Movement accounted for at least some of the differences between their worldviews; however, specific trends of the period served to accentuate the dichotomy between the ascetic, septuagenarian Muslim leader and the baby-boom rebels. For example, Muhammad discouraged black men, especially Fruit of Islam, from wearing Afros, beards, and dashikis. "When you let the hair of face and head grow long, you are wearing the style of ancient traditional people," he declared in the July 4, 1969, edition of *Muhammad Speaks*. "I am not going to adopt any of those jungle styles of our people" in Africa. Muhammad was also critical of the miniskirt and felt that black men who allowed their wives and daughters to "show their nude selves to the public" should be incarcerated. In a June 1968 edict, he warned that female believers who wore "traditional African tribal styles and garments with gay colors" faced summary expulsion from the Nation. Perhaps more so than "gay colors," the Muslim leader viewed homosexuality as a particularly disturbing phenomenon that he hoped to steer his followers away from. He roundly condemned men and women who were "falling upon their own" and warned parents to be wary of non-Muslim, single-sex schools. Aware that image was as powerful as substance in the age of high-tech communications, Muhammad cautiously held firm to the traditional mores that had been the cornerstones of the Muslim movement for decades.[7]

While his influence was ubiquitous, Muhammad was not able to police every quarter of his nationwide movement, and some trends among segments of believers were clearly aberrant. Marijuana, popular among many

American youths during this period, attracted some Muslims, who secretly sought highs outside of the spiritual realm. It was not a widespread practice among believers; however, according to one of Muhammad's indulgent grandsons, he was certainly not the only Muslim guilty of "polluting [his] mind with marijuana." For many, marijuana may have been a passing fancy—a brief experiment inspired by peer pressure, youthful rebelliousness, or boredom. Others, especially the indiscreet and the nominally committed, may have become addicts and smoked themselves right out of the Nation. Initially, Muhammad was probably not aware of marijuana use among some of his followers. It was, of course, in the interests of offenders to avoid being discovered, lest they face excommunication back into the grave. Nonetheless, by 1975 when his own son Nathaniel was arrested on a drug charge, Muhammad, and the public, had become privy to enough criminal drug cases involving Muslims to have no illusions about the existence of drug users and suppliers in the Nation. Their presence, even in the "royal family," is not surprising given the widespread availability of various illegal substances in the United States since the 1960s. What is remarkable is that so few Muslims succumbed to the lure of a hallucinogenic escape from reality or to the temptation to make a fast dollar in the increasingly lucrative drug trade. The great majority of Muslims were drug-free individuals who followed their ascetic code of conduct to the letter.[8]

While not necessarily out of sync with the rest of the Black Power Movement in subordinating women, the Nation was certainly going against the grain of societal changes. Though gender issues were becoming more salient in discourse throughout the black community and the larger society, the Nation made no significant efforts to liberalize its doctrines or practices regarding the masculine hold on power in the movement. To be sure, nothing suggested that female believers as a group were discontented with the arrangement of authority and privilege in the Nation. No general desertion of mosques by women occurred even in the wake of the Women's Movement. The Nation continued, however, to be rigidly stratified into two different gender spheres, with women directing the MGT-GCC and the domestic- and family-oriented programs that were traditionally associated with it, and men controlling everything else. In some progressive locales, women perhaps wielded considerable power within the confines of their limited duties. Elsewhere, mirroring longstanding community norms, the influence of female believers on the affairs of the mosque could be negligible, and their treatment even more despairing.[9]

In some Southern settings, ministers laughed in the faces of women who complained of abuse at the hands of their Muslim husbands. Older members of these mosques sometimes informed the national headquarters about beatings inflicted upon female members, but apparently to little avail. Such complaints may never have reached Muhammad. New York Muslims, on the other hand, reportedly tolerated little of this, and an offense as serious as rape might lead to the thrashing of the accused—or worse. Muhammad was not against the corporal punishment of followers, even women who did not know "their place," but would probably have opposed patterns of spousal abuse, which were at odds with Muslim teachings. As in the larger movement, Black Power in the Nation did not always translate into black woman power. Consequently, while the official policy of respecting and protecting black womanhood did seem attractive to potential converts, it actually masked gender inequalities and biases that were as old as the Nation itself.[10]

Despite the ideological and programmatic idiosyncrasies of the Muslim movement, most Black Power spokespersons and organizations lionized Muhammad and his followers. They were widely viewed as forerunners of the new black nationalism. Individuals such as Stokely Carmichael sought meetings with the Messenger of Allah as if he were a medieval caliph whose blessings were needed before a crusade could be launched against the infidels. The Black Panther Party, though critical of the racial chauvinism of groups such as the Muslims, held Muhammad and his followers in "the highest esteem." Panthers who disrespected the Muslims were ostracized by top party officials and labeled pawns of the white establishment. The notoriety of the Nation cut across ideological boundaries, and even African-American leaders and groups only marginally associated with the Black Power Movement were offering praise by the late 1960s. In June 1969, the National Society of Afro-American Policemen honored Muhammad at an award ceremony at the Waldorf-Astoria in New York. The citation was given "as a token of our appreciation and esteem for the people of the Nation of Islam." The impact of the Muslim leader on black America during the period was probably best stated by the Reverend Jesse Jackson, an associate of Dr. King's: "During our colored and Negro days, he was black," an assertion that could be appreciated by this time. Like his nationalist contemporaries, Muhammad put forth his own definition of Black Power, which was, of course, consistent with his theology. During an interview on August 15, 1968, he made it plain for everyone who was listening: "Black Power means the black people will rule the white people on earth as the white people have ruled the black people for the past six thousand years." Unlike in earlier years, few African-Americans voiced opposition to his interpretation of their destiny.[11]

Muhammad relished the spotlight that the Black Power Movement had provided for him. He could rightly claim to be the inheritor of Garvey's mantle, having recognized that black was beautiful long before the slogan appeared. He could also point to the businesses and schools of the Nation and argue that his version of Black Power had practical, material value, beyond mass rallies and fiery speeches. On occasion, Muhammad returned the compliments of other groups, as in the favorable coverage that he extended to James Farmer's CORE in *Muhammad Speaks* during early 1966. More often than not, he preferred not to share the spotlight, since he believed that he alone had been commissioned by God to lead the Black Nation to "freedom, justice, and equality." Consistent with the Muslim propaganda campaigns of the late 1950s and early 1960s, Muhammad attempted to decimate the images of rival leaders so as to enhance his own reputation among blacks and to boost the membership of the Nation. His favorite targets remained Dr. King and the late Malcolm X, both of whom had reputations in the black community that Muhammad would find hard to impugn.

Though he had met King in 1966 and agreed to a "common front," Muhammad routinely maligned him as "a lover of white people" who was ignorant of the knowledge required to resolve the race question. Somewhat disingenuously, the Muslim leader criticized King for teaching blacks "to submit to the white man and to become one of them." Muhammad was unrelenting in his condemnation of civil disobedience and saw only folly in the efforts of King and others to be the "slavemaster's brother." The murder of the preacher in Memphis in April 1968 did touch Muhammad. In the April 12 edition of the Muslim newspaper, a letter of sympathy was printed for "a great and courageous black man who died in the effort to get for his people that which belonged to them—FREEDOM." Still, Muhammad resumed his castigation of King after his death, often in tasteless terms. In essence, the Muslim leader sought to depict the lifework of King as irrevocably tainted by the tricknology of the white man. He saw no value in the preacher's leadership and sacrifices and made strenuous efforts to discredit him in the eyes of African-Americans. In a sweeping indictment during his 1971 Saviour's Day address, he denounced all Christian ministers as the devil's disciples. His final opinion was that King had gone to hell "trying to satisfy his white enemies."[12]

Muhammad was hardly any kinder to his former national minister, Malcolm X. In various statements, the Muslim leader and his proponents assailed the slain black nationalist as a hypocrite, a traitor, and a deceiver of black people. Malcolm was portrayed as being a tool of the white man in his war against the righteous. The quasi-divine status that Malcolm attained in Black Power circles disturbed Muhammad, who believed that whites were using his image to "lead [black people] astray against me." All of the honors that the slain minister received posthumously, from streets bearing his name to Malcolm X University in Chicago, were criticized by Muslim spokesmen as part of a conspiracy "to weaken the leadership position of Messenger Muhammad or to embarrass him." The life and work of Malcolm was viewed as worthless by hard-line Muslims, except for the seventeen years he had devoted to the ministry of Elijah Muhammad.[13]

Malcolm X would always be a sore spot for Muhammad and many of his advocates. The same envy that had led to the isolation and demise of the former minister motivated much of the later contempt for his image and ideas. Muhammad never managed to reconcile himself to the fact that "the Honorable Malcolm X" had become the patron saint of the Black Power Movement even though "the Honorable Elijah Muhammad" had allegedly taught him all that he knew of value. In time, the Muslim leader would realize that he could not dismantle Malcolm's legacy through a protracted smear campaign. Eventually, he decided to try to ignore the looming presence of Malcolm's memory, informing his nostalgic disciples that "I do not give two cents for you following Malcolm.... You will get divine death and destruction." By 1972, he declined even to discuss Malcolm X with journalists, though he rarely granted interviews. In a January press session in his home, he told one inquisitive reporter, "I would not lose any time with a man that has been talked and talked about for years." The newsman, dismayed by the response, respected the leader's wishes and did not press the issue. Ironically, Muhammad, until his own death in 1975, would have to coexist with Malcolm X and live partially in his shadow for a decade after the assassination.[14]

The efforts of Muhammad to enhance his image as a viable black leader were not limited to denunciations of civil rights rivals and dead apostates. During this period, shuffling of personnel in the Nation reflected his perennial concerns regarding the loyalty of his inner circle. Wallace Muhammad, who had been reinstated during Saviour's Day 1965, still found it difficult to pretend. The heterodox Islam of his father was no more palatable to him now than it had been during the early 1960s. Primarily, financial problems and intimidation by Fruit of Islam were responsible for his continuing membership in the Nation.

Between 1965 and 1971, Wallace was expelled from the movement at least two more times for failing to honor Fard Muhammad as Allah. During one of his suspensions, he was dropped from the organizational payroll and forbidden contact with family members. Wallace survived in the grave as best he could, securing jobs as an upholsterer, a painter, and a factory worker. When his financial situation was most uncertain, he probably appealed to his father for readmission into the Nation. Elijah Muhammad was not bothered by the ideological waffling of Wallace—at least not enough to send Fruit of Islam after him. By the late 1960s and 1970s, especially in the era of Black Power, the actions of a minister, even a relative, with no personal following in the Nation only marginally affected the appeal of Muhammad and his message. The Muslim movement grew with and without Wallace; his impact on membership figures was minuscule considering the hundreds who left with Malcolm X in 1964. Perhaps few believers were even aware of Wallace's status at any given time, for he almost never received coverage in *Muhammad Speaks*. Undoubtedly, Muhammad had the upper hand in the renewed struggle with his heir apparent and, at least for a time, could afford to wait until Wallace made up his mind. The Muslim leader made few concessions to orthodox Islam during this period, and the Nation did not seem to be worse off for it.[15]

All things considered, Wallace was a minor player in the politics of the Nation of Islam prior to the mid-1970s. Several others, such as Herbert Muhammad and Raymond Sharrieff, wielded more power in the movement than Wallace had ever had access to. These were the individuals whom Elijah Muhammad trusted most and delegated the greatest measure of authority to. These men were also the ones whom he watched closest, for he was acutely aware of the disaster he would face if any of them betrayed him. John Ali, the national secretary of the Nation, was one of the power brokers among national officials. He had held his office since the early 1960s, managing resources, people, and crises on behalf of the Messenger of Allah. However, by 1970, pressure was certainly being placed on Muhammad to replace him, for some believed he had exhausted his usefulness to the inner circle in Chicago.

In a statement to the press in May 1970 Raymond Sharrieff announced that Ali was to be replaced by someone who was "more competent." Charges that Ali had mishandled Muslim finances were denied. Possibly the need for more professional, accountable bureaucrats to manage the expanding Muslim financial empire dictated the dismissal of Ali. Perhaps the national secretary had, like Malcolm X, made too many enemies in high places to remain in a coveted position of power. Definitely, the rumors regarding his FBI connections were played up by his critics. Whatever the cause, Ali was jettisoned, and in his place, Abass Rassoull, the manager of the Nation-affiliated Salaam Restaurant, was appointed and filled the post until 1975.[16]

In addition to John Ali, Muhammad Ali was another prominent victim of the housecleaning of Muhammad during the late 1960s. Since early 1964, Muhammad Ali had risen swiftly in the ranks of the Muslim movement. His prestige as a boxing-champion-turned-believer had been good for recruitment, and his deep pockets were also beneficial to the organization. Like Malcolm X before him, Ali helped make the Muslim movement attractive to young African-Americans who might otherwise have rejected its conservatism in favor of nationalist groups with more political agendas. Ali, to a lesser degree than Malcolm, became one of the public personas of the Nation. He routinely talked to reporters about what "the Honorable Elijah Muhammad" had taught him and waved his copy of *Message to the Blackman in America* before the cameras for emphasis. The Muslim leader, ever image conscious, allowed Ali to have his fun with news-hungry journalists, but set perimeters to protect the movement's reputation from any damage that the boxer's harangues and secular career might cause. Illustratively, Muhammad demanded the driver's license of Ali in early 1966 after learning that his driving had frequently attracted police scrutiny. "Muhammad ain't playing, man!" Ali exclaimed in a *Sports Illustrated* interview. "When he catch you, boy, you caught!"[17]

Elijah Muhammad had an ambivalent attitude toward Muhammad Ali. The Muslim leader appreciated the publicity and finances that the boxer brought to the Nation; he may even have liked Ali's boisterous style, when it did not reflect poorly on the Nation. However, Muhammad did not care for the occupation of his young disciple and on numerous occasions denounced boxing as a "very wicked sport." As in most other matters, the Muslim leader was pragmatic in his detestation of boxing, aware that he had personally benefited from its financial rewards. Though he frequently stated he wanted to see Ali give up sports to proselytize for the Nation, he nonetheless did not want to see the champion leave the ring "until someone whips him." Paradoxically, he conceded that he never wanted Ali to be defeated. Perhaps in a vicarious way, Muhammad admired the boxer's confidence and athletic abilities. He was careful not to attend the fights of the champion or to permit him to acquire the kind of personal following that Malcolm X had garnered in the Nation. Yet, for several years, he allowed Ali to have a platform in the movement, despite his participation in the world of "white sport and play." He even allowed his son Herbert to become Ali's manager, ostensibly to protect the boxer from the influences of "a crooked business."[18]

Actually, the ambivalence in the relationship between Muhammad and Ali went both ways. From his first flirtations with the Nation of Islam back in 1961 until Muhammad's death in 1975, Ali was enthralled by the Messenger of Allah as both a father figure and the patriarchal leader of the Muslim movement. He had passed up an alliance with Malcolm X to stay in the good graces of Muhammad and had even risked the wrath of Hoover's FBI to be loved by the believers. He donated untold wealth to the Nation and paid Herbert handsomely as his manager. But despite his devotion to the vision of his spiritual teacher, Ali maintained a life outside of the strictures of the movement. He often collected the telephone numbers of coquettish groupies, drove his black Cadillac even after Muhammad had "revoked" his license, and continued to pursue his boxing career. Initially, this defiance was conveniently overlooked by the Muslim leader, who perhaps believed that the youthful rebelliousness of the athlete was a tolerable evil given his value to the Nation. In time, however, Ali's relevance to the program of Muhammad gradually diminished, and he, like Malcolm X, John Ali, and others, was cut loose like so much ballast that was now, in the leader's view, hindering the rise of the movement.[19]

Muhammad Ali was read out of the Nation in April 1969 editions of

Muhammad Speaks. His suspension, which was to last a year, was both public and humiliating—an object lesson for the believers. "Muhammad Ali . . . is out of the circle of the Brotherhood of the followers of Islam under the Leadership and Teachings of Elijah Muhammad," the Muslim leader declared in his statement. "Mr. Muhammad Ali shall not be recognized with us even under the Holy Name, Muhammad Ali. We will call him Cassius Clay." Deprived of contact with the believers, the boxer was back in the grave "until he proves himself worthy" of readmission. Supposedly, Muhammad had acted against Ali in response to the latter's public acknowledgment in early 1969 that he would return to the ring if the financial rewards were adequate. But much more was behind the sanction than this excuse disclosed. Since 1967, Ali had been suspended from boxing due to his refusal to abide by selective service orders. Until 1970, he would be embroiled in a costly legal battle to stay out of prison. Along with his declining tithes and loss of the heavyweight title, the draft controversy probably convinced Muhammad to minimize his losses while he was ahead. In essence, Ali had become a liability for the Nation, which was already feeling the sting of enhanced counterintelligence operations launched by the FBI in 1967.[20]

That Ali's stated desire to be financially rewarded for his boxing talents was all of a sudden offensive to Muhammad is not credible. For the past five years, the fighter had made his living in the sport. By 1969, Muhammad's tolerance of the exceptionality of Ali among his followers was simply no longer necessary. In the era of Black Power, the boxer was no longer an essential factor in the appeal of the Nation to young African-Americans, and his ouster would not have a significant impact on membership. On another level, the suspension of Ali was reminiscent of the isolation of Malcolm X during 1964. It seemed to raise many of the same issues of authority, generational tensions, and jealousies. Arguably, the punishment was meant to be a reassertion of Muhammad's dominion over the Nation—a reminder to followers who had become a bit too enamored of Ali.

Unlike Malcolm X, the suspended boxer, lacking both the leadership talents and ambitions of the former minister, simply bided his time until both his name was cleared (the Supreme Court threw out the draft conviction in June 1970) and his boxing privileges restored. Though he suffered a major defeat in a multimillion-dollar title bout against Joe Frazier in March 1971, Ali was able to make himself once again palatable to Elijah Muhammad. On the front page of the December 1, 1972, issue of the Muslim newspaper, pictures of the two men were prominently featured under the caption "Two Spotlights of the World!" The lead article indirectly suggested that Ali was again welcome in the Nation, since he was "a great spiritual man" who had "shown very great care for his opponents in the ring." In the months to come, the boxer resumed his public role as an advocate of the Messenger of Allah, minus much of the flamboyance and controversy that had surrounded him during the 1960s. More mature and settled, he became deeply involved in the economic ventures of the Nation, spearheading the campaign to raise funds for a Muslim hospital.[21]

While Muhammad Ali and others were falling out of favor with Elijah Muhammad during the 1960s, others were gaining his confidence and thus a measure of influence in the Nation. Chief among them was Minister Louis X of the Boston mosque. Raised by a single West Indian mother in the Roxbury section of Boston, Louis Eugene Walcott had been a precocious child and, at the age of five, learned to play the violin. Since the aspirations of young Louis outpaced the family's finances, he gave up on ever being able to study at Juilliard and instead enrolled in a teaching program at a small black college in Winston-Salem, North Carolina. Louis completed only two years of college before dropping out in 1953. The reasons for his withdrawal are not altogether clear, but certainly meager finances, the pressures of Southern race relations, and a pregnant girlfriend—whom he would later marry—played some part.[22]

Louis was raised Episcopalian, and his mother, Mae Clark, tried to instill in him values that would be appreciated by others. However, by the late 1940s, he found himself smoking marijuana and out in the nightlife of Boston. Fortunately, his musical talent was multidimensional, and he had little trouble finding work as a calypso singer in various clubs. His stage name was the Charmer, which was not wholly inappropriate. Apparently, he was popular enough to record a single entitled "Belly to Belly, Back to Back." But the odds of making it big in show business were poor, and Louis never became a musical phenomenon. In February 1955, a friend persuaded him to attend the Saviour's Day convention in Chicago. Thereafter, Louis, whose mother had been a Garveyite, became engrossed in the message of the Nation of Islam. Having registered with the New York organization, Louis X advanced swiftly through the ranks of Temple No. 7, eventually becoming a lieutenant of the Fruit of Islam. He had the best of tutors, Malcolm X, who helped him to learn the intricacies of Muslim doctrine and protocol. Given his background, Louis contributed greatly to the artistic side of the Nation and produced plays, such as *The Trial* and *Orgena* ("a Negro" spelled backward). He also penned what would become the theme song of the movement, "A White Man's Heaven Is a Black Man's Hell." By 1957, Louis's talent for oratory had been refined to the point that Elijah Muhammad saw fit to appoint him head of the Boston believers. At age twenty-four, he was one of the youngest ministers in the Nation. Over the next four decades, he would become the most controversial of all.[23]

During the 1964–65 war between Malcolm X and the Nation, Louis proved himself a most valuable resource to Elijah Muhammad. Though allegedly approached, he refused to depart with his suspended mentor and remained loyal to the Chicago leadership. He could not see following "a student of the teacher" on an uncertain journey, even though Malcolm had brought him into the Muslim fold. Instead, Louis cast his lot with Muhammad and became an outspoken critic of the former national spokesman. In the pages of *Muhammad Speaks*, the Boston minister excoriated his former mentor as a hypocrite and a traitor "worthy of death." As he would admit years later, he helped create the atmosphere that led to the assassination. While perhaps stunned by the murder, he recalled in a 1994 interview that "I can't say that I approved and I really didn't disapprove" of the killing. "I was numb." Despite the emotional paralysis of Louis, Muhammad was pleased with the triumph over Malcolm and lavishly rewarded the Boston minister for his loyalty and assistance. In a real sense, the rise of Louis X in the Nation coincided with the fall of Malcolm X, and the Boston minister readily acknowledged this on at least one occasion. "Because [Malcolm] died, I have a chance to live," he asserted in a 1980 speech in Harlem. The assassination had, indeed, opened up opportunities.[24]

Louis X, christened Louis Farrakhan during the late 1960s, was appointed minister of the prized Mosque No. 7 shortly after the death of Malcolm X. The position placed Farrakhan in the powerful inner circle of the Nation of Islam. In 1967, he was named national representative of the movement and, a year later, became the radio spokesman of Elijah Muhammad. Like the man whom he had replaced, Farrakhan had reached the upper echelon of the Nation in twelve years. Young, charismatic, and intelligent, he with his passionate orations could not help but conjure up images of Malcolm X, and he had obviously been deeply influenced by his slain mentor. Although he was employed by Muhammad to attract the same youthful, nationalistic constituency that Malcolm had mesmerized, Farrakhan was no cheap carbon copy of his former teacher. Their differences were substantial enough to permanently place one man at the right side of the Messenger of Allah and arguably to send the other to an early grave.[25]

Farrakhan stayed close to the heterodox Islam of Elijah Muhammad, carefully avoiding the political activism that Malcolm had embraced by the early 1960s. The media, though drawn to Farrakhan, did not pay him as much attention as it had Malcolm. The militant pronouncements and actions of individuals such as Huey P. Newton, H. Rap Brown, and Stokely Carmichael commanded more coverage during the Black Power period than the racial theology and capitalist strivings of the Nation. Unlike Malcolm, Farrakhan was not essential to the growth of the Muslim movement during the late 1960s and 1970s. While his predecessor had been instrumental in transforming the Nation from a tiny sect to a national phenomenon, Farrakhan became prominent at a time when the sprawling Muslim movement did not have to rely on individual personalities to prosper. The economic successes of the Nation and the enduring authority of Muhammad, blended with the popularity of his message by the late 1960s, greatly diminished the likelihood of a successful internal assault against his leadership. The failure of Malcolm X to sustain a substantial challenge to Muhammad had set a formidable precedent that few Muslims of even equal talents dared question. Consequently, Farrakhan—or John Ali or Muhammad Ali or others—could be dumped by Muhammad at any time and in any manner with minimal loss of membership. The Nation had reached the point where offices and titles were not inextricably tied to the individual associated with them, with the exception of Muhammad himself. The power structure of the movement had become more bureaucratic, institutional, and holistic; that is, it was no longer merely the sum of its component personalities.[26]

The selection of Farrakhan as minister of Mosque No. 7 and as national representative was not simply a reward for meritorious service. In fact, his appointments were part of a grand strategy of Muhammad designed to broaden the demographic appeal of the Nation. The class, age, and regional foundations of the movement had been shifting since World War II. By the mid-1950s, Southern migrants, at one time the primary constituency of the Nation, were being surpassed in number and influence by the younger, urban-born element. While persons with criminal backgrounds poured into the movement at this time, educated, middle-class individuals were also being attracted by Muslim models of economic self-help and moral reformism. Spokesmen like Farrakhan, to a greater degree than Malcolm X, epitomized the kind of believer whom Muhammad sought to bring into the fold during the late 1960s and 1970s. Young, college-educated, articulate, and talented, the ideal convert would be able to offer something to the movement to promote its image and prosperity. Professionals, in particular, were encouraged to apply for membership at their local mosque and "get together in unity." During a 1972 meeting with several hundred black business people and others, Muhammad exhorted, "Come all of you men and women who have professions and degrees. I have untold amounts of material to help you build them up!" Increasingly, skills and expertise were emphasized along with obedience and tithing. Nepotistic networks of privilege and a measure of corruption did continue even at the upper levels of the organization; however, the qualifications and expectations of key personnel were higher during this period than ever before.[27]

The search for professionals is quite understandable in light of the outburst of Muslim economic activity during the Black Power era. Burgeoning membership and collection baskets made it possible for the leadership to venture into a number of financial realms that had heretofore only been marginally explored. Muhammad now tried to build national industries, all be they autocratically controlled, for the African-African community. There were many notable successes. For example, commercial contacts with the Peruvian fishing industry led to a retail trade that netted the Nation millions of dollars in revenue by the mid-1970s. A four-story, sixty-thousand-square-foot building was purchased and renovated at a cost of a million dollars to house *Muhammad Speaks,* and a Chicago restaurant-supermarket center was secured for another million. To supply the latter operation, a lamb slaughterhouse was acquired for one hundred thousand dollars. Several thousand acres of farmland in Michigan, Georgia, and Alabama produced beef, eggs, milk, and grain, and a Muslim trucking system carried these goods to inner-city markets. If Elijah Muhammad could not claim the religious loyalty of black America, his entrepreneurship and economic nationalism were certainly applauded by many nonbelievers.[28]

While the late 1960s inaugurated a period of tremendous growth in the Muslim financial empire, the early 1970s seemed to confirm that the economic boom that the Nation was experiencing had few limits. In May 1972, the Muslims purchased a former Greek Orthodox church for $4.4 million and converted it into the new Temple No. 2. The acquisition was monumental, for the building was reportedly one of the ten largest houses of worship in the United States. In December, the organization secured a controlling interest in the Guaranty Bank and Trust Company. Though it had been alleged that the Chicago institution had been involved in scandals during the 1960s, its president, Oscar Williams, asserted that the bank had $10 million in assets by 1975. To Muhammad, the procurement of "a bank for the blackman" was a milestone. Now, the Muslims had a medium through which they could channel investments into other areas while servicing the financial needs of the black South Side. Even if Guaranty Bank never became a black Chase Manhattan or Bank of America, as its president predicted it would, the leadership of the movement thought big and invested big during this period. In 1974 at a cost of over a million dollars, the Nation purchased a Lockheed Jet Star Executive jet for Muhammad's personal use, allowing him, in true high-echelon corporate style, to fly "from coast to coast and from border to border" at speeds in excess of five hundred miles per hour.[29] By this time, the Muslim leader controlled the richest black organization in American history.

An Islamic University, which the Muslims had dreamed about since the 1950s, was vigorously pursued during this time. The center of learning, meant to accommodate ten thousand students, was to include a hospital, a technical college, and a nursery. The $50 million required to bring Muhammad's educational vision to fruition turned out to be beyond his reach. There were simply not enough profits from Muslim businesses, proceeds from fund-raisers, or donations from followers—though seventy-five thousand dollars was collected at the 1972 Saviour's Day convention alone—to cover the staggering cost of the black Mecca that he sought to create in Chicago. On a less grand scale, the Nation was able to maintain the forty-seven existing Universities of Islam, which were affiliated with various mosques. Moreover, small Muslim-owned businesses sprang up in almost every major city to the extent that the slogan "Do something for self" was familiar to many, if not most, African-Americans. Ultimately, the successes of the Muslims in other high-profile endeavors seemed to offset their failure to construct an educational center. The economic wherewithal of the Nation of Islam in the 1970s earned it the admiration of many people who had at one time dismissed it as an extremist aberration.[30]

Given the general inexperience of the Muslims in big business, there were some costly failures, especially in farming. The Michigan farm of the Nation was the only viable venture in agriculture. By 1971, roughly one hundred cows were being milked every day, and twenty thousand chickens were producing enough eggs to keep the Chicago retail operations well supplied. Also forthcoming was a range of vegetables and fruits. Farther south, however, the story was very different. The huge 4,350-acre Temple Farms complex near Bronwood, Georgia, represented a grandiose attempt by Muhammad to provide jobs and food for blacks in his native state and elsewhere. On paper, the farm was impressive. It consisted of a large dairy, a cannery, seven hundred head of cattle, and almost a thousand acres of corn, soybeans, and peanuts. Despite these assets, modestly trained farmers failed to manage the operation in an efficient and rational manner. "They tried to grow without irrigation," the former proprietor of the land told reporters, "and even good farmers would fail under those conditions." In this instance, the Nation paid the price for the inexperience of its personnel.[31]

In Pell City, Alabama, the Muslims again failed, but not due to a lack of skills. In a systematic campaign of state and vigilante intimidation, the $750,000 Muslim farm, consisting of nine hundred acres of land, was subjected to cattle poisonings and shootings, lawsuits, and anonymous threats of destruction. For a while, Muhammad ordered the believers to hold the line, and some promised retribution in the event the farm was invaded. By early 1970, as cattle deaths mounted and the white community became even more hostile toward black nationalist farmers in their midst, the Muslims decided to quit Pell City and move their operation to predominantly black Green County. "No use staying where people ain't civilized," the Muslim farm manager acknowledged after the decision to relocate was made. But combined with the foundering farm in Georgia, the debacle in Pell City was disastrous financially. According to a 1973 audit, the Nation had lost $682,000 in failed agricultural schemes. The calamities did not only affect the treasury of the Nation; being chased out of Pell City and self-destructing in Georgia did nothing for the image of the organization. As was the case in so many Muslim endeavors of the period, the sacrifices and expenses that the movement incurred while trying to employ African-Americans in the Deep South have not been matched by any black organization since.[32]

The impact of fiscal mismanagement and excesses on Muslim enterprises is difficult to determine, but there was enough of both to figure in as factors in the failure of at least some economic ventures. Access to extraordinary wealth tended to weaken the forbearance of top officials even more than before, and Muhammad himself spent millions of dollars on lavish personal expenses. The complex of five extravagant homes constructed during the 1970s for members of the "royal family"—at a reported expense of $2 million—was illustrative. During a 1972 lecture, the leader acknowledged that he was a millionaire, but counseled his audience to have faith in trickle-down economics and "wait until I pull you up." For the most part, the believers did just that and continued to feel that he had their best interests at heart. Of course, the federal government, bent upon sharing in his wealth, paid close attention to the income and expenditures of Muhammad. By the end of the year, the Tax Division of the Department of Justice had filed a tax-claim suit against the Muslim leader, no longer convinced that religion should shield his empire from the tax man.[33]

The shadow of extravagance, and sometimes avarice, was cast over many of the financial dealings of the Chicago leadership during this period. While the materialism of some officials contrasted sharply with the moral asceticism inherent in Muslim doctrine, the two themes were not mutually exclusive or necessarily inconsistent in the eyes of most believers. Illustratively, during his 1974 Saviour's Day address, Muhammad was comfortable enough with his affluence to wear a jewel-studded fez allegedly worth $150,000. In keeping with the separatist tradition of the Nation, he reminded his followers that "I can't wear a crown with no country." Unfortunately, the amount of money that passed through Muhammad's hands while he led the Nation, or just during the 1970s, cannot be determined. Muslim records began to reflect the total income of the organization only a few years before his death in 1975. Would the money invested in expensive homes, bloated personal bank accounts, gaudy headgear, and other items have made a decisive difference in the Georgia farming scheme or the fund-raising campaign for the Islamic University? Maybe. Nonetheless, materialism was so entrenched among national leaders by the 1970s that few would sacrifice comfortable standards of living for the sake of ambitious agricultural and educational pursuits that were often risky propositions at best.[34]

Although all of the specific causes behind the failure of some Muslim enterprises cannot be known, the compromises that the Chicago leadership had to make to further its economic objectives are quite clear in many cases. Since the 1950s, Elijah Muhammad had paid at least lip service to orthodox Islam. Depending on the intensity of pressures to conform to traditional Muslim beliefs, he often embraced certain elements of the Middle Eastern faith while ignoring others. His hajj in December 1959 was the watershed event in his search for acceptance among orthodox Muslims. Yet once the tremendous popularity of the Nation during the early 1960s became clearly associated with its race-based Islam and black nationalism, Muhammad saw little need to turn to Mecca for spiritual guidance. Theologically, nothing really changed under his leadership during the late 1960s and 1970s. However, as Muslim economic aspirations became broader in scope and more expensive to realize, the leader found it necessary, and pragmatic, to at least say some of the things that influential Arab OPEC countries wanted to hear.

The appeal for funds from the East was both subtle and direct. For example, around 1970 Muhammad instructed his followers to start observing the month of Ramadan in accordance with the Islamic calendar. Historically, they had commemorated this period of fasting in December to coincide with the Christian celebration of Christmas. Perhaps more significantly, Muhammad reportedly requested that Ali Baghdadi, an orthodox Muslim who wrote editorials for *Muhammad Speaks,* conduct the marriage ceremonies of his grandchildren in line with traditional Islamic rites. Like his hajj, these symbolic overtures did not represent a fundamental change in the theology of the Nation. They were simply trappings employed to make the movement more acceptable to influential Eastern Muslims. The most substantial appeals of Muhammad to the Islamic world for assistance were largely behind the scenes and likely involved promises and pacts that were mutually beneficial.

Editorial criticism of Israel became commonplace in issues of the Muslim newspaper by the late 1960s, and Muhammad himself frequently asserted that Israel "belongs to the Arabs and not to the Jews." Anti-Zionist pronouncements by the Nation had a noticeable impact on Arab listeners. One orthodox Muslim compared Muhammad to a lion who was not afraid to stand up against what he viewed as Jewish imperialism in the Middle East. Another Muslim of some importance, Libyan President Muammar al-Gadhafi, was even more impressed with the Nation and established informal diplomatic relations with the movement. In May 1972, Tripoli gave the Nation a zero-interest loan of $3 million, payable over a three-year period. That same month, Muhammad applied the money to the purchase of the Greek Orthodox church that was converted to the new Mosque No. 2.[35]

While Eastern Muslims certainly placed pressures on Muhammad to take the Nation in a more orthodox direction, monetary assistance from Arab-Islamic countries such as Libya and Abu Dhabi, which gave $125,000 to the movement in late 1972, did little toward revolutionizing his theology. The leader did exhibit a greater willingness to recognize the existence of "white Muslims" who might be spared Allah's wrath during the Armageddon. Nonetheless, his teachings remained largely consistent with what he had learned from his mentor, Fard Muhammad, back in the 1930s. Interestingly enough, Muhammad claimed that he had again been in contact with "Allah in Person" in September 1971. Moreover, only months after the Libyan loan was secured, he stated during a talk at the new Chicago mosque that the Nation would eventually receive "a new Book" to replace the Bible and the Qur'an. The ability of Muhammad to obtain assistance from Middle Eastern nations while remaining true to his basic convictions is a testament to both the theological independence of the Nation and its ongoing loyalty to its primary constituency—the black Muslim population of the United States. The fact that the money was forthcoming anyway suggests that doctrinal conformity was less important to Gadhafi and others than access to the movement's expanding influence and audience.[36]

In addition to reaching out to the Islamic world, during this period Muhammad also toned down his public animosity toward whites. The more conciliatory attitude was more tactical than anything else as economic expansion was creating tensions with the ideology of the movement. For example, while Muhammad continued to call for a separate black state, he was investing more and more funds into projects located throughout white America. The grand nature of some of his plans necessitated appeals to white institutions for aid, such as the request he made for a $10-million loan in the May 17, 1968, edition of *Muhammad Speaks*. After Richard Nixon was elected in late 1968, the Muslim leader hoped to tap into the enterprise zones that the president was touting as a solution to the economic underdevelopment of the African-American community. When no real government policy materialized, Muslim emissaries approached federal officials directly in July 1970 to request tens of millions of dollars in aid to train workers in auto mechanics, printing, and other trades. For anyone who knew the history of Muslim-white relations, these appeals for assistance must have appeared to be the ultimate irony. However, given Muhammad's propensity to tolerate some contradictions for what he viewed as the best interests of the Nation, an alliance of convenience with even "devils" would not have been wholly surprising.[37]

Again, there was no general liberalization of the Nation's racial chauvinism under Muhammad's leadership. During a 1972 lecture, he insisted that "I don't care if [Vietnamese] kill Americans.... Let them fight and let them kill off as many of each other as they can." As late as his 1974 Saviour's Day address, he told a Muslim crowd that nature did not put a thirst for justice, freedom, and equality in whites and that blacks should not look for these qualities in them. These kinds of statements were made more frequently than racially moderate ones. Still, during the 1970s Muhammad was more likely to seek detente with the white community than at any other time. In a few instances, he went so far as to thank the U.S. government for feeding, clothing, and educating blacks and told his followers to respect whites as long as they were in power. The leader himself lived in an integrated community to supposedly prove "that I can live in their neighborhood just as cleanly and noiselessly as they do." Such rhetoric and gestures were aimed at creating an atmosphere of tolerance and economic cooperation between a capital-hungry Nation of Islam and a society that had historically been suspicious of its intentions. Along with advancing his economic program, the occasional racial temperance of Muhammad was also designed to lessen the destructiveness of the counterintelligence war against the Nation that the FBI had escalated in 1967 to include all "black nationalist hate groups."[38]

Richard Nixon was never very popular among black people. Conversely, he did not seem to think much of African-Americans as a racial group or as a political constituency. His career as a politician had been built on the bedrock of anti-Communism that had undergirded American culture since the Great Depression. His politics in the late 1960s had been opposed to the liberal agendas of his presidential predecessors. At bottom, his electoral appeal was based on "law and order" themes that resonated among voters who felt that the government had done far too much for blacks and that it was time to get tough with urban rioters. Ultimately, he hoped to gain the loyalty and votes of the so-called "silent majority" of Americans who he believed had been alienated by civil rights protests, antiwar demonstrations, and the emergence of the New Left.[39]

Ample evidence suggests that Nixon was personally against integration in principle, not to mention legally mandated remedies that forced reluctant whites into compliance. His Southern political strategy required him to distance his administration from the issue altogether, leaving matters of race to the Supreme Court. To him, maintaining the sympathy of white Republicans who might otherwise be swayed by the racist appeals of political opponents such as George Wallace depended upon him staying on a conservative—but not extremist—course regarding desegregation. Yet, despite his politics and beliefs, during the Nixon presidency affirmative action and busing were first introduced to redress racial inequities in education and employment. Many of the decisions of the Warren Burger Court regarding race dismayed the president, but he did not overtly try to obstruct the enforcement of the law. Throughout his time in office, Nixon's view of black America vacillated between cautious concern and subtle hostility. According to White House chief of staff H. R. Haldeman, the president, at his most moderate, sought to "limit all our support and communication to the good blacks and totally ignore the militants." For the most part, Nixon succeeded in doing just that during his six years as president.[40]

One person who did ignore "the good blacks" in favor of paying rapt attention to "the militants" was J. Edgar Hoover. The FBI of the late 1960s was much more aggressive in its search for subversives than in previous years, motivated by the increasing boldness of war protesters and Black

Power advocates. In response to seemingly ubiquitous dissent, Hoover—presumably with the consent of President Johnson—had started a new counterintelligence program on August 25, 1967, to, in the words of the bureau

> neutralize militant black nationalists . . . prevent the coalition of militant black nationalist groups, prevent the rise of a leader who might unify and electrify these violence-prone elements, prevent these militants from gaining respectability and prevent the growth of these groups among America's youth.

This surveillance initiative (code-named COINTELPRO) was the most comprehensive ever. Hoover's favorite organizational target was the Black Panther Party, which was virtually destroyed by FBI informants, bureau-supported police raids, and a calculated campaign of misinformation. But as always, the director was absorbed most by his fixation on Martin Luther King Jr., even until those tragic days in Memphis. In truth, Hoover did not believe that Elijah Muhammad was much of a threat to the kind of America that he wished to reconstruct. The Muslim leader had turned seventy in October 1967, and his advancing age and conservatism were cited by bureau officials as a reason to discount him as a danger to national security. Nonetheless, for the sake of certainty, the Nation was targeted for a dose of counterintelligence anyway. The fear of a black nationalist jihad, of Elijah Muhammad summoning hordes of Fruit of Islam to destroy the white world "with the snap of his finger," still seemed to disconcert Hoover and those around him.[41]

The COINTELPRO offensive against the Nation was nasty and direct. Little was too vile or uncivil. Letters documenting the extramarital affairs of Muhammad were again mailed to Clara. This time, his adult daughters even received copies. Anonymous notes were also sent to "key followers" detailing the affluent lifestyles of their Chicago leaders. Concurrently, proposals to examine the tax returns of Herbert Muhammad were seriously considered, since the FBI believed him to be "merciless, cunning and an ego maniac"—somehow a threat to domestic stability. On a much more sinister note, bureau operatives tried to cause the Nation of Islam and the Black Panther Party "to direct their hatred toward one another" by disseminating unsigned letters that warned Panther newspaper hawkers against posing a challenge to the popularity of *Muhammad Speaks*. Unfortunately, this particular tactic may have been successful, for in February 1971, two members of the organizations fought over who would sell newspapers on a downtown Atlanta street corner. In addition to the tactics described here, countless other FBI counterintelligence ploys will never be disclosed to the public. Declassified documents undoubtedly reveal only those COINTEL-

PRO activities that are least damaging to the reputation of the bureau and its parent agencies.[42]

The tapping of Muhammad's phones, both in Chicago and Phoenix, was officially discontinued in June 1966. To the chagrin of the FBI, the six years of electronic surveillance became public knowledge in 1969. Though the more politically conservative Nation was spared the kind of search-and-destroy campaign that was inflicted upon the left-leaning Panthers, the bureau kept constant tabs on the activities of Muhammad and others, even following him to the Bahamas during a vacation trip in January 1971. Some relief came when Hoover died in 1972 and congressional committees finally began to acknowledge what the federal government had allowed him to do to American civil liberties. Still, the director's legacy would endure beyond his death, given his forty-eight-year tenure as the head of the FBI. For the Nation, there was little change in its relationship with the law enforcement community. Where federal agencies slacked off, local police departments often stepped up the pressure on the more active mosques. In the end, the bureau, even without Hoover, did not lose interest in Muhammad and his Muslims. Up until the leader's death in February 1975, agents and informants still contributed regularly to the voluminous "Black Muslim Movement" file.[43]

The surveillance activities of the FBI and other agencies greatly irritated Muhammad. Occasionally, he could not help but editorially denounce both the "ever-evil snoopers" who "tap our telephones, eavesdrop and follow us around" and the "evil, blind, dead and dumb Black People" who purposely attempted to discredit the reputation of the Nation. Since the 1930s when the FBI first became interested in the movement, Muhammad was aware of at least some of the methods that the bureau had used to hinder its growth, but he never knew the exact extent to which his organization had been infiltrated by informants and agents provocateurs. Uncertainty about the influence of unseen enemies sometimes led to paranoia, which, in a few instances, was translated into organizational policy. For example, after the New York mosque was raided by policemen in April 1972, Muhammad ordered the expulsion of black law enforcement officers from the Nation, a number of whom had been members since the 1950s. Certainly, not all, and probably not even most, black policemen who were in the movement were informants, but the leader, cognizant of the damage that COINTELPRO was causing, was prepared to take extreme measures to protect his mosques from manipulation. As he had always done, Muhammad continued to distance the movement from activities that might encourage government censure. Shaken by the police murders of Fred Hampton and Mark Clark in 1968, he carefully avoided any ties with the Black Panther Party, which he considered "dangerous" and ill-conceived, and reportedly prohibited coverage of its activities in *Muhammad Speaks*. While ruffled by the intrusiveness of COINTELPRO, he did not allow his anger to manifest itself in ways that might jeopardize the many projects, especially in finance and real estate, that the Nation was becoming involved in.[44]

During the 1960s and 1970s, Muhammad often reiterated his opposition to Muslim participation in the American political process. He consistently wrote off electoral politics as laden with corruption. He saw no difference between the two major parties since "the die is always set against us" and continued to believe that white people would rule regardless of how black votes were cast. Characteristically, he remained adamant that blacks were not truly citizens of the United States and that they should "vote for Allah" as he had done in 1942 when ordered to register for the draft. As more African-Americans than ever before were being elected and appointed to local and national offices, Muhammad reasserted that his mission was not a political one "as long as he, the white man, lives." On the surface, his stated aversion to politics was simply a recitation of long-held religious principles. On other levels, his repudiation of the world of "crooked politics" laid bear the conservative, pragmatic, nonactivist values behind his leadership. To the end of his life, Muhammad made strenuous, though largely unsuccessful, efforts to keep the Nation out of the sights of government agencies. He, like all other icons of the Black Power Movement, was sorely aware that the FBI, IRS, and other groups were looking for new ways to "neutralize militant black nationalists," especially those with allegedly subversive agendas.[45]

By the late 1960s, Muhammad had stopped making trips to Phoenix on a regular basis, even for medical reasons. He spent some time in the city during the latter part of 1967, but mainly for recruitment. To be sure, bronchial asthma and other ailments still crippled him on occasion. In 1970, he had cataracts removed from his eyes, an operation that temporarily required him to wear sunglasses. Despite these afflictions, he still had to curtail visits to Phoenix. Beginning in 1971 and continuing through 1973, a number of Muslim mosques were weakened by internal fighting. In a few instances, competition for influence in the Nation led to injuries and deaths. The conflict was related to Muhammad's age and incessant health problems, as some Muslims perhaps desired to gain advantage before a war over succession broke out. Also, the internecine struggles were related to resurgent ideological issues that pitted idealistic Young Turks against the conservative, acquisitive Old Guard. By the time the violence reached Mosque No. 2 in October 1971, Muhammad seldom left Chicago for extended periods of time. The fear of being absent during a coup d'état was very real for him, as it had been since his forced flight from the city in 1935.[46]

Much of the discontent of the dissidents was aimed at national officials such as Fruit of Islam head, Raymond Sharrieff. The affluent lifestyle and broad authority of the Supreme Captain symbolized to some the corruption that had become endemic in some quarters and the hierarchical arrangement of power in the movement, which naturally minimized the influence of the rank and file on organizational policy. The rebels did not have a clearly defined agenda, and their resources and support were negligible. Apparently, no organized leadership was directing the insurrection. Factions operating in New York, Oakland, and Baton Rouge seemed to be loosely connected at best; some claimed to still revere Elijah Muhammad as their spiritual leader, while others seceded from the Nation altogether. If the motivations and objectives of the renegade groups—variously known as the Young Muslims, Saudi Arabia, and El Colistrand—were vague, their methods were stark enough to seize the attention of the national media. Throughout the early 1970s, the dissenters plunged the Nation into a costly civil war that took lives and jeopardized the hard-earned respectability of the movement among African-Americans.[47]

The Supreme Captain had been victimized before; in 1970 he was robbed of twenty-three thousand dollars at gunpoint by intruders who broke into his home. But he had never faced a wave of assaults like the one he encountered during 1971–72. A botched assassination attempt on his life by dissenters in October 1971 set off the violence. Whether a retributive order was given by Elijah Muhammad is unclear, but four of the conspirators were found dead soon after—one slain in his Chicago apartment and three others in San Francisco. In apparent retaliation, one of the assistants of the Supreme Captain was injured by gunfire while in a restaurant. A little while later, Sharrieff's secretary narrowly escaped being shot down when a bullet was fired into the offices of *Muhammad Speaks*. The violence continued into 1972, claiming the lives of up to ten Muslims, including two killed in a January shootout with police while trying to stir up support in Baton Rouge. (Predictably, Muhammad publicly distanced the Nation from this episode, which had also resulted in the deaths of two law enforcement officers.) By year's end, murderous infighting posed the greatest threat to the stability of the Nation since the departure of Malcolm X in 1964. Insulated from the carnage by heightened security measures, Elijah Muhammad maintained general control over his factious Nation. Yet, he failed to resolve the divisive issues of privilege and doctrine that had fueled the clashes.[48]

The brutality of the infighting descended to new depths in 1973. On January 20, a Muslim was found executed, shot twice in the head, in Los Angeles. Four months later, Hakim A. Jamal, a relative of the late Malcolm X and the leader of the Malcolm X Foundation, was killed in his Boston home by four gunmen. Jamal, a former member of the Nation, had been a vocal critic of Elijah Muhammad and was known in the black community for his "loose-lipped" tirades against the Muslim movement. In September, more people turned up dead. James Shabazz, ministerial head of the Newark mosque, was ambushed at his home by two assailants. The bullet that killed him penetrated his brain after entering his left eye. The assassins were not apprehended at the scene, but at least eight members of a splinter group were found guilty of the killing. The Shabazz slaying was followed two weeks later by the double murders of Roger and Ralph Bankston, twin brothers whose links to the Shabazz assassination are hard to discern. In October, the bodies of the two Muslims who police believed killed the Bankstons were found decapitated in a vacant lot a block away from the Newark home of James Shabazz. With every month that passed, the victims of Muslim intra-organizational politics and intergroup rivalries escalated in number, and the methods of their killers became commensurately more morbid. By 1974, it seemed that any member might be found dead, anywhere. In May, police attributed a string of mysterious murders in San Francisco to a secret cell of Muslims who allegedly called themselves Death Angels. Unlike in all of the other killings, the victims in this case were whites, who had apparently been randomly selected for extermination.[49]

Grisly though they were, none of the aforementioned killings matched the mass murder of the Hanafi Muslims in merciless cruelty. Hamaas Abdul Khaalis, the leader of the orthodox-leaning group, had been the secretary of Chicago Mosque No. 2 during the 1950s. As mentioned in Chapter 6, a confrontation with the Nation's leadership over questions of nepotism resulted in his resignation from the movement in 1958. Over the next decade, Khaalis started his own Hanafi Madh Hab Muslim community based in Washington, D.C., which claimed one thousand members by the early 1970s. The group was large enough now to compete with Mosque No. 4 and other branches of the Nation for converts in the African-American community. However, Khaalis overplayed his hand. Around this time, he sent copies of an inflammatory letter to each of the Nation's mosques, criticizing Elijah Muhammad as "a lying deceiver" and Fard Muhammad as a "slightly cockeyed" criminal. The followers of the Nation were denounced as "eaters of their dead brothers' flesh" who were destined to roast in a "violently hot flame." Rhetorically, Khaalis asked Muslim ministers, "What madness is in your leader and teacher Muhammad, what kind of minds do you have?" Later in the letter, he answered the query himself, asserting that Muhammad's teachings had produced "polluted minds." Shortly after his letters were dispatched, Khaalis received a response to his questions and charges. Nothing could have prepared him for what would take place on the afternoon of January 18, 1973.[50]

At around 4 P.M., two men arrived at the four-story Hanafi headquarters on Sixteenth Street N.W. One of the men identified himself as "Tommy," the same person who had called earlier and made an appointment to purchase some literature on the Hanafi movement. When Daud, the young man who answered the door, went to retrieve change for a bill that Tommy had given him, the two callers entered the house and announced, "This is a stickup." Immediately, five or six other men, at least some of whom were armed, came into the house and began tying up the occupants. Daud was executed first by gunfire on the third floor of the dwelling. Another Hanafi man, Abdul Nur, was shot to death in a bedroom. Next, Bibi, Khaalis's twenty-six-year-old wife, was seized by the intruders and forced to watch as they drowned two of her children, a one-year-old girl and a newborn boy, in a bathtub. She was then dragged to the basement to witness the drowning of Tasibur, her nine-day-old step-granddaughter, in a sink. As if to relieve her shock, the killers turned their guns on Bibi and left her for dead before murdering her toddler, Abdullah, in a powder room. Rahman Uddein, the ten-year-old son of Khaalis, met his fate on Daud's bed. Almina, Daud's mother and one of the few survivors, was forced into a closet and then shot in the head. Apparently, the intruders stayed around long enough to rob the house of "a considerable amount" of money before leaving. According to Khaalis, who was not at home during the rampage, they even gave hints about their identities. "Don't mess with Elijah!" one of the fleeing assailants reportedly warned. "Hamaas should've expected this when he wrote those letters!"[51]

The atrocities were a scene from a most horrific version of hell. Little in recent memory measured up to the cold deliberateness of the terror. The killing of actress Sharon Tate and several others by disciples of Charles Manson four years earlier perhaps came close in the eyes of the public, but even these murders did not involve infant children. Actually, words cannot begin to capture the sentiments that produced the ghastly deeds of that Thursday afternoon in 1973. Khaalis, having lost four children and a granddaughter in the massacre, was quick to accuse Elijah Muhammad and his followers of the crimes. "You know by the slaughter of women and children that they do not believe in Allah," he announced at a press conference. Kareem Abdul-Jabbar, a professional basketball player and member of the Hanafi group, seemingly concurred with Khaalis's assessment, adding that "they were so threatened [by the letters] that they had to take the lives of children." Indeed, the temporal relationship between the mailing of the anti-Muhammad letters and the murders did seem to suggest causality.[52]

Despite what the aggrieved Hanafis may have thought, no clear evidence linked Elijah Muhammad to the killings. He could only reasonably be accused of helping to stir up the hatred that inspired the acts by occasionally printing editorials that denounced "the hypocrites." The February 2 edition of *Muhammad Speaks* denied that the Nation was involved in the murders and labeled Khaalis a "modern-day 'Uncle Tom.'" Farrakhan argued that the killers were government operatives who were trying to discredit the Muslim movement. Ultimately, at least four men claiming affiliation with Philadelphia Mosque No. 12 were convicted of the crimes and each sentenced to seven consecutive life sentences. If Farrakhan's contention regarding government involvement was unsubstantiated, few could argue with his conclusion that "no sane Muslim" could have been responsible for the killings.[53]

By the end of 1973, the murderous infighting and interorganizational violence that had racked the Muslim community were finally declining in frequency and destructiveness. Those youthful dissidents who had tried to forcibly reform the Nation from within had either seceded and formed new organizations, died in the power struggle, or resolved to bide their time until the odds for success improved. External challenges to the status quo of the Nation, such as those posed by the Hanafis and others, were never really a threat to the leadership of Elijah Muhammad, but were still minimized by the apparent willingness of some of his followers to mete out punishments in his name. None of the violence touched the Muslim leader, and none of the injuries and deaths can be traced directly to him—at least available sources do not implicate him. Nonetheless, he came out on top of it all, and his position as head of the Nation of Islam was as solid in early 1974 as it had been following the death of Malcolm X. As it turned out, the question of succession was settled during the bloody years of 1971–73. When the shootings, beheadings, and drownings ended, Muhammad was still in a position to name his successor, if he chose to name one at all. No one would come close to toppling him during this period, or even posing a credible challenge to his revered position as the Messenger of Allah. This truism was now even clear to the dissenters in whose blood it had been written.

In the midst of the fighting, death also claimed Clara. At least two weeks prior to her passing in August 1972, doctors had diagnosed her with a terminal illness that could not be treated. She chose to perish at home among family rather than hope for a miracle cure at Mercy Hospital. Her death, according to one report, left Muhammad "considerably distraught." There had been much turbulence in the marriage—and emotional scars that probably never went away despite a later life of comfort and material security. Still, the relationship endured for fifty-three years, even given Muhammad's imprisonment, infidelities, and organizational commitments. Stricken with ailments himself, Muhammad perhaps gained a greater sense of his own mortality in the wake of his wife's passing.[54]

As one might expect for the first lady of the Nation of Islam, her funeral was memorable, and little expense was spared. She was dressed in fine silk and placed in a metallic coffin valued at five thousand dollars. The last rites were given in Arabic in the spacious new Mosque No. 2. Naturally, Muhammad led the two-hundred-car cavalcade to her final resting place at the family burial site at Thornton, Illinois, where his mother, Marie, was interred. Her grave was copper-trimmed, and she was laid to rest in what one of the funeral directors called the "ultimate in burial vaults for earth interments." Given their decades of marriage, it is hard to imagine that anyone would miss her more than her husband, Elijah, but as an icon of the Nation, her death was viewed as a tragedy for all Muslims.[55]

PART FOUR

EQUALITY JUSTICE
ISLAM FREEDOM

JUDGMENT

CHAPTER 10

IN THE LAST DAYS

*I would not refer to my father as a god. . . . I want
to get rid of all this spiritual spookiness.*

*Our purpose is the revival and restoration of the
pure Islam. . . . God does not eat, he does not drink. . . .
The Prophet Mohammed is the seal of the prophets,
and the Koran is the last book.*
—Wallace D. Muhammad, 1976–77 [1]

*We who are the disciples of the Honorable Elijah
Muhammad should bring that program back—stand on
it, don't alter it, don't change it, don't
corrupt it.*
—Louis Farrakhan, 1978 [2]

Elijah Muhammad held his last press conference on January 14, 1972. The leader had never been fond of allowing often hostile reporters to grill him, even in the privacy of his own home, and had not granted the privilege to journalists since the assassination of Malcolm X. However, a number of issues were confronting him that needed to be hashed out publicly—issues that were too important and sensitive for his spokesmen to address on his behalf. The violence among competing factions in the Muslim community was beginning to escalate and may have been the primary reason for Muhammad's decision to speak to the press. As always, he denied involvement in the bloodshed and asserted that he would triumph over his enemies.

"They [the dissenters] always will be striving to be something of their own," Muhammad conceded, "but I do not pay them any attention because I know they will never be successful." On the question of doctrine, he spoke vaguely about a "new Islam," which would be racially exclusive and "led by Black Muslims, only." Predictably, he affirmed his continuing allegiance to the theology of Fard Muhammad, whose voice he still occasionally heard "all of a sudden out of a blue sky, like thunder." The touchiest questions asked dealt with succession, and the reporters almost insisted upon Muhammad's naming an heir. Given his traditional aversion to public discussions of such divisive matters, Muhammad answered the query as he always had. "There will be no successor," he stated candidly. "There is no need for a successor when a man has got the Divine truth and has brought you face-to-face with God." The newsmen had to be satisfied with his reply and wisely moved on to other issues during the one-and-a-half-hour interview. Of course, Muhammad's dodging of the succession question did not resolve the dilemma; if anything, his maneuvering heightened expectations.[3]

While the future of the Nation was by no means clear during the early 1970s, the movement exhibited both promise and prosperity. The membership rolls of local mosques, which numbered seventy-six in February 1975, told part of the story. The Chicago headquarters still attracted believers by the hundreds during regular services, and on Saviour's Days, crowds well over ten thousand strong flooded both the new flagship mosque and local meeting facilities. Los Angeles Mosque No. 27, traditionally a hot spot in the Nation's decades-long troubles with law enforcement agencies, had at least one thousand registered members when Abdul Karim became the new minister in 1971. This figure does not include Muslim cells that had sprung up in Compton and Long Beach. In the South, where the Nation had historically enjoyed only a token presence, the emergence of the Black Power Movement fostered a number of flourishing mosques. The Durham, North Carolina, organization could boast a membership of a couple hundred families—a respectable achievement in a city with fewer than one hundred thousand residents. The oldest branch of the Nation in the Deep South, Atlanta Mosque No. 15, had five hundred registered members in 1973. By 1976, membership figures, according to the estimate of an assistant minister, had quadrupled, commensurate with the city's burgeoning African-American population. Mosques in Southwestern cities such as Dallas and Phoenix also increased in size during the late 1960s and 1970s, but not at the accelerated rates of growth experienced by many other local branches in urban areas heavily populated by African-Americans.[4]

The largest mosque continued to be New York Mosque No. 7, which now comprised a network of Muslim meeting houses sprawled across the city. The Harlem mosque (7A), administered by Louis Farrakhan, may have reached a membership high of five thousand believers, though the nucleus of long-term followers was somewhat smaller. Other organizations in the New York web could attract formidable crowds during any given week, including the Brooklyn mosque (7B), under Minister Arthur 14X, which served the spiritual needs of roughly eight hundred men and six hundred women. In all, twenty constituent mosques (lettered from 7A to 7T) made up the New York section of the Nation of Islam. Outside of Chicago, this East Coast stronghold was the most powerful subunit of the Muslim movement and produced some of its brightest talent. Elijah Muhammad was fond of noting that "there is gold in New York," a reference to the vast recruitment opportunities. Arguably, the state of affairs among the Muslims of Mosque No. 7 was as important as the situation in Chicago. History had already proven it to be integrally linked to the popularity and economic advancement of the entire Nation.[5]

As to the economic empire of the Nation, it would not begin to contract until after Muhammad's death. Holdings in real estate, retail industries, and other areas expanded during the mid-1970s, though the debts of the organization were climbing, due largely to failed ventures and mismanagement. The last big dream of Muhammad was a three-hundred-bed hospital on the South Side of Chicago that would be black owned and operated. The facility, proposed as a new construction, would serve "all the sick and wounded of the area." Initial costs would run well into the millions of dollars. With the exception of the Islamic Center, which was also to include medical facilities, Muhammad desired a hospital more than anything else. Despite fifty-dollar-per-plate dinners, alliances with black businessmen, and even an anonymous five-hundred-thousand-dollar donation to the "Elijah Muhammad Hospital Fund," the contributions were not enough to bring the project to fruition. Like his wife and many other black Chicagoans, the Muslim leader would have to spend most of his last days at Mercy Hospital and Medical Center, surrounded by white administrators and staff members. To be sure, a black hospital was within the realm of possibility for the Muslims. However, its realization would have required more financial resources, technical assistance, and friends in high places than the movement could call upon at the time.[6]

If it was any consolation, the Nation was at least doing well in other areas. Fish sales by various mosques had become lucrative, with profits outpacing expenses by more than a million dollars in 1975. Issues of *Muhammad Speaks* came off the presses by the hundreds of thousands each week, and mandatory sales quotas for Fruit of Islam guaranteed Chicago a substantial share of proceeds. Still, as had been the case for several years, the aura of avarice and graft dogged the Muslim image even as the economy of the Nation boomed. It was all too easy to spot "Superfly" ministers "wearing pimp's clothes and preaching nation building." As Wallace Muhammad observed, some officials fancied "full-length chinchilla coats" and "the hat[s] to match." Unfortunately, one too commonly read about Muslims-turned-criminals who preyed upon the unsuspecting, black and white. Incidents such as the armed robbery of a Kansas City church in October 1974 by six men—three identified as Muslims—did nothing to endear the Nation to the general public. Muslim officials, chagrined by the recidivism of some followers, could only disavow complicity in such acts and promise to ostracize known offenders.[7]

By the mid-1970s, Muhammad had little control over the everyday affairs of various mosques and could not reasonably be held accountable for every instance of lawless behavior on the part of a few of his followers. The tremendous growth of the movement over the past decade, and his advancing age and illnesses, had forced him to delegate greater authority to national officials and trusted subordinates in other states. In a sense, the Muslim leader had become a figurehead, though his word remained the bottom line in all substantial policy matters. To some outside of the movement, he came to represent a kind of venerable iconoclast who had accomplished some positive things in the black community, despite his racial theology. Factors such as his age, his honored role in the Black Power Movement and the African-American community in general, and his thorough embrace of mainstream values—from entrepreneurial capitalism to puritanical morals—made him acceptable to many who had been apprehensive about the Nation in the past.

It was strange how much the situation had changed in only the span of a decade. For example, the Illinois state legislature, which had contemplated closing the University of Islam years earlier, passed a resolution in 1973 recognizing "the Honorable Elijah Muhammad and his organization for a distinct, positive community program." A year later, Mayor Richard Daley, never unaware of the importance of strategic political support, officially declared March 29 as "Honorable Elijah Muhammad Day in Chicago." The motives of Daley and others in these instances are hard to pinpoint, beyond a willingness to acknowledge that the Nation was more of a religious self-help organization than the vanguard of a coming revolution. Whatever the case, the compliments illustrated just how consistent the Muslim work ethic, moral vision, and ethnic solidarity were with American values and practices. Even FBI agents felt comfortable enough to approach Muhammad for an interview on November 12, 1974, and were pleased to hear him state that "he believed in law and order . . . and loved America very much." Undoubtedly, some of the compliments from whites were preliminary eulogies for the Muslim leader, whose health was steadily declining. Others were perhaps subtle apologies for the historical racism, discrimination, and brutality against blacks that had produced Elijah Muhammad and his Nation of Islam in the first place. Typically gracious when praised by nonfollowers, the Muslim leader returned kindness with kindness. To Daley and the Illinois state government, he wrote, "My followers and I will try with all our efforts to prove worthy of the respect and honor given to us from you as good citizens of Chicago, and of Illinois." In all likelihood, he was being totally sincere.[8]

Perhaps to some, the Nation of Islam appeared to be a tolerable American institution by the mid-1970s. It had not only distinguished itself as a model for black economic initiative and cultural rejuvenation; it had also survived challenges from many quarters. With each triumph over his opponents, be they orthodox enemies such as Talib Dawud and Hamaas Khaalis, civil rights critics such as Martin Luther King Jr. and Roy Wilkins, apostates such as Malcolm X and Wallace Muhammad, or Hoover's meddlesome FBI, the Muslim leader strengthened his hold on the reins of the movement. Of course, he attributed his success in these feuds to the will of God—an explanation that few of his followers questioned. Even to the nonbeliever, Muhammad's staying power over the past four decades bordered on miraculous, considering the ubiquity of the opposition against him. Certainly some, such as Daley, had simply become used to the Nation's being around and were thankful that it had not gone the "radical" route of the Black Panthers and others. The Muslim movement, at least as long as Muhammad lived, seemed indestructible and capable of adjusting to most any circumstance. When the Muslim leader told reporters at the 1972 press conference that he routinely ignored dissenters, he may only have been slightly exaggerating.

While Muhammad could perhaps afford to overlook young rebels, he could not disregard his own mortality and its implications for the future of the Muslim movement. The potentially explosive issue of succession had been around since the early 1960s when Muhammad was combating his bronchial asthma with annual trips to Phoenix. The jealousies that had helped cause the Malcolm X crisis were largely centered around the questions of who would inherit the movement and in what directions would he take it. Publicly, the leader, fearful of triggering a Muslim civil war, refrained from appointing an heir apparent. "I have nothing to do with who will succeed Me," he told an audience at Mosque No. 2 in 1972. "Whether there will be one to succeed Me or not is up to Allah." However, in private, he was aware that the Nation could not afford to face his death without a new captain at the helm, lest it crash and sink in the chaos of infighting. During his last months of life, Muhammad shrewdly groomed potential successors, but was careful not to elevate any single believer in a decisive manner. Contenders relished even the most indirect compliments that he gave them and ingratiated themselves accordingly.[9]

Of the top aspirants for the throne of the Nation of Islam, Wallace Muhammad arguably had the favor of his father more than anyone else. As mentioned earlier, Wallace had been in and out of the organization since 1964, periodically accepting and disavowing the teachings of the Muslim movement. By 1974, he was back in the Nation and was allowed to teach at the main mosque in Chicago, ostensibly without restriction. During the year, Wallace visited various branches of the movement throughout the country to solidify his support among the believers. At a meeting of Fruit of Islam in Harlem Mosque No. 7 in January 1975, he plainly told Minister Farrakhan, National Secretary Abass Rassoull, and others gathered that he would be taking over the Nation upon his father's death. He even went so far as to warn the New York minister that he would "sit him down" if he failed to "live up to the requirements and the demands" of Wallace's future reign over the Nation. Undoubtedly, Elijah Muhammad had allowed Wallace the leeway necessary to become a prominent influence in the movement during this time. Moreover, he ceded Wallace enough authority to dictate to powerful officials such as Farrakhan, Rassoull, and others. However, he did not embrace the Sunni Islamic teachings of his son, despite his previous overtures to Arabs and whites. Nor did he ever officially appoint Wallace as a successor publicly or otherwise, as the latter would concede later. Nonetheless, Muhammad's seventh child did seem poised to follow in his father's footsteps. It is entirely possible that the Messenger of Allah intended this.[10]

The only major player in the succession intrigue outside of the Muhammad clan was the national spokesman of the Nation, Louis Farrakhan. The New York minister was one of the top five most powerful men in the movement, along with Supreme Captain Raymond Sharrieff, Herbert Muhammad, Wallace Muhammad, and Elijah Muhammad himself. He ruled over the organization's largest mosque and had held the position of official spokesman much longer than Malcolm X had. But Farrakhan, despite his charisma, intellect, and adherence to the original teachings, was an outsider not only in a familial sense, but also in relation to the all-important circle of power that governed the movement from Chicago. The minister influenced the power center, but geography and the lessons of history—Malcolm's challenge to Chicago was still a recent memory—precluded him from encroaching upon the domain of other officials who were based at the headquarters. Few people who had been in the Nation for any length of time could reasonably believe that Elijah Muhammad would look outside of his kinship and advisory networks in Chicago for a successor. Such a course of action would probably have led to the disintegration of the Nation into competing regional and ideological factions.

Regardless of whether he was aware of his dilemma, Farrakhan was in earnest and tried to position himself for the ultimate appointment anyway. Though he promised Wallace his allegiance in the event of Elijah's death as late as January 1975, the New York minister took great comfort in being recognized by Muhammad during a 1972 lecture series as "a very good minister" who could sit in the seat of the messenger and lead the people. In early 1975, two of Farrakhan's daughters married a grandson and a nephew of the Muslim leader, and *Muhammad Speaks* announced joyously, "Two Great Families Unite!" In the wake of Muhammad's death, the minister and his partisans reportedly held late-night strategy sessions to determine how best to outsmart the opposition. Despite the maneuvering of the national spokesman, obstacles were in place to keep him from succeeding Muhammad. Dynastic forces had been watching him for years and were well prepared to deal with any bid for power that he might make. According to Elijah Muhammad Jr., the order "to keep an eye on" Farrakhan had come directly from the top. If that was indeed the case, the New York minister never had a chance at all.[11]

The fatal breakdown of Muhammad's health came all at once. No one who had been keeping up with his recent medical history should have been surprised, but the rapidity of his physical deterioration contrasted sharply with his tenacious, protracted struggles against bronchial asthma, high blood pressure, diabetes, and other ailments. Since late 1973, *Muhammad Speaks* had sporadically been printing articles that reminded readers of Muhammad's age, apparently in a subtle effort to condition the believers for the inevitable. Reports of his advancing senility and the constant presence of doctors at his bedside were leaked to the mainstream media, and even some public episodes of forgetfulness occurred, such as when Muhammad failed to recall the birth year of Fard Muhammad during his 1973 Saviour's Day address. The sudden collapse of his health during early 1975 seemed all the more alarming since his medical condition during the previous year had not been entirely debilitating. In fact, he was still able to address the faithful during the annual Saviour's Day convention, even though he sounded fatigued and weak. At least one story reached the press at this time alleging that he planned to marry one of his secretaries. Nothing, however, became of the rumor. In addition to officiating at Saviour's Day, 1974, the leader was strong enough to travel abroad during the year. In December, just before he was struck fatally ill, he had been vacationing in Morelos, Mexico, where he had reportedly acquired another resort home.[12]

The final ordeal began on January 29, 1975, when Muhammad, using an alias, entered Mercy Hospital for what his son Herbert called a "routine checkup." His condition turned out to be much more serious than his family had perhaps anticipated. On February 8, the Muslim leader suffered congestive heart failure and was immediately admitted to the intensive cardiac unit of the hospital. Over the next several days his situation degenerated, and medical officials labeled his status critical on February 17. The chances for survival waned precipitously, and preexisting maladies such as bronchial asthma and diabetes mellitus complicated the acute case of arteriosclerotic heart disease that had caused his heart to fail. Any suffering was confined to a week. At 8:10 on the morning of February 25—Saviour's Day eve— Elijah Muhammad was pronounced dead at the age of seventy-seven.[13]

There was neither an autopsy nor a prefuneral public display of the body. Instead, Muhammad's corpse was discreetly delivered to Griffin Funeral Home on King Drive for preparation. Upon hearing the news of his death, publications throughout the country printed obituaries and eulogies. Foreign dignitaries and even a representative of the Ford administration made their way to Chicago to pay their last respects. *Jet* magazine, based in Chicago, described the lifework of Muhammad as a "great legacy of pride and respect." *Newsweek* honored him as "a kind of prophetic voice in the flowering of black identity and pride." Graciously, William Raspberry, writing for the *Washington Post,* credited the leader with inculcating "pride in thousands of black derelicts, bums, and drug addicts, turning outlaws into useful, productive men and women." All of these commentaries were reasonable interpretations of Muhammad's significance and could have been supplemented with further accolades. For the skeptics who needed verifiable proof of these statements, they need only to have been in Chicago on Friday morning, February 28, when grief-stricken Muslims by the thousands gathered to mourn the passing of their Messenger of Allah.[14]

Funeral services were held in Mosque No. 2 and lasted only twenty-five minutes. Mourners who were able to find seats stood and faced east as the last rites were chanted in English and Arabic. Columns of believers, unable to get inside the packed house of worship, braved the brittle Chicago winter winds long enough to join the cavalcade of five hundred cars that escorted Muhammad's body to Glenwood Cemetery, twenty-five miles south of downtown Chicago. The burial of the Muslim leader was befitting of a king, and those who knew him best fully expected him to go to the grave first-class. His coffin, valued at twenty thousand dollars, was lined with silver. On the top of the casket, a National was rendered with a red and white background, and the star and crescent colored in gold. At the burial site, Muhammad's remains were lowered into a bronze-copper vault designed to be electrically sealed. Some Fruit of Islam, while standing at attention, could not help but touch the magnificent casket as it was prepared to descend. James Shabazz, minister of the Chicago mosque, gave a ten-minute address before the interment. He could not have said much that would have strengthened the belief among many present that the honored dead had been the closest thing to God on earth. As Wallace Muhammad, the newly selected leader of the Nation, headed back toward the family car, others stayed behind. Some simply would not leave until the inscription on the coffin, "Elijah Muhammad—1897–1975," could no longer be seen.[15]

Two days before the burial of Elijah Muhammad, earthly matters regarding the immediate future of his Nation of Islam were peacefully and publicly resolved. Saviour's Day, 1975 was not different simply because the Messenger of Allah had died a day earlier; the structure and tone of the ceremony were noticeably changed from the past. Apparently, Wallace Muhammad had been chosen to assume command over the Nation prior to his father's death on February 25, for by the time of his keynote address at the convention, his authority over the movement was already being recognized by the Chicago inner circle and other powerful players. Officially, a five-member board, consisting of Muhammad Ali, Herbert Muhammad, Louis Farrakhan, Raymond Sharrieff, and Elijah Muhammad Jr., had been impaneled to assist him in administering the Nation. Moreover, Wallace assumed the unpretentious title of Mujeddid, meaning "one to watch over the new Islam." As the future would reveal, the five-man committee was largely advisory, and the new leader's title was scarcely indicative of his real authority. On matters of policy, Wallace had been invested with power that closely resembled the autocratic sovereignty of his father.[16]

Actually, Wallace held court at the 1975 convention like a feudal monarch announcing divine rights to succeed an ancestor. Orderly, public displays of loyalty began the event, punctuated by occasional eulogies. First, Raymond Sharrieff and Muhammad Ali swore fealty to the new Supreme Minister. Then Jesse Jackson, Nathaniel Muhammad, and Prof. Ali Baghdadi, a teacher at the University of Islam, extolled the memory of Elijah Muhammad, followed by a number of other mourners and sympathizers. Louis Farrakhan shed tears for his deceased teacher, but did not forget the primary reason he had been called upon to speak. In carefully chosen words, he informed the audience of twenty thousand that "I, like all the rest, submit and yield to see that the work of Elijah Muhammad is carried on by his son Wallace D. Muhammad." To some who had been privy to his role in the political intrigue surrounding Muhammad's illness and death, the New York minister was as much conceding defeat as he was pledging allegiance.[17]

The keynote speech itself was uninspired and hard to follow. The frequent use of symbolism and allegories often obscured many of the points Wallace was trying to make. The overall purpose of the talk was to publicly display Muslim unity and to praise the work of Elijah Muhammad. Quite notably, however, the address omitted references to a number of traditional themes, such as racial separation, economic self-help, and white devilry, which had been mainstays of previous conventions. On the topic of whites in particular, Wallace was careful not to denounce white skin as inherently embodying evil. Instead, he criticized the mentality of white supremacy and the "grafted, strange mind" of whites. The distinction here is important. Starting on Saviour's Day, 1975, Wallace gradually disentangled physical whiteness from white racism and the historical burdens it had placed on black people. In essence, he was purging the Nation's theology of the myths that had breathed life into the Yacub story as well as the group's cult of blackness.[18]

The show of unity at Saviour's Day was easy compared to what Wallace had to do next. The economic domain of the Nation was not quite as healthy as many observers had assumed. In an unprecedented disclosure of Muslim financial strength, the Supreme Minister told the press in June that the assets of the movement totaled about $46 million, $30 million less than news agencies had estimated. A more shocking revelation was that the Nation had run up $4.6 million in debt due to failed enterprises and lavish spending. By the time Elijah Muhammad died in February, taxes were in arrears to the extent that the IRS launched an investigation of the movement to determine how much of its holdings were taxable. Wallace told the press that "my father felt he should not pay taxes or honor other federal obligations because we were not treated by the government as a religious group." This was, indeed, the truth, but it impressed neither the Nation's creditors nor federal auditors.[19]

To combat these economic woes, Wallace launched an austerity program that called for a restructuring of the group's assets and more accountability of top officials. Except for the fishing enterprise, the Muslim newspaper, and most of the farming projects, everything else would go to the highest bidder. Muslims who worked in the businesses were given the first chance to acquire the properties, and the Chicago headquarters offered assistance to prospective buyers to secure loans through the Small Business Administration. Doing what was unthinkable during his father's reign, Wallace began scrapping the most prominent symbols of the Nation's vitality and appeal during the summer of 1976. Undoubtedly, the decision to sell was necessary to prevent creditors from dismantling the Nation in a piecemeal fashion. However, the intangible costs of restructuring in terms of organizational credibility and morale must have been steep.[20]

Even before he addressed the advancing insolvency of the Nation, Wallace had had to address another financial crisis immediately after the death of his father. Elijah Muhammad died intestate, and perhaps only his closest relatives and advisers were privy to his desires regarding the financial future of the Muslims. Given the facts that Muhammad had been ill for so long and that he certainly had access to legal counsel, he more than likely intended to die without a will. A living will, especially one made public, would surely have complicated the succession issue. Lavish gifts and large lump-sum payments to family members and confidants could only have worsened and prolonged the violent infighting that shook the Nation during the early 1970s and would have confirmed charges of corruption and nepotism. After all, what better ammunition could a "purist" faction have to justify seceding from the movement than a publicized, official transfer of expensive properties to Muhammad's friends and relatives? Additionally, dying intestate would baffle, for a while, the IRS and others who would inevitably step forward to stake a claim against the Nation's resources. The tax man would eventually get something, but not before untangling assets and accounts that were an auditor's nightmare. Muhammad left the government and ambitious dissidents with estimates and speculation, and little else. Cleverly, he handed the entire matter over to Wallace and the family to settle discreetly and to their advantage.

The estate of Elijah Muhammad was eventually handled to Wallace's liking, but not without hitches. Upon his father's death, Wallace immediately had $3.2 million in assets transferred from the Honorable Elijah Muhammad's Poor Fund to Wallace Muhammad's Poor Fund. The First Pacific Bank of Chicago, where the money was deposited, allowed the conversion, assuming, like Wallace, that the money had been organizational property and should not be counted as part of the estate of Elijah Muhammad. According to the estimate of the Chicago leadership, the Messenger of Allah had died with real and personal property totaling only $200,000, divisible between his eight legitimate children. (This figure was revised upward to $363,000 by 1979.) Predictably, litigation started almost without delay. The thirteen illegitimate children of Muhammad filed a joint suit against the estate of their father, first to force a redivision of his property that would include them, next to lay claim to the $3.2 million in assets converted by Wallace in 1975. During a decade of court battles, the plaintiffs were able to show that the Poor Fund had been used by Elijah Muhammad as if it were his own personal bank account and not group assets. Wallace, however, won a seemingly conclusive victory on December 31, 1987, when an Illinois appellate court ruled that $5.7 million in principal and interest accrued in the Wallace Muhammad Poor Fund was organizational property and thus did not belong to Elijah Muhammad or his twenty-one children. Unpleasant by any standard, the struggle over money was a sad bottom line in the history of a religious organization that had been fundamentally shaped by economic concerns since the 1940s.[21]

Wallace dealt not only with the Nation's finances. Under the guise of ushering in a "New Islam," the Supreme Minister revolutionized much of the structure and message of the Nation of Islam. Given Wallace's past leanings toward Sunni Islam, his stated desire to bring the Lost-Found Nation of Islam in the West into "the great, vast, universal Nation of Islam all over the world" was not unexpected. Yet, the quick succession of changes that he initiated to accomplish this could hardly have been predicted. He intended not only to change the soul of the Nation, but also to alter its countenance. For example, seats were taken out of mosques so that believers could prostrate for prayer in the manner of orthodox Muslims. *Muhammad Speaks* was renamed *The Bilalian News* on November 1, 1975, dedicated to being "the Voice of Truth for all people of the world." Additionally, sales quotas for Muslim men were dropped, which caused the weekly circulation of the newspaper to plummet roughly to fifty thousand. In Wallace's view, believers should not have to buy a single issue of the paper if they did not desire to. In an attempt to rid the movement of coercive and violent elements, Wallace abolished the Fruit of Islam. Instead of serving as enforcers for the Nation, male members, along with women, were encouraged to register to vote and to discard the racial separatism of the past. In a hurried but calculated way, Wallace was priming his followers to embrace the totality of al-Islam.[22]

It seemed as if new reforms were being announced every week, and apparently nothing was too sacred to escape scrutiny. By the summer of 1975, Wallace had altered the Nation's racial ideology to the point that the organization would be open to people of all races. This was possible because the attributes of devils were no longer associated with "something physical." Now, according to Wallace, a devil was "the person within the physical body" and represented the mentality of the individual, not the pigmentation of his or her skin. This revision was a hard sale, and more than a few believers left the fold after a handful of whites trickled into the movement. Still, the policy withstood the test of time and transformed the Nation of Islam into a multiracial entity. Since the goal was to immerse the movement into the waters of al-Islam, in October 1976 Wallace renamed the organization the World Community of Islam in the West (WCIW), effectively terminating the Nation of Islam. Seven months later he completed the revolution by publicly discounting his father's claim to be the divinely commissioned Messenger of Allah. In accordance with traditional Islamic teachings, the Prophet Muhammad was upheld as the last messenger, and the Qur'an revered as the last holy book. For a time, it appeared that Wallace had been able to do peacefully what others had failed to do through internecine violence, media smear campaigns, and counterintelligence programs: disassemble the Nation of Islam. Later events would prove, however, that the Nation of Islam was more resilient than he had realized.[23]

The splintering of the Nation of Islam, and later the WCIW, was a foreseeable consequence of the broad changes that Wallace had enacted. At no time in the history of the movement had significant ideological shifts taken place without triggering rebellions and factionalism. The worst schisms occurred during the 1930s following the disappearance of Fard Muhammad and the resultant scramble to claim his mantle and define his theological legacy. But other secessions and apostasies had occurred during times of doctrinal tensions such as the mid-1960s and the early 1970s. Given the gulf between the WCIW and the Nation of Islam in structure, ideology, and objectives, the emergence of malcontents longing for the familiarity of the old order was inevitable. The only real question was what would be the character and impact of the insurrections once they finally broke out.

Like an uncertain prince who distrusted his father's advisers, Wallace tried to preclude a crisis over succession and ideology by shaking up the leadership of the Nation. Powerful top officials such as Raymond Sharrieff and Abass Rassoull were summarily dismissed, and a number of ministers were either deposed or assigned to other cities. A few leaders, such as Min. Jeremiah Shabazz of Philadelphia and Silas Muhammad of San Francisco, chose to quit the Nation rather than submit to its new ruler. The latter official even started his own Muslim faction in August 1977 to revive the original teachings. Casually, Wallace disregarded them all as being more interested in the economic side of the movement than religious affairs. However, as a probable precaution against usurpation, he had the body of Elijah Muhammad exhumed and buried elsewhere. Presumably, he wanted no one to be able to come forward and say that the Messenger of Allah had visited him posthumously and chosen him to lead, pointing to the empty Glenwood grave as proof.[24]

None of the dissatisfaction with Wallace had a notable impact on his reforms. Disaffected believers who chose to leave typically did so quietly without slander or violence. No significant counterreform movement occurred in the WCIW, but at least one secession of dissidents, led by Min. Louis Farrakhan, warrants comment. After assuming control of the Nation, Wallace had been careful not to alienate the national spokesman or to allow him much room to maneuver within the confines of the new order. Only weeks following his father's death, the Supreme Minister appointed Farrakhan international representative of the Nation and relocated him to Chicago. Officially, the appointment was supposed to be a promotion that would allow the minister to spread "to the Caribbean and elsewhere . . . the word and work of the Nation." But less frequent coverage of Farrakhan in *Muhammad Speaks* and *The Bilalian Times* seemed to belie this rationale. The reassignment probably reflected Chicago's concern about keeping Farrakhan "under close surveillance," as one inside source put it, rather than an interest in international expansion. Whatever the case, Farrakhan was stripped of command of the treasured Mosque No. 7—which Wallace renamed Malcolm Shabazz Temple No. 7 in honor of Farrakhan's predecessor—and incorporated into the Chicago bureaucracy in mid-1975.[25]

Farrakhan stayed in the Nation of Islam and the WCIW for approximately three years following the death of Elijah Muhammad. Though he had sworn loyalty to Wallace Muhammad before a crowd of thousands at Saviour's Day, 1975, the new leader's economic reforms and ideological innovations disenchanted Farrakhan to the point that he embraced apostasy. The break was largely ideological; Farrakhan had simply not lost faith in the Islam of the Messenger of Allah, which he had preached for twenty years. Beneath doctrinal tensions, however, issues of ego and pride would probably not allow him to continue following the man who had beaten him in the competition for the crown of Elijah Muhammad. Wallace practically begged the minister to stay—even offering to reinstate him at Mosque No. 7—but did not mobilize a propaganda campaign against Farrakhan when he departed nor send forces out to punish him. Yet, there was bitterness on both sides: Farrakhan allegedly vowed not to "be a prostitute for anybody anymore," and Wallace promised to attack all who sought to change "the minds of this community." By 1978, the former national spokesman had begun giving speeches based on the original teachings. The following year, he had gathered together enough dissidents to launch his own organization, sentimentally naming it the Nation of Islam. For better or for worse, the disciples of Elijah Muhammad went their separate ways. Perhaps, the late leader had meant for things to turn out that way.[26]

By the time of his death in February 1975, Elijah Muhammad had lived the better part of a century. Like other prominent men, his life had been a conduit through which the societal influences and values that had shaped his leadership were transmitted to countless others. In retrospect, it was hard to imagine in the 1970s that the leader of the most prosperous black organization in American history had been born to sharecroppers in Georgia, educated in storefront churches, and condemned to prison for his beliefs during World War II. His four-decade reign over the Nation of Islam is even more fascinating to ponder, given the constant internal and external opposition to him. Muhammad commonly argued that his long tenure as the Messenger of Allah had been divinely arranged and that the devil, the hypocrites, and other enemies could not triumph against the will of God. Notwithstanding this explanation, events and circumstances had certainly allowed him to leave an indelible impression on the world of the twentieth century.

The significance of Elijah Muhammad is primarily ideological and secondarily programmatic, though the two themes are interrelated. In essence, his life was dedicated to equating blackness with power and initiative. No other historical personality has had the kind of prolonged impact on black consciousness that he has had, and no recent group in the African-American community has promoted—largely by example—economic self-help, cultural regeneration (or redefinition), and moral living more vigorously than his Nation of Islam. The Muslims were "black" before it became fashionable to be labeled as such, and the Black Power Movement and all subsequent African-American protest styles, from the rhymes of the nationalistic rap group Public Enemy to the raison d'être of the Million Man March, are undeniably offshoots of the legacy of Elijah Muhammad. Interestingly, while he fought the influence of orthodox Islam for most of his life, the Nation of Islam is almost single-handedly responsible for making African-Americans aware of the Eastern faith. Most of his major Islamic adversaries, including Hamaas Abdul Khaalis, Malcolm X, and his own son Wallace Muhammad, had been under his philosophical wing at one time or another. Ironically, they were able to find a voice in al-Islam only after he had awakened them spiritually with the heterodox teachings of Fard Muhammad.

The ideology of the Nation of Islam, though fiercely enunciated by various spokesmen, was thoroughly conservative. Little of what Elijah Muhammad said, and even less of what he actually did, fundamentally challenged the status quo of the United States. In some ways, his theological and social views neatly meshed with the prevailing mores of his times. Illustratively, he counseled against black participation in electoral politics, railed against the Civil Rights Movement, encouraged racial separation, wrote off much of Africa as uncivilized, and did not question the basic operation of American capitalism. In extreme instances, he even appeared reactionary in his flirtations with white supremacist and fascist groups and in his tolerance of gender inequalities in the Nation. Only his support for the racial supremacy of the Original People, denunciation of Christianity, and opposition to African-American participation in U.S. wars went against the grain of American values and practices. Otherwise, his Nation of Islam was as homegrown as the NAACP or the Ku Klux Klan, despite its anti-American appearance. By the 1970s, it had become clear to most that Elijah Muhammad and his Muslims were more interested in capitalist pursuits and the moral health of the black community than revolution, and his overtures to the white community for assistance confirmed as much. But a curious mix of racial chauvinism, organizational militarism, and religious inventiveness had, for many people, obscured the basic conservatism of the Muslim movement for most of its existence.

In its program and actions, the Nation of Islam mirrored the personality and experiences of its leader. The entrepreneurial enterprises of the organization were directly inspired by Muhammad's rural agrarian background and his journeys through urban, industrial America. The acquisition of farms, fishing interests, and other businesses during the postwar period reflected the value that he, and most other blacks, placed on land ownership and economic independence following Reconstruction. His admiration for the self-sufficiency and technical modernism of FCI Milan and other institutions and trends of the Cold War period also played a role in the economic shift in the Nation's program. Organizational advances in business were accompanied by a growing and more diverse membership, largely as a result of gifted ministers, conflicts with ideological opponents, and nationwide media exposure. With the improving finances of the movement came an unfortunate degree of avarice and corruption by the 1950s, especially in its upper echelons.

There were some contradictions. Often, Muhammad, who had elevated himself above the judgment of his flock, counseled restraint. But on a number of occasions, he practiced self-indulgence to an extent that would have led to the excommunication of rank-and-file offenders. Difficulties with government agencies, which he strenuously avoided, made him appear Christlike to the believers, who felt that he was being punished for simply preaching "Truth." Yet, his conflicts with apostates such as Malcolm X showed that he could be the persecutor as well as the persecuted. Despite this, the mystical, autocratic role of Muhammad as the Messenger of Allah still accorded him a measure of sanctity in the eyes of his followers. His struggles against counterintelligence programs, paternity suits, persistent sickness, and "the hypocrites" only nurtured his lifelong sense of persecution and sacrifice and further endeared him to the faithful.

Notions of mission and destiny remained with Muhammad to the end, and pressure from others to change his theology and racial views did not ever seem to work. His unique brand of black nationalism and Islamic revisionism may have appeared obsolete in a society becoming more open to African-American participation than ever before. Nonetheless, his movement still had enough momentum and relevance to outlive his forty-year reign. Regardless of personal flaws and other impediments, Elijah Muhammad had saved thousands from drug abuse, prostitution, thievery, and self-destruction. He had clearly constructed for them a functional identity. In many ways, his life was an admirable effort to show black people how to appreciate and realize themselves.

EPILOGUE

ELIJAH MUHAMMAD IN AMERICAN MEMORY

Few American leaders have been more misunderstood than Elijah Muhammad. While working on this book, I found that the general public has an inconsistent, confused image of him at best, distorted mostly by the misinformation of his detractors and the self-interested depictions of his life and message offered by his advocates. The lack of interest in the Nation of Islam on the part of academia, and the resultant dearth of published studies on the subject, are at least partially responsible for this. However, the level of ignorance exhibited by the person on the street (and in the university and the mosque) regarding his life and significance have appalled me, especially given the resurgence of interest in Malcolm X and other Black Power icons over the past few years. It is interesting to note just how many Elijah Muhammads I have encountered while preparing this book. Most of the people I have talked with had an opinion about the leader, but not one that was well grounded in the historical record—or much else.

Misconceptions about Elijah Muhammad and the Nation of Islam freely cross generational, gender, and philosophical boundaries, though people in large urban areas tend to be marginally more knowledgeable than their rural counterparts. During a talk with a distant relative of the leader's in Sandersville, Georgia, I found that the African-American community there had done nothing to distinguish the town as the birthplace of the Muslim leader. No street signs, monuments, schools, or markers would give you any sense that there had ever been an Elijah Poole. Only the county probate court contained any information about the family's background, but the white, middle-aged probate judge was clueless regarding my topic. The best she could do was offer an unsolicited apology for the historical enslavement of blacks in the South ("That's just how things were") and assure me that Poole was a popular name in the area. Recently, when I told a curious male relative in his sixties that I was writing a book on Muhammad, his inquisitiveness instantly turned to indignation, and he demanded to know, "Boy, why are you writing a book on him? He and that old Malcolm X were racists, talking about killing people and what not." I had never heard that tone of voice from him before, though I have known him all my life. I did not risk further stirring up his displeasure by talking to him at length about the book.

In some instances, race seemed to be significant regarding one's awareness of Elijah Muhammad. Nonetheless, I have talked to enough blacks and whites about the leader to conclude that ignorance and distortions can emanate from anywhere regarding the life of Muhammad. During a visit to Chicago, I stopped by the Cook County Probate Court to view the estate records of the leader. The white clerk seemed eager and willing to serve until I stated, "I would like to see the estate documents relating to Elijah Muhammad, the leader of the—" Before I could finish the sentence, the clerk snapped, "I know who he is." Based on the not-too-subtle hostility behind his reply, I got the distinct impression that he was not an admirer and could not see beyond the unflattering media images of Muhammad. (He would perhaps have been surprised to know that the building in which we were standing was named after a cordial acquaintance of Muhammad's, Richard Daley.) Yet, he was not the only one apprehensive about my study. In February 1994, I aroused the ire of a number of black students at the university at which I teach after I did not blindly praise Muhammad during a Black History Month presentation. Few of my youthful critics had been more than infants when the leader died in 1975, but just knew that I had gotten it all wrong. Perhaps more because of bureaucratic indifference than anything else, my written request for pictures of Muhammad from the Library of Congress netted me a number of photocopies of prints of Malcolm X, and only a few of my subject. A note included in the parcel reminded me that the pictures of the former national spokesman were copyrighted, as if to suggest that I had requested them. Apparently, to them, the two men were virtually one and the same.

Finally, indifference, even hostility, toward a scholarly evaluation of Muhammad's life and message showed up in some unlikely places. I had heard that the Coalition for the Remembrance of Elijah Muhammad (CROE) in Chicago had some materials on the life of the leader that might be of use to me. However, in my telephone conversation with one of the curators of the "archives," I found that he harbored many of the same sentiments that some of the students who had attended my Black History Month talk had. In a most candid tone, he asked me, "What can you say in your book that the Honorable Elijah Muhammad has not already said or wrote?" He did not want to hear anything about objectivity or historical perspective. Following a lecture about his wariness regarding how CROE's materials were used, he offered to sell me videotaped speeches and a twenty-five-dollar "study group" membership. Dismayed, I respectfully declined his offers and marked the repository off my list of places to visit.

To its credit, CROE would at least speak with the general public. A number of groups who are now claiming to represent the legacy of Elijah Muhammad showed no interest in talking with me about the leader. Their staffs would quickly encourage me to buy their literature and other wares, but my requests to talk with knowledgeable people about Muhammad invariably went unfulfilled. Twenty years after his death, the generation of youths born since 1975 know little about the Muslim leader, and the blame for this can be evenly divided between the indifference of academia, the romanticized portraits offered by his present-day partisans, and a media drawn more to image than substance. Sadly, this legacy of neglect and distortion starkly revealed itself to me during a final exam that I recently administered to an undergraduate history course. Halfway through an essay question on the Nation of Islam, a female student raised her hand and whispered sheepishly, "Do I have to write about Elijah Muhammad? I don't remember much about him." Judging from the number of her classmates who suddenly looked up at me for an answer, she was not alone.

APPENDIX

TERMINOLOGY OF THE NATION OF ISLAM

blind, deaf, and dumb: The state of being unaware of the teachings of the Nation of Islam.

chastisement: An affliction believed to be imposed by God to punish violators of the laws of the Nation of Islam. Can range from the "burning of the brain" to death.

the devil: White people collectively. Also referred to as Yacub's race of devils, made-man, mankind, the Adamic race, and the (former) slave master.

East Asia: The Middle East and Northeastern Africa. It is believed to have been the cradle of the world's oldest civilization and a sort of paradise on earth.

fishing: The search for new converts by Nation of Islam members.

Fruit of Islam: Male members of the Nation of Islam. Also, individual members responsible for organizational security and enforcing discipline.

the grave: The world outside of the Nation of Islam; secular society; the white world.

hypocrite: A Nation of Islam apostate.

icehouse: The Christian church. (*Icemakers* are clergymen.)

laborer: A member of the Nation of Islam.

lost-found: A member of the Nation of Islam.

mental resurrection: The attainment of an awareness of Nation of Islam teachings.

messengership: The organizational office of Elijah Muhammad in the Nation of Islam, which embraced the notions that he had met God in the person of W. Fard Muhammad and that he was the sole living intermediary between man and the divine.

Mother Plane: A circular ship capable of space travel. It is believed to carry fifteen hundred smaller ships designed to destroy America and England with bombs during the Judgment.

Muslim Girls Training and General Civilization Class (MGT-GCC): The branch of the Nation of Islam devoted to female members and their socialization into the culture of the movement.

the National: The Islamic star and crescent and the official flag of the Nation of Islam.

Original People: Black people, especially those believed to be responsible for the earth's first civilization.

our own: The cultural and territorial legacy of black people believed to include Islam, Arabic language and customs, and a homeland in Africa and the Middle East.

Poison Book: The Bible.

seed planter: A person engaged in activities designed to arouse suspicion, division, and/or rivalry in the Nation of Islam.

spook: Refers to the belief of Westerners and Christians that God is noncorporeal, eternal, and spiritual as opposed to human, mortal, and comprehensible.

temple: A place of worship for Nation of Islam members. Later changed to *mosque*.

Tribe of Shabazz: One of the original thirteen tribes of black people, which eventually held sway over East Asia.

tricknology: All manners of deceitful, treacherous, and abusive behavior practiced by whites to maintain their dominance over black people.

Truth: The teachings of the Nation of Islam. Also known as *the knowledge of self and others*.

West Asia: Europe or the area where whites were forced into exile after their expulsion from Mecca, East Asia, six thousand years ago.

the wilderness (of North America): The United States of America, analogous to the wilderness roamed by Old Testament Jews.

X: Letter given to replace the European surname of Nation of Islam members until an "original" (usually Arabic) name is bestowed upon the convert. Believed to be the ultimate indicator of one's break with his or her non-Islamic past.

NOTES

Chapter 1: 26,000 Years

1. *Cotton to Kaolin: A History of Washington County, Georgia, 1784–1989* (Sandersville: Washington County Historical Society, Inc., 1989), 152–53.

2. Washington County was larger during this time than it is now, and the Pools' land was probably located in what is now Baldwin County. Washington County, at that time, probably contained parts of what are now Baldwin, Wilkinson, and Johnson Counties. Lydia Pool, telephone conversation with author, 19 August 1994.

3. "Sources of Information on E. P. Newsom File Cards" (in possession of author); Grace Poole, letter to author, 20 August 1994.

4. Ibid.; "Middleton Pool," *Division of Estates,* Book A: 1829–1871, Washington County Probate Court (WCPC), 196–97; and "Middleton Pool," *Wills Book B.*, 1852–1903, WCPC, 160.

5. James M. McPherson, *Ordeal by Fire: The Civil War,* vol. 2 (New York: McGraw-Hill, Inc., 1993), 460; Burke Davis, *Sherman's March* (New York: Random House, 1980), 75–77; and *Cotton to Kaolin,* 152.

6. While Elijah Muhammad stated one hundred years later that his father, William Pool, "just missed slavery by one year," the census records of Washington County for the years 1880 and 1900 list William's age as twelve and thirty-two, respectively. Apparently, he was born sometime between 1866 and 1868. Washington County 1880 and 1900 Censuses for the 100th Militia District, WCPC; " 'We Live in the Times of a Change of Worlds,' " *Muhammad Speaks,* 9 September 1966, 7; Edmund L. Drago, *Black Politicians and Reconstruction in Georgia* (Baton Rouge: Louisiana State University Press, 1982), 31; and Donald L. Grant, *The Way It Was in the South: The Black Experience in Georgia* (New York: Carol Publishing Co., 1993), 138, 146.

7. Eric Foner, *A Short History of Reconstruction, 1863–1877* (New York: Harper & Row, 1990), 183–85; Grant, *Way It Was,* 140; Hatim A. Sahib, "The Nation of Islam" (Master's thesis, University of Chicago, 1951), 87; "Marriage License," *Marriage Records F, 1885–1890,* Court of Ordinary, WCPC; Elijah Muhammad, *History of the Nation of Islam* (Cleveland: Secretarius Publication, 1994), 46–47 (originally, an interview of Elijah Muhammad conducted by the *New York Herald Tribune* in January 1965).

8. *Cotton to Kaolin,* 154, 157; Department of the Interior, Census Office, *Report on Population of the United States, Eleventh Census: 1890—Part 1* (Washington, D.C.: Government Printing Office, 1895), 494; Grant, *Way It Was,* 140–41, 145–56; and Olin B. Adams, "The Negro and the Agrarian Movement in Georgia, 1874–1908" (Ph.D. diss., Florida State University, 1974), 243–44.

9. The author is not sure when the Pools changed the spelling of their surname to *Poole*. Ostensibly, the new spelling was meant to distinguish the black Pooles from the white Pools.

10. Malcolm X, *The Autobiography of Malcolm X* (1965; reprint, New York: Ballantine Books, 1988), 205; William Worthy, "The Angriest Negroes," *Esquire*, February 1961, 105.

11. "The Family of Elija Poole," 1900 Census—100th Militia District of Washington County, Georgia (two-page list in possession of author); Jabril Muhammad, *This Is the One: The Most Honored Elijah Muhammad, We Need Not Look for Another!* vol. 1 (Phoenix: Jabril Muhammad, 1993), 166; and "An Interview with Sister Annie Muhammad," *Muhammad Speaks*, 11 July 1975, S-1. Elijah Muhammad never knew the exact date of his birth, but chose October 7 as a substitute for the unknown day. "Muhammad Meets the Press!" (part 3), *Muhammad Speaks*, 11 February 1972, 3.

12. Malcolm X, *Autobiography*, 205; "The Family of Elija Poole"; Grant, *Way It Was*, 141; and E. Muhammad, "Anti-Christ," *Muhammad Speaks*, 12 December 1969, 16.

13. I was first told of Elijah Muhammad's half brother, Lonnie, by Mrs. Katie Smith Poole, a current resident of Sandersville. Throughout my research, most sources have described Elijah as one of thirteen children. However, an FBI document based on an interview of Muhammad lists two extra siblings, including a Jarmin (Lonnie?) whose name appears without comment, unlike the other fourteen names. Elijah's sister Tommie is erroneously listed twice in the FBI report. Katie Smith Poole, interview with author, Sandersville, Georgia, 6 July 1994; "The Family of Elija Poole"; and Report—"Biographical Data," SAC New York, 26 February 1968, sec. 12, p. 4 (Elijah Muhammad FBI file, 105-24822).

14. Daughters of the American Revolution (Fort Early Chapter), *History of Crisp County* (Cordele, Georgia, 1916), 5–6, 12–13.

15. Sahib, "Nation of Islam," 87–88, 190; E. Muhammad, *The Theology of Time*, transcribed by Abass Rassoull (Hampton, Va.: U.B. & U.S. Communications Systems, 1992), 69, 143, 296; and Steven Barboza, *American Jihad: Islam After Malcolm X* (New York: Doubleday, 1993), 99.

16. Sahib, "Nation of Islam," 90; Malcolm X, *Autobiography*, 205–6; and E. Muhammad, *Theology of Time*, 297–98.

17. E. Muhammad, *Message to the Blackman in America* (Chicago: Muhammad Mosque of Islam No. 2, 1965), 178; "Muslim Cult of Islam," 21 February 1957, 3 (Wallace D. Fard FBI file, 25-330971); Wallace H. Terry, "Black Muslim Elijah's Lowly Start," *Washington Post*, 12 December 1960, A3; Arna Bontemps and Jack Conroy, *Anyplace but Here* (New York: Hill and Wang, 1966), 223; Malcolm X, *Autobiography*, 205; Louis E. Lomax, *When the Word Is Given* (Cleveland: The World Publishing Co., 1963), 51–52; and Department of Commerce, Bureau of the Census, *Thirteenth Census (1910)*, vol. 2 (Washington, D.C.: Government Printing Office, 1913), 402. Later, Elijah Muhammad would discount anything he may have learned in Cordele, maintaining that "the only knowledge I really have today had come to me through Mr. Fard," his spiritual teacher of the early 1930s. According to Sahib's interviews of Muhammad during the late 1940s, he only attended school for a half term at age twelve. Sahib, "Nation of Islam," 89.

18. Sahib, "Nation of Islam," 88–89; Terry, "Black Muslim," A3.

19. Sahib, "Nation of Islam," 93; E. Muhammad, "Slavery in Alabama and Mississippi," *Muhammad Speaks*, 30 August 1968, 18–19.

20. E. Muhammad, *Theology of Time*, 227.

21. Adams, "Negro and the Agrarian Movement," 243–44; Grant, *Way It Was*, 294; and "Unknown Negro Is Lynched," *Atlanta Constitution*, 17 October 1903, 2.

22. E. Muhammad, "We Face Divine Truth," *Muhammad Speaks*, 11 November 1964, 1, 3; Sahib, "Nation of Islam," 89; and Terry, "Black Muslim," A3.

23. Lomax, *When the Word Is Given*, 51–52; "Cordele Negro Quickly Lynched," *Atlanta Constitution*, 1 December 1912, 7B; E. Muhammad, *Message*, 178; E. Muhammad, "Negro," *Muhammad Speaks*, 7 February 1969, 21; Sahib, "Nation of Islam," 88; and Malcolm X, *Autobiography*, 206.

24. Grant, *Way It Was*, 292–95.

25. Ibid., 141, 290, 294; John Dittmer, *Black Georgia in the Progressive Era, 1900–1920* (Urbana: University of Illinois Press, 1977), 188–89.

26. E. Muhammad, *Theology of Time*, 440; "Muslim Cult of Islam," 21 February 1957 (W. D. Fard FBI file); Ida Young, Julius Gholson, and Clara N. Hargrove, *History of Macon, Georgia* (Macon: Lyon, Marshall, and Brooks, 1950), 454, 546; Grant, *Way It Was*, 282, 308; Dittmer, *Black Georgia*, 28; and Memo—"Elijah Poole," 15 July 1959, sec. 3, p. 2 (E. Muhammad FBI file).

27. "Elijah Poole," 2 (E. Muhammad FBI file); E. U. Essien-Udom, *Black Nationalism: A Search for an Identity in America* (Chicago: University of Chicago Press, 1962), 75; Wallace D. Muhammad, *As the Light Shineth from the East* (Chicago: WDM Publishing Co., 1980), 24–25; and Report—"Biographical Data," SAC New York, 26 February 1968, sec. 12, p. 4 (E. Muhammad FBI file).

28. In 1919, James Grant, a veteran, was lynched in Cordele, and a number of black churches and other buildings were burned. Grant, *Way It Was*, 308; Sahib, "Nation of Islam," 89; and E. Muhammad, "The Might of Arms Is the God of This World," *Muhammad Speaks*, 20 July 1973, 16.

29. According to Malcolm X, Elijah left Georgia to "avoid trouble" with a white employer who had cursed him. Malcolm X, *Autobiography*, 206. Surprisingly, given the town's history of racial oppression, the Cordele branch of the National Association for the Advancement of Colored People (NAACP) was established in 1920. Grant, *Way It Was*, 312; E. Muhammad, *Message*, 178; and "Man of Myth and Fact," *New York Times*, 29 June 1964, 32. It is interesting to note that another well-known African-American, Berry Gordy Jr., has roots in Sandersville. Berry Gordy Sr. was born in rural Washington County around 1888 and attended high school in the city. In 1922, he left Georgia for Detroit on a train out of Macon, probably the same route taken by the Pooles a year later. Ester Edwards, the daughter of Berry Gordy Sr., recently told the author that Elijah and the father of the Motown founder may have attended school together in Sandersville; however, this possibility is very unlikely given that the Pooles moved to Cordele when Elijah was only three. What is possible is that the Pooles and the Gordys were related in some way. Especially considering the small size of the black population of Washington County, it would not be far-fetched to suggest that the two families knew one another well, even if there were no familial ties. Berry Gordy Sr., *Movin' Up: Pop Gordy Tells His Story* (New York: Harper & Row, 1979), x, xii, 19, 85; Berry Gordy Jr., *To Be Loved: The Music, the Magic, the Memories of Motown* (New York: Warner Books, 1994), 11–15; Ester Edwards, telephone conversation with author, 6 September 1995; and Michael Dixon, telephone conversation with author, 6 September 1995.

Chapter 2: An Original Man, Lost and Found

1. Gay Talese, *Thy Neighbor's Wife* (New York: Bantam, 1985).

2. Richard W. Thomas, *Life for Us Is What We Make It: Building Black Community in Detroit, 1915–1945* (Bloomington: Indiana University Press, 1992), 26–27, 39; Bureau of the Census, *Thirteenth, Fourteenth, and Fifteenth Censuses of the United States:*

Population (Michigan) 1910, 1920, and 1930, vols. 1, 2, and 3, part 1 (Washington, D.C.: Government Printing Office, 1913, 1922, and 1932), 948, 496, and 1147, respectively.

3. For businesses controlled by blacks in 1929, see Fred B. Jones (letter and questionnaire) to Irving Johnson, 6 August 1929, Box 1, Detroit Urban League (DUL) Papers, Michigan Historical Collection, University of Michigan, Ann Arbor, Michigan. Mayor's Interracial Committee, *The Negro in Detroit* (Detroit, 1926), reprinted in Normal Miles, "Home at Last: The Urbanization of Black Migrants in Detroit, 1916–1929" (Ph.D. diss., University of Michigan, 1978), 74, 100; B. J. Widick, *Detroit: City of Race and Class Violence* (Detroit: Wayne State University Press, 1989), 26; and John C. Dancy to Chas. S. Johnson, 16 July 1929, and Dancy to Robert L. Cruden, 11 February 1929, Box 1, DUL Papers.

4. Miles, "Home at Last," 135.

5. Widick, *Detroit,* 23, 27–28; Sahib, "Nation of Islam," 90–91.

6. Sahib, "Nation of Islam," 90; Report—"Biographical Data," SAC New York, 26 February 1968, sec. 12, pp. 4–5, and Report—"Elijah Muhammad," 18 September 1953, sec. 1, p. 2 (E. Muhammad FBI file).

7. "Elijah Muhammad," 2 (E. Muhammad FBI file); "Muslim Cult of Islam," 21 February 1957 (W. D. Fard FBI file); and August Meier and Elliott Rudwick, *Black Detroit and the Rise of the UAW* (New York: Oxford University Press, 1979), 5–8.

8. Warith D. Mohammed interview with Elaine Rivera, *Muslim Journal,* 20 May 1994, 15; Wallace D. Muhammad, *As the Light,* 199; and C. Eric Lincoln, *The Black Muslims in America* (Boston: Beacon Press, 1961), 181. During his first year of residence in Michigan, Elijah Muhammad saw two blacks killed by policemen, which convinced him that "the difference [between the North and the South] is that they do not hang them up to the trees but they kill them right here on the streets!" Between January 1, 1925, and June 30, 1926, twenty-five blacks were killed by Detroit law enforcement officers as compared to twenty-four whites. Sahib, "Nation of Islam," 90; Wilma V. Henrickson, ed., *Detroit Perspectives: Crossroads and Turning Points* (Detroit: Wayne State University Press, 1991), 328. During the depression, Clara helped support the family by taking jobs as a domestic worker. Zafar I. Ansari, "W. D. Muhammad: The Making of a 'Black Muslim' Leader (1933–1961)," *American Journal of Islamic Social Sciences* 2.2 (December 1985): 249. According to one of his grandsons, Elijah routinely gambled and drank away the money that he earned while employed. In one instance, family members had to retrieve him after he collapsed on a railroad track, too drunk to comprehend the gravity of his situation. Barboza, *American Jihad,* 273.

9. Sahib, "Nation of Islam," 91. Except in the cases of quotations and titles, the words *Muhammad* and *Muslim* will be used throughout this work instead of the anglicized *Mohammed* and *Moslem* since Elijah Muhammad and the Nation of Islam preferred the former spellings.

10. J. Muhammad, *This Is the One,* 164.

11. Michael A. Gomez, "Muslims in Early America," *Journal of Southern History* 60.4 (November 1994): 682, 695–96.

12. Ibid., 706–7.

13. Richard B. Turner, "Islam in the United States during the 1920's: The Quest for a New Vision in Afro-American Religion" (Ph.D. diss., Princeton University, 1986), 181–87; Lincoln, *Black Muslims,* 220–21; and Essien-Udom, *Black Nationalism,* 311, 311 n. 26.

14. Turner, "Islam in the United States," 181–87.

15. Clifton E. Marsh, *From Black Muslims to Muslims: The Transition from Separatism to Islam, 1930–1980* (Metuchen, N.J.: Scarecrow Press, 1984), 41–49. The ideologies of the MSTA and Marcus Garvey as they relate to that of the Nation of Islam are expounded upon in Chapter 3 of the present work.

16. For the most detailed account of Fard's teachings, see Elijah Muhammad's *Message to the Blackman in America*.

17. "Records Los Angeles Police Department," 5 March 1965; Report—"W. D. Fard," SAC Chicago to SAC Detroit, 31 July 1957 (W. D. Fard FBI file). According to Hazel Osborne, a former common-law wife, Fard had always been, despite his criminal record, "morally a good man" and had not been known for indulging in alcohol, tobacco, or games of chance. However, when he visited her in 1932, she learned that he had embraced an even more ascetic lifestyle. As she recalled years later, Fard had grown his hair out "long and full in the back" and "was only eating one meal a day," which was the primary tenet of the dietary code of the Nation of Islam. Report—*"Changed:* W. D. Fard," SAC Los Angeles to FBI director, 18 October 1957, 2–5; "Background Information on Wallace Dodd," SA Edwin O. Raudsep to SAC, 8 March 1965; and Report—"W. D. Fard," SAC San Francisco to FBI director, 27 August 1957 (W. D. Fard FBI file).

18. Sahib, "Nation of Islam," 65–66, 118.

19. Insofar as the meeting hall on Hastings Street could accommodate only about four hundred people, Elijah Muhammad's claim that thousands attended may be exaggerated. Nonetheless, enough people came to hear Fard that it became necessary for him to hold meetings twice a day, four times a week. Sahib, "Nation of Islam," 68, 91, 121; "Muslim Cult of Islam," 21 February 1957 (W. D. Fard FBI file).

20. If the account of the FBI regarding Fard's imprisonment is true, while in San Quentin he identified himself as white. "Records Los Angeles Police Department," 5 March 1965 (W. D. Fard FBI file). There has been much speculation about Fard's racial background. He has been variously described as "an Arab and Syrian," "a Jamaican Negro whose father was a Syrian Moslem," a "Turco-Persian," a mulatto, and a white man. Erdmann D. Beynon, "The Voodoo Cult Among Negro Migrants in Detroit," *American Journal of Sociology* 43.6 (May 1938): 895; Lincoln, *Black Muslims*, 12; Akbar Muhammad, "Muslims in the United States," in *The Islamic Impact*, eds. Yvonne Y. Haddad, Byron Haines, and Ellison Findly (Syracuse: Syracuse University Press, 1984), 201; and E. Muhammad, *Our Saviour Has Arrived* (1974; reprinted, Newport News, Va.: United Brothers Communications Systems, n.d.), 183. Perhaps coincidentally, almost all subsequent national leaders and spokesmen for the Muslims after Fard would be fair-skinned men, including Elijah Muhammad, Malcolm X, Wallace D. Muhammad, and Louis Farrakhan. Sahib, "Nation of Islam," 92; E. Muhammad, *History*, 6–7; Wallace D. Muhammad, *As the Light*, 27; and Barboza, *American Jihad*, 100.

21. Sahib, "Nation of Islam," 91–92; E. Muhammad, *History*, 2.

22. Sahib, "Nation of Islam," 92–93; E. Muhammad, *Message*, 17.

23. Sahib, "Nation of Islam," 92; E. Muhammad, *History*, 2–3.

24. This information can be found in the article "History," in "Muhammad University of Islam–No. 2—1973" yearbook, 24, reprinted in Report—"Elijah Poole," SAC Chicago, 26 November 1973, sec. 15, pp. 5–6 (E. Muhammad FBI file). Also see Malcolm X, *Autobiography*, 209. The subsequent use of the term *Muslim* will refer to the Nation of Islam and its membership unless otherwise specified.

25. E. Muhammad, *History*, 4.

26. Beynon, an early researcher of the movement, states that Fard sold "original names" for ten dollars each. Beynon, "Voodoo Cult," 901, 906; "Intended Voodoo Vic-

tims' Number Still Mounting," *Detroit Free Press*, 27 November 1932, 1, 4; and Wallace D. Muhammad, *As the Light*, 199–200.

27. Sahib, "Nation of Islam," 78–79, 96.

28. "Muslim Cult of Islam," 21 February 1957 (W. D. Fard FBI file); E. Muhammad, *History*, 4; E. Muhammad, *Theology of Time*, 81, 84; and J. Muhammad, *This Is the One*, 165.

29. Though Fard periodically attempted to tone down the godly image that his minister was presenting of him, he further instructed that, at a later date, "when I am gone . . . then you can say whatever you want to about Me." E. Muhammad, *History*, 3; Nathaniel 10X, "Muslim Pioneers Remember the Early Years of Islam,"*Muhammad Speaks*, 16 March 1973, 4; Sahib, "Nation of Islam," 92–93; Marsh, *From Black Muslims*, 108–9; E. Muhammad, *Our Saviour*, 36–37; and Lincoln, *Black Muslims*, 109–10.

30. The Nation of Islam Lessons are also known as the "Secret Ritual of the Nation of Islam" and "Teachings of the Lost Found Nation of Islam in a Mathematical Way." Like other converts with limited education, Elijah Muhammad did not comprehend the lessons in their entirety and as late as the 1940s could still not understand four or five of the problems discussed in the "Lost Found Moslem Lessons." Nation of Islam Lessons (in possession of author); Sahib, "Nation of Islam," 219–20, 241. The emphasis of the lessons on mathematical measurements of the earth and its movement and the Nation of Islam's preoccupation with large numbers in its teachings may reflect efforts to give the organization a kind of mystique based on privileged insider knowledge. These elements of the Muslims' teachings may also be designed for the more practical purpose of instructing members in basic arithmetic and rudimentary scientific concepts, which many undereducated believers may not have been exposed to prior to joining the movement.

31. In addition to holy texts, Fard also drew his message from the contemporary world histories of James H. Breasted and Henrik Willem Van Loon, works on Freemasonry, and books and speeches authored by Christian leaders such as Judge Rutherford, Frank Morris (a Baptist minister), and others. Elijah Muhammad would later state that it took him six hours to tell an audience what Fard had taught him. Beynon, "Voodoo Cult," 900; Sahib, "Nation of Islam," 67, 69–70, 97, 135–37, 232.

32. Fard himself would have a number of aliases including Wali Farrad, Professor Ford, Mr. Farrad Mohammed, and Mr. F. Mohammed Ali. Sometimes his chosen name was prefaced by *prophet* or *master*. The FBI compiled a list of over fifty names that it identified Fard by. Beynon, "Voodoo Cult," 896, 901; Report—"Biographical Data," 15 February 1958, 4 (W. D. Fard FBI file); Sahib, "Nation of Islam," 93–94; Lincoln, *Black Muslims*, 110–11; Essien-Udom, *Black Nationalism*, 100, 203–5; and Peter Goldman, *The Death and Life of Malcolm X* (Urbana: University of Illinois Press, 1979), 46.

33. Sahib, "Nation of Islam," 142; Essien-Udom, *Black Nationalism*, 77 n. 37.

34. The activities of ministers and the upkeep of the temple were largely funded by one-dollar donations collected once per month from the membership. "Laws Governing the Officials of Islam and Their Respective Duties," SAC Chicago to FBI director, 30 October 1957, 43 (W. D. Fard FBI file); Beynon, "Voodoo Cult," 902; and Sahib, "Nation of Islam," 87, 250.

35. Sahib, "Nation of Islam," 250; Beynon, "Voodoo Cult," 902.

36. Though Takahashi's influence on the Nation was fleeting, Elijah Muhammad, in line with the Muslim view of the Japanese and other nonwhites as members of the Black Nation, stated in 1933 that the Japanese nationalist had been sent to teach "the black people . . . that the Japanese were brothers and friends of the American Negroes." Takahashi's assessment of the character of Abdul Muhammad was made about this time

when the two roomed together in Detroit. Sahib, "Nation of Islam," 96; "Muhammad University of Islam–No. 2—1973" yearbook, 26 November 1973, sec. 15 (E. Muhammad FBI file); Ernest Allen Jr., "Satokata Takahashi and the Flowering of Black Messianic Nationalism," *Black Scholar* 24.1 (winter 1994): 37; and Report—"*Changed*," SAC Chicago to FBI director, 30 October 1957, 3–4 (W. D. Fard FBI file).

37. Sahib, "Nation of Islam," 85, 237.

38. "Cult Killer Bares Plot on Mayor," *Detroit Evening Times*, 23 November 1932, 1–2; "Leader of Cult Admits Slaying at Home 'Altar,'" *Detroit Free Press*, 21 November 1932, 1–2; and "Leader of Cult Called Insane," *Detroit News*, 22 November 1932, 4.

39. "Dole Aides Stunned by Voodoo 'King's' Death," *Detroit Evening Times*, 22 November 1932, 2; "Leader of Cult Admits Slaying," 1; "Negro Leaders Open Fight to Break Voodooism's Grip," *Detroit Free Press*, 24 November 1932, 1; and "Pastors Decry Growth of Cult Practices Here," *Detroit Evening Times*, 28 November 1932, 1–2.

40. "Dole Aides Stunned," 2; "Cult Killer Bares Plot," 1–2; and "Leader of Cult Called Insane," 4.

41. "Negro Leaders Open Fight," 1–2.

42. Ibid., 1–2; NOI Lessons, "Lost Found Moslem Lesson No. 1," question and answer 10; Sahib, "Nation of Islam," 75–76, 95; and Beynon, "Voodoo Cult," 894 n. 2, 903–4. In the 1970s, one individual did reportedly carry out this teaching to its literal, bloody conclusion. According to Ali K. Muslim, a member of the Newark mosque, a man "thoroughly confused about Elijah Muhammad's teachings" approached temple officials and tried to exchange a sack for a star-and-crescent pin and a trip to Mecca. To the horror of the Muslims, the bag contained four severed heads. The police were immediately called, and the executioner was arrested and presumably tried for murder. Barboza, *American Jihad*, 115–16.

43. According to his wife, Harris had been insane for a while and had threatened on several occasions "to cut off her head and also to kill their two children, Rudy, 9 years old, and Arsby, 12." "Leader of Cult Called Insane," 4; "4 Suspects Held for Quiz in 'Voodoo' Altar Slaying," *Detroit Evening Times*, 24 November 1932, 2; "Voodoo King's Sanity to Be Tested," *Detroit Evening Times*, 26 November 1932; "Voodoo Reign Here Is Broken," *Detroit Free Press*, 7 December 1932, 7; "New Human Sacrifice With a Boy as Victim Is Averted by Inquiry," *Detroit Free Press*, 26 November 1932, 1–2; "500 Join March to Ask Voodoo King's Freedom," *Detroit Free Press*, 25 November 1932, 1; Beynon, "Voodoo Cult," 897 n. 10; "Negro Leaders Open Fight," 1; "Voodoo Killer Tied Up After Starting Fire," *Detroit Sunday Times*, 27 November 1932, 2; and "Intended Voodoo Victims' Number," 4.

44. "Voodoo Reign Here Is Broken," 7.

45. E. Muhammad, *Our Saviour*, 23; J. Muhammad, *This Is the One*, 166; Essien-Udom, *Black Nationalism*, 128; E. Muhammad, *History*, 4; and E. Muhammad, *Message*, 179–80.

46. "Banished Leader of Cult Arrested," *Detroit Free Press*, 26 May 1933, 10; Sahib, "Nation of Islam," 70–71; "Background Information on Wallace Dodd," 8 March 1965 (W. D. Fard FBI file); and E. Muhammad, *The Supreme Wisdom*, 1st ed. (1957; reprint, Newport News, Va.: National Newport News and Commentator, n.d.), 14.

47. Elijah Muhammad described Fard Muhammad's departure as "one of the greatest tragedies that he has ever seen among the Negro community." Sahib, "Nation of Islam," 71, 76–77; E. Muhammad, *Our Saviour*, 36.

48. Beynon, "Voodoo Cult," 903–4; Malcolm X, *Autobiography*, 209; Sahib, "Nation of Islam," 77; Ted Stewart, "Who Will Inherit the $80 Million Black Muslim Empire?" *Sepia*, May 1975, 19, 20; and Marsh, *From Black Muslims*, 109.

49. After searching the Scriptures, Elijah Muhammad concluded that Fard Muhammad would not return until "He can secure the kingdom. Then He returns to the people He had made Himself manifest to." E. Muhammad, *History*, 4, 8–9; E. Muhammad, *Theology of Time*, 379; Sahib, "Nation of Islam," 70–71, 76–77, 98; E. Muhammad, *Supreme Wisdom*, 1st ed., 15; Beynon, "Voodoo Cult," 906–7; "Muhammad University of Islam–No. 2—1973" yearbook, 26 November 1973, sec. 15 (E. Muhammad FBI file); E. Muhammad, *Our Saviour*, 35, 145; and Essien-Udom, *Black Nationalism*, 45–46. It is unfortunate that the list of 104 books assigned to Elijah by Fard Muhammad is not available for study by researchers. It would surely shed more light on the ideological origins of the Muslim movement.

50. Beynon, "Voodoo Cult," 903–4, 906–7; E. Muhammad, *Message*, 212–13; and Sahib, "Nation of Islam," 76–77, 79.

51. Beynon, "Voodoo Cult," 903–4; "What Approaches Will Be Dreadful," *Muhammad Speaks*, 8 December 1967, 7; and Report—"Elijah Poole," SAC Detroit to FBI director, 9 August 1957, sec. 2, p. 1 (E. Muhammad FBI file).

52. James R. Grossman, *Land of Hope: Chicago, Black Southerners, and the Great Migration* (Chicago: University of Chicago Press, 1991), 123–27; Bureau of the Census, *Sixteenth Census of the United States: Population (Illinois) 1940*, vol. 2, part 2 (Washington, D.C.: Government Printing Office, 1943), 643.

53. Grossman, *Land of Hope*, 123–27, 130, 259–60, 264–65; John H. Franklin and Albert A. Moss, *From Slavery to Freedom*, 7th ed. (New York: McGraw Hill, Inc., 1994) 386, 471.

54. The rates of unemployment and relief work are based on the numbers of people of both races and sexes counted in the Chicago labor force by the census of 1940. Bureau of the Census, *Sixteenth Census: Population and Housing (Illinois) 1940* (Washington, D.C.: Government Printing Office, 1943), 39, 58; Bureau of the Census, *Sixteenth Census: Population (Illinois) 1940*, vol. 2, part 2, 643.

55. As early as the 1920s, some groups in Chicago, such as the Abyssinians and the Ancient Order of Ethiopian Princes, were separatist, critical of terms such as *Negro* and *colored*, hostile to the white world, and millennial in their view of history. The Chicago Commission on Race Relations, *The Negro in Chicago: A Study of Race Relations and a Race Riot* (Chicago: University of Chicago Press, 1922), 480–81, 487–88; Wallace D. Muhammad, *As the Light*, 15; "Gulam Bogans," 1 June 1942, 3, and Report—"Changed," SAC Chicago to FBI director, 30 October 1957, 32 (W. D. Fard FBI file); Sahib, "Nation of Islam," 87; and E. Muhammad, *How to Eat to Live*, book 2 (1972; reprint, Newport News, Va.: Newport News and Commentator, n.d.), 169.

56. "Moors Battle in Court; 40 Hurt," *Chicago Defender*, 9 March 1935, 1–2; Karriem Allah, "The Early Days of Islam,"*Muhammad Speaks*, 1 February 1974, 3; "Cultists Riot in Courts; One Death, 41 Hurt," *Chicago Daily Tribune*, 6 March 1935, 1, 10; Karriem Allah, "The Early Days of Islam: The 'Glorious Past,' " *Muhammad Speaks*, 24 August 1973, 18; and "Convict 40 'Moors' in Courtroom Riot," *Chicago Defender*, 16 March 1935, 24.

57. Some of the sources regarding the courtroom incidents in March and April convey the impression that the two events were either closely related or one and the same. E. Muhammad, *Message*, 213–14; Sahib, "Nation of Islam," 86–87.

58. Malcolm X, *Autobiography*, 209; E. Muhammad, *Message*, 257, 264; J. Muhammad, *This Is the One*, 173; Sahib, "Nation of Islam," 80–81; and "Muslim Cult of Islam," 21 February 1957 (W. D. Fard FBI file).

Chapter 3: The Knowledge of Self and Others

1. Malcolm X, *Malcolm X: February 1965, The Final Speeches,* ed. Steve Clark (New York: Pathfinder Press, 1992), 208–9.

2. E. Muhammad, *Our Saviour,* 39–40, 43, 146; E. Muhammad, *Theology of Time,* 92, 95; and E. Muhammad, *Message,* 290.

3. Elijah Muhammad believed that icy Pluto symbolized the plight of the African-American, who has for four hundred years been separated "from our people, frozen-up in the power of the white man. We could not rotate according to the light and power of the wisdom of our Own God." E. Muhammad, *Our Saviour,* 44–46, 53; E. Muhammad, *Theology of Time,* 269, 387–88; E. Muhammad, *History,* 14; E. Muhammad, *How to Eat to Live,* book 2, 7; and E. Muhammad, *Supreme Wisdom,* 1st ed., 47.

4. E. Muhammad, *Our Saviour,* 96; E. Muhammad, *Theology of Time,* 19, 96, 278; NOI Lessons, "Student Enrollment," answers 1, 9; and Malcolm X, *The End of White World Supremacy,* ed. Benjamin Goodman (New York: Merlin House, Inc., 1971), 47.

5. David Y. Hughes and Harry M. Geduld, *A Critical Edition of The War of the Worlds: H. G. Wells's Scientific Romance* (Bloomington: Indiana University Press, 1993), 238, 245–46; Jenny Randles and Peter Warrington, *Science and the UFOs* (New York: Basil Blackwell, Inc., 1985), 4; and E. Muhammad, *The Fall of America* (1973; reprint, Newport News, Va.: National Newport News and Commentator, n.d.), 237.

6. E. Muhammad, *Theology of Time,* 113–14, 373; E. Muhammad, *Our Saviour,* 97–98.

7. E. Muhammad, *Supreme Wisdom,* 1st ed., 36; E. Muhammad, *Message,* 70; and E. Muhammad, *Our Saviour,* 26, 35.

8. E. Muhammad, *Theology of Time,* 275–76; E. Muhammad, *Our Saviour,* 56; E. Muhammad speech in Atlanta, 1961, in Lomax, *When the Word Is Given,* 114; Malcolm X, *End of White World Supremacy,* 47; and E. Muhammad, *Message,* 31.

9. Malcolm X, *End of White World Supremacy,* 48; E. Muhammad, *Supreme Wisdom,* 1st ed., 33.

10. E. Muhammad, *Supreme Wisdom,* 1st ed., 33–34; E. Muhammad, *Message,* 31, 104; Malcolm X, *End of White World Supremacy,* 48; and Wallace D. Muhammad, *As the Light,* 26. In fact, the belief in Africa as being uncivilized died hard among the Muslims. As late as 1970 when the study of African history was becoming popular among African-Americans, Elijah Muhammad still felt it necessary to remind Muslims that the "ignorance and savagery here and there in Africa must be removed and replaced with the modern civilization of Islam." NOI Lessons, "Lost Found Moslem Lesson No. 1," answer 7; Essien-Udom, *Black Nationalism,* 197–98; and E. Muhammad, "The Angry Nations, 100% Dissatisfaction," *Muhammad Speaks,* 20 March 1970, 15. The theme of African savagery in black separatist thought is discussed in Claude A. Clegg, "Supermen, Savages, and the Divine Promise: The Image of Africa in Nineteenth-Century Black Separatist Thought," unpublished seminar paper, University of Michigan, and Wilson J. Moses, *The Golden Age of Black Nationalism, 1850–1925* (Camden, Conn.: Archon Books, 1978).

11. NOI Lessons, "Student Enrollment," answer 10; E. Muhammad, *Supreme Wisdom,* 1st ed., 44; E. Muhammad, *The Supreme Wisdom,* vol. 2 (1957; reprint, Newport News, Va.: United Brothers Communications Systems, n.d.), 53; and E. Muhammad, *Our Saviour,* 32–33.

12. E. Muhammad, *Message*, 107; E. Muhammad, "Indians in America," *Muhammad Speaks*, 12 October 1973, 12.

13. E. Muhammad, *Message*, 110–12; E. Muhammad, "Mr. Muhammad Speaks," *Pittsburgh Courier*, 19 April 1958, 14.

14. E. Muhammad, *Message*, 111–12; E. Muhammad, *Our Saviour*, 51.

15. E. Muhammad, *Message*, 113–14. Elijah Muhammad viewed Yacub's persecution as akin to his own as leader of the Nation of Islam and even admired "our Brother" Yacub, though he had "no good nor truth" in him. In the Muslims' program of the 1960s, Muhammad asked white Americans for the same arrangement that the mythical Yacub received from the Meccans: a separate territory and supplies and provisions for the next twenty to twenty-five years. Ibid., 161; E. Muhammad, *Our Saviour*, 58, 77.

16. E. Muhammad, *Message*, 114–16; NOI Lessons, "Lost Found Moslem Lesson No. 2," answers 28, 30, 31; E. Muhammad, *History*, 21, 54; and E. Muhammad, *Our Saviour*, 58. During the six hundred years of grafting on Pelan (which the Muslims identify as the island of Patmos in Revelation 1: 9), major racial and ethnic groups such as the Chinese were created in addition to the white race. E. Muhammad, *Our Saviour*, 52.

17. NOI Lessons, "Lost Found Moslem Lesson No. 2," answer 32; E. Muhammad, *How to Eat to Live*, book 1 (1967; reprint, Newport News, Va.: National Newport News and Commentator, n.d.) 72; E. Muhammad, *Message*, 102, 116; E. Muhammad, *Our Saviour*, 110–11; and E. Muhammad, "Mr. Muhammad Speaks," *Pittsburgh Courier*, 25 July 1959, 14.

18. E. Muhammad, *Message*, 91, 116–18, 133; Malcolm X, *End of White World Supremacy*, 60–61; E. Muhammad, *Fall*, 225; E. Muhammad, *Theology of Time*, 19; and NOI Lessons, "Lost Found Moslem Lesson No. 1," answer 4. The Muslims believed that the story of the expulsion of Adam and Eve from the Garden of Eden was an allegorized version of their history of the white race's ouster from Mecca. Adam is actually considered a white murderer in Nation of Islam lore, and Yacub's race of devils, rooted in murder and lies, was also known as the Adamic people.

19. The assertion that whites lived in caves was probably gleaned from a book by Henrik Van Loon that states that the "great-great-grandfathers [of Europeans lived] in caves" while the "valley of the Nile had developed a high stage of civilization thousands of years before." Fard Muhammad cited this work occasionally and referred his followers to it. Elijah Muhammad pointed to the surah in the Qur'an entitled "The Cave" as additional (allegorical) proof that whites "turned into apes and swine as a divine curse." E. Muhammad, *Message*, 103–4, 119–20; Malcolm X, *End of White World Supremacy*, 62–63; Henrik Willem Van Loon, *The Story of Mankind* (New York: MacMillan Co., 1923), 16; and Beynon, "Voodoo Cult," 900.

20. E. Muhammad, *Message*, 119–20; E. Muhammad, *Theology of Time*, 375–76; E. Muhammad, *History*, 97; and NOI Lessons, "Lost Found Moslem Lesson No. 1," answer 4.

21. E. Muhammad, *Message*, 120; E. Muhammad, *Our Saviour*, 33.

22. According to the Muslim history of Jesus, Joseph was married to another woman when he fathered Jesus by Mary. E. Muhammad, *Supreme Wisdom*, 1st ed., 27; NOI Lessons, "Lost Found Moslem Lesson No. 1," answer 5; and E. Muhammad, "Mr. Muhammad Speaks," *Pittsburgh Courier*, 7 September 1957, 10.

23. According to Nation of Islam doctrine, a council of twelve men over the course of the last several thousand years have purposely kept the knowledge of God secret from the world. E. Muhammad, *Our Saviour*, 50, 61, 86, 157, 172, 192, 204; E. Muhammad, *Supreme Wisdom*, 1st ed., 13, 16; and E. Muhammad, *Supreme Wisdom*, vol. 2, 20–21.

Compare the language that Fard Muhammad and the early Muslims used to describe Christianity (the white man "uses his [Jesus'] name to shield his dirty religion, which is called Christianity") to the denunciation of the state of Israel by Louis Farrakhan over fifty years later (the Jew uses "God's name as a shield for your dirty religion"). NOI Lessons, "Lost Found Moslem Lesson No. 1," answer 5; "Excerpts of Interview with Louis Farrakhan," *Washington Post,* 1 March 1990, A16.

24. For the Quranic version of the birth, life, and physical departure of Jesus from human affairs, see surahs 4:157–59 and 171, 9:30, and 19:20–23 and 30–33, in *The Meaning of the Holy Qur'an,* trans. Abdullah Yusuf Ali (Brentwood, Md.: Amana Corporation, 1993), 235–36, 239–40, 446, 748–49, 750–51.

25. E. Muhammad, *Message,* 94.

26. Much of Fard Muhammad's teachings on Islam, ancient Egypt, and the Crusades probably came from a history book by James Breasted that he sometimes cited in his talks. James H. Breasted, *The Conquest of Civilization* (New York: Harper & Brothers Publishers, 1926); E. Muhammad, *Message,* 116; E. Muhammad, "Mr. Muhammad Speaks," *Pittsburgh Courier,* 3 January 1959, 14; and Beynon, "Voodoo Cult," 900.

27. NOI Lessons, "English Lesson, No. C1," no. 27–36; Beynon, "Voodoo Cult," 900–901; E. Muhammad, *History,* 39–40; E. Muhammad, *Supreme Wisdom,* 1st ed., 15–17; E. Muhammad, *Message,* 244; and E. Muhammad, *Our Saviour,* 93.

28. E. Muhammad, *Supreme Wisdom,* vol. 2, 47; E. Muhammad, *Our Saviour,* 99; E. Muhammad, *Message,* 34–35, 49, 65–66; Sahib, "Nation of Islam," 141; E. Muhammad, *Supreme Wisdom,* 1st ed., 12–13; NOI Lessons, "Lost Found Moslem Lesson No. 2," answer 9; and E. Muhammad, "Christianity vs. Islam," Philadelphia, Penn., 1962 (audiotape).

29. NOI Lessons, "Lost Found Moslem Lesson No. 2," answers 14, 35; E. Muhammad, *Message,* 267–68; Sahib, "Nation of Islam," 97; E. Muhammad, *Our Saviour,* 99; E. Muhammad, "Mr. Muhammad Speaks," *Pittsburgh Courier,* 21 March 1959, 14; and E. Muhammad, *Supreme Wisdom,* 1st ed., 17.

30. For information on John Hawkins, see Franklin and Moss, *From Slavery to Freedom,* 43; David B. Davis, *Slavery and Human Progress* (New York: Oxford University Press, 1984), 68; and Milton Meltzer, *Slavery: From the Rise of Western Civilization to Today* (New York: Dell Publishing Co., 1972), 176–78. Even as recently as February 1995, some Muslims, including Louis Farrakhan, maintained there was an unrecorded sixty-four-year history of African slavery in North America between 1555 and 1619. Louis Farrakhan, "Jesus Saves," International Amphitheater, Chicago, Illinois, 26 February 1995 (audiotape).

31. Essien-Udom, *Black Nationalism,* 126–27; E. Muhammad, 1958 Saviour's Day Address (audiotape); E. Muhammad, *History,* 6–7; E. Muhammad, *Message,* 19–20; Sahib, "Nation of Islam," 94; and E. Muhammad, *Our Saviour,* 132, 183. According to Elijah Muhammad, the name Fard means "an independent One and One Who is not on the level with the average Gods (Allahs).... One whom we must obey, or else He destroys us." E. Muhammad, *Our Saviour,* 57.

32. As recollected by Elijah, Fard Muhammad claimed to be "from the royal dynasty of the Hashimide Sheriffs of Mecca, who were the kings of Hejaz until the first world war." Sahib, "Nation of Islam," 69; Beynon, "Voodoo Cult," 896–97; and E. Muhammad, *History,* 5.

33. According to Nation of Islam lore, Fard Muhammad matriculated either at the University of California (at Los Angeles?) or the University of Southern California. E. Muhammad, *History,* 5; Beynon, "Voodoo Cult," 896–97; E. Muhammad, *Message,* 165; and Sahib, "Nation of Islam," 65–66, 118.

34. E. Muhammad, *History*, 8–9.

35. Elijah Muhammad was critical of orthodox Muslims who challenged his messengership and at one time stated that "it makes you look like a fool for no brother Muslim should say anything against another brother Muslim especially in the presence of an enemy of Islam and for the sake of that enemy, speak evil against your own brother. You are not given any credit by Allah." E. Muhammad, "I am the Last Messenger of Allah: A Defense of Messenger Elijah Muhammad's Messengership Against Orthodox Muslims," transcript (Cleveland: Secretarius Publications, 1992), 3; E. Muhammad, *Theology of Time*, 6–7; E. Muhammad, *Message*, 171, 306; E. Muhammad, *Supreme Wisdom*, 1st ed., 39; E. Muhammad, "The Benefit Party," *Muhammad Speaks*, 28 August 1970, 16; and E. Muhammad, *Fall*, 205, 246.

36. The Muslims believed that in eating one meal per day "we would live over 100 years. Eating one meal every two days would lengthen our lives just that much longer. . . . [We] would never be sick, eating one meal every three days." On Fard Muhammad's advice, Elijah Muhammad reported later that he cleaned out his medicine cabinet during the 1930s. He also claimed that his wife, Clara, did not use any drugs to bear children during this period. E. Muhammad, *How to Eat to Live*, book 1, 11–12, 14–15, 19–20, 25, 32–33, 35, 70, 98, 110; Sahib, "Nation of Islam," 216–17; E. Muhammad, *Our Saviour*, 83; and E. Muhammad, *Message*, 47, 50, 54–55, 179–80, 185.

37. E. Muhammad, *Our Saviour*, 2, 8; E. Muhammad, *Supreme Wisdom*, 1st ed., 35–36; and E. Muhammad, *Message*, 155–56.

38. Germany and England would also be singled out for divine retribution. E. Muhammad, *Message*, 267–72, 282; E. Muhammad, *Theology of Time*, 357, 517; " 'We Live in the Time of a Change,' " 5; E. Muhammad, *Fall*, 50–53, 103, 130, 132, 154–56; and E. Muhammad, *Supreme Wisdom*, 1st ed., 47–49. By the 1970s, when the Muslims were moderating some of their rhetoric, Muhammad was willing to concede that "good done by any person is rewarded and these white people who believe in Islam will receive the Blessing of entering into the Hereafter." E. Muhammad, *Supreme Wisdom*, 1st ed., 35; E. Muhammad, "Days of Allah," *Muhammad Speaks*, 25 December 1970, 16–17; E. Muhammad, *Fall*, 55; E. Muhammad, *History*, 54–55, 58; and E. Muhammad, *How to Eat to Live*, book 2, 159.

39. E. Muhammad, *Supreme Wisdom*, 1st ed., 35; E. Muhammad, "Days of Allah," 16–17.

40. According to Muslim theology, the biblical Ezekiel saw the Mother Plane as did Canadians in the 1930s. E. Muhammad, *Supreme Wisdom*, 1st ed., 14; E. Muhammad, *Fall*, 236–42; E. Muhammad, *Theology of Time*, 512–13; E. Muhammad, *Message*, 290–91; Wallace D. Muhammad, *As the Light*, 15–16; and Sahib, "Nation of Islam," 95.

41. England is bombed in Fard Muhammad's tale perhaps as punishment for its long imperial history and its support of the Balfour Declaration of 1917, which advocated a Jewish homeland in the Middle East. E. Muhammad, *Theology of Time*, 278, 511, 516–17, 535; E. Muhammad, *Our Saviour*, 105–6, 126–27, 162; and "The Black Separatists: Elijah Muhammad on the Philosophy of the Black Muslims," interview by Ben Anderson, Phoenix, Arizona, 1964 (audiotape), in Undergraduate Library, University of North Carolina at Chapel Hill.

42. Larry H. Addington, *The Patterns of War since the Eighteenth Century* (Bloomington: Indiana University Press, 1984), 166–67; Russell F. Weigley, *The American Way of War* (Bloomington: Indiana University Press, 1977), 247.

43. E. Muhammad, *Message*, 291.

44. The activities and whereabouts of black people during the thousand-year burning and cooling of America were not elaborated on by Elijah Muhammad or other Muslim

leaders. E. Muhammad, *Fall*, 133, 143; E. Muhammad, *Theology of Time*, 499; E. Muhammad, *Our Saviour*, 79, 81–83, 92, 110–12, 117, 124–27; E. Muhammad, *History*, 14; E. Muhammad, *Supreme Wisdom*, 1st ed., 25–26; and NOI Lessons, "Lost Found Moslem Lesson No. 1," answer 38.

45. Karen E. Fields, *Revival and Rebellion in Colonial Central Africa* (Princeton: Princeton University Press, 1985), 6.

46. Fard Muhammad may also have been influenced by Druze, Ismaili, and other Islam-inspired doctrines that emphasized secrecy, private revelation (for initiates only), successive incarnations of Allah, cyclical history, and messianism. According to Elijah Muhammad's youngest son, Akbar, Fard Muhammad was "somewhat versed in medieval Islamic astrology, and a deviant form of Protestantism, and held a number of Bahai and Shiah views." Monroe Berger, "The Black Muslims," *Horizon* (winter 1964): 61; A. Muhammad, "Muslims in the United States," 201; and E. Muhammad, *Message*, 97.

47. For a brief, general discussion of the differences between the Nation of Islam and orthodox Muslims, see Mustafa El-Amin, *The Religion of Islam and the Nation of Islam: What Is the Difference?* (Newark, N.J.: El-Amin Productions, 1991). Though Muslims would later evoke, in a self-serving manner, the Quranic acceptance of polygamy to defend Elijah Muhammad against charges of marital infidelity in the 1960s, historically the Nation of Islam has not accepted polygamy as moral or permissible among the believers. Interestingly, Erdmann Beynon, who studied the movement in the 1930s, states that ministers in the organization were then allowed to participate in "extra-marital sex relations." However, he cites no sources to support this curiously phrased contention. Throughout the history of the movement, Elijah Muhammad routinely imposed severe penalties on those who engaged in illicit sexual activities. Additionally, he did not claim for himself, at least not as far as the present author is aware, any special prerogative regarding multiple partners until, of course, his own liaisons were publicly disclosed in the 1960s. This matter is discussed at length in Chapters 7 and 8. Beynon, "Voodoo Cult," 902; Essien-Udom, *Black Nationalism*, 207–8; Benjamin Karim, *Remembering Malcolm* (New York: Carroll & Graf Publishers, Inc., 1992), 154; and Malcolm X, *Autobiography*, 294–99.

48. The racial designation *black* was also denounced by the Moorish-Americans, for they believed it had been forced on them by Europeans in 1774. According to Noble Drew Ali, the Moors were olive-skinned. Noble Drew Ali, *The Holy Koran of the Moorish Science Temple of America* (1929), 58–59; Marsh, *From Black Muslims*, 41–49. During the early period, members of the Nation of Islam were known for their extravagant attire, which putatively reflected "their original high status" in the Tribe of Shabazz. Beynon, "Voodoo Cult," 906.

49. Ali, *Holy Quran*, 5–8, 56.

50. "Memorandum for the Attorney General," 15 May 1942 (W. D. Fard FBI file); Yvonne Y. Haddad and Jane I. Smith, *Mission to America: Five Islamic Sectarian Communities in North America* (Gainsville: University of Florida, 1993), 86–87; and Arthur H. Fauset, *Black Gods of the Metropolis* (1944; reprint, Philadelphia: University of Pennsylvania, 1971), 42–43, 48. Though Elijah Muhammad maintained that neither he nor Fard Muhammad were ever members of the MSTA, they both had high opinions of Noble Drew Ali, a Muslim whose work "we are only trying to finish up." Essien-Udom, *Black Nationalism*, 63 n. 1; E. Muhammad, *History*, 76–77; and E. Muhammad, *Supreme Wisdom*, vol. 2, 84.

51. E. Muhammad, *Supreme Wisdom*, vol. 2, 84; Daniel Burley, "Foreword," in E. Muhammad, *Message*, xxiii; and Marcus Garvey, *More Philosophy and Opinions of Marcus Garvey*, eds. E. U. Essien-Udom and Amy Jacques-Garvey (Totowa, N.J.: Frank Cass, 1977), 242. Though corroborating evidence is elusive at best, a number of people have claimed that Elijah Muhammad was affiliated with the Garvey Movement before

joining the Nation of Islam. In one of her writings, Amy Jacques-Garvey, the widow of Marcus Garvey, described Muhammad as a corporal in the Chicago division of the UNIA during the 1920s. J. Charles Zampty, who was familiar with the Detroit UNIA, has portrayed Muhammad as "an active member" of the Motor City branch. These assertions are not supported by documentation and, of course, contradict Muhammad's own story. However, it is possible that Muhammad did try to attract Garveyites to the Nation by giving speeches in the Chicago UNIA Liberty Hall during the early 1930s. John Henrik Clarke, ed., *Marcus Garvey and the Vision of Africa* (New York: Vintage Books, 1974), 372; Tony Martin, *Race First: The Ideological and Organizational Struggles of Marcus Garvey and the Universal Negro Improvement Association* (Dover, Mass.: Majority Press, 1976), 76, 80.

52. Randall Burkett, *Garveyism as a Religious Movement: The Institutionalization of a Black Civil Religion* (Metuchen, N.J.: Scarecrow Press, Inc., 1978), 16, 23–25, 28–29, 47, 50–53, 61–63. Also, see Marcus Garvey, *Philosophy and Opinions of Marcus Garvey*, ed. Amy Jacques-Garvey (1923; reprint, New York: Atheneum, 1986); Marcus Garvey, *Marcus Garvey: Life and Lessons*, eds. Robert A. Hill and Barbara Bair (Berkeley: University of California Press, 1987); and Robert A. Hill, ed., *The Marcus Garvey and Universal Negro Improvement Association Papers,* vol. 1 (Berkeley : University of California, 1983), xxxv–xc.

53. Jill Watts, *God, Harlem U.S.A.: The Father Divine Story* (Berkeley: University of California Press, 1992), 26–71, 115–16, 167–70.

54. Ibid., 69–70, 105, 115, 167–70.

55. Elijah Muhammad was a member of the Masons between 1924 and 1931. William A. Muraskin, *Middle-Class Blacks in a White Society: Prince Hall Freemasonry in America* (Berkeley: University of California Press, 1975), 199; Sahib, "Nation of Islam," 90; Essien-Udom, *Black Nationalism,* 100–101; and E. Muhammad, *The Secrets of Freemasonry* (Cleveland: Secretarius Publications, 1994): 3, 10, 13, 15, 23, 30–31.

56. E. Muhammad, *Theology of Time,* 282–83. During his speech at the Million Man March in Washington, Louis Farrakhan referred often to numerological mysteries, Freemasonry, and biblical prophecy. Louis Farrakhan, speech at the Million Man March in Washington, D.C., C-Span, 16 October, 1995.

57. *Enduring to the End: Jehovah's Witnesses and Bible Doctrine* (Schaumburg, Ill.: Regular Baptist Press, 1987), 22, 25, 29, 162; E. Muhammad, *Supreme Wisdom,* 1st ed., 41; Barbara G. Harrison, *Vision of Glory: A History and a Memory of Jehovah's Witnesses* (New York: Simon & Schuster, 1978), 173–74, 178; Harold Bloom, *The American Religion: The Emergence of the Post-Christian Nation* (New York: Simon & Schuster, 1992), 159–70; E. Muhammad, *Message,* 83, 267–72; and Sahib, "Nation of Islam," 97.

58. According to Elijah Muhammad, Judge Rutherford and a number of government officials believed that Fard Muhammad was God. E. Muhammad, *Fall,* 57, 165; E. Muhammad, *Message,* 323; E. Muhammad, *Our Saviour,* 49–50; and J. Muhammad, *This Is the One,* 171.

Chapter 4: Tabernacle in the Wilderness

1. Ali, *Meaning of the Holy Qur'an,* 853.

2. Joe W. Trotter Jr., *Black Milwaukee: The Making of an Industrial Proletariat, 1915–1945* (Urbana: University of Illinois Press, 1988), 148, 150, 176, 179.

3. Ibid., 1–2, 9, 148, 152, 155–56.

4. J. Muhammad, *This Is the One*, 173; Trotter, *Black Milwaukee*, 177; and Malcolm X, *Autobiography*, 209.

5. Malcolm X, *Autobiography*, 209; J. Muhammad, *This Is the One*, 172–73; Sahib, "Nation of Islam," 80, 97; and "The Greatest Life Ever Lived in Modern Times," *Muhammad Speaks*, 19 January 1968, 3.

6. Benjamin X would later become the minister of Temple No. 24 in Richmond, Virginia. James C34X, "Through Divine Black Leadership," *Muhammad Speaks*, 14 March 1975, 7; Barboza, *American Jihad*, 80. For a good discussion of the response of black leadership to the Roosevelt administration and the New Deal, see John B. Kirby, *Black Americans in the Roosevelt Era* (Knoxville: University of Tennessee Press, 1982). The African-American population figures for Washington, D.C., are for 1940. Bureau of the Census, *Sixteenth Census of the United States: Population (District of Columbia), 1940*, vol. 2, pt. 1 (Washington, D.C.: Government Printing Office, 1943), 956.

7. "The Greatest Life," 3; Malcolm X, *Autobiography*, 209; J. Muhammad, *This Is the One*, 173; "Muslim Cult of Islam," 21 February 1957, 4 (W. D. Fard FBI file); E. Muhammad, *Theology of Time*, 56–58; and "Appendix," 27 September 1966, sec. 11, p. 4 (E. Muhammad FBI file).

8. Sahib, "Nation of Islam," 82; Nathaniel 10X, "Pioneers Remember Early Years of Islam," *Muhammad Speaks*, 20 April 1973, 19. Regrettably, there are no published critical analyses of women in the Nation. Besides a few pieces by insiders that tout the Muslim view of the place of women in the family and society, this area of study is still relatively untouched by writers. Hopefully in the future, Muslim women will be as willing to publicize their experiences as former female members of the Black Panthers have been.

9. Wallace D. Muhammad, *As the Light*, 19; Beynon, "Voodoo Cult," 905; Sahib, "Nation of Islam," 81; and "Muslim Cult of Islam," 21 February 1957, 7 (W. D. Fard FBI file).

10. Abdul Muhammad, an early rebel against the leadership of Elijah Muhammad, died in October 1938 of tuberculosis. He may have spent his last days confined in an insane asylum. Report—"Changed," SAC Chicago to FBI director, 30 October 1957, 3–5, and Report—"W. D. Fard," SAC Detroit to FBI director, 31 January 1958, 2 (W. D. Fard FBI file); Essien-Udom, *Black Nationalism*, 77 n. 37; and Sahib, "Nation of Islam," 74–75. Anti-welfare-state literature produced by the Nation contained statements such as: "Roosevelt gave you a social security number just to hold you, and now he's getting ready to call in these numbers and give you a stamp. . . . He's going to put a stamp on you, the mark of the beast. You signed up with the devil and he gives you the filthy crumbs from his table like the rich man gave the man Lazarus." Bontemps and Conroy, *Anyplace but Here*, 224–25; Beynon, "Voodoo Cult," 904–5; Marsh, *From Black Muslims*, 106; and Report—"Biographical Data," SAC New York, 26 February 1968, sec. 12, p. 22 (E. Muhammad FBI file).

11. According to Benjamin X, Muhammad's host at this time, the Muslims in Washington, D.C., first held meetings in his home. Later, they gathered in "storefront Baptist churches" before securing their own building. Barboza, *American Jihad*, 80. In addition to the entry of the United States into World War II, A. Philip Randolph's threat to lead African-Americans in a march on Washington at this time probably heightened the sensitivity of the American government to the Nation of Islam and other black "radical" groups in the country's capital and elsewhere. Kirby, *Black Americans in the Roosevelt Era*, 173–74.

12. In regard to individuals imprisoned for World War II draft violations, "over onefourth of all convictions of conscientious objectors resulted in sentences of from 4 to 5 years. . . . About 30 percent of these delinquents were sentenced from 2 to 3 years and

nearly 20 percent from 1 to 2 years." Selective Services, *Conscientious Objection*, vol. 1 (Washington, D.C.: Government Printing Office, 1950), 261, 264–65; Lewis B. Hershey, *Selective Service in Peacetime: First Report of the Director of Selective Service, 1940–41* (Washington, D.C.: Government Printing Office, 1942), 188, 190, 245; Hershey, *Selective Service in Wartime: Second Report of Selective Service, 1941–42* (Washington, D.C.: Government Printing Office, 1943), 279, 286, 289, 292, 605; and E. Muhammad, *Message*, 179.

13. Bernard C. Nalty, *Strength for the Fight: A History of Black Americans in the Military* (New York: The Free Press, 1986); Franklin and Moss, *From Slavery to Freedom*, 433–60.

14. "Memorandum to the Attorney General," 15 May 1942 (W. D. Fard FBI file); Report—"Elijah Poole," SAC Chicago, 14 November 1955, sec. 1, p. 13 (E. Muhammad FBI file); and "Moslem Leader Nabbed" (picture caption), *Washington Afro-American*, 16 May 1942, 26.

15. Supposedly among the Nation of Islam material confiscated by the FBI was a document that accurately detailed the future of China. J. Muhammad, *This Is the One*, 178; "The Greatest Life," 3; "Third Moslem Cultist Nabbed on Draft Count," *Washington Afro-American*, 23 May 1942, 5; and Report—"Biographical Data," SAC New York, 26 February 1968, sec. 12, pp. 7–8 (E. Muhammad FBI file).

16. The Muslims arrested in Detroit denied ever discussing the selective service act in the temple. Their leader, William Muhammad, was fifty years old in 1942, definitely too old to register for the draft. Deborah 3X, " '73 Graduate Tells of Messenger's Hard Trial in Washington, D.C.," *Muhammad Speaks*, 9 March 1973, 18; "Third Moslem Cultist Nabbed," 5; "Dark Islam," *Newsweek*, 1 June 1942, 29; and "Gulam Bogans," 13 June 1942, 2–3 (W. D. Fard FBI file).

17. "The Greatest Life," 3; Deborah 3X, " '73 Graduate," 18; and "FBI Holds Moslem Chief on Draft-Evasion Charge," *Washington Afro-American*, 9 May 1942, 1.

18. J. Muhammad, *This Is the One*, 173; Wallace D. Muhammad, *As the Light*, 24–25; Deborah 3X, " '73 Graduate," 18; Essien-Udom, *Black Nationalism*, 75; and Ansari, "W. D. Muhammad," 251.

19. According to one Muslim account of the incident, the order to have Elijah Muhammad arrested came from President Roosevelt himself. "The Greatest Life," 3; "FBI Holds Moslem Chief," 26; and Report—"Biographical Data," SAC New York, 26 February 1968, sec. 12, pp. 7–8 (E. Muhammad FBI file).

20. E. Muhammad, *Supreme Wisdom*, 1st ed., 15. In regard to leaving Washington, D.C., Elijah Muhammad would later state that "I felt relieved to be out of all that strain, although I was not afraid because I had not done anything." "The Greatest Life," 3.

Chapter 5: Public Enemy

1. *The Confessions of Nat Turner* (Baltimore: 1831), reprinted in Thomas R. Frazier, *Afro-American History: Primary Sources* (New York: Harcourt Brace Jovanovich, Inc., 1971), 40.

2. The average temperature for July 1942 in Chicago was seventy-five degrees Fahrenheit compared to eighty-three in New Orleans, eighty-one in Nashville, and eighty-three in Charleston, South Carolina. B. R. Mitchell, *International Historical Statistics: The Americas and Australasia* (London: MacMillan Press, Ltd., 1983), 31–32; "Muslim Cult of Islam," 21 February 1957, 7 and Report—"Allah Temple of Islam," 15 August 1942 (W. D. Fard FBI file).

3. "Allah Temple of Islam"; Sahib, "Nation of Islam," 172; Report—"Biographical Data," SAC New York, 26 February 1968, sec. 12, p. 22 (E. Muhammad FBI file); and "Another Negro Fanatic Seized as Plot Leader," *Chicago Daily Tribune*, 23 September 1942, 8.

4. Report—"Biographical Data," SAC New York, 26 February 1968, sec. 12, pp. 7–8 (E. Muhammad FBI file); E. Muhammad, *Theology of Time*, 511–12; "12 Negro Chiefs Seized by FBI in Sedition Raids," *Chicago Daily Tribune*, 22 September 1942, 9; and Essien-Udom, *Black Nationalism*, 67.

5. "12 Negro Chiefs," 9; Report—*"Changed,"* SAC Chicago to FBI director, 30 October 1957 (W. D. Fard FBI file); "Takahashi's Blacks," *Time* 5 October 1942, 25; and "Seize 84 Negroes in Sedition Raids," *New York Times*, 22 September 1942, 4.

6. "12 Negro Chiefs," 9; "U.S. Indicts 38 Cult Members," *Chicago Defender*, 3 October 1942, 1; and "Another Negro Fanatic," 8.

7. "Sedition: Race Hate Used by Tokio to Lure 85 Nabbed by FBI," *Chicago Defender*, 26 September 1942, 4.

8. E. Muhammad, *Theology of Time*, 18, 511–12; Report—"Biographical Data," SAC New York, 26 February 1968, sec. 12, pp. 7–8 (E. Muhammad FBI file).

9. E. Muhammad, *Message*, 322–23; "12 Negro Chiefs," 9.

10. "U.S. Indicts 38," 1.

11. "Cultists 'Guilty'; 32 Given Jail Sentences," *Chicago Defender*, 10 October 1942, 1, 5; Report—"Biographical Data," SAC New York, 26 February 1968, sec. 12, p. 22 (E. Muhammad FBI file); "U.S. Studies Seized Cult Literature," *Chicago Defender*, 17 October 1942, 5; Hershey, *Selective Services in Wartime*, 286; and *Survey of Racial Conditions in the United States* (Washington, D.C.: Federal Bureau of Investigation, 1943), 578.

12. "Five Face U.S. Sedition Charges in Court Monday," *Chicago Defender*, 28 November 1942, 1; Report—"Biographical Data," SAC New York, 26 February 1968, sec. 12, pp. 7–8 (E. Muhammad FBI file); and *Racial Conditions*, 23. Nationally, as many as one hundred of Muhammad's followers served time in prison during this period for draft violations and other offenses inspired by religious conviction. E. Muhammad, *Message*, 321–22.

13. Essien-Udom, *Black Nationalism*, 67; Wallace D. Muhammad, *Religion on the Line* (Chicago: W. D. Muhammad Publications, 1983), 133; E. Muhammad, *Theology of Time*, 47; Bontemps and Conroy, *Anyplace but Here*, 224; and E. Muhammad, 1954 Saviour's Day Address (audiotape).

14. Report—"Biographical Data," SAC New York, 26 February 1968, sec. 12, pp. 7–8 (E. Muhammad FBI file); *Racial Conditions*, 23; and James L. Stokesbury, *A Short History of World War II* (New York: William Morrow and Co., 1980), 285–86, 292–96.

15. Franklin and Moss, *From Slavery to Freedom*, 453; "23 Dead, 650 Hurt As Violence Grows," *Chicago Defender*, 23 June 1943, 1; and Report—"Biographical Data," SAC New York, 26 February 1968, sec. 12, pp. 7–8 (E. Muhammad FBI file).

16. The author was not able to locate information on the ratio of black prisoners to white inmates for the early 1940s, but according to one source, FCI Milan housed 651 African-Americans in 1940, a figure that seems extremely high given population statistics for later years. The number of blacks in federal prisons in 1942 was 3,306, out of an overall federal prison population of 16,630. Bureau of Prisons, *Federal Offenders, 1940* (Leavenworth, Kans.: Federal Prison Industries, Inc. Press, 1941), 204, 207, 209; John W. Roberts (Federal Bureau of Prisons), letter to author, 8 April 1994, 2–4; and Jack

Germond, "Federal Correctional Institution: Milan, Michigan" (Washington, D.C.: U.S. Bureau of Prisons, 1960), 1, 4.

17. In March 1942, FCI Milan produced 150 beds per day. Bureau of Prisons, *Gearing Federal Prisons to the War Effort* (1943?); Bureau of Prisons, *Federal Offenders, 1940,* 209; and Germond, "Federal Correctional Institution," 10–11.

18. By the 1950s, those inmates who tested below fifth-grade scholastic achievement were automatically enrolled in the general educational program. Germond, "Federal Correctional Institution," 6, 12–13.

19. Federal Correctional Institution (Sandstone, Minnesota), "Supplementary List of Authorized Correspondents" (Wallace D. Mohammed), 4 January 1962, Reg. No. 4577-SS, National Archives; Germond, "Federal Correctional Institution," 4; and Report—"Elijah Poole," SAC Chicago, 27 January 1958, sec. 2, p. 5 (E. Muhammad FBI file).

20. "Elijah Poole," 6; Germond, "Federal Correctional Institution," 12; and J. Muhammad, *This Is the One,* 183.

21. According to one report, "virtually all inmates gain weight during their stay at Milan," due to the allegedly wholesome diet. This was probably not the case for Muhammad and many of his followers. Germond, "Federal Correctional Institution," 8, 12–13; E. Muhammad, *Theology of Time,* 366–67; Lester X Anthony, "Muslim, Messenger Jailed in 1942 on Phony Charge," *Muhammad Speaks,* 8 April 1966, 25; E. Muhammad, *How to Eat to Live,* book 1, 27–28, 54–55; E. Muhammad, *Message,* 298–99; "Muhammad University of Islam–No. 2—1973" yearbook, 26 November 1973, and Report—"Elijah Poole," SAC Chicago, 27 January 1958, sec. 2, p. 5 (E. Muhammad FBI file).

22. In addition to Clara, Muhammad also corresponded regularly with his mother and younger brother John, who had served in a number of positions, such as treasurer and principal of the Detroit University of Islam during Fard Muhammad's leadership of the Nation. John Muhammad, "My Aims, Purposes, and Plans," *Muhammad Speaks Continues,* November 1994; 31; Report—"Elijah Poole," SAC Detroit to FBI director, 9 August 1957, sec. 2, pp. 4–5 (E. Muhammad FBI file); Marsh, *From Black Muslims,* 117–18; "Muhammad University of Islam–No. 2—1973" yearbook, 26 November 1973, sec. 12 (E. Muhammad FBI file); Ansari, "W. D. Muhammad," 253; and Essien-Udom, *Black Nationalism,* 67–68. According to one source, Clara Muhammad experienced a "nervous breakdown" during her husband's imprisonment. The author is not aware of the exact cause(s) or extent of this psychological collapse, if it indeed did take place. See E. Muhammad to U.S. Board of Parole (petition), March 25, 1945, cited in Bruce Perry, *Malcolm: The Life of a Man Who Changed Black America* (Barrytown, N.Y.: Station Hill Press, 1992), 146, 434.

23. Report—"Allah Temple of Islam," 23 October 1943, 43 (W. D. Fard FBI file); Sahib, "Nation of Islam," 81; Report—"Elijah Poole," SAC Chicago, 27 January 1958, sec. 2, p. 5 (E. Muhammad FBI file); Essien-Udom, *Black Nationalism,* 69; and Wallace D. Muhammad, *As the Light,* 22.

24. Muhammad was supervised by the Probation Office of Chicago until the expiration of his term on December 17, 1947. During this period, his "adjustment" to civilian life was deemed "satisfactory" by his parole officer. FCI (Sandstone, Minnesota), "Supplementary List," National Archives; E. Muhammad, *Theology of Time,* 18; Malcolm X, *Autobiography,* 211; and Report—"Elijah Poole," SAC Detroit to FBI director, 9 August 1957, 2, and Report—"Elijah Poole," SAC Chicago, 27 January 1958, sec. 2, p. 5 (E. Muhammad FBI file).

25. Ansari, "W. D. Muhammad," 249–52; Bruce M. Gans and Walter L. Lowe, "The Islam Connection," *Playboy,* May 1980, 180, 200.

26. Wallace D. Muhammad, *As the Light,* 19–20; Marsh, *From Black Muslims,* 117.

27. A few of Muhammad's relatives were employed in the Nation's businesses, including his daughter Ethel Sharrieff and his son Wallace. Essien-Udom, *Black Nationalism,* 167; Karriem Allah, "The Early Days," *Muhammad Speaks,* 23 June 1974: 3, 19; Sahib, "Nation of Islam," 73 n. 1, 82–84, 134; and Wallace D. Muhammad, *As the Light,* 20.

28. The ten donations requested by the Muslims were for Elijah Muhammad, his family, the University of Islam, the restaurant, the farm, the minister, the secretary, the laborers, emergencies, and the general treasury. Sahib, "Nation of Islam," 112, 171, 175.

29. Ibid., 145; Report—"Elijah Poole," SAC Chicago, 27 December 1957, sec. 1, p. 25 (E. Muhammad FBI file). The annual income of Muhammad during this time would be equivalent to $137,000 in 1993 dollars.

30. Of the 286 members in the Chicago temple around 1950, 172 were male. Although dated, the master's thesis of Hatim Sahib is still the most detailed work on the Muslim movement during the late 1940s. Much of the present discussion of this period (and the earlier years) is drawn from this account. Sahib, "Nation of Islam," 57, 99–100, 106–8.

31. None of the members employed by the Nation and its businesses received regular salaries except Elijah Muhammad and the General Secretary. Still, the compensation paid to select members of the organization for their services accounted for the majority of funds consumed by the movement. Ibid., 108–9, 112, 170.

32. Outsiders were usually allowed to attend Sunday services. On occasion, the younger members of the Nation held dances and parties, probably with adult supervision. Ibid., 175–76, 188, 215–16, 218.

33. Ibid., 175–76, 217, 220.

34. Ibid., 110–11; E. Muhammad, 1959 Saviour's Day Address (audiotape).

35. According to Sahib's survey, most of the Muslims over twenty-five years of age claimed previous affiliation with the Masons. Sahib, "Nation of Islam," 104–6.

36. In the Muslim version of events, the National was hidden in the White House until Fard Muhammad came to reclaim it. Ibid., 141, 218; E. Muhammad, *Supreme Wisdom,* vol. 2, 78; and E. Muhammad, *Message,* 237–40. Some have interpreted the *I* in the National as standing for "Islam." Minus the lettering, the flag of the Nation of Islam resembles the Turkish national standard.

37. Sahib, "Nation of Islam," 177–78.

38. Thirteen- to eighteen-year-old boys were organized into the Junior Fruit of Islam, which mostly performed military drills. Ibid., 140, 172–73; Essien-Udom, *Black Nationalism,* 150–51, 154–57, 207–8; Report—"Gulam Bogans," 6 August 1942 (W. D. Fard FBI file); and Karim, *Remembering Malcolm,* 154. According to Malcolm X, Muhammad punished officials more quickly than new converts, because an offender who held an office "betrayed both himself and his position as a leader and example for other Muslims." Malcolm X, *Autobiography,* 288–89.

39. Temples No. 5 through 12 were organized respectively in Cincinnati, Baltimore, New York City, San Diego, Youngstown (Ohio), Atlantic City, Boston, and Philadelphia. Essien-Udom, *Black Nationalism,* 343; Malcolm X, *Autobiography,* 215.

40. During the Korean War, the Nation of Islam supported the Chinese and North Koreans apparently because of their opposition to Western imperialism and influence in Asia. Sahib, "Nation of Islam," 134, 145, 169–70, 219, 225; Lincoln, *Black Muslims,* 193; and Essien-Udom, *Black Nationalism,* 145–46.

41. Sahib, "Nation of Islam," 174–75; Wallace D. Muhammad, *As the Light,* 19; and William G. Nunn, "Muhammad Blasts 'Intellectuals,'" *Pittsburgh Courier,* 8 March 1958, 7.

42. During 1950, Clara Muhammad was offered a Chrysler New Yorker by the Washington, D.C., temple as a gesture of appreciation and reverence. Sahib, "Nation of Islam," 134, 174–75; "CG Investigative Summary Rpt.," 16 May 1952 (W. D. Fard FBI file); E. Muhammad, 1954 Saviour's Day Address (audiotape); and Report—"Malcolm K. Little," SAC New York, 7 September 1954, sec. 1 (Malcolm X FBI file, 100–399321), in Clayborne Carson, *Malcolm X: The FBI File* (New York: Carroll & Graf Publishers, 1991), 104.

43. According to one poorly documented source, Elijah Muhammad may have roomed with Malcolm's half sister, Ella Collins, during his wanderings along the East Coast between 1935 and 1942. Louis E. Lomax, *To Kill a Black Man* (1968; reprint, Los Angeles: Halloway House, 1987), 59. Both of Malcolm's parents, Earl and Louise Little, were members of the Omaha, Nebraska, chapter of the UNIA during the 1920s. Walter Dean Myers, *Malcolm X: By Any Means Necessary* (New York: Scholastic Inc., 1993): 12, 14–15; Malcolm X, *Autobiography,* 6–7, 10, 21, 38, 99, 118–21, 125, 142–45, 154–55, 171; and Carson, *Malcolm X,* 58–60.

44. Malcolm X, *Autobiography,* 36, 154–56, 159–60, 162, 169–70, 173, 183, 189–90.

45. Carson, *Malcolm X,* 60; Malcolm X, *Autobiography,* 169, 185–89, 191–96, 212.

46. Malcolm X, *Autobiography,* 183; E. Muhammad, *Supreme Wisdom,* 1st ed., 49.

47. Malcolm X, *Autobiography,* 196–97.

48. Ibid., 198–201, 204. Elijah Muhammad's own father, Wali Muhammad (formerly William Poole), died shortly after his son's return from prison. As the younger Muhammad recalled it, "Death struck him at the age of 81 while he was in the Temple. He was applauding Me. Then he got up and threw up his hands at Me for the last time. He walked out and never returned anymore. He died the next day. Nobody ever knew he was dead until the nurse went in to see him. When the nurse felt him she was the first one to announce he was dead. He made no struggle at all, he just slept away just like that." E. Muhammad, *Theology of Time,* 299.

49. Malcolm X, *Autobiography,* 212–15; Carson, *Malcolm X,* 61.

50. Report—"Malcolm K. Little," 18 November 1954, sec. 1 (Malcolm X FBI file), in Carson, *Malcolm X,* 105–7.

Chapter 6: Messenger of Allah

1. Quoted in "The Black Supremacists," *Time,* 10 August 1959, 25.

2. Robert H. Ferrell, ed., *The Twentieth Century: An Almanac* (New York: World Almanac Publications, 1985), 330–31.

3. Lerone Bennett, *Before The Mayflower,* 5th ed. (New York: Penguin Books, 1988), 549–50; Richard H. Rovere, *Senator Joe McCarthy* (New York: Harper & Row, 1959), 229–31.

4. On February 28, 1957, the Chicago headquarters was legally renamed "Muhammad's Temple #2 of the Holy Temple of Islam." Notarized Application of Incorporation, Document No. 16432414, filed 29 November 1955; Notarized Amendment to Affidavit of Incorporation, Document No. 16846736, filed 12 March 1957; and "Copy of Resolutions of the Members of Muhammad's Temple #2 of the Holy Temple of Islam, A Religious Corporation," pp. 1–4, 6 (all in the estate records of Elijah Muhammad, Pro-

bate Division, Cook County Circuit Court, Chicago). Also, see Essien-Udom, *Black Nationalism*, 68–69, 148, 166.

5. The fifteen-unit apartment building was purchased at a cost of between $115,000 and $140,000 and carried a $70,000 mortgage in 1958. Temple No. 2 and the Chicago University of Islam were paid for at this time, having cost $92,500. William G. Nunn, "Chicago Moslems Show the Way," *Pittsburgh Courier* (Magazine Section), 15 March 1958, 5; Report—"Elijah Poole," SAC Chicago, 27 January 1958, sec. 2, p. 10 (E. Muhammad FBI file); and Essien-Udom, *Black Nationalism*, 166–67.

6. Malcolm X, *Autobiography*, 224–25, 262–63.

7. E. Muhammad, "Mr. Muhammad Speaks," *Pittsburgh Courier*, 22 August 1959, 12.

8. Ibid., 12; E. Muhammad, *Supreme Wisdom*, vol. 2, 39.

9. One of the young professionals attracted to the movement during this time was Dr. Abdulalim Shabazz (formerly Lonnie X. Cross), a professor of mathematics at Atlanta University. More than anything else, the message of the Nation and its struggles to educate black children attracted him to the movement. In a recent conversation with the author, Dr. Shabazz described his conversion experience: "Truth attracted me. Initially, I became interested in the Nation after reading newspaper reports about an attack on the University of Islam in Detroit in 1959. I was distressed by these efforts by the city to keep our people from educating our own children. In 1960, I went to a meeting in Atlanta to hear the Honorable Elijah Muhammad speak at the Magnolia Ballroom. I was converted on the spot." In 1962, Dr. Shabazz became an assistant minister in the Atlanta mosque and was later promoted to minister of Temple No. 4 in Washington, where he presided for twelve years (1963–75). Abdulalim A. Shabazz, telephone conversation with author, 19 September 1995; E. Muhammad, "Mr. Muhammad Speaks," *Pittsburgh Courier*, 22 August 1959, 12; Malcolm X, *Malcolm X: February 1965*, 203; and Aubrey Barnette, "The Black Muslims Are a Fraud," *Saturday Evening Post*, 27 February 1965, 27.

10. According to Essien-Udom, who studied the movement firsthand around 1960, Lottie Muhammad, Elijah's youngest daughter, led the MGT-GCC. In 1964, Malcolm X described her as the head of the Chicago and Detroit Universities of Islam. Essien-Udom, *Black Nationalism*, 76, 145–46; Malcolm X, *Autobiography*, 264; "University of Islam Graduates, Tomorrow's Leaders," *Muhammad Speaks*, April 1962, 13; Betty Shabazz, "Malcolm X as Husband and Father," *Malcolm X: The Man and His Times*, ed. John H. Clarke (1969; reprint, Trenton, N.J.: Africa World Press, 1990) 138; and Marsh, *From Black Muslims*, 61.

11. As of early 1958, Muhammad owed six or seven thousand dollars on the apartments that were occupied by his two daughters. Report—"Elijah Poole," SAC Chicago, 27 January 1958, sec. 2, p. 4 (E. Muhammad FBI file); E. Muhammad, *Supreme Wisdom*, vol. 2, 40; and "Organizational Study," (1958?), 13 (E. Muhammad CIA file). The bakery, restaurant, and grocery store of Temple No. 2 were also listed in John Hassan's name by December 1956. Report—"Elijah Poole," SAC Chicago, 27 December 1957, 8, 25; Report—"Changed—Elijah Poole . . . ," SAC Chicago, 14 November 1955; and Report—"Elijah Poole," SAC Chicago, 15 February 1959, sec. 3, p. 4 (E. Muhammad FBI file). According to Muhammad, "The reason I drive a Cadillac is obvious. Negroes place a high value on things like this. Personally, I would prefer any little old car that would take me to places. But if I did so, Negroes would begin to say, 'Islam made him poor.' On the contrary, they can see for themselves that Islam doesn't make one poor." Essien-Udom, *Black Nationalism*, 76, 153.

12. E. Muhammad, *Supreme Wisdom*, vol. 2, 27, 72, 77; E. Muhammad, "Mr. Muhammad Speaks," *Pittsburgh Courier*, 16 August 1958: 14.

13. During a 1958 interview, Elijah Muhammad told FBI agents that there were approximately 165 children in the Chicago University of Islam. Report—"Changed—Elijah Poole ...," SAC Chicago, 8 July 1957, sec. 2, p. 6, and Report—"Elijah Poole," SAC Chicago, 27 December 1957, sec. 1, p. 10 (E. Muhammad FBI file); "Muslim Cult of Islam," 21 February 1957, 4 (W. D. Fard FBI file); Lincoln, *Black Muslims*, 177–78; "Organizational Study," (1958?), 18 (E. Muhammad CIA file); Essien-Udom, *Black Nationalism*, 70; and Malcolm X, *Autobiography*, 290.

14. According to Essien-Udom, the active membership of Temple No. 2 numbered about one thousand in 1960. Peter Goldman estimated that the Harlem temple peaked at two thousand members in the early 1960s. A September 1959 news report placed the membership of Temple No. 27 in Los Angeles at three thousand, which may be inflated. Essien-Udom, *Black Nationalism*, 4, 5; Goldman, *The Death and Life*, 64; Lincoln, *Black Muslims*, 98; Malcolm X, *Autobiography*, 410; Louis E. Lomax, *The Negro Revolt* (New York: Harper & Row, 1962), 168; "Is New York Sitting on a 'Powder Keg'?" *U.S. News & World Report*, 3 August 1959, 50; and Lomax, *When the Word Is Given*, 18. In 1942, Elijah Muhammad told FBI interrogators that there were more than twenty-five thousand Moslems over "the United States and about four hundred to five hundred in the city of Chicago." The figures for that particular period of the movement's development were definitely much lower if he was referring only to Muslims in his own organization. "Muslim Cult of Islam," 21 February 1957, 4 (W. D. Fard FBI file); James H. Laue, "A Contemporary Revitalization Movement in American Race Relations: 'The Black Muslims,'" in *The Black Church in America*, eds. Hart M. Nelsen, Raytha L. Yokley, and Anne K. Nelsen (New York: Basic Books, 1971), 228; Barnett, "The Black Muslims," 26; and Alfred Balk and Alex Haley, "Black Merchants of Hate," *Saturday Evening Post*, 26 January 1963, 74. During a 1990 interview, Wallace D. Muhammad stated that active "membership hardly ever went over maybe ten thousand people. That was for the whole Nation of Islam. Under the Honorable Elijah Muhammad, the membership was transient. People were coming in and going out regularly." Barboza, *American Jihad*, 103.

15. Lomax, *When the Word Is Given*, 24; Lincoln, *Black Muslims*, 22–23; and Karim, *Remembering Malcolm*, 103–4.

16. Ted Watson and Paul E. X. Brown, "Moslems Stage Goodwill Tour," *Pittsburgh Courier*, 15 September 1956, 19; Report—"Malcolm Little," SAC New York, 30 April 1958, sec. 3 (Malcolm X FBI file), in Carson, *Malcolm X*, 141–44; *The Messenger Magazine* 1.1 (1959), in C. Eric Lincoln Papers, Special Collections, Clark Atlanta University, Atlanta, Georgia; Malcolm X, *Autobiography*, 237–38; and John Woodford, "Testing America's Promise of Free Speech: *Muhammad Speaks* in the 1960s, a Memoir," *Voices of the African Diaspora* 7.3 (fall 1991): 9; and Essien-Udom, *Black Nationalism*, 168.

17. James H. Cone, *Malcolm & Martin & America* (Maryknoll, N.Y.: Orbis Books, 1991), 98; Taylor Branch, *Parting the Waters: America in the King Years, 1954–63* (New York: Simon & Schuster, 1988), 32. Malcolm and the New York Muslims would later sue the police department on Hinton's behalf. The result was a seventy-thousand-dollar award, the biggest settlement ever paid by the City of New York for police misconduct. Evelyn Cunningham, "Moslems, Cops Battle in Harlem," *Pittsburgh Courier*, 4 May 1957, 20; Malcolm X, *Autobiography*, 233–35, 291, 295; "Moslem Announces $ Million NY Suit," *Pittsburgh Courier*, 9 November 1957, 7; Essien-Udom, *Black Nationalism*, 172; and Report—"Malcolm Little," SAC New York, April 30, 1958, and Report—"Malcolm K. Little," SAC New York, 17 November 1960, sec. 6 (Malcolm X FBI file), in Carson, *Malcolm X*, 139, 197–98.

18. When Elijah Muhammad approached the podium to deliver his 1960 Saviour's Day address, one visitor admitted, "I could not believe my eyes. I was waiting to see a really black man. But who came in? A Chinese. He looks very much like an Oriental." Essien-Udom, *Black Nationalism*, 75 n. 32; Worthy, "The Angriest Negroes," 105; E. Muhammad, *Message*, xv, xxii; Malcolm X, *Autobiography*, 252–53; E. Muhammad, *Su-*

preme Wisdom, vol. 2, 3; Goldman, *Death and Life,* 36, 289; "Dark Islam," 29; Lincoln, *Black Muslims,* 184–85; and James Baldwin, *The Fire Next Time* (New York: Dell Publishing Co., 1962), 88–89.

19. During his first attendance at a Saviour's Day convention in February 1955, Louis Farrakhan recently described himself as "taken aback" by Muhammad's "splitting of verbs" and "misuse of the language." Farrakhan, "Jesus Saves" (audiotape). According to Louis Lomax, Muhammad spoke "with a disturbing lisp." The present writer has not been able to detect this speech defect in any of the recorded addresses used as sources for this work. Lomax, *Negro Revolt,* 168; Relman Morin, "'All Whites Evil': Top Black Muslim" (undated article from unnamed newspaper in C. Eric Lincoln papers); Bontemps and Conroy, *Anyplace but Here,* 235; and Peter Goldman and Martin Weston, "The Founding Father," *Newsweek,* 10 March 1975, 21. According to Lincoln's observations, Muhammad was "calm and temperate" at home. His discourse was "at a level consistent with his appraisal of the visitor. To be sure, Muhammad has an uncamouflaged hostility against the white man, but this hostility does not dominate his private conversation." Lincoln, *Black Muslims,* 112, 184–86; Baldwin, *Fire Next Time,* 91; George Breitman, Herman Porter, and Baxter Smith, *The Assassination of Malcolm X* (1976; reprint, New York: Pathfinder Press, 1991), 22; and Hakim A. Jamal, *From the Dead Level: Malcolm X and Me* (New York: Random House, 1972), 108–12.

20. According to Muhammad's grandson Ozier Muhammad, the paternal role that the leader played in the Nation was quite conspicuous. "My grandfather *acted* like he was reverential. He acted like he was *everybody's* grandfather." Barboza, *American Jihad,* 107. For an interesting, though rambling, discussion of the charisma of Elijah Muhammad, see Leon Forrest, *Relocations of the Spirit* (Wakefield, R.I.: Asphodel Press, 1994), 64–116.

21. Malcolm X, *Autobiography,* 238; "'Be Polite, Courteous, Respectful,'" *Pittsburgh Courier,* 18 January 1958, 6; "Mr. Muhammad Calls for 'United Front of Black Men' at New York City Rally," *Pittsburgh Courier,* 19 July 1958, 8; "Messenger Blasts Self-Made Leaders, Intermarriage; Call Negro Lost Race," *Pittsburgh Courier,* 16 August 1958, 6; and Report—"Nation of Islam," SAC Chicago to FBI director, 11 December 1958, sec. 3, and Report—"Elijah Poole," SAC Chicago, 15 February 1959, sec. 3, p. 3 (E. Muhammad FBI file). For typical columns of Muhammad's teachings published during the late 1950s, see "Mr. Muhammad Speaks," *Pittsburgh Courier,* 1 February 1958, 3 May 1958, 9 August 1958, 6 September 1958, and 1 November 1958, 14, 14, 14, 14, and 12, respectively.

22. E. Muhammad, 1959 Saviour's Day Address (audiotape).

23. The security provided by Washington, D.C., surprised Muhammad. He expressed his gratitude in glowing terms: "Thanks to the wise and well-trained police department of the nation's capital. . . . My followers and I want them to know that we appreciated this great service. Allah will ever reward those who do good to others." E. Muhammad, "Mr. Muhammad Speaks," *Pittsburgh Courier,* 13 June 1959, 14; E. Muhammad, *Theology of Time,* 338; and Louis Lomax, "10,000 Moslems Hold Meeting in Washington," *Pittsburgh Courier,* 6 June 1959, 1, 9.

24. E. Muhammad, "Mr. Muhammad Speaks," *Pittsburgh Courier,* 24 June 1959, 14; Report—"Elijah Muhammad," deputy CIA director to FBI director, 10 February 1960, 2 (E. Muhammad CIA file, C5CI-3/758, 545); E. Muhammad, *Supreme Wisdom,* vol. 2, 33; and "Justification for Continuation of Technical or Microphone Surveillance," 30 October 1959, June mail, p. 1 (E. Muhammad FBI file).

25. According to one report, Muhammad's speech was interrupted twenty-two times by applause. Lomax, "10,000 Moslems," 9; Malcolm X, *Autobiography,* 248–51; and E. Muhammad, Uline Arena Address, Washington, D.C., 31 May 1959 (audiotape).

26. Lomax, "10,000 Muslims," 9; E. Muhammad, Uline Arena Address (audiotape).

27. Lomax, "10,000 Muslims," 9.

28. E. Muhammad, *Supreme Wisdom*, vol. 2, 18, 25, 39, 77, 78; Report—"Biographical Data," SAC New York, 26 February 1968, sec. 12, p. 27 (E. Muhammad FBI file).

29. E. Muhammad, *Supreme Wisdom*, 1st ed., 27, 32–33, 40, 41, 44; " 'Be Polite, Courteous, Respectful,' " 6.

30. "Mister Muhammad's Message to African-Asian Conference!" *Pittsburgh Courier*, 18 January 1958, 6; "Nasser Answers Muhammad Cable," *Amsterdam News*, 15 February 1958, 17; and Report—"Elijah Poole," SAC Chicago, 12 August 1958, sec. 3, p. 1 (E. Muhammad FBI file).

31. Essien-Udom, *Black Nationalism*, 238, 318–19; "Muslim Cult of Islam," 21 February 1957, 50–51 (W. D. Fard FBI file); Warith D. Mohammed speech at the University of Massachusetts at Amherst, 16 November 1993 (videotape in possession of author); "CG Investigative Summary Rpt.," 16 May 1952 (W. D. Fard FBI file); E. Muhammad, 1954 Saviour's Day Address (audiotape); Report—"Elijah Poole," SAC Chicago, 14 November 1955, sec. 1, p. 1 (E. Muhammad FBI file); and E. Muhammad, *Supreme Wisdom*, 1st ed., 44–47.

32. Lomax, *When the Word Is Given*, 20. According to Malcolm X, Marie Muhammad "had as large a funeral as Chicago has seen." Malcolm X, *Autobiography*, 204, 206, 223–24; Sahib, "Nation of Islam," 142–43; and "Elijah Muhammad's Mother Is Buried," *Pittsburgh Courier*, 31 May 1958, 3.

33. Although estimates vary, one researcher has concluded that roughly 7,420,000 Africans were exported into Arab lands by way of the trans-Saharan slave trade between 650 and 1900 C.E. This figure does not include the millions of Africans who were victims of the East Coast and Red Sea trade. Meltzer, *Slavery*, 345–50; Murray Gordon, *Slavery in the Arab World* (New York: New Amsterdam Books, 1989), 148–49, 159, 232–34; and E. Muhammad, *Supreme Wisdom*, 1st ed., 29–30, 37. For a brief, but insightful, discussion of the history of racial attitudes toward black Africans in the Arab world, see Bernard Lewis, *Race and Color in Islam* (New York: Harper & Row, 1971). This book contains a number of illustrations from the early Islamic period that bolster the author's thesis that racial prejudice against blacks has a long history in the Arab world.

34. Among the other stated reasons, it is also possible that Malcolm did not visit Mecca in order to avoid seeing the holy city before Muhammad did. Perry, *Malcolm*, 206; Abdel B. Naaem, "Malcolm X's Cordial Reception in Cairo," typescript dated August 5, 1959, in C. Eric Lincoln papers; "Arabs Send Warm Greetings to 'Our Brothers' of Color in U.S.A.," *Pittsburgh Courier* (Magazine Section), 15 August 1959, 1; and Report—"Malcolm K. Little," 17 November 1959, sec. 5 (Malcolm X FBI file), in Carson, *Malcolm X*, 178–80.

35. Naaem, "Malcolm X's Cordial Reception"; "Arabs Send Warm Greetings," 1; and Malcolm X, *Malcolm X: The Last Speeches*, ed. Bruce Perry (New York: Pathfinder Press, 1989), 106.

36. In his autobiography, Malcolm X devotes only a small paragraph to his trip to the Middle East in 1959. He says nothing about its impact on his views. Malcolm X, *Autobiography*, 238; Lomax, *To Kill a Black Man*, 95–96.

37. Malcolm X, *Autobiography*, 238; "The Hate That Hate Produced," *News Beat*, WNTA-TV (Channel 13), New York City, July 1959 (videotaped reprise of July 13–17 series in possession of author). For transcripts of selected parts of the series, see Report—"Nation of Islam," SAC New York to FBI director, 16 July 1958, and Report—"Nation of Islam," SAC New York to FBI director, 21 July 1959, sec. 4 (Malcolm X FBI file), in Carson, *Malcolm X*, 159–70.

38. "The Hate That Hate Produced" (videotape).

39. Ibid.; Malcolm X, *Autobiography,* 288, 291; and Bontemps and Conroy, *Anyplace but Here,* 232.

40. "The Hate That Hate Produced" (videotape); Malcolm X, *Autobiography,* 238.

41. Mike Wallace made two unsuccessful attempts to enter the arena, where only African-American reporters were allowed. "Moslems Fight Back; Bar White Press," *Amsterdam News,* 1 August 1959: 1, 31. When later questioned about the exclusion of whites from the gathering, Muslim officials argued that "with so many of our people inside there just wasn't any room left for the whites." "Muhammad at Rockland Palace Sunday," *Amsterdam News,* 15 August 1959, 3.

42. "The Black Supremacist," 24–25; "Is New York Sitting," 50–51; "Black Supremacy Cult in U.S.—How Much of a Threat?" *U.S. News & World Report,* 9 November 1959, 112; and Lincoln, *Black Muslims,* 143.

43. The Michigan State Department of Public Instruction had unsuccessfully tried to close the Muslim school as far back as the early 1950s. "Trouble Is Old Stuff for Secret Cult," *Detroit Free Press,* 14 August 1959, 3; "Cult Seeks New Site: Race-Hate School Evicted by City," *Detroit Free Press,* 15 August 1959, 3.

44. Elijah Muhammad was not able to appear at the Rockland Palace meeting due to fatigue caused by his schedule. "Muslims' Critics Tell Falsehoods," *Pittsburgh Courier,* 29 August 1956, 6; "Moslems Fight Back," 1, 31.

45. For editorial criticism of black leaders, especially ministers, see E. Muhammad, "Mr. Muhammad Speaks," *Pittsburgh Courier,* 3 May 1958, 18 October 1958, 4 April 1959, and 22 August 1959: 14, 14, 14, and 12, respectively.

46. "Roy Wilkins Hits Racists for Aid," *Chicago Defender,* 8 August 1959, 1; "Marshall Calls 'Moslem' Leaders 'Lawless Thugs,'" *Chicago Defender,* 24 October 1959, 1; and Balk and Haley, "Black Merchants," 68.

47. Ironically, in December 1959, King met with NAACP officials to mend divisions that had arisen between that organization and his own group, the Southern Christian Leadership Conference. Adam Fairclough, *To Redeem the Soul of America: The Southern Christian Leadership Conference and Martin Luther King, Jr.* (New York: New American Library, 1982), 246; Cone, *Martin & Malcolm & America,* 256.

48. E. Muhammad, "Mr. Muhammad Speaks," *Pittsburgh Courier,* 22 August 1959, 12.

49. E. Muhammad, *Supreme Wisdom,* vol. 2, 78; Lincoln, *Black Muslims,* 153; Malcolm X, *Autobiography,* 243–44; E. Muhammad, "Mr. Muhammad Speaks," *Los Angeles Herald Dispatch,* undated, in "The Truth," book 2. (This is a compilation of Muhammad's editorials taken from the *Los Angeles Herald Dispatch* and distributed by the African-American Genealogy Society of Compton, California.)

50. "Fire New Blasts at 'Moslems,'" *Chicago Defender,* 5 December 1959, 1, 2.

51. According to Khaalis, who would become one of Elijah Muhammad's most bitter foes, he joined the "gang in Chicago" at the insistence of a Pakistani acquaintance who told him that the followers of the Nation "were being deceived and I should try to help them." Ivan C. Brandon, "Hanafi Moslem Chief Quit Key Muslim Post," *Washington Post,* 2 February 1973, A1, A4; "Muslim Cult of Islam," 21 February 1957, 50–51 (W. D. Fard FBI file).

52. Bontemps and Conroy, *Anyplace but Here,* 227; "Moslems Fill Rockland, Leader Fails to Show," *Amsterdam News,* 22 August 1959, 21.

53. E. Muhammad, "Mr. Muhammad Speaks," *Pittsburgh Courier*, 15 August 1959, 14; "Muslim Leader Calls Moslem Leader 'Phony,' " *Amsterdam News*, 30 October 1959, 11.

54. In regard to the differences between the Islam of the Nation and Eastern Muslims, Elijah Muhammad conceded the inevitability of doctrinal conflict. In 1957, he wrote, "I cannot . . . blame them if they differ with me in certain interpretations of the message of Islam. In fact, I do not even *expect* them to understand some of the things I say unto my people here." E. Muhammad, *Supreme Wisdom*, 1st ed., 4; "Muslim Leader Calls Moslem," 11.

55. James O'Gara, "Muslims, Black and White," *Commonweal*, 18 January 1963, 428.

56. Naaem, "Malcolm X's Cordial Reception"; Malcolm X to Mr. Handler, 23 September 1964, Alex Haley Papers, Schomburg Center for Research in Black Culture, New York Public Library.

57. Memo—"Elijah Muhammad," 5 February 1959, sec. 3, p. 1; Report—"Nation of Islam," SAC Chicago to FBI director, 26 May 1959, sec. 3, p. 2; Report—"Elijah Muhammad," SAC Chicago to FBI director, 9 July 1959, sec. 3, p. 2; Report—"Elijah Muhammad," SAC Chicago to FBI director, 3 June 1959, sec. 3; Report—"Elijah Muhammad," SAC WFO to FBI director, 19 June 1959, sec. 3, p. 1; Report—"Elijah Muhammad," SAC Chicago to FBI director, 18 June 1959, sec. 3, p. 3; and Memo—"Elijah Muhammad," FBI director to SAC Chicago, 1 July 1959, sec. 3 (E. Muhammad FBI file).

58. The New York City Muslims raised as much as three thousand dollars for Muhammad's hajj. Malcolm X to "Holy Apostle," 3 November 1959, Aliya Hassan Papers, Michigan Historical Collection, University of Michigan, Ann Arbor, Michigan. Report—"Elijah Poole," SAC Chicago, 3 March 1960, sec. 5, p. 20, and "Teletype," SAC New York to director and SAC Chicago, 21 November 1959, sec. 4 (E. Muhammad FBI file).

59. Bernard Lewis, *The Emergence of Modern Turkey* (New York: Oxford University Press, 1968), 310, 416–17; John P. McKay, Bennett D. Hill, and John Buckler, *A History of World Societies*, 3rd ed. (Boston: Houghton Mifflin Co., 1992), 1080.

60. McKay, Hill, and Buckler, *History of World Societies*, 1080; Lewis, *Emergence*, 312–14, 418–24; Ferell, ed., *Twentieth Century*, 162, 353; and Brian Lapping, *End of Empire* (New York: St. Martin's Press, 1985), 341–349.

61. Lewis, *Emergence*, 202–3, 216, 405; E. Muhammad, *Supreme Wisdom*, 1st ed., 4; E. Muhammad, "I Am the Last Messenger," transcript, 3–6; E. Muhammad, *Our Saviour*, 89; and E. Muhammad, *Theology of Time*, 210, 475.

62. According to Muhammad, a man he met in a Syrian airport told him that he knew of the plight of African-Americans and desired "the chance to go to America so I could fight for you all until I die." Report—"Elijah Muhammad," SAC WFO to FBI director, 1 June 1965, sec. 10, pp. 1–2 (E. Muhammad FBI file); Afaf Lutfi Al-Sayyid Marsot, *A Short History of Modern Egypt* (New York: Cambridge University Press, 1992), 109–21.

63. Malcolm X, *Malcolm X: Speeches at Harvard*, ed. Archie Epps (New York: Paragon House, 1991), 126; E. Muhammad, *Theology of Time*, 78.

64. E. Muhammad, "The Sudden Death of President Nasser of Egypt," *Muhammad Speaks*, 9 October 1970, 17; E. Muhammad, *Theology of Time*, 78–79.

65. Report—"Elijah Muhammad," legal attaché (Madrid) to FBI director, 15 January 1960, sec. 4 (E. Muhammad FBI file).

66. George S. Schuyler, "The World Today," *Pittsburgh Courier*, 19 December 1959, 20.

67. Tim Niblock, *Class & Power in Sudan* (Albany: State University of New York Press, 1987), 143–55, 217–24; Bill Freund, *The Making of Contemporary Africa: The Development of African Society Since 1800* (Bloomington: Indiana University Press, 1984), 249.

68. Freund, *Making of Contemporary Africa,* 210; Roland Oliver and J. D. Fage, *A Short History of Africa* (New York: Penguin Books, 1985), 272–73.

69. Niblock, *Class & Power,* 87–99, 149–50; Harold G. Marcus, *Haile Selassie I: The Formative Years, 1892–1936* (Berkeley: University of California Press, 1987), 30–31, 59–60; and Meltzer, *Slavery,* 352–53.

70. Fouad Al-Farsy, *Modernity and Tradition: The Saudi Equation* (New York: Kegan Paul International, 1990), 4, 9; E. Muhammad, "Elijah Muhammad's Trip to Mecca," *Salaam,* July 1960, 32.

71. Describing this experience thirteen years later, Muhammad stated, "I kissed the Little Black Stone but I didn't like it because I know what it meant. It means that the people will bow to the real Black Man that is coming up out of an uneducated people who do not have the knowledge of the Bible and Holy Qur'an. That is why they made that Stone an unknown stone. He will be uneducated. So there I was kissing the sign of Myself and I didn't want to tell the Sheik, 'This is Me you are talking about here.' " E. Muhammad, *Theology of Time,* 31; E. Muhammad, "Elijah Muhammad's Trip," 32–33; and Robert Payne, *The History of Islam* (New York: Noble & Barnes, 1959), 4–5, 79.

72. Payne, *History of Islam,* 5; Frances E. Peters, *The Hajj: The Muslim Pilgrimage to Mecca and the Holy Places* (Princeton: Princeton University Press, 1994): xxv–xxvii; E. Muhammad, *Theology of Time,* 22–23; E. Muhammad, "Elijah Muhammad's Trip," 32–33; and Lomax, *When the Word Is Given,* 69.

73. E. Muhammad, *Message,* 59; Rounaq Jahan, *Pakistan: Failure in National Integration* (New York: Columbia University Press, 1972), 51–57.

74. E. Muhammad, *Theology of Time,* 541; Report—"Elijah Muhammad," SAC WFO to FBI director, 1 June 1965, sec. 10 (E. Muhammad FBI file); and A. Muhammad, "Muslims in the United States," 205.

75. Malcolm X, *Autobiography,* 263; A. Muhammad, "Muslims in the United States," 205; Warith Muhammad, speech at University of Massachusetts (videotape); David E. Long, *The Hajj Today: A Survey of the Contemporary Makkah Pilgrimage* (Albany: State University of New York Press, 1979), 115–16, 118; and E. Muhammad, *History,* 47.

76. A. Muhammad, "Muslims in the United States," 205; Malcolm X, *Malcolm X: February 1965,* 189; and Malcolm X, *Malcolm X: The Last Speeches,* 125.

Chapter 7: Trials and Tribulations

1. Laurence J. Peter, *Peter's Quotations: Ideas for Our Time* (New York: Bantam Books, 1980), 43.

2. William H. Chafe, *Civilities and Civil Rights: Greensboro, North Carolina, and the Black Struggle for Freedom* (New York: Oxford University Press, 1981), 71–72, 80–86; Sitkoff, *Struggle,* 87–91, 97–113; and Lapping, *End of Empire,* 243.

3. Fairclough, *To Redeem the Soul,* 85–109; Sitkoff, *Struggle,* 125–26; and David Steigerwald, *The Sixties and the End of Modern America* (New York: St. Martin's Press, 1995), 44–51.

4. "Muhammad Holds Non-Racial Press Meet on West Coast," *Chicago Defender,* 20 February 1960, 6.

5. "Muhammad Demands Separate States," *Mr. Muhammad Speaks*, September 1960, 3.

6. "Jack Hails Leader of Negro Moslems," *New York Times*, 1 August 1960, 5; "5,000 Here Listen to Negro Muslims," *New York Times*, 28 August 1961, 32; "Muslim Repeats Request for Negro Area in U.S.," *New York Times*, 13 August 1962, 25; E. Muhammad, 1962 Saviour's Day Address (audiotape); E. Muhammad, *Message*, 317; Terry, "Black Muslim," A3; and Lomax, *Negro Revolt*, 173.

7. Elijah Muhammad quoted in Essien-Udom, *Black Nationalism*, 261.

8. E. Muhammad, *Supreme Wisdom*, vol. 2, 24–25; E. Muhammad, "Christianity vs. Islam," 1962 (audiotape); and E. Muhammad, *History*, 43.

9. A month after the Muslim-Klan meeting, the main faction of the Georgian KKK applied for and received a charter in Fulton County. The group now called itself "the Invisible Empire, United Klans, Knights of the Ku Klux Klan of America, Inc." Wyn C. Wade, *The Fiery Cross: The Ku Klux Klan in America* (New York: Simon & Schuster, 1988), 312; "Malcolm K. Little," SAC New York, 17 May 1961, sec. 5 (Malcolm X FBI file), in Carson, *Malcolm X*, 203–4; and Malcolm X, *Malcolm X: The Last Speeches*, 123.

10. Major Robinson and Carl Nesfield, "Were Secret Muslim-KKK Talks Held in Atlanta?" *Pittsburgh Courier*, 20 February 1965, 1, 4; David Chalmers, *Hooded Americanism: The History of the Ku Klux Klan* (Durham, N.C.: Duke University Press, 1987), 375.

11. Rockwell, whose American Nazi Party never reached more than a couple hundred active members, had grandiose plans regarding a prospective alliance with the Muslims. In an enthusiastic letter to his followers, he asked, "Can you imagine a rally of the American Nazis in Union Square protected from Jewish hecklers by a solid phalanx of Elijah Muhammad's stalwart black stormtroopers. Oi, oi, oi!" James Farmer, *Lay Bare the Heart: An Autobiography of the Civil Rights Movement* (New York: Penguin Books, 1985), 226.

12. John George and Laird Wilcox, *Nazis, Communists, Klansmen, and Others on the Fringe: Political Extremism in America* (Buffalo, N.Y.: Prometheus Books, 1992), 349, 354–55; Malcolm X, *Malcolm X: The Last Speeches*, 124; "'You're Brainwashed,' Malcolm X Tells 8,000," *Afro-American*, 9 July 1961, 8; E. Muhammad, 1962 Saviour's Day Address (audiotape); Baldwin, *Fire Next Time*, 112; and Dan Burley, "We Must Have Some of This Earth," *Muhammad Speaks*, April 1962, 3 (see picture and caption).

13. Interestingly, like Rockwell, Stoner acknowledged an admiration for the "Black Supremacists" and encouraged African-Americans to seek nationhood in Ghana or the West Indies. For reprints of Stoner's letter and Muhammad's reply, see "White Filth Crusader Aims Guns at Moslems," *Pittsburgh Courier* (Magazine Section), 22 March 1957, 6; "Mr. Muhammad Answers White Filth Crusader," *Pittsburgh Courier* (Magazine Section), 30 March 1957, 6; and E. Muhammad, *Message*, 330–41. In 1959, Stoner changed the name of his group to the Christian Knights of the Ku Klux Klan and proclaimed himself "Imperial Wizard." For background on Stoner, see Wade, *The Fiery Cross*, 282–83, 302–03; Chalmers, *Hooded Americanism*, 343–44; and Michael Newton and Judy Newton, *The Ku Klux Klan: An Encyclopedia* (New York: Garland Publishing, Inc., 1991), 543–45.

14. For a brief discussion of Garvey's dealings with the KKK, see Martin, *Race First*, 344–47.

15. "Rockwell & Co.:—They Speak for All White" (picture caption), *Muhammad Speaks*, April 1962, 3. In a recent interview, Louis Farrakhan commented that, among white supremacists, "I'm probably the most respected black man in America. Among them. And the reason for that is they don't want to see black men with white women.

They don't want to see integration and mongrelization of the races. They want to see black folk separate. In that sense we have some common ground. But that's all there is to that." In September 1985, Tom Metzger, leader of the White American Political Association, attended a Farrakhan rally in Los Angeles and donated one hundred dollars to his cause. Barboza, *American Jihad*, 147; Katharine Macdonald, "Farrakhan Connection to Ex-Klan Chief Alleged," *Washington Post*, 5 October 1985, All; and "Brothers in Bigotry," *Time*, 14 October 1985, 41.

16. E. Muhammad, *Message*, 36. For a similar discussion of how Muslim theology justified the racial status quo, see Essien-Udom, *Black Nationalism*, 286–87.

17. Black journalist Louis Lomax reported in 1968 that a Muslim minister had informed him of a contract placed on the reporter's life as far back as 1962. Apparently, by the time Lomax found out, the order had been rescinded. Lomax, *To Kill a Black Man*, 97–98; Bontemps and Conroy, *Anyplace but Here*, 236; "Organizational Study" (1958?), 10, 19 (E. Muhammad CIA file); Barnette, "Black Muslims," 23–24, 28; and Malcolm X, *Malcolm X: The Last Speeches*, 132–33.

18. Claude Lightfoot, a black Communist leader based in Chicago, was sympathetic to the Muslim movement, but believed that it exhibited reactionary tendencies and was on a "harmful and divisive course." Claude Lightfoot, "Negro Nationalism and the Black Muslims," *Political Affairs* 41.7 (July 1962): 3–20; Terry, "Black Muslim," A3; "Black Muslim Debates James Baldwin, C. Eric Lincoln, Eric Goldman" (1962?) (audiotape), Undergraduate Library, University of North Carolina at Chapel Hill; "Malcolm K. Little," SAC New York, 17 November 1960, sec. 6 (Malcolm X FBI file), in Carson, *Malcolm X*, 112; and Rosemari Mealy, *Fidel & Malcolm: Memories of a Meeting* (Melbourne, Australia: Ocean Press, 1993), 22, 36–37, 43, 48, 54.

19. Muhammad's most thorough exposition of his economic philosophy during the 1960s is in his *Message to the Blackman in America* (in particular, pages 34–41, 169–77, and 192–203).

20. Ibid., 170, 193–94, 198. For the economic doctrines of Washington and Garvey, see Booker T. Washington, *Up From Slavery* (1901; reprint, New York: Penguin Books, 1987), 148–55, 218–25; Louis R. Harlan, *Booker T. Washington: The Making of a Black Leader, 1856–1901* (New York: Oxford University Press, 1975), 64–65, 140–45; Marcus Garvey, *Marcus Garvey: Life and Lessons*, 252–58; and Martin, *Race First*, 22–37, 151–67. According to every major indicator (including unemployment, occupation, and earnings), the economic gap between blacks and whites was wider in 1960 than at the close of World War II. William H. Harris, *The Harder We Run: Black Workers Since the Civil War* (New York: Oxford University Press, 1982), 131.

21. Viola Key, the former proprietor of a home bought by Muhammad in Phoenix, continued to stay in the residence, an arrangement that Muhammad apparently agreed to. "Muhammad to Speak in Washington, D.C.," *Chicago Defender*, 10–16 June 1961, 4; and Report—"Elijah Poole," SAC Chicago to FBI director, 14 April 1963, sec. 7, and Report—"Elijah Poole," SAC Chicago, 12 October 1965, sec. 10, pp. 17–18 (E. Muhammad, FBI file).

22. For sketches of the proposed Islamic Center, see "Exclusive: Architect's Drawing of Chicago Mosque," *Mr. Muhammad Speaks*, September 1960, 19; "A Center of Faith," *Salaam*, July 1960, 36; and "An Education Center," *Muhammad Speaks*, 15 January 1965, 12–13. Residents of the Chatham-Avalon Park community where Muhammad planned to build the $20-million complex tried to halt construction by claiming that public land designated for a park had been illegally sold to the Muslims. However, since the city could not afford to secure the land for this purpose, the sale could not be legally contested. "Fight Proposed Muslim 'Mosque,'" *Chicago Defender*, 9 July 1960, 2. The newspaper *Muhammad Speaks* started off as *Mr. Muhammad Speaks* and was produced by Malcolm X and others in New York. By December 1961 when the paper was begin-

ning to be printed regularly, the name was changed and production was moved to Chicago. Malcolm X, *Autobiography*, 237–38; Report—"Elijah Poole," SAC Chicago, 5 April 1963, sec. 7, p. 29 (E. Muhammad FBI file); Essien-Udom, *Black Nationalism*, 97–99, 176–77; and John Woodford, "Falsehood and Hypocrisy!" *Muhammad Speaks*, 28 May 1971, 16.

23. Muslims selling *Muhammad Speaks* in Chicago (by April 1963, in Illinois in general) were not as burdened financially by the newspaper as those living in other states, who had to buy the paper at twenty cents a copy. Goldman, *Death and Life*, 82; Barnette, "Black Muslims," 28; Muhammad's Mosque of Islam (MMI), "Your Orientation Brochure" (estate records of E. Muhammad); Roland E. Worseley, *The Black Press, U.S.A.* (1971; reprint, Ames: Iowa State University Press, 1990), 90; and Karim, *Remembering Malcolm*, 149. Ghayth Kashif, an editor of *Muhammad Speaks* during the 1960s and 1970s, recently told the author that often only half of the papers printed ever reached the public. Ghayth Kashif, telephone conversation with author, 26 September 1995. According to John Woodford, the editor of *Muhammad Speaks* during the late 1960s, the newspaper was ironically first published by the Lerner printing house, a Jewish company. Woodford, "Testing America's Promise," 13.

24. Barnette, "Black Muslims," 24, 27; Malcolm X, *Malcolm X: February 1965*, 202–3. Some women of humble means, at least in the Newark mosque, made their own uniforms. This apparently was acceptable as long as the homemade outfits were well tailored. Cynthia S. West, "Nation Builders: Female Activism in the Nation of Islam, 1960–1970" (Ph.D. diss., Temple University, 1994), 108.

25. West, "Nation Builders," 203; Shabazz, "Malcolm X as a Husband," 138.

26. MMI, "Your Orientation Brochure," 10–11; Report—"Elijah Poole," SAC Chicago to FBI director, 19 September 1961, sec. 6, pp. 2–3 (E. Muhammad FBI file); Alfred P. Klauser, "Muslim Rally," *Christian Century*, 22 March 1961, 372; Karim, *Remembering Malcolm*, 150; and Goldman, *Death and Life*, 82.

27. Karim, *Remembering Malcolm*, 151; Barnette, "Black Muslims," 27; and MMI, "Your Orientation Brochure," 11.

28. George and Wilcox, *Nazis, Communists, Klansmen*, 229–33; Jamal, *From the Dead Level*, 248; Baldwin, *Fire Next Time*, 111–12; Lomax, *To Kill a Black Man*, 108; and Malcolm X, *Malcolm X: The Last Speeches*, 125.

29. Bruce Perry's discussion of financial corruption in the Nation appears well-informed, although the author is biased against Muhammad and his followers and has a penchant for depicting poorly supported speculation as fact. Perry, *Malcolm*, 218–25; "Muhammad Son Says Muslims Threatened Him," *Chicago Daily Defender*, 8 July 1964, 3, in Michael Friedly, *Malcolm X: The Assassination* (New York: Carroll & Graf Publishers, 1992), 195–96; Malcolm X, *Malcolm X: The Last Speeches*, 125; Hedrick Smith, "Elijah's Son Quits as Black Muslim," *New York Times*, 15 January 1965, 19; Report—"Malcolm K. Little," SAC New York to FBI director, 7 July 1964, sec. 12 (Malcolm X FBI file), in Carson, *Malcolm X*, 294; Ghayth Kashif, telephone conversation, 26 September 1995; Na'im Akbar, telephone conversation, 27 September 1995; and Karim, *Remembering Malcolm*, 149–51. For a picture of Ethel Sharrieff in furs and jewels, see "Sister Ethel Sharrieff" (picture caption), *Pittsburgh Courier*, 15 March 1958, 5.

30. Report—"Nation of Islam," SAC Phoenix to FBI director, 6 May 1963, sec. 8, pp. 1–22 (E. Muhammad FBI file).

31. Barnette, "Black Muslims," 29.

32. E. Muhammad, "What Is Un-American?" *Muhammad Speaks*, December 1961, 4.

33. Frank Donner, *Protectors of Privilege: Red Squads and Police Repression in Urban America* (Berkeley: University of California Press, 1992), 90–92. According to Leon Forrest, an editor of *Muhammad Speaks* during the late 1960s, some members of the Chicago Police Department were rumored to be subsidized by Elijah Muhammad. "The cops who worked in the area near the Lamb's house were well remembered at Christmas time and during the rest of the year as well." Forrest, *Relocations*, 79.

34. In his memoirs, Frank Sullivan, a former press secretary for the Daley administration, described Elijah Muhammad as a friend of the mayor's. Frank Sullivan, *Legend: The Only Inside Story about Major Richard J. Daley* (Chicago: Bonus Books, 1989), 205.

35. "Hint Muslim Parents Could Be Prosecuted," *Chicago Defender*, 19–25 May 1962, 1.

36. At the time, about three hundred elementary and twenty-six high school students were enrolled in the school. Ibid., 2; E. Muhammad, *Message*, 313–14.

37. Abdul Rahman Muhammad, the captain of the Fruit of Islam in the Miami mosque between 1961 and 1968, recently described to the author the founding of Mosque No. 29: "In Miami, we bought a building. Blacks, our own people, petitioned against us. They did not want us in the community. This prompted the Honorable Elijah Muhammad to buy a much bigger place in the center of town. Those same blacks were sorry when we did this." Abdul Rahman Muhammad, telephone conversation with author, 22 September 1995. African-American resistance to the Nation of Islam in the South was not unique to Miami. Na'im Akbar, an assistant minister in Mosque No. 15 during the 1970s, related to the author similar problems faced by Muslims in Atlanta. He attributed anti-Islamic feelings among some Southern African-Americans to their strong "Christian fundamentalist" backgrounds. Na'im Akbar, telephone conversation, 27 September 1995. As of December 1959, some thirty official mosques and several other smaller groupings had not received numbers. By September 1971, the Nation had over fifty local organizations with Denver Mosque No. 51 being the latest official addition. Essien-Udom, *Black Nationalism*, 343–45; "Visit Muhammad's Mosques of Islam," *Muhammad Speaks*, 17 September 1971, 31.

38. E. Muhammad, *Message*, 170–71; Washington, *Up From Slavery*, 221–22; Nell I. Painter, *Exodusters: Black Migration to Kansas after Reconstruction* (New York: W. W. Norton & Co., 1979), 137–45; and Martin, *Race First*, 361–73. For a good discussion of Turner and his views, see Henry McNeal Turner, *Respect Black: The Writings and Speeches of Henry McNeal Turner*, ed. Edwin S. Redkey (New York: Arno Press, 1971), and John Dittmer, "The Education of Henry McNeal Turner," in *Black Leaders of the Nineteenth Century*, eds. Leon Litwack and August Meier (Urbana: University of Illinois Press, 1988), 253–272.

39. "Defers Decision in Muslim Case," *Chicago Defender*, 25–31 March 1961, 2; "Muhammad's Son Imprisoned: Courts Jail Muslim Ministers; Taught Negroes in Faith of Islam Religion!" *Muhammad Speaks*, December 1961, 32.

40. "La. Grand Jury Scores U.S.; Indicts Muslim," *Chicago Defender*, 3–9 June 1961, 3; "La. Muslim Leader Sentenced to 10 Years," *Chicago Defender*, 11–17 November 1961, 1; "Muhammad's Son Imprisoned," 32; and "Black Muslims Denied Review," *Pittsburgh Courier*, 17 November 1962, 1.

41. Joint Legislative Committee on Un-American Activities (State of Louisiana), *Activities of "The Nation of Islam" or the Muslim Cult of Islam, in Louisiana*, Report No. 3, 9 January 1963, Baton Rouge, 106–8.

42. Ibid., 38, 108.

43. Though the Burns Committee was named after Sen. Hugh Burns, Richard Combs controlled its operation. Donner, *Protectors of Privilege*, 63–64.

44. Lincoln, *Black Muslims*, 177–78; E. Muhammad, "What Is Un-American?" 1, 4, 27, 31; and E. Muhammad, *Message*, 177–86.

45. E. Muhammad, "What Is Un-American?" 31.

46. Donner, *Protectors of Privilege*, 248–52.

47. Ibid., 3, 249.

48. "Cultist Is Slain Battling Police," *New York Times*, 29 April 1962, 72; "Coast Muslims Face Riot Charges," *Pittsburgh Courier*, 12 May 1962, 7; and "L.A. Muslims Face Trial Over 'Riot,'" *Pittsburgh Courier*, 15 December 1962, 1. For the Muslim version of events, see E. Muhammad, *Message*, 211–12; "Muhammad Calls for United Black Front!"; "Eyewitness: 'Saw Cops Kill Muslim'"; and "L.A. Was Like Nazi Germany or Algiers," *Muhammad Speaks*, June 1962, 1–3.

49. "Bury Slain Muslim in Simple Dignity," *Muhammad Speaks*, July 1962, 7; Gordon Parks, "'What Their Cry Means to Me'—a Negro's Own Evaluation," *Life*, 31 May 1963, 31; and "Black Muslim Inquiry Begun," *New York Times*, 16 May 1962, 32.

50. "L.A. Was Like Nazi Germany," 2; "National Leaders Blast L.A. Police Brutality . . . ," *Muhammad Speaks*, July 1962, 5; "Mayor Yorty Says Cult Backs 'Hate,'" *New York Times*, 27 July 1962, 8; Jamal, *From the Dead Level*, 220–24; and Karim, *Remembering Malcolm*, 135–36.

51. Encouraged by Muhammad in the wake of the Stokes killing, Muslims reportedly sold a phenomenal four hundred thousand copies of the July edition of *Muhammad Speaks*. This issue, which covered the funeral of the murdered Muslim, was the last monthly issue of the newspaper. Henceforth, *Muhammad Speaks* was published biweekly. "Newspapers Circulation Up, *Muhammad Speaks* Leads," *Muhammad Speaks*, 15 July 1962, 10; Jamal, *From the Dead Level*, 221.

52. Jamal, *From the Dead Level*, 223–24; Karim, *Remembering Malcolm*, 138; and Lomax, *To Kill a Black Man*, 97.

53. During the early 1960s the litigation of Muslim inmates gradually broadened the religious freedoms of all prisoners. Christopher E. Smith, "Black Muslims and the Development of Prisoners' Rights," *Journal of Black Studies* 24.2 (December 1993): 138–41; "Suit by Prisoners," *New York Times*, 25 March 1962, sec. 4, p. 6; and "Black Muslim Gives Testimony in Court," *New York Times*, 24 October 1962, 8.

54. "Plea Denied in Draft Case," *New York Times*, 1 November 1961, 79. Perhaps in a symbolic gesture, Muhammad avenged the shootings of Los Angeles Muslims by filing a lawsuit in Phoenix against the federal government on the day of the Stokes killing. The suit called for monetary compensation for Muhammad and passengers who were riding with him when a Bureau of Indian Affairs bus struck his 1959 Cadillac on January 25, 1962. Muhammad sought $5,200 to have his automobile repaired, and his four passengers sued for a total of $172,700 to cover personal injuries. Report—"Elijah Poole," SAC Chicago, 5 April 1963, sec. 7, p. B (E. Muhammad FBI file). On June 10, 1961, Muhammad had been involved in another automobile accident in which he had struck two pedestrians while driving in Chicago. He would later be sued for negligence. Memo—"Elijah Poole," SAC Chicago, 31 October 1967, sec. 11 (E. Muhammad FBI file).

55. "11 Muslims Guilty, 2 Cleared on Coast," *New York Times*, 15 June 1963, 23; Lee C. White (assistant special counsel to the president) to Mildred Hull Ahlen, 1 August 1963, White House Name File, "Black M" folder, Box 223, John F. Kennedy Library, Boston.

56. Kenneth O'Reilly, *"Racial Matters": The FBI's Secret File on Black America, 1960–1972* (New York: The Free Press, 1989), 5, 39–40, 46; Kenneth O'Reilly, *Black*

Americans: The FBI File, ed. David Gallen (New York: Carroll & Graf Publishers, 1994), 9–10.

57. According to Malcolm X, some government informants in the Nation of Islam were touched by the message of the movement and voluntarily revealed their missions to the Muslim leadership. However, other spies remained loyal to the government and dutifully reported what they learned. Malcolm X, *Autobiography*, 258; Donner, *Protectors of Privilege*, 47; and Report—"Nation of Islam," SAC Chicago to FBI director, 19 February 1963, 1–2 (W. D. Fard FBI file). Journalist Louis Lomax maintained in his two books on the Nation of Islam that John Ali, the national secretary of the movement, had previous ties to the FBI. The accuracy of this assertion, which Lomax claimed was "based upon persistent reports and information," is difficult to confirm; however, Elijah Muhammad allowed Ali to retain his position in the movement for a number of years after Lomax publicized his claim. Lomax, *When the Word Is Given*, 95; Lomax, *To Kill a Black Man*, 199.

58. O'Reilly, *"Racial Matters"*, 39; David Caute, *The Great Fear: The Anti-Communist Purge Under Truman and Eisenhower* (New York: Simon & Schuster, 1978), 89–90, 94, 100–103; "May Probe Muslims," *Chicago Defender*, 4–10 August 1962, 1; and *Congressional Record*, 87th Cong., 2nd sess., 1962, House Resolution 743, vol. 108, pt. 13.

59. "Committee Told Bias, Br[u]tality of L.A. Police," *Muhammad Speaks*, 15 October 1962, 3; "Justification," SAC Phoenix to FBI director, May 28, 1963, June mail, p. 1 (E. Muhammad FBI file).

60. Bureau of the Census, *Statistical Abstract of the United States: 1994*, 114th ed. (Washington, D.C.: Government Printing Office, 1994), 238–45; "The Black Separatists," 1964 (audiotape).

61. Bradford Luckingham, *Phoenix: The History of a Southwestern Metropolis* (Tucson: University of Arizona Press, 1989), 175; Franklin J. James, Betty L. McCummings, and Eileen A. Tynan, *Minorities in the Sunbelt* (Rutgers: State University of New Jersey, 1984), 41–42; and Bureau of the Census, *Census of Population: 1960 (Arizona)*, vol. 1, pt. 4 (Washington, D.C.: Government Printing Office, 1963), 4–31 (table 21).

62. It is possible that Muhammad's trip to the arid Middle East during late 1959 influenced him to seek dry climates during the winter months once he returned to the United States. Malcolm X, *Autobiography*, 289; "Muhammad Says 'Jesus' Prophet, Not Son of God," *Chicago Defender*, 3–9 February 1962, 7; and Report—"Elijah Poole," SAC Chicago to FBI director, 8 December 1961, and Memo—"Nation of Islam," 3 August 1961, sec. 6 (E. Muhammad FBI file).

63. E. Muhammad, *Message*, xxii–xxiii; Anne Ali, "What Manner of Man Is Mr. Muhammad?" *Muhammad Speaks*, 31 October 1969, 19.

64. Rev. Nathan Wright, the minister of the Harlem church that Louis Farrakhan attended before joining the Nation of Islam, met with Muhammad in 1968. He found the leader to be "most gracious" in his reception of guests, even the white insurance-company official who had accompanied Wright to the Chicago residence. Wright was most impressed by the "etiquette and human decency" that Muhammad showed his guests, in addition to his "basic sense of equanimity." Nathan Wright, telephone conversation with author, 3 October 1995. According to Alauddin Shabazz, the former minister of the mosque in Pensacola, Florida, Muhammad had occasionally allowed white reporters to dine and spend the night at his home. Alauddin Shabazz, telephone interview with author, 27 September 1995. In 1970 during an interview with a reporter from *Ebony* magazine, Muhammad chided, "Don't pick the ugliest pictures of me for publication like the white papers always do . . . not that I think I'm pretty or anything like

that." Hans J. Massaquoi, "Elijah Muhammad: Prophet and Architect of the Separate Nation of Islam," *Ebony*, August 1970, 82.

65. Lincoln, *Black Muslims*, ii, v; Essien-Udom, *Black Nationalism*, x–xi; and E. Muhammad, *History*, 78. In 1963, Louis Lomax published his first book on the Muslim movement, entitled *When the Word Is Given: A Report on Elijah Muhammad, Malcolm X, and the Black Muslim World*. This work is useful for anecdotal information regarding the Nation but has a journalistic bent and lacks the scholarly insight of the works of Lincoln and Essien-Udom.

66. Malcolm X, *Autobiography*, 384–87; Ghayth Kashif, telephone conversation with author, 26 September 1995; and Lincoln, *Black Muslims*, 186.

67. Muhammad's plans to publish a booklet were perhaps also derailed by a failure to work out a mutually satisfactory agreement with the Cross Type Setting Company, the Chicago firm that he had approached with the idea. Report—"Elijah Poole," SAC Chicago, 5 April 1963, sec. 7, pp. B, C (E. Muhammad FBI file); advertisement for *Message to the Blackman in America*, *Muhammad Speaks*, 22 October 1965, 14.

68. Malcolm X, *Autobiography*, 264–65; Memo—"Nation of Islam," 3 August 1961, sec. 6 (E. Muhammad FBI file); Lincoln, *Black Muslims*, 196–99; Essien-Udom, *Black Nationalism*, 80–82; and Malcolm X, *Autobiography*, 386.

69. Essien-Udom, *Black Nationalism*, 81; Marsh, *From Black Muslims*, 109; and "The Black Separatists" (audiotape).

70. "Black Muslim Debates James Baldwin" (audiotape); Malcolm X, *Autobiography*, 204, 291.

71. Malcolm X, *Autobiography*, 265, 289.

72. According to Armiya Nu'man, an assistant minister in Mosque No. 7 during the early 1970s, Malcolm X was actually the second national minister. The first had been Sultan Muhammad, minister of Milwaukee Mosque No. 3 during the early period. Armiya Nu'man, telephone conversation with author, 20 September 1995; Malcolm X, *Autobiography*, 232, 284–85, 292–93; Goldman, *Death and Life*, 110; and "Malcolm X: The Real Story," CBS News video, 1992.

73. "Negro Cultist's Son Convicted," *New York Times*, 24 March 1960, 14; "Plea Denied in Draft Case," 79; Herbert Muhammad, "An Interview with Elijah Muhammad's Successor," *Amsterdam News*, 9 April 1975, A16; and Ansari, "W. D. Muhammad," 258, 260. In 1980, Wallace Muhammad stated that his father had forced him to refuse the assignment at the hospital and was thus responsible for his imprisonment. Gans and Lowe, "The Islam Connection," 200.

74. Gans and Lowe, "The Islam Connection," 256; H. Muhammad, "An Interview," A16; Wallace D. Muhammad, *Religion on the Line*, 43–44; Barboza, *American Jihad*, 110; and Report—"Elijah Poole," SAC Chicago to FBI director, 9 October 1964, sec. 8, p. 21 (E. Muhammad FBI file).

75. Wallace D. Muhammad, *Religion on the Line*, 44.

76. Ibid., 44; H. Muhammad, "An Interview," A16; Lomax, *To Kill a Black Man*, 99–100; and Malcolm X, *Autobiography*, 298.

77. Howard Pulley, "Muslims a Fraud, Dakota, Hubby Charge," *Chicago Defender*, 2–8 June 1962, 1, 2; "Muslim vs. Muslim! Malcolm X Fires Salvo at Dakota," *Pittsburgh Courier*, 27 September 1962, 1, 4.

78. "Muslim vs. Muslim! Ahmadiyya Head Raps Muhammad," *Pittsburgh Courier*, 27 September 1962, 1, 4.

79. Memo—"Elijah Muhammad," 24 July 1961, sec. 6, p. 2 (E. Muhammad FBI file); Bob Queen, "Muhammad Bars 2 Orthodox Muslims," *Pittsburgh Courier*, 20 October 1962, 2; and E. Muhammad, *Message*, 327–29.

80. Mr. and Mrs. Hajji Talib Dawud to President Johnson (teletype), 27 December 1963, White House Name File, Lyndon B. Johnson Library, Austin, Texas.

81. E. Muhammad, *Message*, 327–28.

82. In the interest of privacy, only the names of women who publicly charged Elijah Muhammad with fathering their children will be specified in this book. All of the women and their children are listed in "Banks Must Pay $4.6 Million to Elijah Muhammad Heirs," *Jet*, 8 March 1982, 12. Also, see Memo—"Elijah Muhammad," A. H. Belmont to J. F. Bland, 20 May 1960, sec. 5 (E. Muhammad FBI file); Malcolm X, *Autobiography*, 296–97.

83. Malcolm X, *Malcolm X: February 1965*, 207; Malcolm X, *Autobiography*, 295; "Banks Must Pay," 12; and Report—"Elijah Poole," SAC Chicago, 5 October 1962, sec. 7, p. D, and Report—"Elijah Poole," SAC Chicago to FBI director, 9 October 1964, sec. 8, p. 24 (E. Muhammad FBI file).

84. Apparently, at least one of the women usually spent time with Muhammad in Phoenix. Report—"Nation of Islam," SAC Phoenix to FBI director, 19 December 1961, sec. 6; Report—"Elijah Poole," SAC Phoenix to FBI director, 20 March 1962, sec. 6; Report—"Elijah Poole," SAC Phoenix to FBI director, 19 June 1962, sec. 7, pp. 1–3; Report—"Elijah Poole," SAC Chicago, 6 April 1962, sec. 7, p. B; and Report—"Elijah Poole," SAC Chicago, 5 October 1962, sec. 7, pp. B, C (E. Muhammad FBI file).

85. The two women who left their children at the Chicago residence of Muhammad were surprised to find out that Raymond Sharrieff turned the matter over to the local police, who kept the children until they were claimed by their mothers. According to an FBI informant, the women "indicated extreme disgust" over the incident and vowed to "take further actions against Muhammad." Memo—"Nation of Islam," F. J. Baumgardner to W. C. Sullivan, 14 July 1962, sec. 7, p. 1; Report—"Elijah Poole," SAC Phoenix to FBI director, 19 July 1962, sec. 7, pp. 1–3; Report—"Elijah Poole," SAC Chicago, 5 October 1962, sec. 7, pp. B, C; Report—"Elijah Poole," SAC Chicago, 6 October 1961, sec. 6, p. B; and Report—"Elijah Poole," SAC Chicago, 6 April 1962, sec. 7, pp. B, C (E. Muhammad FBI file).

86. E. Muhammad, *Message*, xvii–xix, 58–59, 64–67, 71, 192; E. Muhammad, *Supreme Wisdom*, 1st ed., 22, 48; E. Muhammad, *Supreme Wisdom*, vol. 2, 56–58; Essien-Udom, *Black Nationalism*, 208; E. Muhammad, 1959 Saviour's Day Address (audiotape); E. Muhammad, "Babies Murdered," *Muhammad Speaks*, 19 February 1971, 16–17; E. Muhammad, *Theology of Time*, 153; Malcolm X, *Autobiography*, 229, 295; and E. Muhammad, *Our Saviour*, 56.

87. Report—"Elijah Poole," SAC Chicago, 6 April 1962, sec. 7, pp. B, C (E. Muhammad FBI file).

88. Apparently, Elijah Muhammad was not the only highly placed Muslim official suspected of engaging in extramarital activities during this period. His son Herbert made front-page news after allegedly attacking his white mistress. Among other injuries, her jaw was broken in four places after she attempted to end her affair with Herbert. The Muslims later denied the allegations and held that the woman was not white. "White Girl Accuses Muslim of Beating," *Chicago Defender*, 13–19 October 1962, 1, 2; "Muslims Blast 'False Charges,' " *Chicago Defender*, 20–26 October 1962, 1.

89. While waiting to speak with Muhammad at his Chicago home in the early 1960s, James Baldwin may have seen one of the leader's newborns. "On one side of the room sat half a dozen women, all in white," the author wrote later. "They were much occupied

with a beautiful baby, who seemed to belong to the youngest of the women." Baldwin, *Fire Next Time*, 85. Wallace's statements are quoted from "Malcolm X: Make It Plain," PBS documentary, 26 January 1994.

90. According to his widow, Betty Shabazz, Malcolm actually witnessed the pleading of three of the women for child support during one of his frequent visits to Muhammad's home in Chicago. "Malcolm X," PBS documentary; Malcolm X, *Autobiography*, 294–98; Malcolm X, *Malcolm X: February 1965*, 207; and Karim, *Remembering Malcolm*, 153.

91. Malcolm X, *Autobiography*, 294–98.

92. "First Lady Visits Son in Cairo," *Muhammad Speaks*, June 1962, 3. For an interesting picture of Clara seated beside one of the erstwhile mistresses of Elijah Muhammad during the 1963 Saviour's Day convention, see "Empty Chair" (picture caption), *Muhammad Speaks*, 18 March 1963, 4. "Justification . . . ," SAC Chicago to FBI director, 29 April 1960, June mail, p. 2a; Report—"Elijah Poole," SAC Chicago to FBI director, 23 May 1962, sec. 7; Report—"Nation of Islam," FBI director to SAC Chicago, 26 April 1962, sec. 7, pp. 1–2; Memo—"Nation of Islam," Sullivan to Baumgardner, 14 July 1962, sec. 7; and Memo—"Nation of Islam," FBI director to SAC Chicago, 25 July 1962, sec. 7 (E. Muhammad FBI file).

93. "Justification . . . ," SAC Phoenix to FBI director, 23 May 1963, June mail, p. 2a (E. Muhammad FBI file); Malcolm X, *Autobiography*, 296.

Chapter 8: Rumors of War

1. Report—"Nation of Islam," SAC Phoenix to FBI director, 6 May 1963, sec. 8, p. 20 (E. Muhammad FBI file); telegram of Elijah Muhammad, *Muhammad Speaks*, 18 March 1963, 3.

2. "Keynote Speaker Blasts Parson," *Muhammad Speaks*, 18 March 1963, 3–4; Malcolm X, *Autobiography*, 298. According to an FBI source, Muhammad was pressured by family members to order Malcolm X out of Chicago after the New York minister "made numerous appearances and speeches" around the city following Saviour's Day. Report—"Malcolm K. Little," SAC New York, 16 November 1962, sec. 8 (Malcolm X FBI file), in Carson, *Malcolm X*, 222.

3. Report—"Justification," SAC Phoenix to FBI director, 28 May 1963, June mail, p. 22 (E. Muhammad FBI file); M. S. Handler, "Muhammad Predicts Final Victory for Muslims," *New York Times*, 17 June 1963, 14.

4. Malcolm X, *Autobiography*, 298–99; Report—"Elijah Poole," SAC Chicago to FBI director, 14 April 1963, sec. 7, p. 2 (E. Muhammad FBI file).

5. Apparently, Louis X was among the East Coast Muslims who reported Malcolm X to Chicago as a seed planter. "Of course I mentioned it to the Honorable Elijah Muhammad, which I told Malcolm I was going to," he acknowledged in a 1985 interview. "Now some may call that opportunistic, I don't know, but I am a loyal man to my father." David Jackson, "Ascent and Grandeur," *Chicago Tribune*, 15 March 1995, 22.

6. According to FBI eavesdroppers, Malcolm X stated in June 1964 that ministers in the Chicago and Boston mosques were teaching that the love children of Elijah Muhammad were "divine babies" who would bless the nations of the earth. Elsur Logs, 26 June 1964, 2:30 A.M. (Malcolm X FBI file, 105-8999-Sub 1), in Carson, *Malcolm X*, 478–79; E. Muhammad, *Supreme Wisdom*, 1st ed., 13.

7. E. Muhammad, *Theology of Time*, 6–7, 72; E. Muhammad, *Message*, xxv–xxvi.

8. Surah 4:3; "Denies Paternity Charges," *Amsterdam News*, 11 July 1964, 2; E. Muhammad, "Memo: From Desk of Muhammad, To: The Original Black People!" *Mu-

hammad Speaks, 11 September 1964, 15; and Isaiah Karriem, "Cites 20-Year Association with Messenger of Allah," *Muhammad Speaks*, 11 September 1964, 4.

9. Currently, at least two of Muhammad's children by a former columnist of *Muhammad Speaks* serve as ministers in Farrakhan's Nation of Islam. The woman herself is also closely associated with his organizational organ, *The Final Call*. Tynetta Deanar, "Women in Islam Striving for Self," *Muhammad Speaks*, 27 April 1973, 19; "Banks Must Pay," 12; Cook County Vital Statistics, "Medical Certificate of Death," (Elijah Muhammad), 27 February 1975, Chicago; Yusef Salaam, "Wives of the Late Elijah Muhammad Speak Out at Illinois Muslim Event," *Amsterdam News*, 20 March 1993, 9, 49; and Barboza, *American Jihad*, 146–47.

10. For four months, Malcolm X was the minister for both New York Mosque No. 7 and the Muslims in the capital. In September 1963, he was replaced by Lonnie X. Cross as the Washington, D.C., minister. Abdulalim A. Shabazz, telephone conversation with author, 19 September 1995; M. S. Handler, "Malcolm X Starting Drive in Washington," *New York Times*, 10 May 1963, 1, 14; Report—"Justification," SAC Phoenix to FBI director, 28 May 1963, June mail, p. 2b (E. Muhammad FBI file); and Report—"Malcolm K. Little," SAC New York, 15 November 1963, sec. 9 (Malcolm X FBI file), in Carson, *Malcolm X*, 243.

11. Queen, "Muhammad Bars 2," 2; Robert S. Bird, "Ten Negroes," *Herald Tribune*, 30 April 1963, 10; and E. Muhammad, *Message*, 318–19.

12. Bird, "Ten Negroes," 10; E. Muhammad, *Message*, 217–18; and M. S. Handler, "Malcolm X Terms Dr. King's Tactics Futile," *New York Times*, 11 May 1963, 9.

13. E. Muhammad, *Message*, 241–42, 308; Garrow, *Bearing the Cross*, 357, 368.

14. Arvarh E. Strickland, *History of the Chicago Urban League* (Urbana: University of Illinois Press, 1966), 243; "Muhammad Calls for United Black Front!" 3; and "Black Muslims Get Jersey Mosque Site," *New York Times*, 1 June 1963, 8.

15. Powell appeared on the front page of the March 27, 1964, edition of *Muhammad Speaks*. "The Honorable Elijah Muhammad Tells Why We Must Elect Our Own Candidates," *Muhammad Speaks*, 18 March 1963, 3; E. Muhammad, *Message*, 130, 173; "Quotations from the Messenger," *Muhammad Speaks*, 2 August 1963, 9; "Build Own Society," *Muhammad Speaks*, 28 August 1964, 1, 3, 8; and " 'Put Muslim Program to Congress': Messenger," *Muhammad Speaks*, 9 October 1964, 3.

16. E. Muhammad, *Message*, 235.

17. F. J. Baumgardner to W. C. Sullivan, 30 July 1963 (W. D. Fard FBI file). Much of the information contained in the Fard article would have been available only in FBI records. For photocopies of the articles, see "Black Muslim Founder Exposed as White," *Los Angeles Herald Examiner*, 28 July 1963, 1–2 and "Muslim Founder White Masquerader," *Record American*, 28 July 1963, 16, in W. D. Fard FBI file.

18. Muhammad's contention that Muslims did not give money to W. Fard Muhammad contrasts sharply with later statements concerning the issue. During a 1972 lecture, he stated, "I gave My last dime when I first heard Islam. I gave My last dime and I had a wife at that time sitting home hungry." E. Muhammad, *Theology of Time*, 81; E. Muhammad, "Beware of Phony Claims," *Muhammad Speaks*, 16 August 1963, 1; and Report—"Nation of Islam," SAC San Francisco to FBI director, 17 June 1963, and Report—"Wallace Dodd Ford," SAC Chicago to FBI director, 31 July 1963 (W. D. Fard FBI file).

19. "Muslims Halt Rally As Police Ask Entry," *New York Times*, 28 October 1963, 18; E. Muhammad, *Message*, 215; and Report—"Nation of Islam," SAC Phoenix to FBI director, 7 November 1963, sec. 8 (E. Muhammad FBI file).

20. It does not appear that anything ever became of the two lawsuits, if they were actually filed. Report—"Nation of Islam," SAC Phoenix to FBI director, 26 November 1963, sec. 8 (E. Muhammad FBI file).

21. Report—"Nation of Islam," SAC Phoenix to FBI director, 2 December 1963, sec. 8, p. 3; Report—"Nation of Islam," SAC Phoenix to FBI director, 20 November 1963, sec. 8; and Report—"Justification . . . ," SAC Phoenix to FBI director, 13 December 1963, June mail, p. 2b (E. Muhammad FBI file).

22. E. Muhammad, *Fall,* 33–34, 117–18.

23. "Mr. Muhammad's Statement on the President's Death," *Muhammad Speaks,* 20 December 1963, 3; Malcolm X, *Autobiography,* 300–301; and "Malcolm X Scores U.S. and Kennedy," *New York Times,* 2 December 1963, 21.

24. According to Malcolm X, his trip to Chicago on December 2 fell on the date that he usually made his monthly visit to the Muslim leader. Malcolm X, *Autobiography,* 301; "Malcolm X Scores U.S.," 21; and Perry, *Malcolm,* 240–41.

25. Jack V. Fox, "Negro Leaders Lambaste Malcolm X's Delight in Death of Atlanta Whites," *Chicago Defender,* 14–20 July 1962, 5; Report—"Internal Security—Nation of Islam," SAC New York, 16 November 1962, sec. 8 (Malcolm X FBI file), in Carson, *Malcolm X,* 220–21; and Malcolm X, "Message to the Grassroots," Afro-American Broadcasting and Recording Co., sound recording on LP record, 10 November 1963.

26. Malcolm X, *Autobiography,* 301–2; E. Muhammad, *History,* 32–33; and "The Black Separatists" (audiotape).

27. According to one member of the New York organization, officials in Chicago (perhaps John Ali or Raymond Sharrieff) instructed them to give Malcolm "a job washing dishes in the restaurant" if he tried to return to the mosque after his suspension. Karim, *Remembering Malcolm,* 156; Malcolm X, *Autobiography,* 302; "Elijah Suspends Malcolm," *Amsterdam News,* 7 December 1963, 1, 2; and "Mr. Muhammad's Statement," 3.

28. Malcolm X, *Autobiography,* 302; Report—"Nation of Islam," SAC Phoenix to FBI director, 6 December 1963, sec. 8, pp. 4, 7; and Report—"Nation of Islam," SAC Phoenix to FBI director, 13 December 1963, sec. 8, pp. 6–7 (E. Muhammad FBI file).

29. Report—"Nation of Islam," SAC Phoenix to FBI director, 27 January 1964, sec. 8, pp. 1–3 (E. Muhammad FBI file).

30. Karim, *Remembering Malcolm,* 158–59; Malcolm X, *Autobiography,* 302–3, 305.

31. Report—"Nation of Islam," SAC Phoenix to FBI director, 27 January 1964, sec. 8, p. 3 (E. Muhammad FBI file).

32. Report—"Malcolm K. Little," SAC New York to FBI director, 5 February 1964, sec. 10 (Malcolm X FBI file), in Carson, *Malcolm X,* 252–53.

33. Report—"Elijah Poole," FBI director to SAC Chicago, 11 July 1973, sec. 14 (E. Muhammad FBI file); Report—"Nation of Islam," SAC Chicago to FBI director, 19 February 1963, 1–2 (W. D. Fard FBI file).

34. Report—"Nation of Islam," SAC Phoenix to FBI director, 23 January 1964, sec. 8, pp. 1–5 (E. Muhammad FBI file).

35. Ibid., 1–5.

36. Rumors of the imminent replacement of Malcolm X as head of Mosque No. 7 were in the air as early as the first week of December. However, James Shabazz was not believed to be a favored choice according to the sources of the *New York Times.* "Malcolm Expected to Be Replaced," *New York Times,* 6 December 1963, 27; Marsh,

From Black Muslims, 112; Barboza, *American Jihad*, 102; Goldman, *Death and Life*, 135–36; Malcolm X, *Autobiography*, 305; Malcolm X, *Malcolm X: February 1965*, 213; Report—"Nation of Islam," SAC Phoenix to FBI director, 23 January 1964, sec. 8, p. 6; and Report—"Nation of Islam," SAC Phoenix to FBI director, 27 January 1964, sec. 8, p. 4 (E. Muhammad FBI file).

37. According to a Muslim version of the meeting, Malcolm confessed that he had used his knowledge of Muhammad's affairs for selfish purposes and begged the leader to allow him to rectify his actions. Goldman, *Death and Life*, 125.

38. Report—"Nation of Islam," SAC Phoenix to FBI director, 27 January 1964, sec. 8, pp. 7–8 (E. Muhammad FBI file).

39. Ibid., 6; Malcolm X, *Autobiography*, 302–3, 305, 308–9, 381; Karim, *Remembering Malcolm*, 158–59; and "Malcolm X Tells of Death Threats," *Amsterdam News*, 21 March 1964, 50.

40. Malcolm X, *Autobiography*, 303–9.

41. Elijah Muhammad, 1964 Saviour's Day Address (audiotape); "Bar Malcolm X from Muslim Chi Convention," *Amsterdam News*, 15 February 1964, 1, 2; M. S. Handler, "Malcolm X's Role Dividing Muslims," *New York Times*, 26 February 1964, 39; and M. S. Handler, "Malcolm Absent As Muslims Meet," *New York Times*, 27 February 1964, 23.

42. Thomas Hauser, *Muhammad Ali: His Life and Times* (New York: Simon & Schuster, 1991), 97; Don Atyeo and Felix Dennis, *The Holy Warrior: Muhammad Ali* (New York: Simon & Schuster, 1975), 52–53; Malcolm X, *Autobiography*, 303–8; and Goldman, *Death and Life*, 127. According to Cassius Clay, he had joined the Nation as early as 1961. Hampton and Fayer, *Voice of Freedom*, 325.

43. "Cassius Sends Greetings to Savior's Day," *Muhammad Speaks*, 13 March 1964, 6.

44. Pictures and articles relating to Muhammad Ali appeared in the following 1964 editions of *Muhammad Speaks:* March 13, April 10, June 19, July 31, August 28, September 11, September 25, and December 4. "Clay Puts Black Muslim X in His Name," *New York Times*, 7 March 1964, 15; Barboza, *American Jihad*, 105; and "Walk the Way of Free Men!" (picture caption), *Muhammad Speaks*, 10 April 1964, 1.

45. Goldman, *Death and Life*, 128–29; Shabazz, "Malcolm X as a Husband," 140; and Barboza, *American Jihad*, 105.

46. M. S. Handler, "Malcolm X Splits With Muhammad," *New York Times*, 9 March 1964, 1, 42.

47. Ibid., 1, 42; "Telegram to Muhammad," *Amsterdam News* 14 March 1964, 1; Malcolm X, *Malcolm X Speaks: Selected Speeches and Statements*, ed. George Breitman (New York: Grove Press, 1965), 20; and Malcolm X, *Malcolm X: February 1965*, 213.

48. James Booker, "Malcolm X: 'Why I Quit and What I Plan Next,'" *Amsterdam News*, 14 March 1964, 51; "Telegram," 1; Malcolm X, *Autobiography*, 409; and Report—"Nation of Islam," SAC Phoenix to FBI director, 12 March 1964, sec. 8, p. 1 (E. Muhammad FBI file).

49. Malcolm X, *Autobiography*, 297.

50. Report—"Malcolm K. Little," SAC New York, 18 June 1964, sec. 11 (Malcolm X FBI file), in Carson, *Malcolm X*, 285–86; Report—"Nation of Islam," SAC Phoenix to FBI director, 12 March 1964, sec. 8, p. 2 (E. Muhammad FBI file).

51. E. Muhammad, "Beware of False Prophets," *Muhammad Speaks*, 31 July 1964, 8.

52. Karim, *Remembering Malcolm*, 160.

53. Malcolm X, "The Ballot or the Bullet," Detroit, Michigan, March 1964 (audiotape).

54. George Breitman, *The Last Year of Malcolm X: The Evolution of a Revolutionary* (New York: Pathfinder Press, 1967), 105–24.

55. Report—"Malcolm K. Little," transcript of WUST *Focus* radio interview, 12 May 1963, sec. 9 (Malcolm X FBI file), in Carson, *Malcolm X*, 237; Malcolm X, *Malcolm X: The Last Speeches*, 86.

56. Malcolm X, *Autobiography*, 318, 338–42; Lomax, *To Kill a Black Man*, 95–96.

57. "Malcolm Exposed by His Brother," *Muhammad Speaks*, 10 April 1964, 3, 4; "Hit Malcolm X as 'Judas,' " *Chicago Defender*, 28 March 1964, 1.

58. James Shabazz, "Obey Divine Messengers, Find Life of Truth," *Muhammad Speaks*, 10 April 1964, 1, 3, 9; Louis X, "Minister Who Knew Him Best—Part I: Rips Malcolm's Treachery, Defection," *Muhammad Speaks*, 8 May 1964, 13; and Louis X, "The Truth About Fall of a Minister," *Muhammad Speaks*, 5 June 1964, 8.

59. Report—"Nation of Islam," SAC Phoenix to FBI director, 23 March 1964, sec. 8, p. 1 (E. Muhammad FBI file); "On My Own" (cartoon caption), *Muhammad Speaks*, 10 April 1964, 3. The theme of decapitation appeared in a number of Muhammad's pronouncements. For examples, see E. Muhammad, "Mr. Muhammad Speaks," *Pittsburgh Courier*, 24 January 1959, 14; E. Muhammad, *Message*, 166; and E. Muhammad, " 'We Live in the Time of a Change,' " 6.

60. "Malcolm X Flees for Life; Muslim Factions at War," *Amsterdam News*, 20 June 1964, 1, 2; "Muslims Rally to Muhammad," *Amsterdam News* 4 July 1964, 1, 2.

61. According to the estimate of the *Amsterdam News*, over twelve thousand Muslims attended Muhammad's speech. Malcolm's talk at the Audubon Ballroom was attended by a thousand people. "Muslims Rally to Muhammad," 1, 2; Joseph Lelyveld, "Elijah Muhammad Rallies His Followers in Harlem," *New York Times*, 29 June 1964, 1, 32.

62. "Ex-Sweetheart of Malcolm X Accuses Elijah," *Amsterdam News*, 11 July 1964, 1, 2.

63. Evelyn Williams had been engaged to Malcolm X prior to his marriage to Betty X. "Ex-Sweetheart of Malcolm X," 1, 2.

64. Report—"Elijah Poole," SAC Chicago to FBI director, 9 October 1964, sec. 8, p. 24 (E. Muhammad FBI file); "Malcolm X on Islam, US, Africa," *Egyptian Gazette*, 17 August 1964, in U.S. Department of State records on Malcolm X, microfilm 8701149, sec. 1; and Elsur Logs, 7 June 1964, 3:25 P.M. (Malcolm X FBI file), in Carson, *Malcolm X*, 470.

65. George Curry, "Farrakhan," *Emerge*, August 1990, 32.

66. Report—"Changed Malcolm K. Little," SAC New York, 20 January 1965, sec. 14 (Malcolm X FBI file), in Carson, *Malcolm X*, 323–35.

67. E. Muhammad, "Memo: From Desk," 5, 14–15, 20; E. Muhammad, "Beware of False Prophets," 8; and Memo—"Malcolm K. Little," SAC New York to FBI director, 7 July 1964, sec. 12 (Malcolm X FBI file), in Carson, *Malcolm X*, 294.

68. Malcolm X, *Malcolm X: The Last Speeches*, 136–37.

69. Stewart, "Who Will Inherit," 21; "Muhammad Son Says," 3; and Report—"Elijah Poole," SAC Chicago to FBI director, 9 October 1964, sec. 8, p. 21 (E. Muhammad FBI file).

70. Hassan Sharrieff is the son of Raymond and Ethel Sharrieff. He greatly admired his uncle Wallace and decided to follow him out of the Nation of Islam. Clarence Page, " 'New Muslims': Success Amid Strife," *Chicago Tribune*, 7 January 1979, sec. 1, p. 6; Gans and Lowe, "The Islam Connection," 180, 200; and Barboza, *American Jihad*, 110, 114.

71. "Muhammad Son Says," 3; Gans and Lowe, "The Islam Connection," 201.

72. Hassan had gone to the FBI as early as June 23. Report—"Nation of Islam," SAC New York to FBI director, 17 August 1964, sec. 8, p. 20, and Report—"Elijah Poole," SAC Chicago to FBI director, 9 October 1964, sec. 8 (E. Muhammad FBI file); Gans and Lowe, "The Islam Connection," 201; "Muhammad Son Says," 3; Stewart, "Who Will Inherit," 21; and Ansari, "W. D. Muhammad," 258.

73. E. Muhammad, "Beware of False Prophets," 8.

74. According to one report, Malcolm X had talked with Akbar in August 1964 while visiting Cairo. *Arab Observer*, 24 August 1964, in U.S. Department of State records on Malcolm X, microfilm 8701149, sec. 1; Report—"Nation of Islam," SAC New York to FBI director, 17 August 1964, sec. 8 (E. Muhammad FBI file); and Smith, "Elijah's Son Quits," 19.

75. "Decree Akbar Muhammad," *Muhammad Speaks*, 1 January 1965, 9.

76. Smith, "Elijah's Son Quits," 19; E. Muhammad, *Theology of Time*, 406–7. According to Wallace, he received "special treatment" during his incarceration because he was the son of Elijah Muhammad. Warith D. Mohammed interview with Ayesha K. Mustafaa, *Muslim Journal*, 23 February 1996, 15.

77. Report—"Nation of Islam," SAC Phoenix to FBI director, 2 November 1964, sec. 9, p. 1 (E. Muhammad FBI file).

78. M. S. Handler, "Malcolm Rejects Racist Doctrines," *New York Times*, 4 October 1964, 59; "Malcolm's Plans Irk Muslims Here," *New York Times*, 8 November 1964, 48; and Memo—"Elijah Muhammad," SAC Chicago, 27 November 1964, sec. 9 (E. Muhammad FBI file).

79. "Elijah Muhammad," SAC Chicago, sec. 9; "Malcolm Ordered to Move from Black Muslim House," *New York Times*, 3 September 1964, 16. Joseph X denied any mosque involvement in the killing of the former Muslim, though he conceded that the two accused men had attended services at Mosque No. 7. Les Matthews, "Muslims Charged in Death," *Amsterdam News*, 14 November 1964, 1, 2; Louis X, "Boston Minister Tells of Malcolm—Muhammad's Biggest Hypocrite," *Muhammad Speaks*, 4 December 1964, 11–15; and "Nation of Islam Warns Malcolm X," *Crusader*, 12 December 1964, 3, quoted in Report—"Nation of Islam," SAC Chicago, 15 December 1964, sec. 13 (Malcolm X FBI file), in Carson, *Malcolm X*, 307–8.

80. E. Muhammad, *History*, 32; E. Muhammad, "Victory of the Apostle," *Muhammad Speaks*, 15 January 1965, 3; "The Black Separatists," 1964 (audiotape); " '65, the Crucial Year," *Muhammad Speaks*, 29 January 1965, 9; and Jamal, *From the Dead Level*, 251.

81. Muhammad, who would probably not have ordered the deliberate destruction of organizational property, blamed Malcolm X for the razing of the $16,200 home. Austin C. Wehrwein, "Muhammad Says Muslims Played No Part in Slaying," *New York Times*, 23 February 1965, 20; "Malcolm Ordered to Move," 16; and Report—"Nation of Islam," SAC Los Angeles to FBI director, 24 March 1965, sec. 9 (E. Muhammad FBI file). Malcolm had been allowed to stay in the Queens residence beyond the January 31 deadline because of a pending appeal. On February 15, he lost the appeal and was ordered out of the partially damaged house. M. S. Handler, "Malcolm X Flees Firebomb Attack," *New York Times*, 15 February 1965, 1, 21; "Malcolm Accuses Muslims of Blaze;

They Point to Him," *New York Times*, 16 February 1965, 18; and Malcolm X, *Malcolm X: The Last Speeches*, 126, 131–32.

82. Handler, "Malcolm Rejects Racist Doctrines," 59; E. Muhammad, *Message*, 308; and Malcolm X, *Malcolm X: The Last Speeches*, 131.

83. Barboza, *American Jihad*, 108.

84. Wehrwein, "Muhammad Says Muslims," 1, 20; Salaam, "Wives of the Late Elijah," 49. In 1974, Muhammad Ali echoed the sentiments of Louis X before a British audience. "Malcolm X had to be punished. . . . When you talk against a man who is so loved, the man himself don't have to put the word out to get you, the people themselves are going to get you. The love for that man will get you killed." Atyeo and Dennis, *Holy Warrior*, 54.

85. For in-depth investigations of the assassination of Malcolm X, see Peter Goldman, *The Death and Life of Malcolm X;* Michael Friedly, *Malcolm X: The Assassination;* George Breitman, Herman Porter, and Baxter Smith, *The Assassination of Malcolm X;* Zak A. Kondo, *Conspiracys: Unraveling the Assassination of Malcolm X* (Washington, D.C.: Nubia Press, 1993); and Karl Evanzz, *The Judas Factor: The Plot to Kill Malcolm X* (New York: Thunder's Mouth Press, 1992). Though Hayer claimed that he was not a member of the Nation of Islam, the prosecution introduced photographs during the trial which showed him practicing karate in the Newark mosque. "Defendant Admits Killing Malcolm X," *New York Times*, 1 March 1966, 33.

86. Report—"The Nation of Islam," SAC Phoenix to FBI director, 27 January 1964, sec. 8, pp. 7–8; Report—"Nation of Islam," SAC Phoenix to FBI director, 23 March 1964, sec. 8, p. 1 (E. Muhammad FBI file).

87. In fear of his life, Wilfred X, one of Malcolm's pro-Muhammad brothers and the minister of the Detroit mosque, went into hiding following the assassination. "Police Guarding Muhammad's Home Here," *Chicago Tribune*, 22 February 1965, 2; "Malcolm X Assassinated: Black War Eminent?" *Pittsburgh Courier*, 27 February 1965, 1; "Police Alerted: Black Nationalist Civil War Looms," *Charlotte Observer*, 23 February 1965, 1A; "Crate Delivered to Muslim Chief," *Charlotte Observer*, 25 February 1965, 1A; and "Death of a Desperado," *Newsweek*, 8 March 1965, 24–25.

88. Only hours after the assassination of Malcolm X, the Chicago apartment of Muhammad Ali caught fire. Apparently, the blaze had accidently been set by tenants on a lower floor and was unrelated to the death of Malcolm X. Will Grimsley, "Malcolm X Reprisal Doesn't Scare Clay," *Charlotte Observer*, 24 February 1965, 14A; "Death of a Desperado," 24; Peter Kihss, "Mosque Fires Stir Fear of Vendetta in Malcolm Case," *New York Times*, 24 February 1965, 1, 31; "Setting the Record Straight," *Muhammad Speaks*, 12 March 1965, 9; "Who Sent 10G Check to Malcolm X Slaying Suspect," *Amsterdam News*, 13 March 1965, 2; "Police Guarding Muhammad's Home," 1; and "Close Guard Kept," 1.

89. Wilfred X, preface to 1965 Saviour's Day Address of Elijah Muhammad (audiotape); Austin C. Wehrwein, "Muhammad Says Muslims Must 'Protect' Themselves," *New York Times*, 27 February 1965, 1; and transcript of Saviour's Day Address, *Muhammad Speaks*, 12 March 1965, 1.

90. Wallace D. Muhammad, preface to 1965 Saviour's Day Address of Elijah Muhammad (audiotape). According to Elijah Muhammad, Wallace had been trying to get back into the Nation since January. E. Muhammad, *History*, 35.

91. E. Muhammad, 1965 Saviour's Day Address (audiotape).

92. "Black Supremacists" (audiotape).

93. Earl Grant, "The Last Days of Malcolm X," *Malcolm X: The Man and His Time,* ed. Clarke; "Harlem Is Quiet As News Spreads," *New York Times,* 22 February 1965, 2; and Malcolm X, *Autobiography,* 454.

94. At the 1965 Saviour's Day convention, Willie Grier, a known critic of Elijah Muhammad, was denied entrance into the Chicago Coliseum and severely beaten by Fruit of Islam. "They don't like me," he acknowledged after his ejection. "That's why they beat me. They kicked me all over." "Muhammad Talks On Despite Death Threats," *Chicago Defender* (national edition), February 27–March 5, 1965, 1; Bontemps and Conroy, *Anyplace but Here,* 240. As late as the 1990s, Louis Farrakhan was still being pressed by interviewers to answer questions regarding the Nation's role in the assassination of Malcolm X. For recent interviews posing these questions, see Curry, "Farrakhan," 32–33; Barboza, *American Jihad,* 146–47; and Louis Farrakhan, interviewed by Barbara Walters, *20/20,* ABC, 22 April 1994.

Chapter 9: A Nation of Shopkeepers

1. Report—"Elijah Poole," SAC Chicago, 12 October 1965, sec. 9, pp. 3, 5; Report—"Tynnetta Alethia Nelson," SAC Phoenix to FBI director, 5 May 1965, sec. 9; Report—"Elijah Muhammad," SAC Chicago to FBI director, 20 May 1965, sec. 9 (E. Muhammad FBI file).

2. Donald Janson, "2,000 Guardsmen on Chicago Alert," *New York Times,* 15 August 1965, 1; Gladwin Hill, "Coast Riot Area Gets $1.7 Million for Cleanup Job," *New York Times,* 19 August 1965, 1; and Report—"Elijah Poole," SAC Chicago, 12 October 1965, sec. 10, p. 25 (E. Muhammad FBI file).

3. Report—"Nation of Islam," SAC Phoenix, 11 February 1965, sec. 9, p. 2; Report—"Nation of Islam," SAC Chicago to FBI director, 5 August 1965, sec. 10, pp. 1–3 (E. Muhammad FBI file). For the comments of Muhammad, King, and others on the meeting, see Jim Bishop, *The Days of Martin Luther King, Jr.: A Biography* (New York: Barnes & Noble, 1971), 420; Goldman, *Death and Life,* 65; E. Muhammad, *Theology of Time,* 353–54; E. Muhammad, *Fall,* 23–24; "Meeting with Muhammad," *New York Times,* 24 February 1966, 75; and "First Major Address of 1966: Muhammad, King Meet on Eve of Saviour's Day," *Muhammad Speaks,* 4 March 1966, 3.

4. For writings by and about Dr. King, see Taylor Branch, *Parting the Waters: America in the King Years;* David J. Garrow, *Bearing the Cross: Martin Luther King, Jr., and the Southern Christian Leadership Conference;* Adam Fairclough, *To Redeem the Soul of America: The Southern Christian Leadership Conference and Martin Luther King, Jr.;* Michael Friedly and David Gallen, *Martin Luther King, Jr.: The FBI File;* Stephen B. Oates, *Let the Trumpet Sound: The Life of Martin Luther King, Jr.;* Jim Bishop, *The Days of Martin Luther King, Jr.: A Biography;* James H. Cone, *Martin & Malcolm & America: A Dream or a Nightmare;* and James M. Washington, ed., *A Testament of Hope: The Essential Writings and Speeches of Martin Luther King, Jr.* (New York: HarperCollins, 1986).

5. In regard to education, Muhammad was critical of Negro History Week. He did not believe that it was "complete, sufficient or comprehensive enough to enable my people to learn the true knowledge of themselves." E. Muhammad, *Message,* 34, 246–47; E. Muhammad, *Our Saviour,* 48–49; E. Muhammad, *Fall,* 92, 150; E. Muhammad, *Supreme Wisdom,* vol. 2, 58; and E. Muhammad, *How to Eat to Live,* book 1, 86.

6. In a 1972 editorial, Muhammad warned his followers that there were behaviors that even the so-called Pygmies of Africa would not tolerate. "You can go to the jungle

and the pygmy will not want [obnoxious neighbors]. Late at night he and a gang of monkeys will come out and beat you up." E. Muhammad, "Every Nation Has a Term," *Muhammad Speaks*, 15 September 1972, 16–17; E. Muhammad, *Theology of Time*, 54, 320; E. Muhammad, "The Judgment of America," *Muhammad Speaks*, 22 May 1970, 16–17; E. Muhammad, "The Black Man's Confusion," *Muhammad Speaks*, 9 August 1968, 16–17; E. Muhammad, "The Angry Nations," 15; E. Muhammad, "Robbed of Self!" *Muhammad Speaks*, 19 June 1970, 17; Barbara Reynolds, "Leader Scorns Jackson, King," *Chicago Today*, 10 February 1970, 12; and Kathleen X, "Shun the Afro," *Muhammad Speaks*, 12 September 1969, 24. For a good discussion of the "civilizing" trend in nineteenth-century black nationalist thought, see Moses, *The Golden Age of Black Nationalism*. This trend can be traced through the 1920s when Garvey's UNIA proclaimed its intention "to assist in civilizing the backward tribes of Africa." Garvey, *Marcus Garvey: Life and Lessons*, 207.

7. E. Muhammad, "Beards," *Muhammad Speaks*, 4 July 1969, 5; E. Muhammad, *Message*, 192, 277; E. Muhammad, *Fall*, 127–28; E. Muhammad, "To the Black Woman in America," *Muhammad Speaks*, 4 September 1970, 16–17; and E. Muhammad, "Warning to M.G.T. and G.C.C. Class," *Muhammad Speaks*, 28 June 1968, 4.

8. Barboza, *American Jihad*, 112; Paul Delaney, "Black Muslims, Amid Changes, Consider Sale of Much Property," *New York Times*, 26 February 1976, 14; and Perry, *Malcolm*, 225.

9. In the Newark mosque, a woman could be suspended for ninety days for voicing her opinion. West, "Nation Builders," 139.

10. Woodford, "Testing America's Promise," 14; Sterling X Hobbs, "Miracle Man of the Muslims," *Sepia*, May 1975, 28. The Newark mosque was similar to the New York organization in regard to violence against women. According to one female believer, "In the sixties in Newark, New Jersey, you could not disrespect a Muslim woman, oh no, you'd better be walking a straight line when you walked pass a sister, or some brother would snatch you up." West, "Nation Builders," 144.

11. Though it had been shunned earlier, the term *Black Muslims* was embraced by Muhammad during this period. "Sure, we are Black Muslims!" he declared in a 1969 editorial. "Of course it started at first from the press. But we do not get indignant about being called Black for that is what we are.... Our very Nation is Black People. Our Creator was a Black God." E. Muhammad, "Are We the Black Muslims?" *Muhammad Speaks*, 7 February 1969, 20–21; Austin C. Wehrwein, "Carmichael Plans Black Unity Talks with Muslims," *New York Times*, 29 July 1966, 13; "FBI Raids Panther Office in Chicago," *Muhammad Speaks*, 13 June 1969, 33–34; Rudy Johnson, "Negro Policemen Laud Black Muslims and Give Award to Elijah Muhammad," *New York Times*, 16 June 1969, 29; Goldman and Weston, "The Founding Father," 21; and Report—"Elijah Poole," SAC Chicago, 17 October 1968, sec. 12, p. 7 (E. Muhammad FBI file).

12. Muhammad was also critical of Rev. Jesse Jackson and his organization, Operation Bread Basket. "The position of a beggar of bread for his people is the most humiliating and disgraceful style he could have assumed for himself, in this modern time. And the white man is laughing up his sleeve at the poor Rev. Jesse Jackson." E. Muhammad, "The Angry Nations," 17; E. Muhammad, *Theology of Time*, 355; E. Muhammad, *Our Saviour*, 34; E. Muhammad, "To: The Family of Dr. Martin Luther King," *Muhammad Speaks*, 12 April 1968, 3; E. Muhammad, 1971 Saviour's Day Address (audiotape); E. Muhammad, "Destruction of America's Education," *Muhammad Speaks*, 5 June 1970, 16–17; and E. Muhammad, *Fall*, 23–24, 225–26.

13. E. Muhammad, "Destruction of America's Education," 16–17; John Ali, "Whiteman and the Hypocrites Love Malcolm," *Muhammad Speaks*, 3 October 1969, 20; E. Muhammad, "Lull Before the Storm," *Muhammad Speaks*, 19 February 1971, 16; and E. Muhammad, *Theology of Time*, 356.

14. E. Muhammad, "Destruction of America's Education," 16–17; "Muhammad Meets the Press!" (pt. 3), 4.

15. Wallace has given two different accounts of his post-1965 suspensions. During a 1977 interview, he stated that he had been expelled "at least three or four times" during the 1960s, but remained in the Nation after his father readmitted him in 1970. In contrast, he commented in 1980 that he was banished from the movement twice—in 1969 and 1971—but reinstated in 1974. Marsh, *From Black Muslims*, 112–13; Gans and Lowe, "The Islam Connection," 203.

16. "Muslim Ouster Denied," *Chicago Daily Defender*, 9–15 May 1970, 1; Lomax, *When the Word Is Given*, 95; Lomax, *To Kill a Black Man*, 199; Abass Rassoull, "Introduction," in E. Muhammad, *Theology of Time*, xxix–xxx; and Delaney, "Black Muslims, Amid Changes," 14.

17. James Olsen, "Learning Elijah's Advanced Lesson in Hate," *Sports Illustrated*, 9 May 1966, 51.

18. Robert Lipsyte, "Elijah Speaks of Clay, Boxing and Black Muslims," *New York Times*, 24 September 1966, sec. 5, pp. 1, 7; Massaquoi, "Elijah Muhammad," 84. Initially, Herbert's salary was to be based on a sixty-forty division of earnings in favor of Ali. Herbert would be responsible for expenses. In 1967, less than a year into the two-year contract, Ali added an amendment that entitled him to two-thirds of the earnings after expenses were paid from the gross proceeds. Hauser, *Muhammad Ali*, 155–56.

19. Atyeo and Dennis, *Holy Warrior*, 48; Olsen, "Learning Elijah's Advanced Lesson," 51.

20. E. Muhammad, "We Tell the World We're NOT With Muhammad Ali," *Muhammad Speaks*, 4 April 1969, 3; E. Muhammad, "Classification of Action Taken by Messenger Muhammad Against Muhammad Ali's Action," *Muhammad Speaks*, 11 April 1969, 2–3; Massaquoi, "Elijah Muhammad," 84; Reynolds, "Leader Scorns Jackson, King," 12; and Hauser, *Muhammad Ali*, 194.

21. Eugene Majied, "Two Spotlights of the World," *Muhammad Speaks*, 1 December 1972, 1–2; Emmett George, "Black Muslim Hospital Planned in South Shore," *Chicago Tribune*, 28 February 1974, sec. 1, p. 5; Charles 67X, "More Than 1,900 Honor Messenger Muhammad at Dinner," *Muhammad Speaks*, 12 April 1974, 3, 17.

22. Louis was able to attend the black teachers college on a track scholarship. Howard Fineman and Vern E. Smith, "An Angry 'Charmer,'" *Newsweek*, 30 October 1995, 34–35; Malcolm Gladwell, "Louis Farrakhan's Journey," *Washington Post* (national weekly edition), 22–28 January 1996, 6–7; Barboza, *American Jihad*, 132; Hobbs, "Miracle Man," 26, 28; and Arthur J. Magida, *Prophet of Rage: A Life of Louis Farrakhan and His Nation* (New York: Basic Books, 1996), 24, 27.

23. Barboza, *American Jihad*, 132; Jackson, "Ascent and Grandeur," 22; Gladwell, "Louis Farrakhan's Journey," 6–7; Hobbs, "Miracle Man," 28; Magida, *Prophet of Rage*, 29; and Henry L. Gates Jr., "A Reporter at Large: The Charmer," *New Yorker*, 29 April and 6 May 1996, 120.

24. Curry, "Farrakhan," 32–33; Louis X, "Boston Minister Tells of Malcolm," 15; Barboza, *American Jihad*, 147; Louis Farrakhan, interviewed by Barbara Walters, *20/20*, ABC, 22 April 1994; and Lawrence Mamiya, "Black Muslim to Bilalian; The Evolution of a Movement," *Journal for the Scientific Study of Religion* 21.2 (June 1982): 142.

25. Jackson, "Ascent and Grandeur," 22; Karim, *Remembering Malcolm*, 103–4.

26. For a representative sampling of Farrakhan's speeches during this period, see Louis Farrakhan, *7 Speeches* (Newport News, Va.: Ramza Associates, n.d.).

27. "Saviour's Day Meeting," *Muhammad Speaks*, 13 May 1970, 3, 16–17. A number of the professionals who attended the Chicago meeting sponsored by Muhammad on 1 October 1972, were offended by some of his criticisms. One New Yorker, Dr. Robert Browne, later stated, "I would not have flown all the way here [Chicago] just to hear a lecture." Paul Delaney, "Black Professionals Hear Muslim Plea for Unity," *New York Times*, 2 October 1972, 24; Brother Nathaniel, "Intellectuals Fill New Temple No. 2," *Muhammad Speaks*, 13 October 1972, S-8; and E. Muhammad, *Our Saviour*, 150.

28. According to the estimate of *Time* magazine, the Nation invested $6 million dollars in economic pursuits in 1968, concentrating most of the funds on projects in Chicago. Revenues from fish sales for 1973 and 1975 (estate records of E. Muhammad); "The Nation of Islam Mourns Elijah Muhammad," *Ebony*, May 1975, 78–79; "The Original Black Capitalists," *Time*, 7 March 1969, 21; Frank McCoy, "Black Business Courts the Japanese Market," *Black Enterprise*, June 1994, 216; "Black Capitalism in the Muslim Style," *Fortune*, January 1970, 44; Bernard E. Garnett, *Invaders from the Black Nation: The "Black Muslims" in 1970* (Nashville: Race Relations Information Center, 1970), 20–21; "Muhammad Leaves Great Legacy of Pride and Respect," *Jet*, 13 March 1975, 7; and "Negroes Build Farm Empire," *U.S. News & World Report*, 21 September 1970, 83–84.

29. Unfortunately, a four-engine plane owned by the Nation was destroyed in a crash in Gary, Indiana, on September 24, 1973. It had been carrying produce back to the Midwest after unloading a shipment of *Muhammad Speaks* in California. None of the five people aboard were seriously injured. "Five Escape Crash in Gary," *Chicago Tribune*, 25 September 1973, sec. 3, p. 16; Lonnie Kashif, article on new mosque, *Muhammad Speaks*, 9 June 1972, 3, 4; E. Muhammad, *Theology of Time*, 313; Stewart, "Who Will Inherit," 20; Pamela Zekman, "Black Muslims Buy Bank on South Side," *Chicago Tribune*, 9 January 1973, sec. 1A, p. 7; "A Bank for the Blackman in America" and Charles 67X, "Bank President's Promise: Progress," *Muhammad Speaks*, 19 January 1973, 1–2; and Charles 67X, "A Jet for Muhammad!" *Muhammad Speaks*, 16 August 1974, 4–5.

30. "Islamic University," *Muhammad Speaks*, 12 June 1970, 15; E. Muhammad, "Benefit Party," 16; Angela Parker, "Black Muslims Told to Buy South Side," *Chicago Tribune*, 27 February 1972, sect. 1A, p. 14; "The Original Black Capitalists," 21; and Stewart, "Who Will Inherit," 20.

31. Nathaniel 10X, "Knowledge, Pride Speed Growth," *Muhammad Speaks*, 29 October 1971, 8–9; "Negroes Building Farm Empire," 84; and "On Georgia Farm, Nation of Islam Seeks to Replow Old Ground," *Chicago Tribune*, 12 March 1995, 16.

32. E. Muhammad, *Fall*, 84–86; "The Muslims' Farm," *Newsweek*, 8 December 1969, 57; "Muslims in Alabama," *Time*, 2 February 1970, 12–13; and "The Cattle Poisoners," *Newsweek*, 30 March 1970, 24.

33. The new nineteen-room estate of Muhammad, "distinguished by its high stained-glass windows and Moorish-style dome," may alone have cost a million dollars. "The Nation of Islam Mourns," 79; "Who Will Inherit," 21; "Muhammad Meets the Press!" (pt. 2), *Muhammad Speaks*, 4 February 1972, 3; "Black Muslims: Muhammad Speaks," *Newsweek*, 31 January 1972, 23; E. Muhammad, *Theology of Time*, 432; and Report— "Nation of Islam," G. C. Moore to E. S. Miller, 12 December 1972, sec. 14 (E. Muhammad FBI file).

34. During this period, Muhammad continued to market collections of his speeches and writings to disseminate his teachings and to earn revenue for the Nation. His most significant works, *The Fall of America* (1973) and *Our Saviour Has Arrived* (1974), were largely comprised of old editorials from *Muhammad Speaks*. Volume one of his book *How to Eat to Live* (1967) was sold in the same manner as the Muslim newspaper was. The Fruit of Islam were required to purchase thirty to forty copies of the book monthly

(at a cost of two dollars each) until there were no surplus copies. Report—"Nation of Islam," SAC Chicago to FBI director, 11 June 1968, sec. 12, p. 2 (E. Muhammad FBI file); Atyeo and Dennis, *Holy Warrior*, 54; and E. Muhammad, 1974 Saviour's Day Address (audiotape).

35. Marsh, *From Black Muslims*, 114; Ali Baghdadi, questionnaire to author, 17 September 1995; Mary Eloise X, "Two Great Families Unite!" *Muhammad Speaks*, 14 February 1975, S-4; E. Muhammad, "The Worst Is Yet to Come," *Muhammad Speaks*, 12 September 1969, 21; E. Muhammad, *Fall*, 171; and Charles Bartlett, "Big Libyan Loan for Muslims Here," *Chicago Sun-Times*, 8 May 1972, 48. After finding repayment difficult, the Nation negotiated with Libya a six-year amortization. Nathaniel 10X, "Loan to Nation of Islam Reduced by Libyan Brother," *Muhammad Speaks*, 20 October 1972, 7.

36. According to Muhammad, "The Old Testament and the New Testament have served their purpose so now we have to remove them and get a third Book and a fourth Book. There are two more to come. One is for you and one is for the Orthodox Muslim world. It takes a little more for them than you since they are the fountain of scripture and you never had any. Think over that." E. Muhammad, *Theology of Time*, 64, 210, 379; Nathaniel 10X, "Muslim Nation of Abu Dhabi Unites to Help Nation of Islam," *Muhammad Speaks*, 20 October 1972, 6.

37. E. Muhammad, "God Helps Those Who Help Themselves!" *Muhammad Speaks*, 17 May 1968, 3; E. Muhammad, "Muslims Seek Six Million Dollar Loan!" *Muhammad Speaks*, 4 December 1970, 17; Forrest, *Relocations*, 91; and Art Petacque, "Muslims Seek U.S. Aid on Job Training Plans," *Chicago Sun-Times*, 30 July 1970, 16.

38. While he did not want blacks to participate in the Vietnam War, Muhammad did not sympathize with the Vietnamese people insofar as they were not Muslims. "I wish that My God would allow Me to get one of these nuclear bombs and one of these planes, to fly over [Vietnamese] territory," he fantasized in 1972. "I would show you how long they would be here. I don't love you (Hindus) Myself." E. Muhammad, *Theology of Time*, 474–76; E. Muhammad, 1974 Saviour's Day Address (audiotape); E. Muhammad, *Our Saviour*, 37; and E. Muhammad, "God Helps Those," 3. Regarding his white neighbors, Muhammad stated in 1972 that "I live next door to devils but they never find Me coming out, morning or evening, trying to get a chance to speak to them. I never speak to them unless they speak to Me. I am not seeking their love nor friendship whatsoever. No. I don't want it." E. Muhammad, *Theology of Time*, 425; E. Muhammad, "Every Nation Has a Term," 16–17. In addition to moderating his own racial rhetoric, Muhammad instructed his followers to do the same. According to his fiery national spokesman, Louis Farrakhan: "The Honorable Elijah Muhammad called me on the telephone [in 1972 or 1973] and said, 'I wish you'd stop throwing trash in a well that I am trying to get a drink of water out of!' And he hung up the phone. . . . I guess the well is that there is something of value in America that can be extracted for the good of our people. And you can't consistently keep throwing trash in a well, lest nobody will be able to drink at all." George E. Curry, "Farrakhan, Jesse & Jews," *Emerge*, July/August 1994, 34.

39. David Farber, *The Age of Great Dreams: America in the 1960s* (New York: Hill and Wang, 1994), 225–29; Steigerwald, *Sixties*, 278–84.

40. H. R. Haldeman, *The Haldeman Diaries* (New York: Berkley Books, 1995), 66, 141, 152, 172, 220, 490; Farber, *Age of Great Dreams*, 226–28; and Gerald S. Strober and Deborah Hart Strober, *Nixon: An Oral History of His Presidency* (New York: HarperPerennial, 1994), 24, 112–14.

41. Memo—"Counterintelligence Program . . . ," G. C. Moore to W. C. Sullivan, 27 February 1968, sec. 1; "Airtel," FBI director to SAC Albany, 4 March 1968, sec. 1, p. 3 (Black Extremists/Black Nationalist—Hate Groups file, 100-4480006); O'Reilly, *"Racial Matters,"* 241, 260, 276–78, 293–324; Friedly and Gallen, *Martin Luther King, Jr.*, 21–

99; and U.S. Congress, Senate Select Committee to Study Government Operations with Respect to Intelligence Activities, *Supplementary Detailed Staff Reports on Intelligence Activities and the Rights of Americans*, bk. 3, 94th Cong., 2d sess. (Washington, D.C.: Government Printing Office, 1976), 20 n. 90.

42. Report—"Nation of Islam," SAC Chicago to FBI director, 22 April 1968, sec. 2, pp. 2–7; Memo—"Counterintelligence Program . . . ," SAC Richmond to FBI director, 13 November 1970, sec. 22, pp. 1–2 (Black Extremists/BNHG file); and "Two Blacks Come to Blows, a Melee Flares in Atlanta," *New York Times*, 16 February 1971, 37.

43. "Teletype," FBI director to SAC Chicago, 23 June 1966, June mail; Report—"Elijah Poole," SAC Chicago to FBI director, 19 January 1971, sec. 13 (E. Muhammad FBI file); and Martin Waldron, "Muslim Wiretap Clarified by F.B.I.," *New York Times*, 6 June 1969, 24. The "Black Muslim Movement" file, consisting of approximately 46,600 documents, has not been declassified for public scrutiny. It may not be available to researchers before the turn of the century. J. Kevin O'Brien (Freedom of Information Privacy Acts Section of the FBI) to Claude Clegg, 23 June 1993.

44. E. Muhammad, *Fall*, 47; E. Muhammad, "Solve the Problem," *Muhammad Speaks*, 7 November 1969, 17; George Goodman Jr., "Muslim Minister Assails Police Action," *New York Times*, 16 April 1972, 56; and "Patrolmen, 31, Shot in Harlem Mosque, Dies of His Wounds," *New York Times*, 21 April 1972, 77. The purging of policemen from the Nation was also triggered by public statements made by a black law officer who claimed that he had infiltrated both the Muslim movement and the Black Panther Party. Apparently, the expulsions also affected mosques outside of New York. "Muslims Purge Police Members," *New York Times*, 29 October 1972, 20; James S. Tinney, "Black Muslims: Moving into Mainstream?" *Christianity Today*, 10 August 1973, 44; Report—"Elijah Poole," SAC Chicago, 19 October 1970, sec. 13, p. 20 (E. Muhammad FBI file); Forrest, *Relocations*, 89; and E. Muhammad, *Theology of Time*, 216.

45. Herbert Muhammad Jr., the grandson of Elijah, was arrested on 5 March 1971, for violating selective service orders. "Muslim's Grandson Seized," *New York Times*, 6 March 1971, 54; E. Muhammad, *Fall*, 36; E. Muhammad, *Theology of Time*, 33; and E. Muhammad, *Our Saviour*, 48.

46. Racial violence in Phoenix may have played a minor role in Muhammad's decision to make fewer trips to Arizona. In 1967, two hundred people were arrested during a civil disturbance in the city. Luckingham, *Phoenix*, 178; "Muhammad Meets the Press!" (pt. 3), 3; Teletype—"Elijah Muhammad," SAC Phoenix to SAC Chicago and FBI director, 15 September 1967, sec. 11 (E. Muhammad FBI file); "Phoenix Residents Treated to Milk, Kosher Lamb, Beef," *Muhammad Speaks*, 8 December 1967, 3; and Massaquoi, "Elijah Muhammad," 82.

47. "Black Muslims: Muhammad Speaks," 23; William Mullen, "Black Muslim Feud Marked by Signs of Growing Terrorism," *Chicago Tribune*, 28 January 1973, sec. 1, p. 18; and "Holy War?" *Newsweek*, 5 February 1973, 41.

48. In August 1971, Muhammad reported to police that twenty thousand dollars had been stolen from his home. Merv Block, "Elijah Muhammad—Black Paradox," *Chicago Sun-Times*, 26 March 1972, sec. 2, p. 4; Mullen, "Black Muslim Feud," 18; "Black Muslims: Muhammad Speaks," 23; "Holy War?" 41; Jon Nordheimer, "4 in Baton Rouge Are Slain in Clash," *New York Times*, 11 January 1972, 1, 24; Jon Nordheimer, "Racial Tension Rises in Baton Rouge as Versions of Shootout That Killed Four Vary," *New York Times*, 12 January 1972, 27; and "Baton Rouge," *Muhammad Speaks*, 21 January 1972, 2.

49. "Back of Killings? Religious Split Among Blacks," *U.S. News & World Report*, 5 February 1973, 83; "Holy War?" 41; "Black Leader Slain by Boston Gunmen; Muslim Feud Hinted," *New York Times*, 3 May 1973, 26; Tinney, "Black Muslims," 44; "Black

Muslim Leader Shabazz Slain in Trap," *Chicago Tribune*, 5 September 1973, sec. 1, p. 1; "Black Muslim Leader in Newark Shot to Death; Two Men Sought," *New York Times*, 5 September 1973, 50; Philip Wechsler, "Decapitated Bodies of 2 Found in a Newark Park," *New York Times*, 19 October 1973, 47; Richard Phalon, "11 Sect Members Arrested in Newark Muslim Slaying," *New York Times*, 25 October 1973, 32; Wallace Turner, "7 Arrested Men Tied to Muslims," *New York Times*, 3 May 1974, 13; Wallace Turner, "4 Blacks Indicted in Coast Killings," *New York Times*, 17 May 1974, 27; and "3 Black Muslims Convicted of Murder in Coast Killing," *New York Times*, 11 November 1974, 39.

50. Brandon, "Hanafi Moslem Chief," A4; "Back of Killings?" 83; John Hanrahan and Ivan Brandon, "Muslims Attacked in Letter," *Washington Post*, 24 January 1973, C1, C8; and "Holy War?" 41.

51. Paul Delaney, "Survivor Tells How 7 Moslems Died in Washington," *New York Times*, 25 January 1973, 25; Alfred E. Lewis and Timothy S. Robinson, "Seven 'Executed' in District's Biggest Mass Murder," *Washington Post*, 19 January 1973, A1, A10; Paul Delaney, "7 Slain at Muslim House in Capital; 5 Are Children," *New York Times*, 19 January 1973, 1, 13; "Suspects Sought in Capital Slayings of 7 Muslims," *New York Times*, 20 January 1973, 62; Paul Delaney, "Black Muslims Accused by Rival Sect in 7 Killings," *New York Times*, 23 January 1973, 1, 77; "Holy War?" 41; and "Back of Killings?" 83.

52. "Holy War?" 41.

53. Shirley Hazziez, "All Blacks Are Muslims, Believe It or Not," *Muhammad Speaks*, 2 February 1973, 15; Eugene L. Meyer, "Black Muslim 'Traitors' Warned of Vengeance," *Washington Post*, 5 April 1974, B1, B6; and "Muslim Sentenced to 140 Years in Jail," *New York Times*, 8 January 1975, 13. For articles denouncing "the hypocrites" and others, see *Muhammad Speaks* for November–December 1970; 30 April 1971; 18 May 1971; 4 June 1971; 3 September 1971; and 3 December 1971.

54. Elijah's older sister, "Tommie" Bogans, died in 1967 at the age of seventy-three. "Hold Muslim Rites for Sister of the Messenger," *Muhammad Speaks*, 1 September 1967, 18; "2,000 Attend Muslim Rites for Mrs. Elijah Muhammad," *Jet*, 31 August 1972, 12–14.

55. "2,000 attend," 12–14.

Chapter 10: In the Last Days

1. Barbara Reynolds, "Changes in Black Muslims: Why the Surprise?" *Chicago Tribune*, 7 March 1976, 38; "Conversion of the Muslims," *Time*, 14 March 1977, 59.

2. Jackson, "Ascent and Grandeur," 22.

3. "Rare Interview with Messenger Muhammad!" *Muhammad Speaks*, 28 January 1972, 3; "Muhammad Meets the Press!" (pt. 2), 4; and "Muhammad Meets the Press!" (pt. 3), 4.

4. "Visit Muhammad's Temple of Islam," *Muhammad Speaks*, 21 February 1975: 23; Charles 67X, "18,000 Hail Muhammad's Address," *Muhammad Speaks*, 9 March 1973, 3; Robert Davis, "Muhammad Speaks: Thank the Whites," *Chicago Tribune*, 27 February 1974, sec. 3, p. 18; Wali Muhammad, telephone conversation with author, 2 October 1995; Kenneth Muhammad, telephone conversation with author, 25 September 1995; and Na'im Akbar, telephone conversation with author, 27 September 1995.

5. Hobbs, "Miracle Man," 24, 26; Armiya Nu'man, telephone conversation with author, 20 September 1995. In late 1974, the FBI estimated that the Nation of Islam

was "a 10,000-member black separatist group." Given the number of mosques in existence at that time and the membership figures of some of the larger ones, this estimate is almost certainly too low. Teletype—"Elijah Poole," SAC Chicago to FBI director, 21 November 1974, sec. 15, p. 2 (E. Muhammad FBI file).

6. Charles 67X, "More than 1,900 Honor Messenger Muhammad at Dinner," *Muhammad Speaks,* 12 April 1974, 22; "Fete Muhammad at Dinner to Help Build New Hospital," *Jet,* 18 April 1974, 54.

7. Revenue from fish sales for 1973 and 1975 (estate records of E. Muhammad); Wallace D. Muhammad, *As the Light,* 110; and James S. Tinney, "Black Muslims: Billing the Baptists?" *Christianity Today,* 25 October 1974, 49–50.

8. Memo—"Nation of Islam," SAC Chicago to FBI director, 19 June 1973, sec. 14; Report—"Elijah Poole," SAC Chicago, 29 November, 1974, sec. 15, p. 1a (E. Muhammad FBI file); Lillian Williams, "Dinner for Funds for Hospital to Honor Elijah Muhammad," *Chicago Sun-Times,* 29 March 1974, 20; and E. Muhammad, open letter to Daniel Walker and Richard J. Daley, *Muhammad Speaks,* 12 April 1974, 1.

9. E. Muhammad, *Theology of Time,* 41; "Muhammad Meets the Press!" (pt. 2), 4.

10. According to Wallace, Elijah Muhammad told him in 1974 that he could present him (Elijah) as the "god figure" upon his death. He also allegedly suggested that he (Wallace) could become the new messenger. This plan was supposed to be a last resort to prevent schisms in the Nation after Muhammad's death. Wallace, whose account of this conversation cannot be independently verified, declined the offer. Warith D. Mohammed, "The History of the African-American Experience in Islam," University of Arkansas, Little Rock, date unknown; Marsh, *From Black Muslims,* 113–14; Wallace D. Muhammad, address at Fruit of Islam meeting, Mosque No. 7, Harlem, New York, 18 January 1975; and Barboza, *American Jihad,* 99.

11. According to Elijah Muhammad Jr., "My father told me to keep an eye on him [Farrakhan] because he was trying to use the family." Jackson, "Ascent and Grandeur," 22; Wallace D. Muhammad, address at Fruit of Islam meeting; Nathaniel 10X and Samuel 17X, "Muhammad's Eighth Lecture on Theology of Time!" *Muhammad Speaks,* 28 July 1972, S-10; Alauddin Shabazz, telephone conversation with author, 27 September 1995; and Mary Eloise X, "Two Great Families Unite!" S-4.

12. For articles that refer to the age of Elijah Muhammad, see *Muhammad Speaks* for December 1973 and January 1974. Paul Delaney, "Black Muslim Group in Trouble from Financial Problems and Some Crime," *New York Times,* 6 December 1973, 37; E. Muhammad, 1973 and 1974 Saviour's Day Addresses (audiotapes); Irving Kupcinet, "Kup's Column," *Chicago Sun-Times,* 28 January 1974, 52; and Teletype—"Elijah Poole," FBI director to Legat. Mexico City, 24 December 1974, sec. 15, p. 1 (E. Muhammad FBI file).

13. During a hospital visit in September 1974, Muhammad was admitted under the assumed name "Charles Evans." Teletype—"Nation of Islam," SAC Chicago to FBI director, 17 September 1974, sec. 15, p. 3 (E. Muhammad FBI file); Simon Anekwe, "Muslims Say Ailing Muhammad Is Stronger," *Amsterdam News,* 15 February 1975, A1; "Muslim Ruler Elijah Muhammad Dies," *Chicago Tribune,* 26 February 1976, sec. 1, p. 1; Gregory Simms, "Nation Mourns Muslim Leader," *Jet,* 13 March 1975, 15; and Cook County Vital Statistics, "Medical Certificate of Death" (Elijah Muhammad).

14. "Medical Certificate of Death"; "The Nation of Islam Mourns," 81; "7,000 Mourn Muhammad," *Chicago Tribune,* 1 March 1975, sec. 1, p. 4; "Muhammad Leaves Great Legacy," 6; "The Founding Father," 21; and William Raspberry, "The Miracle of Elijah Muhammad," *Washington Post,* 28 February 1975, A23.

15. "The Nation of Islam Mourns," 81; "7,000 Mourn," 4.

16. Herbert Muhammad Jr. was the only family member who publicly opposed Wallace as a successor. Simon Anekwe, "Grandson of Muhammad Defies Son's Leadership," *Amsterdam News*, 8 March 1975, A1, A2; Herbert Muhammad, "Muhammad Speaks: Exclusive Statement," *Amsterdam News*, 22 March 1975, A1, A10; Simms, "Nation Mourns," 53; and "New Muslim Leader Tells Why Muslims Bar Whites," *Amsterdam News*, 16 April 1975, A1, A2.

17. Wallace D. Muhammad, 1975 Saviour's Day Address (audiotape); Simms, "Nation Mourns," 15, 18, 52–53.

18. Wallace D. Muhammad, 1975 Saviour's Day Address (audiotape).

19. As of June 1975, the Nation owned $14.5 million in property in Chicago and twenty-five thousand acres of farmland elsewhere, valued at $6.2 million. The seafood enterprise was reportedly a $22-million-a-year business. Susan C. Cowley and Martin Weston, "'Yesterday's Message,'" *Newsweek*, 30 June 1975, 71; Dennis A. Williams and Elaine Sciolino, "Rebirth of the Nation," *Newsweek*, 15 March 1976, 33; Barbara Reynolds, "Muslims $5 Million in Debt, Under IRS Probe: Leader," *Chicago Tribune*, 1 March 1976, sec. 1, p. 1; and "White Muslims?" *Time*, 30 June 1975, 52.

20. Williams and Sciolino, "Rebirth of the Nation," 33; Clarence Page, "Muslims Act to Sell Empire," *Chicago Tribune*, 15 August 1976, sec. 2, p. 13.

21. "The Honorable Elijah Muhammad's Poor Fund," bank statement, 6 March 1975, the First Pacific Bank of Chicago; Gail Muhammad to the First Pacific Bank of Chicago, 3 March 1975; "Memorandum in Opposition to Motion to Strike and Dismiss Counterclaim as to Wallace D. Muhammad and Third Party Complaint as to Gail Muhammad a/k/a Hafeeza Bahar and the Nation of Islam and Its Successors," Docket 806, No. 75 P 4128, Circuit Court of Cook County, Illinois Probate Division, filed 11 August 1981 (estate records of E. Muhammad); "Elijah Muhammad Wills $200,000 Estate to Kids," *Jet*, 26 June 1975, 6; "Elijah Muhammad's 13 Illegitimate Children Must Share Estate, Court," *Jet*, 25 January 1979, 8; "Transfer of Funds to Muslims Voided," *New York Times*, 18 February 1982, 2; "Banks Must Pay," 12; Charles Mount, "Muhammad's Heirs to Share in Fortune," *Chicago Tribune*, 11 July 1986, 1, 2; and "Muslim Mission Wins $5.7 Million Appellate Ruling," *Washington Post*, 2 January 1988, A11. Before his death, Muhammad gave four expensive homes (valued at $120,000 each) to relatives as nontaxable gifts. However, the IRS determined in 1990 that the residences were bestowed "in contemplation of death and are subject to gift tax." *Wall Street Journal*, 2 May 1990, A1.

22. Wallace D. Muhammad, "The Lost-Found Nation of Islam in the West," *The Bilalian News*, 14 November 1975, 20; "Conversion of the Muslims," 59; Wallace D. Muhammad, "Special Announcement," *Muhammad Speaks*, 31 October 1975, 1; Gans and Lowe, "The Islam Connection," 203; Nathaniel Sheppard Jr., "Black Muslim Movement Divided in Dispute Over Doctrinal Changes," *New York Times*, 7 March 1978, 18; and Joel D. Weisman, "Muslims Break With Past, Authorize Members to Vote," *Washington Post*, 29 February 1976, A2.

23. Wallace D. Muhammad, "The Destruction of the Devil," *Muhammad Speaks*, 11 July 1975, 13; "Nation of Islam: The Alternative Culture for America," *Muhammad Speaks*, 25 July 1975, 16; Paul Delaney, "Black Muslims Will End Longtime Ban on Whites," *New York Times*, 17 June 1975, 9; "Nation of Islam Changes Name to Fight Black Separatist Image," *New York Times*, 19 October 1976, 33; and "Black Muslims Revise View of Former Leader," *Washington Post*, 3 May 1977, A4. At least a few Caucasians had been affiliated with the Nation of Islam since the late 1960s. Seifullah Ali Shabazz, who was informally "tutored" by Min. James Shabazz of Newark as early as 1969, attended the Saviour's Day convention of that year with the permission of Elijah Muhammad. Another white Muslim, Dorothy 13X, began openly attending mosque functions in the wake of Elijah Muhammad's death. Her husband, Donald 12X Dorsey, had

converted her back in 1970. Seifullah A. Shabazz, telephone conversations with author, 2 October 1995 and 19 November 1995; Barbara Reynolds, "First White Woman Becomes a Muslim," *Chicago Tribune*, 2 March 1976, sect. 4, p. 12.

24. Delaney, "Black Muslims, Amid Changes," 14; Page, " 'New Muslims,' " 6; Peter Noel, "One Nation?" *Vibe*, February 1996, 72–73; and "Muhammad's Body Moved," *Washington Post*, 9 March 1975, A5.

25. Joe Walker, "Growth of 'Baby Nation' Shown in Muhammad Speech," *Muhammad Speaks*, 18 July 1975, S-1; Barboza, *American Jihad*, 101; and Charlayne Hunter, "Black Muslim Temple Renamed for Malcolm X; Move Reflects Acceptance of Slain Ex-Leader," *New York Times*, 1 February 1976, 1.

26. Farrakhan later purchased the home of Elijah Muhammad and Mosque No. 2, which he renamed Mosque Maryam. Barboza, *American Jihad*, 101, 133; Sheppard, "Black Muslim Movement Divided," 18; Jackson, "Ascent and Grandeur," 22; Paul Delaney, "Radical Changes by New Leader Leave Many Muslims Disaffected," *New York Times*, 25 December 1978, 16; and Page, " 'New Muslims,' " 6.

Bibliography

1. Louis E. Wright, "The Political Thought of Elijah Muhammad: Innovation and Continuity in Western Tradition" (Ph.D diss., Howard University, 1987); William A. Marshall, "Education in the Nation of Islam during the Leadership of Elijah Muhammad, 1925–1975" (Ed.D. diss., Loyola University of Chicago, 1976); and Walter Abilla, "A Study of Black Muslims: An Analysis of Commitment" (Ph.D. diss., Case Western Reserve University, 1972). E. Curtis Alexander's book, *Elijah Muhammad on African-American Education* (1981; reprint, New York: ECA Associates, 1989), is one of the few published specialized accounts of the Nation. The work surveys the educational and economic elements of the philosophy and program of Elijah Muhammad, but is not as much about education as the title might lead one to believe. The book is heavily reliant on extensive quotes from other works and is uncritically laudatory in its analysis of Elijah Muhammad and the Muslim movement.

2. Adib Rashad, *Elijah Muhammad: The Ideological Foundations of the Nation of Islam* (Newport News, Va.: U.B. & U.S. Communications Systems, 1994).

3. Fahim Knight, *In Defense of the Defender: The Most Honorable Elijah Muhammad* (Durham, N.C.: Fahim and Associates, 1994).

4. The author has found former high-ranking members of the Nation under Elijah Muhammad particularly hard to contact regarding interviews for this project. Elijah's brother John Muhammad, who has started an offshoot of the Nation in Detroit, has replied to correspondence but has provided little information. Louis Farrakhan has been extremely difficult to get in touch with through numerous certified letters and telephone calls, though the *Final Call* newspaper did graciously provide useful photographs for this project. Warith D. Mohammed (formerly Wallace D. Muhammad) has not replied to correspondence or telephone calls, although conversations with his national representative, Abdul Malik Mohammed, have led the author to believe that he is interested in works relating to his father. Another son of the leader, Elijah Muhammad Jr., informed the author that he no longer grants interviews. During a telephone conversation, Akbar Muhammad, Elijah's youngest child (by Clara), offered to assist the author through correspondence, but never responded to subsequent letters or telephone messages. Regretfully, former national secretary Abass Rassoull has been of no assistance whatsoever. John Muhammad to Claude Clegg, 4 October 1995; Richard Muhammad to Claude

Clegg, 11 April 1996; Abdul Malik Mohammed, telephone conversation with author, 24 October 1995; Elijah Muhammad Jr., telephone conversation with author, 2 October 1995; Akbar Muhammad, telephone conversation with author, 7 September 1995; and Abass Rassoull, telephone conversation with author, 13 October 1995.

BIBLIOGRAPHY

A Note on Sources and the State of Research*

Prior to 1960, an article and a master's thesis, both from a sociological perspective, were the main scholarly accounts of the Nation of Islam. Erdmann D. Beynon's piece, entitled "The Voodoo Cult Among Negro Migrants in Detroit" (in *The American Journal of Sociology*, May 1938), describes the obscure origins of the movement, concentrating mostly on general ideology and the socioeconomic character of the membership. This article succeeds, at least partially, in capturing the initial dynamics of the movement among immigrant blacks in Detroit, but is short on historical antecedents and does not situate the organization within the history of black nationalism or Islam in the United States. The second major piece, a master's thesis by Hatim A. Sahib entitled "The Nation of Islam" (Sociology, University of Chicago, 1951), does an excellent job critiquing the development of the movement immediately following World War II and contains firsthand observations and extensive interviews of Elijah Muhammad. Also, this study deals at length with the attraction of the movement to African-Americans and the psychological needs it fulfilled. However, the work is strictly rooted in the sociological theories of the period and only minimally ventures into the historical and ideological environment that sired the Nation. Together, the works of Beynon and Sahib give the reader only a snapshot of the movement and its leaders at selected times in its history and do not construct spatial or historical contexts necessary for fully understanding Muhammad or the Muslims.

Among the few available monograph-length published works on the Nation, C. Eric Lincoln's *The Black Muslims in America* (1961) is the seminal study. Unlike most subsequent works, this book is balanced in its assessment of the Nation of Islam and is not skewed by the personal and organizational conflicts that surrounded the departure of Malcolm X. Lincoln's work, however, is mainly sociological and is not very concerned with the early history of the organization beyond establishing a broad context for his study, which focuses on the late 1950s and early 1960s. His conclusions that the Nation of Islam was extremist, escapist, and dysfunctional unduly

*Notes for the Bibliography section are on pages 542–43.

characterize the organization as a mere deviant reaction to the racism and segregation that prevailed in American society. Additionally, his book predates the publication of *The Autobiography of Malcolm X*, the declassification of government (especially FBI) documents relating to the Nation, and subsequent important works, including Muhammad's own magnum opus, *Message to the Blackman in America* (1965). Lincoln's focus is more on the mechanics of the organization, the nature of its membership, and its implications for American race relations than on Elijah Muhammad or his central role in the movement.

The second major scholarly work to appear on the Muslims was *Black Nationalism: A Search for an Identity in America* (1962) by E. U. Essien-Udom. This book complements the work of Lincoln and is an ethnographic look at the Nation, with an emphasis on the nationalism of the organization and the demographic makeup of its membership. The author argues that the Muslims did fill important psychological needs among blacks who were disenchanted with the Civil Rights Movement and their second-class status in America. Like *The Black Muslims*, Essien-Udom's treatment of the early history of the Nation (prior to the mid-1950s) is cursory, though the latter does a better job in situating the Muslims in the broader historical tradition of black separatism. This work, while both sympathetic to the Muslims and critical of problematic features of the group, generally benefits from being a firsthand, pre-schism study of the Nation. Still, like Lincoln's study, *Black Nationalism* is dated and does not focus on Elijah Muhammad beyond a glance at his early life and his organizational and theoretical development during the late 1950s and early 1960s.

The book by journalist Louis Lomax, *When the Word Is Given* (1963), has a journalistic flavor, though it does not sensationalize the Nation of Islam. It contains a good discussion of the essence and historical purpose of religion (and religious intolerance), but is as much about Malcolm X as it is about Elijah Muhammad and the Muslim movement. Lomax includes useful transcripts of speeches by the two leaders, but deprives the reader of footnotes. Furthermore, his work is less scholarly than those of Essien-Udom and Lincoln (whom he relies upon) and cannot be considered a researched study. Despite these problems, *When the Word Is Given* does make an admirable attempt to capture the "Muslim moment" in the sweep of African-American history.

After a generation of neglect, recent book-length examinations of the Nation of Islam have been few and largely disappointing. Clifton E. Marsh's *From Black Muslims to Muslims: The Transition from Separatism to Islam, 1930–1980* (1984) is a good overview of Islam in the black community from the 1920s to the 1970s. The reader with only a general interest in the history of the Nation of Islam should begin here. However, the serious researcher will find the book void of any new interpretations or points not made elsewhere. No overarching theoretical framework holds the book together. The source material used by Marsh is quite limited and subsequently hampers his analysis of themes pertinent to the evolution of the Nation.

The work of Martha E. Lee, *The Nation of Islam: An American Millenarian Movement* (1988), is written in a vein similar to Marsh's study, giving a broad survey of the Nation from its inception to the 1980s. This piece emphasizes the millenarian aspects of the Nation's "Fall of America" prophecy and therefore captures only a part of the group's (and Muhammad's) significance. Lee relies heavily on newspaper articles and the major books of Nation historiography (i.e., *Message to the Blackman* and *The Autobiography of Malcolm X*), but neglects other important sources such as FBI records and subsequent publications by Muhammad (i.e., *The Fall of America, Our Saviour Has Arrived, The Supreme Wisdom*, and numerous *Muhammad Speaks* editorials). Moreover, the historical context of the book is not fleshed out as well as it could be. Both Marsh and Lee try to cover fifty years of the Nation's development in 140 pages or less and limit their discussions of Elijah Muhammad and the Muslim movement prior to 1963 to thirty pages or less. Overall, their treatments of the leader and the movement are too cursory and deprive the reader of much that is relevant.

A welcome trend in recent literature on the Nation that has borne mixed fruit is the appearance of specialized studies that highlight selected facets of the movement. In general, these works tend to be doctoral dissertations—though there are some published works—that cover one feature of the Muslim organization from a particular perspective, be it sociological, educational, political, or otherwise. Few of these dissertation have been published since the publication of C. Eric Lincoln's *The Black Muslims* in 1961, and few, if any, are the work of historians. Of the approximately one dozen or so dissertations on Elijah Muhammad and the Nation of Islam, typical titles suggestive of their focus include "The Political Thought of Elijah Muhammad: Innovation and Continuity in Western Tradition" by Louis E. Wright (political science, Howard University, 1987); "Education in the Nation of Islam during the Leadership of Elijah Muhammad, 1925–1975" by William A. Marshall (education, Loyola University of Chicago, 1976); and "A Study of Black Muslims: An Analysis of Commitment" by Walter Abilla (sociology, Case Western Reserve University, 1972). The general tendency in these works is to compartmentalize the Nation and the leadership of Elijah Muhammad into categories and frameworks that necessarily strip away the larger context(s) within which the leader and the movement operated. Hopefully in the future, further research and writings by graduate students will demonstrate an awareness of the multifaceted nature of the Nation's evolution and a willingness to analyze the whole as well as to anatomize the parts.[1]

Besides the works of scholars, a number of books have been written about the Nation by participants and former members. Many of these works were published in or after 1965 and are often subject to the biases created by the 1963–64 schism and the assassination of Malcolm X. The most useful and factual literature begins with *The Autobiography of Malcolm X* (1965) by Malcolm X (with Alex Haley). This account contains substantial biographical material on Elijah Muhammad and the history and inner operations of the Nation during the 1950s and early 1960s. The ideology of the movement is laid out well by the author, and Haley's epilogue is quite insightful. A second book of importance to the researcher is *As the Light Shineth from the East* (1980) by Wallace D. Muhammad (now, Warith D. Mohammed). This work traces the ideological development of the Nation and is more objective in its analysis of the movement and its leadership than most other works by insiders. In the form of a memoir, this piece contains biographical material on the life of Elijah Muhammad that cannot be found elsewhere.

Finally, on the bottom end of the writings on the Nation are several defenses of Elijah Muhammad, some of which are cloaked in the guise of scholarship. The best known is *This Is the One: The Most Honored Elijah Muhammad, We Need Not Look for Another!* (1993) by Jabril Muhammad (formerly Bernard Cushmeer). The author, a true believer, is harshly critical of the critics of Elijah Muhammad, laments the scarcity of favorable coverage that the leader and the movement have historically received, and excoriates integration and its advocates. At several points, this work digresses into tedious theological and metaphysical discussions and contains extensive quotes from other sources. *This is the One,* while quite polemical, does contain some useful biographical material on Elijah Muhammad, especially from the 1930s and 1940s. However, the reader should read with caution since the book has a pronounced agenda.

Similarly, Adib Rashad's *Elijah Muhammad: The Ideological Foundation of the Nation of Islam* (1994) is another recent eulogy of Muhammad and his life's work. It is written in the same defensive/laudatory manner as Jabril Muhammad's book and suffers from the same lack of objectivity and critical analysis. Rashad has a distracting tendency to drift into discussions that seem unrelated to the titles and stated purposes of the chapters and the book itself. Also, there are some inaccuracies, and many of the points made are based on weak evidence or missing citations. On a positive note, Rashad has a firm grasp on the history of Islam, and at least two of the contributors to the volume (Sulayman S. Nyang and Na'im Akbar) offer insightful articles that approach a balanced view of Muhammad's life. The author is not a member of the Nation of Islam, but he is deeply sympathetic to its cause.[2]

Additionally, *In Defense of the Defender: The Most Honorable Elijah Muhammad* (1994) by Fahim A. Knight rarely rises above the level of a panegyric appraisal of Muhammad and Louis Farrakhan. Although little here is new, the author does resist the temptation of damning Malcolm X as a hypocrite, which too few writers partial to the Nation of Islam have been able to do. Knight uses more source materials than Muhammad and Rashad and includes citations for many of his points. However, he begins with the premise that Elijah Muhammad is "a divine messenger," and there is little pretense toward objectivity. Taken together, these three works and others like them do contain tidbits of information hard to find elsewhere, but are not works of serious scholarship or products of meticulous research.[3]

Critiquing the literature as done above reveals the limitations of previous works on Elijah Muhammad and the need for a balanced, contextual account of his life and importance. Especially at the present time, historical research regarding the leader and the Muslim movement is beneficial and pertinent. The historian today, while still faced with the perennial problems of gaining access to the personal papers of members and obtaining interviews of prominent Muslim leaders, does have at his/her disposal a plethora of angles from which to view the life of Muhammad and the history and operation of the Nation. Several published books by the leader, collections of published speeches and other pronouncements, periodicals, declassified government (especially FBI) documents, recently published insider accounts, preserved audiotape and videotape records, and a number of other sources make it possible for the serious historical researcher to comprehend Muhammad and the movement from different perspectives. When examined together, these materials provide an opening into the movement large enough to counterbalance the closed nature and anti-outsider bias of the organization regarding disclosure of its internal operation. In addition to being an almost pristine area of research, historical work on Elijah Muhammad and the Muslims also lends further context to a number of subjects that have enjoyed much greater scholarly attention, such as the Civil Rights Movement and the evolution of contemporary black separatism. Undoubtedly, all future studies of these historical phenomena and many others would profit from an appreciation of the significance of Elijah Muhammad and the Nation of Islam in shaping the ethos and aspirations of African-Americans in the twentieth century.[4]

Newspapers

Amsterdam News (New York), Atlanta Constitution, The Bilalian News, The Charlotte Observer, The Chicago Defender, The Chicago Sun, Chicago Sun-Times, Chicago Today, Chicago Tribune, Chicago's American, The Detroit Free Press, The Detroit News, Detroit Times, The Final Call, Herald Tribune (New York), The Los Angeles Herald Dispatch, The Michigan Chronicle, Muhammad Speaks, Muhammad Speaks Continues, Muslim Journal, The New York Times, News & Record (Greensboro, NC), The Pittsburgh Courier, Salaam, The Wall Street Journal, The Washington Afro-American, The Washington Post.

Manuscript Collections

Detroit Urban League Papers. Michigan Historical Collection. The University of Michigan, Ann Arbor.

Alex Haley Papers. Schomburg Center for Research in Black Culture. The New York Public Library.

Aliya Hassan Papers. Michigan Historical Collection. The University of Michigan, Ann Arbor.

Lyndon B. Johnson Papers. Lyndon Baines Johnson Library, Austin, Tex.

John F. Kennedy Papers. John Fitzgerald Kennedy Library, Boston, Mass.

C. Eric Lincoln Papers. Special Collections. Clark Atlanta University, Atlanta.

Oral History Research Office. Columbia University in the City of New York.

Books

Addington, Larry H. *The Patterns of War since the Eighteenth Century*. Bloomington: Indiana University Press, 1984.

Alexander, E. Curtis. *Elijah Muhammad on African-American Education*. New York: ECA Associates, 1989.

Al-Farsy, Fouad. *Modernity and Tradition: The Saudi Equation*. New York: Kegan Paul International, 1990.

Ali, Noble Drew. *The Holy Koran of the Moorish Science Temple of America*. 1929.

Anderson, Benedict. *Imagined Communities: Reflections on the Origin and Spread of Nationalism*. New York: Verso, 1990.

Atyeo, Don, and Felix Dennis. *The Holy Warrior: Muhammad Ali*. New York: Simon & Schuster, 1975.

Baldwin, James. *The Fire Next Time*. New York: Dell Publishing Co., 1962.

Barboza, Steven. *American Jihad: Islam After Malcolm X*. New York: Doubleday, 1993.

Bishop, Jim. *The Days of Martin Luther King, Jr.: A Biography*. 1971. Reprint, New York: Barnes, & Noble, 1994.

Blackstock, Nelson. *COINTELPRO: The FBI's Secret War on Political Freedom*. New York: Vintage Books, 1975.

Bloom, Harold. *The American Religion: The Emergence of the Post-Christian Nation*. New York: Simon & Schuster, 1992.

Bontemps, Arna, and Jack Conroy. *Anyplace but Here*. New York: Hill and Wang, 1966.

Branch, Taylor. *Parting the Waters: America in the King Years, 1954–63*. New York: Simon & Schuster, 1988.

Breasted, James H. *The Conquest of Civilization*. New York: Harper & Brothers Publishers, 1926.

Breitman, George. *The Last Year of Malcolm X: The Evolution of a Revolutionary*. New York: Pathfinder, 1967.

Breitman, George, Herman Porter, and Baxter Smith. *The Assassination of Malcolm X*. New York: Pathfinder Press, 1976.

Brotz, Howard, *The Black Jews of Harlem*. 1964. Reprint, New York: Schocken Books, 1970.

Burkett, Randall K. *Garveyism as a Religious Movement: The Institutionalization of a Black Civil Religion*. Metuchen, N.J.: Scarecrow Press, 1978.

Carson, Clayborne, ed. *Malcolm X: The FBI File*. New York: Carroll & Graf Publishers, 1991.

Cashman, Sean D. *African-Americans and the Quest for Civil Rights, 1900–1990*. New York: New York University Press, 1991.

Caute, David. *The Great Fear: The Anti-Communist Purge under Truman and Eisenhower*. New York: Simon & Schuster, 1978.

Chafe, William H. *Civilities and Civil Rights: Greensboro, North Carolina, and the Black Struggle for Freedom*. New York: Oxford University Press, 1981.

Chalmers, David M. *Hooded Americanism: The History of the Ku Klux Klan*. Durham, N.C.: Duke University Press, 1987.

Clarke, John H., ed. *Malcolm X: The Man and His Times*. 1969. Reprint, Trenton, N.J.: Africa World Press, 1990.

———, ed. *Marcus Garvey and the Vision of Africa*. New York: Vintage Books, 1974.

Cone, James H. *Martin & Malcolm & America: A Dream or a Nightmare*. Maryknoll, N.Y.: Orbis Books, 1991.

Cotton to Kaolin: A History of Washington County, Georgia, 1784–1989. Sandersville, Ga.: Washington County Historical Society, 1989.

Daughters of the American Revolution (Fort Early Chapter). *History of Crisp County*. Cordele, Ga.: 1916.

Davis, Burke. *Sherman's March*. New York: Random House, 1980.

Davis, David B. *Slavery and Human Progress*. New York: Oxford University Press, 1984.

Dittmer, John. *Black Georgia in the Progressive Era, 1900–1920*. Urbana: University of Illinois Press, 1977.

Donner, Frank. *Protectors of Privilege: Red Squads and Police Repression in Urban America*. Berkeley: University of California Press, 1992.

Drago, Edmund L. *Black Politicians and Reconstruction in Georgia*. Baton Rouge: Louisiana State University Press, 1982.

Drake, St. Clair, and Horace R. Cayton. *Black Metropolis*. 2 vols. New York: Harper & Row, 1945.

Draper, Theodore. *The Rediscovery of Black Nationalism*. London: Secker & Warburg, 1970.

Dumenil, Lynn. *Freemasonry and American Culture, 1880–1930*. Princeton: Princeton University Press, 1984.

Dyson, Michael E. *Making Malcolm: The Myth & Meaning of Malcolm X*. New York: Oxford University Press, 1995.

El-Amin, Mustafa. *The Religion of Islam and the Nation of Islam: What Is the Difference?* Newark, N.J.: El-Amin Productions, 1991.

Enduring to the End: Jehovah's Witnesses and Bible Doctrine. Schaumburg, Ill.: Regular Baptist Press, 1987.

Esedebe, P. Olisanwuche. *Pan-Africanism: The Idea and Movement, 1776–1963.* Washington, D.C.: Howard University Press, 1982.

Essien-Udom, E. U. *Black Nationalism: A Search for an Identity in America.* Chicago: University of Chicago Press, 1962.

Evanzz, Karl. *The Judas Factor: The Plot to Kill Malcolm X.* New York: Thunder's Mouth Press, 1992.

Fairclough, Adam. *To Redeem the Soul of America: The Southern Christian Leadership Conference and Martin Luther King, Jr.* Athens: University of Georgia Press, 1987.

Farber, David. *The Age of Great Dreams: America in the 1960s.* New York: Hill and Wang, 1994.

Farmer, James. *Lay Bare the Heart: An Autobiography of the Civil Rights Movement.* New York: Penguin Books, 1985.

Farrakhan, Louis. *A Torchlight for America.* Chicago: FCN Publishing Co., 1993.

———. *7 Speeches.* Newport News, Va.: Ramza Associates, n.d.

Fauset, Arthur H. *Black Gods of the Metropolis.* 1944. Reprint, Philadelphia: University of Pennsylvania Press, 1971.

Ferrell, Robert, ed. *The Twentieth Century: An Almanac.* New York: World Almanac Publications, 1985.

Fields, Karen E. *Revival and Rebellion in Colonial Central Africa.* Princeton: Princeton University Press, 1985.

Finkle, Lee. *Forum for Protest: The Black Press during World War II.* Rutherford, N.J.: Fairleigh Dickinson University Press, 1975.

Foner, Eric. *A Short History of Reconstruction, 1863–1877.* New York: Harper & Row, 1990.

Forrest, Leon. *Relocations of the Spirit.* Wakefield, R.I.: Asphodel Press, 1994.

Franklin, John H., and Alfred A. Moss. *From Slavery to Freedom.* 7th ed. New York: McGraw-Hill, 1994.

Freund, Bill. *The Making of Contemporary Africa: The Development of African Society Since 1800.* Bloomington: Indiana University Press, 1984.

Friedly, Michael. *Malcolm X: The Assassination.* New York: Carroll & Graf Publishers, 1992.

Friedly, Michael, and David Gallen. *Martin Luther King, Jr.: The FBI File.* New York: Carroll & Graf Publishers, 1993.

Gallen, David, ed. *Malcolm X: As They Knew Him.* New York: Carroll & Graf Publishers, 1992.

Garrow, David J. *Bearing the Cross: Martin Luther King, Jr., and the Southern Christian Leadership Conference.* New York: Vintage Books, 1986.

Garvey, Marcus. *Marcus Garvey: Life and Lessons.* Eds. Robert A. Hill and Barbara Bair. Berkeley: University of California Press, 1987.

———. *More Philosophy and Opinions of Marcus Garvey.* Eds. E. U. Essien-Udom and Amy Jacques-Garvey. Totowa, N.J.: Frank Cass, 1977.

---. *Philosophy and Opinions of Marcus Garvey*. Ed. Amy Jacques-Garvey. 1923. Reprint, New York: Atheneum, 1986.

George, John, and Laird Wilcox. *Nazis, Communists, Klansmen, and Others on the Fringe: Political Extremism in America*. Buffalo, N.Y.: Prometheus Books, 1992.

Ginzburg, Ralph. *100 Years of Lynching*. New York: Lancer Books, 1969.

Goldman, Peter. *The Death and Life of Malcolm X*. Urbana: University of Illinois Press, 1979.

Gordon, Murray. *Slavery in the Arab World*. New York: New Amsterdam, 1989.

Gordy, Berry, Jr. *To Be Loved: The Music, the Magic, the Memories of Motown*. New York: Warner Books, 1994.

Gordy, Berry, Sr. *Movin' Up: Pop Gordy Tells His Story*. New York: Harper & Row, 1979.

Gosnell, Harold. *Negro Politicians: The Rise of Negro Politics in Chicago*. 1935. Reprint, Chicago: University of Chicago Press, 1967.

Grant, Donald L. *The Way It Was in the South: The Black Experience in Georgia*. New York: Carol Publishing Co., 1993.

Grossman, James. *Land of Hope: Chicago, Black Southerners, and the Great Migration*. Chicago: University of Chicago Press, 1989.

Haddad, Yvonne Y. *Muslim Communities in North America*. Albany: State University of New York Press: 1994.

---. *The Muslims of America*. New York: Oxford University Press, 1991.

Haddad, Yvonne Y., and Jane I. Smith. *Mission to America: Five Islamic Sectarian Communities in North America*. Gainesville: University Press of Florida, 1993.

Haddad, Yvonne Y., Byron Haines, and Ellison Findly, eds. *The Islamic Impact*. Syracuse, N.Y.: Syracuse University Press, 1984.

Haldeman, H. R. *The Haldeman Diaries*. New York: Berkley Books, 1995.

Hall, Given K. *A History of Deepstep, Georgia*. Deepstep, Ga.: Mayor and Council of Deepstep, 1991.

Hamilton, Charles V. *Adam Clayton Powell, Jr.: The Political Biography of an American Dilemma*. New York: Macmillan Publishing Co., 1991.

Hampton, Henry, and Steve Fayer (with Sarah Flynn). *Voices of Freedom: An Oral History of the Civil Rights Movement from the 1950s through the 1980s*. New York: Bantam Books, 1990.

Harris, William H. *The Harder We Run: Black Workers Since the Civil War*. New York: Oxford University Press, 1982.

Harrison, Barbara G. *Visions of Glory: A History and a Memory of Jehovah's Witnesses*. New York: Simon & Schuster, 1978.

Hauser, Thomas. *Muhammad Ali: His Life and Times*. New York: Simon & Schuster, 1991.

Henrickson, Wilma W. *Detroit Perspectives: Crossroads and Turning Points*. Detroit: Wayne State University Press, 1991.

Hill, Robert A., ed. *The Marcus Garvey and Universal Negro Improvement Association Papers*. Vol. 1. Berkeley: University of California Press, 1983.

Hughes, David Y., and Harry M. Geduld. *A Critical Edition of The War of the Worlds: H. G. Wells's Scientific Romance*. Bloomington: Indiana University Press, 1993.

Jabara, Robert. *The Word: The Liberation Analects of Malcolm X*. Atlanta: Clarity Press, 1992.

Jahan, Rounaq. *Pakistan: Failure in National Integration*. New York: Columbia University Press, 1972.

Jamal, Hakim A. *From the Dead Level: Malcolm X and Me*. New York: Random House, 1972.

James, Franklin J., Betty L. McCummings, and Eileen A. Tynan. *Minorities in the Sunbelt*. Rutgers: State University of New Jersey, 1984.

Karim, Benjamin. *Remembering Malcolm*. New York: Carroll & Graf Publishers, 1992.

Kedourie, Elie, ed. *Nationalism in Asia and Africa*. New York: New American Library, 1970.

Kirby, John B. *Black Americans in the Roosevelt Era*. Knoxville: University of Tennessee Press, 1982.

Kly, Y. N. *The Black Book: The True Political Philosophy of Malcolm X*. Atlanta: Clarity Press, 1986.

Knight, Fahim A. *In Defense of the Defender: The Most Honorable Elijah Muhammad*. Durham, N.C.: Fahim and Associates, 1994.

Kondo, Zak A. *Conspiracys: Unravelling the Assassination of Malcolm X*. Washington, D.C.: Nubia Press, 1993.

Lee, Martha E. *The Nation of Islam: An American Millenarian Movement*. Lewiston, N.Y.: Edwin Mellon Press, 1988.

Lemann, Nicholas. *The Promised Land*. New York: Alfred A. Knopf, 1991.

Lewis, Bernard. *The Emergence of Modern Turkey*. New York: Oxford University Press, 1968.

———. *Race and Color in Islam*. New York: Harper & Row, 1971.

Lincoln, C. Eric. *The Black Muslims in America*. Boston: Beacon Press, 1961.

Litwack, Leon, and August Meier, eds. *Black Leaders of the Nineteenth Century*. Urbana: University of Illinois Press, 1988.

Lomax, Louis E. *The Negro Revolt*. New York: Harper & Row, 1962.

———. *To Kill a Black Man*. 1968. Reprint, Los Angeles: Halloway House, 1987.

———. *When the Word Is Given*. Cleveland: World Publishing Co., 1963.

Long, David E. *The Hajj: A Survey of the Contemporary Makkah Pilgrimage*. Albany: State University of New York Press, 1979.

Luckingham, Bradford. *Phoenix: The History of a Southwestern Metropolis*. Tucson: University of Arizona Press, 1989.

McCartney, John T. *Black Power Ideologies*. Philadelphia: Temple University Press, 1992.

McKay, John, Bennett D. Hill, and John Buckler. *A History of World Societies*. 3rd ed. Boston: Houghton Mifflin Co., 1992.

McPherson, James M. *Ordeal by Fire: The Civil War*. Vol. 2. New York: McGraw-Hill, 1993.

Magida, Arthur J. *Prophet of Rage: A Life of Louis Farrakhan and His Nation.* New York: Basic Books, 1996.

Malcolm X. *The Autobiography of Malcolm X* (as told to Alex Haley). 1965. Reprint, New York: Ballantine Books, 1988.

———. *The End of White World Supremacy: Four Speeches by Malcolm X.* Ed. Benjamin Goodman. New York: Merlin House, 1971.

———. *Malcolm X: By Any Means Necessary.* Ed. George Breitman. New York: Pathfinder Press, 1970.

———. *Malcolm X: February 1965, the Last Speeches.* Ed. Steve Clark. New York: Pathfinder Press, 1992.

———. *Malcolm X: The Last Speeches.* Ed. Bruce Perry. New York: Pathfinder Press, 1989.

———. *Malcolm X on Afro-American History.* New York: Pathfinder Press, 1970.

———. *Malcolm X Speaks: Selected Speeches and Statements.* Ed. George Breitman. New York: Grove Press, 1965.

———. *Malcolm X: Speeches at Harvard.* Ed. Archie Epps. New York: Paragon House, 1991.

———. *Malcolm X Talks to Young People: Speeches in the U.S., Britain, and Africa.* Ed. Steve Clark. New York: Pathfinder Press, 1991.

Marsh, Clifton E. *From Black Muslims to Muslims: The Transition from Separatism to Islam, 1930–1980.* Metuchen, N.J: Scarecrow Press, 1984.

Martin, Tony. *Race First: The Ideological and Organizational Struggles of Marcus Garvey and the Universal Negro Improvement Association.* Dover, Mass.: Majority Press, 1976.

Marsot, Afaf Lutfi Al-Sayyid. *A Short History of Modern Egypt.* New York: Cambridge University Press, 1992.

Mealy, Rosemari. *Fidel & Malcolm X: Memories of a Meeting.* Melbourne, Australia: Ocean Press, 1993.

Meier, August, and Elliott Rudwick. *Black Detroit and the Rise of the UAW.* New York: Oxford University Press, 1979.

Meltzer, Milton. *Slavery: From the Rise of Western Civilization to Today.* New York: Dell Publishing Co., 1972.

Mitchell, B. R. *International Historical Statistics: The Americas and Australasia.* London: MacMillan Press, Ltd., 1983.

Mohr, Clarence L. *On the Threshold of Freedom: Masters and Slaves in Civil War Georgia.* Athens: University of Georgia Press, 1986.

Mordechai, Abir. *Saudi Arabia in the Oil Era: Regime and Elites; Conflict and Collaboration.* Boulder, Colo.: Westview Press, 1988.

Moses, Wilson J. *Black Messiahs and Uncle Toms.* University Park: Pennsylvania State University Press, 1982.

———. *The Golden Age of Black Nationalism, 1850–1925.* Camden, Conn.: Archon Books, 1978.

Muhammad, Elijah. *The Fall of America.* 1973. Reprint, Newport News, Va.: National Newport News and Commentator, n.d.

———. *History of the Nation of Islam.* Cleveland: Secretarius Publication, 1994.

———. *How to Eat to Live.* Bk. 1. 1967. Reprint, Newport News, Va.: National Newport News and Commentator, n.d.

———. *How to Eat to Live.* Bk. 2. 1972. Reprint, Newport News, Va.: National Newport News and Commentator, n.d.

———. *Message to the Blackman in America.* Chicago: Muhammad Mosque of Islam No. 2, 1965.

———. *Our Saviour Has Arrived.* 1974. Reprint, Newport News, Va.: United Brothers Communication Systems, n.d.

———. *The Secrets of Freemasonry.* Cleveland: Secretarius Publications, 1994.

———. *The Supreme Wisdom.* 1st ed. 1957. Reprint, Newport News, Va.: National Newport News and Commentator, n.d.

———. *The Supreme Wisdom.* Vol. 2. 1957. Reprint, Newport News, Va.: United Brothers Communications Systems, n.d.

———. *The Theology of Time.* Transcribed by Abass Rassoull. Hampton, Va.: U.S. Communications Systems, 1992.

Muhammad, Jabril. *This Is the One: The Most Honored Elijah Muhammad, We Need Not Look for Another!* Vol. 1. Phoenix: Jabril Muhammad, 1993.

Muhammad, Wallace D. *As the Light Shineth from the East.* Chicago: WDM Publishing Co., 1980.

———. *Religion on the Line.* Chicago: W. D. Muhammad Publications, 1983.

Muraskin, William A. *Middle-Class Blacks in a White Society: Prince Hall Freemasonry in America.* Berkeley: University of California Press, 1975.

Myers, Walter D. *Malcolm X: By Any Means Necessary.* New York: Scholastic, 1993.

Nalty, Bernard C. *Strength for the Fight: A History of Black Americans in the Military.* New York: Free Press, 1986.

Nelsen, Hart M., Raytha L. Yokley, and Anne K. Nelsen. *The Black Church in America.* New York: Basic Books, 1971.

Newton, Michael, and Judy Newton. *The Ku Klux Klan: An Encyclopedia.* New York: Garland Publishing, 1991.

Niblock, Tim. *Class & Power in Sudan.* Albany: State University of New York Press, 1987.

Oates, Stephen B. *Let the Trumpet Sound: The Life of Martin Luther King, Jr.* New York: New American Library, 1982.

Oliver, Roland, and J. D. Fage. *A Short History of Africa.* 1962. Reprint, New York: Penguin Books, 1985.

Onwuachi, P. Chike. *Black Ideology in African Diaspora.* Chicago: New World Press, 1973.

O'Reilly, Kenneth. *Black Americans: The FBI File.* Ed. David Gallen. New York: Carroll & Graf Publishers, 1994.

———. *"Racial Matters": The FBI's Secret File on Black America, 1960–1972.* New York: Free Press, 1989.

Painter, Nell I. *Exodusters: Black Migration to Kansas after Reconstruction.* New York: W. W. Norton & Co., 1979.

Payne, Robert. *The History of Islam.* 1959. Reprint, New York: Barnes & Noble, 1992.

Perry, Bruce. *Malcolm: The Life of a Man Who Changed Black America.* Barrytown, N.Y.: Station Hill Press, 1991.

Pinkney, Alphonso. *Red, Black, and Green: Black Nationalism in the United States.* New York: Cambridge University Press, 1976.

Porter, Frances E. *The Hajj: The Muslim Pilgrimage to Mecca and the Holy Places.* Princeton: Princeton University Press, 1994.

Randles, Jenny, and Peter Warrington. *Science and the UFOs.* New York: Basil Blackwell, 1985.

Rashad, Adib. *Elijah Muhammad: The Ideological Foundation of the Nation of Islam.* Newport News, Va.: U.B. & U.S. Communications Systems, 1994.

Rovere, Richard H. *Senator Joe McCarthy.* New York: Harper & Row, 1959.

Sherwin, Mark. *The Extremists.* New York: St. Martin's Press, 1963.

Spear, Allan H. *Black Chicago: The Making of a Negro Ghetto, 1890–1920.* Chicago: University of Chicago Press, 1967.

Steigerwald, David. *The Sixties and the End of Modern America.* New York: St. Martin's Press, 1975.

Stokesbury, James L. *A Short History of World War II.* New York: William Morrow and Co., 1980.

Strickland, Arvarh E. *History of the Chicago Urban League.* Urbana: University of Illinois Press, 1966.

Strober, Gerald S., and Deborah Hart Strober. *Nixon: An Oral History of His Presidency.* New York: HarperPerennial, 1994.

Sullivan, Frank. *Legend: The Only Inside Story about Mayor Richard Daley.* Chicago: Bonus Books, 1989.

Theoharis, Athan G., and John S. Cox. *The Boss: J. Edgar Hoover and the Great American Inquisition.* Philadelphia: Temple University Press, 1988.

Thomas, Richard W. *Life for Us Is What We Make It: Building Black Community in Detroit, 1915–1945.* Bloomington: Indiana University Press, 1992.

Trotter, Joe W., Jr. *Black Milwaukee: The Making of an Industrial Proletariat, 1915–1945.* Urbana: University of Illinois Press, 1988.

Turner, Henry McNeal. *Respect Black: The Writings and Speeches of Henry McNeal Turner.* Ed. Edwin S. Redkey. New York: Arno Press, 1971.

Tuttle, William M., Jr. *Race Riot: Chicago in the Red Summer of 1919.* New York: Atheneum, 1982.

Unger, Irwin, and Debi Unger. *America in the 1960s.* St. James, N.Y.: Brandywine Press, 1988.

Van Loon, Henrik W. *The Story of Mankind.* New York: MacMillan Co., 1923.

Wade, Wyn C. *The Fiery Cross: The Ku Klux Klan in America.* New York: Simon & Schuster, 1988.

Washington, Booker T. *Up From Slavery.* 1901. Reprint, New York: Penguin Books, 1987.

Washington, James M., ed. *A Testament of Hope: The Essential Writings and Speeches of Martin Luther King, Jr.* New York: HarperCollins, 1986.

Washington, Joseph R., Jr. *Black Sects and Cults.* Garden City, N.Y.: Doubleday & Co., 1972.

Watts, Jill. *God, Harlem U.S.A.: The Father Divine Story.* Berkeley: University of California Press, 1992.

Waugh, Earle H., Baha Abu-Laban, and Regula B. Qureshi. *The Muslim Communities in North America.* Edmonton: University of Alberta Press, 1983.

Widick, B. J. *Detroit: City of Race and Class Violence.* Detroit: Wayne State University Press, 1989.

Wilmore, Gayraud S. *Black Religion and Black Radicalism.* 2nd ed. Maryknoll, N.Y.: Orbis Books, 1991.

Wish, Harvey, ed. *The Negro Since Emancipation.* Englewood, N.J.: Prentice-Hall, 1964.

Wolfenstein, Eugene V. *The Victims of Democracy: Malcolm X and the Black Revolution.* London: Free Association Books, 1989.

Wolseley, Roland E. *The Black Press, U.S.A.* 1971. Reprint, Ames: Iowa State University Press, 1990.

Wood, Joe, ed. *Malcolm X: In Our Own Image.* New York: St. Martin's Press, 1992.

Wynn, Neil A. *The Afro-American and the Second World War.* New York: Holmes & Meier Publishers, 1975.

Young, Ida, Julius Gholson, and Clara N. Hargrove. *History of Macon, Georgia.* Macon: Lyon, Marshall, and Brooks, 1950.

Journal Articles and Pamphlets

Allen, Ernest, Jr. "Satokata Takahashi and the Flowering of Black Messianic Nationalism." *Black Scholar* 24.1 (winter 1994): 23–46.

Ansari, Zafar I. "Aspects of Black Muslim Theology." *Studia Islamica* 53 (1981): 137–76.

———. "W. D. Muhammad: The Making of a 'Black Muslim' Leader (1933–1961)." *American Journal of Islamic Social Sciences* 2.2 (December 1985): 245–62.

Battle, V. DuWayne. "The Influence of Al-Islam in America on the Black Community." *Black Scholar* 19 (January/February 1988): 33–41.

Beynon, Erdmann Doane. "The Voodoo Cult Among Negro Migrants in Detroit." *American Journal of Sociology* 43.6 (May 1938): 894–907.

Caldwell, Wallace F. "A Survey of Attitudes Toward Black Muslims in Prison." *Journal of Human Relations* 16.2 (1968): 220–38.

Garnett, Bernard E. *Invaders from the Black Nation: The "Black Muslims" in 1970.* Nashville: Race Relations Information Center, 1970.

Gomez, Michael A. "Muslims in Early America." *Journal of Southern History* 60.4 (November 1994): 671–710.

Hatchett, John F. "The Moslem Influences Among American Negroes." *Journal of Human Relations* 10.4 (1962): 375–82.

Jones, Oliver, Jr. "The Black Muslim Movement and the American Constitutional System." *Journal of Black Studies* 13.4 (June 1983): 417–37.

Kearney, Reginald. "Japan: Ally in the Struggle Against Racism, 1919–1927." *Contributions in Black Studies* 12 (1994): 117–28.

Khalifah, H. Khalif. *The Legacy of the Honorable Elijah Muhammad.* Newport News, Va.: United Brothers Communications Systems, 1988.

Lightfoot, Claude. "Negro Nationalism and the Black Muslims." *Political Affairs* 41.7 (July 1962): 3–20.

Mamiya, Lawrence H. "From Black Muslim to Bilalian: The Evolution of a Movement." *Journal for the Scientific Study of Religion* 21.2 (June 1982): 138–52.

Record, Wilson. "Extremist Movements Among American Negroes." *Phylon* 17.1 (1956): 17–23.

Smith, Christopher E. "Black Muslims and the Development of Prisoners' Rights." *Journal of Black Studies* 24.2 (December 1993): 131–46.

Tyler, Laurence L. "The Protestant Ethic Among the Black Muslims." *Phylon* 27.1 (spring 1966): 5–14.

White, Abbie. "Christian Elements in Negro American Muslim Religious Beliefs." *Phylon* 25.4 (winter 1964): 382–88.

Woodford, John. "Testing America's Promise of Free Speech: Muhammad Speaks in the 1960s, a Memoir." *Voices of the African Diaspora* 7.3 (fall 1991): 3–16.

Magazine Articles

"Back of Killings? Religious Split among Blacks." *U.S. News & World Report*, 5 February 1973, 83.

Balk, Alfred, and Alex Haley. "Black Merchants of Hate." *Saturday Evening Post*, 26 January 1963, 68–75.

"Banks Must Pay $4.6 Million to Elijah Muhammad's Heirs." *Jet*, 8 March 1982, 12.

Barboza, Steven. "A Divided Legacy." *Emerge*, April 1992, 26–32.

Barnette, Aubrey. "The Black Muslims Are a Fraud." *Saturday Evening Post*, 27 February 1965, 23–29.

Berger, Monroe. "The Black Muslim." *Horizon*, winter 1964, 49–64.

"Black Capitalism in the Muslim Style." *Fortune*, January 1970, 44.

"Black Muslims: Muhammad Speaks." *Newsweek*, 31 January 1972, 23.

"Black Muslims on the Rampage." *U.S. News & World Report*, 13 October 1962, 6.

"The Black Supremacists." *Time*, 10 August 1959, 24–25.

"'Black Supremacy' Cult in U.S.—How Much of a Threat?" *U.S. News & World Report*, 9 November 1959, 112.

"The Black Wasps." *Trans-Action*, May 1969, 8–9.

"Brothers in Bigotry." *Time*, 14 October 1985, 41.

Brown, Warren, and James M. Stephens, Jr. "Police Probe Killings in Baton Rouge." *Jet*, 27 January 1972, 6–9.

"The Cattle Poisoners." *Newsweek*, 30 March 1970, 24, 29.

"Conversion of the Muslims." *Time,* 14 March 1977, 59.

Cooper, Clarence L., Jr. "Aftermath: The Angriest Negroes Revisited." *Esquire,* June 1961, 164–66.

Cowley, Susan C., and Martin Weston. "Yesterday's Message." *Newsweek,* 30 June 1975, 71.

Crawford, Marc. "The Ominous Malcolm X Exits from the Muslims." *Life,* 20 March 1964, 40–40A.

Curry, George E. "Farrakhan." *Emerge,* August 1990, 28–37.

———. "Farrakhan, Jesse & Jews." *Emerge,* July/August 1994, 28–41.

"Dark Islam." *Newsweek,* 1 June 1942, 29–30.

"Death of a Desperado." *Newsweek,* 8 March 1965, 24.

"Elijah Muhammad Wills $200,000 Estate to Kids." *Jet,* 26 June 1975, 6.

"Elijah Muhammad's 13 Illegitimate Children Must Share Estate: Court." *Jet,* 25 January 1979, 8.

"Enter Muhammad?" *National Review,* 2 July 1963, 519–21.

"Fete Muhammad at Dinner to Help Build New Hospital." *Jet,* 18 April 1974, 54.

Fineman, Howard, and Vern E. Smith. "An Angry 'Charmer.'" *Newsweek,* 30 October 1995, 32–35, 38.

Ganns, Bruce M., and Walter L. Lowe. "The Islam Connection." *Playboy,* May 1980, 118–20, 130, 180, 200–201, 203.

Gates, Henry L., Jr. "A Reporter at Large: The Charmer." *New Yorker,* 29 April and 6 May 1996, 120.

Goldman, Peter, and Martin Weston. "The Founding Father." *Newsweek,* 10 March 1975, 21.

Haley, Alex. "Mr. Muhammad Speaks." *Reader's Digest,* March 1969, 100–104.

Henry, William A., III. "Pride and Prejudice." *Time,* 28 February 1994, 21–27.

Hentoff, Nat. "Elijah in the Wilderness." *Reporter,* 4 August 1960, 37–40.

Hobbs, Sterling X. "Miracle Man of the Muslims." *Sepia,* May 1975, 24–30.

"Holy War?" *Newsweek,* 5 February 1973, 41.

"'I Like the Word Black.'" *Newsweek,* 6 March 1963, 27–28.

"Is New York Sitting on a 'Powder Keg'?" *U.S. News & World Report,* 3 August 1959, 48–51.

Klausler, Alfred P. "Muslim Rally." *Christian Century,* 22 March 1961, 372.

Lincoln, C. Eric. "The Meaning of Malcolm X." *Christian Century,* 7 April 1965, 431–33.

———. "A Visit with Muhammad." *Negro Digest,* April 1964, 75–80.

McCoy, Frank. "Black Business Courts the Japanese Market." *Black Enterprise,* June 1994, 212–16.

Makdisi, Nadim. "The Moslems of America." *Christian Century,* 26 August 1959, 969–71.

"Malcolm X Slain: Vendetta by Rivals Feared." *Senior Scholastic,* 11 March 1965, 21.

Massaquoi, Hans. "Mystery of Malcolm X." *Ebony,* September 1964, 38–48.

Morrison, Allan. "Who Killed Malcolm X?" *Ebony,* October 1965, 135–42.

"Muhammad Leaves Great Legacy of Pride and Respect." *Jet,* 13 March 1975, 6–9.

"The Muslim Message: All White Men Devils, All Negroes Divine." *Newsweek,* 27 August 1962, 26–27, 30.

"Muslim Rivalry." *Christianity Today,* 16 February 1973, 53–54.

"The Muslim Way." *Newsweek,* 25 September 1972, 106, 109–10.

"The Muslims' Farm." *Newsweek,* 8 December 1969, 52, 57.

"Muslims in Alabama." *Time,* 2 February 1970, 12–13.

Nadle, Marlene. "Burying Malcolm X." *Village Voice,* 4 March 1965, 1, 10.

———. "Malcolm X: The Complexity of a Man in the Jungle." *Village Voice,* 25 February 1965, 1, 6, 19.

"The Nation Mourns Elijah Muhammad." *Ebony,* May 1975, 74–81.

"Negroes Building Farm Empire." *U.S. News & World Report,* 21 September 1970, 83–84.

"A New Move by the Black Muslims." *U.S. News & World Report,* 11 March 1963, 18.

Noel, Peter. "One Nation?" *Vibe,* February 1996, 70–73.

"Now It's Negroes vs. Negroes in America's Racial Violence." *U.S. News & World Report,* 8 March 1965, 6, 8.

O'Gara, James. "After Malcolm X." *Commonweal,* 26 March 1965, 8.

———. "Muhammad Speaks." *Commonweal,* 26 April 1963, 130.

———. "Muslims, Black and White." *Commonweal,* 18 January 1963, 428.

Olsen, Jack. "Learning Elijah's Advanced Lesson in Hate." *Sports Illustrated,* 9 May 1966, 37–38, 43–44, 46, 51–53.

Parks, Gordon. "The Violent End of the Man Called Malcolm X." *Life,* 5 March 1965, 26–31.

———. " 'What Their Cry Means to Me'—a Negro's Own Evaluation." *Life,* 31 May 1963, 26–27, 31–32, 78–79.

"Peking and Malcolm X." *New Republic,* 27 March 1965, 8.

Plimpton, George. "Miami Notebook: Cassius Clay and Malcolm X." *Harper's,* June 1964, 54–61.

"Recruits Behind Bars." *Time,* 31 March 1961, 14.

Russell, Carlos E. "Exclusive Interview with Brother Malcolm X." *Liberator,* May 1964, 12–13, 16.

Sackett, Russell. "Plotting a War." *Life,* 10 June 1966, 100–102, 104, 106, 109–10, 112.

Shabazz, Betty. "The Legacy of My Husband, Malcolm X." *Ebony,* June 1969, 172–74, 176, 178, 180, 182.

———. "Loving and Losing Malcolm." *Essence,* February 1992, 50–52, 104, 107, 109–110, 112.

Simms, Gregory. "Nation Mourns Muslim Leader." *Jet,* 13 March 1975, 15–16, 18, 52–53.

Southwick, Albert B. "Malcolm X: Charismatic Demagogue." *Christian Century,* 5 June 1963, 740–41.

Stewart, Ted. "How Rich Are the Black Muslims." *Sepia,* May 1972, 14–18, 20.

———. "Who Will Inherit the $80 Million Black Muslim Empire?" *Sepia,* May 1975, 18–23.

Sykes, Ossie. "The Week That Malcolm X Died." *Liberator,* April 1965, 4–7.

"Takahashi's Blacks." *Time,* 5 October 1942, 25–26.

Tinney, James S. "Black Muslims: Billing the Baptists?" *Christianity Today,* 25 October 1974, 49–50.

———. "Black Muslims: Moving into Mainstream?" *Christianity Today,* 10 August 1973, 44–45.

Turque, Bill. "Playing a Different Tone." *Newsweek,* 28 June 1993, 30–31.

"2,000 Attend Muslim Rites for Mrs. Elijah Muhammad." *Jet,* 31 August 1972, 12–14.

"White Muslims?" *Time,* 30 June 1975, 52.

"Why Black Muslims Are Focusing on the Nation's Capital Now." *U.S. News & World Report,* 27 May 1963, 24.

Wiley, Charles W. "Who Was Malcolm X?" *National Review,* 23 March 1965, 239–40.

Williams, Dennis A., and Elaine Sciolino. "Rebirth of the Nation." *Newsweek,* 15 March 1976, 33.

Worthy, William. "The Angriest Negroes." *Esquire,* February 1961, 102–5.

Dissertations and Theses

Abilla, Walter. "A Study of Black Muslims: An Analysis of Commitment." Ph.D. diss., Case Western Reserve University, 1972.

Adams, Olin B. "The Negro and the Agrarian Movement in Georgia, 1874–1908." Ph.D. diss., Florida State University, 1974.

Clegg, Claude A., III. "An Original Man: The Life and Times of Elijah Muhammad, 1897–1960." Ph.D. diss., University of Michigan, 1995.

Jones, Oliver, Jr. "The Constitutional Politics of the Black Muslim Movement in America." Ph.D. diss., University of Illinois, 1978.

McCloud, Beverly. "A Method for the Study of Islam in America Through the Narratives of African American Muslim Women." Ph.D. diss., Temple University, 1993.

Marshall, William A. "Education in the Nation of Islam during the Leadership of Elijah Muhammad, 1925–1975." Ph.D. diss., Loyola University of Chicago, 1976.

Miles, Norman. "Home at Last: The Urbanization of Black Migrants in Detroit, 1916–1929." Ph.D. diss., University of Michigan, 1978.

Sahib, Hatim A. "The Nation of Islam." Master's thesis, University of Chicago, 1951.

Turner, Richard B. "Islam in the United States in the 1920's: The Quest for a New Vision of Afro-American Religion." Ph.D. diss., Princeton University, 1986.

West, Cynthia S. "Nation Builders: Female Activism in the Nation of Islam, 1960–1970." Ph.D. diss., Temple University, 1994.

Wright, Louis E. "The Political Thought of Elijah Muhammad: Innovation and Continuity in Western Tradition." Ph.D. diss., Howard University, 1987.

Government Documents

Black Extremists/Black Nationalist–Hate Groups File (#100-4480006). Federal Bureau of Investigation. 26 sections. 6,106 documents.

Bureau of Prisons. *Federal Offenders, 1939.* Leavenworth, Kans.: Federal Prison Industries, Inc. Press, 1940.

———. *Federal Offenders, 1940.* Leavenworth, Kans.: Federal Prison Industries, Inc. Press, 1941.

———. *Gearing Federal Prisons to the War Effort.* Washington, D.C. (1943?)

———. *Manual of Policies and Procedures for the Administration of the Federal Penal and Correctional Service.* Washington, D.C., 1942.

———. *Milan.* Washington, D.C., 1960.

———. *Operating the Culinary Department.* Washington, D.C., 1950.

Censuses for the 100th Militia District. Washington County Probate Court, Sandersville, Ga.

Chicago Commission on Race Relations. *The Negro in Chicago: A Study of Race Relations and a Race Riot.* Chicago: University of Chicago Press, 1922.

Cook County Vital Statistics. "Medical Certificate of Death" (Elijah Muhammad). 27 February 1975. Chicago.

Division of Estates. Book A: 1829–1871. Washington County Probate Court, Sandersville, Ga.

Estate Records of Elijah Muhammad. Probate Division. Cook County Circuit Court, Chicago.

W. D. Fard File. Federal Bureau of Investigation. 1 section. 372 documents.

Germond, Jack. "Federal Correctional Institution: Milan, Michigan." Washington, D.C.: U.S. Bureau of Prisons, 1960.

Hershey, Lewis. *Selective Service in Peacetime: First Report of the Director of Selective Service, 1940–41.* Washington, D.C.: Government Printing Office, 1942.

———. *Selective Service in Wartime: Second Report of the Director of Selective Service, 1941–42.* Washington, D.C.: Government Printing Office, 1943.

Joint Legislative Committee on Un-American Activities (State of Louisiana). *Activities of "The Nation of Islam" or the Muslim Cult of Islam, in Louisiana.* Report No. 3, January 9, 1963. Baton Rouge.

Malcolm X File. Central Intelligence Agency.

Malcolm X File. U.S. Department of State.

Marriage Records F, 1885–1890. Court of Ordinary, Washington County Probate Court, Sandersville, Ga.

Elijah Muhammad File. Central Intelligence Agency.

Elijah Muhammad File (#105–24822). Federal Bureau of Investigation. 16 sections (plus index and "June Mail"). 2,798 documents.

Elijah Muhammad File. Department of State.

Selective Service. *Conscientious Objection*. Vol. 1. Washington, D.C.: Government Printing Office, 1950.

Survey of Racial Conditions in the United States. Washington, D.C.: Federal Bureau of Investigation, 1943.

U.S. Congress. *Congressional Record*.

U.S. Congress. Senate. Select Committee to Study Governmental Operations with Respect to Intelligence Activities. *Final Report—Foreign and Military Intelligence*. Book 1. 94th Cong., 2nd sess. Washington, D.C.: Government Printing Office, 1976.

———. *Intelligence Activities and the Rights of Americans*. Book 2. 94th Cong., 2nd sess. Washington, D.C.: Government Printing Office, 1976.

———. *Supplementary Detailed Staff Reports on Intelligence Activities and the Rights of Americans*. Book 3. 94th Cong., 2nd sess. Washington, D.C.: Government Printing Office, 1976.

U.S. Department of Commerce. Bureau of the Census. *Population of the United States*. 1910–1960.

———. *Statistical Abstract of the United States: 1994*. 114th ed. Washington, D.C.: Government Printing Office, 1994.

U.S. Department of Interior. Census Office. *Population of the United States*. 1890–1900.

U.S. Department of Labor. *Negro Migration in 1916–17*. Washington, D.C.: Government Printing Office, 1919. Reprint, Negro Universities Press, 1969.

Wills Book B., 1852–1903. Washington County Probate Court, Sandersville, Ga.

Audiotapes, Records, and Transcripts

"Black Muslim Debates James Baldwin, C. Eric Lincoln, Eric Goldman." (1962?) Undergraduate Library, University of North Carolina at Chapel Hill.

"The Black Separatists: Elijah Muhammad on the Philosophy of the Black Muslims." Interview of Muhammad by Ben Anderson. Phoenix, Arizona. 1964. Undergraduate Library, University of North Carolina at Chapel Hill.

Farrakhan, Louis. "Jesus Saves." International Amphitheater. Chicago, Illinois. 26 February 1995.

Malcolm X. "The Ballot or the Bullet." Detroit, Michigan. March 1964.

———. "Message to the Grassroots." 10 November 1963. Afro-American Broadcasting and Recording Co. Sound recording on LP record.

Mohammad, Warith D. "The History of the African American Experience in Islam." University of Arkansas, Little Rock. Date unknown.

———. "Islam and Nationalism, How They Influence Each Other." Malcolm X College, Chicago. 7 January 1994.

Muhammad, Elijah. "Christianity vs. Islam." Philadelphia, Pa. October 1962.

———. "Explanation of Master Fard Muhammad." n.d.

———. "I Am the Last Messenger of Allah: A Defense of Messenger Elijah Muhammad's Messengership Against Orthodox Muslims." Transcript. Cleveland: Secretarius Publications, 1992.

———. "Opposition Against Truth Punished." 14 March 1964.

———. Saviour's Day Addresses. Chicago. 1954, 1957–59, 1962, 1964–65, 1967–68, 1971, 1973–75.

———. "The Tricknology of the Enemy." Transcript. Cleveland: Secretarius Publications, 1992.

———. Uline Arena Address. Washington, D.C. 31 May 1959.

Muhammad, Wallace D. Address at Fruit of Islam Meeting. Mosque No. 7., Harlem, N.Y. 18 January 1975.

Videotapes and Televised Broadcasts

Louis Farrakhan. "After the Million Man March, Now What? Guidance and Instruction to the Year 2000." University of Illinois, Chicago Pavilion, Chicago. C-Span. 26 February 1996.

Louis Farrakhan. Interviewed by Mike Wallace. *60 Minutes*. CBS. 14 April 1996.

Louis Farrakhan. Interviewed by Barbara Walters. *20/20*. ABC. 22 April 1994.

Louis Farrakhan. Speech at the Million Man March in Washington, D.C. C-Span. 16 October 1995.

"The Hate That Hate Produced." *News Beat*. WNTA-TV Channel 13, New York. July 1959.

"Malcolm X: Make It Plain." PBS documentary. 26 January 1994.

"Malcolm X: The Real Story." CBS News video. 1992.

Warith D. Mohammed. Speech at the University of Massachusetts at Amherst. 16 November 1993. (Videotape in possession of author.)

Letters, Questionnaires, Conversations, and Interviews

Akbar, Na'im. Telephone conversation with author, 27 September 1995.

Baghdadi, Ali. Questionnaire to author, 17 September 1995.

Edwards, Ester. Telephone conversation with author, 6 September 1995.

Goldman, Peter. Telephone conversation with author, 19 May 1993.

Hakim, Nasir. Telephone conversation with author, 20 September 1995.

Islam, Khalil. Telephone conversation with author, 2 October 1995.

Kashif, Ghayth. Telephone conversation with author, 26 September 1995.

Knight, Fahim A. Letter and questionnaire to author, 27 August 1995.

Lee, Paul. Letter to author, 17 June 1993.

Lincoln, C. Eric. Letter to author, 17 May 1993.

Mohammed, Abdul Malik (national representative of Warith D. Mohammed). Telephone conversation with author, 24 October 1995.

Muhammad, Abdul Rahman. Telephone conversation with author, 22 September 1995.

Muhammad, Akbar. Telephone conversation with author, 7 September 1995.

Muhammad, Chloe (representative of Silis Muhammad). Telephone conversation with author, 4 September 1995.

Muhammad, Elijah, Jr. Telephone conversation with author, 2 October 1995.

Muhammad, John. Letter to author, 4 October 1995.

Muhammad, Kenneth. Telephone conversation with author, 25 September 1995.

Muhammad, Sophia (representative of Louis Farrakhan). Telephone conversation with author, 6 November 1995.

Muhammad, Wali. Telephone conversation with author, 2 October 1995.

Nu'man, Armiya. Telephone conversation with author, 20 September 1995.

Pool, Lydia B. Letter to author, 14 September 1995.

———. Telephone conversation with author, 19 August 1994.

Poole, Grace. Letter to author, 20 August 1994.

Poole, Katie Smith. Interview with author, Sandersville, Ga., 6 July 1994.

Rashad, Adib. Telephone conversation with author, 25 September 1995.

Rassoull, Abass. Telephone conversation with author, 13 October 1995.

Roberts, John W. (Federal Bureau of Prisons). Letter to author, 8 April 1994.

Shabazz, Abdulalim A. Telephone conversation with author, 19 September 1995.

Shabazz, Alauddin. Telephone conversation with author, 27 September 1995.

Shabazz, Betty. Telephone conversation with author, 13 October 1995.

Shabazz, Seifullah A. Telephone conversations with author, 2 October 1995 and 19 November 1995.

Sharrieff, Akbar H. Telephone conversation with author, 2 October 1995.

Veal, Nonie C. (Genealogy Committee of Sandersville, Ga.). Letter to author, 1 August 1994.

Woodford, John. Telephone conversation with author, May 1993.

Wright, Nathan. Telephone conversation with author, 3 October 1995.

INDEX

Abdul-Jabbar, Kareem, 263
Abortion, 186
Abu Dhabi, 255
Affirmative action, 257
Afro-Descendant Society of Upliftment, 224
Afro hairstyle, 241
Agricultural ventures, Muslim, 253, 278
Ahmad, Mirza Ghulam, 18–19, 143
Ahmadiyyas, 18–19, 21, 143, 183
Aiken, Allah Ben, 90
Al-Azhar University, 189, 224
Algeria, 109
Ali, John, 161, 165, 166, 171, 176, 187, 191, 200, 220, 226
   Malcolm X and, 203–204, 205, 207
   replaced as national secretary of Nation of Islam, 246
Ali, Muhammad (Cassius Clay), 118, 246–249, 276, 277
   draft conviction, 248
   given original name, 211
   as heavyweight champion, 210
   loses title to Frazier, 248
   Malcolm X and, 118, 208, 210, 212
   Elijah Muhammad and, 210–212, 246–249
Ali, Noble Drew (né Timothy Drew), xii, 19, 29, 184
Ali, Othman, 29
Ali, Ugan, 31, 32
American Nazi Party, 153–154
American Nut Company, 16
American Red Cross, 84
American Wire and Brass Company, 16
Amharic people of Ethiopia, 140
Amsterdam News, 116, 220
Armenian Christians, Turkish massacres of, 137
Arthur 14X, Minister, 270
Autobiography of Malcolm X (Haley), 178

Badshahi Mosque, 142
Baghdadi, Ali, 255, 277
Bahar, Pauline, 81, 92
Banking, 252
Bankston, Ralph, 262
Bankston, Roger, 262
Barnette, Aubrey, 156
"Belly to Belly, Back to Back," 249
Bengalee, Mutiur Rahman, 19
Berry, Edwin, 196
Bethel Baptist Church, 154
Bilalian News, The, 279
Birmingham, Alabama, 195–196
Birth control, 186
Black Muslims in America, The (Lincoln), 177–178
Black nationalism, 41, 60, 70–71, 102, 121–122, 133, 135, 150–52, 153, 155, 166, 239
Black Nationalism: A Search for Identity in America (Essien-Udom), 177–178
Black Panther Party, 233, 243, 258, 259
Black Power Movement, 234, 240–241, 250, 270, 282, 285
   ascendancy of, 236, 238
   beliefs about black history, 240–241
   FBI surveillance of, 257–260
   image of Elijah Muhammad and, 239, 243
   Malcolm X's reputation in, 244, 245
   women and, 243
Black Stone, 141–142
Bold Spring Baptist Church, 6
Boston Record American, 197–198
Briggs Body and Chevrolet Axle Company, 16
Brotherhood of Liberty for the Black People of America, 90
Brown, Earl, 119
Brown, H. Rap, 250
Buddhism, 47, 48
Bunche, Ralph J., 110
Burns Committee, 168–169
Butler, Norman 3X, 229

California Fact Finding Committee on Un-American Activities, 168
Carmichael, Stokely, 233, 238, 243, 250
Cassius Clay, *see* Ali, Muhammad (Cassius Clay)
Castro, Fidel, 156
Catholic Church, criticism of, 73
Challouehliczilczese, Wyxzewixard S. J., 37
Charlotte Observer, 230
Chicago, Illinois, 37–40, 88–89, 164–165, 272
  black employment and housing in, 37, 38
  racial riots in, 235, 237
Chicago Board of Education, 164–165
Chicago Defender, 223
Chicago Urban League, 196
Chisholm, Shirley, 235
Christian Anti-Communist Crusade, 170
Christian Anti-Jewish Party, 154
Christianity, 69
  among black slaves, 18, 58
  Muhammad's childhood and, 7–8
  Nation of Islam and, 27, 41, 57, 60, 63, 121, 122, 123, 131, 283
    Jesus in creation myth of, 54–56
    Yacub myth, 50
Citizenship, U.S., rejection of, 70, 197, 260
Civil Rights Act of 1964, 235
Civil rights legislation, 149, 235, 236, 238
Civil Rights Movement, 110, 134, 149, 150, 173, 195, 235, 236, 283
  Birmingham, Alabama, 195–196
  Freedom Summer, 211
  leadership of, Nation of Islam and, 128–131, 144, 195–197, 237–238, 244, 272
  Malcolm X and, 180, 190, 216
  Selma, Alabama, 235, 238
  subversives and, 163–164
  see also names of individual leaders
Civil War, 3, 4–5
Clark, Mark, 259
Coalition for the Remembrance of Elijah Muhammad (CROE), 286
COINTELPRO, 258–260
Colonialism in Africa and Asia, 135, 149
Combs, Richard E., 168–169
Communism and communist hunters, 156, 167–170, 173, 174–175, 183
Communist Party, U.S., 110
Congress of Racial Equality (CORE), 149, 233, 244

Conscientious objection, 83
Coptic Christianity, 141
Cordele, Georgia, 7–10
Costin, John T., 5
Cross, Dr. Lonnie X, 191
Crusades, 57
Cuba, 149

Daley, Richard, 164, 272, 273, 286
Davis, Benjamin O., Jr., 110
Dawud, Talib Ahmad, 132–133, 134, 136, 139, 182–184, 272
Deanar, Tynetta, 191
Death Angels, 262
Delany, Martin R., 151
DePriest, Oscar, 38
Detroit, Michigan, 14–37 *passim*, 128
  black employment and housing in, 14–15
  racial violence in, 93
Detroit Copper Company, 16
Detroit Free Press, The, 33, 128
Diab, Jamil, 122–123, 131–132, 134, 181, 282
Diggs, Charles C., Jr., 110
Draft, the, *see* Military service
Drew, Dr. Charles R., 84
Du Bois, W. E. B., 149

"East Asia":
  connection of blacks to, 45–46, 48, 123–124, 140–141
  see also Middle East
Eberspacher, Edward, 164–165
Education:
  deficient, 175, 235
  desegregation of, 108–109, 195, 235
  Universities of Islam, *see* Universities of Islam
Egypt, 109, 124, 138–139, 140
  ancient civilization of, 45, 46
Egyptian Gazette, 220
Eisenhower administration, 120
Employment discrimination and unemployment, 12, 16–17, 24, 25, 38, 78, 175, 235
Enterprise zones, 256
Eritrean nationalists, 140
Essien-Udom, E. U., 114, 177–178
Ethiopia, 140, 141
Europe, creation myth and history of Nation of Islam and, 52–53, 54, 57–58

INDEX 369

Fard, W. D., *see* Muhammad, Fard
Farmer, James, 149, 233, 244
Farrakhan, Louis (formerly Louis X), xii, 249–251, 270, 276
　background of, 249
　denunciation of Malcolm X, 218, 226, 228, 249–250
　launch of his own organization, 281–282
　Malcolm X as mentor of, 249–250
　on murder of Hanafi Muslims and, 263–264
　name change, 250
　as orator, 249, 250
　rise in Nation of Islam, 249, 250
　sexual indiscretions of Elijah Muhammad and, 192, 194
　as spokesman of Elijah Muhammad, 250
　Wallace Muhammad's succession to head of the Nation of Islam and, 273, 274–275, 277, 281
Fascism, 155–157, 283
Father Divine (George Baker Jr.), 71
FBI, 20, 84–85, 86, 89–91, 97, 120, 129, 152, 173–174, 184, 199, 209, 215, 224, 236, 246, 247, 248, 272, 273
　assassination of Malcolm X and, 229, 233
　counterintelligence efforts in late 1960's, 257–260
　downfall of Malcolm X and, 205
　exposé on Fard Muhammad, 197
　letters to Clara Muhammad about Elijah's romances, 189, 258
　telephone tap on Elijah Muhammad, 175, 203, 229, 259
Federal Correction Institute (FCI), Milan, Michigan, 93–97, 107, 223, 283
Final Call to Islam, 38
First Pacific Bank of Chicago, 279
Flag:
　American, saluting the, 72
　of Nation of Islam, 102–103
Ford administration, 275
Frazier, Joe, 248
Freedom Rides, 149
Freemasonry, 71–72
Fruit of Islam, 28, 88, 100, 117, 119, 171, 198, 219, 230, 249, 258, 271
　abolishing of, 279
　Malcolm X and, 209, 221, 226
　described, 103–104, 156
　leadership of, 113

　at Elijah Muhammad's funeral, 276
　Wallace Muhammad's charges regarding, 223, 224
　physical appearance, standards for, 241
　responsible directly to Elijah Muhammad, 181

Gadhafi, Muammar al-, 255, 256
Garvey, Marcus, xii, 20, 70, 151, 155, 158
Garvey Movement, 41, 70–71, 166
Georgia:
　black suffrage in, 5
　civil rights movement and, 149
　Elijah Muhammad's childhood in, 3–13
　Great Migration of black labor from, 11–12
　slavery in, 4
Ghana, 121
Glenwood Cemetery, 276
Gottschalk, Arthur, 164–165, 172
Great Depression, 14, 24, 77
Great Migration, 11–12, 14, 37
Guaranty Bank and Trust Company, 252

Hagia Sophia, 136, 137
Haldeman, H. R., 257
Haley, Alex, 178, 179
Hall, Ellen, 5
Hall, Mariah, *see* Poole, Mariah (née Hall) (Elijah Muhammad's mother)
Hampton, Fred, 259
Hanafi Muslims, 262–263, 264
Harris, Robert, 30–32
Hassan, John, 159
Hassan, Lemuel, 107
Hassan, Rosie, 39
"Hate That Hate Produced, The," 125–27, 128, 136
Hawkins, John, 58, 59
Hayer, Talmadge, 229
Hayes, Robert, 164
Henry X, 208
Hinduism, 47, 48
Hinton, Johnson, 116
Hitler, Adolf, 80, 153, 156
Homosexuality, 241
Hoover, J. Edgar, 87, 90, 120, 173–174, 184, 189, 233, 236, 247, 257, 273
　death of, 259
　downfall of Malcolm X and, 205

Hoover, J. Edgar, (Cont.)
  exposé on Fard Muhammad, 197–198
  Martin Luther King Jr. and, 258
  racial prejudices, 173
House Un-American Activities
    Committee (HUAC), 174–175,
    183
Housing:
  laws banning segregation in, 235
  segregation in, 15, 37, 38, 77, 78, 175,
    235, 236
Hunt, Haroldson L., 161–162

Inonu, General Ismet, 136
Internal Revenue Service, see Taxation
International Railroadmen's Benevolent
    Industrial Aid Association, 12
Islam, 17–18
  history of, in U.S., 18–21
  Nation of Islam, see Nation of Islam
  orthodox, 41, 217, 255, 282
    beliefs and practices of, 68–69, 137
    relationship to Nation of Islam, see
      Nation of Islam, orthodox Islamic
      groups and
Islamic Center of Chicago, 131, 159, 161
Islamic News, The, 116
Islamic University, dream of building, 252
Israel, 255

Jack, Hulan, 119
Jackson, Reverend Jesse, 243, 277
Jamal, Hakim A., 261–262
James 3X, 159
Japan, 29, 66, 82
Jeffries, Edward J., 31
Jehovah's Witnesses, 72–73
Jeremiah X, 152, 153, 210
Jet magazine, 275
Jews and Judaism, 57, 138, 153, 155
  anti-Zionist pronouncements of
    Muhammad, 255
  creation myth of Nation of Islam and,
    53–54
  Garvey and, 70
Jim Crow, 6
John Birch Society, 170
Johnson, Lyndon B., 183–184, 258
Johnson, Thomas 15X, 229
Johnson administration, 184, 235, 238
Jones, David, 92
Joseph, Edward, 198
Joseph X, Captain, 202, 203–204, 206,
    207, 213

Judaism, see Jews and Judaism
Justice Department, U.S., 166, 173, 199,
    254

Karim, Abdul, 270
Karriem, Elijah, see Muhammad, Elijah
Karriem, Isaiah, 194
Karriem, Len, 88–89, 92
Kelly, James C., Jr., 167, 168
Kemal, Mustafa, 136
Kennedy, John F., 173, 199–200
  assassination of, 199, 200
    Malcolm X's remarks following, 200–
      202, 218
  civil rights and, 149, 196, 200
Kennedy, Robert F., 166
Kennedy administration, 164, 199
Khaalis, Bibi, 263
Khaalis, Hamaas Abdul, 132, 134, 262–
    263, 272, 282
Khan, Ayub, 142
King, Dr. Martin Luther, Jr., 116, 127,
    129–30, 149
  ascendancy of Black Power and role
    in civil rights struggle, 238–239
  assassination of, 244
  criticism of Vietnam War, 238
  J. Edgar Hoover and, 258
  Malcolm X and, 130, 216
  Elijah Muhammad and, 195, 196, 237–
    238, 244, 272
  Nobel Peace Prize, 196
Korean War, 104
Ku Klux Klan, 5, 152, 154, 155, 162

Liberia, 166
Library of Congress, 80, 87, 286
Libya, 255, 256
Life, 150
Lincoln, Charles Eric, 114, 177–178
Liston, Sonny, 210, 212
Little, Malcolm, see Malcolm X
Lockheed Jet Star Executive jet, 252
Lomax, Louis, 114, 125–27, 128, 136
Los Angeles:
  racial riots in, 235, 237
  shootings at mosque in, 168–173, 183
Los Angeles Herald Dispatch, 116
Los Angeles Herald-Examiner, 197–198
Los Angeles Police Department, 170,
    171, 172, 237
Louisiana legislative Committee on Un-
    American Activities, 167–168
Louis X, see Farrakhan, Louis

Lucius X, 159, 195
Lumumba, Patrice, 149
Lynchings, 6, 11
  witnessed by Muhammad, 10, 12–13

McCarthy, Joseph, 110
Malcolm X, 105–108, 110, 112, 156, 161, 285
  Muhammad Ali and, 118, 208, 210, 212
  assassination of, 156, 228–232, 234, 239
  climate surrounding, 208, 209, 212, 219, 222, 226–228, 250
  FBI and, 229, 233
  legal authorities and, 229
  autobiography written by Haley, 178
  background of, 105–107
  charisma of, 115, 215
  children of, 180
  Civil Rights Movement and, 180, 190, 216
  departure from Nation of Islam, xi, 208, 212–228
  downfall of, 192, 200–210
    remarks following Kennedy assassination, 200–202, 218
    "trial," 207
  firebombing of his house, 227
  as fund-raiser, 116, 180
  hierarchy of Nation of Islam and, 190, 192, 195
  placement of Muhammad family members in, 112, 113
  succession issue and, 180–181
  integration and, 152–153
  Martin Luther King Jr. and, 130, 216
  legacy of, 233–234
  the media and, 126, 180, 201, 204, 221
    after departing Nation of Islam, 213
  as mentor of Farrakhan, 249–250
  Middle East, tours of, 124–125, 127, 135, 136, 217, 226
  Elijah Muhammad and, 116, 118, 178, 180, 233, 234, 273, 282, 283
    appointment of Malcolm X as minister over Washington, D.C., 195
    appointment of Malcolm X as national minister, 181
    assassination of Malcolm X and, 208, 209, 222, 228, 229–232, 234
    departure of Malcolm X from Nation of Islam and ensuing events, 212–228
    downfall of Malcolm X, 200–209
    first encounters, 106–108
    loyalty, 180, 206
    posthumous criticism, 244, 245
    sexual indiscretions of Elijah and, 188, 191–192, 202, 207, 220–221, 227
  name change from Malcolm Little, 108
  as orator, 108, 115–116, 120, 131, 153, 190–191, 200
  Organization of Afro-American Unity and, 216, 219
  political activism and, 215–216
  political process and, 180, 215–216
  posthumous reputation, 244–245, 285
  rise in Nation of Islam, 108
  as spokesman of Nation of Islam, 16, 126, 128, 131, 171, 172, 180, 183, 184
  succession issue and, 180–181
Malcolm X Foundation, 261–262
Malcolm X University, 244
Malik X, 40
Marijuana, 241–242, 249
Marshall, Thurgood, 129, 131
Mecca, 45, 51, 124, 141–142, 143, 217, 226
Medina, 142
Mercy Hospital and Medical Center, 271, 275
Meredith, James, 195
Message to the Blackman in America (Muhammad), 178–179, 196, 246
Messenger Magazine, The, 116
Michigan State Board of Education, 36–37
Middle East:
  creation myth of Nation of Islam and, 45–46, 48, 123–124, 140–141
  Elijah Muhammad's hajj to, 135, 136–144, 254
    lasting effects of, 143–144
  funds for Nation of Islam from, 255, 256
  Malcolm X's tours of, 124–125, 127, 135, 136, 217, 226
  Muhammad's beliefs about, 123–124
  OPEC, 255
  recognition by Muslims of American Islamic groups seeking, 133
  slavery in, 123–124, 141, 144
Military service, 82–84
  racial discrimination and, 83–84

Military service *(Cont.)*
  rejection of obligation of, 70, 72–73, 82, 90, 91, 283
  Wallace Muhammad imprisoned for draft evasion, 172, 181, 182, 187
Million Man March, 282
Milwaukee, Wisconsin, 77–80
Miniskirts, 241
Miscegenation, 152–153
Mitchell, Benjamin, 79–80
Mohammed, Warith D., xii
Monroe, Louisiana, 166–167, 172
Montgomery, Ed, 197
Moorish Science Temple of America (MSTA), 19–20, 29, 80
  compared to Nation of Islam, 69–70
  founding of, 19
  ideology of, 19, 20
  influences on Nation of Islam, 41
Moslem Sunrise, The, 19
Mount Zion Baptist Church, 176
"Mr. Muhammad Speaks," 116, 118, 128
Muhammad, Brother Abdul, 17, 29, 35, 209
Muhammad, Akbar (son of Elijah Muhammad), 86, 98, 113
  education in Egypt, 189, 224
  leaves Nation of Islam, 162, 224–225
  Middle East tour, 136–144
  returns to Nation of Islam, 162
Muhammad, Augustus, 40
Muhammad, Clara (née Evans) (wife of Elijah Muhammad), 23, 79, 113, 119, 190
  birth of, 12
  courtship, 12
  death and funeral of, 264–265
  Elijah's imprisonment and, 85, 86–87, 96–97
  move to Detroit, 13
  sexual indiscretions of Elijah and, 172, 185, 186, 188–189, 258
  travel to Middle East, 189
  as wife and mother, 16, 17, 35, 40, 86, 194
Muhammad, Elijah:
  African civilization, views about, 240–241, 283
  ancestry, 3–6
  appearance, 117
  arrest and imprisonment, 37, 84–87, 90–98, 107, 223, 282
  birth of, 6
  Black Power Movement and image of, 239, 243
  as ceremonial figure, 104, 118, 272

childhood:
  interest in religion, 7–8
  in rural Georgia, xiii, 3–13, 282
conservatism of, 258, 282–283
conversion to Islam, 23–25
death of, 275–276
death threats against, after assassination of Malcolm X, 230
diabetes, 236
drinking, 17, 24
education, 8–9
estate of, 278–279, 286
exhumation and reburial of, 281
exile to Eastern states for seven years, 79–80, 87, 260
extramarital exploits and illegitimate children, 172, 184–189, 206, 207, 227, 258, 284
  affect on membership, 191
  exposure of, 220–221
  litigation of Elijah's estate, 279
  rationalizations of, 192, 193–194, 239
Fard and, *see* Muhammad, Fard, Elijah Muhammad and
FBI telephone tap, 175, 203, 229, 259
finances, 100, 157–162, 162, 234
  affluent lifestyle, 104, 113, 254, 252
  conversion to Islam and, 24–25
  taxation, *see* Taxation, of Muhammad and Nation of Islam
genealogy of, vii
health, 119, 175, 187, 225, 236–237
  bronchial asthma, 96, 104, 117, 172, 176, 179, 190, 260, 275
  cataracts, 260
  diabetes, 275
  in mid-1970s, 272
interviews with, 121, 125–126, 150, 177, 195, 196, 227, 243, 245, 272
joblessness, 16–17, 24, 25
as laborer, 9, 10–11, 12, 15–16
as leader of Nation of Islam, 35–40, 78–276 *passim*
legacy of, 282–284, 285–287
loyalty of his followers to, 104–105, 155–156, 187
mental evaluation, 95–96
Message to the Blackman in America, 178–179, 196, 246
as Messenger of Allah, 35, 36, 62, 63, 118, 156, 187, 264, 280
Middle East tour, 135, 136–144
military service and, 12, 73

Muhammad, Elijah: *(Cont.)*
  as misunderstood, 285–287
  move to Detroit, 13
  names:
    aliases, xi, 79, 82, 84
    Elijah Muhammad, 33–34
    Karriem, 23–24
    "slave name" of Poole, xi, 23
  newspaper column, *see* "Mr. Muhammad Speaks"
  obituaries, 275–276
  pastoral aspirations, 16, 17, 23
  persecution and sacrifice, feelings of, 87, 93, 95–96, 117, 209, 234
  Phoenix home, 175, 176
  race relations in the South and, 9–10, 12–13
  seventieth birthday, 258
  "slave name" of Poole, xi, 23
  speeches, 107, 117–118, 118–119, 127, 150, 153–154, 176, 208–209, 219, 244, 256
    after assassination of Malcolm X, 231–232
    "Islam vs. Christianity," 183
    radio, 176
    at Uline Arena, 119–121, 126
  staying power of, 273, 282
  succession issue, 179–180, 191, 264, 269–270, 273–277
  as Supreme Minister, 23–24, 25, 33
  first sermon, 25
  typical day in 1960s, 176, 179
  women, view of, 186, 241
  see also Nation of Islam
Muhammad, Elijah, Jr. (son of Elijah Muhammad), 113, 176, 274–275, 276
Muhammad, Emmanuel (son of Elijah Muhammad), 13
  birth of, 12
  prison sentence as conscientious objector, 92, 96
Muhammad, Ethel (daughter of Elijah Muhammad), *see* Sharrieff, Ethel (daughter of Elijah Muhammad)
Muhammad, Fard, 157
  arrested, 20–21, 31–33, 34, 35
  background of, 20–21, 198
  beginning of preachings, 20
  departure from Detroit, 34–35
  divinity of, self-proclaimed, 22, 26, 31, 33, 60–62
  Elijah Muhammad and, 25–28, 32, 33, 79, 80, 144, 256, 269
    first encounters, 17–18, 21–23
  last meetings, 34–36
  naming of Elijah Muhammad as Supreme Minister, 23–24, 25, 62
  surname Karriem, Elijah's receipt of, 23, 33–34
  FBI exposé, 197
  FBI's search for, 174
  finances, 25
  renaming himself as Wallace Fard Muhammad, 33
  "the Truth" preached by, *see* Nation of Islam, creation myth and history of *and* ideology of
Muhammad, Herbert (son of Elijah Muhammad), 113, 176, 189, 246, 274, 275, 276
  birth of, 16
  as manager of Muhammad Ali, 247
  Middle East tour, 136–144
  tax returns, proposal to examine, 258
Muhammad, Kalot (brother of Elijah Muhammad), 28, 40, 209
Muhammad, Lottie (daughter of Elijah Muhammad), 16
Muhammad, Nathaniel (son of Elijah Muhammad), 277
  birth of, 16
Muhammad, Silas, 280
Muhammad, Sultan, 85, 92
Muhammad, Wallace (son of Elijah Muhammad), 98, 127, 128, 162, 181, 190, 206, 271, 273, 282
  birth of, 35
  imprisoned for draft evasion, 172, 181, 182, 187
  as leader of Nation of Islam, 276–281
    changes instituted by, 279–280
    renaming the organization the World Community of Islam in the West, 280
  reinstated in Nation of Islam, 231, 232, 245
  revolt against his father and Nation of Islam, 222–224, 245–246
  sexual indiscretions of his father and, 187, 188, 192, 222
  succession to head of Nation of Islam, 179–180, 181, 273–277
  Sunni Islam and, 181–182, 207, 222, 224, 274, 279
Muhammad, William, 85
Muhammad ibn Abdullah, 56–57, 122, 280
Muhammad Speaks, 116, 159–160, 169, 175, 179, 181, 194, 198, 202, 210, 211, 215, 216–217, 218, 219, 221–222, 225, 226, 227, 230, 241,

Muhammad Speaks (Cont.)
    244, 246, 248, 250, 255, 256,
    258, 259, 263, 271, 274, 275,
    278
  building housing, 251–252
  renaming of, 279
Murphy, Frank, 31
Muslim Brotherhood, Inc., 132, 183
Muslim Girl's Training and General
    Civilization Class (MGT-GCC),
    29, 88, 100, 242
Muslim League, 143
Mussolini, Benito, 156

NAACP Legal Defense and Education
    Fund, 129
Nasser, Gamal, 109, 122, 124, 136
  Elijah Muhammad's meeting with, 138–
    139
National Association of Colored People
    (NAACP), 129, 130, 196, 216
Nationalism, black, *see* Black nationalism
National Muslim Improvement
    Association of America, 183
National Society of Afro-American
    Policemen, 243
Nation of Islam:
  anthem of, 103
  as anti-Communist, 156
  Christianity and, *see* Christianity,
    Nation of Islam and
  Civil Rights Movement leadership
    and, 128–131, 144, 195–197, 237–
    238, 244, 272
  civil war within, 260–264, 269
  creation myth and history of, 41–67
    "East Asia," connection of black
      Americans to, 45–46, 48, 123–
      124, 140–141
    enslavement of Original People in
      America, 57–60
    Jesus, 54–56
    Mars, intelligent life on, 42, 43–44
    Musa (or Moses), 53–54
    the Original People, 20, 24, 42–43
    red-skinned Indians and, 47–48
    relocation of Tribe of Shabazz to
      Africa, 46–47
    stereotypes about Africa and
      Africans, 240–241
    white race, creation of, 50–52
    Yacub myth, 49–52
  early scandals, 30–32
  economic and material concerns of, xii–
    xiii, 98–100, 105, 110–114, 144,
    150, 157–163, 171, 179, 187, 243,
    272, 282, 283
    agricultural ventures, 253, 278
    avarice of leadership, xii–xiii, 113,
      157–158, 157–163, 190–191, 194,
      254, 258, 271, 283
    banking, 252
    "Do something for self," 239, 253
    misuse of finances, 100, 253–254
    fishing industry, 251, 271, 278
    hospital project, uncompleted, 271
    in late 1960s and 1970s, 239, 251–
      254, 255–256, 260, 271
    new Temple No. 2, 252, 255
    "Three-Year Economic Program,"
      158
    under Wallace Muhammad, 277–
      279
  enforcement arms, *see* Fruit of Islam
  expansion into the Deep South, 165
  flag of, 102–103
  foreign aid to, 122, 255, 256
  founding of, xii
  Fruit of Islam, *see* Fruit of Islam
  government surveillance and
    persecution of, xiii, 25, 35, 36–37,
    39, 82–86, 88–93, 97, 98, 120,
    163–175, 184, 197–199, 205, 209,
    233, 248, 283, 284
    in late 1960s, 257–260
  hierarchy of, 28, 88–89, 103, 110, 245–
    246, 250–251
    family members controlling, 110,
      112–113, 144, 155, 171, 176,
      251
    rivalries among, 29–30, 35, 36, 40,
      81–82, 190, 191, 192, 195, 203–
      204, 206, 212, 260–264, 273
    succession issue and, 179–181, 191,
      273–277
  ideology of, 20, 24, 41–73
    afterworld, 66–67
    black supremacy, 20, 24, 52, 54,
      127, 130, 144, 283
    changes instituted by Wallace
      Muhammad, 279–280
    divine destruction of white world,
      20, 64–66, 69, 82, 98, 179, 239
    Fard as divine, 20, 22, 27
    major influences on, 67–73
    modifications by Elijah Muhammad
      of, 105, 255–256
    moral and dietary rules, 24, 63, 68–
      69, 100, 102, 240, 242, 282, 284
    Mother Plan story, 65–66, 69
    nationalism, *see* Black nationalism

Nation of Islam: *(Cont.)*
　racial separatism, 98, 121–122, 133, 134, 144, 150–152, 165–166, 179, 197, 208, 239, 279, 283
　self-defense, armed, 121, 122, 171
　white devilry, 20, 52, 98, 125, 134, 150, 179, 237–238, 239
　women's role, 29, 100–101, 186, 242–243
　incorporation of, 110
　initiation rituals, 26–28
　journalistic interest in, xi–xii, 177–178
　media coverage of, 125–28, 136, 144, 176–179
　membership, 89, 100, 108, 110, 144, 154, 157, 163, 245, 270, 283
　　in 1930s, 80–81
　　demographics of, 111–112, 251
　　estimates, 114–115, 125
　Elijah Muhammad as leader of, 35–40, 78–276
　Muslim Girl's Training and General Civilization Class, *see* Muslim Girl's Training and General Civilization Class (MGT-GCC)
　naming of initiates, 27–28, 69, 108, 157
　orthodox Islamic groups and, 122–123, 131–136, 150, 182–184, 209, 232, 246, 254–255, 282
　renamed the World Community of Islam in the West, 280
　structure of authority and obligations, 28, 155
　succession issue, *see* Muhammad, Elijah, succession issue
　terminology of, 289–290
　theme song, 249
　"the Truth," *see this entry under* creation myth and history of; ideology of
　Universities of Islam, *see* Universities of Islam
　conflict involving violence, 234, 260–264, 269
　voodooism and, 32, 33, 37
　see also Malcolm X; Muhammad, Elijah; Muhammad, Fard
Nation of Islam (Farrakhan's organization), 281–282
Native Americans, 47–48, 57–58, 175
Nativism, 73
Nazis, 153–154, 157
Negro World, 71
News Beat, 125–27, 128, 136
Newsweek, 275–276, 1550
Newton, Huey P., 250

New York Herald Tribune, 195
New York Police Department, 215, 229, 233
New York Times, The, 225
Nixon, Richard, 256, 257
Nur, Abdul, 263

OPEC, 255
Organization of Afro-American Unity, 216, 219
Original People, the, 20, 24, 42–43

Pakistan, 142–143, 183
Pakistan University of Engineering and Technology, 142
Palczynski, Joseph, 39
Parker, William, 169–170, 172, 237
Peace Mission movement, 71
Peace Movement of Ethiopia, 90
Pell City, Alabama Muslim farm, 253
Philbert X, 105, 214, 218, 231
Phoenix, Arizona, 175–176, 191
Pittsburgh Courier, The, 116, 128, 139, 230
Playboy, 178
Poll taxes, 235
Polygamy, 69, 136
Pool, Irwin, 4–5
Pool, James, 3
Pool, Middleton, Jr., 3–4
Pool, Middleton, Sr., 3
Poole, Annie (sister of Elijah Muhammad), 6
Poole, Charlie (brother of Elijah Muhammad), 18
Poole, Elijah, *see* Muhammad, Elijah
Poole, Fornie (Tommie) (sister of Elijah Muhammad), 6
Poole, Hattie (sister of Elijah Muhammad), 6
Poole, Lonnie, 7
Poole, Lula (sister of Elijah Muhammad), 6
Poole, Mariah (née Hall) (Elijah Muhammad's mother), 5, 6, 13, 16
　as laborer, 6–7
　last rites for, 123
　renamed Marie Muhammad, 34
Poole, Peggy, 5
Poole, Vinnie, 7
Poole, William, Jr. (Billie) (brother of Elijah Muhammad), 6, 17, 82
Poole, William (Elijah Muhammad's father), 13, 17

Poole, William *(Cont.)*
  birth of, 5
  as laborer, 15–16
  as preacher, 5, 7
  renamed Wali Muhammad, 33–34
Poor People's Campaign, 238
Powell, Adam Clayton, Jr., 196–197
Public accommodations, laws banning segregation in, 235
Public Enemy, 282
Puffer, Noble J., 165
Punjab region, Pakistan, 18, 142–143

Ramadan, observance of month of, 68–69, 255
Raspberry, William, 276
Rassoull, Abass, 246
  dismissal of, 280
  Wallace Muhammad's succession to head of Nation of Islam and, 273, 274
Reconstruction, 5
Reginald X, 105, 106
Rockwell, George Lincoln, 153–154, 155, 162
Rogers, William, 170
Rosary, Lucille, 220, 221, 227
Rozier, Theodore, 37, 81, 82
Rutherford, Judge, 73

Sadat, Anwar, 124
Salaam Restaurant, 246
Sandersville, Georgia, 3–7, 285
Saudi Arabia, 124, 141–142
Saviour's Day conventions, 104–105, 119, 123, 153–154, 161, 190–191, 208, 231, 244, 249, 252, 254, 256, 270, 275, 277
Segregation, 7, 152–153, 235
  in armed services, 84
  desegregation of education, 109, 195, 235
  in housing, 15, 37, 38, 77, 78, 175, 236
  in prisons, 94
Selassie, Haile, 37, 140
Selective Training and Service Act of 1940, 82–83
Selma, Alabama, 235, 238
Senegal, 139
Shabazz, Betty (wife of Malcolm X), 229
Shabazz, Minister James, 176, 191, 207, 218, 226, 276
  slaying of, 262
Shabazz, Minister Jeremiah, 280
Shabazz, Minister John, 169, 171
Shah, Azzim, 81
Shalimar Gardens, 142–143
Shaltuat, Grand Sheikh, 138
Sharecropping, 6, 7
Sharrieff, Ethel (daughter of Elijah Muhammad), 12, 13, 113, 162
Sharrieff, Hassan, 223, 224
Sharrieff, Raymond, 89, 104, 113, 159, 166, 176, 220, 226, 246, 261, 274, 276, 277
  assassination attempt on life of, 261
  dismissal of, 280
  Malcolm X and, 203–204, 205, 207
Sherman, General William, 4–5
Slavery:
  in Arab countries, 123–124, 141, 144
  reparations for, 122
  in Southern states, 4, 9, 18
Small Business Administration, 278
Smith, James, 30, 32
Soofi, Abdul Ghefoor, 183
South Africa, 149
Southern Railroad Company, 12
Sports Illustrated, 247
Spousal abuse, 242–243
Staton, Dakota, 132, 133, 183
Stokes, Ronald, 170, 171, 172, 196
Stoner, Jesse B., 154
Student Nonviolent Coordinating Committee (SNCC), 149, 233
Sudan, 139–140, 141
Suez Canal crisis of 1956, 138
Sufism, 138
Sunni Islam, 132, 134, 228
  Wallace Muhammad and, 181–182, 222, 224, 274, 279
Supreme Court, 109, 248
Supreme Wisdom, The (Muhammad), 123, 179, 193
Swint, Jane Irwin, 4
Sylvia, Sister, 102
Syria, 138

Takahashi, Satokata, 29
Taxation:
  exemption of blacks from, proposal for, 114
  of Muhammad and Nation of Islam, 162–163, 180, 254, 278
  FBI proposal to have returns of Herbert Muhammad examined, 258
Temple Farms complex, Georgia, 253

Temple People, 35, 36, 38–40, 85, 86, 88
  see also Nation of Islam
Tenney, Jack, 168
Time, 127, 128, 150
Trial of Orgena, The, 249
Troy X, 166, 167
Turkey, 136–137
Turner, Bishop Henry McNeal, 151, 166

Uddein, Rahman, 263
Unemployment, *see* Employment discrimination and unemployment
Union Baptist Church, 6
United Arab Republic, 138
United Press International, 224
Universal Negro Improvement Association (UNIA), 70–71, 155, 166
Universities of Islam, 98, 101, 113, 125, 128, 239–240, 243, 252
  described, 29
  legal authorities and, 36–37, 39, 164–165, 172
University of Mississippi, 195
U.S. News & World Report, 127, 230

Venable, James, 166, 167
Vietnam, 109, 149, 200, 236, 256
  King's criticism of the war, 238
Voting by blacks, 5, 37, 197, 215–216, 260, 279, 283
  civil rights legislation and, 235
Voting Rights Act of 1965, 235

Walcott, Louis Eugene, *see* Farrakhan, Louis (formerly Louis X)
Wallace, George, 257
Wallace, Mike, 114, 125–27, 128, 136
Walter, Francis E., 174

War on Poverty, 236
Washington, Booker T., 158, 165
Washington, D.C., 79–80
Washington Post, 276
Watts, California, 235
"What Is Un-American?," 169
Wheeler, Joe, 4
White Citizens Councils, 109–110
"White Man's Heaven Is a Black Man's Hell, A," 249
Whites:
  as devils, *see* Nation of Islam, ideology of, white devilry
  Elijah Muhammad's moderation of his views on, 197, 256
  Wallace Muhammad's position on, 277
White supremacists, 153–155, 157, 283
Wilfred X, 107, 231
Wilkins, Roy, 129, 196, 272
Williams, Evelyn, 220, 221, 227
Williams, Jerry, 220
Williams, Oscar, 252
Willis, Benjamin C., 165
WNTA, 121, 125–27, 128
Women:
  Black Power Movement and, 243
  Elijah Muhammad's view of, 186, 241
  Nation of Islam's view of role of, 29, 100–101, 186, 242–243
  spousal abuse, 242–243
Women's Army Corps, 83
Women's Movement, 242
Woodson, S. Howard, 196
World Community of Islam in the West (WCIW), 280–281
World Muslim Council, 226
World War I, 11
World War II, 73, 82, 93

Yemen, 138
Yorty, Samuel W., 168, 171, 172, 237
Yorty Committee, 168

www.ingramcontent.com/pod-product-compliance
Lightning Source LLC
Chambersburg PA
CBHW030104010526
44116CB00005B/92